Cognition

Arnold Glass

THOMSON

Australia · Canada · Mexico · Singapore · Spain · United Kingdom · United States

Cognition
Arnold Glass

Executive Editors:
Michele Baird, Maureen Staudt &
Michael Stranz

Project Development Manager:
Linda deStefano

Sr. Marketing Coordinators:
Lindsay Annett and Sara Mercurio

Production/Manufacturing Manager:
Donna M. Brown

Production Editorial Manager:
Dan Plofchan

Pre-Media Services Supervisor:
Becki Walker

Rights and Permissions Specialists:
Kalina Hintz and Bahman Naraghi

Cover Image
Getty Images*

The Adaptable Courseware Program consists of products and additions to existing Thomson products that are produced from camera-ready copy. Peer review, class testing, and accuracy are primarily the responsibility of the author(s).

Cognition
Arnold Glass

ISBN 978-1-4266-2568-8
(1-426-62568-5)

International Divisions List

Asia (Including India):
Thomson Learning
(a division of Thomson Asia Pte Ltd)
5 Shenton Way #01-01
UIC Building
Singapore 068808
Tel: (65) 6410-1200
Fax: (65) 6410-1208

Australia/New Zealand:
Thomson Learning Australia
102 Dodds Street
Southbank, Victoria 3006
Australia

Latin America:
Thomson Learning
Seneca 53
Colonia Polano
11560 Mexico, D.F., Mexico
Tel (525) 281-2906
Fax (525) 281-2656

Canada:
Thomson Nelson
1120 Birchmount Road
Toronto, Ontario
Canada M1K 5G4
Tel (416) 752-9100
Fax (416) 752-8102

UK/Europe/Middle East/Africa:
Thomson Learning
High Holborn House
50-51 Bedford Row
London, WC1R 4LS
United Kingdom
Tel 44 (020) 7067-2500
Fax 44 (020) 7067-2600

Spain (Includes Portugal):
Thomson Paraninfo
Calle Magallanes 25
28015 Madrid
España
Tel 34 (0)91 446-3350
Fax 34 (0)91 445-6218

Table of Contents

Chapter 1
Introduction   1

Chapter 2
Action   15

Chapter 3
Vision   41

Chapter 4
Attention   71

Chapter 5
Recognition and Language   115

Chapter 6
Infant and Language Learning   153

Chapter 7
Semantic Learning   175

Chapter 8
Categorization and Mnemonics   199

Chapter 9
Retrieval   219

Chapter 10
Episodic Memory   253

Chapter 11
Reasoning   275

Chapter 12
Problem Solving and Intelligence   299

Bibliography   321

Index   377

Chapter 1

INTRODUCTION

I t has happened many times. Someone asks me what I do. I say that I am a psychology professor and they get all interested. Then I say that I study cognition, the mouth drops, a blank expression takes over the face, and I hear the person say, "oh" in a disappointed tone. But this is the response of ignorance. Without cognition there would be no personality, no beliefs or feelings, normal or abnormal.

All your mental abilities are organized into a complex system, the overall function of which is termed **cognition**. The branch of psychology that studies human cognition is called cognitive psychology. Fundamentally, **cognitive psychology** is the study of how people use knowledge to guide their actions. So the study of cognition begins with action.

COGNITION AND ACTION

One of the fundamental dimensions on which living things differ is whether or not they can move themselves. Many life forms, including virtually all plants, have little or no such ability. I am talking about *internally* generated **motor actions** like wiggling a flagella or fin, as opposed to merely being blown about in the wind or carried by a current. Motor actions give a creature certain advantages in dealing with the world, enabling the creature (or a body part) to move away from danger and towards nourishment.

In animals, two specialized systems are involved in making motor actions possible: the muscle system that actually causes the movement through contracting body parts, and the nervous system that initiates an action by transmitting a signal to the muscle. Why does motor action require two systems instead of one? Mere movement does not necessarily confer an advantage on a creature. In fact, it may be a disadvantage. Flailing about aimlessly uses up energy for no purpose. Lying still might leave one just as well off. In order for movement to confer some benefit it must be based on information, typically information about the world beyond the creature. There is no point in trying to move forward if one has run into a wall. In such a case, the ability to detect something one has bumped into through physical contact, i.e., touch, may provide useful information on which direction to go. In order for a muscle system to be useful, it has to be connected with a system that directs it on the basis of information. Thus the nervous system contains both a sensory subsystem for collecting information and a motor subsystem for initiating movements in response to it. Notice that action may also be based on information about the internal state of a creature: A hungry creature may be better off moving around looking for food, but a satisfied creature may be better off lying still out of the way of prey.

As creatures evolved in size and complexity, their nervous systems evolved along with them. Diverse kinds of information about the world and oneself may be useful for survival. The sensory system evolved in a variety of different ways to detect all kinds of information through touch, smell, hearing, and sight. As the sensory subsystems became more complex, their detection functions became differentiated from their control functions. For example, when light falls on the retina of the eye it causes the pupil to contract. This simple reflex is an example of the detection and control functions associated with the light input being one and the same. The light stimulus causes the motor response of pupil contraction. In contrast, when a hungry creature moves towards something that it sees, the visual image does not cause the movement. In this case, the visual input provides **guidance** for the movement, but the **initiation** of the movement is controlled by the creature's internal state (e.g., hunger). The same creature in a different state (e.g., satiated) may not have moved toward the object.

Furthermore, there was an evolution from mere detection to representation. For example, big things may be potential predators (danger) and little things may be potential prey (nourishment). To determine the size of something in the world the nervous system evolved so that information from many different sensory receptors was combined and simple computations were performed . At this point the nervous system that carried out the computations had grown so large that we must give it a special name. This information processing subsystem of the nervous system is called the brain. Brains contain representations of things in the world. When a creature is aware of this **representation** we call this process **perception**, (but that is getting a little ahead of the story).

A motor-control subsystem of the nervous system also evolved so that many different muscle movements could be coordinated to perform sophisticated actions like sucking, biting, swallowing, swimming, and walking. These sophisticated actions gave the organism an advantage over simpler creatures in the battle for survival. The ability to perform a sophisticated activity like swimming required a complicated motor-control system that directed a large number of muscles to contract at precise time intervals. So the motor-control (or, simply, **motor**) **system** must contain a representation of the entire action. We will call the representation of the temporal sequence of muscle contractions necessary to perform a particular action the **motor program** of that action.

Notice that even though the **perceptual system** and **motor system** were distinct subsystems, they had to evolve in tandem, for they served a common purpose. The evolution of a specific action requires both more precise perceptual information to guide the muscle movements and more control over the muscles to make them. There is no point in being able to swim in any direction you chose if you do not have access to sufficient sensory information to know where to go. Conversely, there is no point in knowing where to go if you do not have sufficient control over your muscles to swim in that direction.

In a routine and predictable world it may be necessary to do only a very few things well. However, in the variable, sometimes dangerous worlds, that many creatures inhabit, there may be an advantage in doing many things well and in performing particular actions appropriate to each situation. The motor-control system became elaborated into a more general control system that selected the most appropriate action to a situation. The control system causes a motor program to be executed in response to either an external input (e.g., something that appears big) or an internal state (e.g., hunger). The selection of an action is called **attention** and the more common name of the control system is the **attention system**. In order to make available the necessary information for selecting the best action, the perceptual system became capable of providing more information to the brain about the world.   Eventually, the perceptual system became capable of providing more information than the brain could possible process at one time.

A subsystem of the attention system evolved for selecting among the perceptual inputs those most likely to be helpful to the creature. Where did the ability to select from among perceptual inputs come from? It evolved out of the motor system. The most primitive way of controlling the flow of perceptual, e.g., visual, information is by simple motor movements: raising and lowering your eyelids and turning your head. So the most primitive perceptual-selection system is comprised of set of physical actions, head turning, eyes opening and closing, etc., that sample information from different parts of the environment. A more sophisticated way of controlling the flow of visual information is by inhibiting the flow of visual information within the nervous system itself. So a physical motor action was supplemented by a nonphysical mental action. In the course of evolution, some "motor" program evolved that inhibited the flow of information within the nervous system itself rather than causing some muscle external to the nervous system to contract. Hence, it was no longer a motor program at all because the action it performed was a completely nonphysical mental action.

Here we come to the organizing theme of this book. The purpose of cognition is to perform effective actions in the world. Prior to an effective physical motor action, a great many nonphysical mental actions are performed. For example, before you get out of bed, wash up and make breakfast, you first think about what you are going to do.

Mental actions are similar to motor actions not only in purpose but in kind. Throughout evolution the elaborate mental machinery that evolved first for performing sophisticated motor movements provided an opportunity for mental actions to evolve as well. The same neural subsystems that first evolved to perform the elaborate calculations necessary to perform fine motor movements could later be recruited into systems that performed purely mental actions as well.

As brains became larger and more complex, the control of actions became more sophisticated. It became possible to execute a related set of actions sequentially over a period of time to perform a specific function like hunting or courting. Such a sequence of actions that are initiated for a common purpose is called a **behavior**. With this growing sophistication, the relationship between a creature's internal states, its input from the environment, and its behavior, became more abstract and complex. Interactions developed between the internal states of a creature and its sensory system. A looming object might activate an internal state we may gloss as "fear," which in turn might initiate a program directing attention to the location of the looming object in the environment. Among animals with the most complex nervous systems, many of the internal states that motivate purposeful behaviors are perceived as emotions. The emerging **emotional system** played a fundamental role in the control of behavior. Notice that the relationship between motivation and attention is abstract, so that different emotions can motivate the same action. For example, the act of running is involved in both chasing and fleeing.

Many creatures achieved a competitive advantage by living together. A herd can explore more territory in search of food than a single creature. Also, being a member of a herd may increase each individual member's chance of detecting a predator and of avoiding it or fending it off. But this advantage cannot be exploited unless members of the herd can communicate where the food or predator is. Hence, perceptual and motor systems were adapted to a new function: communication. Squealing and screaming are clearly actions and hearing a squeal or scream is perception.

As creatures became more complex, the world they inhabited became more complicated. The greater the variety of actions all creatures could perform the greater the number of challenges any one creature had to face. One way of equipping a creature with the abilities to cope with all the challenges it will ever face in its lifetime is build in all the abilities it will need at birth. The only effect of the environment is to provide stimuli that trigger the behavior appropriate for each situation. Insects are a good example of such biological robots.

The problem with building in everything in advance of birth is that the world is just not routine enough to know at birth everything that you will encounter in your lifetime. The one thing that building in behaviors at birth cannot prepare you for is the challenge of the novel. Novel situations may require novel actions. In order for a creature to be able to **learn** to perform novel actions, the sensory and motor systems evolved so that the motor system could be adjusted on the basis of experience. This again requires an increase in the brain's complexity. In order for a creature to learn to do or not to do something, there must be feedback from the result of the action that either increases or decreases the probability that the action will be performed again. In order to be able to do something better a creature must first be able to guide an action on the basis of sensory information the way; for example, a sense of balance is used to remain upright while walking. Second, the creature must be able to use feedback from the result of its action to alter the action it performs on the basis of the same sensory input, as a very young animal does as it learns to walk. Third, the change in how the action is performed must be permanent so that it is subsequently more accurate. So once an animal learns to walk, it does not forget it.

It would of course be simpler for a creature to be born knowing how to walk rather than having to learn it for itself. But a creature that can learn to walk can learn to walk on any surface in the world, hard or soft, muddy, sandy, or icy slick, as well as climb, crawl, and swim if necessary. Compare any walking creature with a motorized vehicle, even a so called "all terrain vehicle". The vehicle has its "response" built in and as a result there is always some place, up a slope or in the water, that it can't go, that a creature that can learn to use its legs can.

The ability to learn creates the opportunity to learn something new. The more efficient the system for learning how to perform an action, the less of the action that needs to be represented at birth. But this creates a "chicken and egg" problem. If there is no representation of an action in your motor system, how do you do it for the first time? The answer is that you need an additional level of the motor system that allows you to create ad hoc representations of new actions you want to try. Such actions are, by definition unlearned. Necessarily, they must be performed more slowly than learned action because the sequences of movements must be planned out first before the action is attempted. Also, the action is likely to be less precise or accurate than a learned action, whether we are talking about the first time you tried to walk, or write, or drive a car. However, as imperfect as it is, the ability to do new things that you were not born to do gives you tremendous power over the world. You can learn to use tools, drive a car, and fly an airplane. An unlearned ad hoc action has a special name. It is called a **voluntary action**. Voluntary action requires you to construct a plan of the action before you execute it. In order to construct a plan of a purposeful action you must make use of detailed representations of both the world around you and your own body. The planning and execution of a voluntary action you experience as **consciousness**. All the representations involved in planning and controlling of the voluntary action, including representations of the world and representations of internal states, such as emotional states, are part of the conscious experience. The representations of the world contributing to the making of voluntary actions you experience as **perception**.

Consciousness makes you aware of your immediate surroundings. It also connects you with the past and future. Again, systems that first evolved to construct and execute physical actions became available for constructing mental actions as well. Consider the behavior of a hunting predator. A sequence of actions must be planned in advance in order to track, hunt and kill the prey. This requires a representation of an anticipation of events in the immediate future, so that the future must be represented as well as the present in planning action. A hunter may be guided by past success. When in a familiar place, not only does a perceptual representation of it enter awareness, but also entering awareness are representations of things you did or saw or heard on previous occasions when you were there. A representation of the present may access a representation of the past, which may be used to construct a representation of the future.

Organizing and connecting the awareness of the past, present, and future is a sense of self. Human ancestors were social creatures, as we are today. Survival depended not only on acting on one's own plans to satisfy one's own motives, but in understanding the motives and plans of others. For in societies, whether animal or human, the survival of the individual is determined by the success of group action as well as individual action. Paradoxically, in order to perceive the motives of others, group members first had to be able to perceive their own motives. A sense of self evolved so that motive and action could be contained within a single representation. Sense of self is a new level of representation in which we are not only aware of our plans and actions but also of ourselves as actors.

Human cognition is the mental activity that guides human action. Specifically, this mental activity is information processing. That is, human cognition is the information processing that governs human action. Since information processing is itself a kind of activity, human cognition consists of some actions that govern other actions. However, this does not imply an infinite regress. Rather, it implies a continuous, interactive, processing sequence in which information leads to action, which produces more information, which can be used to direct further action. So let us consider what information is and how it is used to guide action.

BASIC PROCESSES OF COGNITION

Any pattern or organized sequence contains information. Consider the endless sequence ...010101... Suppose that the digits were painted on a sidewalk, one digit per square. If you were standing on a zero, you would know that the digits ahead and behind are ones. This predictability is **information**. Information can be used to direct action. For example, the notes on a sheet of music direct a musician about what movements to make to play her instrument. Also, when a pattern has certain correspondences with an object in the world, the pattern **represents** the object. For example, Figure 1.1 represents a cup. When a pattern is related to the rest of the world in some way so that its information describes either an action or an object, then the information is called **knowledge**. Describing an action versus an object are two different kinds of knowledge about the world. Knowledge about how to do something is called **knowing how**. Knowing what something looks, sounds, feels like, etc. is called **knowing what**.

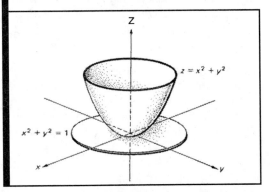

FIGURE 1.1

Alternative codes. This cup and saucer can be represented by equations.

All your waking hours you acquire knowledge by perceiving the world about you. Some of the knowledge is used immediately as when you reach for something under visual guidance. Other knowledge may be stored and used at some point in the indefinite future, as when you answer test questions. Knowledge is so important that the entire purpose of many actions, such as looking and listening, is acquiring knowledge. Furthermore, knowing some things makes it possible to learn others. For example, you don't have to memorize this book in order to use the information in it. But you do need to know how to read, and reading is a skill based on a vast amount of knowledge (e. g., knowing the meanings of thousands of printed words). If you did not have the meanings of these words stored in your memory, or you could not gain access to them rapidly, printed pages would be completely meaningless to you.

As the examples above suggest, knowledge has two essential components: a representation and a **procedure** that operates upon it. The information in a **representation** must be used by some procedure in order for cognitive activity to occur. The notes on a page of sheet music are just a pattern of ink stains until a musician recodes them as a set of finger and hand movements. The words on a page are also just ink stains until they activate representations in the brain of a reader. A representation and the procedures that can be performed on it are inter-related because the form of the representation determines the kind of procedures that can be applied.

MENTAL REPRESENTATION

In order to describe mental representations, a consideration of the details of representations in general is necessary. All representations have three fundamental aspects: content, code, and medium.

Content vs. code. Consider a simple English word like cat. It labels a certain furry household pet that purrs. A word can be encoded as a sound wave or as a printed word. There are different kinds of a printed codes, from block lettering to script. In Morse code a cat is a series of dots and dashes and in Braille it is a pattern of raised dots. Across all these examples the thing being represented, i.e., the word cat, stays the same. The information about this thing is the **content** of the representation. Each different way the information can be expressed is called a representational **code**.

Another example of alternative codes is illustrated in Figure 1.1. This is a picture, i.e., a representation, of a cup. As the figure also illustrates, a cup could also be represented by mathematical equations. The saucer can be represented by $x^2 + y^2 = 1$ (the equation of a circle) and the cup by $z = x^2 + y^2$ (the equation of a paraboloid). Most people find the picture more intuitive than the equations. But if you had to find the volume of the cup, the picture would be far less useful than the equations. While different codes can represent the same information, which code is most useful depends on the use to which the information will be put.

People are able to represent information in many different mental codes, and the mental codes can be quite different from the form in which the information was presented. In a classic experiment, Conrad (1964) found that college students made predominantly verbal errors in remembering visually presented letter strings, indicating that the visually presented letters had in fact been encoded verbally. Later, Neal Kroll and his colleagues (Kroll, Parks, Parkinson, Bieber, & Johnson, 1972) found that when students had to perform a verbal task at the same time as they saw a letter, they remembered the letters visually. This demonstrates that people can encode the same content in more than one code, depending on which code is most convenient for the task they are performing.

Code vs. medium. Words can be printed on paper, blackboards, or computer screens. In each case the code is the same but the physical **medium** containing it is different. Also, words of any language, as well as pictures and mathematical equations, can be all be printed on paper. In these cases the medium is the same but the codes are different. Similarly, the different codes in human memory (e.g., both verbal and visual codes for letters) may be realized in the same neural medium.

Suppose we were able to construct a computer like the various imaginary ones that have starred in science fiction movies. Then we might carry on conversations with the computer in English (a possibility that still remains no more than science fiction). We would want to be able to describe the information shared between the hypothetical computer and us. But we couldn't describe this information in terms of the underlying medium because this medium would be vastly different for people and the computer. In one case the medium would be biological; in the other case it would be electronic. But even though the representational media would differ, both human and computer would be representing information in a common code – English. So even if we knew everything about the nervous system, we would still want to be able to describe information and its representation at the more abstract code level in order to describe the cognitive interaction between the human and the computer. For these reasons, the central subject matter of cognitive psychology is at the level of codes (representations) rather than media.

We do not mean to imply, however, that we can simply ignore the neural bases of cognition. A brain is different from a computer, although they both may be able to add numbers. Furthermore, there are certain details of cognitive processing that are determined by the medium. The physical structure of a medium determines the codes that it can contain. Black ink and white paper are insufficient for encoding colors. Similarly a color-blind individual is limited in the codes the medium of his visual system can represent. Second, the medium determines how long a code is available, what it can be used for, and how rapidly it can be used. A message written in chalk on a blackboard may be immediately available, but not for very long. It contrast it may take a long time to find a passage in the middle of a long book, but it will be there as long as the book exists. We shall see below that, similarly, the media of different subsystems of the brain affect the accessibility of the codes they contain.

MENTAL PROCEDURES

If your knowledge remained passively stored in memory, it would be completely useless to you. In order to use your knowledge, you must execute a procedure. A procedure is a purposeful sequence of overt actions or mental operations. For example, in order to add two single-digit numbers on a calculator you would perform the following simple procedure:

A-1. Press a number key.
A-2. Press the + key.
A-3. Press another number key.
A-4. Press the = key.

Each key you press is an instruction to the calculator to perform a particular action. So in response the calculator performs the following procedure:

B-1. Read the number from the keyboard into memory position 1 (number key).
B-2. Read the number from the keyboard into memory position 2 (number key).
B-3. Add the contents of memory position 2 to the contents of memory position 1 (+).
B-4. Write the contents of memory position1 on the liquid crystal display (=).

(The key press initiating each action is shown in parentheses. Notice that the calculator actually performs the task in a different order from the order of the directions given.)

A procedure consists of one or both of two kinds of actions:
   1) A **recoding operation** transforms information from one code to another. Statements B-1, B-2, and B-4 in the example procedure are recoding operations. The first two steps transfer information from the keyboard to the calculator's memory, and the last step transfers it from the memory to the visual display. Thus the content was transformed from a position code (i.e., a location on he keyboard) to a binary code (i.e., a string of ones and zeros) to a digital code.
   2) In contrast to recoding operations, **intracode operations** change the content within a code in some way. For example, statement B-3 performs the intracode operation of addition. A more common name for intracode operations is **computations**.

In the example the calculator transformed not only the code of the information but its medium as well. Many appliances important in our lives are simply ways of transforming information into a medium that is especially convenient for some purpose. The telephone is a mechanical device that performs a procedure for transforming sound waves into electricity and back again because electricity can be quickly transmitted over long distances. However, transforming information across codes does not necessarily involve a change of medium. For example, as you read, the visual input is transformed through many different codes that all exist within a relatively homogeneous neural medium. In this case the content is transformed to a code that is convenient for some purpose. The act of reading is essentially an elaborate recoding procedure in which the visual patterns on a page activate memories and operations within the brain. It is akin to, though vastly more complicated than, steps B-1 and B-2, which activates memories within a calculator. Human cognition also involves computations. If asked whether an M is an upside-down W you can determine the answer by mentally rotating a visual representation of a W. In fact human cognition requires a great many computations that are hidden from awareness. For example, consider how it is possible that you can experience the world. You can only be directly aware of inputs that impinge directly on your body and activate neurons in your skin, ears, eyes etc. How do these peripheral sensations become your perceptual experiences of a world filled with solid objects and sounds? The answer is that the pattern of sensations across your body provides information about the kinds of objects and events in the world that caused them. By combining many different patterns of sensations your brain can construct a representation of the world around you. Constructing a representation of the world requires many precise computations that combine the spatial and temporal patterns of sensation into a representation of the world.

ORGANIZATION OF THE NERVOUS SYSTEM

The medium of human information processing is the nervous system. It performs all the recoding operations and computations. The nervous system consists of the **peripheral nervous system**, the **spinal cord**, and the brain. The peripheral nervous system is comprised of **sensory neurons** that detect inputs and motor neurons that cause the contraction of muscle fibers (Figure 1.2). Most neurons in the peripheral nervous system connect with neurons in the spinal cord. The exceptions are the neurons that form the **twelve cranial nerves** and connect directly with the brain.

Information processing (the operations of recoding and computation) begins in the **spinal cord**. The spinal cord contains connections between sensory and motor neurons called **reflex arcs**. A simple stimulus may rapidly produce a response, as in a knee-jerk in response to a hammer tap. A reflex arc is a simple action that does not, obviously, involve mental representations.

The most important function of the spinal cord and cranial nerves is to transmit sensory information from the receptors (such as fingers, eyes, and ears) to the brain, and motor commands from the brain to the muscles. Two of the most important cranial nerves for cognition are the **optic nerve** and **auditory nerve** that carry inputs from the eye and ear, respectively. It is these inputs that allow you to see and hear.

The brain performs millions of computations upon the information it receives in order to construct a representation of the body itself, as well as the world beyond the body. This representation is used to plan actions that are then transmitted to the muscles for execution. The brain has an extremely complex organization and many subsystems, each of which has many levels and which are integrated with one another. Its organization reflects its evolution over millions of years.

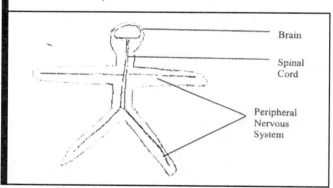

FIGURE 1.2
The nervous system

Brain

Spinal
Cord

Peripheral
Nervous
System

ORGANIZATION OF THE BRAIN

In order to fully understand human cognition it is necessary to understand something of the organization of the brain itself as well as well as the codes and procedures it contains. One unfortunate barrier to understanding the organization of the brain is the strange names of its various components. The various parts of the brain were first identified anatomically and given names that described their appearance or location. Furthermore, they were named in Latin. Today, it really does not help our understanding of the function of the small, critical piece of brain tissue in the motor control system called the substantia nigra to know that its name literally means black substance and that it was given that name because it looks black when stained in particular way. It is too late to invent new names for all the brain structures. So you will just have to learn the ones we have.

Another barrier to understanding the organization of the brain is its sheer complexity. There are several different ways to survey the organization of the brain. It can be examined from bottom-to-top in terms of increasing complexity or from front-to-back or left-to-right in terms of functionally distinct subsystems. Each approach provides a different insight into the process of cognition. A brief description of brain organization is provided here to orient you to the medium of cognitive activity. The structures highlighted here will be referred to throughout the book in conjunction with the representation that each contains or the procedures in which the structures are involved. For descriptive purposes, the human brain can be said to consist of three structures that sit one on top of the other like three scoops on an ice cream cone. At the base is the **brain stem** (Figure 1.3). Surrounding the brainstem is the much larger and more complex **forebrain** (Figure 1.3). Covering the surface of the forebrain is the **neocortex**. The

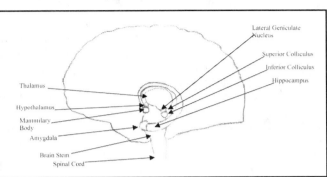

FIGURE 1.3
Left side view of diencephalon and brain stem.

three structures evolved one after the other in the order given. So there are some animal brains that are equivalent to just a brain stem and many more animal brains that are equivalent to a brain without a neocortex. No animal has a neocortex remotely as large as the human neocortex. Each of these three structures is involved in processing both sensory and motor information. However, there is a qualitative difference in the kinds of representations that exist at each level. In the brain stem there is relatively simple sensory control of muscle movements. Moving upward through the forebrain there is an increase in the variety and detail of the sensory and motor representations. At the surface, in the neocortex there are detailed representations of a person's immediate environment, as well as his emotions, intentions, plans, and actions.

Brain Stem

The brainstem consists of two main parts. The lower portion is called the **hindbrain** and the upper portion is called the **midbrain** (Figure 1.4). The brainstem has two functions. First, the brainstem begins the information processing of input from the sensory receptors (such as the fingers and ears) that is transmitted by the cranial nerves and spinal cord. It initiates reflexes in response to particular inputs. Second, the brainstem acts a relay station that transmits sensory information from the receptors to the brain, and motor commands from the brain to the muscles.

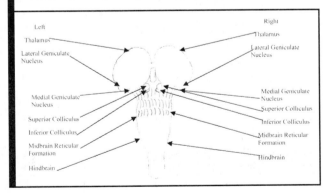

FIGURE 1.4
Rear view of diencephalon and brain stem.

Throughout the brain, groups of neurons are organized into bundles called **nuclei** that have a common function. Nuclei in the hindbrain process input from the ear used in hearing and maintaining balance, and are the location of reflexes regulating the face, eyes, and mouth. The midbrain continues the information processing of input from the spinal cord that is used in motor coordination. Also, the midbrain contains two important structures called the **superior colliculus** and the **inferior colliculus**. These are, respectively, the primary visual and auditory processing areas for those animals with a poorly developed or nonexistent neocortex (fish, reptiles, birds). However, in humans these structures play specialized and secondary roles in perceptual processing. The **superior colliculus** receives input from a branch of the optic nerve that is used to control eye movements. Directly beneath the superior colliculus, the **inferior colliculus** continues the processing of auditory input that it receives from the midbrain.

The most important function of the brainstem is as a relay station. In particular, the **inferior colliculus** is a relay station along a pathway that ultimately transmits auditory information to the auditory neocortex. Brainstem reflexes function as part of integrated perceptual and action systems that are controlled at higher levels of the brain.

Also, much of the brainstem is covered by the **reticular formation**, which participates in arousal, respiration, cardiac control, modulation of reflex muscular activity in the limbs and pain regulation. The reticular formation also ultimately controls states of consciousness, such as sleep and wakefulness, as part of the attention system.

FOREBRAIN

In front and above the midbrain, dwarfing it in size, is the **forebrain**, which contains several brain structures. To begin, immediately in front of the midbrain is the **diencephalon**, which consists of two structures. The **thalamus** is the gateway to the neocortex (Figure1.3). With the exception of some **olfactory** (odor) input, all sensory modalities have relay stations (nuclei) in the thalamus that distribute the input to the primary cortical sensory receiving areas. Directly below the thalamus, the **hypothalamus** receives emotional input from the amygdala and activates the secretion of hormones in the endocrine system through its close connections with the pituitary gland.

As shown in Figure 1.4, the thalamus actually consists of two distinct bodies, a left thalamus with connections to the right side of the body and a right thalamus with connections to the left side of the body. In about two-thirds of individuals, the left and right thalamus are connected by a pathway called the **massa intermedia**, which transmits information between them. Also shown in Figure 1.4 are the relay stations for visual and auditory information transmitted along their respective pathways, the **lateral geniculate nucleus** and **medial geniculate nucleus**, respectively. As shown, there are two of these as well, and this dual structure is maintained throughout the forebrain.

Surrounding the thalamus and brainstem is a complex set of structures called the **medial temporal cortex** or the **limbic system** (Figure 1.3). This structure is mostly **cortex**, which is made up of layers of cell bodies of neurons. Gray in color, it is distinguished from the white axons that form much of the interior of the forebrain. The limbic system contains the **hippocampus**, **fornix**, and **mammilary body**, which control learning and memory, and the **amygdala**, which is the central relay station of the emotional system of the brain.

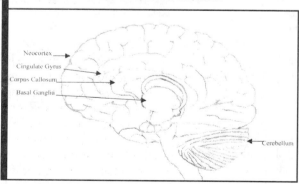

FIGURE 1.5

Interior of neocortex and cerebellum.

Sitting behind the midbrain and beneath the forebrain is the **cerebellum** (Figure 1.5). The cerebellum controls motor movements throughout the body. It is the locus of many reflexes and is a computation center that transforms motor plans constructed at higher levels into programs describing sequences of muscle movements.

Beginning in the midbrain and extending upward and around the thalamus is a collection of integrated forebrain structures collectively called the **basal ganglia**, which are essential for the initiation and control of movement (Figure 1.5). The basal ganglia control motor function in animals with a poorly developed neocortex (reptiles and birds). But in humans the basal ganglia are only part of the motor control system. As we shall see, the basal ganglia receive input from throughout the neocortex and transmit information to the cerebellum and brainstem.

To summarize, in the forebrain are four great switches for four important processing systems. The basal ganglia comprise the switch that controls movement. The thalamus is the switch that controls perception. The hippocampus and connecting structures form the switch that controls learning. The amygdala is the switch that controls emotion. These four switches are all interconnected.

A band of cortex known as the **cingulate gyrus** forms a border between the **medial temporal** cortex and the rest of the brain (Figure 1.5). Surrounding the cingulate gyrus is the **cerebral cortex**, or **neocortex**, which is comprised of two symmetrical hemispheres that consist of large, thin sheets of over 9 billion layered neurons. The two hemispheres are connected at their base by a structure called the **corpus callosum**, which transmits information between them. The surface of the neocortex is shown in Figure 1.6. The surface of the neocortex has deep folds. The folds in the brain matter are called convolutions or **gyri** (the singular is **gyrus**) and the spaces between the gyri are called **sulci** (the singular is **sulcus**). The folds of the cortex make it possible to pack more cortical surface into the skull. Like a giant spreadsheet, the increase in surface area increases the number of computations that may be performed on the input. Here on the cortex are performed the computations involved in perception, language, reasoning, and action.

FOUR PRINCIPAL AREAS OF THE NEOCORTEX

As shown in Figure 1.6, the folds in the cortical surface divide it into four principal areas, or lobes: the **frontal, parietal, temporal,** and **occipital lobes**. Each lobe contains several areas that perform distinct functions. First notice the three white areas in Figure 1.6. The large white area in the frontal cortex is where actions are first planned and then executed by transmitting commands to subcortical structures, which eventually reach the muscles. The small white area at the top of the temporal lobe is the area that receives auditory information from the thalamus. The larger white area comprising most of the occipital lobe is the area that receives visual information from the thalamus. Pathways from the occipital cortex as well as from subcortical structures, transmit visual and tactual information to the parietal lobe (shown in light gray in Figure 1.6), which in turn transmits information to motor areas in the frontal lobe. In the parietal cortex visual and tactual information is combined within a single representation, so things look the way they feel and vice versa. This representation is in turn used to direct the body movements that comprise voluntary actions.

FIGURE 1.6
The surface of the neocortex.

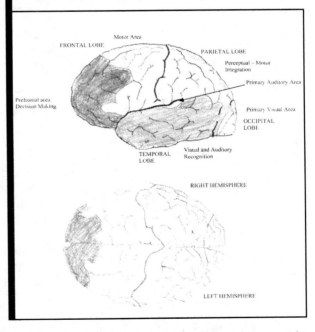

From the primary auditory and visual areas of the cortex, shown in white, pathways carry the perceptual information into the temporal cortex, (shown in darker gray in Figure 1.6), where the perceptual input is matched with representations of sounds and objects and the recognition of sounds and objects takes place. Auditory and visual pathways intersect in the temporal cortex, so that words and messages are understood here. From the temporal cortex pathways carry messages and object information into the frontal cortex. The pathways extend all the way into the front portion of the frontal lobe (shown in the darkest gray in Figure 1.6), which is called the prefrontal cortex. Also, the bottom area of the prefrontal cortex receives input from the amygdala that creates an emotional response to the message and object information sent from the temporal cortex. The prefrontal cortex is where decision-making occurs. The various kinds of information are used to decide on subsequent actions, and these decisions are transmitted along pathways to the motor area of the frontal lobe.

Hence, moving from front to back, we move from output to input: reasoning, planning, and action are all initiated and directed by the frontal lobe, while visual and auditory input is initially processed by the occipital and temporal lobes, respectively. In the temporal lobe both visual and auditory input are used to construct a detailed representation of the world. The pathway to the temporal lobe and from there to the prefrontal area of the frontal lobe underlies knowing what. In contrast, pathways from the primary perceptual areas to the parietal lobe and from there to the motor area of the frontal lobe underlie knowing how. The parietal lobe performs an integrative function. It combines perceptual and motor information to direct action.

As shown in the bottom of Figure 1.6, the neocortex actually consists of two distinct bodies, called the right and left hemispheres. When we compare the functions of the opposite areas of the **left** and **right hemispheres** they generally appear to be identical, but for the opposite sides of space. The left hemisphere processes information from the right side of space and controls the right side of the body and the right hemisphere processes information from the left side of space and controls the left side of the body. However, the one glaring exception is language. Language production is localized entirely in the left hemisphere and language comprehension is predominantly localized in the left hemisphere.

To summarize, the organization of the brain becomes more complex as it proceeds from the spinal cord through the medulla, pons, and midbrain to the diencephalon and cerebral cortex. This organizational complexity increases the number and sophistication of the computations that can be performed on the input and hence enables increasingly complex behaviors.

COGNITIVE PROCESSING

Cognition is an occult process. So it is easy to overlook the feats of intellectual prowess that the most mundane tasks require. For example, reading a page of text like this one poses little apparent difficulty. But a subjectively easy task may require processes of staggering complexity. As a preliminary to our investigation of cognition, let us take a closer look at the task of reading.

While reading a page like this one your eyes move in unison, in brief jumps called **saccades**, from word to word, at the rate of about 4 words per second. In between jumps your eyes fixate on each word for a period of time (Just & Carpenter, 1980). During each fixation, light reflected off the page is focused by the lens of each eye onto its interior surface, called the **retina**. In less than a tenth of second, the input has been sent from the retina to the thalamus, and from there to the primary visual cortex (Riggs, 1971). As you read, the visual cortex is constructing representations of the letter strings in the input and the temporal cortex is comparing them with representations in memory. Matches are activating the meanings of individual words, which are sent to the areas of the temporal and frontal cortex to be assembled into sentences, and ultimately to the frontal cortex to be integrated with other information to construct a representation of the meaning of the entire passage. Matches are also activating an emotional response as the input passes from the temporal cortex to the amygdala to the prefrontal cortex. So, in fact, an easy task like reading may be easy precisely because of the extensive processing that occurs below the level of consciousness.

However, we are not yet done. To understand more fully the process of reading we must examine in detail each cognitive system, including perception, action, attention, memory, emotion, and language, involved in reading. This will take the rest of the book. For no matter how complicated a cognitive process at first appears, when we examine it in more detail it is even more complicated.

The brain imposes order and meaning on the chaos of sensation. Your existence is the product of your brain's activity. Your own body, this book, the words on this page, and their meanings, all exist for you as patterns activated within your brain, which are experienced as consciousness. Cognition involves the constant comparison of the immediate experience against memory. You may construct from representations in memory descriptions of events that have occurred and of events that never occurred. Part of cognition is judging the correspondence between your memories and immediate experiences on the one hand and a presumed real history and objective reality on the other. When a pattern of activation produces an experience that corresponds to how the world really is, it is called **perception**. When your memory or immediate experience does not correspond to the world then it is called an **illusion**. When you deliberately construct a description of the world that does not correspond to your immediate experience then it is called **imagination**.

SUMMARY

- Cognitive processing evolved for the purpose of controlling action. Cognitive processing is itself a form of mental action that does not directly move muscles. Instead, it uses the same systems that evolved for the sensory control of motor movements to create a sense of self, a perceptual representation of the world, and to plan actions in the world.

- Action that requires cognitive processing is called voluntary action. Voluntary action is controlled by processing information about the world into a representation of it and then combining that representation with information about the body to develop a plan of action. Information that represents the world (including our own bodies) in some way is called knowledge. There are two kinds of knowledge:
    - knowing how to do something
    - knowing what something is.

- Knowledge is so important to action that the entire purpose of many mental and physical actions, e.g., looking, listening, reading, studying, thinking, is the encoding of knowledge in preparation for the planning of physical action.

- The mental representation of knowledge has three levels:
    - Content
    - Code
    - Medium

- The code of the mental representation of knowledge has two components:
    - A representation of some action or object in the world
    - A procedure that uses the representation to perform some action.
        * A recoding operation transforms information from one code to another.
        * Intracode operations (computations) change the content within a code.

- In order to fully understand cognitive processing we must consider the physical medium in which it occurs: the brain.
    - The forebrain contains four great switches for four important processing systems.
        * The basal ganglia comprise the switch that controls movement.
        * The thalamus is the switch that controls perception.
        * The hippocampus and connecting structures form the switch that controls learning.
        * The amygdala is the switch that controls emotion.
    - The cerebral cortex consists of two hemispheres that each contains four lobes: frontal, parietal, temporal and occipital. It contains the processing systems for the two kinds of knowledge
        * The occipital – parietal – frontal pathway is the "knowing how" system that engages in attention and action.
        * The occipital – temporal – prefrontal pathway is the "knowing what" system that engages in perception, recognition, and reasoning.

Chapter 2

ACTION

You move about so effortlessly that it is easy to think of action as something simple. It takes the kind of extremely unpleasant surprise that an injury provides to discover just how complex motor control is. A stroke occurs when the blood flow to some brain area is cut off. One day a woman had a stroke that damaged her temporal cortex and her frontal cortex. Her stroke stripped away some of the hidden complexity of the action system and left her with her odd impairment. She discovered that she could no longer use a simple tool like a hammer, a knife, or a key. She could no longer imitate a military salute. But she could imitate a meaningless novel action, like touching her chin with her fist, perfectly (Bartolo, Cubelli, Della Sala, Drei, & Marchetti, 2001). Even though representations long stored in memory no longer correctly directed familiar actions, the ability to perform novel actions was unimpaired. So different subsystems must control novel and familiar action.

The action system is so complex because it builds complicated, precise, and subtle actions out of very simple muscle movements. Ultimately, all human movement is caused by the contraction of a bundle of muscle fibers. Penultimately, all human movement is caused by a signal from a motor neuron to a bundle of muscle fibers, which causes them to contract. A single motor neuron and the bundle of muscle fibers to which it connects form a **motor unit**. All the muscle fibers in a motor unit contract together when signaled by their controlling motor neuron. The motor unit is the smallest unit of analysis in the description of human action. All human movement is the result of sequences of muscle contractions caused by motor units.

Motor units may be recruited for action in either of two ways. On the one hand, a large number of motor units operate independently of one another in response to simple local stimuli. These form the bulk of the involuntary movements. On the other hand, many motor units are regulated to respond in precisely timed sequences to cause complex movements. These form the bulk of the voluntary movements.

All human movement is either involuntary or voluntary. If I flash a light or a puff of air in your face, your eyes will blink. They will blink not because you will them to, but in response to the stimulus of the light or air. The mechanism that causes involuntary movements is called the **reflex**. Of course, you can also blink your eyes any time you feel like it. So an eye blink may be involuntary or voluntary. As we shall see, dual and even multi-level control is a characteristic of human action.

REFLEXES

The simplest reflexes consist of a bundle of sensory neurons and a bundle of motor neurons such that each sensory neuron is connected with a single motor neuron and each motor neuron is connected with a set of muscle fibers. When the sensory neuron is stimulated by its **unconditioned stimulus** it in turn activates the motor neuron, which in turn causes the muscle fibers to contract. The contraction of the muscle fibers causes a ballistic movement of some body part. A **ballistic movement** is one that, once initiated, is not under the continued control of the nervous system. The reflex involves the parallel action of many pairs of sensory and motor neurons. But since the complete circuit for each bit of signal involves exactly one sensory and one motor neuron the reflex is called a two-neuron or **monosynaptic** (one-synapse) reflex. (The "connection" between two neurons is actually a tiny space called a **synapse**. Each neuron signals its successor by sending a chemical signal across the synapse.) An example of a mono-synaptic reflex is the **patellar** or **flexor reflex**. When the knee is struck, the blow stimulates sensory neurons in the knee, which extend their axons up through the leg into the spinal cord, where they activate motor neurons, which extend their axons all the way back down the leg, where they cause muscle fibers to contract, which causes the leg to extend.

Every person is born with essentially the same set of **unconditioned reflexes** to get them going in the world and keep them out of harm. These reflexes are called unconditioned reflexes. An unconditioned reflex provides an innate fast response to a single, simple, stimulus. A reflex can be fast because it involves few sensory neurons, so very little processing takes place and there is only a short processing time before the movement is activated. The stimulus for a reflex is necessarily simple and the reflex always occurs without any conscious decision to perform the action. Speed is an advantage. A hand pulls away from a burning stimulus before the person even feels the pain. But simplicity is a limitation. We do not have reflexes to visual patterns because the recognition of visual patterns requires millions of sensory neurons, and so we do not have reflexes that utilize vision to keep us from putting our hands where they do not belong in the first place.

Below the level of awareness, reflexes perform four different functions. Imagine that you go out for a walk on a beautiful winter's day. First, some reflexes withdraw the body from stimuli that may damage it and hence protect it from harm. For example, as you step out into the bright sun, your eyes blink to protect them from the glare off of the snow. Second, some reflexes vary body parameters in order to maintain performance in changing conditions. For example, as you move into bright light, your pupils contract. Later, as you walk to the shelter of trees and the light dims, your pupils dilate. As a result, your retina always receives just enough light to see most clearly. As the terrain you walk upon changes, motor reflexes contract muscles in response to the pull of gravity throughout your body to keep you in balance. Furthermore, not all reflexes are simple local movements. As you move about you agitate the fluid in the semicircular canals in your ears. The movement of the fluid signals the tilt of your body and activates compensatory **vestibular** reflexes in the brain stem and cerebellum that keep you from falling. More generally, the vestibular system keeps track of the orientation of the body and this information is used by the motor system in making both reflexive and voluntary movements.

Not all vestibular reflexes are concerned with balance. Consider what happens if you move your head up and down while reading this page. As you move your head you disturb the fluid in your inner ear. A sensory neuron that detects the motion of the fluid extends to the cerebellum, where it signals a motor neuron controlling the muscle fibers fixing the eyeball in your skull (see Figure 2.1). As you move your head in one direction, the **vestibular-ocular reflex** causes your eyeballs to roll in their sockets in the exact opposite distance and direction that your head is moving. As a result, the image of this page remains fixed on your retina and you can see it clearly. But suppose instead of moving your head you use your hands and arms to move this book up and down. There is no reflex that moves the eyes to compensate for the motion of the book, so the image of the page is smeared across your retina and you can no longer read it.

Some reflexes move a body towards an informative or potentially help-ful stimulus. For example, as you walk along, a reflex in the inferior colliculus moves the head and eyes towards a sound you hear. Similarly, a reflex in the superior colliculus moves the head and eyes toward

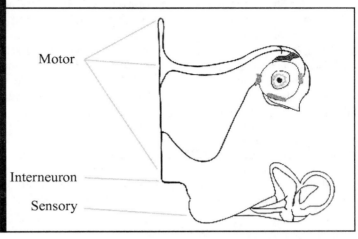

FIGURE 2.1
Vestibular-ocular reflex (House & Pansky, 1967).

Motor

Interneuron

Sensory

light. These reflexes are part of a larger **orientation reaction** that draws attention to a novel input. That is why the flashing lights and siren of an emergency vehicle always attract your attention. Finally, as the cold air rubs against your skin it raises goose bumps all over the exposed portions of your body. The pur-pose of the goose bumps is to fluff out your pelt so that your hair will better hold your heat against your body. But where is your pelt? An ancestor lost it long ago. Only the now useless goose bumps remain. So some reflexes serve no current function at all.

Other stimuli besides the unconditioned stimulus can also come to elicit a reflex. To see how this occurs, consider the following simple unconditioned reflex. A puff of air (or any light pressure) on the eye causes the eye to blink. The puff of air is an unconditioned stimulus. If the eye is made to blink repeat-edly by air puffs in a room with a clicking sound every half a second then the eye will not be conditioned to blink when a click is heard. But suppose that the room is usually silent and the click is only heard half a second before each puff of air. In this case the click is a **novel, alerting stimulus** that attracts your attention (Rescorla &Wagner, 1972), and, after a few click-puff pairings, the click will also cause the eye to blink (Reynolds, 1945). When this occurs the click is called a **conditioned stimulus** and the click-blink pair is called a **conditioned reflex**. A conditioned reflex is the occurrence of an innate, fast response to the usual context of the unconditioned stimulus.

Conditioning is useful because it permits useful actions to be performed a little sooner than they otherwise would be. Often, making a conditioned response before the unconditioned stimulus occurs is an advantage. When your mouth waters at the sight of a delicious meal, you are ready that much soon-er to enjoy it. However, the usefulness of conditioned reflexes is limited. First, the potential for a condi-tioned reflex depends on how your nervous system is organized. In order for the alerting stimulus to cause the response it must activate an interneuron connected to the motor neuron of the reflex. Second, the number of mundane situations in life that are predictable enough for a useful conditioned reflex to devel-op is limited.

Some psychologists have believed that conditioning is a precursor of learning, and it has been studied intensively since the famous experiments of Ivan Pavlov (1927) in which dogs were conditioned to salivate in response to a bell. However, conditioning is quite different from what we normally mean by learning because conditioning is totally involuntary. The type of learning that we usually think of as mean-ingful and useful is the result of voluntary action. Also, conditioning is often transient in a way that learn-ing is not. When the conditioned stimulus is no longer paired with the unconditioned stimulus, the response undergoes extinction. That is, after a number of unpaired trials the unconditioned stimulus no longer elicits the response.

Not all reflexes are simple motor movements. The sensory neuron may also activate a motor neuron in the spinal cord called a **central pattern generator** that activates a set of other motor neurons, which in turn cause a complex sequence of motions. For example, at birth human babies possess a swimming reflex. If a newborn infant is placed in a pool of water the infant will vigorously kick until he reaches the side. However, no matter how finely suited to a specific situation, we can always imagine a slightly different situation in which that reflex is not as effective. The perfect reflex for catching mice would not be quite as effective for catching birds or fish. Yet a cat can do all three. For our line of ascent, evolution has chosen a different approach to the infinite variety of life from the endless multiplication of specific reflexes. The swimming reflex disappears a few weeks after birth, as do other reflexes, in order to make way for a much more complex method of controlling action.

SUMMARY OF REFLEXES

- Reflexes are rapid, unlearned responses to specific stimuli. Many different reflexes play vital, if subordinate, roles as components of the action, perceptual, and emotional systems.

VOLUNTARY ACTIONS

When you go out to play in the snow, there are many different things that you may choose to do. You may walk forward, rolling the snow ahead of you to form a snowman, flop down on your back to imprint a snow angel, or pack some snow in your hands and throw a snowball at a tree nearby. Or, if you are at the beach during the summer then you can perform most of these actions in the sand and throw a Frisbee rather than a snowball. All of these are voluntary actions. Using the snowball as an example, let us consider the three abilities a voluntary action entails (Table 2.1). First, in order to throw a snowball at a tree, you need to see the tree. You need to perceive the target. So perception is a prerequisite for voluntary action. Without a perceptual system to create a representation of the world we cannot begin to talk about moving about it. Perception does not involve the mere detection of stimulation but the use of that stimulation as information to construct a representation of the world. As discussed in the next chapter, this is a computationally intense process, so already voluntary motion is many orders of magnitude more complicated than reflexive motion. Second, you need an awareness of your own body in space. In particular you need precise information about the locations of your movable body parts, your fingers, hands, arms, and limbs. This information must be constantly updated as these body parts move. Third, you need to be able to control the movements of your body parts so that you can aim them to perform your intended functions. To bend over, pack snow between your hands, stand erect, aim, and hurl the ball at the designated tree requires the activation of thousands of motor units in a precisely timed sequence. There is also a fourth and a fifth ability that are part of human action and that make human actions much more adaptable. The fourth is the ability to detect errors. Hence, if you miss the tree, you know it. The information you receive from your motor system and perceptual system about how your body has moved and what has been accomplished in the world is called feedback. Fifth, you can use **feedback** as information to alter your motions. You keep adjusting later tosses toward the tree until you hit the target.

TABLE 2.1
Component Abilities of Voluntary Action

1. Ability to perceive target (Perception).
2. Awareness of locations of body parts (Kinesthesia).
3. Ability to control movements of body parts.
4. Ability to detect the results of body movements (Feedback).
5. Ability to alter body movements on the basis of feedback (Learning).

THE MOTOR SYSTEM

The performance of a voluntary action requires multiple levels of control, and the motor system extends literally from top to bottom throughout the central nervous system, as shown anatomically in Figure 2.2. Before we begin our description of how voluntary actions are planned and executed, let us unpack the system in the brain that performs these functions. All parts of the motor system are shown in shades of gray. At the bottom of the figure, we see the spinal cord and brain stem, which are involved in both executing reflexes and muscle movements programmed at higher levels. Also shown is the cerebellum, which translates a motor plan describing body part movements into a motor program describing the sequence of muscle movements necessary to move those body parts. Not shown in the figure (though it is part of the motor system) is the thalamus because instead the basal ganglia, which wrap around it, are shown. The basal ganglia initiate and terminate the body part movements specified in the motor plan. Also shown are the layers of cortex above the basal ganglia that are part of the motor system.

In the top panel of Figure 2.2 we see the surface of the neocortex. All parts of the **motor system** are shown in shades of gray. At the rear of the frontal lobe, in almost the exact certain of the brain, the motor area is shown in the lightest shade of gray. This is where most voluntary movements are first executed. The motor area

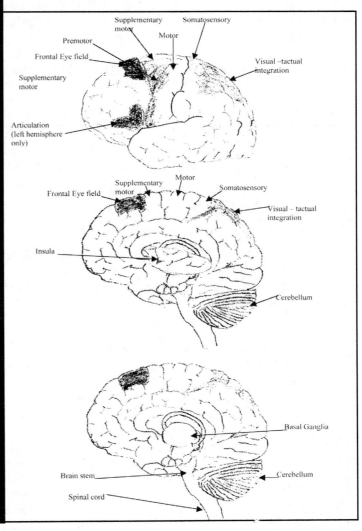

FIGURE 2.2
The motor system.

receives input from the motor planning areas to the left and right of it, shown in darker shades of gray, and sends commands for the movement of specific body parts to the subcortical structures below. To the left of the motor area in the front of the parietal cortex is a strip of cortex, shown in the next lightest shade of gray, called the **somatosensory area**. This area provides feedback about the location of body parts during motor movements.

To the left of the motor area, at the extreme top of the frontal lobe, there is a strip of cortex called the **supplementary motor area**, which is shown in a light shade of gray. This area plans actions that do not require perceptual information. For example, you do not require perceptual information to shake your head or wave your hand effectively in the way that you do to eat soup with a spoon. In contrast, below the supplementary motor cortex is the **premotor cortex**, shown in a darker shade of gray. This area plans actions on the basis of visual and tactual information. It receives this information from the parietal cortex extending beyond the somatosensory cortex, also shown in a darker shade of gray. Finally, extending to the left of the supplementary and premotor cortex into the prefrontal cortex are areas involved in the planning of two very specialized actions, shown in the darkest shades of gray: eye movements and speech articulation. As indicated in the figure, the areas devoted to planning speech exist only in the left hemisphere.

The middle and lower panels show that the motor areas extend below the surface of the cortex. Furthermore, the middle panel shows another band of cortex that is above the basal ganglia but below the surface of the cortex. This area is called the **insula**. It is also involved in speech articulation.

PLANNING, GUIDANCE, INITIATION, PROGRAMMING, AND EXECUTION

The motor system is shown schematically in Figure 2.3. Voluntary action begins with a goal generated in the prefrontal cortex. This area of the cortex is outside of the motor system proper but is the focal point for purposeful behavior in general. We will take it as the starting point for the idea to do something, whether it is to throw a snowball or a Frisbee. The prefrontal cortex communicates this intent to the motor areas of the cortex, which plan actions designed to accomplish the intended purpose. Often a sequence of actions has a single purpose. In order to throw a Frisbee you must grasp it, pick it up, pull it back, and fling it forward while releasing it. These are four separate actions but we refer to them as if they were one. Treating a sequence of actions with a single purpose as a single action is not just a figure of speech. The **motor plan** specifies the sequence of actions to be

FIGURE 2.3

The action system is organized into a multilevel heterarchy: aspects of the motor plan are sent to other parts of the action system for the guidance, programming, initiation, and execution of the action.

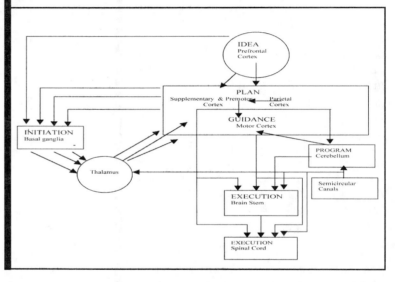

taken, i.e., the movement of the hand into a grasping position, the movement of the arm to place it in contact with the projectile, the lifting of the arm to place it in the initial throwing position, and the force and direction of the toss. In order to effectively fling a Frisbee and hit, or a least get close to, a target, the motor plan must be constructed on the basis of perceptual information describing both the Frisbee and the location of the target. The premotor cortex constructs such a motor plan on the basis of visual and tactual information provided by the parietal cortex, as shown schematically in Figure 2.3. The motor plan describes a sequence of actions to be carried out by one or more body parts. It is important to keep in mind here that the motor plan is specified in terms of body parts, at a higher level of abstraction than individual muscle contractions.

When the motor plan is complete, the premotor cortex communicates aspects of it to three other parts of the action system that together accomplish the plan as shown schematically in Figure 2.3. The direction of the body part's movements is computed in the motor cortex. We will call this **guidance**. The precise temporal sequence of muscle contractions necessary to perform the body part movements specified in the motor plan is computed in the cerebellum. We call the representation of the sequence of muscle contractions the **motor program**. Finally, the precise moment that the action is initiated and terminated is determined by a large collection of structures beneath the frontal cortex called the basal ganglia. We will call this function **initiation**. Finally, under the direction of input from premotor cortex, motor cortex, cerebellum, and basal ganglia, the action is performed by motor units responding to signals transmitted to the brain stem and spinal cord. We will call this **execution**.

When an action is executed it generates feedback, which is used to guide all but the simplest movements. The primary sources of feedback are the visual system, the vestibular system, and the **kinesthetic** system. The kinesthetic system detects body movements. Neurons in your joints keep track of where your arms, legs, and fingers are as you move them. Information about the location of body parts is called **proprioceptive** feedback. Feedback is used at multiple levels of the motor system to direct an action once it has been initiated. Vestibular and proprioceptive feedback is used by the cerebellum to refine muscle movements. Concurrently, visual feedback to the parietal cortex may be used by the motor and premotor cortex to modify the action as it is being performed.

The motor heterarchy. In summary, the motor system contains multiple levels of control that are all engaged when a voluntary action is made. On the one hand, there is a hierarchy of control: planning by the premotor and parietal cortices, guidance and initiation of body part movements by the motor cortex and basal ganglia, respectively, programming of motor unit contractions by the cerebellum, and execution by the brainstem and spinal cord. On the other hand, at each stage different sources of control may operate in parallel. Both kinesthetic and visual information may influence the construction of the plan. During execution the movements are under the combined control of the motor cortex, basal ganglia, and cerebellum. Notice that in Figure 2.3 information flows both ways: between the cortex and the basal ganglia and between the cortex and the cerebellum. The cerebellum not only recodes the plan into a program but also contains many reflexes, like the vestibular-ocular reflex, which operate in response to the voluntary movements and contribute to the success of the action. At the lower levels, spinal and cerebellar reflexes maintain body posture and help maintain fixation on the target. The motor system may be called a **heterarchy** to reflect the fact that it is partly hierarchical while at the same time several parts of it must function in parallel. Motor movements generate vestibular, kinesthetic, and visual feedback that is used to guide an action during execution. Vestibular feedback reaches the cerebellum. Proprioceptive feedback reaches the brain stem and cerebellum. Finally, visual feedback reaches the parietal cortex. Cross-talk among the parts of the motor system is necessary to synchronize the adjustments made by the different control systems on the basis of feedback.

Obviously, the fact of multiple levels of control makes the action system quite complicated. However, there is an important reason for multiple levels of control, which applies to other moving systems as well. For example, a plane is under control of the pilot, but at the same time it is under the control of the navigator and the air traffic controller on the ground. Each level of control has a special function. The navigator keeps the plane pointed in the correct direction, the air traffic controller keeps it from crashing into other airplanes, and the pilot deals with the details of moving the rudder and flaps to adjust air speed and angle of descent in response to input from the navigator, air traffic control, and immediate wind and weather conditions. All these levels of control must be exerted simultaneously in order to safely fly and land a plane. When you perform purposeful actions, you do not want to perform actions that are too vigorous or too weak and you do not want to collide with obstacles along the way. The cortical areas tend to provide the directional plans and maps. The subcortical structures, i.e., the basal ganglia and cerebellum, tend to provide the temporal schedules necessary for movements to accomplish purposeful actions. However, this distinction between the spatial maps versus temporal scheduling is only a rough one. As shown in Figure 2.3, there is cross-talk between the various components of the action system, just as there is cross-talk between components of the air traffic control system.

When you turn the page of this book, you do not have the sense that first you planned to do it and then you followed the plan. Actions seem to occur simultaneously with intentions. However, the existence of motor plans is revealed when the time to initiate and perform a sequence of voluntary actions is carefully measured.

Evidence of motor plans. When you perform an action the movement appears to be coincident with the thought, if there is any thought at all. There is not a conscious experience of first planning and then executing the action. Nevertheless, when the times it takes to make a sequence of motor movements are precisely recorded, the planning-execution cycle becomes evident. This is particularly evident in keyboarding, in which several keystrokes are planned, then executed, at a time. A pause is observed between

FIGURE 2.4

When the same repetitive motor sequence is learned in two different orders, the time to initiate a movement is determined by its position in the learned sequence   (Povel & Collard, 1982).

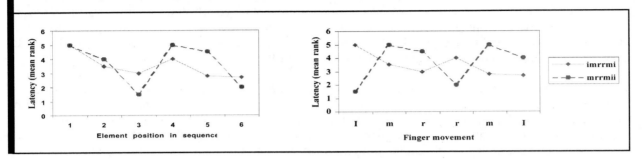

sequences of keystrokes while the next sequence is planned.   Sternberg, Knoll, and Wright (1978) found that when pre-specified sequences of different lengths had to be typed to a signal, the latency from the signal to the first stroke increased with the length of the sequence. Longer sequences took longer to plan before the first movement of the sequence was initiated.

Povel and Collard (1982) cleverly demonstrated the role of planning in keyboarding by instructing people to repeat exactly the same tapping sequence according to two different plans and showing that the pauses came in different places. They had subjects learn the same sequence of finger movements as two different pairs of sub-sequences. One pattern was index (i), middle (m), right (r), right, middle, index. The other pattern was middle, right, right, middle, index, index. The left panel of Figure 2.4 shows the initiation latencies for the finger movements coded in order of sequence position for both patterns. In each case, the latency is largest for the first and fourth positions, indicating that each pattern is composed of two three-movement sub-sequences. When people were told to repeat imrrmi they first planned and executed imr and then rmi. For this set of sub-sequences, the first pause came before the first index finger stroke and the second pause came before the second ring finger stroke. When people were told to repeat mrrmii they first planned and executed mrr and then mii. With this different set of sub-sequences, the first pause came before the first middle finger stroke and the second pause came before the second middle finger stroke. The important point is that when the person was repeating either sequence over and over, the movements of the first and second sequences were identical except for the very first finger movement. Thus, when the sequences are repeated both contain the subsequence imrrmi. The right panel of Figure 2.4 shows the data from the left panel re-plotted for the sequence imrrmi. The latency profile is different for exactly the same sequence of movements when produced according to two different plans.

PLANNING

The supplementary motor cortex, premotor cortex, and other specialized areas shown in Figure 2.2 are where motor plans are constructed. As the specialized areas in the figure indicate, the motor system is comprised of four sub-systems, each of which controls a different set of body parts that have distinct functions. Each sub-system makes use of its own pathways to control its actions. The **locomotion** system makes it possible to move about through control of the legs and trunk. Motor plans and programs make crawling, walking, running, jumping, and skipping possible. The **manipulation** system makes pointing, reaching, grasping, throwing, catching, and writing possible through control of the arms and hands. These actions are planned in the supplementary motor cortex and premotor cortex. The **visuomotor** system directs and focuses the eyes to where you wish to look so that you can track a moving object, examine a face, or read a book. As shown in Figure 2.2, it makes use of a special frontal cortical area, anterior to the other motor areas, called the **frontal eye field**. Many tasks require that an action be planned by more than one subsystem, which then must perform the action in an integrated manner. For example, many actions require hand-eye coordination. It is the integration of the manipulation and visuomotor systems that makes hand-eye coordination possible. Finally, the **vocalization/ingestion** system makes speech and eating possible through control of the mouth and vocal apparatus. As shown in Figure 2.2, speech production requires specialized cortical areas in the left hemisphere directly anterior to the premotor cortex. So unlike all other actions, speech is not under bilateral control but is produced by the left hemisphere alone.

Notice that the four subsystems differ in other ways besides the body parts that they control. They differ in the extent to which actions are planned on the basis of perceptual input; i.e., input from beyond the body. Perceptual input is central to the planning of eye movements, locomotion, and manipulation, all of which involve movement in the world. However, it plays a limited role in eating and no role in the planning of speech. Recall that planning is done in the premotor and supplementary motor areas. The premotor area receives proprioceptive input from the cerebellum and visual input from the parietal lobe. It is likely that this is where both novel and learned actions are planned and controlled under the guidance of perceptual information. The supplementary motor area receives input from the basal ganglia but not from the perceptual system. It may be here that learned actions are planned by retrieving posture representations unmodified by current perceptual information.

One challenge to motor planning is selecting the most efficient plan of action. There is often more than one way to move your body toward a particular target. Suppose that you want to pick up a pencil just out of reach. To reach the pencil, you may lean your entire body towards it, or stretch out your arm, or perform some combination of these two actions. Also, you may reach with your right hand or your left. Therefore you first select a particular constellation of body parts for performing the action, such as the right hand, right arm, and torso. Second, you select the final postures that the body parts will take when each movement is complete. Third, you specify the sequence of movements that must be performed to move the body parts into their final postures. To retrieve the pencil there are at least two actions that must be performed: the first is reaching out and grasping the pencil, the second is lifting it and bringing it to a point close to your body. Each action is represented in the motor plan by the posture of the body when the action is completed. In the motor plan to pick up the pencil, the action sequence is represented by two body postures: the arm extended and the fingers of the hand first grasping the pencil, and the arm retracted with the pencil, still in the grasp, close to the body.

Posture plans. Planning of a posture has three steps. First, representations of how the action was performed in the past are retrieved from memory. Second, criteria derived from the current situation are used to select the representation most efficient for the current situation. Third, the selected representation is modified to bring it into alignment with the current target.

Each posture is constrained to some extent by the larger action sequence of which it is a part and the environment in which it is performed. Sometimes the constraints are so tight that there is only one possible posture. Consider Povel and Collard's (1982) finger-tapping task. The movement of a single finger is tightly constrained. The only option the actor has is to rapidly move a specific finger up and down at a specific point in time. There is some choice in how fast and hard the finger may be moved, but that is it.

Other times several postures are possible within the task's constraints. Consider the action of picking up a pencil. Here the constraints are much less than a tapping task. The pencil might be grasped between the thumb and one other finger or grasped with all four fingers except the thumb and rolled into the palm of the hand. If grasped between the thumb and one other finger, that finger might be the index, middle, or ring finger. All these options are available to the action system, but they are not equally available. You were born with a motor program that already contained representations of certain efficient ways of doing things. You did not have to figure out the **pincer grip** between the thumb and index finger for yourself. It was already built into you, waiting to be discovered.

However, other decisions must be made in applying the grip. Shall the pencil be grasped at one end or the other or near the middle? To what degree shall the wrist be tilted when the pencil is grasped? Of course, when you pick up a pencil you do not consider any of this anymore than you ponder whether to use the familiar pincer grip or employ a more novel grip for a change. You simply grab the pencil. However, during the planning of the grasp the action system uses a set of internal constraints that tend to increase the accuracy and decrease the effort (hence increasing the overall efficiency) of the action, as described by David Rosenbaum and his colleagues (Rosenbaum, Meulenbroek, Vaughan, & Jansen, 2001). The description of posture planning below was based not only on their own work but the imaginative work of several other researchers cited in their report.

The steps in planning the simple action of reaching out and grasping a pencil are shown in Figure 2.5. To begin, as shown schematically at the top, representations of postures used to grasp pencils in the past are retrieved from memory. Next the grasping posture that best satisfies the task constraints is selected, as shown in the next panel down. According to Rosenbaum et al. (2001), two general kinds of constraints are used to select the best final grasp posture for the hand and then the best final posture for the extended arm. Except for the contact points between the fingers and the pencil, the hand and arm must be occupying what at the start of the movement is empty space. If more than one posture satisfies the basic location constraints then the one that involves the least twisting and turning is selected. More specifically, six constraints are applied to the set of hand and arm postures retrieved from memory in the following order:

FIGURE 2.5

Four steps in planning a grasping action. Representations of grasping hand postures are retrieved from memory (top panel). The hand posture providing the closest fit to the target is selected (second panel). Representations of arm extensions are retrieved from memory (third panel). The arm extension providing the best fit with the grasp posture and its location is selected (bottom panel). (Rosenbaum et. al, 2001.)

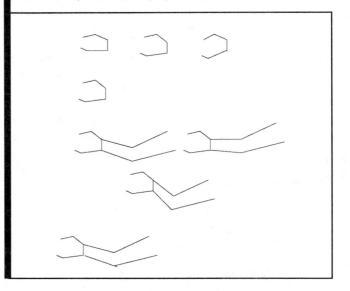

1. Hand constraints
    a. The hand is not in the same location as the target object or any other object.
    b. The hand is grasping the object near the center between the thumb and index finger.
    c. The amount that the finger and thumb have to be turned from their starting positions is less than for any other final posture that satisfies a. and b.
2. Arm constraints
    a. The arm is not in the same location as the target object or any other object.
    b. The position of the wrist allows the hand to assume the position described in 1.
    c. The amount that the shoulder, elbow, and wrist have to be turned from their starting positions is less than for any other final posture that satisfies a. and b.

So after the hand posture is selected, representations of arm postures consistent with it are retrieved from memory, as shown in the third panel of Figure 2.5. Finally, as shown in the bottom panel of Figure 2.5, the best arm posture is selected. Notice that in planning a complicated action, the posture of the body part requiring the finer adjustment is selected first and then is used to constrain the postures of the rest of the body parts. In this example first the hand posture is selected and then the arm posture. This will be called **Planning By Components (PBC)**. Finally, the selected posture-representation is modified to bring it into precise alignment with the target, i.e., the pencil.

Performance. As shown in Figure 2.3, once the motor plan is complete the frontal cortex sends commands to the motor cortex, the basal ganglia, the cerebellum, the brain stem, and the spinal cord to initiate and control the performance of the planned action. Guidance, initiation, programming and execution all occur at the same time and together control the performance of the action.

GUIDANCE

In order for the various areas of the brain to communicate with each other each area must contain a precise map of the human body, so that when a hand action is planned in the premotor cortex commands are sent to the areas of the motor cortex controlling the direction of the fingers and the wrist. So body maps play a central role in the planning and performance of actions.

The supplementary motor or premotor cortex sends the sequence of body postures that must be generated to the motor cortex. As shown on the left side of Figure 2.6, the motor area contains a detailed, if distorted representation of voluntarily movable human body parts. The map is distorted so that body parts, such as the tongue and hands, which require fine control, have large areas devoted to them and areas that require only gross control, like the trunk, have small areas devoted to them.

Once each final posture has been selected, the path the body part must take from the initial posture position to reach it must be planned. For example, in reaching for the pencil you may use an underhand, overhand, or straight-line path. The motor cortex plans the path that each body part follows to move from one posture to the next. The path selected is the one most consistent with the posture constraints listed above that does not cause any part of the body to bump into an obstacle along the way. Heterarchical control is used to plan movements around obstacles. When an obstacle is in front of a target, two distinct movements are encoded in parallel in the motor cortex: one towards the target and the other around the obstacle. The actual direction represented as the result of this dual control moves the body part around the obstacle to the target.

Apostolos Georgopoulos (1995) used single-cell recordings to investigate how direction is encoded in the motor cortex. In this method, an extremely thin wire is inserted in a single neuron in the brain of a monkey in order to record its activity while

FIGURE 2.6

Body map in motor area of frontal cortex (left) and somatosensory area of parietal cortex (right). (Penfield & Rasmussen, 1950)

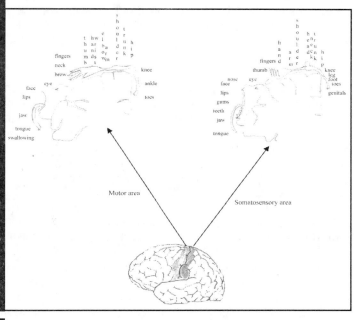

FIGURE 2.7

Representing limb direction in the motor cortex. Each motor neuron responds to a wide range of directions but has a greatest response for a particular direction of movement away from the body (top panel). A direction is represented on an area of the cortex by activation of many neurons, represented by the straight lines. The length of line represents the strength of the neuron's activation and the orientation of the line is the direction the neuron encodes. The average of the activation of all the neurons is the direction that the body part moves, shown by the arrow (bottom panel). (Georgopoulos, 1995.)

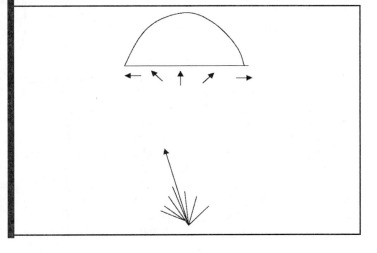

the monkey is performing a motor task. He also reported similar results using noninvasive recording methods with humans. Recall that each sub-area of the motor area controls a different body part. Within each body-part sub-area, there are neurons that direct that body part to move in various directions. Each neuron in the sub-area for a body part directs the body part in a particular direction. However, these neurons are broadly tuned, as shown in the top panel of Figure 2.7. Each neuron will be somewhat active if a movement is made within 90 degrees of the one caused by its strongest response. That is, a neuron that is most active when the hand is moving straight away from the body will only be a little less active when it is moving forward to the right or left. Each possible direction is represented by many neurons in the area. When direction is represented in the motor area, many of the direction neurons for the body part are active so that the direction actually specified is the average of the directions indicated by all the individually active neurons, as shown in the bottom panel of Figure 2.7.

Damage to any part of the body map in the motor area causes the loss of voluntary control over whatever body part is represented in that portion of the map. Effectively, the part of the body represented by the map becomes paralyzed. As discussed below, the left hemsiphere controls the right side of the body and vice versa. So damage to the left motor cortex results in paralysis on the right side of the body and vice versa. This paralysis is called **hemiplegia**.

INITIATION AND THE BASAL GANGLIA

One advantage of separating planning from performance is the ability to make your move at the right moment. For example, a cat increases its success if it waits until its prey comes in range before it pounces. Likewise, you are able to drive a car safely because you can prepare to turn the wheel before you actually reach the corner. The holding of the motor plan in the cortex in preparation for initiation of the execution of the plan can be seen in brain scan studies: When monkeys were cued as to the direction of a response and then given a go signal after a fixed interval, the activation of the direction neurons in the motor cortex was maintained throughout the interval (Georgopoulos, 1995).

Fine motor control requires that partly opposing muscle movements are initiated at precise time intervals. When we move from the cortical to the subcortical levels of the motor system we move from the where to the when of motor control. The basal ganglia and cerebellum perform the recoding operations to construct temporal representations of muscle contractions from spatial representations of limb movements.

The basal ganglia appear to play an important role in the fine control of actions that require precise, complex muscle movements. The basal ganglia influence cortical processing by inhibiting the flow of activation from the thalamus to the cortex (Figure 2.8). Thus, the basal ganglia can make fine corrections by increasing inhibition of the cortex, hence braking what would otherwise be excessive movement, or by decreasing inhibition of the cortex, hence increasing what would otherwise be inadequate movement. Entire sequences of movements may be regulated, such as those involved in writing, eating, and driving. The basal ganglia contain an elaborate set of parallel inhibitory

FIGURE 2.8

The circuit between the cortex, basal ganglia, and thalamus. The basal ganglia regulate the flow of activation from the thalamus to the cortex by inhibiting the thalamus (a). In Huntington's disease the ability of the basal ganglia to inhibit the thalamus is impaired (b). In Parkinson's disease the basal ganglia over-inhibit the thalamus (c).

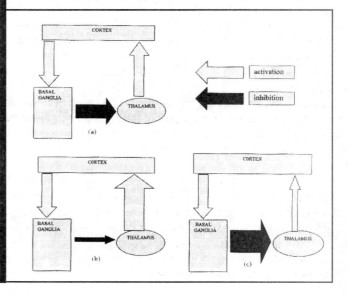

and excitatory pathways that respond to feedback in adjusting the final inhibitory output to the thalamus. Much of what is known of basal ganglia function is inferred from the disorders that result from damage to different pathways.

Huntington's disease is a largely hereditary disorder. Deterioration of the nuclei in the anterior part of the basal ganglia, called the **striatum**, which receives input from the rest of the cortex, ultimately results in decreased inhibition to the thalamus, which results in increased stimulation of the motor plan in the cortex. The end result is the jerky, involuntary movements that are a defining characteristic of the disorder (Figure 2.8 (b)). As the deterioration proceeds, the person's ability to make voluntary movements becomes more impaired, until she is unable to make deliberate actions at all.

Parkinson's disease results from damage to the part of the basal ganglia extending into the midbrain, called the **substantia nigra**. The damage may be caused by environmental toxins. Damage to the substantia nigra ultimately increases inhibition to the thalamus, which reduces the activation from the thalamus to the motor cortex (Figure 2.8 (c)). When the damage is severe the behavioral effect is **endo-akinesia**, the inability to make a voluntary movement without an external stimulus. If unattended, a person with Parkinson's disease will sit or lie still indefinitely. But if you put a bar of soap in his hand, he will wash himself. If you put a toothbrush in his hand, he will brush his teeth. As the disorder becomes more severe, more extreme stimulation is required to elicit a response.

Damage to other parts of the basal ganglia will have other effects. The rare disorder called **hemiballismus** results from damage to the part of the basal ganglia between the midbrain and thalamus, called the **subthalamic nucleus**. Damage here disrupts the usual inhibition sent to the thalamus. So instead of a precise voluntary action, a violent flinging motion occurs. Yet another basal ganglia disorder is **Tourette's syndrome**. Voluntary action may be unaffected, but as the result of a decrease in inhibition from the basal ganglia, involuntary movements occur in the form of twitches and tics. One rare but particularly unpleasant symptom is involuntary vocalization, including barks and curse words.

PROGRAMMING

At the same time that the motor plan is transmitted from the frontal cortex to the motor area and basal ganglia it is also transmitted to that vast super computer called the cerebellum. The cerebellum translates the motor plan into a motor program that specifies the precisely timed sequence of muscle contractions necessary to implement the plan and produce smooth movements (Braitenberg, 1967). At the level of the motor program, there is no tree, no snowball, no hand, and no arm. There is just a long, precisely ordered sequence of motor units that must contract in order to implement the plan. When the cerebellum is damaged, and hence the timing of the muscle movements is coarsened, voluntary movements become less precise and the ability to rapidly alternate movements that require antagonistic muscles is lost (Holmes, 1939). Richard Ivry and Steven Keele (1989) directly tested the role of the cerebellum in timing by having patients with cerebellar damage perform both a motor and a perceptual timing task. The patients' performance was more variable than normal when they tried to tap to a beat of 550 milliseconds. They were also less accurate than normal at discriminating two short (less than half second), slightly different temporal intervals defined by pairs of tones. When the timing of muscle movements is impaired the individual suffers from a motor coordination problem, called **ataxia**. Walking becomes wobbly, reaching attempts lead to overshoots, and it becomes difficult to touch your finger to your nose. Alcohol causes these symptoms because it disrupts cerebellar activity.

The cerebellum is comprised of three parts. It is the **neocerebellum** and **spinocerebellum** that turn motor plans into motor programs and transmit the motor programs to the spinal cord. The **vestibulocerebellum** contains the reflexes mentioned above for maintaining balance and coordinating eye movements, like the vestibular-ocular reflex. As we can see, these reflexes rapidly make many small adjustments that facilitate voluntary movement. Finally, the motor program is transmitted from the cerebellum to the brain stem and spinal cord, which contains the motor neurons that execute the motor unit contractions that cause the movement.

The control of action is complicated by the bifurcated nature of the brain and the need to control movements on both sides of the body. The left cortex is connected with the right cerebellum, which is connected with the right side of the body. The right cortex is connected with the left cerebellum, which is connected with the left side of the body. So each cortex plans the movements of the opposite side of the body. But during the actual execution of the plans, movements on both sides of the body must be coordinated. During execution it appears that one cortex is ultimately responsible for cross body coordination. Cross body coordination keeps you from getting in your own way and makes it possible to coordinate different movements on each side of the body, (for example in playing an instrument or swinging a bat or racquet). Since one hemisphere or the other normally takes control of coordinating cross-body coordination, it is normally difficult to move opposite body parts independently. For example, point your index fingers towards each other and then try to twirl one finger towards you and one away from you. You will find them both going in the same direction.

Cross body coordination is normally assisted by the **corpus callosum**, which transmits information between the left and right cortex, and the **massa intermedia**, which transmits information between the left and right thalamus. Nonetheless, the cognitive functioning of the many individuals born without a massa intermedia is indistinguishable from everyone else. Similarly, when the corpus callosum was severed in a few individuals as a treatment for intractable epilepsy, the operation did not impair their motor coordination. However, it did make it possible for them to make more independent hand movements than are seen in normal individuals, such as copying two different pictures at the same time. Since cross-body coordination is rarely a problem, there must be redundant pathways for it.

EXECUTION

An advantage of the motor system heterarchy is that it provides redundant sources of control. In different situations, you may perform exactly the same action under the control of either the premotor or supplementary motor cortex. An action may be performed under the external control of both proprioceptive and visual feedback, or the **external control** of either proprioceptive or visual feedback, or **under internal control** without any feedback at all!

Feedback. When a movement is executed feedback is generated that ultimately reaches all the areas where the action was planned and programmed. So the information pathways in the motor system are circuits. The motor control circuits maintain control of the motion through both visual and proprioceptive feedback. You can type under visual control or under proprioceptive control. For example, West (1967) showed that experienced typists detected 50 percent of their errors even when they could not see what they were typing. Rabbitt (1967, 1968) reported even higher error detection rates for a simpler key-pressing task. You can make accurate hand movements in the dark, hence without visual feedback, or wearing a blood pressure cuff tightened to eliminate proprioceptive feedback.

Information about the locations of body parts is conveniently located in the body map of the **somatosensory area**, located conveniently adjacent to the motor area where body-part movements are guided, as shown on the right in Figure 2.6. The somatosensory area is divided into sub-areas that each receives input from a specific part of the body. Activation of neurons in this area produces the sensation of feeling in some part of the body. So this is where you experience the sensation of your own body. When you shake hands, the sensory neurons in the hand send proprioceptive signals that ultimately arrive at the part of the somatosensory cortex corresponding to your hand in your body map. It is the activation of these cortical neurons that produce the feeling of having a hand. Proprioceptive and/or visual input to the hand area in the somatosensory cortex is used to plan and execute the hand movements

The body maps in the motor area and somatosensory area were discovered before the body maps in the basal ganglia and cerebellum. The discoverer of the body maps, Wilder Penfield (Penfield & Rasmussen, 1950) first drew a little caricature to show how the control of the body is laid out on the cortex. This tradition is continued in Figure 2.6. But you should be clear that there is not a little person inscribed on your brain. The figure merely gives an indication of how the body map is laid out.

Phantom limbs. Suppose that a person is unfortunate enough to lose a body part, such as a finger, hand, arm, or leg. The person is surprised to discover that after the amputation he still feels like he has the missing limb. Often he feels that he is able to move the phantom limb as easily as a fleshy one. Everything is just the way it was before the amputation. It is just that the limb is no longer there. Why this is so was demonstrated by the physician and psychologist, V. S. Ramachandran. Under normal circumstances, neurons in the body map receive signals from sensory neurons in the body part they represent. Of course, once that body part is lost this can no longer be so. The neurons in the cortex that represent your right hand can not be receiving signals from neurons in your right hand once it has been cut off. But if your hand is cut off, within hours the neurons that transmit information to immediately adjacent areas extend their processes into the cortical area previously receiving input from the right hand. So the neurons in the body map for the right hand continue to receive sensory information. It is just that it is no longer coming from the right hand. If you look again at Figure 2.6 you will see that the area in the body map for the hand is next to the area for the face. When Ramachandran reached out and touched the cheek of a man whose arm had been amputated, the patient reported that Ramachandran had not only touched his cheek, but also his phantom hand (Ramachandran, Rogers-Ramachandran, & Stewart, 1992).

Ramachandran and his colleagues (Ramachandran, Rogers-Ramachandran, & Cobb, 1995) made use of the fact that limb movements can be guided by purely visual feedback to diagnose and treat an usual kind of pain. Recall that the amputation of a limb often leaves the sensation of a phantom limb behind. Some people feel like they can move this phantom limb, while others feel like they are unable to move their phantom limb. For this latter group, it feels like the limb is curled into an uncomfortable position, and the individual feels excruciating pain. Ramachandran cut two holes in a box and had such an individual insert his remaining hand through one hole and his phantom hand through the other. On the other side of the box was a mirror that reflected an image of the remaining hand, so when he looked over the top of the box he saw two hands: the remaining hand and its reflection in the position of the phantom hand. Ramachandran told the patient to try to move his two hands in some cooperative pattern, clapping, twirling, etc. Suddenly, under visual control, the patient discovered that he could move his phantom hand perfectly well, and when he could move it the pain went away.

In fact, some well-learned tasks that are normally performed under the guidance of feedback can be performed accurately without any feedback at all. Evidence that actions that manipulatory movements may be made without feedback comes from a rare disability called a **neuropathy** in which a patient loses the sensory neurons in a limb, so there was no proprioceptive feedback to guide movement (Rothwell, Traub, Day, Obeso, Thomas, & Marsden, 1982); however, the motor neurons are preserved. Such a patient was still able to make a complex hand movement such as tracing a circle in the air in the dark, even though no visual or proprioceptive feedback was available.

Fitts' Law. There are two kinds of proprioceptive feedback: gross short loop feedback from the spinal cord and brain stem and fine long loop feedback from the cerebellum. The short loop feedback allows rapid, approximate corrections to the motion of the limb. Proprioceptive feedback can reach the brain from a variety of muscles in less than 25 milliseconds and from tongue and eye muscles in only 4-6 milliseconds (Adams, 1976, p. 215). The long loop feedback allows slower, fine corrections to the motion of the limb. When a grasping action is filmed and examined in detail it is found to have two components. Most of the distance to the target is covered by a rapid ballistic phase. The hand is simply pointed at the target and a series of motor units are contracted that cause a rapid movement of the limb that places the hand close to the target. Then the hand is guided, under the control of feedback, over the remaining short distance to the target.

Hence, the control of a guided movement during its execution is not continuous. Rather, the maximum control is exerted at the beginning of the action and at the end. Thus the speed profile of a guided movement is not much different from the speed profile of an airplane. Just as an airplane speeds up at take-off and slows down at landing, a guided movement speeds up at the beginning and slows down at the end. Just as the airplane is under the finest degree of control at landing (the rest of the time it is only necessary to point the plane in the correct direction and leave it on autopilot), a guided movement is under the finest degree of control just before it reaches the target. As was the case for the airplane, the rest of the time it is only necessary to point the body part in the correct direction and move it as fast as possible without feedback. It is the time it takes to process the long loop feedback at the end of a guided movement and to make any necessary motor adjustment that slows the movement at the end. Since most of the distance traveled by a guided movement consumes only a small portion of its travel time, the total movement time increases only modestly as a function of distance. The relationship between movement time and the distance and size of the target:

$T = a + B \log_2 (2D/W)$
T = movement time
a,B = constants
D = distance of movement from start to target center
W = width of the target

is called Fitts' Law after the psychologist who formulated it, Paul Fitts (Fitts, 1954). Movement time changes as the log of the distance, reflecting the fact that movements to targets farther away do not take much longer than movements to close targets. The constants a and B in the equation are determined by the body part that is being moved. As we move from finger to wrist to arm the effect of distance on movement time increases. Notice that the more cortical area devoted to a body part, hence the finer control of it, the less effect that distance has. Fitts' Law has practical significance for the design of tools and work spaces because it allows us to predict in advance how rapidly someone will be able to perform a task requiring guided movements (Proctor & Van Zandt, 1994; Sanders & McCormick, 1993).

APRAXIA

Damage to the parietal, premotor, or supplementary motor areas of the cortex, to subcortical pathways connecting them, and to the basal ganglia, may all impair the ability to carry out routine actions. Even though the person can still move her hands, arms, and legs she has difficulty combining movements to perform a purposeful action. For example, a person may no longer be able to get dressed. Somehow, everything gets all tangled up, with the arm in the wrong sleeve and the blouse inside out. Using a knife and fork, piling up a pile of blocks, writing a brief note, may all now be insurmountably complex. Sometimes a parietal injury results in an action being performed in a less efficient way. For example, a person who has lost the fine control for grasping objects now overshoots them and must search the area with a cupped hand before the target is obtained. The normal cutting of meat may be replaced with a rapid sawing motion. Sometimes some actions are impaired while others are not. Though the symptoms vary with location of the damage, all these disorders are sometimes collectively referred to as **apraxia**. However, all apraxic disorders are not the same and milder forms seem to reveal specific stages of the operation of the action system (Cubelli, Machetti, Boscolo, & Delaa Sala, 2000; Rothi, Ochipa, & Heilman, 1997). Apraxic disorders have been categorized in three ways.

First, the external versus internal control distinction mentioned above has been used to distinguish between actions involving a tool or object, e.g., using a toothbrush, and actions not involving an object, e.g., waving or pointing. Actions that make use of tools are called **transitive** and actions that do not use tools are called **intransitive**. Some patients are apraxic for only transitive actions, while others are apraxic for only intransitive actions, which tends to support this distinction. On the other hand, it is has not been established that apraxia for transitive actions is associated with parietal, premotor, and cerebellar injuries and apraxia for intransitive actions is associated with supplementary motor and basal ganglia injuries (Cubelli, et al., 2000). So if the external and internal control subsystems exist, the basis for them remains murky.

Second, if we consider only actions that use tools, some patients are able to perform a familiar action when given the appropriate tool but unable to pantomime it. For example, a patient who cannot pantomime how to use a knife and fork may perform adequately when the actual utensils are placed in her hand. The patient can still turn a screwdriver correctly, but when she attempts to pantomime it she fails to put her hand in a grasping posture before turning. This deficit suggests that the representation of the action is intact in memory but the patient has difficulty retrieving it and needs the strong cue of the tool to do so. Some patients are able to both perform and pantomime familiar actions, such as using a knife and fork, correctly, but are unable to imitate novel actions. This deficit suggests that the representations of familiar actions can still be retrieved to direct action, but connections with the parietal cortex for translating visual information into actions have been damaged, which makes the imitation of novel actions impossible (Bartolo, et al., 2001). Finally, as mentioned at the beginning of the chapter, a woman became unable to perform familiar actions, though she could imitate novel actions perfectly. In this case it seems the performance of familiar actions was still under the control of memory, but either the representations of the actions or the selection of the correct representation was impaired.

Third, we may distinguish between being able to recognize an action and being able to perform it. Apraxia only implies being impaired in performing the action. Many apraxic patients can recognize an action, such as using a spoon or toothbrush, if someone demonstrates it. However, sometimes not only is the action performed incorrectly, but also the patient does not recognize the correct action when he is shown it (Heilman, Rothi, & Valenstein, 1982). In contrast, some patients can imitate the action correctly but cannot recognize it. This related disorder, called visual agnosia, is discussed in the chapter on recognition.

SUMMARY OF VOLUNTARY ACTIONS

- Initially, a voluntary action is planned in the premotor, the supplementary motor cortex, or some other specialized area of the frontal cortex.
  - The premotor cortex makes use of perceptual information from the parietal cortex.
  - Planning an action involves three steps:
    * Retrieving representations of final body postures for completing each movement from memory.
    * Selecting the representation that best fits the current situation.
    * Modifying the representation as necessary. First the posture of the body part closest to the target of the action is planned, e.g., the hand in a grasping action, and then the adjacent body parts, i.e., the arm. Hence, planning by components (PBC) occurs.

- The performance of a voluntary action is in the control of a heterarchy.
  - There is a hierarchical command structure from the cortex to the sub-cortex to the brain stem to the spinal cord, but at each level there is more than one source of control exerted in parallel. Aspects of the plan are communicated from the premotor cortex in parallel directly to:
    * the motor cortex, which provides guidance for the direction of the limb movements, including the movement around obstacles, and also communicates with the basal ganglia and brain stem.
    * the basal ganglia, which initiate the sequence of actions through pathways down to the brain stem and through the thalamus back to the premotor cortex.
    * the cerebellum, which programs the sequential muscle movements necessary for the action and also communicates with the brain stem.
    * the brain stem and spinal cord, which execute the muscle movements that comprise the action.
  - Communication among the various structures of the action system is facilitated by the existence of body maps within each structure such that each area within a map represents and controls a particular body part.
  - The right premotor cortex communicates with the left cerebellum, which directs the left side of the body and vice versa. In this way the control of the body is divided, with each cortex controlling body parts on the opposite side. In addition, one cortex takes responsibility for coordinating the movements on each side of the body.

⚬ Actions may be executed under the control of both visual and proprioceptive feedback, under the control of either visual or proprioceptive feedback, or without feedback at all.

      * The internal control system, comprised of the supplementary motor cortex and basal ganglia, does not appear to make use of feedback. The external control system in the premotor cortex makes use of visual and proprioceptive feedback from the parietal cortex and the cerebellum to select or modify an action representation or to construct one from scratch.

      * Actions are executed under the control of short-loop feedback to subcortical structures that make quick adjustments possible and long-loop feedback to cortical structures that make finer adjustments possible.

⚬ Damage to a part of the motor system may impair the ability to carry out some kind of routine action. An impairment of this kind is called apraxia.

SKILL LEARNING

The multiple levels of redundant control that make the motor system so complicated have a purpose. They are what make skill learning possible, as control is passed from voluntary to automatic control systems through the creation of a detailed plan and program that may be retrieved rather than constructed. A **skill** is an action that has come to be performed faster and more accurately as the result of practice. Pure motor skills, like snapping ones fingers, may be distinguished from perceptual-motor skills, like using a spoon. As their name implies, perceptual-motor skills make use of some sort of perceptual information to guide the action. However, both motor skills and perceptual skills are learned in the same way so it will not be necessary to distinguish between them here. In fact, the categories overlap because some actions can be performed both with and without perceptual guidance.

STAGES

We may broadly distinguish among three stages in skill learning (Fitts & Posner, 1967). Initially, when someone tries to walk, or ride a bicycle, or sew, or catch a baseball for the first time, there is no plan for the action in memory. Rather, the entire action requires the construction and execution of many small motor plans for the individual movements comprising it. Many of the attempts to perform the action result in failure. So constant attention is required to determine whether each movement is correct. This was originally called the **cognitive** stage of skill learning but is now called the **declarative stage**. Skill learning was called knowing how in Chapter 1 and is also called **Procedural Memory**. Knowing what is also called **Declarative Memory**. Declarative memory implies conscious awareness of what you know. For example knowing what something looks like implies being able to describe it. The first stage of skill learning is called the declarative stage because you do in fact have a declarative representation of the action in memory. You know what you are supposed to do. You could recognize the action if someone else performed it. However, you do not yet have a procedural representation of the action. You do not yet know how do to it yourself.

      With practice, as the result of feedback, multiple representations of slightly different versions of movement are stored in memory. As a result, the movements required to perform an action become more accurate and fewer corrections are necessary. For example, every time you reach out and grasp something, the object is in a slightly different position in relation to your body, so a slightly different final posture is encoded in memory. With practice, an infant builds up a collection of reach and grasp posture representations for different objects in different locations. The next time a similar action must be taken, the posture of the most similar successful action is retrieved and used to guide the new movement. In the **associative** stage, the amount of attention to the action is reduced because to construct a plan it is only necessary to modify the posture representation of a previous action. It is not necessary to start from scratch. Because of the need for modifications, the skill still requires attention.

Over repeated trials, a repertoire of successful postures for similar actions is built up in memory so that almost all new actions are similar to some previous successful action. In the **autonomous** stage the posture of an identical previous action is retrieved and used as the plan. Since the action no longer requires planning, some other activity that requires planning may be carried out simultaneously. This is how you can carry on a conversation while walking, reaching for something, feeding yourself at dinner etc., since none of these well-practiced actions require planning. The representations being retrieved to guide performance only contain information relevant to making accurate motor movements. Hence they are procedural representations.

RELATIONSHIP BETWEEN DECLARATIVE AND PROCEDURAL (ASSOCIATIVE AND AUTONOMOUS) STAGES OF MOTOR LEARNING

During the declarative stage of motor learning the novel action is under the control of the declarative system as the person recalls what to do first, what to do second, etc. Each time the task is performed under the control of the declarative system, a representation of how the action was performed is encoded as part of the procedural system. After sufficient repetitions a procedural representation has been formed (hence the associative stage of learning has been reached.

Marc Jeannerod (1994) has studied the relationship between declarative and procedural motor learning and found evidence of two distinct but interrelated systems. For example, he and his colleagues (Slachevsky, Pillon, Renie, Levy, Jeannerod, & Dubois, 2003) compared the performance of normal individuals and those with frontal lobe damage on a novel motor task. The task was to trace over a straight line on a computer screen. The participant moved a stylus over a graphics tablet that was placed underneath the computer screen so that the participant could not see her or his hand or the path of the line he was drawing when he moved the stylus across the tablet. Without informing the participant, the computer displaced the angle of motion produced by the participant to the right when plotting it on the computer screen. Therefore, in order to trace the line shown on the screen a participant would have to displace his angle of motion to the left (see Figure 2.9). Eighteen normal participants performed the task, as well as 20 individuals with frontal lobe damage. None of the 20 individuals with frontal lobe damage was impaired in the control of the hand used to perform the task. Participants performed the task repeatedly and on each trial the size of the displacement angle added to the path was increased.

As can be see from Figure 2.9, at the end of each trial the line that the participant was drawing emerged from under the masking screen and the participant could compare it with the line that he was supposed to be tracing. All the normal participants explicitly reported the correct strategy to correct for the added right angle displacement (move the hand at an angle to the left of the target) in order to trace the line before trial 5. After the sixth trial they were able to

FIGURE 2.9

The target is a vertical line. With a 22 degree angular displacement to the right, when a participant attempts to trace the target by drawing a vertical line as shown in 1, the line drawn emerges from under the mask as shown in 1'. When the participant compensates by drawing a line with a 22 degree angular displacement to the left as shown in 2, the line drawn emerges from under the mask as shown in 2' (Slachevsky et al., 2003).

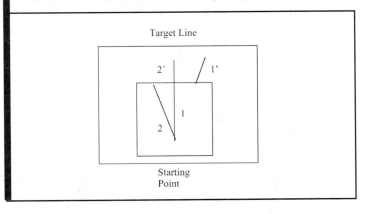

implement the strategy and trace over the target line by displacing the hand motion to the left. However, recall that a participant could not see his hand, or the precise angle of the pathway he took, because these were masked by the screen. When the participants selected from a set of alternatives the path their hands followed to reproduce the target line, they severely underestimated the displacement angle of the pathway. Hence, normal individuals were able to create a declarative representation of the strategy necessary to trace the target line. They were able to implement this strategy in a procedural representation that accurately produced a trace of the line. However, the proprioceptive feedback from performing this motion was inadequate for creating an adequate declarative representation of it. Even though the individuals were accurately moving their hands under the mask to trace the target line, they did not know accurately the angle at which they were moving their hands.

Nine of the individuals with frontal lobe damage also reported the correct strategy to transfer the lines before trial 5, and the performance of these participants was indistinguishable from the normal participants. However, six individuals with frontal lobe damage took longer than five trials to report the correction strategy, and five individuals with frontal lobe damage were never able to report the correction strategy at all (though all individuals noticed that their lines deviated from the target above the mask). Though these individuals showed some improvement on the task, their performance was significantly worse than for the 27 individuals who were immediately able to state the correction strategy. These results demonstrate the importance of declarative representation in learning. It is first necessary to understand what has to be done and to repeatedly make conscious efforts to do it, in order to encode an accurate representation of how the motion should be made.

EXPONENTIAL LAW OF PRACTICE

Complex movements are built up from simple ones through the creation of hierarchically organized motor programs and motor plans. For example, consider writing. Initially, each letter must be laboriously created by executing a sequence of strokes. However, with enough practice a single motor program can be created for an entire letter so that the entire letter is planned and executed. Similarly, with enough repetition a letter group program can be created, enabling more than one letter to be planned and executed at a time. Given enough practice, these programs can be embedded into still larger programs and whole words can be planned at once. The advantage of the large motor program is speed. A pianist's fingers can execute movements only 60 milliseconds apart.

When sequences of smaller movements are hierarchically organized into larger ones, each subsequence of the hierarchy is called a **chunk**. Hierarchically arranging a lot of small chunks into one large one greatly decreases the time to plan and execute an action because only one large chunk must be retrieved and executed instead of a lot of little ones. During the associative phase of learning, as the number of chunks required to plan and execute an action decrease, the time to perform the action rapidly decreases. For example, a British psychologist, E. R. F. W. Crossman (1959) measured the performance of the operators of cigar-making machines of different years of experience. Figure 2.10 shows the results of his study. The figure shows an initial large decrease in cigar rolling time for novice workers and after that an apparently negligible decrease for experienced workers. However, it is not really possible to tell from Figure 2.10   whether

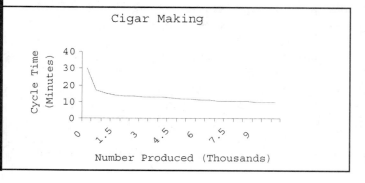

FIGURE 2.10
The effect of practice on the time to roll cigars plotted on a linear time scale (Crossman, 1959). The function is the average cycle-time for making a cigar over one week's production for one operator. The x-axis is the total production by the operator since beginning work.

experienced workers continue to improve because their speeds are compressed into a narrow range when compared with those for novice workers. Figure 2.11 shows exactly the same data re-plotted on a graph in which the production and time scales are logarithmic scales rather than linear ones. From Figure 2.11 it is clear that even during the autonomous phase, practice on a skill continues to improve performance for years. He found that the time to operate a cigar-rolling machine decreased for at least two years and three million cycles, at which time the operator approached the mechanical operating limit of the machine. Figure 2.11 illustrates the **exponential law of practice** (Heathcote, Brown, & Mewhort, 2000). This is described by the function:

$$T = A + Be^{-aN}$$

T = time to perform task
N = number of times task has been performed
A = asymptotic time to perform action
B = change in time as function of learning

The equation describes the function shown in Figure 2.11 . This is the precise function predicted by the chunking explanation of motor learning described above. As can be seen in the figure, the improvement in performance between successive repetitions of a task decreases as the number of repetitions increase. Exponential functions are always plotted on a logarithmic time-scale axis, as in Figure 2.11 , rather than on a linear time-scale, as in Figure 2.10 , so that the small differences that continue with extended practice can be seen on the graph. However, even though the function approximates a straight line when plotted on a log scale, do not lose sight of the fact that the actual relationship between speed of performance and practice is as shown in Figure 2.10 .

Until Heathcote et al.'s (2000) review, a slightly different function called the **power law of practice** (Proctor & Van Zandt, 1994) was believed to best describe motor skill. All older books and journals that describe skill learning, as well as some more recent writings, describe this function instead of the exponential function.

Notice again that in Figure 2.11 the practice function only appears to flatten when it reaches the cycle time of the cigar-making machine. Though the improvement in the performance of a motor skill with practice eventually becomes tiny, as far we know there is no point at which improvement in

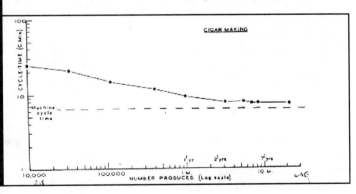

FIGURE 2.11
The effect of practice on the speed of cigar making plotted on a logarithmic time scale. Same data as Figure 2.8. (Crossman, 1959.)

task performance, however slight, ceases altogether. The asymptote (A) is never quite reached in motor skill learning. There is always improvement with practice. Once a motor skill is learned, it is never forgotten. The familiar example is that no one ever forgets how to ride a bicycle. Actually, this has not been tested. But a variety of other motor skills have been tested over retention intervals of up to several years, and no forgetting has been found (Fleishman & Parker, 1962; Hammerton, 1963).

DISTRIBUTED VERSUS MASSED EFFECTS OF PRACTICE

The accumulation of posture representations can account for the general effect of practice on the performance of a skill described by the power law. However, there is one aspect of skill learning that it does not account for. This is the advantage of distributed over massed practice for long-term retention. In the 1970's, when mail was still sorted by humans, the British postal service was faced with the prospect of teaching large numbers of postal workers to type so that they could operate keyboard driven sorting machines. They turned to the Applied Psychology Unit of the Medical Research Council whose director, Alan Baddeley, conducted a study of different practice schemes (Baddeley & Longman, 1978). Trainees were each given one of four different practice schemes: a single one-hour practice session a day, two one-hour practice sessions a day, a single two-hour practice session a day, or two two-hour practice sessions a day. The number of days to learn the keyboard was 35, 22, 22, and 13 for the respective groups. So the more time per day that was spent practicing, the fewer the number of days in which the skill was learned. However, when the same data are examined as a function of the number of hours to learn the keyboard, the results are 35, 43, 43, and 50, for the respective groups. When examined this way it can be seen that the skill was learned with fewer hours of practice when the practice was distributed over more days. Figure 2.12 shows the final level of performance after 60 hours of practice for the single-hour a day group and 80 hours of practice for the other three groups, and the level of performance after **retention intervals** of one, three and nine months. (The retention interval is the period of time between training and test. So no typing was done during this interval.) After nine months, trainees with only a single hour a day of practice had the same level of retention as trainees with more than one hour a day of practice. The postal workers who learned in the fewest number of days had the poorest retention of all. After nine months it appears that the number of days of practice rather than the amount of time spent each day practicing is the most important determiner of retention. Baddeley and Longman's (1978) study of learning to type illustrates two general principles of skill learning. On the one hand, massed practice produces better immediate performance than distributed practice (Shea & Morgan, 1979). On the other hand, distributed practice leads to better long-term retention than massed practice (Magill & Hall, 1990). This leaves the question of why distributed practice is superior. In various later chapters some hypotheses about the short-term superiority of massed learning and the long-term superiority of distributed learning will be presented. However, this is a question that remains to be answered.

FEEDBACK IN SKILLED PERFORMANCE

The four action subsystems differ in the extent to which feedback is required to guide the movement of a body part during the time that an action is being executed. The short rapid movements involved in vocalization and eye movement do not allow for modification during the brief period when the movement is being executed. In contrast, feedback may be useful for the slower movements made in locomotion and essential for the precise movements required by manipulation. In addition to planning, it may be that the premotor area also contributes to the guidance of voluntary actions during their execution in response to feedback.

Adams, Goetz, and Marshall (1972) showed that reducing perceptual information was even more disruptive to skilled performers than to unskilled performers. What is available during training determines the kind of feedback needed during skilled performance. For example, Notterman and Tufano (1980) showed that a repetitive motion learned under visual control required less proprioceptive feedback. Conversely, when Proteau, Marteniuk, and Levesque (1992) had people practice hitting a target without visual feedback they found that later letting them see what they were doing hurt performance. Depending on how it was learned, a skilled movement may make use of both or either of visual and proprioceptive feedback for guidance, or it may be performed without the use of feedback at all.

Even when placed in an environment in which the normal visual-proprioceptive correlations do not apply, for example, one in which

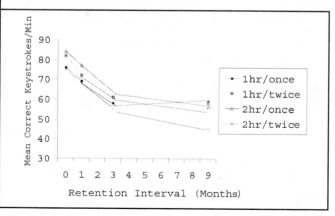

FIGURE 2.12
The retention of typing learned under four different practice schedules. (Baddeley & Longman, 1978)

your hand feels like it is in one place and looks like it is in another, the visual-proprioceptive correlations are recalibrated so that accurate movements can be made.   Perhaps you remember how difficult it was the first time you tried to comb your hair while looking in the mirror.   Nonetheless, after a few attempts it became less disturbing to see your hand move away from you as you moved it away from the mirror. Stratton (1887) demonstrated just how far the motor system could accommodate to the visual system when he wore an inverting lens over one eye (the other eye was patched).   When looking through the lens, down appeared up and right appeared left.   Over a period of days his motor system recalibrated so that he could reach for objects and move about normally.

The ability to recalibrate proprioceptive feedback to be consistent with visual feedback is what makes tool use possible.   A novice carpenter feels the hammer handle in his hand.   A journeyman feels the hammer as part of his hand and can place the hammerhead on the nail as easily as he could pound it with his fist.

RIGIDITY AND FLEXIBILITY IN TRANSFER OF TRAINING

The advantage of chunking many small motor programs into one large one is speed.   The disadvantage of a single large motor program for a complicated action is its inflexibility.   For example, if the notes on a piano or the letters on a computer keyboard were rearranged, you would have to learn a new program. Training on one particular spatial arrangement of keys on the keyboard does not transfer to another spatial arrangement.   So skilled motor performance appears to be ultimately based on a spatial representation of the task that guides the selection of the limb postures during planning.   Consequently, there is no transfer of training to a task in which the spatial arrangement of target objects is different.

On the other hand, as long as the spatial arrangement of targets (e.g., piano keys) is maintained, training does transfer to the same action performed with entirely different muscles.   You can write equally well on a paper by moving your wrist or on a chalkboard by moving your arm.   You can even trace letters with your toes.   All of these motor programs direct entirely different motor units yet translate the same motor plan.   The comedian Harpo Marx demonstrated transfer of training by playing the piano with his elbow!   The degree of transfer depends on the degree of variability in the training materials.   The task dimensions along which training transfers suggest that skilled performance depends on more than retrieving posture representations.   There is also a representation indicating the spatial locations of the targets in relation to the person's body.   As long as new tasks are consistent with the spatial representation, a high degree of transfer occurs, even when the motor movements are quite different.   However, there is a limit to the generalization of a spatial representation across motor programs.   Right-handed people who learn a skill with their right hand cannot then perform it well with their left hand.   However, the skill can be relearned separately with the left hand.

SUMMARY

- There are two ways of planning an action: constructing the plan of a novel action and retrieving the plan of a familiar action
    - Novel actions must be planned over time as representations of the necessary postures are retrieved and combined.
    - Novel actions become familiar because as the result of repeating an action, the representations of the individual postures become hierarchically arranged into a single representation of the entire action.   This is called skill learning.   Skill learning passes through three stages.
        * In the declarative stage there are no representations of the entire action in memory.
        * In the associative stage a number of representations, i.e. chunks, are hierarchically organized into a single representation of the entire action.   As a result, the time to perform the action decreases at an exponential rate.
        * In the autonomous stage a single representation is retrieved and executed without the need for adjustment during planning.

- For a familiar action a single representation of the entire action is retrieved and executed.

- Distributed practice produces retention over a longer interval than massed practice. There is little or no forgetting of a routinely practiced skill even after a long retention interval when no practice was possible.

- Skilled motor performance appears to be ultimately based on a spatial representation of the task that guides the selection of the limb postures to perform instances of the task. Hence, there is transfer of training to a task maintaining the same spatial arrangement, even if it involvements different body parts, but there is no transfer of training to a task in which the spatial arrangement of target objects is different.

SUMMARY OF CHAPTER

- The ability to perform actions is the result of two distinct methods of muscle control:
  - Reflexes are rapid, unlearned responses to specific stimuli. Many different reflexes play vital, if subordinate, roles as components of the action, perceptual, and emotional systems.
    - * Voluntary actions are constructed in response to novel situations and then may be retrieved and repeated if the same circumstances occur again. Voluntary action has two discrete stages: planning and performance.

- The performance of a voluntary action is in the control of a heterarchy in which
  - the action is planned in the prefrontal cortex and performed by the motor cortex, basal ganglia, cerebellum, brain stem, and spinal cord.
  - Spatial representations of body part movements in the prefrontal and motor cortex are recoded as temporal representations of the sequence of body part movements and muscle contractions in the basal ganglia and cerebellum.

- Planning an action involves three steps:
  - Retrieving representations of final body postures for completing each movement from memory.
  - Selecting the representation that best fits the current situation.
  - Modifying the representation as necessary. First the posture of the body part closest to the target of the action is planned, e.g., the hand in a grasping action, and then the adjacent body parts, i.e., the arm. Hence, planning by components (PBC) occurs.

- The brain stem and spinal cord, which execute the muscle movements that comprise the action.
  - Actions may be executed under the control of both visual and proprioceptive feedback, under the control of either visual or proprioceptive feedback, or without feedback at all.
  - Damage to a part of the motor system may impair the ability to carry out some kind of routine action, called apraxia.

- There are two ways of planning an action: constructing the plan of a novel action and retrieving the plan of a familiar action. Skill learning has three stages:
  - Declarative "knowing what to do" stage
  - Associative learning stage
  - Autonomous "knowing how to do it" procedural stage

- Distributed practice produces retention over a longer interval than massed practice. There is little or no forgetting of a routinely practiced skill even after a long retention interval when no practice was possible.

Chapter 3

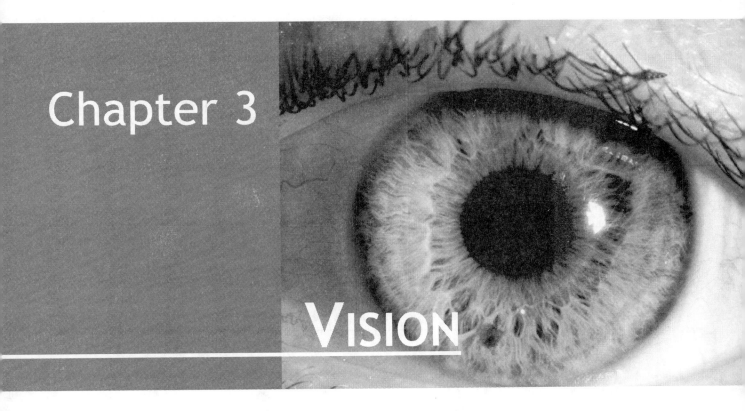

VISION

I n November 1966 a twenty-five-year-old soldier home on leave accidentally suffered carbon monoxide poisoning from leaking gas fumes. This accident was a serious one, since exposure to carbon monoxide can cause brain damage and death. Following resuscitation, the soldier was able at first to converse with relatives. But the next day he lapsed into a coma from which he recovered only slowly. In a month he was alert and talkative again. However, he experienced severe visual problems.

Seven months after the accident the soldier was admitted to Boston Veterans Administration Hospital for extensive tests. Most of his cognitive abilities, such as language use and memory, appeared normal. Most of his perceptual system was also intact. He could readily identify and name things through their feel, smell, or sound. In addition, his most elementary visual abilities were also preserved. He was able to identify colors, discriminate between lights of different intensities, and tell in what direction an object was moving. Nevertheless, the soldier's visual perception was severely impaired. He was unable to recognize objects, letters, or people when he saw them. His impairment was so severe that on one occasion he identified his own reflection in a mirror as the face of his doctor!

A common factor in these recognition failures appeared to be the inability to identify any visual shape or form. To test this hypothesis, two neurologists, D. Frank Benson and John P. Greenberg (1969), gave the soldier a variety of tests in which he had to verbally identify a pattern, copy a pattern, select which two of several patterns were the same, or simply say whether two patterns were the same or different. The results of a typical task are shown in Figure 3.1. In this task the soldier had to mark one of four comparison patterns

FIGURE 3.1

Matching task. The soldier who suffered from carbon monoxide poisoning was unable to mark the appropriate matching figure in any of these examples. (Benson & Greenberg, 1969).

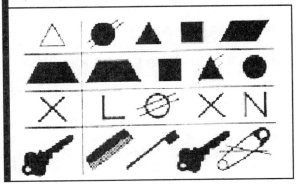

that was the same as a standard pattern on the left. He was unable to match any of them correctly. All of the results from this and similar tests were equally dismal. The soldier was simply unable to distinguish visual shapes from one another. He could not even tell a circle from a square.

The soldier's disorder dramatically demonstrates that pattern perception requires much more than the eye's ability to detect a beam of light. A great deal of cognitive processing is required in order for the observer to figure out whether the light beam was reflected off a square object or a round one. This is an extremely complex task.

RETINAL-IMAGE THEORY

You have good reason to believe that you usually perceive the world accurately. If you look out your window and see a tree, quite likely a tree is really there. This fact is so unremarkable that you hardly ever stop to think about it. Yet the task is quite a formidable one. How do you go about determining the shapes and locations of objects through vision alone? For example, when you see a square, how do you know that it is a square and not a rectangle, a parallelogram, or a trapezoid?

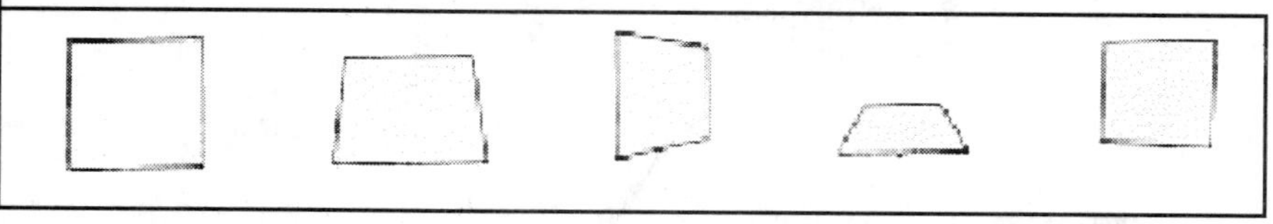

The first step toward answering this question is to realize that the answer is not obvious. That is, you don't simply see the square as a square because that's its shape. The case study of the soldier demonstrates that perceiving light is not equivalent to perceiving the shapes of objects. Figure 3.2 shows the image of an object on the retina. When you look at an object, the light reflecting from the object passes through the lens of the eye, which focuses an upside-down image on the retina at the back of the eyeball. The retina is a curved surface containing light-sen-

FIGURE 3.2
Visual processing begins with an inverted image of an object on the retina

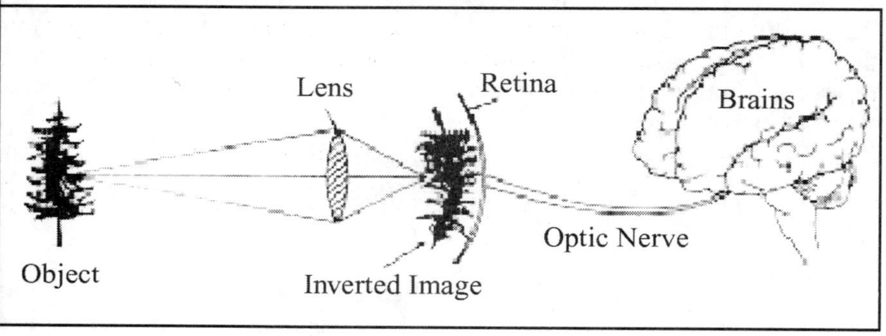

FIGURE 3.3
How a square may appear when viewed from different perspectives.

sitive cells that transmit signals along the optic nerve to the brain. According to the retinal-image theory of pattern recognition, when you look at an object like a square the retinal image is transmitted to the brain, where it is turned right side up and recognized immediately. The problem with this simple theory is that unless you are looking at the square head-on in absolutely even illumination (which is practically impossible to obtain), the image of a square does not fall on your retina. Instead, the image will most likely be some trapezoidal shape because the side of the square closest to you will produce a longer edge in its retinal image (Figure 3.3). Often the shape will be even less square-like, since the square will be broken into light and dark areas by glare and shadow.

When we turn from this artificial example of viewing a single simple shape to the everyday perception of the environment, the problems of a retinal-image theory of perception increase a thousand-fold. Consider what you see when you look around a room. Perhaps you see walls, tables, chairs (all with rectangular surfaces), a round clock on the wall, a picture, and a tree through a window. But if you stop to analyze what the retinal image must be like, you realize that no shape in the retinal image is actually as you perceive it. The right angles you see everywhere as parts of walls, tables, etc., are almost all acute or oblique angles when they fall on your retinas. Similarly, the round clock is likely to be an ellipse in the retinal image.

Colors and sizes also differ between the retinal image and your perception. A shadow falls across an orange couch, yet the entire couch appears to be the same color. One chair of two is closer to you, yet both appear to be the same size. You can easily tell the difference between the picture and the window, though the images they present to your retinas are very similar. The most remarkable aspect of the discrepancies between the retinal image and perception is that usually it is perception, not your retinal sensation, which is veridical. Your eyes lie, but your mind tells you the truth!

OVERVIEW OF VISUAL PROCESSING

Much of what the visual system does is below awareness, which makes it seem effortless. However, the effortlessness of visual perception is misleading. The way you actually see is much more complicated than the effortless process revealed by introspection. It is the result of an enormous number of computations being performed below the level of awareness. Hundreds of millions of years of evolution have endowed you with a super computer that performs millions of computations on the visual input before you are aware that you have seen anything at all.

Figure 3.3 shows that a square can cast many different images on the retina. However, the image that the square casts is determined by its position in relation to the observer. For example, images (b) and (d) occur when the bottom edge of the square is closer to the observer than the top edge, so the square is either above or below the observer. Furthermore, as the relative position of the square in relation to the observer changes, its image changes in a predictable way. For example, if the eyes fixate first to the left, then on the center, then to the right of a square, its image on the retina will successively be as shown in (c), (a), and (e). An accurate three-dimensional representation of a three-dimensional shape can be constructed from two or more two-dimensional images of it when seen from different locations. This is exactly what the visual system does. It constructs a three-dimensional representation from a sequence of pairs of two-dimensional retinal images.

The anatomical locations of the main components of the visual processing system are shown in Figure 3.4. The system is also shown schematically in Figure 3.5. Visual processing begins when light passes through the lens embedded in the front of the eyeball and is focused on the back of the eyeball, called the **retina**. After light falls on the retina, the visual input passes through three stages of processing before perception occurs.

The first stage is the **sensory registration** stage. The retinal images are encoded and sent up the optic pathway to the thalamus. The retinal images are sharpened, and the different kinds of information they contain are sorted out and sent on to specific cortical locations for further processing.

The second stage is **feature analysis**. The most detailed description of the input is sent from the thalamus to the **primary visual cortex** of the occipital cortex. Neurons there extract simple features, such as edges and angles from a single retinal image. Additionally, the two retinal images are combined to form a three-dimensional representation of the visual field encoded on

FIGURE 3.4
Cut-away view of visual system.

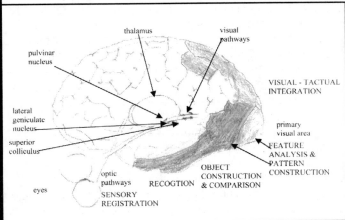

FIGURE 3.5

The visual system is organized into a heterarchy.
Some stages occur sequentially while some stages occur simultaneously

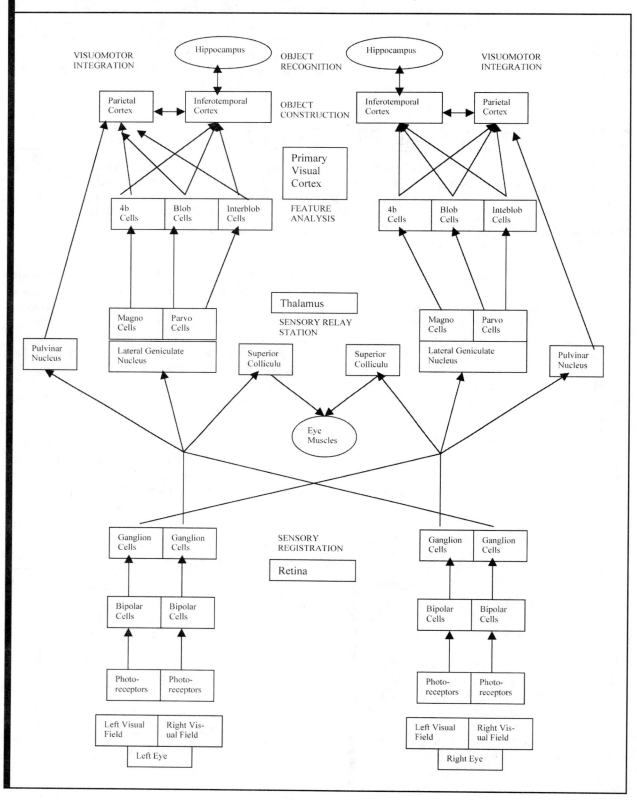

the retina. The processing of the input is continued in adjacent occipital, temporal and parietal regions where the results of the basic analyses on adjacent areas of the image are combined to form patterns that correspond to surfaces in the visual field.

Specifically, the visual processing pathway splits into two processing pathways. One pathway extends upward into the parietal lobe. Here the third stage of processing is the **visual-tactual integration stage**. Visual and tactual information are integrated within a single representation that is used to direct limb movements in such tasks as reaching and grasping, as described in Chapter 2. This visual knowledge is procedural.

The other pathway extends downward into the temporal lobe. Here the third stage is the **object construction stage**. Here pattern representations corresponding to surfaces are combined and compared with memory to construct shape representations. Ultimately, all the shape representations are combined into a single representation of a three-dimensional world filled with three-dimensional objects, which corresponds to your perception of the world. This visual knowledge is declarative.

SENSORY REGISTRATION

When light falls on the **retina** of the eye it stimulates the **photoreceptors** embedded in it. The photoreceptors signal the **bipolar** cells, which in turn signal the **ganglion** cells. Already at the retina there is some sorting out of the signal because different areas of the retina are sensitive to different information. The photoreceptors consist of rod neurons and **cone** neurons, and only the cone neurons are frequency sensitive and hence transmit color information. There are three different types of cone cells, and each type is maximally sensitive to one of three different frequencies that produce either the perception of red, green, or blue, respectively. However, people perceive four, rather than three, primary colors. When observers are presented with a large number of color samples and asked to pick out those which do not appear to be mixtures of other colors they tend to pick out four colors: red, green, blue, and yellow (Bornstein, 1973). Furthermore, the four primary colors can only be mixed in particular ways. You cannot see a reddish-green or a bluish-yellow. This is because input from the three kinds of cones is combined to form red-green, blue-yellow, and lightness pathways within the color lane of the optic pathway.

The cones only exist in the central area of the eye, called the fovea. If you move a crayon across your visual field while keeping your eyes fixated on a point you will find a point at which you can no longer see its color. As a result of the way the cones are arranged, the visual field for color is smaller than the visual field for form. Also, the rods are most numerous immediately outside the fovea and thin out towards the periphery of the retina. If you continue to move the crayon away from the center of your visual field you will find a point at which you cannot see it at all. However, while the rods are too sparse for form detection, motion detection is still possible. If you wiggle your finger at the location where you can no longer see the crayon, you will see something out there. When you fixate on a point in space, light from one side of the point falls on the right side of each retina and light from the other side of the point falls on the left side of each retina. So the right sides of both retinas have images of one half of the visual field and the left sides of both retinas have images of the other half of the visual field. The axons from the ganglion cells that receive the input from the right sides of each retina form the **optic pathway** to the left hemisphere of the cerebral cortex. Similarly, the images from the left sides of the retinas are transmitted to the right hemisphere. So, unsurprisingly, each hemisphere receives visual information from the side of the body that it controls, which is the opposite side of the body it is on (as shown in the right panel of Figure 3.4). Otherwise, there would not be the efficient visual control of motor movement that was described in the last chapter.

In each hemisphere, the optic pathway divides and terminates in three locations. The smallest portion of the pathway terminates in the superior colliculus. The output from this pathway is used to control eye movements. The next largest portion goes to the **pulvinar nucleus** of the thalamus and from

FIGURE 3.6

Eye movements. Left: Picture observed. Right: Record of eye movements made in continuous observation of picture. (Yarbus, 1967).

FIGURE 3.7

Serial position curves for four-letter strings observed for 2400 or 150 milliseconds without an eye movement for identification. (Estes, et al., 1976).

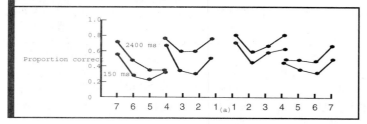

there to the parietal cortex. This is part of the procedural pathway, which constructs a representation that is used to control motor movements involved in reaching and grasping for things you can see. By far the largest portion arrives at the **lateral geniculate nucleus** of the thalamus and from there goes to the primary visual area in the occipital cortex. Most of this pathway continues as the declarative pathway in the temporal lobe, which constructs the visual representation of the world that determines your perceptual experience.

VISUAL ACUITY

As shown in Figure 3.6, about three or four times a second your eyes move in unison, and fixate on the same new location in space (Yarbus, 1967). These jumps are called saccades. A saccade takes anywhere from 20 milliseconds to 300 milliseconds. The duration of the saccade is directly proportional to the distance traveled (Becker, 1991). So most of the time both eyes are fixated on a common point in space. Eye movements are essential in order to see more than a tiny portion of the world in detail. Visual acuity is the amount of detail that can be seen. The number of cones packed together in a given area is the primary determinant of visual acuity, so it is much higher for the fovea than for the rest of the retina. Estes, Allmeyer, and Reder (1976) showed just how important eye movements are for good visual acuity by training observers to hold their eyes still while staring at a fixation point. A string of four letters was shown to the right or left of the fixation points. The observers had either 150 milliseconds or 2.4 seconds to see the string without making an eye movement. They were asked to report all four letters. The results are shown in Figure 3.7. The observers did not always report all four letters accurately. Without making an eye movement, visual acuity is not sufficient to always clearly see a novel letter string of four random letters extending to the right or left of the fixation point.

Everything you can see at a given instant is your **visual field**. You perceive the visual field as having uniform clarity. However, this cannot be the case. The constant motion of the eyes keeps the center of clarity always changing, and what you perceive is actually the integration of several images. There is a peephole of clarity in the center of the visual field with a width of no more than eight letters. Outside of that area only gross changes in brightness are being detected.

The image you perceive as being simultaneously encoded in all directions extending out from your fixation point is in fact a composite constructed over time. The representation you perceive at any given instant is put together from retinal images collected over the past few seconds as your eyes jumped from fixation point to fixation point in the visual field. Images with different fixation points have different peepholes of clarity. When all the different peepholes of clarity are stitched together, an apparently equally clear perception of the entire visual field is constructed and constantly updated.

EYE MOVEMENTS

For you to obtain detailed information about the visual world it is necessary for your eyes to move to fixation points of high information in the visual field. There is an elaborate system to do just this that makes use of visual input in order to control eye movements. Eye movements are controlled by a hierarchical system extending from the midbrain to the cortex.

At the lowest level, it is important that an extraneous head movement does not blur the retinal image the way moving a camera blurs the image in a photograph. So the vestibular-ocular reflex (discussed in Chapter 2) keeps the eyes focused on a point during a fixation even when the head is turning (Brown & Deffenbacher, 1979). At the next level, the superior colliculus moves the eyes to areas of contrast, since these are usually areas of high information that are likely to mark the boundaries of objects and parts of objects. For example, in reading the eyes tend to fixate on the beginnings of words, and in Figure 3.6 you can see that when a face is examined the eyes return repeatedly to specific, high information parts such as the eyes. The superior colliculus is the vestige of a more primitive visual perceptual system that was reduced to controlling eye movements when the ability to process patterns evolved elsewhere in the brain (Levinthal, 1983; p. 58). So it plays a supporting role in presenting a clear sequence of images to the brain for further processing.

The superior colliculus receives input from the basal ganglia, which in turn receive input from the cortex. Ultimately, a circuit containing the **frontal eye fields** and the **posterior parietal cortex** cooperates in the control of eye movements (Figure 2.2). At the highest level, the eye-fields in the frontal cortex may make use of non-visual information, such as the expectations of the viewer, to direct the eyes to particular points. Clearly, the control of eye movements is anything but simple. An eye movement may be directed by some information in the periphery of the visual field, so that, for example, when you read your eyes fixate near the beginnings of words, rather than in between them. But eye movements are also influenced by the difficulty of the reading material. More generally, the difficulty of the visual task and the intentions of the observer influence eye movements. These effects are the result of cortical control. In summary, control of where to jump is shared between a cortical control system responding to the intentions of the observer and a subcortical control system responding to changes in the visual input. Jan Theeuwes and his colleagues (Godijn & Theeuwes, 2002; Theeuwes, Kramer, Hahn, Irwin, & Zelinsky, 1999) found that even when an observer directed his eyes to a distinctly colored target, the eyes were likely to move in the direction of a new input suddenly appearing in the visual field.

Control of when to jump is also shared by different parts of the visual system. Most eye fixations last between 200 and 400 milliseconds. But eye fixation times vary over a wide range from less than 100 milliseconds to greater than a second, depending on the informativeness of the fixation point. As the eyes move from fixation point to fixation point, they must linger at each point long enough to encode all the information there. If the eyes leave a point too soon, then a regression occurs, and they return to the point they have just left.

You are not aware of your eyes moving several times a second nor the many times that you blink, because the threshold for detecting a visual input during a saccade or blink is increased. In other words, you are not aware of any brief blurring of the image or any little moments of darkness. However, even though the increased threshold for an input during a saccadic movement may prevent it from being processed by the visual cortex, and ultimately from being perceived, the visual system still processes the information and uses it to compute the locations to which subsequent saccades are directed. As a result, normal observers may exhibit the bizarre behavior called **blind sight**, in which they can identify the locations of flashes that they claim they have not seen. For example, Skavenski and Hansen (1978) asked observers to strike with a hammer in the dark at very briefly illuminated points presented during the observer's saccades. The observers claimed to be unable to see the targets, yet their hammer strikes were quite accurate. Similarly, Weiskrantz, Warrington, Sanders, and Marshall (1974) described patients with lesions in the visual cortex who could accurately reach in space for targets that they said they could not see.

Modern technology has made it possible for experiments to examine how a composite representation is built up over a sequence of fixations. Currie, McConkie, Carlson-Radvansky, and Irwin (2000) performed an experiment in which an observer scanned a picture of a scene. Elements of the scene were changed during a saccadic movement. The question was whether the observer noticed these changes. During an observer's saccade to a target object, one of three kinds of changes occurred in the scene: the location of just the background was displaced (i.e., moved slightly up or down), the location of just the target object was displaced, or the entire picture was displaced. The results provided evidence of a multilevel integration process that directs eye movements.

The displacement that was detected least often was the displacement of just the background. Observers detected the displacement of the background about 40% of the time. Since visual acuity is good only at the fixation point the visual system did not have sufficiently detailed information about the background to detect a change more than half the time.

The displacement that was detected next most often was the displacement of the entire picture. Observers detected the displacement of the entire picture over 70% of the time. Notice that when the entire picture is displaced, the target's location is displaced. The sensitivity to the change in the target's location suggests that this is the key element in the integration of the successive images. Presumably, when the target was displaced the detection of the change in its location occurred at the feature analysis stage. The posterior parietal cortex detected features indicating an object in the periphery, moved the eyes there, and found no such features when it got there. However, notice that the detection of the displacement of the target was still only 70%. In fact, even under normal viewing the eyes occasionally undershoot the fixation of a target, so a failure to find the target does not signal an image disparity unless its displacement is beyond a critical distance.

The displacement that was detected the most often was the displacement of just the target. When only the target's location was displaced, detection of the displacement increased to over 80% of the time. In this case, it was possible for detection of the displacement to occur at either the feature analysis or object construction stage. Even if the displacement of the target was not detected at the feature analysis stage on the basis of the distance between the fixation point and the target, it could still be detected at the object construction stage because the location of the target object in relation to all the objects in the scene had shifted. The new location of the target object did not correspond to the representation of the scene based on previous saccadic movements.

Eriksen and Collins (1967) studied temporal integration using a different method. They prepared two random dot patterns, like those shown in the top panels of Figure 3.8, which formed a nonsense syllable when superimposed, as shown in the bottom panel of Figure 3.8. When each dot pattern was shown for 6 milliseconds with a 25 millisecond interval between them, the male graduate students observing them saw the nonsense syllable 85% of the time (see also, Brockmole, Wang, & Irwin, 2002). Hence, the visual system combined the information from two images that were encoded 25 milliseconds apart.

Other evidence for temporal integration comes from visual marking. Theeuwes, Kramer, and Atchley (1998) found that when an observer searches the visual field, they preferentially fixate on objects they have not seen before, which means that the visual system is marking objects that it has already seen.

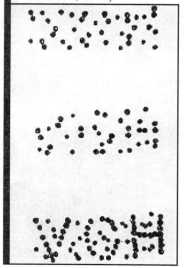

FIGURE 3.8
The upper two dot patterns when superimposed result in the bottom pattern in which the nonsense syllable VOH can be read. (Ericksen & Collins, 1967).

SUMMARY OF SENSORY REGISTRATION

- Visual perception begins when the lens of the eye focuses light on its back wall, called the retina, and activates photoreceptor cells in the retina.
  - Photoreceptors are packed together most densely in or adjacent to a small area in the center of the retina called the fovea. Hence, if you fixate on a string of letters, you can see clearly at most four letters to the right and left of the fixation point.
  - So what you can see at any given moment is quite different from your perception. You perceive the visual field as having uniform clarity. However, this cannot be the case. Rather, there is a peephole of clarity in the center of the visual field with a width of no more than eight letters. Outside of that area only gross changes in brightness are being detected.

- To obtain detailed information about the visual world, it is necessary for the eyes to move to fixation points of high information in the visual field. The image you perceive as being simultaneously encoded in all directions extending out from your fixation point is in fact a composite constructed over time. There is an elaborate system to do just this.
  - About three or four times a second your eyes jump in unison from one fixation point to another.
  - The superior colliculus moves the eyes to areas of high contrast, since these are usually areas of high information. The eye-fields in the frontal cortex make use of non-visual information, such as the expectations of the viewer, to direct the eyes to particular points.
  - When all the different peepholes of clarity are stitched together, an apparently equally clear perception of the entire visual field is constructed and constantly updated.

- The visual information is sent along the optic pathway to the thalamus.

FEATURE ANALYSIS

In this section of the chapter and the next, the declarative pathway of the visual system is followed to its conclusion along the bottom of the temporal cortex, where representations of familiar objects are constructed (as shown in the left panel of Figure 3.4). To begin, Figure 3.5 shows schematically the areas involved in feature analysis. The lateral geniculate nucleus contains two kinds of neurons, **magnocellular** (large) and **parvocellular** (small), which are named for their size, and which project to different layers of the **primary visual cortex** of the occipital cortex (also called the **striate cortex**) for the **feature analysis** stage. Neurons in striate cortex extract simple features, such as edges and angles from a single retinal image. Additionally, the two retinal images are combined to form a three-dimensional representation of the visual field encoded on the retina. From the striate cortex the input is sent to the **secondary visual cortex** (also called **prestriate and extrastriate** cortex) in adjacent occipital, temporal and parietal regions where the results of the basic analyses on adjacent areas of the image are combined to form patterns that correspond to surfaces in the visual field.

The cells in the primary visual cortex that receive their input from magnocellular neurons are called **4b** cells. The parvocellular neurons project to two kinds

TABLE 3.1

Functions of Visual Subsystems

System	4B	P-blob	P-interblob
Contrast	high	high	low
Location	low	low	high
Motion	high	low	middle
Color	low	high	middle
Orientation	middle	low	high

of neurons of the visual cortex. One kind of neuron forms clumps that appear as **blob**s when a small area is stained with a dye. So these are called blob cells. The remaining cells, which fall between the blobs, are called **interblob** cells.

As summarized in Table 3.1, 4b cells, blob cells, and interblob cells are sensitive to three different kinds of information that is available in the visual input. The 4b cells are most sensitive to motion and contrast, and so are responsible for the representation of motion. Blob cells are most sensitive to color and contrast and so are responsible for the representation of color. Interblob cells are sensitive to location and orientation and so are responsible for the representation of form.

Within the 4b, blob, and interblob systems, there are even more specialized subsystems of feature analysis that all operate on the visual input at the same time. At the next stage the results of all these analyses are combined in a single representation. So visual processing is partly hierarchical, as the input moves from registration to feature analysis to construction, and partly parallel, as many separate analyses are carried out simultaneously at the analysis stage. Altogether, the input is simultaneously analyzed in about thirty different ways to extract details of the three-dimensional representation (Gazzaniga, Ivry, & Mangun, 1998; p. 133). To make note of both aspects, the visual system, like the motor system, is called a heterarchy.

Damage to the primary visual area destroys the feature analysis of some part of the visual input. So it generally results in a deficit in form and/or color perception, which is revealed by discrimination and matching tasks. The deficit may vary from mild to severe depending on the extent of the injury. A mild deficit might be loss of color vision or a blind spot in the visual field. A severe deficit would be total blindness.

ORIENTATION AS AN ELEMENTARY VISUAL FEATURE

In the primary visual area of the cortex there are many feature-detector neurons that each receive input from a few cells in the lateral geniculate nucleus (LGN) of the thalamus, which in turn have received input from small adjacent areas on one or both retinas. The retinal area is called the LGN neuron's receptive field. Each receptive field consists of a center and a surround, as shown in Figure 3.9. The LGN neuron responds when the brightness of the center of the receptive field is different from the brightness of the surround. Figure 3.9 shows the center and surround sending input to a single LGN cell. When the center and surround are both illuminated, as in Figure 3.9(a), or both unilluminated, as in Figure 3.9(b), the LGN cell does not respond. But when the center is illuminated and the surround is not, as in Figure 3.9(c) then the LGN neuron responds and sends input to the visual cortex.

A feature-detector neuron responds when it receives input from a sufficient number of LGN neurons with overlapping receptive fields. So ultimately, the response of the feature-detector neuron in the visual cortex depends on the retinal receptive fields of the LGN neurons that provide its input, as shown in Figure 3.10. These fields are organized into several simple shapes called **features**. Among the most common are the orientation **features**, such as the vertical line shown in Figure 3.10(a). The receptive fields of these cortical neurons contain a center that is in the shape of a line in a specific **orientation**. So ultimately a single cortical neuron responds to a line in a single orientation. There are many different cortical feature-detector neurons that are sensitive to many different orientations (Knierim & Van Essen, 1992). For example, cortical receptive fields for a vertical a diagonal, and a horizontal line are shown in Figures 3.9(a), 3.9(b), and 3.9(c), respectively. So the representation is a kind of feature map in which the visual input has been segmented into a large

FIGURE 3.9
The receptive field of an LGN neuron contains a center and surround.

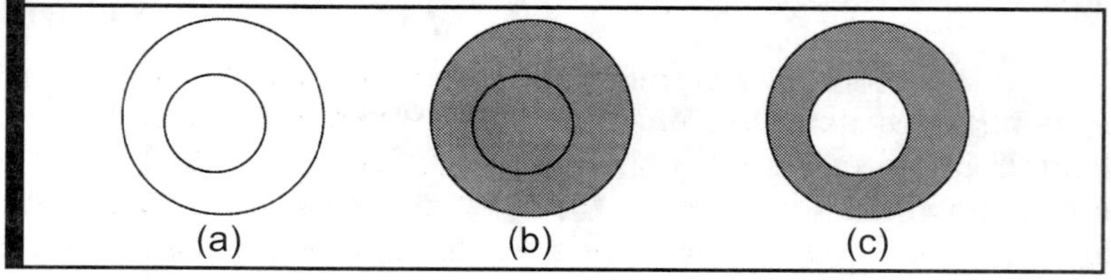

(a)   (b)   (c)

FIGURE 3.10
Receptive fields of orientation neurons

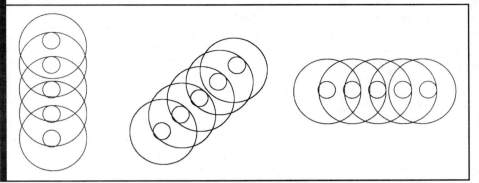

FIGURE 3.11
Edge detection by an orientation neuron

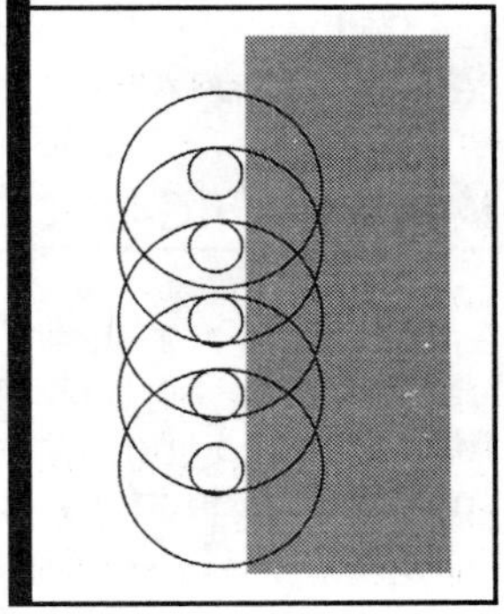

number of highly localized features, each recording the orientation of a line at that location.

An edge is any sharp change in brightness. Notice that if the edge of a bright field moves across the receptive field of an orientation detector that is oriented parallel to the edge it will activate the feature-detector when it passes through its center, as shown in Figure 3.11. Edges in specific orientations activate simple orientation features, and orientation detectors are also called edge detectors. So orientation is one of the basic features out of which both the edges and surfaces of objects are ultimately constructed. As soon as the orientation features are encoded they are combined into more complex features called corners, and shapes (Pomerantz, 1981), as shown in Figure 3.12. A corner is where two or more lines meet as an angle or curve. Corners are further differentiated by the visual system into two-line and three-line corners. A shape is a line with no end, a closed figure. One question that has not been resolved is how many different kinds of features are important for the construction of three-dimensional surfaces. One possibility is that most of the time just simple orientation features are used. A second possibility is that there are a few basic types of features like those shown in Figure 3.12. We shall consider this issue again when shape construction is considered.

FIGURE 3.12
Orientation, corner, and shape features

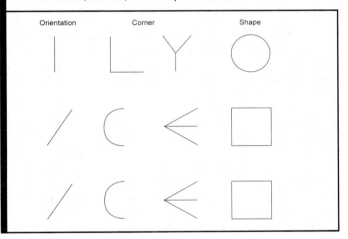

FIGURE 3.13
A triangle made up of illusory contours resulting from closure

The orientation, corner and shape detectors are sufficiently sensitive so that even lines that do not quite meet may activate corner and shape detectors. Hence you experience the phenomenon of **closure**; that is a C is perceived as an incomplete circle. Or, as shown in the third row of Figure 3.12, dotted lines are nevertheless perceived as lines, rather than as unrelated dots. Corner and shape features activated by incomplete input can also be grouped together by the visual system and are experienced as illusory contours. For example, in Figure 3.13 each pair of incomplete circles activates a different orientation feature such that all three orientation features combine to form a triangle that is detected by a shape detector.

VISUAL ORGANIZATION

A **texture** is a pattern made up of adjacent features that all have the same orientation. Texture encoding by the visual system is apparent through the phenomenon of **pop-out**. Just as LGN neurons with overlapping visual fields input to a common feature detector neuron in the visual cortex, feature detector neurons with overlapping fields for a common feature input to a common texture-detector neuron, which is thus activated by a texture consisting of adjacent identical features. So if a visual display contains two textures then the visual system organizes the display into the two areas corresponding to the two textures, so that one texture pops out from the other. For example, in Figure 3.14(a) the one line in a different orientation pops out because the seven lines in the same orientation are combined into a single texture. The visual system not only puts lines in the same orientation together into textures but also features of the same type. In Figure 3.14(b) a corner pops out from among lines, and in Figure 3.14(c) a shape pops out from among corners. The strength of the pop out effect increases with the size of the texture. As shown in Figure 3.15, a stronger pop out effect is experienced for four adjacent vertical lines among diagonal lines than for one vertical line among diagonal lines.

Figure 3.16 provides a striking illustration of how large patterns are created by organizing identical adjacent areas into successively larger areas. First look at the pattern in Figure 3.16(b), which is perceived as a symmetrical black pattern on a white background. In contrast, Figure 3.16(a) appears to be just random noise. In fact, Figure 3.16(a) contains almost the same pattern as Figure 3.16(b). A thin strip of pixels along the vertical and horizontal axes has been replaced by noise, but otherwise the patterns are identical. However, in Figure 3.16(a) there are no adjacent areas with identical features to be detected and combined by a texture-detector neuron. So the fig-

FIGURE 3.14
Pop out as the result of texture segmentation. (a) A distinct orientation. (b) A corner among lines. (c) A shape among corners.

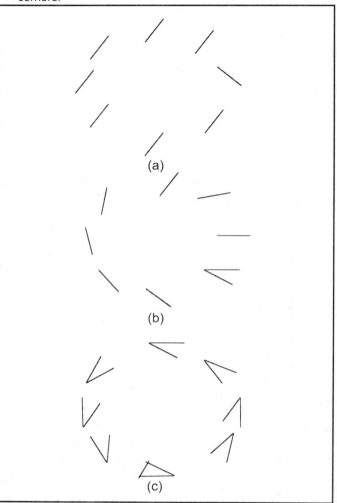

FIGURE 3.15
Finding the single vertical line is more difficult in (a) than finding the four vertical lines together in (b).

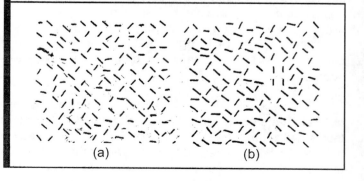

ure is not organized into a pattern and remains random noise. It is only because texture-detector neurons combine corresponding areas with identical features that you perceive Figure 3.16(b) as a symmetrical pattern. Otherwise, it would look as random to you as Figure 3.16(a). The operation of these neurons was impaired in the visual system of the unfortunate soldier described at the beginning of the chapter. So to him patterns in Figure 3.16(a) and Figure 3.16(b) would look the same.

FIGURE 3.16

Pattern perception. (a) Mostly symmetrical pattern, which is difficult to perceive because of central random strip; (b) symmetry pattern, which is easy to perceive. (Julesz, 1975).

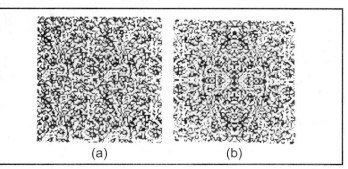

(a)   (b)

VISUAL STRESS

Each feature-detector neuron in the visual cortex ultimately responds to the pattern of light and dark falling on its receptive field in the retina. Each receptive field consists of a central area that excites the neuron and a surround that inhibits it. Light-dark patterns such as stripes that activate the central areas of some neurons but not their surrounds cause the greatest levels of excitation in the visual cortex. Furthermore, the greatest level of excitation in the visual cortex occurs when the thickness of the stripes (technically called their spatial frequency) most closely matches the thickness of the central receptive fields of the maximum number of neurons in the visual cortex. Arnold Wilkins found that the maximum response is to a pattern like that in Figure 3.17. For some individuals, the visual cortex has such a large response to such a pattern that they have a seizure when they look at it (Wilkins, Binnie, & Darby, 1981). That is, the neurons start firing out of control. Less than one per cent of people have such an extreme response. However, many more people find looking at such a pattern uncomfortable. Unfortunately, most books are type set so that the letters form a similar annoying spatial frequency pattern (Wilkins & Nimmo-Smith, 1988). So many people find reading tiring and suffer migraine headaches because of it. They are much poorer readers than they would be if the type were spaced differently. Fortunately, there is a remedy. Neurons that respond to different frequencies of light are not all equally sensitive to the same spatial frequency patterns. By wearing colored glasses while reading, a person can reduce the frequencies to which they are most sensitive and read much more comfortably. The same result can be achieved by reading through covered overlays (Wilkins & Lewis, 1999). This is called the Mears-Irlen effect after its discoverer (Mears) and popularizer (Irlen). The key is to get a proper diagnosis of the frequencies that need to be filtered out.

FIGURE 3.17

This spatial frequency pattern causes maximum firing in the visual cortex and maximum discomfort.

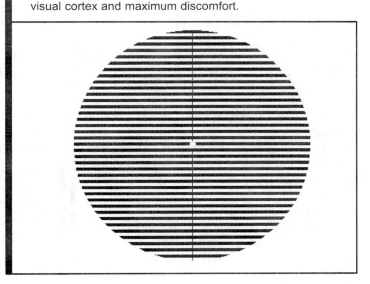

DEPTH CONSTRUCTION

An important problem that needs to be solved in constructing a three-dimensional representation of an object from its two-dimensional image is how far away that object is. Without distance information there is no way to know how large the object is.

Monocular cues. When you look at something, the farther away something is, the smaller the image that it has; that is, the points that comprise the retinal image are closer together. As a result, lines receding from you into the distance that are actually parallel seem to come together in the distance at a vanishing point, as shown in Figure 3.18. This cue for depth is called perspective and is used by the visual system to assign distances and relative sizes to other objects in the visual field. For example, notice that the horizontal line in the foreground looks smaller than the horizontal line in the background even though they are exactly the same size. The effect of perspective is to make the line in the background appear farther away. But since they both are objectively the same size on the paper, and hence have the same retinal images, the line further away must actually be larger, and so is assigned a greater size by the visual system to the line below it. This effect is called the Ponzo illusion, after its discoverer. To see the horizontal lines as the same size it is only necessary to cover the diagonal lines creating the perspective. Another depth cue is size, which is often combined with perspective. Notice that in Figure 3.18 the smaller square appears to be farther away.

FIGURE 3.18

Perspective is a depth cue. Top: The Ponzo illusion. Upper horizontal line looks larger. Bottom: Size and perspective combine to make smaller square look further away.

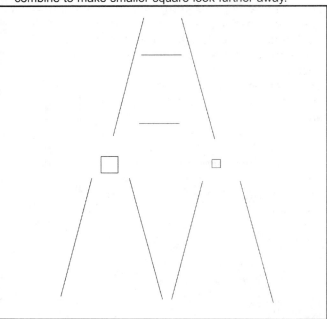

Another perspective illusion is shown in Figure 3.19. Notice that line AB looks shorter than line BC, even though they are both the same size. That is because the line between them creates a corner feature that may be the apex of a pyramid such that BC is receding into the background, hence further away, and AB is projecting into the foreground, hence closer. But if BC is both farther away than AB and has the same retinal image then it must actually be larger, and so is assigned a larger size in the representation of the visual field. To see that AB and BC are actually equal size sides of a triangle it is only necessary to cover the line dividing angle B (Gregory, 1978).

So perspective and size are cues for the relative sizes and distances of objects seen in the visual field. Perspective and size are called **monocular cues** because they are available from only one retinal image. At the same time that orientation features are being combined to form textures other neurons are detecting perspective cues and using them to construct a depth representation. Hence, a texture can be formed by combining patterns that have a common orientation in depth, as shown in Figure 3.20. On both the right and left of Figure 3.20 one pattern is distinguished from the others by the same visual feature. On the left side the patterns are organized into three-dimensional box representations and the distinct feature encodes a different orientation for one box. Hence, it pops out. But on the right side of Figure 3.20 the squares are not organized into shapes in two different orientations in depth by the visual system, so the different square does not pop out.

FIGURE 3.19

Line AB appears shorter than BC because they are the same length but BC appears farther away; hence it must be longer.

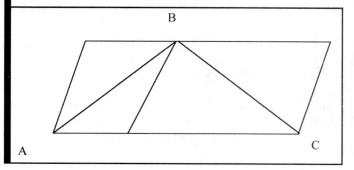

Binocular cues. Many neurons receive input from both the left and right eyes. These neurons are capable of detecting **binocular** cues that require both eyes. At the same time that basic orientation features are being detected and monocular cues are being detected, binocular cues are being detected as well. Some neurons are capable of detecting differences between the right and left retinal images. These differences, called **disparities**, are an important source of depth information. As shown in Figure 3.21, when you fixate on a point from two different locations, such as your left and right eyes, the images cast on each

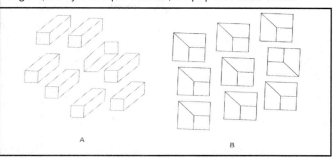

FIGURE 3.20
No form on the right is distinguished by a unique feature, so pop-out does not occur. One form on the lef is distinguished by a unique feature, so pop-out does occur.

eye are slightly different. The closer an object is to you the closer together its retinal images are to the center of the visual field in each retinal image. For example, as shown in the figure, if you look at a larger square with a smaller hole in it, so what you see through the hole is farther away, the retinal images will be as shown in A and B. Conversely, if you look at a larger square with a smaller square in front of it, the retinal images will be as shown in C and D. The combination of these separate images to form a single representation is called **stereopsis**.

With effort, some of you can use Figure 3.21 to see how retinal images are fused for yourself. Place a piece of cardboard between C and D, and place your nose against the cardboard so that your left eye only sees C and your right eye only sees D. If you cross your eyes so that the pictures fuse, and wait a few seconds, then you will see the small square floating in front of the large one in C/D and the small square floating behind the large one in A/B.

Another way to attempt to fuse the images is to attempt to look through the page to a point beyond it. Unfortunately, image fusing under these conditions is not easy. However, there are several ways of making the task easier that you may have experienced. For example, if one picture was printed in red and the other in green, and you looked at them through glasses with one red and one green lens, then each eye would see only one picture and it would be much easier to fuse them. Also, the two pictures could be printed on top of each other. The pattern produced is called an **autostereogram**. If you fixate intently on an autostereogram for awhile your eye muscles become tired, your eyes diverge a little from the fixation point, so the two

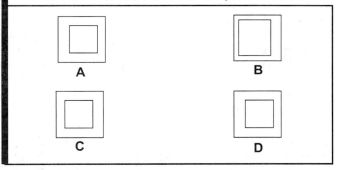

FIGURE 3.21
When you fixate head-on on two objects such that one is directly behind the other their images will be displaced on each retina as shown in A/B if the larger square is in front and as shown in C/D if the smaller square is in front.

retinal images diverge a little and the disparities between them produce the perception of depth, i.e., the small square floating in front of or behind the large one. However, for a small percentage of the population small difficulties in fixation early in life prevented the normal development of binocular vision and for these people the form in the stereogram remains flat (Von Noorden, 1995).

Another depth cue is the angle that each eye must turn to focus on the same point. This angle, called the **convergence**, or **vergence**, of the eyes is greater the closer the fixation point is to you. Also, **occlusion** aids in depth perception. When seen from two different angles slightly more of the occluded object appears in one image than in the other (Anderson & Nakayama, 1994). Finally, depth construction does not only make use of the comparison of simultaneous images in the right and left eyes. It also makes use of successive retinal images from the same eye (Hadani, Ishai, Frisch, & Kononov, 1994).

THE ROLE OF MULTIPLE IMAGES AND CUES IN PERCEPTION

You may have wondered why visual processing is such a complex process, involving many separate images and several different kinds of features and cues. In fact, there are advantages to using multiple images. As we have seen, creating a composite of several foveal images provides more detail since acuity is greatest in the fovea. Also, each retina contains a **blind spot** where the optic pathway exits from it. You do not notice the blind spot for two reasons. First, the blind spot on each retina rarely covers the same area of the visual field, so at least monocular information is received from all parts of the visual field. Second, when the blind spots do line up the visual system fills in the spot with part of an image from an earlier fixation. Finally, multiple images have spatial and temporal disparities that provide cues to depth that are not available in a single image.

There is also an advantage to using multiple cues to construct a representation. As the result of distance and lighting, different cues may be most informative in different visual fields or in different parts of the same visual field. Binocular cues make it possible to compute the absolute distance from you of objects in your visual field. However, binocular cues are only useful for objects a few feet away from you. For distant objects there are no detectable disparities between the retinal images and the differences in vergence are also undetectable. So only monocular cues are available. By combining the information from all the cues the maximum amount of information may be extracted from a scene. In particular, different cues are effective at different distances.

SUMMARY OF FEATURE ANALYSIS

- The feature analysis stage begins when the visual input reaches the occipital cortex. The optic pathway reaching the occipital cortex contains three main sub-pathways that in turn each have several sub-pathways etc. The three main sub-pathways sort out the input into
  - that used for representing color.
  - that used for representing motion.
  - that used for representing shape.

- In the shape pathway, the input is sorted into edges that form simple visual features. An edge is any sharp change in brightness. An edge may be represented as a line in a specific orientation and, in fact, that is how the visual system does represent edges.
  - Orientation is one of the basic features out of which the representations of objects are ultimately constructed.
  - As soon as the edges are encoded, adjacent edges are combined into features.
  - The visual system puts features together into representations of surfaces and textures.

- An important problem that needs to be solved in constructing a three-dimensional representation of an object from its two-dimensional image is how far away that object is.
  - Monocular cues such as perspective and relative retinal image size are cues for the relative sizes and distances of objects seen in the visual field.
  - Retinal disparity gives information about depth.
  - Different cues are effective at different distances. Binocular cues make it possible to compute the absolute distance from you of objects in your the visual field. However, binocular cues are only useful for objects a few feet away from you. For distant objects only monocular cues are available.

SHAPE CONSTRUCTION

In the physical world different surfaces are connected together to form three-dimensional objects. After feature analysis, the next task for the visual system is to identify each representation as a three-dimensional object. To perform this task, the various depth and texture patterns are combined into a single object representation. For example, the top of Figure 3.22 shows a scene filled with objects that are simple geometric forms. The corner and shape features must be combined to form the representations of these three-dimensional forms. Putting together simple edge and texture representations to construct the representations of three-dimensional objects is neither simple nor straightforward because there are a large number of different possible patterns into which the features can be organized.

AMBIGUITY AND CAMOUFLAGE

Individual features can always be organized in more than one way to create a pattern. This is illustrated in Figure 3.23. Notice that the X on the left can be perceived as two vertical lines crossing or as two arrows whose points are touching. Most observers tend to see it as two vertical lines crossing. Also, the hourglass-like figure on the right can be perceived as an X whose top and bottom endpoints are connected by horizontal lines or as two triangles whose points are touching. Most observers tend to see it as two triangles whose points are touching. Each pattern can correspond to more than one mental representation. When a pattern has more than one representation it is called **ambiguous**. In the pattern on the left, the center crossing is represented as two diagonal lines intersecting; but in the pattern on the right, exactly the same center crossing is represented as the tips of two triangular shapes touching. When more than two lines meet at a point there is always more than one possible representation. In each representation different pairs of lines are connected. Only one of the possible representations is selected and incorporated into the perceptual experience.

The way the visual system tends to perform this selection process is illustrated by the two patterns in Figure 3.24. The hexagon on the right is in fact contained in the striped parallelogram on the left. However, this is not apparent because the visual system prefers to organize the line segments of the figure on the left into a representation of a parallelogram whose surface is covered with a striped texture. Neither of these representations (the parallelogram or the striped texture) contains the hexagon. Another way of saying this is that the hexagon is not a **good part** or **gestalt** of the striped parallelogram. When one pattern is contained in but not a good part of another, the hidden pattern is said to be **camouflaged**. Camouflage is the opposite of pop out. A pattern pops out from a visual field when it is assigned a distinct representation. A pattern is camouflaged in the visual field

FIGURE 3.22
A block scene with each surface numbered (Grasselli, 1969).

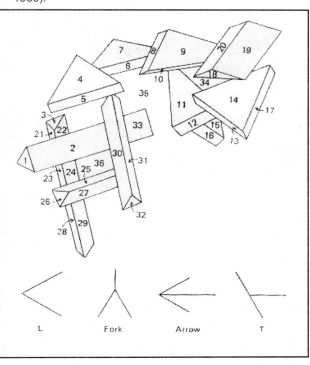

FIGURE 3.23
Crossing is usually perceived as crossing diagonal lines on left but as touching triangle points on right.

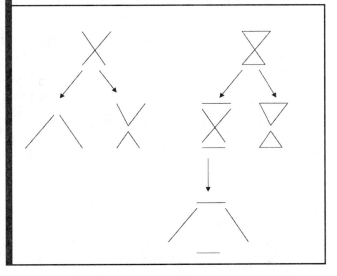

when it is not assigned a distinct representation but instead its elements are partitioned among different features or embedded in a texture.

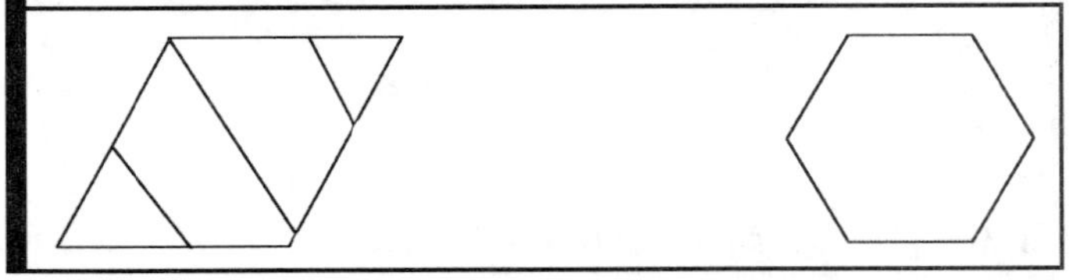

When faced with an ambiguity, the representation that is selected is the one that is consistent with a three-dimensional representation of the entire pattern. For example, in Figure 3.22 we want to connect the edges so that area 29 is connected with area 28, but not area 27. There are many different possible representations that the display at the top of Figure 3.22 could receive. In computing the one that corresponds to the set of three-dimensional forms that you see, the visual system naturally makes use of those features that are most likely to correspond to the edges, corners, and surfaces of three-dimensional forms. A three-dimensional form must contain some convex corners and surfaces. For example, Figure 3.25 is clearly perceived as a star with four points, not as a square with four triangular pieces missing. That is, it is organized into four convex areas that are its points. Look again at Figure 3.22. At the top notice how each distinct numbered surface area can be constructed from corner features and shape features that represent convex areas. The bottom of Figure 3.22 shows four different corner features that define convex areas in the drawing above.

Determining a three-dimensional representation for the entire pattern requires many computations combining corner features to represent convex surfaces. Furthermore, the occlusion of one object by another creates an additional complication. In Figure 3.22 the separated areas 2 and 33 are perceived to be part of the same surface. Let us consider how disjoint areas are combined in a single surface representation.

FIGURE 3.24

Hexagon is camouflaged in striped parallelogram.

FIGURE 3.25

This pattern is perceived as a 4-pointed star, not as a square with 4 missing triangles. Patterns are encoded into convex parts.

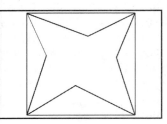

OCCLUSION AND SHADOW

If you put a plate down on a table, the tabletop does not seem to disappear under the plate, making the plate look like it floats unsupported in space. Rather, you see the plate on the table. The representation of the tabletop includes the unseen area under the plate. An important property of the shape representation is that it includes both the parts of the object that can be seen and the parts that are occluded and hence can't be seen.

In constructing a representation of the occluded part of an object, the visual system makes use of closure to complete its shape. Recall that a partial input is sufficient to activate a shape detector. Figure 3.26 illustrates how an occlusion is interpreted. You see this display as one circle partially occluded by another. The striking thing is that this representation seems like the only natural one, even though there are many other possibilities. A few of the alternative completions are depicted in Figures 3.26 (b-e). In each case the occluded portion of the left figure is represented by a dotted line. Figure 3.26 (b) represents the natural interpretation of Figure 3.26 (a) as overlapping circles. But as 3.26 (c) shows, Figure 3.26 (a) might simply be perceived as a chipped circle adjacent to a complete one. Furthermore, as (d) and (e) indicate, the occluded portion of the left figure might have a noncircular completion.

The filling in of missing parts makes it possible to see separated areas as part of the same surface. For example, as mentioned above, in Figure 3.22 the areas labeled 2 and 33 are seen as part of the same surface. For a still more striking example of how the visual system completes occluded objects examine Figure 3.27. There is no occlusion in the top panel of Figure 3.27, just some odd shapes that form no obvious pattern. Now look at the bottom panel of Figure 3.27. Here a new shape has been added that appears to occlude the fragments. So the visual system connects them even though they are not adjacent. When the fragments are connected, the pattern of hidden letters is obvious.

FIGURE 3.26
Overlapping circles? Potential completions.

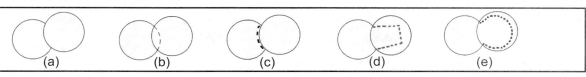

(a) (b) (c) (d) (e)

Finally, when objects are constructed, shadows are distinguished from surface colors and shadow becomes another depth cue. Even though you do not notice the shadow that your telephone casts across your desk, it provides a cue that the telephone rests on the surface of the desk rather than floating above it.

THE ROLE OF MEMORY IN VISUAL PERCEPTION

As we have seen, monocular cues provide information about the relative sizes and distances among objects in the visual field. However, there is not sufficient information to determine any object's absolute size and distance. Without this anchor point, all the objects in the field of vision may be smaller and closer, or larger and farther, within a certain range. You observe ambiguous scenes more often than you realize. When objects are viewed in the distance, or in limited light, or in photographs, depth cues are reduced.   In this case, more than one three-dimensional representation is consistent with the sensory input. The visual system relies on memory to select a single probable three-dimensional representation. What you actually perceive is the three-dimensional representation selected from memory, which you do not experience as ambiguous or indeterminate. For example, under normal illumination you have no difficulty discriminating the different sizes of a real chair and of a much smaller toy chair. But if the visual information is reduced, then the size of a visual object may be determined by the typical size of the object whose memory representation it matches. So size judgments become more difficult and a toy chair may appear to be the size of a real one (Franklin & Erickson, 1969; Schiffman, 1967; Slack, 1956).

Pictures have less information than three-dimensional objects. So pictures are useful for demonstrating ambiguity, illusion, and the effect of memory on visual perception. For example, the shaded circles in Figure 3.28 are ambiguous. They may be images of holes or bumps. In one orientation they look like holes and in the other orientation they look like bumps. The reason is that most of the time in the real world, the light source is from above. The reversal is the consequence of your perceptual experience with the shadows of real holes and real bumps. In each case the ambiguous representation is perceived as the most common representation that it matches in memory. The three-dimensional representation that is selected is the one that would produce the image if illuminated from above. This is a clear example of how memory informs perception.

So when the final three-dimensional object-representation is constructed, the representations of the surfaces of the object built from the visual input are compared with representations of objects in memory, which thus guide the construction process. In fact, as much as possible, visual representations of objects are retrieved rather than constructed. If an input representation is a close enough match to a representation stored in memory, then all the details of the representation in memory become part of the perceptual experience.

FIGURE 3.27
Fragments without a pattern, since there is no information for occlusion (Top Panel). Fragments shown with overlaying pattern creating apparent occlusion (Bottom Panel). (Bregman, 1981).

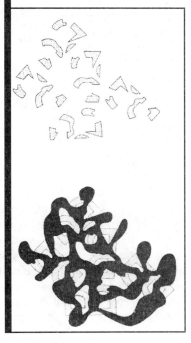

GEONS

Irving Biederman (1985) coined the term **geons** to refer to the representations of convex shapes that are used in object construction. The object representations in memory that guide the construction of the final three-dimensional object-representation are composed of geon representations of the basic geometric forms of which most objects are composed. As we have seen, geons are constructed from corner features, so these should be critical for recognizing objects. Figure 3.29(a) shows line drawings of some familiar objects and Figure 3.29(c) shows the same drawings, with the corner features erased to obscure the geons that comprised them. In Figure 3.29(b) the same amount of erasure, leaving the corner features intact, does not obscure the geons. When shown to students, over 80 per cent of the pictures like those in Figure 3.29(c) were unrecognizable, but less than 5 per cent of the pictures like those in Figure 3.29(b) were unrecognizable.

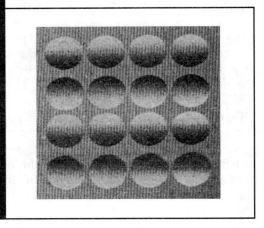

FIGURE 3.28
Depending on shading, semicircle looks like hole or bump. (Ramachandran, 1988).

To provide evidence that geons actually exist, Biederman and Cooper (1991) performed a **priming** task. In this task two **input**s are presented in succession to determine whether the first input, called the prime, influences the processing of the second input, called the **target**. In order to test the geon theory Biederman and Cooper created prime – geon target pairs from line drawings of familiar objects by deleting every other edge and vertex from the drawing to create the prime and using these deleted segments to create the target. In the top row of the panel the picture of a grand piano is divided into two images (left and center) such that each image contains exactly the same set of geons. Notice that the left and center images do not overlap but combined they form the complete original picture of the piano. Biederman and Cooper used one of these images as the prime and the other image as the geon target. In addition, they used 50% of a picture of an upright piano as a semantic target (which will be defined below). Biederman and Cooper also created prime – part target pairs from line drawings of familiar objects by deleting every other object part from the drawing to create the prime and using these deleted parts to create the target. So the two complementary images had different geons, as shown in the bottom row of the top panel of Figure 3.30. Biederman and Cooper used one of these images as the prime and the other as a part target. Again, 50% of a different picture was used as the semantic target. In Biederman and Cooper's experiment college students in an introductory psychology course had to identify the briefly presented picture fragments. The procedure is shown in the bottom of Figure 3.30. Each observer first saw a prime block of trials and then a target block of trials. In the prime block, for each object, the observer first saw a fixation point for 500 milliseconds, then the prime for 500 milliseconds, and then a mask for 500 milliseconds that was a random line drawing. A voice key recorded the onset of the observer's voice when she named the pictured object. The prime block took about 7

FIGURE 3.29
The effect of deletion on perception. The left column shows intact pictures. The middle column shows deletions that preserve convex parts. The right column shows deletions that destroy the convex parts. (Biederman, 1985.)

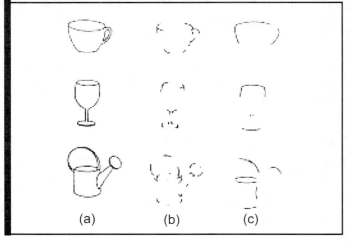

(a)   (b)   (c)

FIGURE 3.30

Prime-target pair at top have same geons but prime-target pair at bottom have different geons (Top Panel). Experimental procedure (Middle Panel). Geon primes produce same results as repetition primes and nongeon primes produce same results as semantic primes (Bottom Panel). (Biederman & Cooper, 1991).

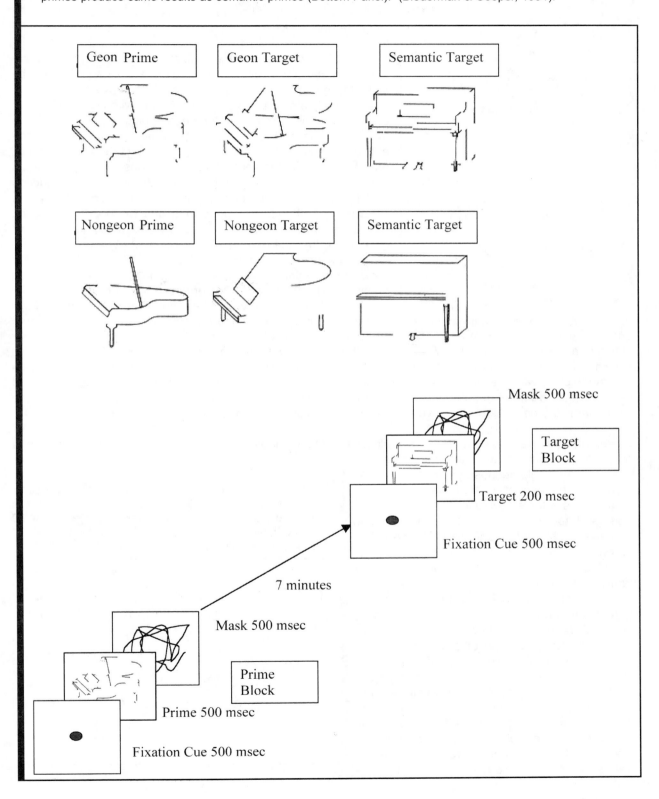

FIGURE 3.30A

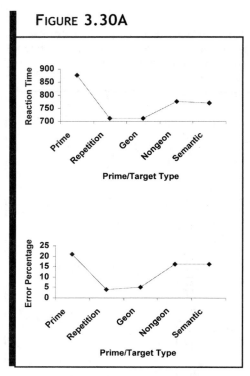

minutes and was followed by the target block. In a target block the sequence of events was the same except that each target was presented for only 200 milliseconds. There were four kinds of target blocks. The targets were identical to the primes, geon targets, part targets, or semantic targets. Each observer saw a single target block.

As we shall see in the next chapter, when the same picture of an object is shown more than once you can name it a little faster the second time, and this is called **repetition priming**. Also, when two different pictures of objects with the same name, e.g., two pianos, are shown, the second picture is named a little faster, and this is called **semantic priming**. In other words, repetition priming occurs for the repeated picture and semantic priming occurs for the second picture that has the same common name as the first picture. In general, there is a larger reduction in naming time for repetition priming than for semantic priming. Figure 3.30A shows that Biederman and Cooper (1991) found this (usual) pattern of naming times: the students named the targets faster than the primes. Also as is typically found in experiments that involve priming, they named the identical targets (repetition priming) faster than the semantic targets (semantic priming). The purpose of Biederman and Cooper's experiment was the comparison between the geon targets and the part targets. They reasoned that if geons existed, then the prime and geon targets would have exactly the same geons. Therefore, the prime and its geon target would activate the same visual representation; i.e., repetition priming would occur. In contrast, since the prime and its part target had different geons they would activate different visual representations of the same object. The part target would function the same as a different picture with the same name, i.e., a semantic target. As shown in the bottom panel, identical and geon targets had the same naming times (shown in milliseconds) and part and semantic targets had the same naming times. As also shown in the figure, the same pattern was found for error rates.

Novel objects. Relying on memory to explain perception muddies the distinction between recognition and perception. If you know that shape across the room is a rectangle because you recognize it as a table, then it cannot be the case that you recognize it as a table because you first perceive that its shape is a rectangle. So how do you perceive the shapes of unfamiliar objects? The answer is that you can perceive the unfamiliar object as a set of connected parts that are familiar geons, but you do not have a spatial description for the entire object that relates the orientation of each part to the others (Johnson, 2001). A frequent test of object perception is to show different objects in different orientations and ask an observer which are different views of the same object. As you can see in Figure 3.31, it is not easy to determine whether you are looking at the two views of the same shape when it is novel. However, even if the overall shape of a novel object is unfamiliar, it is still made up of familiar geons. You recognize the geons and put them together to form a repre-

FIGURE 3.31

Examples of pairs of patterns used for shape comparisons. (a) A "same" pair that differs by an 80 degree rotation in the picture plane. (b) A "same" pair that differs by an 80 degree rotation in depth. (c) A "different" pair that cannot be matched by any rotation. (Shepard & Metzler, 1971).

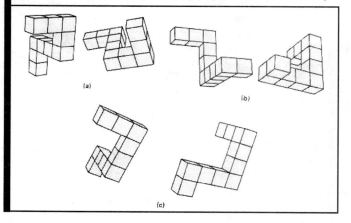

sentation of the entire object. Biederman calls this **recognition by components**. Furthermore, once a spatial representation of the geons of an object has been encoded it will be matched with its representation in memory in any orientation that preserves the representations of its individual geons. Biederman and Barr (1999) called the parts of a figure that generally remain visible in different orientations **non-accidental properties**. They had observers determine whether two briefly presented pictures were of the same novel object or different novel objects, as shown in the center panel of Figure 3.32. First, the fixation point was shown for 500 milliseconds, then the study picture for 400 milliseconds, then a mask for 500 milliseconds, then the test picture for 300 milliseconds, and finally another mask for 500 milliseconds. As shown in the top panel of Figure 3.32, when the objects were different, they either had slightly different dimensions but the same geons, called a metric difference, or they had a different geons, which was called a non-accidental property (NAP) difference. Half the time the test picture was rotated with respect to the study picture and half the time it was not. As shown in the bottom panel of Figure 3.32, when study and test pictures showed the objects in the same orientation error rates were about 20% for different judgments and did not differ for metric and non-accidental property differences. In contrast, when the test picture showed a rotated object the error rate did not change for forms that differed on non-accidental properties but rose to about 60% for those with only metric differences.

As is also shown in the bottom panel of Figure 3.32, even though error rate was not greater for different judgments to rotated objects than for unrotated objects that differed in non-accidental properties from the object in the study picture, response time to make the judgment did increase. An object that has only been seen once before only has one representation in memory. When seen again in a novel orientation it may be necessary for the visual system to first perform computations on the input representation that mentally rotate it to the orientation in which it was just seen in order to match the representation in memory. This mental rotation process adds time to the process of identification (Hayward & Tarr, 1997).

Words and faces. Relying on memory to guide the construction of a visual representation has two advantages. First, retrieving a representation from memory and comparing it with an input in order to determine whether it matches some minimal number of critical features for identification is a faster procedure than organizing all the features of the input into a representation without reference to memory. The features in the input are inherently ambiguous, and when a novel object is presented it takes time to determine which features should be combined to form a representation of the object. However, the representation in memory is not

FIGURE 3.32

Comparison of unrotated and rotated forms. Examples of original form and transformations that preserve (Metric) and alter (NAP) geons that remain visible under rotation (Top). Sequence of events on an experimental trial (Middle). Mean error rates (upper panel) and mean correct RTs (lower panel) as a function of orientation and type of change (same versus NAP difference versus metric (MP) difference) (Bottom). Bars around points show standard errors of the means. (Biederman & Barr, 1999).

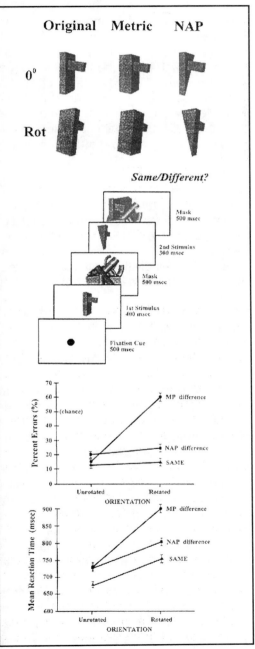

ambiguous. When using memory to produce a visual representation, it is just necessary to determine whether the features of the input representation can be organized the same way as the features in the memory representation. Second, using memory to guide the construction of a visual representation makes it possible to construct a much more detailed visual representation. Recall that visual acuity is good for only a very small portion of the visual field. Nonetheless, you perceive more details of a familiar object than you can actually detect in a single fixation because the remaining details are filled in from memory. Your success in reading and in dealing with the social world depends on fast and accurate recognition of the words and faces, respectively. Many words and faces are very similar to each other so details most be encoded in order to distinguish them. Considerable learning typically occurs for both words and faces because they are seen very frequently, which makes fast and accurate recognition possible.

Recall that you cannot always see four random letters to the right or left of a fixation point (Estes, et al., 1976). However, you have no trouble seeing a four-letter word to the right or left of a fixation point clearly. The role of memory in perception becomes apparent when perception is made more difficult. Suppose a word or letter is presented under conditions that make it very difficult to identify. When a letter is presented in very small type (Prinzmetal & Silvers, 1994) or for a very short time (Reicher, 1969; Wheeler, 1970) it may be identified less often when it is presented by itself than when it is presented as part of a word. The advantage for the letter when part of a word is called the **word superiority effect**. The word superiority effect shows that visual memory contains word representations that are independent of the letter representations, so that the entire word can be perceived without first perceiving the individual letters. The comparison of the input with representations of entire words is called the **whole-word pathway** in contrast to the **letter-sequence pathway**, which first requires the identification of individual letters. Word recognition makes use of both the parallel whole-word and letter-sequence pathways, as will be discussed in detail in Chapter 5.

Recall that when a familiar object is rotated it becomes more difficult to identify. It may still be recognizable because of the non-accidental properties of the representation, but various metric properties are lost. The same effect is observed for inverted words and faces. For example, try turning this book upside down and reading a sentence. It is much more difficult. The letter-sequence pathway still makes it possible because individual letters still match enough of their features to be identified. But the inverted text does not match whole-word representations; so the much faster whole-word pathway is gone

A similar effect is observed when faces are rotated. The representation of an upside-down face contains a sufficient number of individual features (e.g., eyes, nose, and mouth) that can still be matched with representations in memory but the whole-face pathway, which represents spatial relationships among all the features, is gone. An example of the effect of inversion on face perception is presented below.

The effect of inversion on face perception is demonstrated by the Thatcher Illusion (Thompson, 1980), so called because it was first demonstrated with the two upside down pictures of Margaret Thatcher, who was Prime Minister of England at the time, shown in Figure 3.33. Both faces are recognizable through feature matching even though they are upside down. However, when you see a face upside down you do not detect the orientation of parts that you normally encode in right side up faces through the whole-face pathway. That is, though the face remains recognizable, the spatial relations among parts used in normal face perception are lost. The importance of spatial relations encoded in the whole-face pathway in upright face perception becomes apparent when you turn the book around and look at the faces right side up. Murray, Yon and Rhodes (2000) confirmed that spatial relations among features are only represented during the perception of upright faces but individual features are represented during the perception of both upright and inverted faces. They found that when individual features, rather than spatial relations, were distorted the resulting face looked equally bizarre whether upright or inverted.

Notice the similarity between motor learning and perceptual learning. Motor learning relies on the fact that there are two ways of performing an action. Novel actions must be planned over time as representations of the necessary postures are retrieved and combined. For a familiar action a single representation of the entire action is retrieved and executed. Novel actions become familiar when, as the result

FIGURE 3.33
Thatcher Illusion. Invert and notice similarity of faces.

of repeating an action, the representations of the individual postures became hierarchically organized into a single representation of the entire action. Similarly, perceptual learning also relies on the fact that there are two ways of perceiving an object. Representations of novel objects must be constructed from the representations of their individual geons. For a familiar object a single representation of the entire object is retrieved and matched with the input. Novel objects become familiar when, as the result of repeated viewing, the representations of the individual geons become hierarchically organized into a single representation of the object. The similarity between motor learning and perceptual skills is not accidental. The purpose of the visual system is not merely to help you enjoy the world but to act more effectively in it.

Summary of Shape Construction

- You observe ambiguous scenes more often than you realize because when objects are viewed in the distance or in photographs only monocular cues are available. However, you never experience the scene as ambiguous with regard to depth.
  - During the construction of the final three-dimensional object-representation, a three-dimensional representation of the visual input is compared with representations of objects in memory and these representations guide the construction process.
  - In fact, as much as possible visual representations of objects are retrieved rather than constructed. This has the advantage that once you know how big a toaster or a refrigerator is, it always looks the same size to you. It does not seem to shrink or grow when you see it late at night or across the room.
  - Since memory plays a role in perception, ultimately learning must have played a role in perception as well.

- During perceptual learning patterns of features are encoded and hierarchically organized into representations of objects.
  - A novel object is initially encoded by segmenting it into a connected set of geons and then hierarchically organizing the geons into a single representation. This is called recognition by components (RBC).
  - Observation of the object in more than one orientation makes it possible to encode more than one representation of the object so that the object can be recognized in a variety of orientations.

PERCEPTION AND ACTION

Recall that from the primary visual cortex the visual system divides along two distinct pathways. We have followed the perceptual pathway into the lower temporal cortex where shape construction occurs. This is the declarative pathway whose purpose is to identify whatever you are looking at. The representation ultimately constructed determines your perceptual experience. The procedural pathway extends up into the parietal cortex, where it is combined with the input from the pulvinar nucleus of the thalamus that was mentioned above. As we have mentioned, this input is used to guide voluntary movements made by the manipulation and eye-fixation systems. The two pathways were first described in the macaque monkey and were called the "what" and "where" pathways (Ungerleider & Mishkin, 1982). However, while "what" pathway is not a bad nickname for the perceptual pathway "where" is a little misleading for the action pathway because form as well as location information is used to direct action (Goodale & Humphrey, 1998). Since the parietal representation is used to guide motor movements, "how" or procedural pathway is a better name.

While the pathways are anatomically distinct, they are functionally related. In the normal course of events you reach for things that you recognize. Voluntary actions are directed by both perceptual and non-perceptual visual information.

In the parietal lobe, visual and tactual input is compared with the same spatial representation of an object, so cross-modal recognition is possible. You can perceive a three-dimensional shape through touch as well as vision. If you visually examined an object, such as a toy block, before it was thrown into a bag with several blocks of other shapes you would not have difficulty in reaching into the bag and selecting the one that you had seen. Neurons in the parietal cortex respond to both visual and tactile inputs. When you look at the things that you handle, the task of the perceptual system is sensory integration: combining tactile and visual inputs to construct a single representation. But how does information from the different senses come to be integrated? Do things look the way they feel or do they feel the way they look?

A classic experiment answered this question by placing information from the visual and tactual modalities in conflict. Rock and Victor (1964) asked students to grasp a square while simultaneously examining it through a lens that contracted its visual width to half its original size. The hands of the observers were covered with a cloth so they could not see their fingers. Following the examination period the students were asked to pick a match, visually or tactually, from an array of undistorted similar items or else to draw the standard. The students selected or drew a square that was the size that it had appeared visually, rather than its actual size. Thus vision dominated completely over touch-- the square felt the way it looked.

Very strong or complete visual dominance over touch has been demonstrated many times in a variety of perceptual tasks, including judgments of size (Kinney & Luria, 1970; Miller, 1972), curvature (Easton & Moran, 1978), length (Teghtsoonian & Teghtsoonian, 1970), and spatial location (Hay, Pick, & Ikeda, 1965; Warren & Cleaves, 1971). The results of these studies indicate that vision completely predominates over touch in the perception of form. In contrast when there is a conflict between vision and touch with regard to texture, the perceived roughness of the surface is an even compromise between vision and touch (Lederman & Abbott, 1981). Thus the degree of visual dominance depends on the nature of the task. If the conflicting information is a kind that is usually obtained visually, such as shape information, vision dominates completely. But if the conflicting information is of a kind usually obtained tactually, such as texture information, then tactile information also strongly influences the perception.

VISUAL AGNOSIA AND VISUOSPATIAL DISORDERS

Damage to the perceptual versus (visual) action systems leads to distinct deficits. Damage to the perceptual pathway extending down into the inferotemporal cortex causes a deficit in visual recognition, which is called **visual agnosia**. Damage to the visuomotor pathway extending up into the parietal cortex causes a deficit in the visual control of actions, which is called a **visuospatial** or **visuoconstructive disorder**, or **visual ataxia**. Even though a patient with agnosia may not recognize anything, she will not trip over things, have trouble reaching for them, or move clumsily about. In contrast, a patient with visual ataxia may recognize everything, but when it comes to reaching or moving about, her visual guidance of action is poor.

First consider a visuospatial disorder. In mild cases a person may only get the left and the right confused. For example, he might make an error when asked by an examiner facing him to point with his right hand to the examiner's right eye. In more severe cases a person may have difficulty in putting on her clothes and be unable to find her way about (Benton, 1980; Kolb & Whishaw, 1980). Patients with visual ataxia may have difficulty reaching in the correct direction and/or adjusting the orientation of their hand to the object (Perenin & Vighetto, 1988), and/or adjusting their grasp to the shape and size of the object (Goodale et al., 1993) and/or fixating on the object (Milner & Goodale, 1995). Different patients have different difficulties so it appears that different regions of the parietal cortex control different actions.

A revealing task is to show people a simple pattern and then immediately ask them to copy it or draw it from memory (Wechsler, 1945). Visuospatial deficits caused by parietal lobe damage may also be detected by having a person do some simple drawings, like the face of a clock or a daisy (Goodglass & Kaplan, 1972). Patients produce badly distorted drawings like those in Figure 3.35. Butters, Samuels, Goodglass, and Brody (1970) showed a patient a geometric pattern for half a second; then from 0 to 18 seconds later the patient had to select it from a display containing nine patterns. Parietal patients were less accurate in performing this task than patients with frontal lesions (as well as normal controls) at all study-test intervals. There is also the loss of the ability to mentally rotate an object (Butters & Barton; Butters, Barton, & Brody, 1970). Butters et al. (1970) suggested that the visual-retention deficit is the cause of the failure to perform mental rotations, the poor drawing ability, and the confusion of left and right, because all these tasks require a degree of imagery ability that the patient with parietal injury no longer possesses. Notice that the drawings in Figure 3.34 are distorted on the left. When the shape representation is constructed the separate representations of right and left visual space must be integrated within a single hemisphere. For many visuospatial inputs integration takes place in the right hemisphere. So the right hemisphere contains many neurons that respond to visual and tactile inputs from both sides of space. Hence, when the left hemisphere is injured the right hemisphere can take over much of its processing. However, the left hemisphere contains neurons that only respond to visuospatial inputs from the right side of space. So when the right hemisphere is damaged the left hemisphere cannot take over the processing of those neurons and distortions in the left sides of drawings, as shown in Figure 3.34, are one result.

FIGURE 3.34
Drawings indicating parietal injury: A clock with the hands set at 10 past 11 (Left). A daisy (Right).

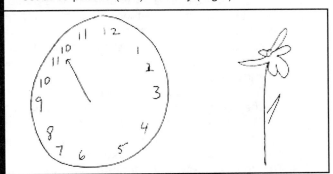

In contrast, consider visual agnosia. A patient with visual agnosia may be able to copy a picture quite well, but be unable to recognize what he is copying (Behrmann, Moscovitch, & Wood, 1995). The recognition deficit in visual agnosia is limited to the visual modality. An agnosic patient who does not recognize his wife standing beside him will recognize her voice as soon as she speaks. An agnosic patient who does not recognize a key lying before him will recognize it tactually as soon as he picks it up and manipulates it and will use it appropriately to open a lock. There are two distinct forms of visual agnosia. One form results from a defect in feature analysis or the integration of visual features in the primary visual cortex. This is sometimes called **apperceptive visual agnosia**. It will be described here. The other form results from a disconnection between the secondary visual cortex and medial temporal cortex (including the limbic system) that prevents the activation of visual memories by visual inputs. This is sometimes called **associative visual agnosia**. It will be described in the chapter on recognition.

Apperceptive agnosia results from bilateral damage to the same small part of the visual processing area in each hemisphere, which can produce a very specific deficit in feature integration or pattern organization that is nonetheless severe enough to disrupt recognition. When the agnosia results from a defect in the integration of features into patterns it is called **simultanagnosia** (Cooper & Humphreys, 2000; Humphreys & Price, 1994). The effect is that only a very small portion of the visual input may be represented at one time. So when looking at a face, an observer can see each eye, the nose, the mouth, etc., all perfectly well. He just cannot see any more than one eye, a nose, etc. at any one time. It is like going through life looking at the world through a narrow tube. Only it is worse. If you look at the world through a tube you can put the pieces together in your memory and eventually recognize what you are looking at. But someone who has lost the ability to integrate the features can never put the pieces together. Since perception is piecemeal, recognition becomes difficult or impossible. For example, the texture formed by the four vertical lines in Figure 3.15(b) does not pop out. In severe cases, like the soldier at the beginning of the chapter, familiar objects become unrecognizable. In a mild case the individual retains enough visual features to recognize things at a general level and so can recognize an object as a face, car, building, or dog. But the person does not retain sufficient features to recognize their own home, car, pet, or face (Benton & Tranel, 1993).

SUMMARY OF CHAPTER

- The central problem of visual perception is how you are able to construct an accurate three-dimensional representation of the world around you from the two-dimensional representation on each retina. The image that the world projects on each retina is distorted with respect to the shapes and sizes of the objects casting the image. Nevertheless, we usually perceive accurately. Your eyes lie but your mind tells the truth!

- Constructing an accurate three-dimensional representation of the world from the information available in the retinal images requires that a great many comparisons within and between images be made across both space and time. The procedure for doing this may be broadly divided into three stages.
    - The first stage is the sensory registration stage. The retinal images are encoded and all the different kinds of information they contain are sorted out for further processing. The optic pathway emerges from the retina and divides into three parts.
        * The smallest part goes directly to the superior colliculus, where its input is used to direct eye movements.
        * The second largest pathway goes first to the thalamus and from there is distributed to parts of the parietal cortex, where its input is used to direct manipulative and other body movements.
        * By far the largest pathway goes first to the thalamus and from there is distributed throughout the occipital cortex. Its input is used to construct the three-dimensional representation of the world that is your perceptual experience.
    - The second stage is the feature analysis stage. The visual system is a heterarchy.
        * There are sequential stages to the processing of the visual input.
        * During the feature analysis stage there are many different patterns being constructed at the same time.
        * These many patterns are combined into single representations in the visual-tactual and object construction stages.
    - The third stage of the procedural pathway is the visual-tactual representation stage. In the parietal lobe a spatial representation is constructed to guide motor movements.
    - The third stage of the declarative pathway is the object construction stage. In the temporal lobe all the patterns are combined into a single representation of a three-dimensional world filled with three-dimensional objects, which corresponds to your perception of the world.

- Visual perception begins when the lens of the eye focuses light on its back wall, called the retina, and activates photoreceptor cells in the retina.
    - Photoreceptors are packed together most densely in or adjacent to a small area in the center of the retina called the fovea.
    - To obtain detailed information about the visual world, it is necessary for the eyes to move to fixation points of high information in the visual field. There is an elaborate system to do just this.
        * About three or four times a second your eyes jump in unison from one fixation point to another.

* The superior colliculus moves the eyes to areas of high contrast, since these are usually areas of high information. The eye-fields in the frontal cortex make use of non-visual information, such as the expectations of the viewer, to direct the eyes to particular points.
  ◦ The visual information is sent along the optic pathway to the thalamus.

- The feature analysis stage begins when the visual input reaches the occipital cortex. The optic pathway reaching the occipital cortex contains three main sub-pathways that in turn each have several sub-pathways etc. The three main sub-pathways sort out the input into that used for representing
  ◦ color.
  ◦ motion.
  ◦ shape.

- In the shape pathway, an edge is any sharp change in brightness. An edge may be represented as a line in a specific orientation and, in fact, that is how the visual system does represent edges.
  ◦ The input is sorted into edges in specific orientations, which are the simplest visual features.
  ◦ As soon as the edges are encoded, adjacent edges are combined into more complex features.

- Some cues used to construct a three-dimensional representation of an object from its two-dimensional image are:
  ◦ Monocular cues such as perspective and relative retinal image size make relative judgments about size and distance possible.
  ◦ Binocular cues such as retinal disparity make depth judgments possible.
  ◦ Binocular cues are only useful for objects a few feet away from you. For distant objects only monocular cues are available.

- Often a scene is ambiguous. That is, more than one representation can be constructed from the visual input.
  ◦ In fact, as much as possible visual representations of objects are retrieved rather than constructed, which resolves most cases of ambiguity. This has the advantage that once you know how big a toaster or a refrigerator is, it always looks the same size to you. It does not seem to shrink or grow when you see it late at night or across the room.
  ◦ Since memory plays a role in perception, ultimately learning must have played a role in perception as well.

- During perceptual learning patterns of features are encoded and hierarchically organized into representations of objects.
  ◦ A novel object is initially encoded by segmenting it into a connected set of geons and then hierarchically organizing the geons into a single representation. This is called recognition by components (RBC).
  ◦ Observation of the object in more than one orientation makes it possible to encode more than one representation of the object so that the object can be recognized in a variety of orientations.

- Damage to a visual pathway results in a characteristic impairment.
  ◦ If some part of the declarative visual pathway is damaged a person can lose the ability to construct visual representations that can be recognized. This disorder is called visual agnosia.
  ◦ If some part of the procedural pathway is damaged a person can lose the ability to use visual information to guide motor movements. This disorder is called visual ataxia.

Chapter 4

ATTENTION

Once upon a time the author of this book was a projectionist for a college film club. Each movie reel is a half hour long and each projection booth has at least 2 projectors. About 5 seconds before the end of a reel a large colored splotch appears in the upper right hand corner of the screen as a signal to the projectionist to be ready to turn on the second projector. This is easy to do, so the audience never notices that the reel has changed. Nor does the audience notice the splotch in the corner of the screen. However, for some years afterward, whenever the former projectionist sat in the audience he always noticed the splotch in the corner. There are two morals to this story. The first is that no one sees everything. The second is that sometimes it is a disadvantage to see too much, and an advantage to see only what is necessary.

DEFINITION

Attention begins with action. In Chapter 2 action was identified with making a motor movement. Though actions often involve movement, they do not have to. Listening for the sound of a starting gun, refusing to move until "Simon says," and trying to remember the answer to a question are all voluntary actions that necessarily require attention but do not require motor movement. Under this more general view of action, at any moment you can do any one of many different things. For example, right now you can continue to read this book or you can stop reading. If you stop reading you may look around the room or close your eyes and relax. However, you can only do one thing at a time. As you make your choice, something becomes the **target** of the task. For example, when you read this book the text is the target. Fundamentally, the target is something to which a voluntary response can be made. The ability to make a voluntary response is the central subject matter of psychology, and there are many names for the experience of performing a voluntary action. When a target enters awareness, just as this sentence is in your awareness, you can do something in response to it. Saying that you are **aware** of some-

TABLE 4.1
Different Ways of Describing
Target of Voluntary Action

Target is in ...
Awareness
Consciousness
Experience
Perception
Working Memory

TABLE 4.2

Differences between Attended and Unattended Input

Effects of Attention and Inattention	Attended Input	Unattended Input
Processing Capacity	Receives what is necessary	Receives what is left over
Part of Present	Yes	No
Procedural Learning	Yes	No
Declarative Learning	Maybe	No

thing, that you are **conscious** of something, that you **experience** something, that you **perceive** something, that something is in **working memory**, and that you can make a **voluntary response** to something are all ways of describing the same thing (Table 4.1).

While these various words tend to be used in different contexts and emphasize different aspects of experience, they do not name different related things, they are all names for the same thing. This can be proven by a test in which any two of the words are selected and we try to imagine whether one can be true of something without the other. For example, you cannot be aware of something without being conscious of it, so awareness and consciousness must be the same thing. So we must avoid the trap of "explaining" consciousness as your experience of something when it is in your working memory. We cannot describe or explain something by simply giving it three different names.

The target of an action is often something in the world, such as the text on this page. This chapter will be concerned with targets in the world, which involve perceptual processing to find them. However, the target of an action may also be a memory or fantasy, such as what you did last weekend or what you plan to do next weekend. In later chapters on learning, retrieval and problem solving actions involving the representations underlying memories and fantasies will be discussed.

There are important consequences of selecting a target representation for a voluntary response (Table 4.2). First, the input to the target representation receives all the processing it needs to be fully analyzed and compare it with memory. Only whatever capacity is left over from processing the attended input is available for processing the unattended inputs. So as you read, you see each word you fixate on clearly, but the words immediately above and below it not at all. Second, the target's representation always locates it within a temporal sequence. Whatever you are perceiving, you are perceiving **now**. An action may or may not be directed to a specific location in space but it always occurs at a particular moment in time. Third, the next time you will process the input a little faster (i.e., procedural learning will occur). Fourth, there is the possibility that the target representation may be encoded in a memory and subsequently retrieved to guide future actions, producing a feeling of familiarity. So declarative learning may occur as well.

At any given moment you can perform any one of many different actions; however, you can only perform one act a time. You may continue to read ahead or you may stop reading or you may go over what you have just read again; but you can only do one of these things at a time. The selection of that one act out of many, the decision of what to do next, is called **attention**. Figure 4.1 shows the parts of the brain involved in selecting a perceptual target or a response to it, i.e., those parts of the brain involved in attention. From the perspective of the brain mechanisms, attention is simply a more general form of motor action. When you chose to look here or there, whether a specific perceptual target is selected by selecting the input along a specific perceptual pathway or by moving your eyes, the same selection mechanism that exerts integrated control over both perceptual pathways and muscles is in play.

FIGURE 4.1

Areas of neocortex involved in attention.

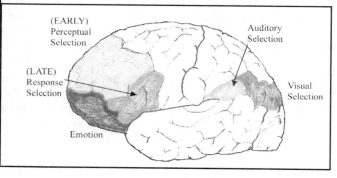

BOTTOM-UP VERSUS TOP-DOWN PROCESSING

The study of attention forces us to address the flow of information in cognitive processing. In the action system commands flow from the top down. The representation of a complete action in the prefrontal cortex is recoded as a representation of sequences of body movements in the motor cortex and basal ganglia, which are recoded as sequences of muscle movements in the cerebellum, which are recoded as executable commands in the brain stem and spinal cord. In a perceptual system such as the visual system, information flows from the bottom up. The sensory representation in the thalamus is recoded as feature, then pattern representations in the occipital cortex, which are finally recoded as object representations in the temporal cortex.

However, action is not entirely **top-down**, nor is perception entirely **bottom-up**. We have already mentioned that voluntary actions may be supported by reflexes. The information flow and control in reflexes is bottom up. We have also mentioned that it is often the case that more than one object representation can be constructed from the same perceptual input; i.e., the input is ambiguous. In this case the various representations are compared with memory and the most likely one is selected. This selection process is top-down. Whether perception is wholly bottom-up or partly top-down depends on details of the perceptual target. When you read this text, word segmentation can be a wholly bottom-up process because the spaces between them are perceptual cues for where one word ends and the next one begins. But suppose that the spaces between the words were eliminated. You could still read this text, but now it would be necessary to generate words from memory and compare them with letter subsequences in the text. This generation-comparison-selection process, where the generation of candidate representations from memory occurs before they are compared with the text, is top-down.

Since the attention system contains both the motor system and the perceptual systems, it is necessarily both top-down and bottom-up. In order to fully describe attention it will be necessary to describe it from four points of view. To begin, we may partition attention into the selection of a target, i.e., perception, and the selection of a response made to it; i.e., action. We may further partition target selection into the top-down selection of a target based on the task's requirements and the bottom-up selection of a target as the result of perceptual organization. First top-down target selection will be described, in the next section, called, "Selective Attention." Then bottom-up target selection will be described, in the second section, called, "Alerting." Similarly, we may partition response selection into problems selecting among competing responses automatically generated by bottom-up processes and problems selecting among competing responses generated by conflicting task demands. Bottom-up response competition and selection will be described in the third section, called, "Interference." Then, top-down response-competition and selection will be described in the fourth section, called, Multitasking."

Finally, voluntary actions are influenced by stimuli that influence performance in involuntary ways. If you are very upset then you may not be able to help yourself, you will just not do as well on an exam. The final two sections of the chapter are concerned with how both target detection and response selection are influenced by your arousal level as well as by your intention.

SELECTIVE ATTENTION

In Chapter 2 we saw that the action system consists of two stages: planning and performance. One advantage of having voluntary movements controlled by a two-stage process is that a planned action can be withheld until just the right moment for execution. For example, a projectionist plans the motion to turn on the second projector and then waits until the second splotch appears.

First the motor plan for turning on the second projector when the second splotch appears is retrieved. When a voluntary action has been prepared, even if it has not yet been executed, the motor plan is said to be in **working memory**. This synonym for consciousness emphasizes both its active nature and the contribution of knowledge in memory. It will be used throughout this chapter. The motor plan contains a representation of the target of the action, i.e., the second splotch. Whenever a motor plan provides access to its target perceptual representation so you know what the target looks like, we say that the target has been specified. That is, the projectionist knows what the splotch looks like before he sees it, which is why he is able to detect it. So the first stage of selective attention will be called **target specification**. When an auditory or visual representation is specified by a motor plan in working memory then perceptual input is directed towards it.

Second, the location of a potential target is identified through the comparison of input with the target representation. This will be called **search**. The search stage ends when the comparison process produces a match and a response indicating that the target has been found. As a result of the match, input from nontarget locations is inhibited and a detailed representation of the potential target enters working memory. The response that places a detailed representation in working memory, thus making it the target of a voluntary action is called the **orienting response**. Hence this final stage of target selection is called **orientation.**

SPECIFICATION: PRIMING AND EXPECTATION

Whatever specifies the target is called the cue. In the example above, the cue for the end of the reel is a colored splotch. Depending on context, a cue may specify what the target is, and where and when it will appear. The splotch specifies all three of these aspects of the target to the projectionist. However, depending on the task, a cue may specify a target to a greater or lesser degree. Consider a lexical decision task, in which an observer must decide whether a string of letters is a word. The definition of the task specifies a target: any word. A second cue may be added by presenting a string of X's at the location that the test item will appear exactly two seconds before it. Specifying the time and location that a target may appear allows an observer to prepare a response and hence respond faster than when such a cue is not presented. The information that the cue provides about the target can be further increased by replacing the string of X's with a form prime or semantic prime (Chapter 3). A form prime is any prime that is a good part of the perceptual representation of the target, like the geons used by Biederman and Cooper (1991).

A form prime for a word would be the first two letters of the word. In Chapter 3 a semantic prime was defined as a pictured object with the same name as the target object, e.g., the prime and object might both be pianos. The definition of a semantic prime may be generalized so that a semantic relationship exists between the prime and target if they are in the same category, e.g., they are both birds. It can be further generalized to include cases where the prime is a category, e.g., *BIRD* and the target is an instance of that category, e.g., *robin*. For example, when the target was *robin*, the cue could be the form prime *ro* or the semantic prime *BIRD*. We shall have much to say about why priming occurs in the Chapter 4. In regards to attention it is necessary to mention that the use of a prime as a cue further reduces the time to respond to a target.

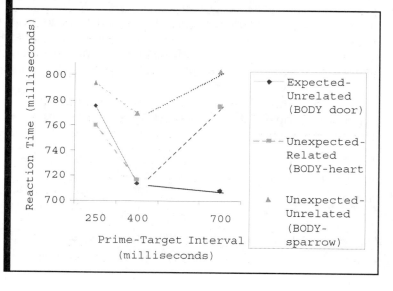

FIGURE 4.2

Relatedness and expectation. As expectations come to influence the processing of an input, the processing of expected targets is facilitated and the processing of unexpected targets is inhibited (after Neely, 1977).

The use of a prime as a cue raises an interesting question. Are cues and primes different things that reduce the time to respond to a target in different ways, or are they really two different names for the same thing? Priming represents an automatic effect of the autonomous processing that results from procedural learning. As we have done before, we may contrast the fast automatic processing that is possible during a familiar task with the slower voluntary processing that is necessary during a novel task. A cue that is not a prime may also reduce the processing of a subsequent target in a novel task. If I tell you that the word *BODY* will be followed by the name of a building part and you believe me, then you have the conscious expectation that after you see *BODY* then you will see the name of a building part. You have an expectation of the target, expressed as specification of the target representation and suppression of **distracter** (i. e., nontarget) representations. In a classic experiment, James Neely (1977) demonstrated the roles of both semantic priming and expectation on target identification.

Neely (1977) used a clever task to distinguish the automatic semantic priming effect from a subsequent expectation response produced by a semantically unrelated cue. Observers were asked to determine as rapidly as possible whether a string of letters was a word (e.g., *robin*) or a nonword (e.g., *rokin*). The letter string was preceded by a cue that was sometimes a word (e.g., *BODY*). When *BODY* appeared, the observers in the experiment knew that two-thirds of the time the word that followed (if the string was, in fact, a word) would be a building part (e.g., *door*) and that only one-sixth of the time would it be a body part. Hence the observers were not expecting a body part. However, as shown in Figure 4.2, when the word followed the semantic prime by only 250 milliseconds body parts were identified faster than building parts. So 250 milliseconds was all the time that was needed for the match of *BODY* to automatically semantically prime body parts. In contrast, when the target followed *BODY* by 700 milliseconds, building parts were identified faster than body parts. The 700 milliseconds were a sufficient interval for a person's expectations to reduce the time to recognize building parts, while suppressing the recognition of body parts. After 700 milliseconds, body parts were identified as words nearly as slowly as words totally unrelated to the priming word, such as bird names.

GATE MODEL OF SELECTION

The brain system for target selection is shown schematically in Figure 4.3. It is sometimes described as a system for opening and closing gates through which the perceptual input must pass. By opening one gate and closing the others, a particular input may be selected for further processing. To the left and top of the figure we have the frontal cortex, parietal cortex, and basal ganglia. We saw in Chapter 2 that areas of these brain structures are parts of the system for performing voluntary motor actions. It is useful to think of attention as an elaboration of the motor system. After all, voluntary actions are often part of a more general shift in attention. When you read this book, as you shift your attention from word to word, your eyes follow and fixate on that word. Moving the eyes to change their fixation point is a motor action that selects a new visual target. As the result of signals from the cortex to the basal ganglia and ultimately to motor neurons directing eye movement, certain muscles contract and the eyes move. It is only one step (though a big one) from using the system that selects a visual target by moving the eyes to adapting that system to select some portion of the visual input after the eyes have fixated.

To the bottom and right of Figure 4.3 we have the thalamus, visual cortex, and temporal cortex. We saw in Chapter 3 that the visual cortex is where the analysis of the visual input into simple features and patterns occurs and the temporal cortex is where these patterns are compared with a representation of the visual target. The superior colliculus regulates eye movements and the parietal cortex marks the spatial location of the visual target. It is in the thalamus that a system of gates distributes perceptual input throughout the visual and parietal cortex. These thalamic gates are controlled by the basal ganglia, which in turn are partly controlled by signals from a variety of pathways from the frontal and parietal cortex. We saw in Chapter 2 that the basal ganglia control motor movements, including eye movements through their influence on the superior colliculus, as shown in the figure. So the basal ganglia that originally evolved for the control of physical action were recruited to become part of a basal ganglia-thalamic system that provides fine control of mental actions such as the selection of a portion of the visual input available at a fix-

FIGURE 4.3

Overview of brain system controlling visual attention.

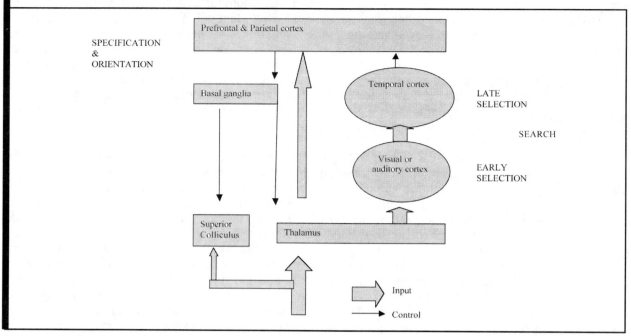

FIGURE 4.4

Attention can be directed by perception to the vertical pattern by the O's. Attention can also be directed by memory to the horizontal letter string that forms the word broth.

O
ZPORF
AQOSG
BROTH
CSOUI
DTOVJ
O

TABLE 4.3

Overview of Selective Attention

Stage	Target
Early or Perceptual	Novel or Perceptually Distinct
Late or Response	Familiar

ation point. Hence, when the cortex signals the basal ganglia, which in turn signals the thalamus, the net effect is that most of the gates in the thalamus slam shut and a single part of the perceptual input is selected for further processing (Desimone, Chelazzi, Miller, & Duncan, 1995; Heilman, Watson, & Valenstein, 1993; Posner & Petersen, 1990).

Two different levels of representation of the input provide two different methods for selecting a target. Having more than one method of selecting a target is useful because a target may differ from its surroundings in a variety of ways. Suppose that in a crowded party you focus on the high-pitched voice, or golden hair, of your companion. It is not necessary (though perhaps pleasurable) to compare the input with a detailed representation of her pretty face or sweet voice to pick her out from the surroundings. When the input has a unique feature defined at the feature analysis stage of the perceptual system (such as pitch or color) then **perceptual selection,** or **early selection**, occurs during search. A single brief search is often sufficient to find a target when early selection of some perceptual feature is possible. Only a single input representation (the one containing the unique critical feature) is compared and matched with the target representation. In contrast, suppose that you search among the voices at a party for someone saying the final score of a baseball game. You were forced to miss the end of the game but you are sure someone in the room did not. When the input has no unique perceptually defined feature it can only be selected by matching it with the specified target representation of the team's names and words about the score. Then **late selection,** or **response selection,** occurs. You must serially orient to several potential target locations and compare the speech input from each location with the detailed specified representation in working memory to find the target. So late selection requires a search-orientation loop to find the target (Table 4.3). For example, in Figure 4.4, attention to the column of O's is an example of early selection. The repeated pattern forms a texture that pops out when the entire visual display is processed in parallel. Attention to the word BROTH in the figure is an example of late selection. It can only be found by serially reading each letter string until it is found.

EARLY SELECTION

As its name implies, early or perceptual selection makes use of perceptual features to reduce the number of input representations that must be compared with memory. Recall that the perceptual system partitions the perceptual input into sub-areas distinguished by different perceptual features. For example, a single red letter among black ones will pop out and enter working memory whether you are looking for it or not. If coincidentally, you happen to be looking for it, this could be described as a case of early selection. Another example of early selection is when each letter of nine different letters is a different color: red, green, blue, yellow, etc. In this case, none of the letters would pop out if you were not looking for any one in particular. However, if you were looking for the red letter, then the gates for all the other color pathways would be closed in the thalamus and only input passing through the red one would be compared with memory. When only the target has a defining perceptual feature, such as a particular color, early selection reduces the number of input representations that must be compared with memory to one, thus reducing the search stage to a single comparison.

A pathway for a specific pitch or location may be used to select an auditory target and a pathway for a specific brightness, location, or color may be used to select a visual target. Early selection can produce perfect selective attention to the target as long as the target is sufficiently discriminable from the distracters, i. e., the target differs sufficiently from the distracters on location, pitch, brightness, etc. One perceptual feature that almost always discriminates both auditory and visual inputs from each other is location. Knowing where to look can reduce the number of comparisons required to find the target to just one. We begin with a discussion of the role of location in early selection and then move on to other auditory and visual features.

Selective attention to a location. Most often you direct your attention to a target at a specific location in space; e.g., you look at someone who is talking to you. When you do this, the entire perceptual system is directed towards that particular location. First, the processing of input from other locations is inhibited and the processing of the input at the attended location is disinhibited. Second, you move your eyes to focus on the attended input. Recall that rods and cones are packed together most densely near the center of the retina. As a result, when a visual input is fixated on it receives a much more detailed analysis than the input being ignored. The detailed analysis is ultimately used to construct a detailed representation.

Similarly, when an auditory input is selected on the basis of location it also receives a much more detailed representation than the input being ignored. In a famous experiment, E. Colin Cherry (1953) had listeners wear earphones while one spoken message was presented to the right ear and another spoken message was presented to the left ear. The listener had to repeat everything he heard in the right ear. This is called "shadowing." Its only purpose was to make certain the listener was selectively attending to the target message in the right ear. The ability to selectively attend to a target in the presence of distracters can be evaluated by measuring how much of both the target and distracters are perceived. The more of the target and the less of the distracters that are perceived, the better is selective attention to the target. Cherry's measure of selective attention was how much of the unattended input in the left ear was remembered. The input in the left ear always began and ended with normal English spoken in a male voice. However, the middle portion of the left ear's input either remained the same or changed to English spoken in a higher-pitched female voice, to reversed male speech (e. g., a segment of tape-recorded speech played backward), or to a single tone. No person was ever able to remember any word or phrase heard in the rejected ear. Furthermore, though all listeners knew the ignored input was speech, some listeners were unable to definitely identify it as English. A few listeners remembered the reversed speech as having something queer about it, but it was thought to have been normal speech by others. Only the change of voice from male to female or the introduction of a tone was almost always noticed. So selective attention on the basis of location was highly effective. Everything in the target message was perceived but very little of the ignored input was perceived.

Early selective attention in audition. Location is not the only perceptual dimension on which you can select. Anne Treisman found that you can select an auditory target if it has a pitch that is different from the distracters so that the auditory system organizes it as a distinct pattern and it pops out. Treisman and Riley (1969) presented one spoken message to each ear of the listener. In this case, both messages were lists of digits that also included an occasional letter spoken in a different voice from the digits. The listeners had to shadow one of the messages, insuring attention to that location. In addition, the listeners were told that when they heard a letter in either ear they should stop shadowing at once and tap their desk with a ruler. The listeners, then, had to selectively attend both to the digits presented in one ear and at the same time to all the letters presented to either ear, which they could do by attending to the distinctive pitch of the voice the letters were spoken in. In fact, Triesman's results showed that nearly all the letters presented to both ears were detected. So a listener can selectively attend to sounds distinguished by their pitch even when she is also attending to sounds distinguished by their location.

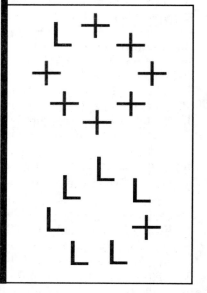

FIGURE 4.5
For even 3-month-old infants, a single plus will pop out from among six Ls and a single L will pop out from among 6 plus signs. (Rovee-Collier, et al., 1992).

Early selective attention in vision. You can select a visual target if it has a unique brightness, color, or other visual feature when compared with the distracters in the visual field, so that the visual system organizes it as a distinct pattern or texture and it pops out. For even 3-month old infants, a single plus sign will pop out from among six Ls and a single L will pop out from among 6 plus signs, as shown in Figure 4.5 (Rovee-Collier, C., Hankins, E. M., & Bhatt, R. S., 1992).

We discussed the role of organization in visual perception in Chapter 3. As described in Chapter 3, when the visual input is organized by the visual system so that some area is segmented from the rest then pop out occurs. When the target pops out, it is called **early selection**. How quickly pop out occurs depends on how different the target is from the surrounding distracters and where visual attention is being directed (Theeuwes, Kramer, & Atchley, 1999).

Early selection of novel inputs. Memory also plays a role in early selection. The visual system will combine adjacent identical letters, such as a field of Zs or Ns, into a single texture. The organization into a single texture is not only influenced by the fact that all the elements have identical features but also by the fact that they all match the same letter representation. When a single character with the same features that does not match the letter representation is inserted in the texture, such as a mirror image Z or mirror image N, it pops out.

FIGURE 4.6

Reaction times as a function of set size when searching for a novel target (mirror-image N among familiar distracters. The slopes for correct target-present and target-absent regressions are shown in parentheses (from Wang et al., 1994).

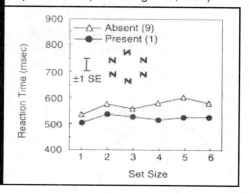

This was shown by Wang, Cavanaugh, and Green (1994), who had observers respond as fast as possible whether 1- to 6-element displays were identical (target absent condition) or contained one different element (target present condition). They systematically varied the familiarity of both the target and the distracters. Figure 4.6 shows an example display and the results for the displays in which a novel target was embedded in a display of familiar elements. In this condition pop out occurred and the number of display elements did not affect the detection of the target. Since a novel target pops out from among familiar ones novel targets are easily found and even novel distracters may be noticed. So the bias of the perceptual system for novelty results in a bias in attention for novelty.

Illusions from rapid presentation. We saw in Chapter 3 that the visual input travels along distinct pathways in the visual cortex and is analyzed into different features that are eventually assembled into the representation of an object. Here we have seen that during early selection a target is selected before its features are assembled into its final representation. This description of early selection implies that if, for example, you are looking for a red gumdrop you will select something as red before you know that it is a gumdrop. A striking illusion demonstrates that this is exactly what happens.

When a sequence of visual inputs occurs one after the other in the same location at a rate greater than 10 per second, the visual system may have difficulty sorting out the features among successive inputs. A task like this is called a **rapid serial visual presentation (RSVP)** task. Suppose an observer in the RSVP task is asked to report a target containing a particular feature, such as an upper case word. The observer detects an upper-case letter by matching a representation of an upper-case letter with part of the input. At the same time, a match between the entire input and a word representation is used to identify the word. Recall that the visual processing system is a heterarchy. So word and letter recognition are performed independently, in parallel, and then subsequently combined in a single representation. However, when 10 words per second are presented, the time it takes to recognize a word is less than the time to determine the case of a letter string, and there is thus no guarantee that the word and letter representations for the same input will be put together. Instead, the upper-case response may be associated with the word response for a different input than the target. When this happens, it is called an **illusory conjunction.** The observer connects the target feature to the distracter presented before or after the target. Lawrence (1971) created such illusory conjunctions between word representations and the cases of their letters. He flashed successive words at observers at rates of up to twenty words a second. At the fastest rate each word was available for processing for 50 milliseconds before it was replaced by its successor. All the words but one were in lower case, and the observer had to report the upper case word. The error rate was 42 per cent for a presentation rate of 20 words per second. Seventy-two per cent of the errors were the reporting of lower case words that were also presented. Of these errors, sixty-nine percent of the time a word following the upper case word was reported and thirty-one percent of the time a word preceding the upper case word was reported.

Using the RSVP technique, Broadbent and his colleagues (Gathercole & Broadbent, 1984; McLean, Broadbent, & Broadbent, 1982) demonstrated illusory conjunctions between digits and their colors, and Intraub (1985) demonstrated illusory conjunctions between pictures and the kinds of frames around them. In each case a feature might be perceived as part of a distracter either preceding or following the target. Using a similar technique, Treisman and Schmidt (1982) presented colored letters and created illusory conjunctions between a letter's shape and color for spatially adjacent colored letters that were presented simultaneously. For example, if a display contained a red B next to a black R, an observer might see a black B. Finally, using the RSVP technique, when a target digit was signaled by an auditory click, distracters that both preceded and followed the target were erroneously reported, indicating an illusory conjunction between the click and the visual presentation of the digit (Weichselgartner & Sperling, 1987). With purely auditory inputs, a similar dissociation is observed for pitch and location (Cutting, 1976; Efron & Yund, 1974).

The illusory conjunctions described above occur because there is insufficient time to suppress all other input when a target feature is detected. As we saw in Chapter 3, the processing of visual input is not continuous but episodic. Discrete snapshots of the visual field are punctuated by saccadic eye movements and shifts in visual attention. It takes a certain amount of time to construct a representation for an input and compare it with representations in memory. As we will see below, during the time that the target's representation is being constructed distracter input is suppressed by closing the appropriate thalamic gates. When the rate of presentation is too great to select only the target's input then various inputs may be combined when the target representation is constructed. In Lawrence's (1971) RSVP experiment, upper-case print was the cue and the target appeared for only 50 milliseconds. Selecting the target meant suppressing all input except for those 50 milliseconds. Correct identification of a target that appears for only 50 milliseconds requires the ability to precisely control the thalamic gates so that only the input during this brief interval is processed. When the temporal control of the thalamic gate is too coarse, so that more than one input gets through; some sort of illusion, such as the illusory conjunction between one word and another word's case, is the result.

LATE SELECTION

When the target does not contain a distinctive auditory or visual feature that a perceptual system uses to segment it from other inputs then all the input representations containing a target feature must be compared with the specified target representation. For example, if you are looking for a white circle and there is more than one white shape in the visual field then all the white shapes may have to be compared with the shape representation for a circle. Late selection runs into two kinds of difficulties not observed with early selection. First, the number of input representations that may be compared with memory is a function of the number of features that must be matched in order to identify them. In the limiting case, such as for word representations, only one input representation may be compared with memory at a time. Since more comparisons have to be made, the duration of the search stage is extended. For example, it is quick and easy to find the word "selection" elsewhere on this page through early selection because it is in bold. But it is tedious and time consuming to find the word "shadow" elsewhere on this page through late selection, because many words have to be read until it is found.   Even if you attempt to speed up the search process for "shadow" by just looking for words that begin with the letter "s" you will read words other than "shadow" that begin with "s."

Late selection in audition. Selective listening becomes difficult when the inputs are similar in pitch and location (Cherry, 1953; Treisman, 1964) and so they are not segmented into distinct sounds. Recall that Treisman and Riley (1969) presented lists of digits that also included an occasional letter to each ear of a listener. The listener had to shadow the list in one ear and detect all the letters. When the letters were spoken in a different voice from the digits, they popped out even before they were identified and were all detected. However, when the letters were spoken in the same voice as the digits they no longer popped out. So each spoken character had to be categorized as a digit or letter by matching it with its representation in memory. When every character presented in either ear had to be compared with memory and identified, the comparison process was overwhelmed and some targets were missed. Thus, late selection was not perfect in Treisman and Riley's (1969) task, as about 75 per cent of the letters presented in the attended ear and only 33 per cent presented in the unattended ear were detected.

Practice and late auditory selection. We saw above that a novel unfamiliar item will pop out from among identical familiar ones because the perceptual system distinguishes the novel item from the familiar ones when it organizes the input. Hence there is early selection for a novel target among familiar identical distracters. On the other hand, we saw in Chapter 3 that the comparison of input to a familiar representation produces a match faster than the construction of a novel representation, so a single familiar item will pop out from among unfamiliar ones. Hence there is rapid late selection for a familiar target among unfamiliar distracters. As a result, late selection for a particular item improves with practice. So the ability to selectively listen to an auditory target increases as its familiarity increases (Poltrock, Lansman, & Hunt, 1982). However, the effect of practice carries a downside. The same practice that makes a specific message, such as a familiar song, easier to recognize also makes it more difficult to ignore (Johnston, 1978). When an unfamiliar target and a familiar distracter are presented together that cannot be distinguished on the basis of early selection, it is the distracter representation that is matched to its input first, which increases the time to find the target.

Late selection in vision. Detecting a visual target also becomes more difficult when early selection is not possible (Duncan & Humphreys, 1989; Northdurft, 1993; Treisman & Gormican, 1988). For example, a target defined by the conjunction of both its shape and color does not pop out from a display containing distracters that have either the same color or the same shape. It can only be selected by either serially examining each display item of the target color to determine its shape or serially examining each display item of the target shape to determine its color. It takes longer to find a conjunction of a letter and a color among colored letters (Duncan & Humphreys, 1992; Treisman, 1991; Treisman, 1992) than to pick out a unique color or a unique letter that pops out. Your visual system organizes the upper panel of Figure 4.7 into a white element in a dark texture by putting all the dark elements together. Since all the dark squares and circles are put together into a single pattern, you can perform early selection on the white circle and the time it takes to detect it is independent of the number of dark squares and circles in the display. Also, your visual system organizes the middle panel of Figure 4.7 into a circle in a texture of squares by putting all the squares together into a single pattern. You can perform early selection so it is quick and easy to find the circle among the squares. But in the bottom panel of Figure 4.7, the white circle does not pop out from among the dark circles and white squares. There is no visual feature that defines all the distracters to enable the visual system to put them together into a texture. The white circle can only be found by comparing the representation of each display element, one at a time, with a representation of a white circle in memory. As a result, the time to find the white circle is proportional to the number of display elements.

Practice and late visual selection. Familiarity has the same effect on late selection in visual attention that it has on late selection in auditory attention. Familiar targets produce matches faster than unfamiliar distracters. For example, letters are not distinguished from numbers by a set of visual features. When unpracticed observers searched for a letter among numbers, the results were as shown in Figure 4.8. The time to find a letter among digits was proportional to the number of distracters in the display because each display element was compared with memory one at a time until the target was found. After 14 days of practicing searching for a letter among digits (during which over 4000 searches were conducted), subjects were able to compare all the display elements with memory at the same time. The target produced a match and a response before any of the distracters. So the time to detect a target was no longer linearly related to the number of display items (Figure 4.8). In fact, if searching for several targets at once has been sufficiently practiced, an observer can scan for any one of several different targets at the same time (Neisser, 1963; Schneider & Shiffrin, 1977; Shiffrin & Schneider, 1977). However, as with audition, there is a downside to practice in vision. When Richard Shiffrin and Walter Schneider (1977) reversed the task, all their practice searching for letters among digits made it difficult for the students to search for digits among letters. The students found that they could not ignore the familiar letters— the former letter-targets kept intruding on their awareness when they tried to search for the digits.

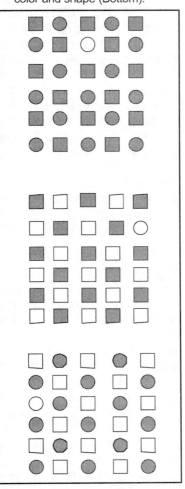

FIGURE 4.7
Selective attention to feature conjunction. White target can be effortlessly selected on the basis of color (Top); round target can be effortlessly selected on the basis of shape (Middle); but white round target requires effort to select on the basis of color and shape (Bottom).

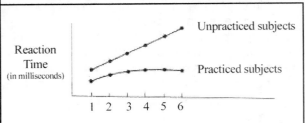

FIGURE 4.8
Performance on an item recognition task for one or more items from a fixed set as function of display size.

Reaction Time (in milliseconds)

Unpracticed subjects

Practiced subjects

1 2 3 4 5 6

Another example of a familiar item being an intrusive distracter comes from proof reading. Practice in reading results in perceptual learning (procedural memory) so that the visual input rapidly matches whole-word representations. So in printed word recognition there are parallel fast whole-word and slower letter-sequence pathways for recognition. This is generally a good thing because it makes reading faster. But the whole-word representation also makes the task of seeing the individual letters more difficult because it does not contain this information (Adams, 1979). Alice Healy (1980) demonstrated this effect of the whole-word pathway by instructing college students to read a prose passage at their normal reading speed and to encircle all the t's they came across. The students missed more t's in common words like *fact* than in rare words like *pact*. Similarly, function words are more frequent than content words, and Schindler (1978) found more letter detection errors on function words than content words. The most common word of all in the English language is *the*. In one passage Healy (1980) found that students missed t's in 38 percent of the *the*'s but only in 20 percent of the other words containing t (see also Corcoran, 1966; Healy, 1976). Similarly, Haber and Schindler (1981) found that misspellings that changed the overall shape of a word were more likely to be detected than ones that did not (see also Holbrook 1978). Because whole-word recognition makes letter detection more difficult, it makes the detection of spelling errors that preserve the overall shape of the word more difficult. Healy (1981) also asked college students to read passages at their normal reading speed but to mark any spelling errors they noticed while reading. She created the spelling errors by substituting one letter for another in the passage. For example, c was substituted for e, creating *studcnts*, and s was substituted for o, creating *absut*. According to the feature analysis hypothesis, c and e differ by only a single feature, the horizontal line that is present in the e but not in the c. However, s and o differ by more than one feature. The students failed to notice 60 percent of the c-for-e substitutions but failed to notice only 5 percent of the s-for-o substitutions. More generally, Healy found that if the substitution maintained the outer configuration of the original, as in c for e or C for G, the student was more likely to fail to detect the substitution than if the outer configuration was changed.

Vigilance. One of the things that you take for granted in a visual search experiment is that you will remember what you are looking for until you find it. However, remembering what you are looking for is not trivial. Adele Diamond (1995) found that infants gradually acquire this ability over the middle months of the first year of life. Memory for an item was assessed by letting an infant see a toy for a period of time and then removing it. After a delay the infant was shown the old toy next to a new toy. Infants have a preference for novelty and they will tend to look at the new toy. If an infant looks more at the new toy than an old one it of course implies that the old toy has been remembered. Diamond found that a 4-month-old infant looked at the novel toy 70% of the time after a retention interval of 10 seconds. A six-month-old infant looked at the novel toy 70% of the time after a retention interval of 3 minutes. By nine months, an infant looked at the novel toy 70% of the time after 10 minutes.

In the case of early selection, it is not necessary to remember what one is looking for to find it because the target will pop out regardless. However, life includes a variety of late-selection tasks that require a person to remember what he is looking for. These are target detection tasks in which the environment must be monitored for an extended period of time. Such a task, called a **vigilance task**, is the assignment of a sentry, lookout, or watchman. During World War II, the vigilance task required of sonar operators stimulated interest in the problem. A small blip on a sonar screen may indicate a school of fish, while a larger blip may be a ship. The operator's task is to alert the rest of the crew if a larger blip is seen. When distracters are sufficiently similar to the target, so that they are only rejected after comparison with the target representation, the target representation is disrupted after a few minutes so the probability of detecting the target is reduced. Therefore, when the similarity among targets and distracters is high, performance deteriorates over time. The seminal study was reported by Norman Mackworth (1948). How long a time passes before the decrement in performance becomes noticeable depends on a host of task variables, environmental variables, and subject variables (Mackie, 1977; Stroh, 1977) that influence the degree of processing of a target. When targets are rare and similar distracters are common, a decrement occurs within 10 minutes of the task's onset (Jerison, 1977; J. F. Mackworth, 1964).

THE ORIENTING RESPONSE AND DIVIDED ATTENTION

When a target representation is matched, several distinct responses are made that are collectively called the **orienting response (OR)**. For example, visual orienting is a two-stage process. First the processing of input from a new location begins and then the eyes move to fixate on the target at that location. A visual OR is made by the brain structures shown in Figure 4.3 (Posner & Petersen, 1990). In the first stage, the frontal cortex and parietal cortex signal the basal ganglia. In turn the basal ganglia signal the pulvinar nucleus of the thalamus and the superior colliculus. The basal ganglia inhibit thalamic processing of input from the old location and disinhibit thalamic processing of input from the new location. Remington (1980) found that the thalamic shift to the new target occurs within 150 milliseconds of its initiation by the basal ganglia. In the second stage, the additional visual information that is gained by the shift is used through the basal ganglia-superior colliculus pathway to guide the eyes to the new location in the eye movement that follows (Fischer & Breitmeyer, 1987; Posner & Cohen, 1984). Notice that visual attention leads rather than follows the eye movement.

After the first stage of a visual OR an observer already has some information about the shape at the target location about 100-150 milliseconds after the OR is initiated. However, complete information about the shape at the target location is not obtained until after an eye movement has been made to fixate on it about 300-milliseconds after the OR is initiated. To determine when visual information is processed during a visual OR, Weichselgartner and Sperling (1987) presented continuous streams of characters at the rate of 10 or 12.5 characters per second at two locations. Observers watched for the presence of the letter C in one location and then reported the first four digits seen in the adjacent location. In fact, the probability of reporting a digit depended on how long after the C it appeared. The first digits detected appeared 100 milliseconds after the C and the probability of reporting a digit peaked at 300-400 milliseconds after the C was shown (Figure 4.9).

Along with the opening and closing of thalamic gates, an OR is accompanied by one or more of several physiological responses. These responses include pupil dilation, contraction of the blood vessels in the limbs, dilation of the blood vessels in the head, and changes in the galvanic skin response and the electrical activity of the brain. The physiological measures are often used as an indirect measure of whether a person has noticed some change in their environment. The measure-

FIGURE 4.9

The probability of a report peaks at 400 milliseconds after the cue to switch attention (from Weichselgartner & Sperling, 1987).

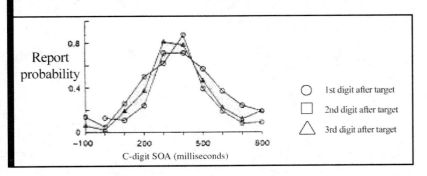

ment of involuntary physiological responses does not require the experimenter to call attention to the change by asking the person about it. For example, you might determine whether a person noticed that her own name was presented in her unattended ear while she was shadowing the message in the other ear by recording whether there was an OR to it.

Another well-known use of the components of the OR is to detect lies. Lie detection is a case of pseudo-psychology run amok. The theory behind the lie detector, or polygraph, is that when a person tells a lie, they feel sufficient anxiety to cause a detectable OR. First, anyone who has ever had the choice between admitting an unpleasant truth or covering up with a convenient falsehood may question whether veracity or mendacity causes more anxiety and therefore whether the theory makes any sense. Second, years of testing (Ben-Shakhar, Lieblich, & Bar-Hillel, 1982; Kleimuntz & Szucko, 1982; Lykken, 1981) have clearly shown that as a practical tool for telling truth from falsehood, the lie detector is useless.

Nevertheless, Epstein (1994) reported that lie detectors are still used, unsuccessfully, by the CIA to look for double agents within its ranks.

DIVIDED ATTENTION

At this point it is useful to make a distinction between a **single target** and a **target sequence** (or **target set,** when more than one target is present at a time). Consider two different tasks. One task is to determine whether there is at least one red one among a pile of M&Ms on the table. The other task is to determine how many red M&Ms there are in the pile on the table. The first task is a selective attention task to a single target and you can use early selection to determine if there is at least one red one in the pile. But since all the red inputs get compared with the same target representation, early selection does not let you know how many M&Ms are red. To count the red M&Ms you must somehow divide your attention among all of them, which are a sequence of targets. Any task that requires that attention be divided among more than one target is a divided attention task.

When there is more than one red M&M visible on the table it is not possible to orient to more than one location at the same time. In divided attention, first attention must be shifted to the location of one target, so that it can enter working memory, and then attention must be shifted to the location of another target so that it can next enter working memory. The representation of a target enters working memory only after the representation has been matched with the target's input, so divided attention to more than one target always requires late selection. Shifting from one location to another takes time and in the interval a briefly presented target may be missed (Duncan, 1980). Divided attention experiments usually make use of briefly presented targets to assess how quickly a person can shift attention among targets.

Divided auditory target detection. Moray, Fitter, Ostry, Favreau, and Nagy (1976) performed an auditory divided attention task. A listener had to detect a target tone of a particular pitch or loudness. The target tone always occurred in one of two locations. The listener had to press one key if the target was heard in one location and the other key when the target was heard in the other location. Also, when target tones were presented simultaneously in both locations the listener was required to attend to both tones and press both keys. The researchers found that when both tones occurred simultaneously the probability of detecting a tone in one location was reduced.

Even though there are misses when independent voluntary responses must be made to simultaneous auditory targets, the probability of responding to both targets is not zero. The time that the representation of an auditory input remains available for further processing is a function of both its intensity and duration and exceeds the period during which it actually occurs. The persistence of the representation of an auditory input after its physical presentation is called its **echo**. Estimates of auditory persistence range from 1 to 5 seconds (Darwin, Turvey, & Crowder, 1972; Glucksberg & Cowan, 1970; Guttman & Julesz, 1963; Kubovy & Howard, 1976; Norman, 1969) depending on how the echo was measured. So if a listener shifts her attention between two locations, she may hear and respond to both of two simultaneously presented tones, though the tones may not be perceived as having occurred simultaneously.

Divided visual target detection. As with audition, when an observer has to make independent responses to simultaneously presented visual targets, one target may be missed. John Duncan (1980) presented a cross consisting of four characters (Figure 4.10). An observer had to look for a digit target among letter distracters. In one experiment there were independent probabilities that a digit could appear in either the vertical or horizontal bar of the cross. Thus, a cross could contain 0, 1, or 2 digit targets. In the single response condition the observer had a single key and was told to press it whenever a cross contained at least one digit. In this condition, even though the observer had to press a key when he saw even a single digit, he was more likely to press it when both the vertical and horizontal bar contained a digit. Thus the probability of pressing the key indicated that when both the vertical and the horizontal bar contained a digit, both targets were seen. Furthermore, it did not matter whether the two bars of the cross were presented simultaneously or successively, a half a second apart.

FIGURE 4.10

Types of visual displays used by Duncan (1980).

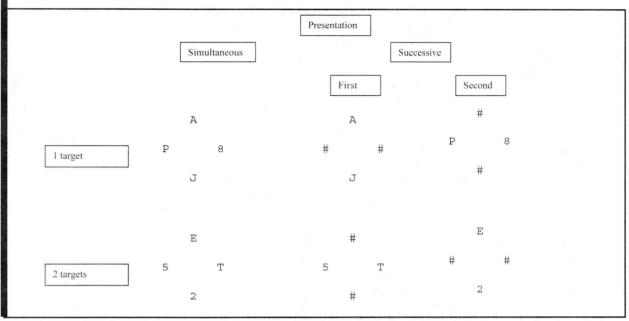

In the dual response condition the observer had one key for the horizontal bar and another key for the vertical bar and had to press the key for the bar where the digit target appeared. Hence, 0, 1, or 2 independent responses might be made to a display. In this condition the probability of detecting a digit target in one bar was negatively correlated with the probability of detecting a digit target in the other bar. Furthermore, performance was better when the bars were presented successively than when they were presented simultaneously. Since the results of the single response condition demonstrated that the observer saw both targets when only one response was required, it must be that in the dual response condition making a response to one target interfered with detecting the other.

This explanation was confirmed by the results of another experiment. Four characters were presented in a square display. In one condition either 0 or 1 target appeared and the observer had to press one of two keys to indicate which. In the other condition either 1 or 2 targets appeared and the observer had to press one of two keys to indicate which. Detection was more accurate in the 0 or 1 condition, presumably because detection of one target requires one response, but the detection of two targets requires two responses. Also, in the 1 or 2 targets condition accuracy was much better when each side of the square was presented successively compared with when the entire square was presented simultaneously.

Duncan and Ian Nimmo-Smith (1996) found a decrement for simultaneously presented targets when the target was selected early on the basis of a variety of features, including color, brightness, texture, length, location, and motion. As was true of auditory targets, though, the probability of responding to both of simultaneous or adjacent visual targets is low, it is not zero. Also, just as it was the case for auditory inputs, the reason the probability is not zero is the persistence of the visual input beyond the interval of its occurrence. George Sperling (1960) demonstrated this persistence of the visual input, called the **icon**, in a classic experiment.

Sperling's task was a little more complicated than a simple detection task. A display of up to twelve letters, such as shown in Figure 4.11, was flashed at an observer for only 50 milliseconds. The display always consisted of three rows of letters. In the whole- (or full-) report condition the observer was simply told to report as many letters as could be recalled. In order to report each letter a distinct verbal

FIGURE 4.11

Kind of display used by Sperling (1960).

TDRX
SVNB
FZLQ

response had to be made to it. So the task was a divided attention task in which a separate verbal response was made to each letter reported. As shown in Figure 4.12, no matter how many letters were presented in the display, people in the whole-report condition were unable to correctly report more than four or five letters on the average.

In the partial-report condition, immediately after the display was terminated the observer heard a high tone, a medium tone, or a low tone. The tone indicated which row of letters had to be reported— high for top, medium for middle, and low for bottom. The observer never knew which row was to be reported until after the display was terminated. Thus, Sperling could use the number of letters reported correctly for the cued row to calculate the total number of letters available to the observer at the time that the cue was presented. (Actually, the number is a lower-bound estimate because some time is needed to process the tone.) The number of letters available is easy to calculate. For example, suppose there are four letters in each row, the second row is cued, and the observer is able to report three of the four letters. Since there were three rows in the display, and the observer presumably could have reported three letters from any one of them, the total number of letters available must have been 3 x 3 = 9. In other words, if the observer could report three out of four letters in one row, we can reasonably assume that nine of the twelve letters in the display were seen.

As illustrated in Figure 4.12, Sperling's partial-report procedure revealed that an observer had been able to see more letters than the whole-report procedure had indicated. The reason that only four or five letters could be reported in the whole-report condition was presumably that the rest of the display had faded from consciousness by the time the names of four or five letters were spoken. This hypothesis was tested by varying the delay at which the tone followed the visual display. When the tone followed the display by up to about a third of a second, more letters were available in the partial-report condition than the whole report condition (Figure 4.13). In other words, even though the display was only presented for 50 milliseconds it remained in consciousness, i.e., an observer still saw it little longer. But if the cue was delayed for a second, the advantage of the partial-report condition disappeared, so by this point the visual input had faded from awareness.

FIGURE 4.12

Results from Sperling's (1960) experiment. The partial report procedure reveals that virtually the entire visual display is still available immediately after it has been terminated.

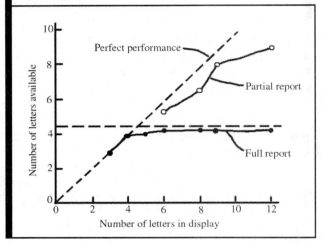

Converging evidence that during the response to one target another target may be missed comes from target detection in the RSVP task. D. E. Broadbent & M. H. P. Broadbent (1987) used the RSVP method to present words at the rate of 80 milliseconds per word (about 12 words per second). The target was either a word in capital letters or an animal name. When two targets were presented within half a second of each other, the probability of reporting the second target was significantly reduced. Furthermore, the likelihood of missing the second target was greater when the first target was detected than when it was missed. So the probability of detecting both targets was very low.

Together, the results of studies on divided visual attention show that there is a period of up to 300 milliseconds when the detection of one visual target impairs the detection of a following target. The period during which the ability to detect a target is momentarily reduced by a previous voluntary response is called a **refractory period**.

FIGURE 4.13

Number of letters available versus time. The number of letters available for the partial report condition decreases with delay of the cue tone.

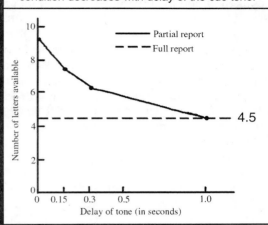

Divided cross-modality attention.   You have distinct visual and auditory working memories. This makes it is easier to divide attention between two inputs in different modalities than it is to divide attention between two inputs in the same modality (Treisman & Davis, 1973). An orienting response by the visual system does not disrupt auditory search and vice versa. Eijkman and Vendrik (1965) and Moore and Massaro (1973) both found little or no decrement in people's accuracy in detecting a simultaneous tone and light pair in comparison with their accuracy in detecting only a single target. Gescheider, Sager, and Ruffolo (1975) found a similar result when using tones and brief vibrations as inputs.

However, even when detection of simultaneous targets in different modalities is not affected, the responses are less than perfect. The two inputs may not be perceived as having occurred simultaneously. If, for example, a light and a tone are presented simultaneously the light is likely to be detected first (Colavita, 1974; Egeth & Sager, 1977). This phenomenon is called **visual dominance** and it occurs in a variety of situations (Posner, Nissen, & Klein, 1976). Tactile targets dominate over auditory targets in the same way that visual targets do (Gescheider et al. 1975). When required to make two separate voluntary responses to two separate inputs in different modalities, most people give priority to the visual input. In fact, if people are given special instructions stressing that they should attend to the auditory input, the difference in the time it takes them to detect the visual and auditory targets is virtually eliminated (Egeth & Sager, 1977).

It turns out that this difficulty in dividing attention between vision and audition has actually been known for centuries. Eighteenth-century astronomers used the ticks of a metronome to time the transits of stars they were observing. It was they who first noticed and recorded the fact that simultaneously occurring visual and auditory targets (a star crossing and a tick) were not perceived as having occurred simultaneously. This observation was confirmed by Wilhelm Wundt, one of the first experimental psychologists, and by 1908 it appeared in a textbook (Titchener, 1908) as the "law of prior entry."

These results generally run contrary to introspection and have therefore been as surprising to psychologists as to anyone else. Experiments on divided attention appear to provide a challenge to our introspection about our ability to perceive simultaneous events. For example, an umpire must both watch for the exact instant a runner touches the base and listen for the sound of the ball hitting the fielder's glove. If the player and the ball arrive simultaneously, the umpire may well see the player touch the base first.

VISUAL SCANNING AS A SKILL

We make an average of four saccades a second. If every eye movement was a voluntary movement, then the refractory period that occurs after every voluntary response would make merely looking out at the world require so much conscious planning that there would be none left for making any other movements at all. However, in fact, eye movements are rarely voluntary. Instead, as mentioned in Chapters 2 and 3, the eye-fixation system includes reflexive, involuntary, automatic, and voluntary control of eye movements by the cerebellum, superior colliculus, basal ganglia, and frontal eye fields. This sophisticated system selects the target location of each eye movement without the need for voluntary control of individual movements. How this system develops is our first example of how ordinary attention is controlled by a mixture of automatic perceptual-motor skills and voluntary actions.

Early development. At two months of age visual attention is focused on a narrow segment of the visual field. But by three months the infant begins to explore her world. In a cleverly designed experiment,

Rovee-Collier, Earley and Stafford (1989) trained 2- and 3-month-old infants to kick to move mobiles. (This task will be described in detail in Chapter 6.) Half of the infants were shown a mobile composed of five identical blocks that each contained a different pattern on each of five sides. The other infants were shown a mobile composed of five different blocks that each contained one pattern on five sides. So both mobiles contained five patterns. However, in the same-side mobile each pattern could be seen on only one block but in the different-side mobile each pattern could be seen on all the blocks. Infants were trained for two days and tested 24 hours later with either the same-side or different-side mobile. If the infant recognized the mobile then she or he kicked to move it. Otherwise, the infant did not kick. The results confirmed that 2-month-old infants scanned less of the visual field during each training session. The 2-month old infants failed to recognize the same-side mobile but did recognize the different-side mobile. Apparently the 2-month-old infants fixated on a single block each session, and if the fixation block differed from session to session they treated the mobile as novel. On the other hand, the 3-month-old infants recognized both mobiles, indicating that they scanned the visual field containing all the different blocks during the training sessions.

So by three months of age infants are already scanning the visual field. At some point early in life, visual scanning becomes an autonomous perceptual-motor skill. A person does not have to voluntarily move his or her eyes three or four times a second. Nevertheless, a person's eyes do not fixate randomly but move to points of contrast that are likely to add some new detail to the input's representation. Furthermore, as experience creates a store of representations of familiar objects and scenes in memory, visual scanning is increasingly guided by these representations.

The further development of visual attention. Performance on both selective attention tasks and divided attention tasks improves all through childhood and peaks somewhere between the ages of 20 and 30. Lane (1980) measured the amount of task-relevant and task irrelevant information remembered after completion of a selective-attention task to measure what was attended during the task. As age increased from childhood to adulthood people recalled more of the inputs to which they were told to attend and fewer of the inputs they were told to ignore. For children, performance on attended and ignored inputs was positively correlated. The more attended inputs that were recalled, the more inputs that were supposed to be ignored were recalled as well. This result implies that the children were not selectively attending to the targets but rather were indiscriminately attending to every input they fixed on. In contrast, for college students, memory for attended and unattended inputs was negatively correlated. The more targets that were recalled, the fewer distracters were recalled. High school and college students remembered fewer distracters than elementary school children (Druker & Hagen 1969; Hagen, Meacham, & Mesibov, 1970; Wagner, 1974). In a measure of divided attention, the number of characters reported from a briefly presented display increased with age (Arnett & DiLollo, 1979; DiLollo, Arnett, & Krunk, 1982), indicating that identification time per character decreases with practice. During adulthood, performance on selective attention tasks remains stable. Once a person passes his or her third decade, performance on divided attention tasks begins a slow, measurable, decline (DiLollo et al. 1982). Whether this is because there is a decreased ability to divide attention or a more general loss of response speed remains controversial (Somberg & Salthouse, 1982).

Reading. The ability to direct visual attention is made possible through a collection of task specific skills. Each visual scanning plan is adapted for its particular input: a pretty face, moving traffic, or a page of text. One particular visual scanning skill that you are using now is reading.

A reading speed of about 300 words a minute is the upper bound on the speed of comprehension. (In comparison, you speak at no more than 120 words a minute.) When you read a page of text, your eyes skip from word to word, briefly fixating on almost every word before going on to the next. During a fixation you can see about four letters to the right of the fixation point clearly, and these are the letters you read. (Input from letters to the left of the fixation point is inhibited.) In addition, you can pick up word length information about fifteen letters to the right (McConkie & Rayner, 1975). Both the length of the word to the right of the fixation area, as well as the frequency of its spelling pattern, particularly the frequency of its initial letter cluster, is used to determine the next fixation point, which is usually about eight letters to the right (Hyona & Bertram, 2004).

FIGURE 4.14

Eye fixations of college students reading scientifc passages. Gazes within each sentence are sequentially numbered above the fixated words, with the durations (in milliseconds) indicated below the sequence number. (After Carpenter & Just, 1980).

1		2	3	4	5		6		7		8		9		1		2		3
1566		267	400	83	267		617		767		450		450		400		616		517

Flywheels are one of the oldest mechanical devices known to man. Every internal combustion

5	4	6		7	8		9		10	11		12		13	14
684	250	317		617	1116		367		467	483		450		383	284

engine contains a small flywheel that converts the jerky motion of the pistons into the smooth

15	16	17		18	19	20	21
383	317	283		533	50	366	566

flow of energy that powers the drive shaft.

On average, you fixate on each word for about a quarter of a second, though this average is misleading because there is great variability in the length of each fixation. Figure 4.14 shows the record of the eyes of a person moving across a line of text. As the figure shows, a fixation can last from less than 100 milliseconds to more than a second (Just & Carpenter, 1980). During a fixation, the meaning of the word is activated by the visual input of the word. That is, you do not have to sound a word out, or identify individual letters, in order for its meaning to be automatically activated. Furthermore, the meaning of the word is integrated with the meaning of the previous text. Conversely, what has been already read is used to predict what is likely to come next. On average, the more predictable a word is from the preceding passage, the less time is spent fixating on it (Ehrlich & Raynor, 1981). However, sometimes a comprehension error occurs during a fixation. During reading, a small number of regressions also occur. That is, the eyes move to the left and fixate on a word for a second time when the wrong representation was selected the first time. A college student makes about 75 forward fixations and 15 regressions to read 100 words of text. From these numbers a gain of 1.33 words per forward fixation can be calculated (Crowder, 1982, p. 9).

SUMMARY OF SELECTIVE ATTENTION

- An act of selective attention has three stages:
  ◦ Target specification
  ◦ Target Search
  ◦ Orientation to the Target

- First a plan that includes a representation of the target is activated in either auditory or visual working memory. This is called **specification**. Subsequent perceptual processing is influenced in two ways.
  ◦ Priming, an automatic effect of the autonomous processing that results from procedural learning. Perceptual and semantic representations related to the target are processed more rapidly.
  ◦ Expectation, expressed as specification of the target in working memory, which results in suppression of distracter representations.

- Second, the location of a potential target is identified through comparison of input with the target representation. This is called **search**. The search stage ends when the comparison process produces a match and a response indicating that the target has been found. There are two stages to the target selection process: early (or perceptual) selection and late (or response) selection.
  ◦ The early (perceptual) selection stage is a system of gates through which the perceptual input must pass.

* Any level of perceptual organization, including features, patterns, object representations and perceptual novelty, may be the basis of selection.
* As the result of perceptual organization, a single target pops out from among all the distracters. Hence all the distracters are processed as part of the background and rejected in parallel.

○ When more than one input passes through a perceptual gate then late selection occurs. In late selection the representation of each input is compared with the target-representation in working memory.
* For late selection you may have to serially orient to several potential target locations and compare each potential target with the representation in working memory before the actual target is found.
* Late selection is influenced by practice. If the target is more familiar than the distracters, then the comparison of its perceptual representation with memory will produce a match in less time than the comparison of the distracter representations, so late selection will be fast and accurate.
* In a vigilance task, the target representation must be maintained over time without a match being found. When the target representation must be compared with many similar distracter representations, it becomes degraded and the probability of detecting it declines.

• As a result of the match, input from nontarget locations is inhibited and a detailed representation of the potential target enters working memory. This is called **orientation**.
  ○ An orienting response need only be made to the first in a sequence of targets in the same location in order to select the entire sequence.
  ○ When each target in a sequence is in a different location and separate orienting response must be made to each target. The number of targets in the sequence that may be detected is limited by the time it takes to make an orienting response to each target.
  ○ Because the visual and auditory systems are largely independent of each other, target detection is greater for a task including both visual and auditory targets than for a task within a single modality.
  ○ As the result of practice, a scanning plan is encoded as part of procedural memory.

ALERTING

At this point it is useful to make a distinction between a target sequence that requires a search for each target in the sequence and a target sequence that does not require a search for each target. Searching for the red candies in the pile or the targets in a video game are examples of the first kind of target sequence. The number, location, and possibly time of appearance of the targets are uncertain. The words on this page are an example of the second kind of target sequence. The location of the next word in each sentence is predictable from the location of the last. There is no uncertainty about when or where the next word will appear.

The first tone of a sequence of tones from the same location, say produced by a beeping horn, is an example of the beginning of a very simple predictable target sequence. Attending to every target in such a predictable sequence is called a **continuous target detection** task. For a continuous target detection task, the task changes after the first target in the sequence is detected. The first target in the sequence requires an orienting response that requires closing and opening the appropriate thalamic gates. It terminates the search process that found the target. Detection of the remaining targets merely requires that the gate through which the target sequence passes be kept open and all other gates be kept shut. The task of **maintaining attention on a predictable target sequence** at a fixed location is easier than detecting the first target because it does not require a search for each target and the resulting orienting response when it is found. Nevertheless, the task is not a trivial one when performed in the presence of competing distracters. For example, when you are driving down the road you scan the road ahead of you for other vehicles and for signals. However, some of the time there are no targets in the visual field that are relevant to driving. At those moments perceptual input may produce a match with a distracter not relevant to driving and so the distracter may enter consciousness. You may see a child run into the street or hear your cell phone ring.

If selective attention were perfect so that all nontarget gates stayed shut and you only detected targets then you would not see the child or hear the phone while driving down the street. However, selective attention is not perfect. Often you do see the child or hear the cell phone ring. A distracter alerting you and interrupting a task may be a good thing or a bad thing depending on the relative importance of the distracter versus the task. On the one hand, seeing the child and avoiding hitting him is a good thing. Slamming into the car stopped at the stop sign in front of you while you answer your cell phone is a bad thing. We shall return to the importance of an unexpected item **alerting** you (i.e., entering consciousness) below. First we shall consider why alerting occurs at all.

A target is selected by shutting the gates on the pathways of all perceptual input lacking the critical target feature used for selection. However, those gates are only swinging doors. When an orienting response closes all the thalamic gates but one, it only closes them for a brief temporal interval that roughly corresponds to the time necessary to respond to the target. If targets are appearing so fast that as a response to one is made the next is detected, then all the distracter gates are repeatedly slammed shut and only the target get is ever open. However, when the targets appear at a slower rate so that when a response to one has been made another has not yet been detected, then the gates on all the perceptual pathways swing open and a competition among all the distracters ensues for which one will enter consciousness.

This competition is not a disorganized one. The same perceptual and comparison and mechanisms that organize selective attention to favor distinct, novel and familiar targets organize alerting to favor distinct, novel and familiar distracters as well. When your driving program is not directing your eye movements down the road control reverts to a more general visual scanning program sensitive to distinct and novel perceptual features. One way to look at this is that driving a car down a road is really a multitask situation. The more primary, more specific driving task, scans a limited portion of the visual field for targets. When none are found there, control of visual attention reverts to a more general visual scanning program that performs the more general task of looking at the world and scans the entire visual field for distinct or novel items. Yet another way to look at this is that when various inputs compete for access to consciousness, the task that you are performing assigns the highest priority to task relevant items and so those are the ones that enter consciousness. In the absence of a task relevant target a distracter may enter consciousness.

The critical balance between being able to maintain attention on task relevant targets and being aware of unexpected but important task irrelevant distracters can be looked at in either of two ways: from the point of view of the primary task or from the alert. First we look at look at the situation from the point of view of the primary task and review the brain mechanisms for shutting perceptual gates. Then we will look at the situation from the point of view of an alert. We will see how the difficulty of the primary task influences whether an alert will succeed. Finally, we look at the three alerting mechanisms: a reflex, novelty (through early selection), and familiarity (through late selection).

CORTICAL CONTROL OF PERCEPTUAL PROCESSING

Figure 4.15 shows that it is the prefrontal cortex that ultimately regulates the processing of input in other parts of the brain. In support of this, Robert Knight and his colleagues found that during normal perceptual processing the prefrontal cortex reduces the processing of both tactual and auditory input in other parts of the brain. They recorded electrical activity (EEG) of the somatosensory cortex and auditory cortex in healthy individuals and individuals with damage to the prefrontal cortex. When pulses were applied to the wrist at the rate of three per second, the electrical activity in the somatosensory cortex in response to each pulse was greater in individuals with prefrontal cortical damage than in normal individuals (Yamaguchi & Knight, 1990). When clicks were presented at the rate of thirteen per second, the electrical activity in the auditory cortex in response to each click was greater in individuals with prefrontal cortical damage than in normal individuals (Knight, Scabini, & Woods, 1989). The increase in electrical activity in the somatosensory cortex and auditory cortex when the prefrontal cortex was damaged suggested that the prefrontal cortex normally reduces their activity. Thus, when the prefrontal cortex was damaged, activity in these areas is increased.

As described above, the prefrontal cortex does not operate alone. Other studies by Knight and his colleagues indicated that the prefrontal and parietal cortical areas cooperate in maintaining selective auditory attention to a target sequence. Electrical activity from both the left and right auditory cortex was recorded in a study in which listeners heard a sequence of clicks in both ears at the same time. The listener was either told to attend to the clicks in the right ear or told to attend to those in the left ear. For normal listeners, the electrical activity was greater in the auditory cortex that received input from the attended ear than in the auditory cortex receiving input from the ignored ear. This is because when you listen to input to the right ear, the processing of input to the left ear is inhibited, and vice versa. For listeners with parietal, or prefrontal damage the difference in electrical activity in the auditory cortex for input from the attended and ignored ears was reduced or eliminated. These results suggest that the parietal cortex and the prefrontal cortex have some control over the selection of auditory input from both the left and right (Knight, Hillyard, Woods, & Neville, 1981; Woods, Knight, & Scabini, 1983).

FIGURE 4.15

The EEG response of the auditory cortex to a sequence of tones is greater for patients with prefrontal cortical damage (bottom) than for normal individuals (top) because there is less inhibition of input to the auditory cortex (Knight et al., 1989).

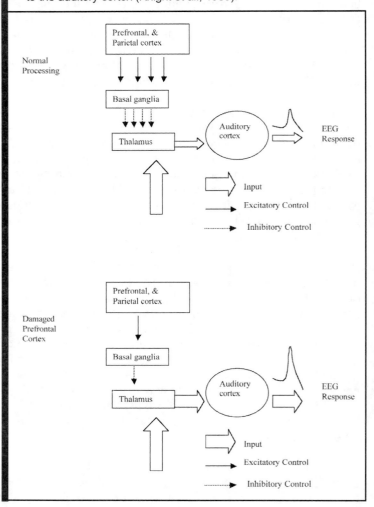

TASK DIFFICULTY AND ALERTING

The probability of an input causing an alert depends in part on the demands placed on working memory by the task that the individual is performing when the input is processed. Recall that voluntary activity suppresses irrelevant perceptual processing. If an individual is maintaining representations in working memory through verbal rehearsal then there is little chance for a distracter to enter working memory and alert him. Hence a very difficult task, requiring voluntary action to maintain representations in working memory, is also more difficult to interrupt than an easier one. Daniel Kahneman (1973, p.14) put it this way:

First try to mentally multiply 83 x 27. Having completed this task, imagine that you are going to be given four numbers, and that your life depends on your ability to retain them for ten seconds. The numbers are seven, two, five, nine. Having completed the second task, it may appear believable that, even to save one's life, one <u>cannot</u> work as hard in retaining four digits as one must work to complete a mental multiplication of two-digit numbers.

Mental multiplication requires a large number of voluntary rehearsals to maintain the intermediate products in working memory during the computation. This continuous voluntary activity reduces the likelihood that a novel input will reach working memory and cause an alert.

An experiment by Zelniker (1971) demonstrated this principle. Zelniker used a very distracting input called **delayed auditory feedback** (DAF). People spoke into microphones while their own speech was played back to them through earphones two-thirds of a second later. DAF is so distracting that people usually stutter and stop when they try to speak under these conditions. Zelniker subjected people to DAF while they were performing an easy task and while they were performing a difficult task. The easy task was to shadow a string of three numbers as they heard them; thus no more than three numbers ever had to be in working memory. The difficult task was to repeat one string of three numbers while at the same time listening for and remembering the next string of three numbers; thus six numbers had to be in working memory. The speech of the participants was much more filled with stutters and stops when they were performing the easy task than when they were performing the difficult one.

The principle that interruptions from unattended inputs can be blocked by conscious concentration on a task has important practical implications. For example, in the Lamaze method of natural childbirth controlled breathing techniques are used to divert attention from the pain of labor. The breathing techniques serve other purposes as well, but pain reduction is the most important one. In using this method the woman takes over conscious control of what is usually an unconscious activity— breathing. Because awareness is directed to the task of breathing in a carefully controlled way attention is less likely to be diverted to the strong pain signals being generated by the contractions of labor.

ALERTING MECHANISMS

When you are reading this book you are not aware of extraneous auditory, tactile, temperature, and visual inputs. It is normally quite satisfactory not to be aware of such inputs, since they are usually not very important. In fact, these extraneous signals receive so little attention that we are tempted to believe that they are not processed at all. However, the complete failure to process such inputs could have disastrous consequences. For example, if you were not processing the temperature, and the room suddenly became very hot, you might be trapped in a fire. If sounds were being totally ignored, then an explosion would bring no response. It would also be inconvenient if you did not hear your name when addressed unexpectedly.

In order to survive, you must be able to detect and respond rapidly to unexpected changes in the environment. Even the input to which you do not attend may be processed to some degree. So attention is not completely under voluntary control. An **alert** is when a distracter involuntarily enters working memory. That is, an orienting response (OR) occurs involuntarily to it. At that point you can continue to search for the target or reconsider your action and perform an action in response to the representation in working memory. So what was a distracter with respect to the old action becomes a target of the new action. For example, if while driving you hear an ambulance and see it in your rear view mirror then you will pull over to the side and let it pass by.

There are several ways in which an unattended input may alert you. You may be distracted from reading this book by a loud noise that elicits a startle reflex. If you are reading in a quiet room and someone begins to speak, her voice is a novel input and may enter your awareness even if it is not loud enough to startle you. This would be an early alert that was caused by the same perceptual organization of the input that makes early selection possible. Finally, if you were reading in a room filled with conversation and someone said your name it might enter your awareness. This would be a late alert that was caused by the same comparison process that makes late selection possible.

Reflexes. Some reflexes provide alerts that shift attention. Recall that some reflexes orient the perceptual system toward new sights and sounds. For example, a reflex in the superior colliculus may move the head and eyes toward light and a reflex in the immediately adjacent inferior colliculus, moves the head and eyes toward sound. Other reflexes that withdraw the body from harmful inputs also provide alerts. If you unexpectedly prick your finger, a flexor reflex not only pulls your hand back, but also sends an alerting signal to the brain so that your hand will become the focus of attention.

Early alerting: Novelty. Not all inputs are so immediately threatening as to require a response before they are even perceived. But they may require immediate investigation. The best response to an input may vary with its environmental context. There may be times when it is useful to turn towards, and other times away, from a sudden sound, depending on what the person is doing and what the sound signifies. If an ordinary person is driving a car and she hears an ambulance siren she may simply pull over to the side of the road and let it go by. But if a lawyer hears the siren he may decide to follow it to see where it is going. Hence, an orienting response merely puts the alerting input in working memory, so that a (voluntary) response to it can be considered. The kind of unattended input that is likely to cause an alert is a perceptually novel one. A remarkably simple system detects novel inputs (Groves & Thompson, 1970).

When a neuron in the peripheral nervous system is repeatedly stimulated, it undergoes **habituation**. The signals it outputs become successively weaker. When the repeated tone is replaced by a tone of a different pitch the new tone is processed by different unhabituated cochlear neurons that send a stronger signal up the auditory pathway that ultimately produces a stronger input to the cortex. So the strength of input is a good indicator of its novelty. Stronger, hence more novel, inputs are less likely to be shut out at the thalamic level. They are more likely to reach the cortex and receive additional processing.

Late alerting: Familiarity. We have just considered how early selection plays an important role in alerting, favoring a perceptually novel input such as a high tone presented among low tones. But this does not mean that late selection plays no role. When Unger (1964) presented a series of numbers in ascending order he observed on OR to a number out of sequence (e.g., 11, 12, 13, 17). The pop out of the 17 indicates just how sophisticated pattern matching is. Familiar visual (Shiffrin & Schneider, 1977) and auditory (Johnston, 1978) distracters are difficult to ignore. Familiar inputs require less time to match a representation in memory and elicit an orienting response. Hence a familiar distracter has a chance of slipping in when a competing task relevant response is not being made. Recall that when a person shadows a message in one ear he remembers little of the message in the other ear (Cherry, 1953). However, when the listener's own name (an extremely familiar input) was part of the message in the unattended ear they sometimes noticed it (Moray, 1959).

HYPNOSIS

Late selection gives you control over what you can selectively attend to. One question that remains to be answered is the extent to which some individuals may become so skilled in the control of attention that they can completely ignore distractions. One measure of an individual's ability to selectively attend is her hypnotic susceptibility. Hypnosis is an exciting topic not because there is anything particularly exciting about hypnosis itself but because it is wrapped in a lurid net of popular mythology. A hypnotic trance is not something that one person, the hypnotist, induces in the other, but rather a selectivity of attention that some people are able to voluntarily attain. People develop no special abilities under hypnosis that they do not have when they are not hypnotized (Barber, 1969; Orne, 1959). Rather, hypnotizable individuals are highly susceptible to suggestion (Kirsch & Braffman, 2001). In fact, a hypnotizable individual will be compliant with a hypnotist's requests whether or not the individual is told he or she is undergoing hypnosis (Orne, 1966).

In a test of hypnotic susceptibility, a person is given a set of suggestions such as that his arm is growing heavy, his eyelids are glued shut, or there is a fly buzzing about. The more suggestions the person translates into a perceptual experience, the more hypnotically susceptible the person is said to be.

There are three standardized tests of hypnotic susceptibility. The Stanford Hypnotic Susceptibility Scale (Weitzenhoffer & Hilgard, 1959; 1962) and the Barber Suggestibility Scale (Barber & Glass, 1962) must be administered to individuals. The Harvard Group Scale of Hypnotic Susceptibility (Shor & Orne, 1962) may be administered to groups. Perhaps 15 percent of all people respond to nearly all the test items and hence are highly susceptible to hypnosis.

What distinguishes the hypnotic state is the kind of perceptual and cognitive experiences the hypnotized individual is capable of having (Orne, 1977). A hypnotized individual may not feel pain from an input that would cause an unhypnotized individual to feel pain (Hilgard & Hilgard, 1975). (Lack of pain is called **analgesia**.) The hypnotic state seems to be an extremely effective form of selective attention, which apparently accounts for the phenomenon of analgesia. The person is able to direct his or her attention to inputs that are not associated with the pain. So the painful input never reaches consciousness. In fact all people can direct attention away from pain to some degree. For example, the Lamaze childbearing technique relies on selective attention to a distracter to reduce pain, and this method can be practiced by anyone.

NEGLECT

A hypnotizable individual may not feel a pain in her left arm because she is selectively attending to her right arm. An individual with damage to his right hemisphere may not feel pain in his left arm for the same reason: he is only attending to his right. Sometimes damage to a part of the brain disrupts scanning so that none of the input that goes first to that part of the brain is ever compared with memory, or none of the targets matched to the input are responded to. Damage to the ability to scan a perceptual field can cause inputs from some locations to be neglected either because they are not perceived or not responded to. Look at Figure 4.16. It shows six self-portraits of the artist Anton Raderscheidt. Portrait (a) was done before he had a stroke in his right hemisphere. Portrait (b) was the first one done after the stroke. Notice that in the first portrait after the stroke he completely neglected to draw the left side of his face. Yet when asked about it he saw nothing odd about it. As he recovered, the neglect lessened in subsequent portraits (b) through (e), and had disappeared by the time he painted portrait (f).

Since, as we have seen, many different brain structures contribute to the control of attention, damage to many different brain structures can cause some form of neglect. Neglect can result from damage to the reticular formation, the thalamus, or the frontal, temporal and parietal lobes. In neglect, there is no damage to the visual cortex, so the patient's problem is not due to a deficit in visual perception. The two major behavioral manifestations of the neglect syndrome are **sensory neglect** and **motor neglect** (Heilman et al., 1993). **Sensory neglect** is the failure to respond to sensory inputs from a particular location. For example, a patient may be unaware of his wife

FIGURE 4.16
Self-portraits of the painter Anton Raderscheidt before and after he suffered a right-hemisphere stroke in October 1967: Self-portrait in 1965 (a); December 1967 (b); January 1968 (c); March 1968 (d); April 1968 (e); June 1968 (f) (from Jung, 1980).

standing to his left but be able to see and hear her when she steps to his right. **Motor neglect** is the failure to make responses with a particular portion of the body. For example, when asked to clap hands a patient may uselessly lift only his right hand in the air. The location of the lesion determines whether sensory or motor neglect is primarily observed.

Neglect to various portions of space has been observed (Rapcsak, Cimino, & Heilman, 1988; Shelton, Bowers, & Heilman, 1990), but usually neglect is observed for either the right or left side of space. Furthermore, neglect of the left, as shown in Figure 4.16, is more common than neglect of the right. The integration of the visuospatial representations of the left and right sides of space usually takes place in the right temporal and parietal cortices, where there are many neurons that respond to inputs from both the left and right. So when only the left hemisphere is damaged the right is often able to immediately compensate and no neglect is observed. Usually, the left hemisphere only responds to inputs from the right. Hence, when only the right hemisphere is damaged the left is not able to immediately compensate and neglect is observed.

The neglect syndrome may be subcategorized into three different levels of severity. In its mildest form, a patient responds to a single input in any location. But when inputs are presented simultaneously to more than one location the patient is unaware of the input in the neglected location. This phenomenon is an exaggeration of a response bottleneck, discussed below, that occurs in perfectly normal individuals when two or more briefly presented targets compete for attention. The interval over which a normal individual may miss a second target is about half a second and there is not an irreversible bias to miss targets in a particular location. In the patient with neglect, briefly presented targets in a particular location are always missed when another, competing target appears in another location.

In its moderate form, a patient will neglect inputs in a particular location even when there is no limitation on the time available to detect it. The moderate form of neglect may involve primarily sensory neglect or primarily motor neglect or a combination of both. For example, if a person with left sensory neglect is asked to put a line through all the letter a's on a page placed in front of her she may cross out only the a's on the right side. However, if the patient's attention is called to the a's on the left by pointing them out, she can momentarily respond appropriately to the neglected side. Similarly, a person with left motor neglect may try to lift a long object using only his right hand.

The neglect extends to visual imagery. Bisiach, Capitani, Luzzatti, and Perani (1981) asked patients with right-hemisphere lesions to describe a location familiar to them: the cathedral square in Milan. The patients first described the features of the square from the vantage point facing the cathedral from the opposite side of the square. Then the patients were asked to describe the square again, this time imagining their vantage point to be the central entrance to the cathedral looking out onto the square. The patients were able to correctly report more details on their right for both perspectives. Heilman et al. (1993) cited evidence that failure to report buildings on the left was the result of inattention to it. When similar patients were asked to turn their eyes to the left during recall, more details from their left sides were reported.

The severest form of the neglect disorder is coupled with **anosognosia**. The patient not only completely ignores some area of space but also denies having a deficit. As a result, the person does not try to compensate for the limited field of vision by moving his or her head from side to side. Not only is the patient only aware of sights and sounds from one side of the environment, but the patient will wash, shave, and comb one side of his or her face and head, eat the food off one side of the plate, etc. For example, Raderscheidt thought the self-portrait shown in Figure 4.16(b) looked perfectly normal. A patient with anosognosia cannot be talked out of it. For example, if you point out to the patient that she cannot move her left arm she will respond that there is nothing wrong with her left arm. If you challenge her to move it you get an evasive reply, such as, 'I am not going to do it just because you told me to.' Eduardo Bisiach reasoned that the only way to break the anosognosia would be to provide a powerful alerting stimulus that would arouse the damaged hemisphere. The vestibular sense, in the inner ear, has much stronger connections to the contralateral hemisphere. So Bisiach and his colleagues (Bisiach, Rusconi, & Vallar, 1992) poured ice water in the left ear of a neglect patient. Cold water in the left ear causes the eyes to move to the left. Sure enough, for about a half hour the patient became aware that half her body was paralysed and that she only perceived part of visual space. V. S. Ramachadran repeated the experiment and wrote a vivid account of it (Ramachandran & Blakesless, 1998; p. 145).

Before he admistered the ice water, Ramachandran asked:
Mrs. M. how are you doing?
Fine.
Can you walk?
Sure.
Can you use your left hand?
Yes
Are both hands equally strong?
Yes.

After administering the ice water he again asked:
Can you use your arms?
No, my left arm is paralysed.
Mrs. M., how long have you been paralyzed?
Oh, continuously, all these days.

This was an extraordinary remark, for it implies that even though she had been denying her paralysis each time I had seen her over these last few weeks, the memories of her failed attempts had been registering somewhere in her brain, yet access to them had been blocked.

Twelve hours later a student of mine visited her and asked,
Do you remember Dr. Ramachandran?
Oh, yes, he was that Indian doctor.
What did he ask you?
He asked me if I could use both my arms.
And what did you tell him?
I told him I was fine.

So the effect of the cold water was temporary. When the shock wore off the denial returned. Fortunately, as is dramatically apparent in the self-portraits shown in Figure 4.16, over a period of weeks, spontaneous recovery from severe neglect is common.

INTERFERENCE

One great advantage of voluntary action is that a quite complicated novel target representation may be built and maintained in working memory. For example, you can follow the direction to make a left at the third traffic signal. You typically maintain the representation of the direction in working memory through **verbal rehearsal**. That is, you silently tell yourself three lights, now two lights, etc. Talking to yourself is a voluntary action. Since you can only perform one voluntary action at a time, we must now consider the effect of maintaining the target representation on ultimately executing the response.

Target-response overlap refers to the degree of overlap between the representation of the target and the representation of the response. For many simple tasks there may be no overlap between the perceptual representation of the target and the motor representation of the response. For example, when you press the accelerator in response to a green light there is no overlap between the processing of the visual system that detects the light and the action system that moves your foot in response. Rather, the action can be described as consisting of two discrete stages: the perceptual stage that detects the target and the motor stage that executes the response to it. However, not all target-response pairs are so simple. You may be trying to follow a complicated set of directions that describe either a quite complicated target, as when you drive someplace new, or a complicated sequence of actions, as when you cook or build something for the first time. Maintaining a target in working memory expands the time you have to respond to a single target, the number and complexity of the targets that you can respond to, and the complexity of the response that you can make. However, since the target representations are maintained in working memory through voluntary action, a response bottleneck occurs there. That is, as we have reiterated, you can only perform one voluntary action at a time. If you are actively maintaining a target in working memory through a voluntary act of rehearsal, then how can you be planning and executing a voluntary response to the target at the same time? This difficulty is normally overcome because you have four different action subsystems that you can operate in parallel for locomotion, manipulation, visual fixation, and vocalization. The actions of different subsystems may be executed in parallel even if they are planned sequentially. In particular, the vocalization and manipulation subsystems provide two different modes of action. In a classic experiment Lee Brooks (1968) showed that modality effects are important when both maintaining the target in working memory and generating the response. Brooks asked students to form either a visual image (e.g., a block letter H) or an auditory image of a simple sentence. For the H the students had to determine which corners were convex as they navigated around a mental image of the H in working memory. For the sentence, they had to report whether or not each word was a noun. The students responded either manually, by pointing to either a y or an n (for yes or no) on a page for each corner or word, or vocally by saying yes or no for each corner or word. The students responded faster vocally than manually for the visual imagery task but faster manually than vocally for the linguistic task. Presumably, forming the visual image of the H interfered with visual control of the manual response and forming the auditory image of the sentence interfered with the construction of the vocal response. This pattern of results is called **selective interference** because forming an image selectively interferes with perception or production in the same modality. For example, as just mentioned, forming a visual image interferes with the scanning of a visual display.

However, as soon as language is learned people develop the skill of recoding visual information in **verbal** working memory. Verbal recoding was demonstrated in the simple but elegant study performed by Conrad (1964), who presented a group of college students with lists of six written letters (e.g., PHKVCR). The students read the letters silently. Then the list disappeared and the students had to report the letters in order. The most interesting results concern the errors people made. Sometimes they would substitute an incorrect letter for one they had seen. If subjects were remembering the letters visually, as they were presented, we would expect them to substitute letters that looked similar to the actual letters (e.g., X for V). But instead Conrad's subjects tended to confuse letters with names that sound alike (e.g., they might substitute B for V). So it appears they were maintaining the letters verbally in working memory.

You routinely maintain visual characters verbally, except when verbal interference is present. In the experiment of Neal Kroll and his colleagues (Kroll et al., 1970), students had to repeat a list of letters as they heard them for 1, 10 or 25 seconds. This is called **shadowing** because each letter is shadowed (i.e., repeated) as it is heard. During the shadowing one letter, which the subjects had to remember, was presented either visually or verbally. As Figure 4.17 shows, the students almost always remembered the letter for 1 second, but they made many errors after 10 or 25 seconds. But note that they made fewer

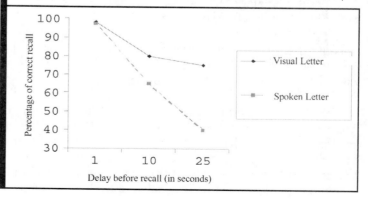

FIGURE 4.17

Shadowing interferes with the recall of a spoken letter more than it interferes with the recall of a visual letter (After Kroll et al., 1970.)

errors when the letter was presented visually than when it was spoken. So you can maintain a letter visually in working memory if necessary.

STIMULUS-RESPONSE COMPATIBILITY

When there is no overlap between the target and the response, compatibility issues between their representations do not arise. For example, as mentioned above, when you press the accelerator in response to a green light there is no overlap between the visual representation used to detect the light and the motor representation that directs your foot in response. However, suppose you come to a detour and see a large arrow pointing to your right. To stay on the road you must turn the car to the right by turning the steering wheel to the right. Now there is overlap between the visual and action representations. The arrow indicates a particular spatial direction and the response must be to move your hands in the same spatial direction. Since both the perceptual system and response system require a spatial response, there is target-response overlap. Once there is such target-response overlap, the issue of target-response compatibility arises. Target-response compatibility is commonly called **stimulus-response compatibility** because that is the name used by Paul Fitts when he and his colleagues first described and named the phenomenon (Fitts & Seegar, 1953). Stimulus-response compatibility refers to the degree to which the target and response have the same features in a representation they share. That is, to respond to the arrow do you turn the wheel in the direction that it points or in the opposite direction? Turning the wheel in the same direction is an example of stimulus-response compatibility. Turning the wheel in the opposite direction is an example of stimulus-response incompatibility. As you might intuit, responding is more difficult when there is incompatibility between the target and response representations. That is why parallel parking requires some effort to learn, and why it is first easier to comb your hair without looking in the mirror.

FIGURE 4.18

A participant had to move a stylus in response to a visual target, in Fitts and Deininger's (1954) study of stimulus-response compatibility. Three different mappings between the location of the target and the direction of the movement were used.

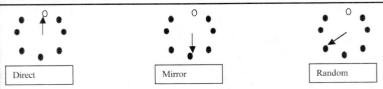

Direct   Mirror   Random

The common representation determining stimulus-response compatibility is usually a spatial one. Fitts and Deininger (1954) placed a stylus at the intersection of eight pathways terminated by lights that were organized like the spokes of a wheel (Figure 4.18). The person's task was to move the stylus to a specified location when a light lit up. In the direct assignment condition, the stylus was moved to whichever light was lit. In the mirror assignment the stylus was moved to the light opposite from whichever light was lit. In the random assignment there was no systematic relationship between where the participant was trained to move the stylus in response to each light. Responses were faster and more accurate with the direct assignment than with the mirror assignment. Reaction times and error rates for the random assignment were over twice those for the mirror assignment. Fitts and Deininger had found a general principle since confirmed by many subsequent studies: responses are faster and most accurate when the response is made towards the location of its stimulus, while responses are next fastest and accurate when there is a simple relationship between the direction or location of the response and its stimulus, and responses are slowest when there is no relationship between the location or direction of the response and its stimulus. Note that it is not the position of a body part that determines the degree of stimulus-response compatibility, but instead it is the spatial location at which the response is made. When a participant crosses his hands so that he controls the right response switch with his left hand and vice versa, it does not decrease stimulus-response compatibility (Anzola, Bertoloni, Buchtel, & Rizzolatti, 1977; Brebner, Shephard, & Cairney, 1972). Furthermore, the spatial representation determining stimulus-response compatibility may be activated through verbal labels. Responses are faster when made to compatible verbal labels like *left* and *right* as well as to compatible visual labels like arrows (Weeks & Proctor, 1990).

RESPONSE CONFLICT

We saw above that in reading, eye movements are automatically guided to the beginning of each word, after which the word's meaning is automatically activated by its visual image. This automatic processing carries a huge advantage. It makes skilled reading rapid and effortless. When the same task is performed again and again, each action comes to prime the next one in the sequence, so that it is prepared and ready to go when its target is selected. This overlap between automatically retrieving the plan for the next action while executing the last one reduces the contribution of planning time to the total response time to essentially zero. This is why whether you are reading, eating, or playing a video game, skilled performance is characterized by the ability to rapidly produce a sequence of task relevant actions. However, automatic processing always carries with it a slight disadvantage. Sometimes you must make a novel response to a target that automatically activates a conflicting response. The most famous example of such a situation is the Stroop Task.

The Stroop effect.   J. Ridley Stroop (1935) showed people a list of color names that were printed in colored ink. Each color name was printed in a color different from the color it named. For example, the word *red* might be printed in blue ink and the word *blue* in green ink. Seventy college students had to read a second list printed in black ink. Stroop found little difference in the reading times for the two lists. Apparently, the students could largely ignore ink color while reading.

A second group of 100 students named the colors of the inks that the color words were printed in and also named the colors of a list of color patches. Stroop found that students required an average of 63 seconds to identify colors on the color patch list but an average of 110 seconds to identify the ink colors on the word list. The students could not avoid reading the words when they tried to name their ink colors and the conflict between the word and the ink color slowed down their responses. The conflict arises because there are two color names in verbal working memory when the person tries to say aloud the name of the ink color. One is the ink color, which is the correct response. The other is the word that is automatically read. Hence if the person does not have to make a verbal response but, rather, indicate in some other way what color the ink is, the interference is greatly reduced (Flowers, Warner, & Polansky 1979; McClain, 1983a, 1983b; Zakay & Glicksohn, 1985).

Colin MacLeod (1991) found that after 700 studies, much about the Stroop effect had been learned. The interfering effect of reading words on another response to the words first appears when children learn to read, and peaks around second grade or third grade (Comalli, Wapner, & Werner, 1962; Schiller, 1966). It then slowly declines (Comalli, et al., 1962; Wise, Sutton, & Gibbons, 1975) as the ability to selectively attend improves until at about 60 years of age, when it begins to rise again as the frontal lobes shrink and the ability to inhibit responses degrades (Comalli, et al., 1962; Cohn, Dustman & Bradford, 1984).

Response interference occurs in a wide variety of other tasks more or less similar to the original Stroop task. For example, interference occurs when a printed word is superimposed on a picture that a person is trying to name (Lupker, 1979; Smith & Magee, 1980). The magnitude of the interference increases with the relatedness of the word's meaning to the color (Klein, 1964) or picture (Lupker & Katz, 1981). Providing an incongruent name for an auditory input, for example calling a low tone, "high," produces interference (Hamers & Lambert, 1972; Zakay & Glicksohn, 1985). Also, naming the number of digits in a row of digits when the digit and row length are incongruent, as shown in Figure 4.19, produces interference (Windes, 1968). As an experiment, try to read aloud, as fast as you can, the number of digits in each row of Figure 4.19. You will find it difficult to ignore the digits as you count them.

FIGURE 4.19

Stroop effect. Say aloud the number of characters in each row as fast as you can.

```
    5   5   5
  1   1   1   1
        2
3   3   3   3   3
      4   4
    5   5   5
  4   4   4   4
    5   5   5   5
        3
      4   4   4
  2   2   2   2
        3   3
      4   4   4
  1   1   1   1
        3
```

Since automatic word reading is itself the effect of practice, with practice a reader should be able to increase his speed on the Stroop task. In fact, Reisberg, Baron, and Kemler (1980) found that with practice on the counting task shown in Figure 4.19, the digits counted interfered less and less with the report of the number of characters on each row. The effect was highly specific. Practice in ignoring the numbers 2 and 4 did not improve performance on rows containing the numbers 1 and 3 or the words "to" and "for." However, consistent with a **semantic** (i. e., word meaning) locus, there was good transfer when the words "two" and "four" had to be ignored. It is worth mentioning that the specificity of transfer to only extremely similar tasks with semantically identical targets is usually an advantage. For example, it would be devastating if practice on inhibiting word reading on some trivial laboratory task carried over into normal reading, which requires automatic processing.

Negative priming. An experiment by Dalrymple-Alford and Budayr (1966) clarified the conditions that produce the Stroop Effect. They compared total color naming time for a list of unrelated color words with that for a list in which each word named the ink color of the next word on the list, e.g., BLUE written in red ink was followed by YELLOW in blue ink. Color naming was slower in the latter condition. Notice that this result implies that there is a delay in executing a correct response that has previously been activated in a context in which it was incorrect. To state this effect more generally, ignoring an item, e.g., the word BLUE, slowed a subsequent response, i.e., saying the word blue. This effect is called **negative priming**, in contrast to the (positive) priming effects described in Chapter 3, in which attending to the prime reduced the processing time of a subsequent target. David L. Strayer and his colleagues (Grison & Strayer, 2001; Malley & Strayer, 1995; Strayer & Grisson, 1999) reported a series of experiments in which negative priming occurred only if the targets were sampled repeatedly from a small set, e.g., the set of color words, throughout the experiment. That negative priming is the result of repeating a small set of items indicates that it only occurs for representations in working memory. That is where task relevant representations that had frequently been repeated would be found. Negative priming occurs for the representation of a response in working memory that is sometimes automatically activated when it is incorrect, such as saying blue in response to the printed word BLUE. To prevent this automatic response from producing fast errors, a verification check is somehow associated with the response so that subsequently, whenever the verbal response blue is activated, a check is made to determine whether it is correct in that context before it is executed. Hence, even though on the very next trial, when YELLOW appears in blue ink, blue is in fact the correct response, its execution is delayed by the verification check. Unfortunately, one thing that the investigators of negative priming agree upon is that the details of the verification check are obscure (Neill & Joordens, 2002; Strayer, Drews, & Albert, 2002; Tipper, 2001). However, the intense work now devoted to negative priming is likely to reveal new details about it in the near future.

MULTITASKING

In real life people are often called upon to do more than one thing at the same time. Suppose that while you are counting lights to a turn while driving your cell phone rings. If you are superhuman then you ignore it until you make the turn. Otherwise, you answer it and reduce the chance that you will drive left when you should. We now consider target-response compatibility in situations in which more than one task is performed at the same time.

Consider again Duncan's (1980) experiment demonstrating that you cannot do two things at once. Recall that a digit target could be in either the vertical or horizontal bar of a cross. An observer had to make an independent response to each digit. When two targets appeared simultaneously, a response to one target reduced the probability of a response to the other target. What would happen if a participant in Duncan's experiment had much more practice responding to two targets? Would the point ever be reached that cross-response interference would disappear? It turns out that four factors determine the degree of cross-response interference when more than one response must be made at the same time. That is, four different conditions must be satisfied to eliminate response conflict:

The first factor is whether the two responses make use of overlapping muscles. Obviously, one cannot say both yes and no at the same time. Performing one of these conflicting responses necessarily delays performing the other.

If there is no motor conflict then the second factor is the predictability of the two kinds of targets. When the targets appear at predictable intervals it is possible to plan their responses in advance.

The third factor is the preparation time for each response, which includes the target detection time and the time for any decision process that must be performed prior to executing the response. Preparation time determines the length of the interval after the target has been detected to initiate a response. If the interval between the cue and the target is sufficient then it is possible to **schedule** the responses so that the planning of one response does not interfere with the planning of the other.

The fourth factor is the amount of practice that a participant has. Even when the first three factors make it possible to plan and simultaneously execute more than one response without conflict, an unpracticed participant will nevertheless perform them sequentially. Only when a skill has developed as the result of practice will response conflict be eliminated.

Studies of the simultaneous performance of two tasks have been of two types. In one type of study the decision processes following target detection for two tasks are simple and neither the motor movements nor representations of the responses overlap, so both responses may be performed at the same time. The question of interest is the degree of interference between responses to simultaneously presented targets. In the other type of study the decision process following target detection is complex and the motor movements for the responses for the two tasks overlap, so it is not possible to respond to more than one target at a time. The question of interest is the time it takes to switch from one task to the other.

COMPATIBLE RESPONSES TO SIMULTANEOUS TARGETS

When two tasks are both easy enough, after sufficient practice, some or all of the participants can perform both tasks together as fast and accurately as either one alone. Schumacher, Seymour, Glass, Fencsik, Lauber, Kieras, and Meyer (2001) performed an experiment to investigate the conditions under which dual task was equivalent to single task performance. They combined an auditory-verbal task with a visual-manual task. In their first experiment the auditory-verbal task was to say "one," "two," or "three" in response to a low, medium, or high tone, respectively. The visual-manual task was to respond with the index, middle, and ring finger to the visual target O—, -O-, and — O, respectively. Half a second after a warning signal either an auditory, visual, or both kinds of targets were presented. Hence, the instant when at least one target would appear was perfectly predicted by the warning signal.

The results of the experiment are shown in Table 4.4. As can be seen from the table, when the participants were

TABLE 4.4

The effect of practice on reaction time (and percent error) for tasks that have different completion times (Schumacher et al., 2001).

Tas	Trial Type	Novice	Practiced
Auditory - Visual	Dual Task	725 (6.5)	456 (5.4)
	Single Task	655 (5.3)	447 (3.3)
Visual - Manual	Dual Task	352 (2.4)	283 (5.6)
	Single Task	338 (1.3)	282 (2.7)

novices their responses were slower and less accurate when two targets appeared (dual task) than when only one appeared (single task). However, after practice, the responses were equally fast whether one or two targets appeared, though still slightly more accurate for a single target. How were the practiced participants able to make two responses as fast as one? Notice from the table that the auditory-verbal task took longer to perform than the visual-manual task. Suppose we assume that the decision processes for the auditory targets could occur in parallel, however, the planning and performance of the verbal and manual responses could only be performed sequentially. As shown in the top of Figure 4.20, practiced participants made use of the fact that the visual-manual task required a much shorter visual decision process (white bar) than the auditory-verbal task, as indicated by the shorter response times for it (entire bar). The practiced participants created a plan to first execute the fast manual response and then the slower verbal response. By the time that the slower decision process for the verbal response was completed, the manual action (button press) had already been initiated. So the first response did not interfere with the second.

TABLE 4.5

The effect of practice on reaction time (and percent error) for tasks that have similar completion times (Schumacher et al., 2001).

Tas	Trial Type	Novice	Practiced
Auditory - Visual	Dual Task	1178 (6.5)	565 (4.8)
	Single Task	821 (2.9)	466 (4.1)
Visual - Manual	Dual Task	965 (10.2)	522 (5.3)
	Single Task	778 (6.9)	466 (6.9)

To test this explanation of the equally fast dual and single task responses, another experiment was performed in which the preparation times for the two responses were equalized by making the visual-manual decision more difficult. Again the auditory-verbal task was to say "one," "two," or "three" in response to a low, medium, or high tone, respectively. This time the visual-manual task was to respond with the ring, index, little, or middle finger to O—-, -O—, —O-, and —-O, respectively. Again a warning signal occurred half a second before one or both targets were presented.

The results of the experiment are shown in Table 4.5. Notice that making the visual-manual task more difficult had the effect of slowing responses in both tasks. Again novice responses were slower and less accurate when two targets were presented than when only one target was presented. This time, though response times decreased, practiced responses to two targets remained slower than responses to one target. These results are consistent with the results of other studies (Ruthruff, Pashler, & Klaassen, 2001) indicating that there is an absolute limit of performing one voluntary action at a time. When a task requires that two voluntary actions be performed at exactly the same time, one or the other must give way, as shown at the bottom of Figure 4.20.

FIGURE 4.20

As shown at the top, when visual preparation takes less time than auditory preparation, the visual response does not interfere with the verbal response. However, as shown at the bottom, when visual decision time is increased and so visual preparation takes the same time as auditory preparation (as indicated by the dotted line), the verbal action is postponed until after the manual action is initiated.

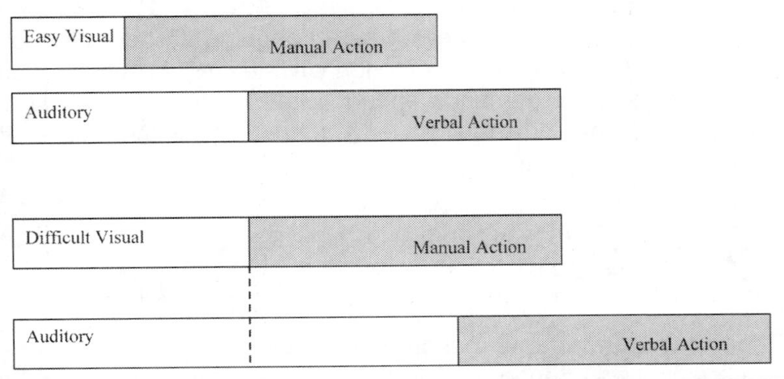

TASK SWITCHING

Until now we have ignored the role of the decision stage in attention. Whenever only a single response is possible, it may be prepared in advance and there is no decision stage; e.g., press the button whenever you see the target. In contrast in the auditory-verbal task above the listener had to decide whether the tone was low, medium, or high and then make the appropriate response. Deciding whether the tone was low, medium, or high is, of course, an example of a simple decision process. In this case, three responses are possible, so a single response cannot be prepared. For the experiment above, Schumacher et al. (2001) selected tasks with non-overlapping auditory-verbal and visual-manual target-detection, decision, and response stages in order to investigate whether two independent voluntary actions could be performed at the same time. It is also possible to select tasks with overlapping decision processes. In a seminal study, Jersild (1927) presented observers with two-digit numbers to which they had to either add or subtract a number. Obviously, you cannot both add and subtract from the same number at the same time. There was no question that addition and subtraction could not be performed simultaneously. Instead the question of interest was how fast a person could switch from addition to subtraction and back again.

Jersild (1927) presented his participants with columns of two-digit numbers. In one condition a participant had to add 6 to each number in the column. In a second condition the participant had to subtract 3 from each number in the column. In the third condition the participant had to alternately add 6 to the first number, subtract 3 from the second number, etc. In order to determine the time to switch from addition to subtraction and back again, the average time to complete the first two homogeneous (all addition and all subtraction) conditions was subtracted from the time for the alternating condition. The difference was the time it took to repeatedly switch from addition to subtraction and back again. Jersild also performed an otherwise identical experiment in which a participant had to add 17 or subtract 13 from each digit. The more difficult computations produced a longer switching time.

Years later, Jersild's (1927) study caught the attention of Spector and Biederman (1976). They proposed that switching time reflected the time required to retrieve from memory the plan for performing the next task. They reasoned that if switching time were the time to retrieve a representation from memory then a cue for that representation would reduce retrieval, hence switching, time. They repeated Jersild's experiment with an easier addition task. This time participants had to add 3 or subtract 3 from each digit. Again performance was slower in the alternating condition. In another alternating condition +3 or −3 was printed next to each number in the column indicating which operation had to be performed. These redundant visual cues reduced switching time, confirming the retrieval hypothesis. Subsequently, other studies found evidence consistent with the retrieval hypothesis. Rogers and Monsell (1995) alternated runs of two or more trials before switching tasks. If switching time represents the time to retrieve the task representation on a "switch" trial, then response time should only increase for the first trial in a run of same-task trials. This is what Rogers and Monsell found.

Daily life may be viewed as an ongoing divided attention task in which task switching is routine. You routinely carry on a conversation while eating a meal or driving a car. Carrying on a conversation on an interesting topic demands enough attention to interfere with braking to a light that has changed from green to red while driving (Strayer & Johnston, 2001). This is why talking on a cell phone increases the danger of driving a car.

AROUSAL

There is more than one reason that a person may scream. A person may scream to deliberately attract someone else's attention or alternatively to distract that person. In this case the scream is another example of a voluntary act. Or, a person may scream because she is scared. Fear is an example of negative emotional arousal, which produces responses that move an organism away from something. The arousal system provides a more primitive alternative to the cognitive system of voluntary action for directing attention to targets and performing responses to them. Voluntary action and arousal sometimes compete and sometimes cooperate in the production of responses. A complete description of the arousal system, including emotional arousal, would require another book as large as this one. Here it will be mentioned in just enough detail to describe how it influences attention.

A person's arousal level is regulated by a complex system called the reticular activating system. The reticular activating system is named after the midbrain reticular formation (Posner & Petersen, 1990), which is connected with all the brain structures involved in attention, including the thalamus, basal ganglia, parietal cortex, and frontal cortex (Heilman, et al., 1993). This system keeps you awake and alert. If enough of an animal's reticular formation is destroyed, the creature falls into a coma from which it cannot be aroused. If only the right half of the reticular formation is destroyed, it appears as if the right hemisphere falls into a coma while the left is intact, and vice versa. For example, in the case of the destruction of the right half of the reticular formation a person or animal shows the neglect syndrome on the left side.

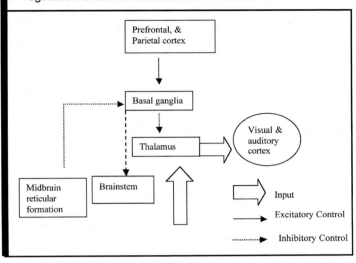

FIGURE 4.21
By inhibiting the basal ganglia, the midbrain reticular formation regulates the flow of information to the cortex.

Attention is regulated by the reticular activating system as shown in Figure 4.21. The basal ganglia, in addition to receiving an activating signal from the cortex above also receive an inhibiting signal from the reticular formation of the midbrain below through the substantia nigra, which is part of both the basal ganglia and midbrain. Normally the reticular activating system inhibits the basal ganglia, which prevents the basal ganglia from inhibiting the thalamus, thus allowing the thalamus to function. But when a voluntary response is made, the signal from the substantia nigra to the rest of the basal ganglia is blocked. The result is that the basal ganglia inhibit the processing of distracters by the thalamus for up to half a second, thereby blocking irrelevant perceptual information during the performance of a voluntary action (Carlsson, 1988). Notice that even though physiological processes embody cognitive operations, the relationship is complex. The reticular formation opens the perceptual gates by inhibiting the basal ganglia. In this arrangement, inhibition at the physiological level can lead to increased processing at the cognitive level.

THE FUNCTION OF SLEEP

The reticular activating system controls the sleep-wakefulness cycle. When your arousal level falls below a certain level you sleep and when it rises above that level you are awake. Human sleep is not a single state but a sequence of five distinct stages, as indicated by brain activity, that repeat in 90-minute cycles throughout the night. The fifth stage is characterized by rapid eye-movements and hence is called **REM** sleep. If awakened during REM sleep, the participant is likely to report the occurrence of dreams (Carlson, 2001). The first four stages of sleep are often referred to as non-REM (**nREM**) sleep to separate them from REM sleep. The four nREM stages begin with two stages that indicate a shift from wakefulness to sleep and then two stages collectively called slow wave sleep (**SWS**) because of the shape of the electrical waves produced by the brain during these stages. Regions of the brain that have the highest activity levels during wakefulness are associated with the lowest levels of activity during SWS, suggesting that the region is resting (Kattler, Dijik, & Borbely, 1994). In the first half of the night, sleep is mostly composed of nREM sleep while the later cycles consist of mostly stage 2 and REM sleep.

Sleep undoubtedly has one or more vital non-cognitive functions. Evidence that sleep performs some vital function comes from the fact that even animals that would appear to be better off without it spend a considerable amount of time asleep. In order to breathe, the Indus Dolphin must constantly swim against the strong current and debris of the Indus River. Pilleri (1979) discovered that the Indus Dolphin has evolved to only take brief naps, between 4-60 seconds each, throughout the day, totaling approximately seven hours of sleep a day. Perhaps the most fundamental non-cognitive function is brain thermoregulation. Overheating is a great risk to the brain, and its functioning can be impaired even by a relatively small change in temperature of 3°C (Horne, 1988). In studies with humans, when brain temperature was increased during wakefulness, slow wave sleep increased during the following night (Horne & Moore, 1985; Horne, 1988). Another likely non-cognitive function is energy conservation. To understand energy conservation it is necessary to turn things around and attempt to describe the function of wakefulness. A creature only needs to be awake in order to perform some vital function. Otherwise, it may remain asleep and conserve its energy.

PARKINSON'S DISEASE

The arousal system influences action through its effect on the basal ganglia. Recall that the basal ganglia receive an activating signal from the cortex above and an inhibiting signal from the reticular formation of the midbrain below through the substantia nigra. Normally, the reticular activating system inhibits the basal ganglia, thus allowing the thalamus to function (Carlsson, 1988).

The basal ganglia operate to shut the thalamic gates and switch off perceptual processing just during the brief moment it might interfere with an ongoing response. As shown in Figure 4.21, they also regulate motor activity by inhibiting the brain stem. But if the switch is damaged and becomes stuck in the off position, it results in a progressive slowing that eventually becomes total inertia. This is the disastrous consequence of the destruction of a small group of dopamine producing cells in the substantia nigra. The destruction of the dopamine synthesizing cells in the substantia nigra eliminates the main source of dopamine in the brain. Dopamine is the neurotransmitter used in the circuit that inhibits the output of the basal ganglia to the thalamus. It is only when the output from the basal ganglia is inhibited that a thalamic gate can open. When the dopamine circuit is destroyed then the basal ganglia continuously inhibit the thalamus. All the thalamic gates are forced shut. The result is an impairment of both motor activity and awareness called Parkinson's disease. A Parkinson's disease patient might first appear to a naive observer to be suffering from muscle damage. A patient first exhibits tremor (caused by the stimulant acetylcholine, another neurotransmitter, which is now present in the brain in excessive quantities because of the missing dopamine). Next there is pronounced slowness of all voluntary movements. The patient walks with slow, short, shuffling steps, arms flexed and held stiffly at sides, and trunk bent forward. Eventually all voluntary movement is lost and the patient is confined to a wheelchair (Zigmond & Stricker, 1989).

But it is not the muscles that have been damaged in Parkinson's disease (reflexes remain normal). It is that the patient is losing the ability to initiate voluntary movement. Furthermore, it is not just movement that is lost but also awareness of the world. When the substantia nigra is destroyed the basal ganglia are no longer inhibited. So the basal ganglia continuously inhibit the thalamus, thus inhibiting perceptual processing (Carlsson, 1988). In 30% of the cases the decline in awareness and activity is accompanied by impairment in a variety of cognitive processes, which is collectively called **dementia**. Temporary relief of these symptoms is achieved by surgical removal of the part of the basal ganglia known as the striatum, since this is the primary source of the inhibitory signal to the thalamus (Obeson, Rodriguez-Oroz, Rodriguez, Macias, Alvarz, Guridi, Vitek, & Delong, 2000). Also, symptoms are alleviated by boosting the production of dopamine by supplying large amounts of the chemical, called levadopa, that the brain makes dopamine from. Finally, a microelectrode is inserted in a part of the striatum and an electric current stimulates the region. This procedure, called **deep brain stimulation,** also reduces the over-inhibition of the thalamus. But as the substantia nigra continues to deteriorate the symptoms eventually return (Guridi, Rodriguez-Oroz, Lozano, Moro, Albanese, Nuttin, Gybels, Ramos, & Obeso, 2000).

However, an occasional input that is extremely significant activates a response. A classic story is of the grandmother with Parkinson's disease who is sitting in a wheelchair with her grandchild in a crib beside her. Suddenly the room catches on fire. The grandmother rises from her chair, grabs the infant, runs to safety, and collapses, again unable to move a muscle. Another story is of a former baseball player confined to a wheelchair in a hospital. One day a doctor throws a baseball toward him. In a single motion the player leaps from the chair, catches the ball in his out-stretched hand, pegs it back to the doctor, and collapses back into the chair. These stories may be apocryphal but similar effects are generated with animals. Today the animal model used for studying Parkinson's disease is the monkey (Obeson, et al., 2000). However, in an early study Levitt and Teitelbaum (1975) produced lethargic behavior in rats by destroying the dopamine producing cells in their brains. When an injured rat was placed in tepid water (neither warm nor cool), the rat sank to the bottom without making an effort to keep afloat. However, if the water was markedly colder, it elicited a vigorous swimming response from the injured rat. In one instance the animal leapt from the water and scampered halfway across the laboratory floor before it again collapsed in an inert heap.

YERKES-DODSON LAW

The effect of the reticular activating system on activity is not all-or-none. Arousal level fluctuates over the course of a day, and there is a very general relationship between arousal and task performance known as the Yerkes-Dodson Law (Yerkes & Dodson, 1908). As shown in Figure 4.22, each task has an optimal level of arousal: that level at which performance is best. The optimal level of arousal is not the lowest level of arousal, at which point you would be asleep, nor the highest level of arousal, but some level in between. If a person's performance on a task is measured at various levels of arousal, performance first increases and then decreases as the level of arousal increases. Furthermore, as shown in Figure 4.22, the more difficult the task, the lower the level of arousal at which performance is optimal.

Why should an increase in arousal be associated with first an increase and then a decrease in task performance? Easterbrook (1959) proposed that as arousal increases, an observer shifts attention among fewer inputs. As arousal increases from low to moderate levels, performance is less likely to be disrupted by the processing of distracters. However, as arousal further increases from moderate to high levels, performance is disrupted because of an inability to process all the targets.

FIGURE 4.22

Yerkes-Dodson law. Performance on easy tasks peaks at a higher arousal level than performance on difficult tasks.

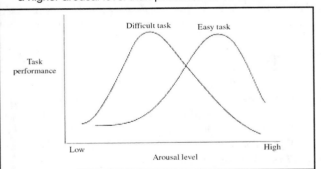

The distribution of attention is usually tested with an experimental paradigm in which a primary task and secondary task are performed concurrently. If increasing arousal restricts the distribution of attention, then as arousal increases there should be more processing of the primary task and less processing of the secondary task, resulting in better performance on the primary task and poorer performance on the secondary task. Most of the experiments that have examined the effect of arousal have used either electric shock or noise to increase it. Easterbrook (1959) reviewed a large number of studies that found that an increase in arousal either improved performance on the primary task or impaired performance on the secondary task. An updated review by Eysenck (1982) found that in 7 of 10 further studies using electric shock and 8 out of 14 studies using noise, performance on the secondary task deteriorated. Also, in 5 of the 14 studies in which noise was used to increase arousal, performance on the primary task improved.

Another task relevant to Easterbrook's (1959) hypothesis is the vigilance task. Recall that in a vigilance task, interference from the distracters degrades the target's representation. Any factor that increases arousal delays the onset of the performance decrement by reducing the number of distracters processed. Arousing factors include noise, paying monetary rewards (Bergum & Lehr, 1964) and telling participants that the task is a selection task for a high-paying job (Nachreiner, 1977).

Fluctuations in arousal and task performance. Things that increase arousal are called **stimulants** and things that decrease arousal are called **depressants**. Arousal tends to increase throughout the day. On the other hand, sleep deprivation decreases the level of arousal. Hence, performance on tasks requiring high arousal is often poorest in the morning and deteriorates as the result of sleep deprivation. Stimulants such as noise (Mullin & Corcoran, 1977) and caffeine (Revelle, Humphreys, Simon, & Gilliland, 1980) have their greatest effects in the morning and counter-act the effects of sleep deprivation (Eysenck, 1982).

Individual differences. In a classic review, Hans Eysenck (1967) identified the personality dimension of introversion—extraversion with a person's average level of arousal. Eysenck proposed that high arousal causes introversion because the introvert shuns external stimuli (such as certain social situations) that further increase the naturally high arousal level. In contrast, low arousal causes extraversion because the extravert seeks external stimuli that increase a low arousal level, as well as engaging in self-stimulation through activity. Introverts and extraverts perform differently on tasks in which performance is affected by level of arousal. For example, extraverts perform more poorly on a vigilance task and show a greater decrement over time (Eysenck, 1982). Also, caffeine, which is a stimulant, causes a performance decrement for introverts, but not extraverts, on a proofreading task (Anderson & Revelle, 1982).

Attention deficit, hyperactive disorder (ADHD) first appears in toddlers and affects an individual throughout his or her life. ADHD individuals suffer from impulsivity, which affects both their social relations and academic performance. A young child who impulsively hits other children when thwarted will soon be ostracized, no matter how remorseful he feels immediately after. A student who selects the first plausible alternative on an exam will never perform well on multiple-choice tests. ADHD is associated with very low arousal. Presumably, the low arousal produces both the distractibility and impulsivity associated with the disorder. The treatment for ADHD includes a stimulant such as Ritalin, which raises the individual's arousal level, combined with behavioral therapy. Unfortunately, behavioral therapy by itself is not an effective way to change arousal. For example, when Holmes (1984) reviewed all the experimental studies that had been done on meditation he found no evidence that people using meditation techniques had more influence over their arousal level than control subjects who were simply told to relax. There is ongoing research on the most effective combination of behavioral and drug therapy for the disorder.

EMOTION

The effect of general arousal on performance is quite crude. A sleeping creature is unresponsive to anything but the strongest alerts. An awake creature at a low level of arousal is **vigilant**. That is, many different inputs have a chance to stimulate a response. A highly aroused creature is focused on a single target, hence primed for action. However, there is more than one source of arousal in the brain (Broadbent, 1971), as anyone knows who has felt both tired and excited while waiting for Santa Claus. The emotional system consists of several subsystems that each act to increase the probability of some actions to specific targets while suppressing the possibility of others. The various responses initiated by the emotional system are collectively experienced as emotional arousal.

FIGURE 4.23
Medial temporal areas involved in emotion.

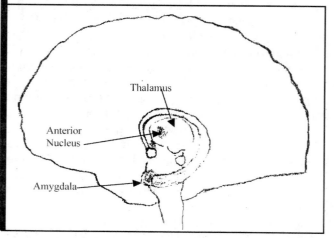

Overview of the emotional system. Figure 4.23 shows the subcortical areas of the brain involved in emotion and Figure 4.1 shows the cortical area. Figure 4.24 shows schematically the principal brain circuits containing the amygdala. The amygdala is the principal switch controlling emotion (LeDoux, 1993). It plays a role in emotion analogous to the role of the thalamus in perception. Just as all sensory inputs that are used to construct perceptual representations first go to the thalamus, which distributes them to the cortex, all sensory inputs that elicit emotional responses go to the amygdala, which initiates those responses. The amygdala may receive input from the representation of a present, imagined, or remembered target. Its anatomical connections suggest that it can be activated by simple features, whole objects,

FIGURE 4.24

The amygdala is at the center of several circuits that control emotional responses.

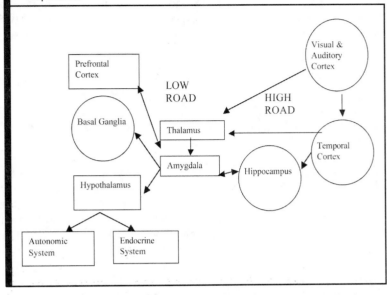

the context in which the objects occur, semantic properties of objects, images and memories of objects, and the like. Any and all of these may serve as the critical trigger information for emotional arousal. The amygdala is at the center of an emotional network comprised of five principal pathways (LeDoux, 1993). Two pathways, from the thalamus and perceptual processing areas of the cortex, direct input to the amygdala. Three pathways from the amygdala, to the hypothalamus, basal ganglia, and hippocampus, make it possible for the amygdala to regulate involuntary responses, voluntary responses, and memory, respectively.

Low road. First, a pathway from the thalamus directly to the amygdala sends sensory input to the amygdala without being first transmitted to the cortex. This pathway is sometimes called the **low road**. The cortex is unnecessary for classical conditioning. However, the conditioning of responses to simple tones and light flashes paired with foot-shocks require an intact thalamus-to-amygdala pathway. Sub-cortical sensory inputs to the amygdala are part of a primitive system passed on from early vertebrates that lacked a well-developed neocortex. These inputs were the main sensory transmission routes to the forebrain in such animals. Recall that unconditioned reflexes are innate. As long as a creature lives in a simple predictable world unconditioned reflexes are all that is needed to survive and flourish. Evolution can gradually select the fittest individuals until all the necessary reflexes are part of the creature's repertory at birth. However, the world is rarely simple or perfectly predictable. The next step in the evolution of cognition is a mental system in which novel inputs are able to elicit reflexes through classical conditioning. For example, imagine a turtle that reflexively withdraws into his shell whenever he sees a looming object. If the appearance of the looming object is reliably preceded by a rustle in the air or water that the turtle can sense, so much the better if the rustle elicits the withdrawal reflex even before the object appears. Hence, at the level of conditioning through the thalamus-to-amygdala pathway the emotional and action systems are one in the same. The amygdala is a key structure in the conditioning of fear to novel stimuli.

In contemporary mammals these pathways are clearly in a secondary position with respect to perceptual processing, since they exit the perceptual system prior to the cortex, where object and event information is represented. However, these pathways continue to function as an early warning system, allowing the amygdala to be activated by simple stimulus features that may serve as emotional triggers. Thus of particular importance is the pathway to the hypothalamus through which the amygdala can set into motion a variety of emotional responses appropriate to the meaning of the stimulus. The hypothalamus initiates endocrine and autonomic responses for the four F's of emotion: fear, fighting, feeding, and sexual activity. Pathways to the hypothalamus initiate autonomic responses and other motor responses asso-ciated with emotional arousal. Pathways to the forebrain and hypothalamic areas are also involved in the control of hormones released by the pituitary gland. This is especially important when rapid responses are required to threatening stimuli. In such situations it may be more important to respond rapidly on the basis of incomplete information from the thalamus than to wait for a complete object representation from the cortex.

Furthermore, an emotional response is more than a set of unconditioned responses to a specific input. In addition, the pathway from the amygdala to the basal ganglia increases the probability that a vol-untary motor action will be taken in response to the mental (cortical) representation of an emotional tar-get. You may reflexively pull your hand back from a hot stove. But you also may pull your hand back from a warm stove if you are afraid that it is hot.

Consider a creature (like a shark) that is born with the tendency to bite things that it sees. Some of the things it bites turn out to be good to eat and others do not. As the result of experience it comes to preferentially attack things good to eat and to ignore those things that are not. But how is this discrimi-nation learned? One approach was the evolution of the emotional system. The shark does not have to have the mental experience of remembering having seen or eaten something before in order to control its behavior. All that is necessary is for some things to look good to eat and for other things to look bad to eat. So if something tastes good, next time it looks good. If it tastes bad, next time it looks bad. The shark may always live within the moment. No conscious memory of past experience is necessary. The advantage of the emotional system is its relative simplicity compared with declarative memory. Detailed representations of specific objects in the world are not required. On the basis of a few simple features, things are merely labeled good or bad, which are cues for approach and avoidance, respectively. However, the simplicity of the emotional system limits its usefulness. The emotional system specifies a limited number of kinds of actions, e.g., feed, fight, or flee.

Two fundamentally different competing systems evolved to make it possible to distinguish between opportunities and threats in the world on the basis of experience. One approach is the evolution of the emotional system, which makes it possible to learn which things in the world are inviting and which are dangerous. The other approach is the evolution of declarative memory. For example, when the shark sees something, it may look good to eat, but he cannot remember that something just like it tasted good. But you can. You can make this kind of decision when ordering from a menu. The advantage of declar-ative memory is that it can provide the information that enables a choice of responses to a target. However, declarative memory is informationally dense and computationally intense. A detailed represen-tation of the experience must first be encoded and then later retrieved, which requires many computations. Such a system took a long time to evolve.

High road. In humans the emotional and declarative memory systems operate together. A pathway for representations of visual objects and auditory messages proceeds forward to the prefrontal cortex and then downward to the amygdala. This pathway is sometimes called the **high road**. In this way, the things you see and hear are imbued with affect that ranges from pleasure to fear to disgust. Also, the amygdala extends into the hippocampus. A target representation that generates a large emotional response is more likely to be encoded in declarative memory. Furthermore, its emotional content is recovered when the input is retrieved from declarative memory. The affect associated with a target strongly influences the action selected in response to it, as first demonstrated by the Kluver-Bucy syndrome. This is a complex set of behavioral changes brought about by damage to the amygdala in primates (Kluver & Bucy, 1937; Weiskrantz, 1956). Following such lesions, animals lose their fear of previously threatening stimuli, attempt to copulate with members of another species, and attempt to eat a variety of things that normal primates find unattractive (e.g., feces, rocks). Weiskrantz proposed that amygdala lesions interfere with the ability to determine the motivational significance of stimuli. A host of subsequent studies has shown that the amygdala is a key structure in the assignment of reward value to stimuli (LeDoux, 1993).

The emotional system and declarative memory system are competing answers to the same prob-lem: the selection of an appropriate action in response to a familiar object or event. Declarative memory provides information about previous experience with the object or event. The emotional system merely lets you know whether it is good or bad. Hypothetically, in a simple enough world an emotional system is all that would be required to select from an innately determined set of actions in all possible situations. However, neither the world nor the creatures that inhabit it have turned out to be that simple. Many creatures have both emotional and memory systems, which often perform complementary, sometimes perform competing, and sometimes perform conflicting roles in the control of action. When you order your favorite dish from a menu, memory and emotion are probably cooperating. When you cannot decide between a satisfying familiar dish or an attractive novel one, memory and emotion may be competing. And when you force yourself to take some particularly unpleasant medicine, then memory and emotion are in conflict.

Often, a high level of emotional arousal prepares an individual to do one thing, either flee, fight, feed, etc. This is useful in the simple world of an animal. But in your world the best way to handle a situation may be to perform a learned or even novel response. If such a situation is an emotional one then emotionally charged distracters may draw attention from your targets and there may be conflict between your considered response and your emotional one. For example, literally running away may not be the best way of escaping danger, and an emotional arousal system that prevents you from considering any other alternative may be deadly. That is why high arousal retards performance by restricting attention to one target, as described by the Yerkes-Dodson law. Alan Baddeley (1972) was initially interested in the performance of deep-sea divers. The original aim of the experiments was to study the effects of nitrogen narcosis on diver performance; nitrogen narcosis is the intoxication that occurs when air is breathed at high pressure. Discrepancies between open-sea results and pressure chamber simulation occurred, and Baddeley subsequently found that the degree of danger was a crucial variable affecting performance. Baddeley was stimulated to review findings on people's performance in dangerous environments, including deep-sea divers, soldiers in combat, army parachutists, and soldiers subjected to extremely realistic, simulated, life-threatening emergencies (see also Weltman, Smith, & Egstrom, 1971). He found that a dangerous situation tends to produce a high level of arousal, i.e., fear, thus reducing target detection and decreasing task performance. Hence, just at the moment that correct performance becomes essential, it becomes most difficult. This leads to the tragedy of an individual in a car stalled on railroad tracks unable to figure out how to open the door while the train approaches.

On the other hand, not all emotional targets and responses are simple. The amygdala responds to complex, socially relevant stimuli (LeDoux, 1993). For social creatures, the emotional system plays an important role in regulating their social behavior. Consider anger. Anger prepares a creature for a fight. It helps regulate behavior within a social group by allowing stronger members to control weaker ones, but rarely leads to serious fighting because weaker members make responses that dissipate the anger of stronger members. When attacked by another member of the same species a display of submission terminates the attack. For example, when dogs are attacked by stronger opponents they bare their throats. This results in cessation of the attack. People are social creatures and so our behavior is regulated by emotion as well. Blair (1995) suggested that for humans as well the perception of distress (i.e., sad facial expression, the sight and sound of tears), initiates a withdrawal response. That is, it is hard to stay angry at someone who is crying. In fact, Camras (1977) has observed that the display of distress cues (a sad facial expression) results in the termination of aggression in 4- to 7-year-olds.

SUMMARY OF CHAPTER

- Attention refers to the process of planning and performing some voluntary action; performing an action in response to some target. Whenever you decide to do something and then do it, you are paying attention. The system for making actions that are responses to targets has three stages:
  - Planning
  - Target Detection
  - Performance

- Planning
  - The time to perform a task is reduced when plans are retrieved in advance of an expected target rather than constructed ad hoc after it appears.
    * Hence, practice improves task performance by reducing planning time.
    * Hence, practice most improves tasks in which targets occur at predictable intervals, so that plans for their responses can be retrieved in advance.
  - Even plans for compatible simultaneous actions may be constructed; so as the result of practice more than one response may be performed at the same time to predictable targets without mutual interference (simultaneous multitasking).
  - When the responses required by different tasks are incompatible, the limiting factor on the time to simultaneously perform the tasks is the time to successively retrieve the plans for the incompatible responses (successive multitasking).

- Target detection. The target detection stage is called selective attention. An act of selective attention has three stages.
  - First a plan that includes a representation of the target in memory is activated in working memory. This is called **specification**. There is both an auditory and visual working memory.
  - Second, the location of a potential target is identified through comparison of input with the target representation. This is called **search**. The search stage ends when the comparison process produces a match and a response indicating that the target has been found. There are two stages to the target selection process: early (or perceptual) selection and late (or response) selection.
    * The early (perceptual) selection stage is a system of gates through which the perceptual input must pass. Any level of perceptual organization, including features, patterns, object representations and perceptual novelty, may be the basis of selection.
    * When more than one input passes through a perceptual gate then late selection occurs. In late selection the representation of each input is compared with the target-representation. For late selection you may have to serially orient to several potential target locations and compare each potential target with the representation in working memory before the actual target is found. Late selection is influenced by practice. If the target is more familiar than the distracters, then the comparison of its perceptual representation with memory will produce a match in less time than the comparison of the distracter representations, so late selection will be fast and accurate.
  - As a result of the match, input from nontarget locations is inhibited and a detailed representation of the potential target enters working memory. This is called **orientation**.
    * An orienting response need only be made to the first in a sequence of targets in the same location in order to select the entire sequence.
    * When each target in a sequence is in a different location and separate orienting response must be made to each target. The number of targets in the sequence that may be detected is limited by the time it takes to make an orienting response to each target.
    * Because the visual and auditory systems are largely independent of each other, target detection is greater for a task including both visual and auditory targets than for a task within a single modality.

- Performance
  - When performance on a task becomes automatic as the result of practice the plan of the response

is retrieved and performed whenever the target is detected, regardless of whether it was expected. Automatic processing produces the fastest and most accurate level of performance; for example, as in reading.
  ◦ When a novel response must be made to a target that automatically elicits another response then conflict occurs, which slows the novel response; for example, the Stroop effect.

• Alerting occurs when a distracter enters working memory. A distracter may enter memory because:
  ◦ of an input eliciting a reflex
  ◦ as the result of perceptual pop out, including the pop out of novel targets
  ◦ as the result of a familiar distracter, perceptually similar to the target, producing a match before the target
  ◦ the greater the complexity of the perceptual representations that must be maintained in working memory to complete a task, the less likely there will be perceptual processing capacity available to process a distracter and cause an alert.

• An increase in arousal decreases the number of perceptual inputs that may be processed in parallel. Thus an increase in arousal may decrease the interruption of a complex task by the processing of a distracter but it also may decrease the probability of fully processing all targets in a simple task.
  ◦ So arousal influences task performance. The relationship between level of arousal and task performance is called the Yerkes-Dodson law. Task performance is best at an intermediate level of arousal, and the intermediate level at which performance is optimal decreases as task difficulty increases.
  ◦ There are individual differences in arousal level and arousal is influenced by emotional state, activity level, stress, and time of day.
  ◦ Emotional arousal increases the probability that particular responses will be performed, depending on which emotion is aroused.

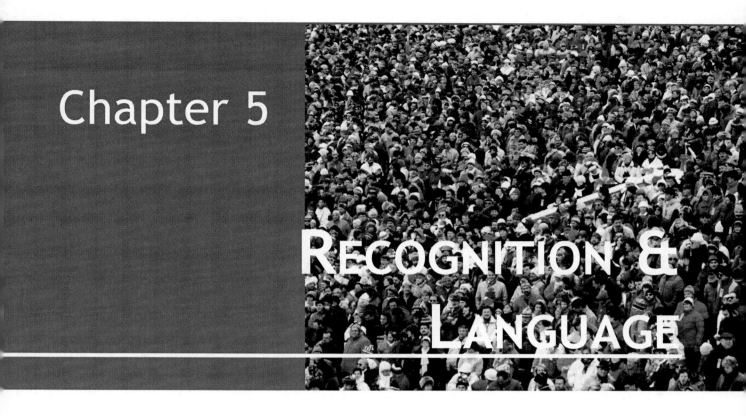

Chapter 5

RECOGNITION & LANGUAGE

John was a corporate executive who went into the hospital for a routine surgical procedure. When he woke up, he found himself in a strange place surrounded by people he did not recognize. One of them took him in a car to another strange place. Terrified, John did not know what had happened to him. He wondered if he had gone crazy and had been taken to the loony bin. But John was not crazy. He was suffering from apperceptive visual agnosia. The strange place he was in was his own home. The unfamiliar person who had taken him there was his wife. When she spoke he recognized her voice and knew who she was. All his intellectual abilities were intact. However, the disruption of one specific step in the process of visual recognition had left him totally disoriented.

This entire chapter is about cognitive processes that take only a few hundredths of a second. That is how long it takes for a perceptual input to activate associated representations in memory. When a perceptual representation enters awareness, it does not come as a mystery. When you sit in class, you do not merely see a room full of objects. All the information you need to make sense of what you see is available as part of the perceptual experience. So you see a familiar classroom, fellow students, and a teacher. Hence, you are oriented to place. John's dilemma shows how central recognition is to your ability to live in the world.

It is the rapidity and sophistication of the recognition system that makes language possible, as well. Because humans are social creatures, communication is an essential part of your existence. Since language also relies on a recognition process that occurs in few hundredths of a second, language will be discussed here as well.

PROCEDURAL VERSUS DECLARATIVE MEMORY

We have already seen that action begins with retrieving a representation of the action you wish to perform from memory. Walking, dressing, eating, writing, etc. are performed efficiently only after practice has encoded the body-part postures from many previous performances. Also, we have already seen that the visual perception of a familiar face or word, or any other object in the visual field beyond a minimum level of complexity, requires retrieving a representation of the object and matching it with the input. If the comparison between the visual input and memory representation is impaired, for example by turning the object upside down (as shown in Chapter 3) then the visual perception of the object is impaired as well. As discussed in earlier chapters, motor learning and perceptual learning are both examples of what is called **procedural memory** and **skill learning**. Procedural learning has also been called: **knowing how** and **implicit memory**. In all these cases a person gets faster and more accurate at something with practice. Procedural memory does not imply remembering the training sessions or training materials. For example, you probably can walk, and probably do not remember learning how to do so.

Motor learning and perceptual learning are often lumped together as examples of procedural memory and we have pointed out the similarities in how motor skills, like writing, and perceptual skills, like reading, are performed. The similarities between motor learning and perceptual learning reflect the analogous operations of two different brain systems. However, there are differences between the motor system and the perceptual system. Motor representations are fundamentally different from the perceptual representations that result in the recognition of inputs. In contrast, perceptual learning is not the product of an entirely different system from recognition but describes the effect of experience on the early stages of the recognition process. Recall that visual learning occurs when the visual system hierarchically organizes smaller patterns as parts of larger ones. This was called recognition by components in Chapter 3. For example, consider reading. Initially, each letter must be laboriously encoded as a set of lines in particular locations and orientations. After a sufficient amount of practice, the entire letter activates a single representation. Similarly, initially a word is a sequence of individual letters. However, with sufficient repetition a single representation of the entire word is encoded. Once a representation of the entire word exists in memory it is retrieved and compared with the input as a unit. This takes less time than retrieving and comparing representations of individual letters.

Hence, the ability to encode a visual representation of an entire word is the result of perceptual learning. When you look down at this page you see more than a white surface with some black marks. You see a book with words that form sentences that you can read and understand. The visual representations of the words activate many additional representations that provide new information about the world. Collectively, the representations of the words and sentences form what is called **declarative memory** to contrast it with procedural memory. It is also called **knowing what** to contrast it with knowing how. It is what we are usually referring to when we speak of memory with no further elaboration. To move from procedural to declarative memory a word must activate more than a visual representation of itself. There are numerous cross-modal connections in the human brain. When you see something you can use these connections to associate the visual representation with representations in other modalities. For example, you can name it. When you give a name to something, its visual representation becomes associated with its verbal representation. You know what a book, a cat, a door, etc. is called when you see it because intermodal activation occurs automatically when visual input matches a visual representation in memory. More generally, all kinds of information become available about something through inter-modal associations when you see it. So when you see a dog, you know it as a dog; i.e., as a barking, friendly kind of animal that you have encountered many times before. To know what something is, is to recognize it, so declarative memory and recognition are one.

KOLERS' EXPERIMENT

Paul Kolers (1976) performed a clever experiment that investigated both perceptual and declarative learning by recording the acquisition of a novel perceptual skill. He had subjects read 200 pages of text in which the typescript was inverted (Figure 5.1). As was the case with learning the motor skill of cigar rolling in Figure 2.9, learning the perceptual skill of reading inverted text follows an exponential function in Figure 5.2. Notice that the function is a straight line because the x-axis is a log scale. At first the readers were extremely slow, as you might expect. The subjects took more than 16 minutes to read their first page of inverted text, as compared with only 1.5 minutes for normal text. But by the time they had finished 200

FIGURE 5.1

Example of geometrically inverted text. (Kolers, 1976).

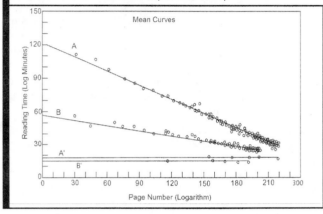

FIGURE 5.2

Reading speed. A and B are for reading inverted text and A' and B' are for normal text (Kolers, 1976).

TABLE 5.1

Actual Occurrence of Passage versus Recognition Response for Inverted-Text Passages Read Once, Twice, Never (From Kolers, 1976).

Actual	Response			
Occurrence	Both	Recent	Old	New
Both	0.49	0.29	0.17	0.05
Recent	0.30	0.55	0.08	0.07
Old	0.06	0.03	0.56	0.35
New	0.0	0.04	0.30	0.66

pages, they were reading inverted text almost as quickly (1.6 minutes per page) as normal text. Kolers retested his subjects a year later. Just as Figure 2.10 showed only a small decline in speed for the motor skill of typing nine months after distributed practice, Figure 5.2 shows almost no decline in speed for the perceptual skill of reading upside down text a year later. The students were still able to read inverted text at about the same speed at which they had left off a year earlier and continued to improve. Furthermore, as was the case with the motor skill of cigar rolling in Figure 2.9, neither normal nor upside down reading speed reaches an asymptote (as shown in Figure 5.2). When the college students' reading speed for normal text was tested at times that were one year apart (A' versus B' in Figure 5.2), their reading speed was faster a year later. So after all the pages you have read in your life, you are still reading a little faster each year.

The increased reading speed of the inverted text was evidence of robust procedural memory for inverted text. This is procedural memory in the service of declarative memory. When you read you recognize the letters, words, sentences and meanings of sentences. Recognizing the meanings of the sentences is the whole purpose of reading. Furthermore, there is a subjective experience when a visual representation activates additional representations and you know what you are looking at. The object appears somewhat familiar. Familiarity is a dimension whose end points are a feeling of complete novelty for something you have never seen before versus detailed recall of a prior occasion on which you have seen something familiar, such as this book. Kolers was interested in how much declarative learning also occurred during his procedural learning task. At the end of the experiment Kolers gave the students all the articles they had read and asked them to sort the articles into four categories: articles they had seen twice, articles they had only seen a year ago, articles they had only seen recently, and articles they had never seen before. Though not perfect the students were able to sort the articles quite accurately (Table 5.1). So there was declarative memory for what they had read as well. How were the students able to know when, if ever, they had seen a particular article before? Obviously, they didn't remember a very long sequence of words. Rather, they recognized the meaning of what they had read, so they were able to infer that they had read the article before. But what is meaning and how is it represented in memory? We begin to look into this question in the next section.

RECOGNITION

In the last two chapters the process of visual perception and recognition was partitioned into five stages: registration, analysis, construction and comparison, response, and decision. In Chapter 3 registration, analysis, and construction and comparison were described. In Chapter 4 the response and decision stages for procedural tasks were described. We now return to the declarative pathway. In this part of the chapter we are now going to consider what happens when the comparison between a representation in memory and a visual input produces a match and a response is made. In the second part of this chapter we describe registration, analysis, construction and comparison, and response selection for audition. The description of the decision stage for both vision and audition will be presented in Chapter 9.

FIGURE 5.3

Neocortical areas involved in recognition. Damage to areas labeled in italics produce an impairment in picture naming, but do not produce aphasia.

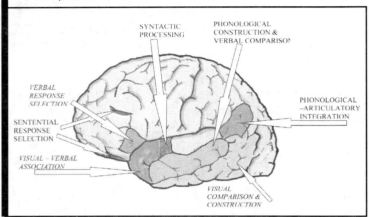

Figure 5.3 shows those cortical areas involved comparison, response and decision-making. These are the temporal lobe and the adjacent areas of the pre-frontal cortex and parietal cortex. The figure is derived from a variety of sources, but particularly work by Hanna Damasio and Antonio Damasio and their colleagues and Nina Dronkers and her colleagues (Damasio, Tramel, Grabowski, Adolphs, & Damasio, 2004; Dronkers, Wilkins, Van Valin Jr., Redfern, and Jaeger, 2004) on the effects of brain damage on naming and sentence comprehension. The lower portion of the temporal lobe, shown in the lightest shade, which extends forward from the visual cortex, is the declarative pathway of the visual system. It compares visual representations with representations of familiar objects like faces and printed words. The middle portion of the temporal lobe, shown in the net lightest shade, which surrounds the primary auditory area, organizes features matching the auditory input into representations of spoken sounds, called **phonemes**, and constructs perceptual representations of the spoken words, called **phonological representations**, as described below. In the front portion of the temporal lobe, shown in the next darkest shade the phonological representations are compared with the representations of words in memory. As we shall see below, in some cases more than one match is found and in this case one alternative is selected. This appears to be the function of adjacent prefrontal areas shown in the same shade. Also, the ability to rehearse speech depends on the integration of phonological and articulatory representations. Shown in the same shade, phonological-articulatory integration is in the area of the parietal cortex adjacent to the end of the middle temporal cortex. Finally, shown in the darkest shade, is one area in the upper temporal cortex and two areas in the prefrontal cortex that construct structural descriptions of sentences.

However, the segregation of the temporal cortex into visual and auditory recognitions regions is partly incorrect. Within the temporal cortex the visual and auditory pathways intersect, so that words can have meaning and things can have names. A fragment of the recognition system for words (in the temporal lobe) is shown in Figure 5.4. Even though this is only a small fragment it initially may appear forbiddingly complex. However, it is made up of only a few basic components that will all become familiar to you by the end of the chapter.

RECOGNITION OF WORDS AND OTHER FAMILIAR THINGS

To begin, in the lower right of the figure, lower case letters, e.g., d, in circles, indicate visual representations of printed letters, letter-sequences, and words. These **intra-modal** pathways are shown connected by single head arrows. The modality of a representation refers to its sensory origin, whether it is visual, auditory, motor, etc. Intra means within, so an intra-modal pathway is within a modality. In the lower right of the figure we see that visual representations of *d* and *og* may combine to form the visual representation of *dog*. In the feature analysis stage, when an input is processed it is analyzed as a set of features and organized into successively more complex patterns. For example, reading the word *dog* activates the visual pattern representations shown in the lower left of the figure. Successively, individual letter (e.g., d), letter sequence (e.g., og), and whole word (e.g., dog) representations are activated by the input.

Inter-modal (between-modality) pathways are shown as two-headed arrows. In the lower right a pathway between the visual representation of *d* and the motor representation of d is shown. Motor representations are shown in mistral type font to distinguish them. Moving upward through the figure, two-headed arrows show inter-modal pathways between the visual representations and auditory representations. The letters between the slash brackets (e.g., /d/) are auditory representations of consonants, syllables, and words. As we have just mentioned, such inter-modal connections between vision and audition are an essential components of recognition. Moving further upward in the figure, there are pathways between the auditory representations and the motor representations that describe their pronunciation.

Logogens. To the left of the figure two-headed arrows connect the visual and auditory representations of *dog* to a circle with two lines through it, labeled by the word *dog* in italics. This is the **logogen** for the word *dog*. This is the point in memory where all the representations of a word come together. It is the point where a word is recognized. Since you know many words, there are many such points in memory. Perceptual representations and logogens are all connected in a network and each point in a network is called a **node**.

The dotted line in the logogen node shows the activation of the logogen. The activation level depends on how well all of its associated representations match the input. When a perceptual represen-

FIGURE 5.4
Logogen for *dog*.

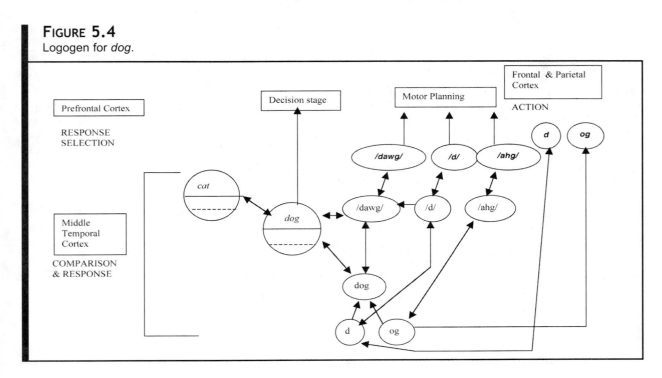

tation matches an input, activation spreads to both other perceptual representations and to the logogen connected to it. This causes the activation level of the logogen associated with the perceptual representation to increase. The more of a perceptual representation that matches the input, the higher the activation of the associated logogen. A logogen is a criterion node that determines when the comparison between an input and a representation in memory has produced a match. For example, the word *dog* causes the activation of the logogen for *dog* to rise. The solid line shows the criterion of the logogen. When the activation exceeds the criterion the word represented by the logogen is perceived and recognized. That is, when the activation of the logogen exceeds its criterion then a response is made. The response is not some motor action; rather, the logogen's response is to make the matching representation a part of working memory. That is, it is only when a logogen makes a response that you perceive a perceptual input. Your perception corresponds to the matching representation in memory that caused the logogen to fire. For example if a visual input causes the *dog* logogen to respond then you see the word *dog*.

Together, the visual and auditory representations form a **polymodal** representation for a word. *Poly* means *several*, referring to the fact that a word has representations in more than one modality. Polymodal representation is what makes naming possible and gives words their meanings. The criterion nodes in memory that are connected with visual and auditory representations of a word are the logogens shown in Figure 5.4. John Morton (1969, 1979) called the criterion nodes associated with the polymodal representations of words, logogens, derived from the Latin logos (word) and genus (birth). Here **logogen** will refer to any criterion node associated with a polymodal representation that makes recognition and understanding possible.

Response stage. Moving beyond the comparison stage we come, for the first time, to the **response stage**. When the comparison process produces a match the criterion of a logogen is exceeded and a perceptual recognition response is made. Your perceptual experience of and identification of the input come bundled together. You don't see or hear anything until the response stage. But when you finally do perceive something, you usually know what it is. The response stage is where you comprehend the world around you by integrating new (perceptual) and old (memorial) information about it. As will be discussed below, when a sequence of inputs causes a set of logogens to fire and consequently a set of perceptual representations to enter working memory, together they may form in working memory a new, larger representation that did not exist in memory before the input sequence was perceived. For example, during language comprehension representations of novel sentences are formed from the representations of familiar words.

Perception and identification become bundled together because of the polymodal nature of the logogen system, which infuses perception with meaning by activating polymodal associations. When the activation of a logogen exceeds its criterion then all the perceptual representations associated with the logogen become available for further processing. So a visual input may activate auditory patterns and vice versa. For example, as shown in Figure 5.4, a word logogen contains both a visual and an auditory representation. So when you see a printed word you become aware of its auditory representation as well. Also, when the criterion of a logogen is exceeded activation spreads to related logogens. For example,

TABLE 5.2
The four stages of Recognition

Sensory Registration	Feature Analysis	Comparison	Response
Sensory information receives initial processing and is passed on to the cortex.	In cortex, sensory input is organized into patterns.	Patterns are compared to memory representations.	Criterion node (logogen) fires; Awareness occurs; Activation spreads to related logogens.

as shown in Figure 5.4, activation will spread from *dog* to *cat*. The four stages of recognition are summarized in Table 5.2. Notice that the first three stages were described in Chapter 3 and that perception and recognition are products of the same process.

Rapid serial visual presentation. The recognition system is remarkably fast and accurate. You are always oriented to person, place, and time, which means that you always know who you are, where you are, and about what time of day and date it is. Orientation to place is the product of the recognition system. Visual recognition of familiar objects takes place in no more than one tenth of a second. For example, Mary Potter (1975, 1976) and Helene Intraub (1980, 1981) had students perform a task using **rapid serial visual presentation (RSVP)** of pictures. They had to detect a target among a sequence of pictures presented for 114 milliseconds apiece, pressing a button when the target appeared. Sometimes the target was defined quite generally, e.g., a picture that is not house furnishings or decorations. Such a definition required the observer to identify every picture in the sequence as either an instance or non-instance of the specified category. Detection accuracy was almost perfect.

Redundant pathways. There are up to three parallel pathways for recognizing a printed word in the recognition heterarchy (Papp, Newson, McDonald, & Schvaneveldt (1982). First, the visual representation of a printed word can activate its meaning directly through a visual whole-word pathway. This is the dog to *dog* pathway in Figure 5.4. Second, the visual representation of the entire printed word can activate an auditory representation of the word, which activates its meaning through an auditory whole-word pathway. This is the dog to /dawg/ to *dog* pathway shown in Figure 5.4. Third, the visual representations of the letters and letter strings activate their pronunciations, which are assembled by the pronunciation system into an auditory representation of the entire word. This pathway is not shown in Figure 5.4, because, as we shall see, it does not exist for the word *dog*.

During reading, all existing pathways are activated in parallel and send inputs to the frontal cortex, where they arrive at slightly different times. Often, the three pathways converge on the same pronunciation and meaning, but this is not always the case. The letter-sequence pathway is governed by spelling-sound correspondences that govern the pronunciation of most (e.g., *barn*, *darn*, *mint*, *hint*, *gave*, *save*, *bog*, *fog*) but not all words. The pronunciation of exception words like *warn*, *pint*, *have*, and *dog* does not follow the usual spelling-sound correspondences. Hence, the inputs from the auditory whole-word and letter-sequence pathways to the pronunciation system are different and only the input from the auditory whole-word pathway is correct. The conflicting information from the whole-word and letter-sequence pathways must be resolved (usually by inhibiting the letter-sequence pathway) before the word can be pronounced. So skilled readers are slower to pronounce exception words than regular words. This **exception** or **regularity effect** is further qualified by word frequency. High frequency words generally show little effect of exceptional spelling-sound correspondences. In contrast, low frequency exception words are typically 25-40 milliseconds slower and more error prone than low frequency regular words (Rastle & Coltheart, 1999a: Seidenberg, Waters, Barnes & Tanenhaus, 1984). This is because for high frequency words the input of the whole-word pathway arrives at the pronunciation system before the letter-sequence input, so that there is no conflict. However, for low frequency words the input from the two pathways arrives together and so the conflict must be resolved.

More generally, in the whole-word pathway all the letters of the word are activated in parallel and every time the whole-word representation is matched to an input it is processed a little faster next time. In contrast, in the letter-sequence pathway the word-representation is constructed by serially scanning its letter sequence from left to right. The speed of construction is not determined by the frequency of the word but by the frequency and regularity of the component letter sequences. Thus word frequency affects the whole-word pathway but not the letter-sequence pathway. The more often a particular word is seen, the faster its particular pronunciation is activated (Baluch & Besner, 1991; McCann & Besner, 1987). In contrast, the number of letters in the word affects the letter-sequence pathway, but not the whole-word pathway (Rastle & Coltheart, 1998; Weekes, 1997). Furthermore, since the representations in the letter-sequence pathway are processed serially from left to right, it follows that the letter-sequence pathway is more likely to produce a conflict with the whole-word pathway when the exceptional letter-sequence occurs early in the word. In fact, this is what is found (Coltheart & Rastle, 1994; Rastle & Coltheart, 1999b).

Having redundant word recognition pathways is an advantage because familiar exception words like *dog* can be recognized rapidly through the visual whole-word pathway while a brand new word that is being encountered for the first time, e.g., *grog*, can still be pronounced through the letter-sequence sound-conversion pathway without ever having been heard before. However, there is a slight downside to redundant pathways. As we have seen, it may take a little longer to pronounce an exception word and it also takes a little longer to detect a homophonic (sound-alike) error. **Homophones** are two different letter sequences that are pronounced the same way, e.g., *cellar* and *seller*, *work* and *werk*. When only one homophone is a word the visual whole-word and auditory letter-sequence pathways produce conflicting responses to the input. In a spelling-error detection task a homophone substitution such as *werk* for *work* was less likely to be noticed than a nonhomophone substitution such as *wark* for *work* (Corcoran, 1966; 1967; Corcoran & Weening, 1968; Mackay, 1968). Also, recall from Chapter 4 that the visual whole-word increases the difficulty of detecting spelling errors that preserve the overall shape of the word; e.g., *studcnt* (Healy, 1981).

Masking and priming. If an input is presented briefly enough, the recognition process begins to break down in an orderly manner. Studies performed using very brief presentations provide further evidence of the distinct recognition pathways. When presentation durations drop below 100 milliseconds, only the faster whole-word pathways but not the slower letter-sequence pathway activate representations . Therefore, at rapid presentation rates, high frequency words are more likely to be recognized than low frequency words (Forster & Chambers, 1973), which are more likely to be recognized than pronounceable nonwords.

Not only recognition, but also perception breaks down when more than one representation is activated within a very brief period of time. You can only see one thing at a time. When two different visual patterns are presented within a single fixation a competition may occur, as each representation attempts to inhibit the other. Ultimately, only one representation may be perceived. The one that is not perceived is said to be **masked**. For example, a 50 millisecond presentation provides enough visual input to read a word. However, suppose that while you are looking at a screen, a word appears for 50 milliseconds and immediately after, a string of x's appears in the same location for half a second. This string is called a **mask**. Under these conditions, the word and mask compete for control of the feature analyzers in the visual system. Since the mask was shown ten times longer it wins the competition and determines the output of the response stage. So you do not see the word at all, only the mask. The effect is called **backward masking** and the mask is called, of course, a **backward mask**. There is also a similar effect called **forward masking**. Suppose that instead the mask is first presented for half a second, and immediately after, in the same location, a word is presented. Again only the mask is seen.

Masking techniques are used in two different tasks that have been used extensively to study **priming**, which you may recall is the facilitating effect of one input upon another. In the **lexical decision task** an observer must report whether a letter string is a word. Both the speed and accuracy of the response are measured. In the **naming task** an observer must read a word or pronounceable nonword aloud. The time to produce the initial speech sound of the word is measured. The word that the observer responds to is called the **target** and the word intended to influence it is called the **prime**. The prime may be presented for a period of time sufficient for it to be visible to the observer, or it may be presented masked so that it is **subliminal**. That is, the prime is not seen at all. The prime is rendered invisible either through a very brief presentation or the use of a forward masking procedure. Notice that when a masked, hence subliminal, prime is presented there is no response stage for the prime. So any effect that the prime has on a subsequent target must occur at the feature analysis or comparison level. Hence masked primes provide a useful tool for studying the early stages of the recognition process.

Repetition and form priming. A subliminal prime can produce both repetition priming and form priming. Repetition priming even occurs when both the prime and target are initially subliminal. Haber and

Hershenson (1965) presented letter strings so briefly (10 milliseconds) that initially no letters could be seen at all. But after several repetitions, the letters began to appear (see also Chastain, 1977). Presumably, each presentation of the input increased the activation of one or more letter representations in memory until they began to exceed criterion. Haber and Hershenson called this the growth of the percept.

Recall that the human perceptual system represents each input as a set of features and organizes the representations in memory by the features they contain. This organization provides an efficient way to compare an input with the representations. For example, suppose the representations of words are arranged in memory alphabetically, somewhat as they are in a dictionary. When you look a word up in the dictionary, you do not open it to the first page and begin comparing the word with every entry until you find a match. Instead, you open the dictionary to the part where you expect to find entries beginning with the same letter. Then you move back and forth over several pages as you successively match the second, third, and fourth letters of the word to entries, until after a very few comparisons you find a match.

FIGURE 5.5

Neighborhood for dog.

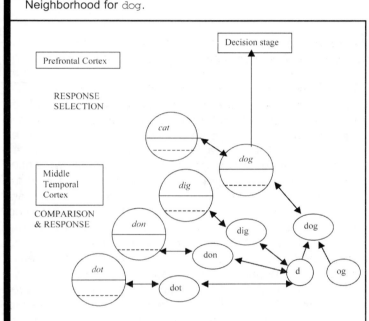

Like the dictionary, human memory is organized by features. Each feature match leads to the retrieval of those representations containing all of the features already matched, so the comparison process is rapidly narrowed to those representations most similar to the target. Just as in the dictionary, human lexical memory is organized by word **onset** (the initial vowel or consonant cluster of a word). For example, as shown in Figure 5.5, the letter *d* is the onset of word-logogens that begin with *d* and a vowel, like *dog*. **Form priming** occurs among words that share one or more letters, including the same onset (Forster & Davis, 1991; Grainger & Ferrand, 1996). The word *dog* causes the activation of the *dot* and *dig* logogens to rise a little, though only the activation of the *dog* logogen rises above its criterion.

Other evidence for letter sequence representations comes from the effect of neighborhood. The neighborhood of a word is the set of words that differ from it by one letter; e.g., *dig*, *dug*, *don*, and *dot* are the neighborhood of *dog*. When a word is part of a large neighborhood its neighbors are also primed and compete with it for recognition. So repetition and form priming effects are larger for hermit words without neighborhoods. Also, words with small neighborhoods may even be form-primed with nonwords (Forster & Taft, 1994). Since the nonword does not have a representation in memory, the priming must be at the level of the letter sequence. Also, there are repetition and form priming effects on nonword targets like *dag* (Perea & Rosa, 2000). So letter (e.g., *d*) and letter sequence (e.g., *ag*), pathways can be primed as well as visual whole-word pathways like *dog*. This is because, though not shown in Figure 5.4, there must be logogens for individual letters and familiar letter sequences whose representations can be assembled to create representations of novel words.

Associative agnosia and related disorders. Sometimes localized damage to some part of the recognition system damages some recognition pathways while sparing others. Associative agnosia results from localized bilateral damage in the temporal cortex. When a recognition pathway is damaged, an associative agnosia specific to that pathway is the result. Associative agnosia can vary from general to specific in the kinds of inputs affected.

Several visual agnosias are specific to reading. Figure 5.6 shows a labeled fragment of the network shown in Figure 5.4, which shows the associations disrupted by specific agnosias. **Deep dyslexia** is the result when the connection between the auditory and visual representations of a word is severed (c). A person can still understand familiar visual words but loses the ability to pronounce them. Such patients even make semantic substitutions when asked to repeat words. For example, a patient might repeat "boat" as "ship." When both path-

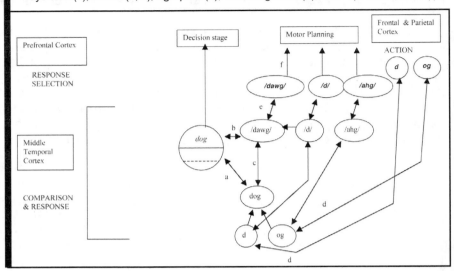

FIGURE 5.6

Fragment shows associations disrupted in agnosias related to language: deep dyslexia (c), alexia (a, c), agraphia (d), verbal agnosia (b), and repetition failure (f).

ways by which the visual representation of a word is recognized are severed (a, c) the result is **alexia**. The person can no longer recognize printed words but can still understand spoken language normally. Since perceptual and motor representations are distinct, production may be spared. In alexia without **agraphia** the person can still write to dictation because pathways b, a, and d from the auditory representation of the word to the motor representation for writing it are intact. But he cannot read his own writing! Conversely, if only pathway d is severed then the person suffers from pure agraphia, which is a form of apraxia. Reading is possible but writing is not. Notice that alexia and agraphia are specific impairments in recognition and execution that can affect any perceptual-motor skill. Recall from the discussion of action in Chapter 2 that many apraxic patients can recognize an action, such as using a spoon or toothbrush, if someone demonstrates it. If we substitute a logogen for an action for the one for dog in Figure 5.6, then pure apraxia is again the result of damage to pathway d. In contrast, when a patient can imitate the action correctly but cannot recognize it (Cubelli, et al., 2000), the patient has a form of visual agnosia, as the result of damage to pathway a. When the action is performed incorrectly, and the patient does not recognize the correct action when he is shown it (Heilman, et al., 1982) this is the result of damage to pathways a and d.

There are also several auditory agnosias that are specific to language. Auditory agnosia is when sound patterns are no longer recognized. Damage to the connections to the auditory cortex in the temporal lobe can cause **verbal agnosia** (Geschwind, 1970). Verbal agnosia is when speech sounds are no longer recognized (b). This is also called **pure word deafness**. Even though the person cannot understand spoken language she can still understand written language. Just like a visual agnosic may be able to accurately copy a picture she can not recognize, a verbal agnosic may accurately repeat a word or sentence she can not understand, as long as pathway e from the auditory representation to the motor representation for pronunciation is intact. Verbal agnosia can also occur without agraphia if pathways c and d from the auditory representation of the word to the motor representation for writing it are intact. So the person can still write to dictation, though she doesn't understand what is being said (Ellis, 1984; Kohn & Friedman, 1986).

Finally, if only the pathway from the phonological representation to the articulatory representation for pronouncing it is severed (f) then the person cannot repeat words and sentences that she can nevertheless understand, which is a form of apraxia. It is the phonological-articulatory loop that makes verbal rehearsal possible. Rehearsal is possible because the content of the phonological code can be recoded into the articulatory code, which, when executed, reproduces the phonological code. Recall from Chapter

4 that verbal rehearsal plays an important role in attention. In Chapter 7 we shall see that it plays an important role in learning as well.

After alexia, the most common form of a specific visual agnosia is the highly specific face-disorder is called **prosopagnosia**. As was mentioned in the last chapter, early in life there is considerable perceptual learning for faces just as there later is for letters and words when a person learns to read. Part of the cortex fills up with representations of faces and facial features, just as it fills up with representations of letters and letter sequences. Again, just as there are redundant, parallel pathways for recognizing words there are redundant parallel pathways for recognizing faces. Recall that in the Chapter 3 we saw that upside-down faces cannot be recognized by the whole-face pathway and must be recognized through the facial feature pathway. In apperceptive agnosia the visual input still matches at least some representations in memory, even though these matches do not activate logogens and produce recognition. Notice that in agnosia, it is not only the case that representations of familiar patterns have been disturbed, but it is also the case that the individual has lost the ability to encode new patterns. In one case, existing patterns were left in place and only the learning process was disrupted. Farah and her colleagues (Tippett, Miller, & Farah, 2000) described a 35-year-old male who could recognize people he knew before his injury but could not learn to recognize any new faces.

On occasion, recognition for something familiar other than faces or printed words is selectively impaired. Glyn Humphreys and Raffaela Rumiata (1998) reported on a 72-year-old female who could not visually recognize familiar objects but was in the normal range for visual recognition of faces and words.

SEMANTIC AND ASSOCIATIVE PRIMING

Declarative knowledge is of two kinds: semantic knowledge and episodic knowledge. Semantic knowledge is knowledge of what something is and episodic knowledge is knowledge of if and when it has been encountered before. Episodic knowledge will begin to be discussed in Chapter 9. We begin the discussion of semantic knowledge here. Whenever we are concerned with knowledge of what something is, declarative memory is more commonly called **semantic memory**. There are three levels of organization in semantic memory: the logogen, which has already been described, and the category node, and the structural description, which will be described here.

As shown in Figure 5.7, there are many different kinds of associations among representations in memory. For example, everything you know about dogs is associated with its criterion node, which is indicated by the label in bold (**dog**). This criterion node is for the concept **dog** rather than the word *dog*. The pictures of a cat and dog represent their visual representations in memory. The concept criterion-node for **dog** and the word criterion-node *dog* are associated by the naming relation, shown as a double-lined arrow. Furthermore, many concepts and words are associated in various relationships that may be called associative or semantic. A relationship is often called **associative** if one item is given as a response to the other; e.g., *cat* is a response to, hence an associate of, *dog*. This relationship is indicated by the two-headed arrow between their word logogens. A rela-

FIGURE 5.7

A fragment of the semantic network.

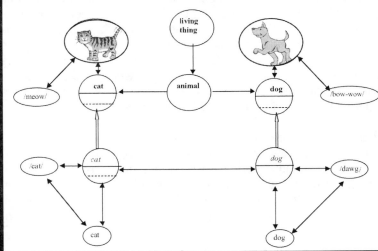

tionship is called **semantic** if there is some obvious connection in the meaning of the items; e.g., *lad* is a synonym of *boy*, though rarely given as a response to *boy*. Obviously, by these criteria, many relationships are both associative and semantic. For example, as shown in Figure 5.7, cats and dogs are both animals, so there is also a semantic relationship between the meanings of **cat** and **dog** as well as an associative one. Relationships like the one between **animal** and **dog** organize semantic concepts into a hierarchy. These are called category-instance relationships, where **animal** is the category and **dog** is an instance. Logogens for different things to which you make a common voluntary response are associated with a common category node. For example, logogens for different foods may be associated with a food category-node. Also, logogens for things with common properties, for which the same set of voluntary responses is appropriate, are associated with a common category node. For example, as in Figure 5.7, the logogens for the **dog**, **cat**, etc. are associated with the category node for **animal**. Categorization will be discussed in Chapter 8.

Priming occurs between words in a variety of relationships. Meyer and Schwaneveldt (1973) first found that when associated words (e.g., *doctor-nurse*) are presented in rapid succession the time to identify the second word is reduced. Fischler (1977) found the same effect for unassociated words that are related in meaning (e.g., *wife-nurse*). Unlike repetition and form primes, which activate sound and letter sequences, and which may be subliminal, associative and semantic primes that activate relationships between whole words must be visible (Adams & Greenwald, 2000). (It is important to note that a subliminal input has an extremely limited effect on perception, hence on behavior, because people (e. g., Packard, 1957) have claimed otherwise, despite the convincing evidence that "subliminal perception" is extremely limited (Vokey & Read, 1985).)

The fact that associative and semantic primes must be visible suggests that the relations they prime are only activated after the activation of a logogen exceeds its threshold and spreads to related logogens. The priming occurs because the response to the prime influences the comparison stage (rather than the feature analysis stage) during the processing of the target. Specifically, after the response to the prime, activation spreads to the target, increasing the activation of the target and making a response to it more likely.

The relationship between associative priming and semantic priming is unclear. It may be that associative primes are simply strong semantic primes or it may be that associative priming occurs at a different level of the recognition process than semantic priming. On the one hand, the magnitude of associative plus semantic priming is larger than the magnitude of semantic only priming (Lucas, 2000). On the other hand, there is no evidence for pure associative (honey-moon) priming between semantically unrelated words (de Mornay Davies, 1998).

Scene perception. Semantic priming influences recognition of an object in even a briefly presented picture. So semantic priming is another aspect of the recognition process that keeps you oriented to place. In one such experiment (Biederman, Mezzanotte, & Rabinowitz, 1982), before each trial an observer was told the name of the target, e.g., hydrant. A fixation point, presented for 500 milliseconds, was followed by a 150-millisecond presentation of a scene, which, in turn, was followed by a cue marking some position in the scene that had just been presented. The observer had to report whether the target had appeared in the location marked by the cue. The question of interest was whether an object that in some way did not fit with the rest of the scene (its context) would be more difficult to detect.

Figure 5.8(a) shows a normal scene in which the target is the fire hydrant. The other scenes in Figure 5.8 have contextual violations. In Figure 5.8(b) the fire hydrant is out of position. In Figure 5.8(c) the hydrant is an improbable object in such a scene. Observers failed to detect the target in an appropriate context, such as in Figure 5.8(a), only 28 percent of the time. They missed it 40 percent of the time when it was involved in a violation, as in Figures 5.8(b) or 5.8(c). Thus within a very brief period of time, less than a fifth of a second, representations of objects in a scene interact to facilitate each other's recognition.

FIGURE 5.8

Scene recognition. (a) The target (hydrant) appropriately positioned in a probable context; (b) the target in a position of violation; (c) the target in a probability violation. (Biederman, et al., 1982).

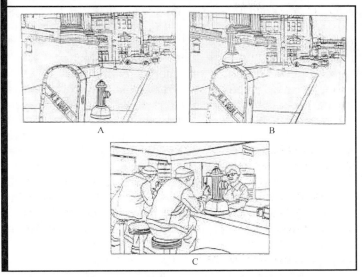

The fact that recognition of the fire hydrant was slower for the scene shown in Figure 5.8(b) demonstrates that the priming did not just depend on an association between a fire hydrant and a general street scene, so that as soon as the mailbox and/or car was recognized the fire hydrant would be recognized as well. If this was all there was to it then the fire hydrant would be recognized as fast in Figure 5.8(b) as it was in Figure 5.8(a) because in both pictures the mailbox and car are equally visible. Since recognition of the fire hydrant was better for Figure 5.8(a) recognition of the scene must have made use of a **structural description** of a scene. A structural description organizes a set of category nodes in a spatial and/or temporal representation. At any given moment the content of working memory is whatever structural description is currently being used to plan a voluntary response. For example, there are visuospatial structural descriptions for faces and scenes and verbal structural descriptions for phrases and sentences.

Figure 5.9 shows a fragment of a visuospatial structural description of a street scene that might have been used to recognize Figure 5.8(a) and Figure 5.8(b). Notice that it organizes the elements of the scene according to their locations. The structural description specifies that the fire hydrant must be on the sidewalk. However, the constraints provided by a structural description are quite broad. The sidewalk could be at the bottom or the middle of the scene and run in almost any direction. So scene identification can only proceed by tentatively retrieving possible representations of different objects. From this set of representations, the largest subset is selected that are all part of a common structural description of a scene. These are the parts of the scene that are perceived first. Novel parts of the scene are only perceived after further comparison with representations that were not part of the structural description of the scene.

FIGURE 5.9

Structural description of street scene.

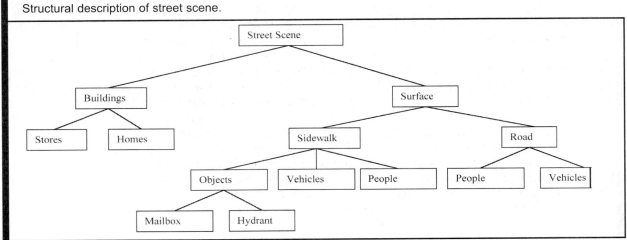

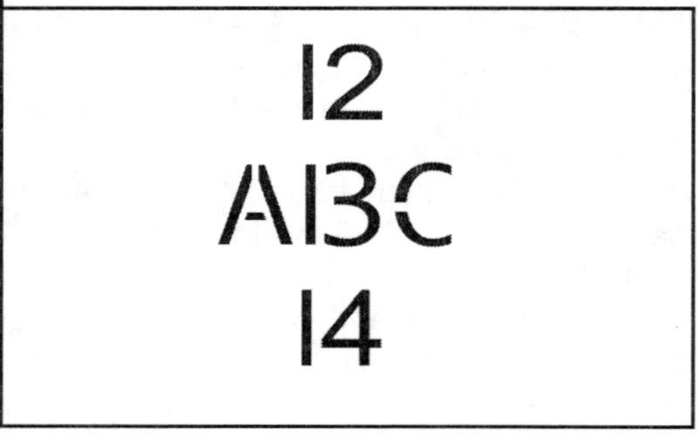

FIGURE 5.10

The same input may be recognized as two entirely different things in different contexts.

12
Al3C
14

FIGURE 5.11

Ambiguous drawing. Man or rat?

FIGURE 5.12

Figures used by Leeper (1935). (a) clock; (b) airplane; (c) typewriter; (d) bus; (e) elephant; (f) saw; (g) shoe; (h) boy with dog; (i) roadster; (j) violin.

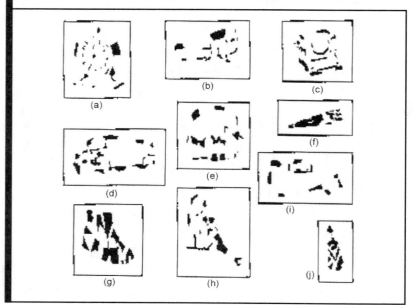

Priming and ambiguity resolution. The combination of structural descriptions and semantic priming keeps you oriented to place by rapidly activating associated representations of things that are normally seen together. Usually the effect of semantic priming is not even noticed. But it can be made apparent through the use of ambiguous inputs. The central element of Figure 5.10 can be either the letter B or the number 13. In an unambiguous context you would never notice the other representation because it would never reach awareness. Another well-known example illustrating this point is the ambiguous drawing shown in Figure 5.11 (Bugelski & Alampay, 1961). If you look at the picture carefully, you will see that it can be interpreted either as a rat or as a man's face. When the rat-man picture is presented alone, as in the figure, most people see it as a man. However, in the context of a series of unambiguous animal pictures, people see it as a rat. Presumably, cross priming among animal logogens increases their activation, giving the rat representation an advantage over the man representation.

Another way to make the effect of semantic priming apparent is by degrading inputs, so they don't match any representation in memory particularly well. The pictures in Figure 5.12 have been degraded so that it is difficult to integrate the elements and perceive what they are. This is probably what integrative agnosia is like. If you were briefly shown a picture in the figure that you didn't recognize and asked to draw what you saw from memory, your performance would be poor. But, as shown in Figure 5.7, there is a pathway from the name of an object to its concept logogen, and from its concept logogen to its visual representation. So reading the name of an unrecognized pictured object activates its visual representation and a match with the picture causes its previously meaningless dark spots to snap into place as they are integrated into the organization of the matching visual representation. Once you can recognize a picture your ability to draw it from memory improves. The dark spots are now meaningful parts that can be generated by searching down from the top of the structural description of an object or scene.

SUMMARY OF RECOGNITION

- There are three levels of semantic organization
  - Logogen—is associated with the representations of objects and words in different modalities. Each logogen has
    - an activation level. When an input matches an associated representation the activation level of the logogen increases.
    - a criterion. When the activation level exceeds the criterion the logogen makes a response and the input is perceived as the representation that it matches.
    - For example, if the input has caused the logogen for the word *dog* to respond then you see the word *dog*.
  - Category node
    - Logogens for different things to which you make a common voluntary response are associated with a common category node. For example, logogens for different foods may be associated with a food-category node.
    - Logogens for things with common properties, for which the same set of voluntary responses is appropriate, are associated with a common category node. For example, the logogens for the dog, cat, etc. are associated with the category node for animal.
  - Structural description—organizes a set of category nodes in a spatial and/or temporal representation like a scene or sentence.
    - Is content of working memory
    - Is used to select among competing logogen responses to same input
    - Is used to plan voluntary response.

- The comparison process that produces word recognition contains three redundant pathways to the logogen:
  - a visual whole-word pathway
  - an auditory whole-word pathway
  - a letter-sequence pronunciation pathway.

- An impairment of any word-recognition pathways produces a distinctive kind of agnosia.
  - Alexia—inability to recognize printed words
  - Pure word deafness—inability to recognize spoken words

SPEECH AND LANGUAGE: PERCEPTION AND RECOGNITION

The early pathways of the auditory system run parallel to the visual pathways and serve similar functions. Both the visual and auditory recognition systems terminate in the temporal cortex with recognition. The ability to comprehend language emerges from and depends on the ability to rapidly recognize words and familiar word sequences and recover their meanings . However, language comprehension requires more than merely the recognition of familiar inputs. As we shall see, a sentence activates a structural description that guides the construction of a representation of the world that constitutes the meaning of the sentence. In this section we will see how the ability to construct the meanings of sentences emerges from more basic visual and auditory recognition abilities.

AUDITORY SYSTEM

Figure 5.13 shows the main brain structures involved in auditory processing and Figure 5.14 shows the same structures schematically. In some general ways the auditory processing sytem parallels the visual processing system, as shown in Table 5.3. Visual processing consists of a registration, analysis, and construction stage, and so does auditory processing. For sensory registration, just as visual input proceeds from the eyes to the superior collicus in the midbrain, to the lateral geniculate nucleus in the thalamus, and from there to the primary visual area in the occipital cortex, auditory input proceeds from the ears to the inferior colliculus in the midbrain, to the medial geniculate nucleus in the thalamus, and from there to the primary auditory area in the cortex.

For analysis, each ear is connected to both hemispheres by a direct neural pathway. Although the connection to the opposite-side hemisphere is stronger, the connection to the same-side hemisphere is strong enough so that a sound input will reach each hemisphere from both ears. So just as visual input from a single source to both eyes is combined in the visual cortex, auditory input to both ears is combined in the auditory cortex. As a result, both visual and auditory processing are stereoscopic. In audition as well as vision, the stereoscopic processing makes it possible to construct a three-dimensional representation that locates the source of the input in three-dimensional space.

Just as for vision, after initial analysis by the primary auditory area the auditory pathway divides into "how" and "what: pathways. The "how" or procedural pathway extends backward along the top of the temporal cortex and upward into the adjacent area of the parietal lobe, as shown in Figure 4.1 (Hickok & Poeppel, 2004; Scott & Wise, 2004). This pathway also extends inward below the surface of the boundary between the temporal and parietal lobes. From there it extends forward to the speech motor areas in the left frontal cortex shown in Figure 2.2. The "what" or declarative pathway extends forward along the upper portion of the temporal lobe, as shown in Figure 5.3 (Hickok & Poeppel, 2004; Scott & Wise, 2004).

FIGURE 5.13
Exploded view of auditory system.

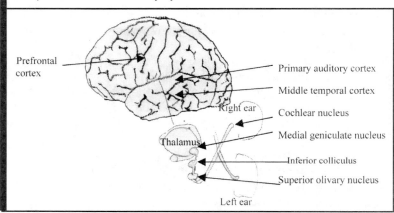

FIGURE 5.14
Schematic of auditory system.

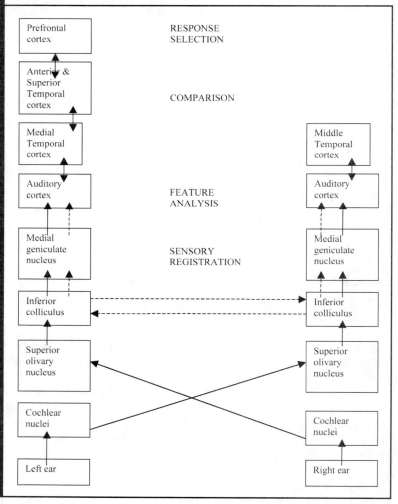

TABLE 5.3
Parallel Pathways in Visual and Auditory Processing.

Visual Processing					
Eyes	to	Superior colliculus (midbrain) and	Lateral geniculate nucleus (thalamus)	to	Primary visual area
Auditory Processing					
Ears	to	Inferior colliculus (midbrain)	to	Medial geniculate nucleus (thalamus)	to	Primary auditory area

For construction, both visual and auditory inputs are compared with memory representations in the temporal cortex and, as we have seen, visual and auditory representations are strongly associated. Finally, these representations are associated with logogens that emit responses when their associated representations match the input. Pathways carry these responses from the temporal to the frontal cortex to complete the recognition process for both visual and auditory recognition.

However, there is an important difference between the visual and auditory systems. The visual system is symmetrical with respect to hemispheric processing of most visual inputs. That is why visual agnosia is the result of bilateral damage to the corresponding areas in both hemispheres. But the left hemisphere dominates the production and perception of speech and language.

EVOLUTION OF THE SPEECH AND LANGUAGE SYSTEMS

Human language is only possible because of four recent evolutionary changes in the human line. First, associative learning between sights and speech sounds makes word meaning possible. No other creature has the rich network of polymodal neuronal connections in the middle of the temporal cortex that make associative learning possible. However, this only gives you the ability to learn individual words. Second, the ability to construct syntactic structural descriptions of word sequences in an adjacent area of the temporal cortex makes it possible to learn to construct and understand sentences (Figure 5.3). These two kinds of codes provide the basis for language. However, in order for speech to be understood it is also necessary to have in place the procedures necessary for recoding auditory input into speech sounds. Three more evolutionary changes were necessary before language through speech was possible.

Larynx.   The larynx is lower in the throats of humans than of other primates. The lower larynx creates a longer the vocal cavity. The longer the vocal cavity the more sounds it is physically possible to create; hence, the greater the variety of human speech sounds possible. The advantage of the longer vocal cavity presumably more than compensates for the one disadvantage of the human anatomy: only humans need an elaborate swallowing reflex to avoid food entering the lungs, causing them to choke on their own food. Infants make the limited kinds of sounds that we call baby speech precisely because their necks and vocal cavities are shorter (Miller, 1982, p. 47).

Specialized speech production areas.   Control of the motor movements that produce speech is localized in specific areas of the frontal cortex and parietal cortex, as shown in Figure 2.2. In particular, as we shall discuss below, in the left hemisphere the subsurface band of cortical tissue called the insular (Figure 2.2) plays an essential role in the articulation of sentences (Dronkers, 1996) in almost all humans. How fast people can speak determines the rate at which information is transmitted in a conversation. In turn, the rate at which people can speak depends on the number of different sounds they can make and the rate at which they can make them. The timing that is required for producing the sounds used in speech pushes the nervous system to its limit. A neuron takes about a millisecond to transmit an impulse. Speech requires successive motor acts that are only a few milliseconds apart. Localization in one hemisphere makes faster production of sounds than would be possible if control were shared between both hemispheres and required back and forth communication across the corpus callosum. If the control of speech were spread across two hemispheres, so that signals had to travel between them to coordinate their commands, the rate at which a person could speak would be significantly slowed. In fact, such slowed commands may be the cause of congenital stuttering, as "echo" commands from the right hemisphere produce the stutter. The phenomenon of stuttering suggests that it is the continuous planning of novel speech that most taxes the speech production system. Stuttering only occurs during spontaneous speech. It does not occur when reciting a rehearsed text. There are professional actors who took up acting as therapy for their stuttering. Also stuttering does not occur during singing.

Interestingly, certain songbirds, including canaries, also have specialized hemispheres. The songs of these birds are under the control of the left hemisphere (Nottebohm, 1977), just as speech is in human beings. Of course, birds are very different from people. However, these findings for birds make salient the advantage of having the production of a complex vocal response lateralized.

The need to create a specialized area for speech processing in the left hemisphere seems to have had a knock-on effect that has resulted in one hemisphere or the other being specialized for aspects of all sorts of processes, including attention and emotion. Also, most human beings are strongly right-handed. In this respect humans are unique, for we are the only animals who show any consistent hand preference as a population (Warren, 1977).   The degree of linguistic lateralization is related to the degree of right-handedness. Non-right-handers tend to make better recoveries from aphasias caused by unilateral lesions in either hemisphere. Thus non-right-handers appear to be less likely to be completely lateralized for language (Rasmussen & Milner, 1977).

With respect to lateralization, human brains appear to be different from the brains of all other creatures (except songbirds). If only one hemisphere of the brain of a nonhuman primate is damaged, the ability to discriminate two shapes, to run a maze, or to avoid shock is influenced in the same way as by an equal amount of damage in the same location in the opposite hemisphere. Neither previously learned abilities nor the acquisition of new abilities is selectively impaired by damage to a single hemisphere (Doty & Overman, 1977; Hamilton, 1977).

Specialized speech perception areas. However, even with these recent motor enhancements, the speech sounds that you actually make are run together and indistinct with respect to the sounds that you intend to make. This is because your muscles cannot keep up with the neural commands to the motor units. So there is a specialized speech understanding area primarily, though not exclusively, in the left temporal lobe (Hickok & Poeppel, 2004; Scott & Wise, 2004) that makes it possible to recover phonemic intent.

LEFT HEMISPHERIC SPECIALIZATION FOR LANGUAGE

Five different kinds of observations of language processing provide independent evidence for the specialization of language processing in the left hemisphere.

Damage to the left hemisphere. To begin with, as mentioned above, visual agnosia is the result of symmetrical bilateral damage to each hemisphere and this is the usual pattern in learning and memory disorders. If bilateral damage is necessary to cause a processing impairment then in all probability the left and right hemispheres contain redundant pathways for whatever process is impaired. However, over 98 percent of all aphasias suffered by right-handed human beings result from injuries to the left hemisphere (Bogen & Bogen, 1976; Russell & Espir, 1961); for ambidextrous and left-handed individuals the percentage is somewhat less (Gloning, 1977; Russell & Espir, 1961). There may be right hemisphere damage as well. But left hemisphere damage alone is sufficient. Language disorders will be considered in more detail after language processing has been examined. First, the other three kinds of evidence of left hemispheric specialization for language will be considered here.

Speech and nonspeech sounds. One can demonstrate the special processing speech inputs receive from the left hemisphere by the simultaneous presentation of artificial sounds that can be interpreted as either speech or nonspeech to both ears (Best, Morrongiello, & Robson, 1981). For example, Rand (1974) split the syllable /ga/ into two components. One piece, the base, consisted of most of the segment, including its vowel. The other part was the portion of the very beginning that determines whether the entire segment is heard as /ga/ or /da/. This segment sounds like a chirp in isolation. When the base segment was presented to one ear and the initial segment to the other, the listener simultaneously heard /ga/ in the base ear and a chirp in the other (see also Liberman 1982; Liberman, Isenberg, & Rakerd, 1981). Hence the same sound input was processed by one portion of the brain as a natural sound and combined with the base by another portion of the brain and processed as a speech sound.

Right and left ear dominance for speech and nonspeech sounds, respectively. Similarly, when different speech sounds are presented simultaneously to each ear (called **dichotic** presentation), there is a bias to hear the sound in the right ear (Kimura 1961, 1967; but also see Bakker, 1970). Interestingly, when Kimura (1974) presented listeners with brief excerpts of classical melodies **dichotically** (to both ears), the results were reversed. The listeners heard the left-ear (right-hemisphere) melody more frequently. However, the results of further studies on the perception of music were quite complex. The advantage of one ear over the other depended on the precise nature of the task (Efron, Bogen, & Yund, 1977; Gordon 1970, 1974; Robinson & Solomon, 1974) and on the musical experience of the listener (Bever & Chiarello, 1974; Gordon, 1980). So the kind of judgment required determines which hemisphere controls the processing of a nonspeech auditory input.

Neuroimagining during language processing. Neurons have electric charges, which play a role in neuronal communication. Hence, neurons generate small magnetic fields and these fields become stronger when the neurons are actively processing information. In functional magnetic neuroimaging (fmri) the magnetic activity of different areas of the brain are measured and used to construct a map of brain activity during a task. Also, during activity a neuron uses more oxygen then when at rest. In order to provide more oxygen, blood flow to the neuron increases. The amount of blood flow to each area of the brain, hence its activity during a task, can be measured by injecting into the blood a harmless amount of a radioactive isotope. In positron emission tomography (PET) scanning the amount of radioactivity emitted by different brain areas is measured and used to construct a map of brain activity during a task. Both kinds of neuroimaging show much more activity in the left temporal lobe and some areas of the frontal lobe during speech and language processing. As will be discussed below, different brain areas have different functions, so which areas show the most activity depends on the specific task being performed (Scott & Wise, 2003).

Split-brain patients. Evidence of the specialized speech and language processing done by the left hemisphere was provided by a surgical procedure that is no longer used. Today epilepsy can be controlled by medication. However, in the recent past that was not always so. Recall that information is transmitted between the hemispheres across the corpus callosum. One surgical procedure occasionally used to control life-threatening seizures was to sever the corpus callosum in order to prevent the seizure from spreading. This operation greatly reduces the size of the seizures, and it leaves the patients with their intellects and personalities relatively intact. In fact, it was only upon careful testing that the cognitive effects of the operation were discovered.

This testing involved presenting an input to only a single side of the body. For example, an object would be placed in either the right hand or the left. Or a sound would be played in either the right ear or the left while a masking sound was played in the other ear. Or while the patient kept his or her eyes on a fixation point, a word or picture would be presented in the right or left visual field. When such an input is presented to a person with an intact brain, the information reaches both hemispheres, because it can cross the corpus callosum from one hemisphere to the other. Even a person with a split brain can still get information to both hemispheres in a normal situation. For example, as a person's eyes scan over an object, it will appear in both visual fields and hence provide direct information for both hemispheres. However, we can thwart these strategies in an experimental situation by blindfolding the person when an object is placed in one hand or by presenting a visual input very rapidly in one visual field so the person doesn't have time to scan it. When these precautions are taken, the stimulus is effectively presented only to one hemisphere of the split-brain patient. This work was begun by R. W. Sperry and was continued by Sperry and his collaborators Michael Gazzaniga, Jerre Levy, and Eran Zaidel.

When most inputs were presented to only a single hemisphere of a split-brain patient, either hemisphere could respond to it by making a motor response. The left hemisphere had good control of the right hand and poor control of the left hand, whereas the right hemisphere had good control of the left hand and poor control of the right. However, if forced to, either hemisphere could make gross movements with either hand. However, this equality of control did not extend to language.

For example, because the connections between them are severed, we can present different visual inputs simultaneously to each hemisphere of a split-brain patient. In a typical experiment, while the patient centers his or her gaze on a fixation point, a word is briefly presented so that half the letters fall to one side of the point and half the letters fall to the other side. As Figure 5.15 illustrates, if the word target were briefly presented, the letters *tar* would fall in the left visual field and be processed by the right hemisphere, while the letters *get* would fall in the right visual field and be processed by the left hemisphere. After such an input is presented, the patient is given a choice of four alternatives and asked to point to the one that was presented. For example, the alternatives might be *tar*, *get*, *cow*, and *pea*.

You might think that since each hemisphere has processed different letters, the person would choose two alternatives and point to *tar* with the left hand and *get* with the right. However, this result did not occur when words were presented to most patients. Instead, the person pointed to the right-visual-field input (e.g., *get*), whether asked to respond with the right or the left hand (Gazzaniga, 1977). Thus the left hemisphere typically controls the response to conflicting linguistic inputs.

FIGURE 5.15

Hemispheric control. If the subject's gaze is fixed on the center of *target*, *tar* falls in the left visual field and *get* in the right.

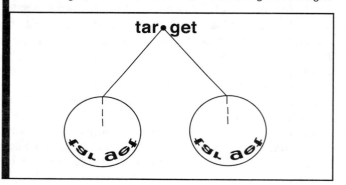

The exceptions were two individuals with early damage to the left hemisphere. When an infant or young child suffers damage to one hemisphere, it appears that the corresponding area in the opposite hemisphere is able to share or take over its function. The two patients who had left hemisphere damage at a young age, hence bilateral linguistic representations, selected both words (Gazzaniga, 1983).

When the patient had an intact left hemisphere, uninjured by the epilepsy that required its corpus callosum to be split, left hemisphere performance on linguistic tasks was essentially normal. For these patients, when a linguistic input, be it word or sentence, was presented in the right visual field (to the left hemisphere), the split-brain patient generally performed the task as well as he or she could prior to surgery. That is, the person could understand sentences presented to just the left hemisphere and produce speech in response to them. However, the linguistic skills of the right hemisphere were much less. (Gazzaniga, 1983 vs. Myers, 1984). When the same words and sentences were presented in the left visual field (to the right hemisphere), most patients were unable to indicate that they understood them in any way. Patients never produced any speech in response to an input just to the right hemisphere. Finally, when tested on Kimura's (1961, 1967) dichotic-listening task for speech sounds, performance for those speech sounds presented in the right ear was normal. In contrast, recognition of left-ear-presented speech sounds was near zero (Milner, Taylor, & Sperry, 1968; Sparks & Geschwind, 1968).

Subsequent examination of three split-brain patients showed considerable right-hemisphere, visual, word identification skills (Gazzaniga, 1983; Zaidel, 1976, 1978a, 1978b), but these patients had little

(Zaidel, 1983) or no (Gazzaniga & Hillyard, 1971) right-hemisphere syntactic comprehension and no right-hemisphere, speech production ability (Gazzaniga, 1983). Two other patients had essentially equal command of production (including speech) and comprehension in the left and right hemispheres (Gazzaniga, 1983). However, one of the patients with right-hemisphere speech production was known and the other was presumed to have suffered left-hemisphere damage early in life (Myers, 1984). As mentioned above, early brain damage radically alters the brain's functional organization, so we cannot draw conclusions about normal organization from these patients.

When conflicting nonlinguistic inputs are presented to the hemispheres, by contrast, it is the right hemisphere that controls the response. Levy, Trevarthan, and Sperry (1972) found that the right hemisphere determines the response to visual patterns such as the one shown in Figure 5.16. Such pictures, made up by putting the right and left halves of two different faces together, were flashed at each of four split-brain patients for 150 milliseconds. They were then asked to select which of three intact faces they had seen. None of these faces was the chimeric one actually presented. However, Levy et al. (1972) reported that patients failed to notice this fact. Instead, when the patients were asked to choose which face had been presented, the half shown in the left visual field (to the right hemisphere) was usually chosen. Patients made approximately the same responses whether asked to respond with the left or right hand, indicating that for this task the right hemisphere had taken control of the motor response mechanism. Similar results were obtained with nonsense shapes and pictures of common objects (Levy & Trevarthan, 1976; 1977).

FIGURE 5.16
Chimeric face (from Levy, et al., 1972).

This balance between the right and left hemispheres can be tipped one way or the other by the precise question asked. When the four split-brain patients were taught names for the three faces used in making up the two-faced stimuli and then asked to respond with the name of the face that had been presented, they most often responded with the name of the face corresponding to the right half of the picture (perceived by the left hemisphere). Similarly, when separate pictures were presented in the right and left visual fields, split-brain patients usually pointed to something visually similar to the left-visual-field input when asked to select what they had seen. However, when they were asked to point to a picture of something with a name that rhymed with that of something they had seen, they pointed to a picture with a name that rhymed with that of the picture presented on the right. Hence the kind of judgment that must be made about the input determines the hemisphere that controls the response.

The work with split-brain patients stimulated the investigation of hemispheric control in normal human brains. In the normal brain information presented to one hemisphere is rapidly transmitted across the corpus callosum to the other. However, the response to input should be a little faster if it arrives first at the hemisphere controlling the response. Using this logic, inputs were presented in specific locations so that they arrived first at the left or right hemisphere. Whether reaction time was faster for left- or right-visual-field presentation depended on the precise nature of the task (Bryden & Allard, 1976; Hellige, Cox, & Litvac, 1979; Zaidel, 1978b). In general, linguistic tasks elicited faster responses with right-visual-field presentations, and visual-pattern analysis tasks elicited faster responses with left-visual-field presentations. (See also Helige, 1980.)

COMPARISON AND RESPONSE SELECTION

The specialization of the left hemisphere for speech processing is the result of the special demands of speech production on cortical processing. First, speech production is localized in specific areas of the left frontal and parietal lobes because speech production requires precise timing of vocal movements that cannot be achieved when control is shared between both hemispheres. Speech perception is localized in the left temporal cortex because the representations used to construct speech must be closely associated with those representations used to recognize it. Sentence understanding requires an articulatory as well as a perceptual representation of the word sequence, as shown schematically in Figure 5.14. As we shall see, speech is recognized in sequences of several words called phrases. In turn, each word is made up of several speech sounds called phonemes. The word comparison process often produces several different matches for short segments of the speech input. For example, the same phoneme sequence may match several different words. These various competing responses are forwarded to the sentence construction stage where they are compared and combined until a single representation of the entire phrase is constructed. Furthermore, as shown in Figure 5.14, there is a pathway back from the response selection stage to the comparison stage. Response selection guides subsequent comparisons through priming.

The role of memory looms so large in speech perception because what is important is not what sounds the speaker actually produced, or what sounds you actually heard, but what sounds the speaker intended to produce in the first place. As we shall see, the sound that reaches your ears is identified with and heard as whatever speech sound makes the most sense in that context. So when you hear speech, the sounds you hear may be closer to what the speaker intended to say than to what she actually produced!

A look at the speech input. Speech perception (and, as a result, language perception) requires specialized processing because the speech that you actually produce is only a noisy approximation of the sounds you intend to produce. Special processing in a listener's brain is required to decode from the speech that was actually produced what the speaker intended to say in the first place. You may have learned as far back as elementary school that a word is made up of syllables and syllables are made up of consonants and vowels. For example, the word lady contains the syllables /la/ and /dy/, which in turn contain the consonants /l/ and /d/ and the vowels /a/ and /e/. These vowels and consonants of English (or any other language) are called phonemes. (Slightly more technically, a **phoneme** is the smallest part of the speech input that makes a difference in a word's meaning.). When you speak your intention is to produce distinct words made up of phoneme sequences. Furthermore, when you listen to someone speak, most of the words sound distinct. That is, each word is perceived as having a definite beginning and ending. The words do not blend into one another. However, that is not what you have actually produced. When you attempt to make a single speech sound, you must adjust your lips, teeth, tongue, vocal cords, and lungs in unison. When you try to speak, the signals for all the successive, distinct sounds that must be made if you are to speak at a reasonable rate come too fast for the vocal apparatus to react separately to each one. Instead, the movements for the various sounds become jumbled up and compromised. As a result, the actual speech produced is not the way it would be if each phoneme were separately articulated.

When the sound input is examined, it often does not contain discrete patterns corresponding to the individual words of a sentence. For instance, Figure 5.17 is a **speech spectrogram** of the sentence *The steward dismissed the girl.* A spectrogram is a visual record of the physical wave pattern you produce when you speak. All the information that the auditory system uses to construct a speech representation is contained in the speech spectrograph. The vertical axis represents frequency (roughly, the pitch of the sound pattern), and the horizontal axis represents time. The darkness of a point on the spectrogram represents the amplitude of that frequency (roughly, its loudness).

As you can see from the spectrogram, there are some relatively white areas. The white areas represent moments of relative silence, and you therefore might imagine that they correspond to breaks between words. However, if you examine the bracketing at the bottom of the figure, you will see that they do not. This bracketing shows approximately where one word ends and another begins. Notice that the word *the* blends into the word *steward* in the higher-frequency ranges. There is no break between the words at all. The first blank area occurs within the word *steward*. Similarly, *steward* blends into *dismissed*, which itself contains two white areas, and the second *the* blends into *girl* in the low-frequency ranges. Hence moments of relative silence are as likely to occur within words as between them. The breaks and

FIGURE 5.17

Spectrogram of *The steward dismissed the girl.*

The   steward   dismissed   the   girl

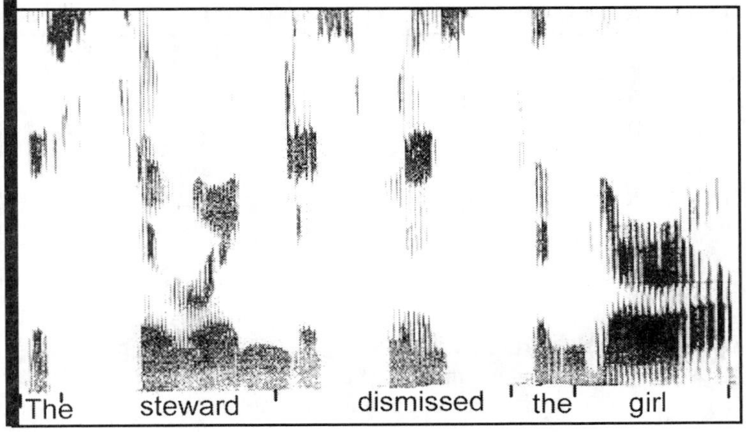

pauses you hear when you listen to speech do not directly correspond to changes in the physical signal at all. In less than a tenth of a second of processing, the continuous input of speech sound is transformed into the discrete intelligible words that are perceived.

To understand spoken language, you need a special phoneme identification system that interprets segments of speech and yields a representation of the sequence of speech sounds that the speaker was trying to produce. For example, when you produce a /p/ or /t/, you momentarily close your vocal tract and stop the flow of air from your lungs. (For this reason /p/ and /t/ are called **stop consonants**.) This stoppage produces a moment of silence in the speech signal. Hence a moment of silence produces the perception of a /p/, /t/, or some other stop consonant when it is part of a speech segment (Liberman, 1982). How the silence is perceived depends on the pattern that contains it. It is the representation produced by the phoneme identification mechanism that is heard.

So in order to perceive speech the input must be analyzed over time. Speech perception can be studied by generating synthetic speech and then determining how different patterns are perceived. If the speech input is segmented into small pieces, so that the temporal context is lost, a single segment may not sound like a speech sound at all but like a nonspeech sound like a whistle (Liberman, Cooper, Shankweiler, & Studdert-Kennedy, 1967). Furthermore, when the beginnings of different syllables containing the same consonant are played, they sound different from each other. For example, the beginning of the tape for /di/ sounds like a rising whistle, while the beginning of the tape for /du/ sounds like a falling whistle (Lieberman et al., 1967). Thus two different sound patterns may be perceived as the same consonant, depending on the following vowel. Also, the same sound pattern may be perceived as different consonants when the vowel context is changed. For example, the identical initial sound will produce /pi/ when paired with /i/ and /ka/ when paired with /a/ (Schatz, 1954).

Syntax and speech perception. In short, how any particular speech input is heard depends on what comes before and after it. When we look at how much of the input before and after a pattern affects its perception, we discover that there must not only be logogens for words but structural descriptions for word-sequences as well. We saw above that scenes have structural descriptions that order semantically related elements by location and that these structural descriptions are used to recognize scenes. Word sequences also have structural descriptions that are used to recognize them. These structural descriptions are called the **syntax** or **grammar** of a language. Structural descriptions are used to recognize the familiar kinds of word sequences we call phrases, clauses, and sentences. We shall examine these below. They apply equally well to spoken and written language. Like the structural descriptions of scenes they are quite abstract; the same structural description can be satisfied by many different word sequences.

There is an advantage to the complex way that speech is perceived. Even speech degraded by extraneous environmental noise may be heard as the speaker intended. The structure of the language restricts the sounds you are likely to hear. First, some combinations of sounds make words and others do not. *John Zuhm an* is not a sentence and *Zuhm,* is not even a word, but *John's a man* is a sentence. Figure 5.18 outlines some of the steps in the processing of the sound sequence that comprises *John's a man*. As shown in Figure 5.18A, the sequence /j/, /ahn/ matches the auditory representation for the word *John*, however, /ahn/ also matches the auditory representation for the word, *on*.

As Figure 5.18B shows, the beginnings of two different phrase descriptions match the sequence /j/, /ahn/, /z/. Structural descriptions are indicated by the square nodes in the figure. Structural descriptions represent the order of their elements. The remaining circular nodes are category nodes. As defined above, a category node is a concept criterion-node associated with a set of instance nodes any of which may match it. For example, the category *Name* is the category of all names, and the name *John* is one of the many inputs that match it. As shown in Figure 5.18B, structural descriptions are associated with category nodes and vice versa when the representation of a word sequence is constructed. A syntactic structural description of two or more words is called a **phrase**. Two different syntactic structural descriptions match a name followed by the sound /z/. Recall that when more than one representation applies to the same input the input is called ambiguous. The one on the right of the second panel is for a possessive noun phrase (POS). As shown on the right, this phrase is completed by a noun. The one on the left is a description is for a contraction of the noun phrase (NP)-verb phrase (VP) pair, *John is*. A phrase that contains a verb phrase is called a **clause**. Clauses, such as the NP-VP clause shown on the left in the second panel of Figure 5.18B, that can be understood without combining their structural descriptions with those of other clauses are called **sentences**. As shown on the right, this sentence is completed by another noun phrase. As is shown in Figure 5.19, the sound sequence /uh/, /m/, /ahn/ matches the structural description of a noun phrase. So the sounds are perceived as grouped according to the organization of that structural description. As another example, *I ate an I scream cone* is not a sentence but *I ate an ice cream cone* is a sentence. The grammatical restrictions on what words may form a sentence and the order they must be in make one interpretation of the auditory input much more probable than the other.

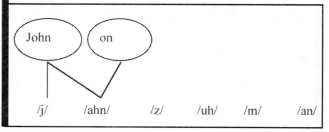

FIGURE 5.18A
Processing speech input.
Logogens matching initial speech input.

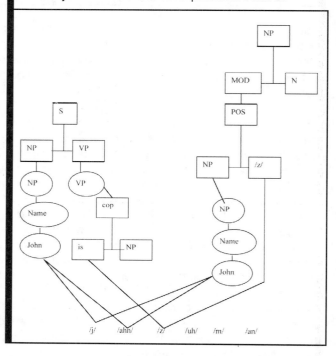

FIGURE 5.18B
Processing speech input.
Two syntactic structural descriptions for John S.

Notice that because structural descriptions refer to category nodes, and each category node may have many different instances, a single phrase description may match many different word sequences. So the category *Name* not only includes *John*, but *Mary*, *Alan*, etc. The number of different word sequences that match a single structural description is determined by the number of different category elements in the phrase and the number of instances in each category. For example, the structural description for a noun phrase contains a modifier element (MOD) and a noun element (N), as shown in Figure 5.18B. One very large subset of the modifier category is the adjective category, e.g., *large*, *small*. So *large men*, *small women*, etc. are all noun phrases. You know over 1,000 adjectives and way over 1,000 nouns, so (using scientific notation) you can recognize as noun phrases many more than $10^3 \times 10^3 = 10^6$ adjective noun combinations. This is over a million two-word combinations. In general, if a structural description has n category elements and there are more than 10^3 instances in each category then 10^{3n} match that structural description. For n greater than 3 the number is more word sequences than you can hear in your entire

FIGURE 5.19

Processing speech input.
Syntactic structural description of *John is a man*.

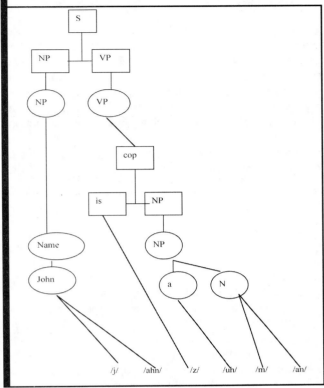

lifetime. Throughout your life many of the word sequences that you process during language comprehension you are hearing for the first time.

Phonemic restoration. One powerful demonstration of how word representations and syntactic structural descriptions combine to influence speech perception is the **phonemic restoration effect**. This effect was first demonstrated by Richard Warren in 1970 and has since been investigated in detail by him and his colleagues (Obusek & Warren, 1973; Warren & Obusek, 1971; Warren & Warren, 1970). In one experiment Warren presented twenty people with a recording of the sentence, "The state governors met with their respective legi*latures convening in the capital city." The asterisk indicates a 0.12-second portion of the recorded speech that had been carefully removed and replaced with the sound of a cough. The subjects were asked if there were any sounds missing from the recording. Nineteen of the twenty subjects said there was no missing sound, and the other subject identified the wrong sound as missing. In fact, Warren himself heard the missing sound. When a larger portion of the word was obliterated and replaced by a tone or a buzz rather than a cough, the word was still perceived as intact. However, the missing portion was noticed if it was replaced simply with silence.

FIGURE 5.20

Processing speech input.
Semantic category relation (left), syntactic structural description (center), logogens (right).

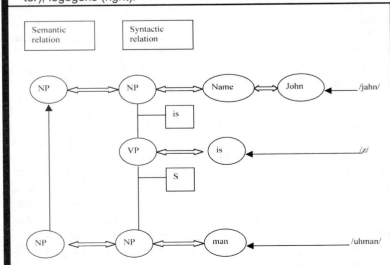

Semantics and speech perception. Of course the purpose of language is to communicate information. Each syntactic description of a phrase is associated with a semantic structural description that defines a relationship among the semantic nodes accessed by the words of the phrase. The fact that sentences usually have meaning further restricts the word sequences that are likely to occur. For example, the Figure 5.20 shows a semantic structural description indicating the categorical relationship between *John* and *man* that is activated by the syntactic structural description of the sentence. Semantic structural descriptions influence speech perception in the same manner that syntactic structural descriptions influence speech perception. The word that ultimately matches a semantic structural description consistent with the rest of the sentence, hence is meaningful, is the one that is selected. Even if the vowel sound produced by the speaker is unclear the most likely word that it is part of may be reconstructed from the rest of the sentence because a listener constructs a speech representation a group of words at a time. For example, *John is a man I know* is a meaningful sentence, whereas *John is a moon I know* is not.

Another way this is put is to say that speech perception is categorical because all the input sounds are sorted into a number of discrete phoneme categories. There is a universal set of phoneme categories for all languages, and each actual language makes use of a subset of the universal set of possible phonemes. So the same speech sound may sound different to people who know different languages. The same two speech sounds that may be placed in the same phonemic category in one language may be placed in two different categories in another language. Native speakers of Japanese, a language that does not distinguish between the English phonemes /r/ and /l/, have great difficulty hearing this distinction.

Warren and Warren (1970) used the phonemic restoration task to demonstrate the effect of semantic context on speech perception. They presented different people with one of the following four sentences:

It was found that the *eel was on the axle.
It was found that the *eel was on the shoe.
It was found that the *eel was on the table.
It was found that the *eel was on the orange.

The only difference among these sentences was the final word spliced onto the end of the tape—*axle, shoe, orange,* or *table*. Depending on the version people listened to, *eel* was perceived as *wheel, heel, meal,* and *peel*, respectively. Hence, even the meanings of words that follow it can influence the perception of a speech sound. So just as semantic priming aids the perception of a degraded visual input, as seen above, it also aids in the perception of a degraded speech input. Since speech inputs are more likely to be degraded than visual inputs, the role of semantic priming in speech perception is correspondingly greater than it is in visual perception. Other studies also suggest that when a word is mispronounced you hear what the speaker intended to say (Cole, 1973; Marslen-Wilson, 1975; Marslen-Wilson & Welsh, 1978); that people often do not even perceive the mispronunciation. When the speech input is processed, each input-sound is matched with one of the phonemes of the language that the listener knows. So even if the match is less than perfect between a particular input and the representation of a particular phoneme in memory, the input is heard as that phoneme if it does not match any other phoneme more closely.

As shown in Figure 5.14, there is a circuit between word comparison and sentence construction. Initial comparisons produce matches that activate particular structural descriptions that increase the activation of particular logogens that increase the probability of them making a response as a result of even a partial match with the input. This cyclical process that converges on a single semantic representation, though many different syntactic and semantic descriptions may be briefly activated early in the process, is called **analysis-by-synthesis** (Townsend & Bever, 2001).

AMBIGUITY AND COMPREHENSION

The whole point of language processing is the construction of the semantic description, i. e., the meaning of the phrase, from the semantic structural description associated with the syntactic structural description of the phrase and the meanings of the words of the phrase. The meaning of a phrase is called a **proposition**. A **proposition** is the smallest unit of meaning that has a truth value. For example, *the red ball* is not a proposition but *the ball is red* is a proposition because only the latter may be true or false. Construction of the proposition is called **comprehension**. Ambiguity greatly complicates the comprehension process. We have already seen in the phonemic restoration example above that the sound at the beginning of *eel was ambiguous. It could have been any one of four different representations and the correct one could only be determined by considering its context. However, this is only the beginning of increased complexity created by ambiguity. Entire words and phrases, as well as individual sound inputs, may activate multiple representations. In each case the one that best fits the context must be selected.

Lexical ambiguity. Many words are ambiguous. This is called **lexical ambiguity**. Just as its visual context selects the most likely object representation in visual processing through semantic priming, the sentential context of an ambiguous word selects the best fitting meaning through semantic priming. Normally, when you hear an ambiguous word in a sentence, you do not recognize that it is ambiguous; you are only aware of the meaning that fits the sentence. For example, for the sentence, *They need a new sink*, you only perceive the noun meaning of *sink* and not the verb meaning. However, Tanenhaus, Leiman, and Seidenberg (1979) showed that both meanings of an ambiguous word are initially activated, and then the appropriate one is selected and integrated into the sentential representation. Tanenhaus et al. found that if *swim* immediately follows, *They need a new sink*, its reading time is still primed. However, if *swim* follows *They need a new sink*, by 200 milliseconds, it is no longer primed. Already, one meaning has been selected (see also Seidenberg, Tanenhaus, Leiman, & Bienkowski, 1982).

Notice that Tanenhaus et al.'s (1979) findings for language comprehension are consistent with Neely's (1977) lexical decision results described in Chapter 4. Neely's and Tanenhaus' findings neatly illustrate the complementary roles that the temporal and prefrontal cortex play in attention and comprehension. First, anything that might be relevant to the target, and hence the task at hand, is rapidly activated in the semantic network in the temporal cortex. Second, working memory contains a structural description that contains particular categories of representations. Newly activated representations that are instances of these categories are incorporated into it and the other representations are inhibited. Hence task relevant information is retrieved from memory through a two-stage process of activation and selection.

If both meanings of *sink* are accessed then the next question to ask is whether they are accessed together or in a particular order. The answer is that the various meanings of an ambiguous word are accessed in an order determined by the frequency of each meaning and the context in which it occurs (MacDonald, Pearlmutter, & Seidenberg, 1994). As we saw above, a particular meaning may be activated through semantic priming from earlier phrases and sentences so that it is the first one accessed. When the wrong meaning is at first selected, a **garden path** misinterpretation occurs. In one study of the detection and resolution of inconsistencies, Carpenter and Daneman (1981) had subjects read "garden path" passages such as the following:

> The young man turned his back on the rock concert stage and looked across the resort lake. Tomorrow was the annual, one-day fishing contest and fishermen would invade the place. Some of the best bass guitarists in the country would come to this spot. The usual routine of the fishing resort would be disrupted by the festivities.

When they read this passage aloud, most people initially pronounced the ambiguous word *bass* in accord with its *fish* meaning, which had been primed by the preceding references to fishing. However, the *fish* interpretation is inconsistent with the immediately following word *guitarists*, which forces the interpretation related to low musical notes. Carpenter and Daneman measured subjects' eye fixations as they read the passage, and they found that people kept their gaze on *guitarists* a relatively long time as the inconsistency was detected, and then they regressed to reread the word *bass*. People thus use the context both to select meanings and to detect inconsistencies as early as possible.

Syntactic and semantic ambiguity. The meaning of the phrase is the conjunction of the meanings of the individual words and the semantic relations among them activated by the syntactic structural description of the phrase. It is necessary to sort out the phrase that the words form from the identification of the words themselves. Human languages make use of two kinds of perceptual features to match word sequences to phrase descriptions. First, the order of the words can determine the relationship between them. Consider the possessive noun phrase, *Fred's radio.* The phrase *radio Fred's* means something entirely different. Second, an inflection in a word or function word between words can mark the relationship between it and another word. In the phrase *Fred's* radio the possessive relation is indicated by the inflection *-s* on *Fred*. Alternatively, in the phrase *the radio of Fred*, the function word *of* marks the possessive relationship between *the radio* and *Fred*. All languages use some mixture of word order, inflections, and function words for marking the relationships between words.

Function words and inflections reduce the number of different structural descriptions that match a word sequence. Hence they reduce the number of comparisons to find a representation of the entire sentence and make it easier to understand. Compare the first two with the last two sentences below. The first two sentences are garden-path sentences. In the first sentence *raced past the barn* can either be the main clause of the sentence or a relative clause. Hence, at this point the sentence is ambiguous. Initially, the more frequently used structural description in English, the main clause is selected (there is one in every sentence). Similarly, in the second sentence *the lawyer* can either be a direct object or the beginning of clause. Hence, at this point the sentence is ambiguous and initially the more frequently used structural description, the object, is selected by the comprehension system. However, when the second verb appears there is no place for it in the description and so the initial representation fails. In contrast, the function word *that* in the last two sentences does not match the incorrect description; as a result these sentences are easy to understand.

> The horse raced past the barn fell.
> Sally warned the lawyer was greedy.

> The horse that raced past the barn fell.
> Sally warned that the lawyer was greedy.

However, function words and inflections only reduce, but do not solve, the problem posed by ambiguity because function words and inflection words are themselves ambiguous. Recall that in Figure 5.18 an inflected noun, e.g., *John's*, matched the beginning of both a sentence and a noun phrase. This ambiguity was resolved by the next word in the sequence. A language has about a hundred function words or inflections that define relationships between words and many of these match more than one syntactic structural description, each one with a different meaning. Consider the meaning of *to* in the following three sentences. As shown below, *went to* matches the beginning of three different phrases. The first phrase ends with a noun phrase, e.g., *the store*, the second phrase ends with a verb phrase, e.g., *get a pencil*, and the third one ends with a verb, e.g., *sleep*. So the structural descriptions for all three phrases must have been matched by the phrase *went to*.

> • Laurie went to the store.
> • Arthur went to get a pencil.
> • Lillie went to sleep.

In all three sentences *to* connects its phrase to the verb *went*, but in each case it marks a different syntactic and semantic relationship between the verb and the following constituent. In the first sentence *to* marks the final location of something after a change in position in space. In the second sentence it marks the purpose of the movement. In the third sentence it marks a change in psychological state. Also, consider the semantic relations activated by the function words *by* and *of* in the following sentences.

> • Lee was seated by the waiter.   Susan was seated by the fire.
> • Vince made a bowl of wood.   Pat made a bowl of soup.

In both these examples the same syntactic structural description, i.e., *by* followed by a noun phrase and *of* followed by a noun, is associated with two different semantic descriptions. A single representation for the entire sentence is selected when each of the meanings of the phrase are compared with the meanings of the individual words. Depending on its context, *by* can refer to an action or a location and *of* can refer to the composition of a bowl or its contents.

VERBAL WORKING MEMORY

We have seen that speech is not processed one sound at a time. Rather, a sequence of sounds that forms an entire word sequence is compared with representations of individual words and syntactic structural descriptions of word sequences until a single matching representation is found. As the phonemic restoration effect demonstrates, the entire sequence of sounds is literally not heard until a single semantic representation is selected. So all the input sounds in the sequence must be preserved until this match is made because they all contribute to the perceptual representation that is finally selected. The set of verbal representations in memory that must remain available for inclusion in the final perceptual representation are collectively said to be in verbal working memory. When verbal working memory is discussed, ordinary memory is called long-term memory to clarify the discussion.

Forgetting of word sequences and syntactic structural descriptions. Since the point of human language is the construction of propositions, it is necessary to only briefly perceive the precise words of a phrase in order to construct its meaning. But once that is done there is no compelling reason to retain the word-sequences or their syntactic descriptions in declarative memory, and this is apparently not done. Jarvella (1970; 1971) demonstrated that word sequences are not retained. He had people listen to passages that contained several clauses. Subjects were instructed that when the passage stopped, they were to write as much of the end of it as they could remember exactly. In one study Jarvella found that people remembered the last clause verbatim 86 percent of the time and the second-to-last clause 54 percent of the time. These results were obtained when the two clauses were part of the same sentence. When the second-to-last clause was not in the same sentence as the final clause, people recalled it verbatim only 20 percent of the time.

A study by Caplan (1972) also provided evidence that only the most recent phrase is in working memory. In this study the subject heard a sentence, at the completion of which a probe word was presented. The subject had to respond as rapidly as possible about whether the probe word appeared in the sentence. For some sentences the probe word (which in this example is *oil*) appeared in the last clause:

- Now that artists are working fewer hours oil prints are rare.

For other sentences it appeared in the next-to-last clause:

- Now that artists are working in oil prints are rare.

As you can see from the examples, the sentences were cleverly constructed so that regardless of whether the probe word was in the last or the next-to-last clause, it was the same number of words from the end of the sentence. If the words of the last clause are maintained in working memory, then a probe word from the last clause should be matched rapidly. If the words of the next-to-last clause are not being maintained in working memory, then the probe word should be matched more slowly because it must first be retrieved from long-term memory. As predicted, the probe word was identified faster when it had occurred in the last clause.

Ambiguity. There are two reasons why you are unaware of the many local ambiguities in sentences or the selection process that resolves them. First, the prior context is usually both a good guide to the appropriate structural description and will have primed it. So if the first structural description that is retrieved is always selected then the correct choice will usually be made. Second, an ambiguous word sequence is usually only one or two or three words. So even if the wrong selection is made initially the alternative interpretation remains available in working memory to replace the initial, incorrect, selection. For example, consider the following pair of sentences:

- When the boys strike the dog kills.
- After the dog bites the man the cat kills.

Warner and Glass (1987) found that college students called both of these sentences grammatical. Notice that each sentence contains a verb, i.e., *strike*, *bites*, followed by a noun phrase, i.e., *the dog*, *the man*, respectively. This creates a local ambiguity because the noun phrase can either be the beginning of a new clause, as in the first sentence, or the object of the verb, as in the second sentence. To distinguish these alternatives with a technical term, the verb is given an **intransitive** interpretation in the first sentence and a **transitive** interpretation in the second sentence. However, the ambiguity is resolved at the end of the sentence. So the length of the ambiguous phrase beyond the noun phrase is one word (*kills*)for the first sentence and three words (*the cat kills*) for the second sentence.

Warner and Glass decided to see what would happen if the ambiguous phrase was made longer, as in the two sentences below:

- Before the boy kills the man the dog bites strikes.
- When the horse kicks the boy the dog bites the man.

The second sentence with the transitive interpretation of the verb was still always called grammatical. However, the first sentence with the intransitive interpretation of the verb was called grammatical less than half the time. In fact, in ordinary spoken and written English the transitive interpretation of a verb followed by a noun phrase is much more common than the intransitive interpretation. So the comprehension system apparently selects the more frequent transitive interpretation of the verb and replaces it with the intransitive interpretation only when conflicting disambiguating information is processed. When the ambiguous phrase is short, as in the first pair of sentences, the re-interpretation is never noticed. However, working memory has a limited capacity. When the ambiguous phrase is long, as in the second pair of sentences, the alternative interpretation is no longer available by the time the conflicting disambiguating information is processed. So a single representation cannot be constructed for the entire sentence and it is perceived as ungrammatical.

Comprehension requires that working memory include all possible representations of a sequence of words until a disambiguating word appears. If the capacity of working memory is exceeded and the wrong representation is selected prematurely then a listener is fooled by a garden path sentence, as in the Warner and Glass (1987) experiment. In this case, the only option is to try to recover the word sequence through the phonological – articulatory loop and to try to construct a new representation from a different word meaning or structural description. Sometimes the number of possible representations of a single sentence fragment exceeds the capacity of working memory. Because the capacity of working memory can be exceeded, it is a limiting factor on language comprehension.

Daneman and Carpenter (1983) made use of a test of verbal working memory they had invented to assess working memory in students with good and poor reading comprehension. In their test a person had to respond true or false to simple statements and also had to remember the last word of each statement. The number of last words correctly recalled was the measure of working memory. People with poorer working memories were poorer readers and had more difficulty with garden path sentences. For example, Daneman and Carpenter (1983) found that poor readers have a great deal of difficulty recovering from a garden path sequence like *There is also one sewer near our home. He makes terrific suits.*

SYNTAX AND MEANING

Notice, as in the example above, each syntactic structural description is associated with a single or small set of semantic structural descriptions, which combine with the meanings of the individual words to form propositions. For example, as discussed in the next chapter, by the age of four children learning English recognize noun-verb-noun syntactic phrases as having agent-action-object semantic structural descriptions. Because the semantic relationship among the words of a phrase is constrained by the syntax of the phrase, even absurd statements like *bicycles push people* can be understood (Slobin, 1966). That people can understand even absurd sentences in a predictable way is a great advantage. It makes possible the creative figurative use of language through metaphor and poetry that expands the kinds of things that can be said and understood.

SCHEMAS, STORY UNDERSTANDING, AND PRAGMATICS

Propositions are not understood in isolation but as segments of conversations, essays, or stories. The structural description of a story is sometimes called a **schema**. A schema represents a temporal sequence of episodes in a hierarchical structure that is similar to the visual descriptions of scenes and the semantic descriptions of phrases. Karl Haberlandt (Haberlandt, Berian, & Sandson 1980) studied how schemas are constructed by measuring the times needed to read individual sentences of simple stories. Each story consisted of a setting (S) and two episodes, where each episode consisted of a beginning (B), reaction (R), goal (G), attempt (A), outcome (O), and ending (E). An example is:

Once upon a time there was a king. The king had three lovely daughters. The king's daughters went for a walk in the woods every day (S). One afternoon a dragon came into the woods and kidnapped the daughters (B). They were frightened by the dragon (R). So they planned to escape from the dragon (G). The daughters tried to distract the dragon by singing songs (A). But they remained the dragon's prisoners (O). The daughters cried desperately (E). Three knights heard the cries (B). They took pity on the daughters (R). They wanted to free the daughters (G). The knights attacked and fought the dragon (A). Finally they killed the fierce monster (O). The knights had saved the king's daughters (E).

Reading times were longest at the beginnings and ends of the episode and declined for sentences in the middle. Haberlandt suggested that at the beginning of an episode the schema activates a new node for integrating the next episode. At the end of the episode the individual sentence propositions are combined into a single proposition for the entire episode, which involves such operations as deleting redundant elements. Cirilo and Foss (1980) found a similar effect on sentence time for somewhat longer and more interesting stories.

We saw above that the visual representation of a fire hydrant is not constructed prior to and independently of the street scene it is part of. Rather, possible representations of different objects are used to constrain each other so that the objects and the scene are perceived together. Similarly, though it is possible to understand individual sentences in isolation, the meaning of each sentence in a story is not determined prior to and independently of its integration into the schema for a story. Rather, details provided by the story may be used to fill in the representation of the sentence. Details that aren't specified by the sentence are filled in through semantic priming and selection. You are so practiced at integrating information across sentences that you don't realize how meaningless individual sentences could be if connections could not be made. However, John Bransford and Marcia Johnson (1973) demonstrated this by ripping some sentences from their contexts. Consider:

- The notes were sour because the seam was split.
- The haystack was important because the cloth ripped.

Understanding them is difficult because you are unable to connect the sentences to anything you already know. But a single word can provide a referent that makes each sentence perfectly comprehensible. The words are *bagpipes* and *parachute*, respectively.

Finally, the ability to understand language in a social setting, such as a restaurant, is facilitated by a structural description of episodes such as being seated, ordering, and paying for a meal. If you call to make a dinner reservation at a restaurant and the host asks, "Do you want smoking or nonsmoking?" The correct answer is not, "yes." These structural descriptions are similar to story schemas, but are sometimes called **scripts** instead of schemas. Also, the contribution of the social setting to language understanding is called **pragmatics**.

STRUCTURAL DESCRIPTON AND COMPREHENSION

The many names for the representations of body parts, objects, utterances, and actions: motor plans, visual structural descriptions, syntactic and semantic structures, propositions, schemas, and scripts reflect differences in their content, not their codes. They are all constructed in the same way, through the comparison-selection circuit. They all are constructed from the same basic motor, visual, and auditory codes. They all hierarchically organize their components in space and time. They all ultimately organize categories of things; hence can be applied to many different instances. Ultimately, scripts must contain schemas, visual structural descriptions, and motor plans. At any given waking moment, the particular schema or script in your working memory insures understanding of each sentence of a story or each request and response in a social situation. It orients you to place and enables you to construct and execute meaningful, relevant, effective actions.

APHASIA

An impairment of the ability to understand language is called **aphasia**. Word finding difficulty, which is called **anomia**, is always a symptom of aphasia. Anomia is caused by damage to visual-auditory connections in the logogen system within the left temporal cortex. An anomic patient has difficulty identifying the referents of familiar words. For example, when asked to touch an ankle, he may not know what to do or may touch his leg instead (Goodglass & Geschwind, 1976). An anomic patient also has difficulty naming familiar objects. When asked the name of a familiar object, such as a spoon, he may be unable to respond or call it a knife. Even if he produces the correct answer, he may take excessive time and be unsure that he was right. Anomia can be assessed by showing the patient pictures of objects that vary in familiarity. An anomic patient is one who can name fewer than normal pictures.

Impaired sentence comprehension is also always a symptom of aphasia. Some individuals with aphasia will have normal comprehension of simple sentences like *The boy is jumping* but all individuals with aphasia will have impaired comprehension for complex sentences like *The girl is kissing the boy that the clown is hugging* (Dronkers, et al., 2004).

If the only language impairments an individual has are anomia and impaired sentence comprehension then the individual is said to have **anomic aphasia**. The patient appears to recognize people and objects, to be aware of her impairment, and can make herself understood through a combination of speech (e.g., this one) and pointing. Even though performance on systematic tests, such as word associations, similarity judgments, and picture naming is below normal it nevertheless is well above chance, indicating that some comprehension is retained. Notice that impaired comprehension of both spoken and written words and sentences is really a syndrome rather than a single disorder. An individual with anomic aphasia has most of the deficits shown in Figure 5.6, including both alexia and word deafness.

Dronkers et al. (2004) identified five areas, the middle temporal cortex, shown in the second lightest shade in Figure 5.3, and four additional areas, shown in the darkest shade in Figure 5.3, as areas where damage produces a sufficiently severe deficit in word and sentence comprehension for the individual to be classified as aphasic. Damasio et al. (2004) identified additional areas, shown in the second darkest shade in Figure 5.3, in which damage produces a limited naming disorder that is not severe enough for the individual to be classified as aphasic.

The reason that damage to a portion of a such a large area of the left hemisphere produces is aphasia is that, as we have seen, language comprehension is a complex process that can be interrupted at many different points. Beyond anomia, cases of aphasia can be classified with respect to kinds of additional symptoms that an individual may have, depending on which speech or language area is damaged and what specific function it has. The three most common specialized forms of aphasia, Conduction aphasia, Wernicke's aphasia, and Broca's aphasia, are described below. In older texts, Broca's aphasia is said to result from damage to an area in the frontal cortex appropriately called Broca's area and Wernicke's aphasia is said to result from damage to an area in the temporal cortex called Wernicke's area. Neither of these areas is shown in Figure 5.3 because it has recently become clear that damage to neither area causes aphasia. It is now clear that the aphasias once attributed to these areas resulted from extended damage that included both these areas and the adjacent language areas shown in Figure 5.3.

Conduction aphasia. An aphasic individual who has lost the ability to repeat sentences is said to have **conduction aphasia**. Conduction aphasia is the result of damage to the phonological-articulatory integration area in the parietal cortex (Figure 5.3 and pathway f in Figure 5.6). Recall that it is the phonological-articulatory loop that makes verbal rehearsal possible. With verbal rehearsal impaired, sentence repetition is no longer possible. A person can still understand simple sentences, but when asked to repeat them gives a paraphrase instead.

Wernicke's aphasia. If the retrieval of information during comprehension is disrupted by widespread damage that includes the middle left temporal lobe then the result is a type of aphasia called **Wernicke's aphasia**, after the German physician Carl Wernicke, who first described it. In Wernicke's aphasia, speech is fluent, though meaningless. Hence the disorder is also called **fluent aphasia.** The patient has poor or no understanding of language. Unsurprisingly, Wernicke's aphasia is often associated with visual agnosia since this disorder is caused by bilateral damage to the adjacent visual processing area in the temporal cortex.

If you casually heard a Wernicke's aphasic speak, you would have the impression that you were listening to someone articulate, amiable, and loquacious. His or her speech would seem to come out rapidly and effortlessly, with normal rhythm and intonation. However, if you listened more closely, your impression would quickly change.

The first thing you would note is that the patient's speech was utterly devoid of content. The patient has difficulty finding words, especially concrete nouns. At best, such speech is filled with pronouns that do not refer to anything (e.g., "He went over there, and did that, and came over here and did this," etc.). At worst, the speech of a posterior aphasic patient is filled with misused content words and nonsense words, run together very rapidly but with normal intonation, so that the speech sounds grammatical but is utterly meaningless. For example, the patient might say (Gardner 1976, p. 68):

> Boy, I'm sweating, I'm awfully nervous, you know, once in a while I get up, I can't mention the tarripoi, a month ago, quite a little, I've done a lot well, I impose a lot, while, on the other hand, you what I mean, I have to run around, look it over, trebbin and all that sort of stuff.

The comprehension of a patient tends to mirror her production in severity. Patients with severe Wernicke's aphasia demonstrate little or no ability to comprehend anything. They exhibit overall poor performance on systematic tests. For example, when Zurif, Caramazza, & Meyerson (1974) asked aphasic patients to sort words into categories severe Wernicke's patients did not appear to be sensitive to even the basic semantic distinction between humans and animals. Thus destruction of the semantic associations seems to be the major component of the disorder. Not only do severe Wernicke's aphasic patients perform very poorly on comprehension tests but they also have anosognosia (Chapter 4); they appear to be largely unaware of their disability. As a result, their responses to situations are frequently inappropriate. The moods of different patients vary from jovial to paranoid.

Broca's aphasia. Broca's aphasia is a syndrome consisting of two distinct deficits that result from damage to two distinct areas in the brain. Sometimes only a single area is damaged and only a single symptom results. Damage to the insular (Figure 2.2) produces in adults the first principal symptom of Broca's aphasia, halting and labored speech, first described by the French physician Paul Broca. Broca's aphasia is also called **expressive** or **nonfluent** aphasia, after this most obvious symptom (Dronkers, 1996).

Recall that the insular is below the surface of the neocortex. If damage is restricted to the surface of the neocortex above the insular then an individual's articulation may be impaired for a brief period following the injury. The impairment rapidly improves (Moss, 1972). But if the damage extends below the surface then the articulation deficit persists (Alexander, Benson, & Stuss, 1989; Mohr, 1973). The patient may initially lose all language use, gradually improving to some permanent level of impairment. In general, the more severe the initial disorder is, the more severe the long-term disorder is likely to be (Mohr, 1976).

The other principal symptom of Broca's aphasia is special difficulty with combining syntactic and semantic structural descriptions into a single representation of an entire sentence. This difficulty greatly reduces the syntactic complexity of the speech that a Broca's aphasic can understand and produce. As shown in Figure 5.3, injury to any one of three distinct areas, one in the temporal cortex and two in the frontal cortex, produces this disorder (Dronkers et al., 2004).

The two principal symptoms of Broca's aphasia may interact so that a person has extreme difficulty in producing certain speech sounds.   The person's speech is filled with pauses and stutters (Goodglass, 1968; 1976; Goodglass & Berko, 1960; Goodglass, Fodor, & Schulhoff 1967; Goodglass, Quadfaseal, & Timberlake, 1964). A person suffering from Broca's aphasia generally has more difficulty pronouncing function words and inflections than pronouncing content words (Gardner 1976, p.63; Geschwind, 1970). Furthermore, Goodglass has shown (Goodglass & Hunt 1958; Myerson & Goodglass, 1972) that one inflection may be harder to produce than another, even when both consist of the same sound. For example, he studied patients who inflected nouns but not verbs. As a result, a person might produce *The boy eats beets* as *The boy eat beets*. The final s would be dropped from the verb (*eat*) but not the noun (*beets*). The same types of errors usually appear when the patient tries to write (Gardner 1976, p. 65).

The tendency to leave out function words and inflections is a symptom of the more general inability to construct and comprehend complex grammatical sentences . Alfonso Caramazza and Edgar Zurif (1976) performed an experiment that demonstrated just how dependent aphasics are on word meanings when interpreting complex sentences. They would read a patient a sentence and ask the person to choose which of two pictures the sentence described. Some sentences could only have one reasonable interpretation on the basis of their lexical items. For example, even if one understands only the four main content words in *The bicycle that the boy is holding is broken*, about the only thing the sentence can mean is that the boy is holding the broken bicycle. In comparison, the sentence *The lion that the tiger is chasing is fat* might be interpreted at least four ways if only the content words were understood: the tiger might be chasing the fat lion, the lion might be chasing the fat tiger, the fat tiger might be chasing the lion, or the fat lion might be chasing the tiger. With this type of sentence the aphasic patients were unable to select the correct picture any more often than would be expected by chance (see also, Bradley, Garrett, & Zurif, 1980).

Though Broca's aphasia leaves people with an inability to combine syntactic and semantic structural descriptions during the comprehension of a sentence, some people with Broca's aphasia can focus on one kind of information or the other. Schwartz, Saffran, and Marin (1980) also found that patients with Broca's aphasia were at chance at understanding who kissed who in sentences like *John was finally kissed by Louise*. But they were 85 to 100 percent accurate at judging which of the following sentences was grammatical:

- John has finally kissed Louise.
- *John was finally kissed Louise.

This finding reveals that the patients retained the ability to recognize grammatical sentences though they could not use this information to help themselves understand the sentences.

Recent research has focused on defining more precisely the nature of the syntactic-semantic integration deficit that impairs the comprehension of complex sentences. It was mentioned above that semantic priming plays a role in sentence comprehension. For example, in the sentence *The gymnast loved the professor from the northwestern city who complained about the bad coffee* the position in the sentence after the word *who* is called a gap. This is because it refers back to the word *professor*. Normally, the comprehension process fills in the gap automatically by activating professor so you know who *who* refers to. One way to demonstrate this is in a priming task in which the listener/observer sees a letter string while hearing the sentence. The task is to respond whether the letter string is a word. When a word appears just after *who* is heard, the normal listener is faster to judge it to be a word if it is semantically related to *professor*, i.e., *teacher*, than if it is unrelated to *professor*, i.e., *address*. Zurif, Swinney, Prather, Solomon, and Bushnell (1993) studied four patients with Broca's aphasia and found that, unlike normal individuals, they were no faster at recognizing *professor* than *address*. However, the normal results were obtained with four patients who had moderate Wernicke's aphasia. So despite the impairment of the semantic network in Wernicke's aphasia, there was still priming in a syntactic context, while in Broca's aphasia there was not.

Of course, as we discussed above, the sentence comprehension is a complex process that may be impaired at several different points. The precise functions of the three parts of the cortex associated with syntactic-semantic integration in sentence processing are not understood. However, these areas have only been recently identified and it is likely that more will be learned of their functions in the near future.

Naming is also a complex process that may be impaired at different points. Like all aphasia, Broca's aphasia includes word-finding difficulty. However, the Broca's aphasic patient retains concrete nouns the best, in contrast to the Wernicke's aphasic patient who retains them the worst (Caramazza & Berndt, 1978). For example, when Zurif, et al. (1974) asked aphasic patients to sort words into categories, the Broca's aphasic patients grouped animal words somewhat differently than normal patients but honored most of the main category boundaries.

Severity. The degree of aphasic impairment varies over the widest range possible, from those individuals whose ability to speak and comprehend is so slightly impaired that it can be detected only by special testing, to those who are mute and understand nothing. At the mild end of the scale aphasia may manifest itself as a limit on the amount the person can comprehend at one time. For example, an aphasic person who will perform each of three simple commands perfectly (e.g., *Put the key in the cup*, *Open the door*, and *Touch your head with your hand*) when given separately, may be unable to perform any when they are given in combination.

One difficulty frequently reported by formerly aphasic patients (Moss, 1972) is that other people seemed to speak to them too fast during the period of aphasia. Another common report is that the speech of other people was not quite comprehensible. Imagine that you are listening to a stream of speech that sounds awfully familiar but that you cannot quite understand. Often a more severe aphasia improves over time to a barely detectable disorder. Nevertheless, a formerly severely aphasic individual may remain uncomfortable in ordinary conversational situations that you take for granted. For example, Schuell (1974, p. 125), related the following sad story:

I once saw a patient who entered the hospital for seizure control two years after a head injury incurred in the war. He showed no obvious aphasia, but an alert resident referred him for examination because there was a history of transient aphasia on his military record. I found a mild word-finding difficulty and a mild reduction of verbal retention span running through all language modalities. I told the patient what I found and said that it was the result of his head injuries. I told him that it was very mild and that I would not have detected it if I had not tested him. I also told him that there were things that he could do at home to improve it if he were interested. Then he began to talk.

He said it would have made all the difference in the world to him if someone had told him this two years before. He said that he had never heard of aphasia before. He did not know he'd been aphasic after his injury. He said that he went back to his hometown, saw people he had known all his life, and could not remember their names. He could not remember addresses or telephone numbers that he had known most of his life. One night he played cards and found that he could not keep score. He tried to balance his checkbook and found he was not able to do this. He read the paper and did not know what he had read. He listened to news on the radio and did not know what he had heard. He thought he was losing his mind and he lived in the terror that if someone discovered this he would most certainly be committed to an institution. He began to avoid people. He did not dare to get a job. He said that he had sat home and watched television for two years.

SEMANTIC DEMENTIA

We may distinguish among cognitive impairments that are temporary, permanent, and progressive. Agnosias and aphasias tend to be temporary or permanent, depending on the severity of the injury. As described above, in such cases the permanent impairment is often quite specific. However, there are also some disease processes that attack the temporal cortex, which are progressive. Though the first sign of the disorder may be a very specific symptom, the number and severity of the symptoms increase as the illness progresses. Alzheimer's disease is the best known of the progressive dementias. Since it attacks other parts of the brain besides the temporal cortex, which produce other symptoms, the description of it will appear later in the book. Here **semantic dementia** is described. This is a variant of **fronto-temporal dementia**, which afflicts either the frontal or the temporal cortex.

Semantic dementia is a common effect of localized temporal lobe damage. It is characterized by a progressive disorder of semantic knowledge, including both verbal and nonverbal material and resulting in severe impairments of naming and word comprehension. Perceptual and reasoning abilities are intact and memory for events is relatively well preserved. As semantic memory degenerates, a fluent aphasia develops. Speech becomes increasingly empty and lacking in substantives, but output is fluent, effortless, and grammaticality correct (Kopelman, 2002).

Warrington (1975) found that knowledge of subordinate categories (e.g., the name of a specific animal) was more impaired than knowledge of superordinate categories (e.g., animals or birds). Similar findings were obtained by Snowden, Goulding, and Neary (1989) and Hodges, Patterson, Oxbury, & Funnel (1992). As will be described in Chapter 6, superordinate categories like *animal* and *bird* form a basic level. They are learned early, are used frequently, and refer to objects that are recognized through a common perceptual representation. When attacked by a degenerative disease, the parts of semantic memory that were (Graham, Lambon Ralph, & Hodges, 1997) or are (Snowden, Griffiths, & Neary, 1995) used most often are the ones that survive the longest.

SUMMARY OF SPEECH AND LANGUAGE PERCEPTION AND RECOGNITION

- The encoding and feature analysis stages of auditory processing
  - Are anatomically parallel and functionally similar to the corresponding stages of visual processing.
  - Make a distinction between speech (left hemisphere) and nonspeech (right hemisphere) sounds for which there is no analogy in vision.

- Speech sounds and the subsequent word and sentence representations require substantial computation
  - A speaker only produces an approximation of the speech sounds that she intends to produce because of the sluggishness of the speech production system. As a result, speech input tends to be ambiguous. That is, small segments of the input approximately match the representations of several different speech sounds and can be put together to match representations of more than one word.
  - However, most of the word sequences that can be constructed are not meaningful utterances. The

speech processing system makes use of syntactic structural descriptions of meaningful word sequences along with other knowledge to constrain the representations of the input to those that are meaningful. As the length of the input sequence increases the number of meaningful representations is reduced until only a single one remains, which is selected as the representation of the input.
- Furthermore, matching structural descriptions prime subsequent comparisons.
- So speech recognition is performed through a repeated process of comparison (temporal cortex) and response selection (prefrontal cortex), sometimes called analysis by synthesis.

- The purpose of speech communication is the construction of a semantic representation that represents the meaning of the sentence. This is called comprehension. There is considerable ambiguity in the meanings of individual phrases that may be resolved through comparison with
  - the meanings of adjacent phrases.
  - the nonlinguistic context of the utterance. Structural descriptions used in comprehension are sometimes called schemas.
  - the general knowledge of the listener. The role of the nonlinguistic context is called pragmatics.

- The speech and language processing system includes
  - Primary auditory cortex in left temporal cortex for feature analysis
  - Middle temporal cortex for feature analysis and comparison at the word level
  - Phonological—articulatory integration area in left parietal cortex for verbal rehearsal
  - Syntactic processing areas in the superior temporal and prefrontal cortex for construction and comparison at the sentence level

- An impairment in language processing is called aphasia. Almost all aphasia
  - is the result of damage to the left hemisphere
  - includes impairments in
    * word comprehension
    * sentence comprehension.

SUMMARY OF CHAPTER

- There are two kinds of knowledge:
  - Procedural memory or skill learning or knowing how
  - Declarative memory or knowing what
    * Semantic knowledge - what something is.
    * Episodic knowledge - if and when it has been encountered before.
  - The two kinds of memory are inter-related because declarative memory requires the exercise of certain perceptual skills. Understanding this passage is an example of the construction of declarative knowledge but the act of reading is a perceptual skill.

- There are three levels of semantic organization
  - Logogen – is associated with the representations of objects and words in different modalities. There are three redundant pathways for word recognition
    * a visual whole-word pathway
    * an auditory whole-word pathway
    * a letter-sequence pronunciation pathway.
  - Category node – dominates logogens for which there is a common response, e.g., foods, animals.
  - Structural description - organizes a set of category nodes in a spatial and/or temporal representation like a scene or sentence.
    * is content of working memory
    * is used to select among competing logogen responses to same input
    * is used to plan a voluntary response

- The encoding and feature analysis stages of auditory processing
    - Are anatomically parallel and functionally similar to the corresponding stages of visual processing.
    - Make a distinction between speech (left hemisphere) and nonspeech (right hemisphere) sounds for which there is no analogy in vision.

- Speech sounds and the subsequent word and sentence representations require substantial computation
    - Speech input tends to be ambiguous. That is, small segments of the input approximately match the representations of several different speech sounds.
    - The speech processing system makes use of syntactic structural descriptions of meaningful word sequences along with other knowledge to constrain the representations of the input to those that are meaningful.
    - Furthermore, matching structural descriptions prime subsequent comparisons.
    - So speech recognition is performed through a repeated process of comparison (temporal cortex) and response selection (prefrontal cortex), sometimes called analysis by synthesis.

- The purpose of speech communication is the construction of a semantic representation that represents the meaning of the sentence. This is called comprehension. There is considerable ambiguity in the meanings of individual phrases that may be resolved through comparison with
    - the meanings of adjacent phrases.
    - the nonlinguistic context of the utterance. Structural descriptions used in comprehension are sometimes called schemas.
    - the general knowledge of the listener. The role of the nonlinguistic context is called pragmatics.
        * The speech and language processing system includes the middle temporal cortex as well as adjacent areas in the parietal, temporal and prefrontal cortex.

Chapter 6

INFANT & LANGUAGE LEARNING

C arolyn Rovee-Collier gave birth to her first son while she was a graduate student. She was faced with the difficulty of taking care of a newborn and writing a dissertation at the same time. As she attempted to write at her desk, her son was in the crib by her side. Of course, every time she tried to write a sentence, her son would cry and she would have to stop writing to shake his mobile for him, which quieted him. Was there any way that she could get her son to entertain himself, so that he would stop interrupting? After all, she was a psychologist. She should be able to think of something.

What she thought of was to tie a ribbon from her son's ankle to the mobile hanging over the crib (Figure 6.1). So now, when the boy squirmed from the colic and moved his leg, the mobile moved as well. The movement instantly caught his attention, distracting and quieting him. Within a few minutes he learned that he could make the mobile shake by moving his leg. This delighted him no end. Transfixed, he would give his leg a quick jerk, observe the result, and belly laugh. Soon he laughed and squealed even before he kicked, anticipating what was going to happen. This left his mother free to complete her work. What was more remarkable was that when Carolyn attached the ribbon to his foot the next day he started kicking straight away. He remembered how to make the mobile move.

This simple tale of infant learning illustrates the close connection between learning and action. Those percepts most likely to be encoded in declarative memory are those that are occasions for action (such as a movable mobile) and those that are the effects of action (such as a moving mobile). Then, in similar circumstances it is possible to act effectively. So every

FIGURE 6.1
Mobile reinforcement, shown here with a 3-month-old. An ankle ribbon tied to the infant's foot is strung to the hook suspending the mobile. When the infant kicks the mobile moves (Rovee & Rovee, 1969).

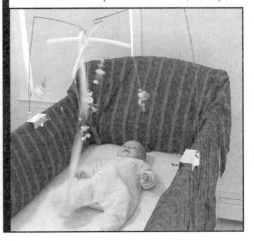

time Carolyn's son saw the mobile to which he had been tethered he tried to move it with a kick. This is the essence of **operant learning**, of which newborn infants are already capable. That is, they are already capable of perceiving things in the world and acting in response to them.

INFANT LEARNING

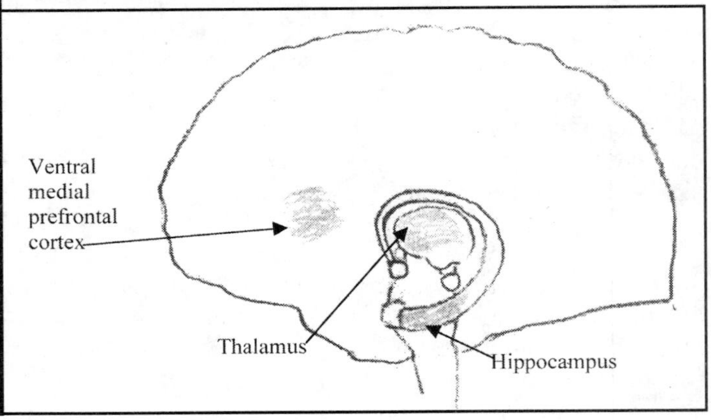

The early learning experiences of the infant are in some ways similar to and in other ways different from the child and adult he later becomes. The brain structures that encode representations in infancy are the same ones that operate throughout a person's life. So the factors that influence learning in infancy, such as the emotionality and frequency of an event, influence learning throughout life. Three overlapping brain mechanisms contribute to learning. The first mechanism is the recognition system (Chapter 5) that terminates in the frontal cortex. Specifically the ability of the recognition system to construct novel representations in working memory begins the learning processing. Recall that novel representa-

FIGURE 6.2
Brain areas involving learning. All are interior areas.

tions are constructed by associating the perceptual input with structural descriptions in long-term memory. Working memory makes it possible to hear a tune, rather than individual notes. It makes it possible to understand a sentence, to plan an action, and anticipate its consequences. Because working memory is where new representations are constructed it is the engine of learning. However, working memory is of limited capacity. Every time something is brought into working memory, something old is pushed out.

The second mechanism is the encoding mechanism. This consists of the thalamus, the medial temporal cortex, and the ventral medial prefrontal cortex, shown in Figure 6.2. The medial areas are the interior areas of the neocortex, far beneath its surface. Here representations constructed in working memory are made a part of long-term memory. Not every representation in working memory is made a part of long-term memory. Rather, there is some probability, depending on factors like the emotional arousal level of the individual, that a representation will be retained. As a result, the more often the representation of an object or action is constructed the more likely it is to become a part of long-term memory. So, there is a bias in the learning system to retain representations of familiar objects and routine actions. Furthermore, the longer the interval over which an object is repeatedly seen or an action performed, the longer its representation will be retained in long-term memory. So even representations of routine events experienced infrequently are retained.

However, more than just routine events are remembered. Some events are so important that they must be remembered the first time they are experienced. The third mechanism is the emotional system. Recall from Chapter 4 that the amygdala, which is the switch for emotional input, directly connects with the hippocampus, which regulates the formation of new representations in memory. When an experience produces a high level of emotional arousal, a permanent representation of the event is encoded. That is, you will remember something that terrifies you.

There is one way that the learning experience is different for the infant than for anyone else. As mentioned in Chapters 3 and 5, perceptual inputs match representations in memory before they reach awareness. New representations are constructed by combining older ones and all learning is an elaboration of prior learning. However, for the first few months of life many experiences are entirely new. For the newborn there are few if any representations for inputs to match. To compensate for his lack of knowledge, the infant is born with some abilities that make it possible to begin to learn without knowledge of the world. To begin with, the infant has innate emotional responses that allow him to communicate with his caregiver from birth. At birth the most useful of the small set of voluntary actions he can perform are emotional responses, like crying. He also has a set of feature analyzers that construct representations of visual and auditory inputs that may innately elicit or become associated with emotional responses. His attention system directs him to novel objects in the short-term and familiar objects in the long-term. These tendencies and abilities are sufficient for learning to begin. During the first six months the infant learns to recognize basic inputs that organize daily life, such as his caregiver and home. Through practice, he develops, through procedural learning, the basic attention and motor skills that make declarative learning effective and useful by giving him the power to direct his attention to the important inputs that his caregiver provides. The infant also has the ability to make speech sounds and to hear the sounds that he makes. This provides him with a model for decoding the speech sounds of his caretakers, which is well underway by five or six months of age. More generally, he has the ability to observe and remember the consequences of his own actions and the ability to imitate the actions of others. Consequently, and infant learns both incidentally as a result of his interactions with the world and intentionally as he tries to learn specific skills, e.g., crawling, walking, talking.

From about six to twelve months of age representations of individual experiences accumulate to the point where **referential communication** with his caregiver becomes possible and language learning begins. That is, the caregiver does not call attention to herself or the infant but directs attention to a third object by pointing or saying its name. Over the next two years the infant is actively learning language. Concurrently, the newly mobile toddler is engaged in the exploration of his world. The repetitive use of language and routine of daily life greatly increase the number and strength of associations between representations into a semantic network. Around three years of age learning assumes a mature form in which learning is the incremental elaboration of a semantic network derived from experience.

INFANT EMOTIONAL DEVELOPMENT

In the course of evolution emotion came to have more than just an evaluative function based on perception of the world. Many creatures are social creatures and living together in groups provides advantages in foraging for food and avoiding predators if group members can communicate with each other. Hence, in social creatures the emotional system took on a communicative function in addition to an evaluative one. For example, emotional communication turns the members on the periphery of a herd into scouts for the entire herd. Suppose that when a herd member on the periphery sees something scary, such as a predator, he utters a cry that makes all of the other herd members fearful as well. They would then all move away from the threat together. Emotional communication links the abilities of all the members of the herd in a single perceptual system that collectively benefits them all.

Notice that emotional communication is often cross-modal and so vision and audition had to first come together in the brain as different stimuli for the same emotional response. Once upon a time, some prehistoric social creature evolved the ability to shriek a warning at the sight of a predator, or perhaps to sing a love cry when it desired a mate. Whichever the case, such an emotional signaling system requires that both a visual and auditory input elicit the same emotion. It may be the fear elicited by both the sight of the predator and the sound of the warning shriek. Or it may be the sexual attraction elicited by first the sound of a potential mate and then further by his or her appearance.

As more complex social organizations developed among animals more sophisticated emotions evolved to regulate these organizations. MacLean (1993) suggested that a critical step was taken in the evolution of emotion when animals began to care for their children for an extended period of time, since a special attachment-dependency emotional system evolved to regulate the interactions between parents and children. According to MacLean, human emotional development begins with the attachment-dependency relationship between a mother and her infant that characterizes all mammals. This relationship exists because of the utterly helpless state of the infant and her complete dependence on the mother. In order for emotions to serve their social function, they must be expressed as well as felt. Within seconds of birth the human baby makes its first emotional communication—a cry. In the early months of life innately specified vocal and visible expressions of emotion enable infants and parents to communicate.

When adults speak to infants their voices always have vocal expression of emotion. This is in contrast to speech to other adults, in which the emotion is usually filtered out (Trainor, Austin, & Desjardins, 2000). Cohn and Tronick (1983) found that when mothers address their three-month old infants with normal emotion the infants are likely to cycle between play, positive expressions, and monitoring. But when the mothers were instructed to address their infants with flat affect the positive expressions decreased and the infants showed more wary expressions and made more protests. Fernald (1993) found that from the age of five months infants can discriminate affective messages indicating approval or prohibition, either in their parents' language, or in a language that their parents do not speak. Infants showed more positive affect to approvals and more negative affect to prohibitions. Also, by two or three months infants appear to smile to express happiness and to make distressed expressions in appropriate circumstances. Lewis, Alessandri, and Sullivan (1990) placed infants two, four, six and eight months old in an infant seat and attached a string to their arms. Pulling the string turned on music for a brief period of time. The infants quickly learned to pull the string to make the music and smiled when the music came on. But when the apparatus was disconnected so that pulling the string no longer initiated the music, the infants made sounds of distress.

By seven months babies can match facial and vocal expressions. Walker-Andrews (1986) showed them filmed expressions of happiness and anger along with adult voices expressing the same or a different emotion. The babies spent longer looking at the film clips of visual expressions that matched the sounds than at expressions that did not match. However, the facial expression of fear, surprise, and anger are not well differentiated as late at eight to twelve months of age (Hiatt, Campos, & Emde, 1979; Lewis, et al., 1990). So all that we can say is that throughout the first year of life infants express, recognize, and undoubtedly feel both happiness and distress in appropriate situations.

Even if it is restricted to happiness and distress, emotion plays an important role in the early learning of the infant. The initial learning episodes of the infant are not the result of instruction but of play. The infant derives pleasure from making things happen and in the process encodes visual and auditory representations that form the basis for all subsequent learning.

INFANT ATTENTION

Recall from Chapter 4 that, depending on the context, an individual's attention may be attracted to either a novel object or a familiar one. Both of these tendencies are already apparent in the infant and both of them facilitate learning.

There is not much that a young infant can do, but one thing she can do is look. As mentioned in Chapter 4, one technique of assessing an infant's attention is to show her a pair of pictures or objects, one familiar and one novel, and record which she looks at longer (Fantz, 1956). Which one the infant looks at depends on how familiar the familiar item is, which in turn depends on how much time she has had to see it previously. Typically, immediately after a short study trial, the infant looks more at the familiar item whereas after a long study trial she looks longer at the novel one (Bahrick & Pickens, 1995). The number of seconds of study time required to produce a novelty preference decreases with age (Rose, Gottfried, Melloy-Carminar & Bridger, 1982). One way of explaining this pattern is that if the study time has been short, then infant has not finished examining and so continues to look at the study item when a novel item is placed next to it. But if the study time has been sufficient to examine the study item and encode a presentation of it then the perceptual system picks out the novel item and that is now the one the infant examines. However, as the retention interval between study and test is increased, the infant's preference for the novel over the familiar item disappears and then reverses. Over retention intervals of one day to two weeks, looking time is divided equally between items moving in a familiar and a novel pattern ((Bahrick & Pickens, 1995) and listening time is divided equally between familiar and novel nursery rhymes (Spence, 1996). At a retention interval of 3 months the infant looks longer at the familiar items in the familiar motion. The change in the distribution of looking times has been explained by assuming that the infant will examine a picture for which there is an initial feeling of familiarity until a complete representation of the picture has been retrieved from memory. Immediately after study retrieval is immediate and so the infant spends most of her time examining the novel picture. A few days later more time is required to retrieve the representation of the familiar representation, which reduces the time for looking at the novel picture, so looking times are equal. At 3 months it takes so long to retrieve the representation of the familiar picture that more time is spent looking at it than the novel picture (Bauer, 2002).

INFANT OPERANT LEARNING

By two months of age an infant enjoys making things happen, such as pulling a string to make music (Lewis, 1990). Furthermore, the infant remembers the consequences of her actions. Learning to do something purposeful is a form of declarative learning called **operant learning**. Rather than make it possible for an infant to hear music by pulling on a string with her arm, the more usual procedure for studying operant learning is to attach the leg of an infant to a mobile hanging above her crib (Rovee & Rovee, 1969). Within a few minutes she learns that she can make the mobile move by kicking her foot. As was mentioned above, infants love to do this. Rovee-Collier tested the infant's memory by taking the mobile away and bringing it back at a later time. If the infant began to kick when she merely saw the mobile again then the kicking demonstrated that she had remembered it. Figure 6.3 shows how infant memory was measured. Baseline is a measure of how often the infant kicked to the mobile before she had ever been connected to it. During acquisition, her foot was tied to the mobile by a ribbon so she moved it when she kicked. During the immediate and (delayed) tests, the ribbon was no longer tied to the mobile. If the infant kicked more often during test than during baseline it demonstrated that the infant remembered moving the mobile during acquisition and was still trying to do so. Furthermore, if the infant kicked as often during the delayed test as the immediate test it suggested that no forgetting had occurred during the retention interval.

An infant who has learned that she can move a specific mobile will only kick when she sees that mobile. So the amount of detail in the infant's memory of the training mobile can be determined by showing the infant a very similar novel mobile that differs in some specific detail from the training mobile. If the infant does not kick to the novel mobile then we can conclude that the infant's representation of the training mobile contains the detail that discriminates between the training and novel mobiles. Rovee-Collier examined the specificity of infant memory by varying the details of painted-block mobiles. She found that an infant has a very specific and detailed memory of the characters painted on the blocks hanging from

FIGURE 6.3

General design of mobile reinforcement paradigm (Rovee & Rovee, 1969).

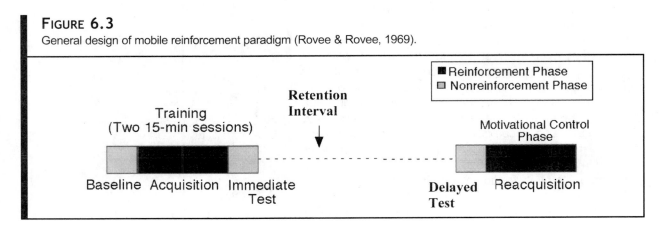

the mobile's arms. At 2-6 months of age, infants did not respond 24 hours later to a test mobile even slightly different from the training mobile (Hartshorn, Wilk, Muller, & Rovee-Collier, 1998). Both two- and three-month-olds did not kick to a 5-block mobile when more than a single block on it was different from the training mobile (Fagen, Rovee, & Kaplan, 1976; Hayne, Greco, Earley, Griesler, & Rovee-Collier, 1986). They could even detect a mobile that differed by only a single block when it was sufficiently different in color to pop out from the others (Gerhardstein, Renner, & Rovee-Collier, 1999).

In other experiments all of the blocks on the novel mobile were painted differently than the test mobile, but the difference was quite small. Infants did not kick to a test mobile with characters just 25% different in size then on the blocks of the training mobile. Three- month-old infants did kick to 7-block test mobile with T's or pluses (+) on all the blocks when the training mobile had L's (Adler & Rovee-Collier, 1994; Bhatt, Rovee-Collier, & Weiner, 1994). Finally, when three-month-old infants were trained with mobiles that had red A's painted on yellow blocks, they did not kick to a mobile that had red 2's painted on yellow blocks, or a mobile with black A's painted on yellow blocks, or a mobile that had red A's painted on green blocks. So both the size and specific visual features of the blocks are part of the training mobile's representation. Moreover, when trained with a mobile with red A's painted on yellow blocks they did not even kick to a test mobile that had yellow A's painted on red blocks (Bhatt & Rovee-Collier, 1994).

The ability to discriminate a similar novel mobile from the training mobile demonstrates that even in the first months of life infants encode detailed visual representations. The ability to encode such detailed visual representations is obviously of great value in learning about the world. The infant can encode a detailed enough representation to recognize her own caregiver, and to represent objects in the world to which the caregiver refers.

Furthermore, at three months of age the memory is highly context-dependent. The infant would not kick to the training mobile at test if the liner of his crib was different from the training session (Butler & Rovee-Collier, 1989; Rovee-Collier, Griesler, & Earley, 1985), if the mobile was shown in a different room from the training room, or if the infant was in a different crib from the training crib (Hayne, Rovee-Collier, & Borza, 1991). These findings indicate that infants are not only capable of encoding detailed visual representations, but that they also make use of this ability to remember a great many details about their environment.

Context-dependence only occurs when a distinctive context is uniquely associated with a distinctive learning event. When infants were trained on the same mobile in two different contexts they kicked to it in a third context (Amabile & Rovee-Collier, 1991; Rovee-Collier & Dufault, 1991).

Once the child is 6 months old, she can sit up in a high chair. So instead of a mobile, Hartshorn & Rovee-Collier (1997) placed a toy train before the child that she could make move by pressing a lever (Figure 6.4). Bar presses replaced foot kicks as evidence of remembering, but otherwise the task remained the same. By combining the results of the two tasks Rovee-Collier and her colleagues were able to investigate how long a toy was remembered over the first 18 months of life. With the same amount of training older children were able to remember the mobile or train for a longer period of time. At 2 months the memory remained available for one day, but at 18 months it remained available for twelve days (Figure 6.5). Also, recall from Chapter 2 that when learning the perceptual-motor skill of typing distributed training resulted in a longer retention interval than massed training. The same effect is found in infants. Hartshorn, et al. (1998) gave 3-month old infants three training sessions and tested retention 21 days after the final session.

FIGURE 6.4

Operant train task, shown here with 6-month-old. Each lever press moves the toy train for 1-2 seconds during acquisition.

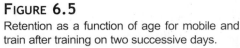

FIGURE 6.5

Retention as a function of age for mobile and train after training on two successive days.

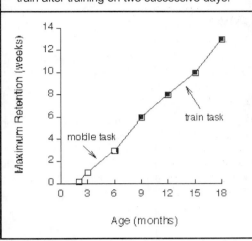

Infants who received training on days 0, 1, and 2 did not recognize the training mobile at test. But infants who received training on days 0, 2, and 8 did recognize the training mobile at test. Only the distributed training produced retention at an interval of 21 days. Of course, there is a limit to how far apart training sessions can be spaced in the distributed condition. When they are spread so far apart that the last session is forgotten before the next one occurs, there is not a cumulative effect of the training session. This was seen for infants who received training on days 0, 4, and 8 did not recognize the training mobile at test. By the time of the second training session on day 4 the training on day 0 was forgotten.

Notice that distributed training was used by Hartshorn et al. (1998) somewhat differently, and more effectively, than by Baddeley and Longman (1978) in their typing study. Baddeley and Longman provided training sessions at equal intervals. In contrast, Hartshorn et al. (1998) provided training sessions at systematically increasing intervals. Each training session more than doubled the retention interval over which the mobile was remembered. This is a very useful property of distributed training. However, it is not known why the retention interval increases in this way.

The mobile and train experimental paradigms demonstrate that for at least the first 6 months of life, learning may be very much learning by doing. An infant's actions have the effect of encoding representations of the target, the response, and its consequence, in long-term memory. Recall from Chapter 4 that Diamond (1995) found that when a six-month-old infant was merely shown a toy, the infant indicated that she remembered the toy (by preferring to look at a new one 70% of the time) up to three minutes later. In contrast, when the six-month-old infant was given the opportunity to play with the toy, she indicated that she remembered it for at least 10 minutes (by preferring to reach for a new one 70% of the time).

EXPLORATION, IMITATION, AND EMOTION

At 6 months an infant can sit up and move around on his own. At this point the infant can explore the world. The infant also begins to learn from other people through observation (Meltzhoff, 1988). For example, if the infant sees someone else playing with a novel toy, taking a mitten off of a puppet and finding a bell, then the infant is likely to repeat the novel action when given the toy. Furthermore, the infant can remember and perform the action even if not given the toy until the next day (Barr, Dowden, & Hayne, 1996). In contrast to the immobile infant who tends to see the same thing in a single context, the toddler can carry the same toy to many contexts. So once the child becomes a toddler his memories are no longer context-dependent. By 18 months, an infant who sees a novel action performed with a rabbit puppet in a day care center will repeat the same action with a mouse puppet at home (Hayne, Boniface, & Barr, 2000).

Once a child begins to move around and do things the effect of distributed practice on learning becomes important because the child will remember an action performed at different times almost indefinitely. When a child repeats an action that she has previously imitated this is called **reenactment**. Hudson and Sheffield (1998) varied the interval between immediate imitation and reenactment to compare the effects of massed with distributed training. Eight boys and 10 girls approximately 18 months of age saw an adult perform eight activities with target objects in a playroom; e.g., find fish food and shake it over a fish tank. One third of the children (0-week group) were given the opportunity to reenact the activities 15 minutes after they had first imitated them. One third of the children (2-week group) were given the opportunity to reenact the activities two weeks later and one third of the children (8-week group) were given the opportunity to reenact the activities 8 weeks later.

All children were brought back to the playroom eight weeks after their reenactment. Upon entering the playroom, children were allowed to play with the toys and props for 8 min. without any instruction. Thereafter, the experimenter used verbal prompts to direct the children to the target activities: "What did we do with the fish? Where do we keep our fish food?" Six months later the children were brought back to the playroom and again both spontaneous and prompted imitation was observed. The results are shown in Figure 6.6. As can be seen from the figure, the 0-week group, which had the massed training, performed more poorly than the other groups and had significant forgetting during the 6-month retention interval between the first and second tests. In contrast, both the 2-week and 8-week distributed-training groups had smaller decreases in spontaneous imitation after the 6-month retention interval than the massed-training group. Furthermore, when imitation was prompted, the 8-week distributed-training had forgotten nothing over the 6-month retention interval.

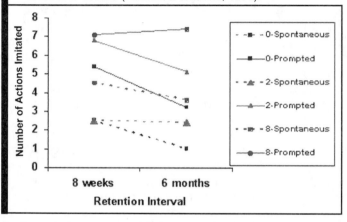

FIGURE 6.6
Eighteen-month-olds imitated actions of an adult with 8 toys in a playroom and then reenacted the actions 15 minutes (0-weeks), 2 weeks, or 8 weeks later. Eight weeks and 6 months later they were tested for spontaneous and prompted recall of te actions (Hudson & Sheffield, 1998).

Also, after 6 months the infant can follow pointing gestures (Butterworth & Itakura, 2000). After 8-10 months an infant has developed fine enough motor control to use the thumb and forefinger in a pincer grip to lift things and begins to point to communicate as well (Franco & Butterworth, 1996). Communication through pointing leads to communication through spoken language. The age of pointing onset predicts both the number of gestures produced and the number of sounds comprehended at 14 months (Butterworth & Morissette, 1996). Pointing eventually gets incorporated in language as **deictic** words like *this* and *that*. Finally, associative learning makes possible the learning of words through sound-image associations. So language learning begins some time after ten months of age and emerges from general communication skills. Nonverbal communication skills at 13 months predict language ability up to 5 years of age (Ulvund & Smith, 1996).

When the child becomes ambulatory, her emotional system develops along with her motor system to keep her safe from harm. What distresses infants changes over the first year of life. Scarr and Salapatek (1970) exposed infants between two months and two years to a variety of things that might distress them, including a jack-in the-box, a moving toy dog, loud noises, a visual cliff, strangers, and someone wearing a mask. They found that the items fell into three categories in regard to the ages at which they distressed children. Few children under seven months showed marked expressions of fear or distress to anything. Their fear of a loud or sudden movement and of unfamiliar toys began around seven months, reached a peak at the end of the first year and then declined in intensity. Fear of the visual cliff also began at seven months and by one year of age all children feared the visual cliff. However, fear of the visual cliff did not then decline with increasing age. Finally, beginning at seven months, the infants showed fear of strangers and masks. Wariness of strangers is associated with distress on separation from the caretaker. Separation distress peaks between 15 and 18 months, then declines, so that by three years of age very distressed reactions to separation are rare. After twelve months children respond to another's distress by comforting, bringing a parent, or offering an object, thus clearly demonstrating that they experience the emotion themselves (Zahn-Waxler, Radke-Yarrow, Wagner, & Chapman, 1992).

Beyond ten months, an infant may look at a parent's face for emotional information before taking action with respect to an ambiguous elicitor (Walden & Ogan, 1988). For instance, Sorce, Emde, Campos, and Klinnert (1985) exposed one-year-old babies to a visual cliff adjusted to a height that did not evoke clear avoidance. Seventy-four per cent of babies crossed when their mother showed a happy expression but none crossed when their mother showed a fearful expression. The residue of the emotional system in adult speech are sarcastic utterances, in which the emotional features of the vocalization are deliberately not filtered out. Sarcastic utterances are possible because the emotional content of voice always dominates word meaning.

SUMMARY OF INFANT LEARNING

- Infant Learning
  - Shortly after birth the infant is already able to make emotional responses, such as cries, and to orient towards emotional targets, such as soothing voices.
  - By three months of age an infant can learn to move a mobile attached by a ribbon to her ankle by kicking her foot.
  - During the first six months
    * the infant learns to recognize basic things that organize daily life, such as his caregiver and home.
    * Through practice, he develops the basic attention and motor skills that make learning possible.
    * The emotional system and attention system together facilitate identification of and communication with the caregiver.
  - After six months the infant is able to
    * sit up, then crawl, and finally walk, enabling the child to explore the world and learn about it.
    * reach for and grasp objects and can learn through imitation of actions she has observed.
  - Some time around ten months she begins to point and understand the function of pointing. Pointing provides an avenue of communication with a caregiver, hence facilitating learning, including language learning.

- Early Memory During the First Months of Life
  - Detailed visual representations are already being encoded.
  - Generalization and category formation already occurs
  - Retention interval is a function of the number and distribution over time of the training/study materials.

LANGUAGE LEARNING

Even before spoken language is learned, infants are already able to communicate through emotional utterances and through pointing. It is within this existing communication system that spoken language is learned. However, as we saw in the last chapter, producing and understanding spoken language requires special brain mechanisms that evolved for that purpose. These play a crucial role in language learning.

When newborn infants are laid down to rest, most of them turn their heads to the right (Turkewitz & Birch, 1971). Furthermore, both infants and adults show more electrical activity in the left hemisphere for some speech inputs but more electrical activity in the right hemisphere for some visual inputs, as measured by EEG recordings (Molfese, Nunez, Seibert, & Rammanaiah, 1976; Wada 1977). So even before language is learned, a specialized speech-processing mechanism begins to develop within the left hemisphere.

The ratio of aphasias caused by left-hemisphere vs. right-hemisphere lesions is almost as large for children as it is for adults (Woods & Teuber, 1978). However, children make much fuller recoveries from aphasia than adults usually do. In fact, in general, children make much better recoveries from brain damage than adults do. When the brain is still young, another section can apparently take over the function of a part that has been lost. Dennis and her colleagues examined the limits of cortical plasticity by comparing the effects of left and right hemidecortication on children (Dennis, 1980; Dennis & Kohn, 1975; Dennis & Whitaker, 1976). In this operation most of the cortex of either the right or left hemisphere is removed. They found that after the removal of either cortex, the children's acquisition of language still approached normal limits. Therefore the right hemisphere does have the capacity to acquire language, if necessary.

THE SOCIAL CONTEXT OF LEARNING TO UNDERSTAND SPEECH

Around 5 or 6 months of age the learning of spoken language begins in the context of nonverbal communication. Furthermore, infants learn to speak by actively engaging in conversation even before they understand what is being said. In many cultures, babies that are still too young to talk are often treated as if they could carry on a conversation. A parent may carry on a "dialog" with an infant in which the adult does all the talking, while treating the baby's burps, yawns, and smiles as "turns" in the conversation (Snow, 1977). By the time the child is a year old, he or she will actually be using one-word utterances in conversational context. When deaf parents have a child who hears normally, they may leave their radio or TV on constantly so that the child will be exposed to speech. However, such children typically know much less language than other children do at the time they enter school, although they will quickly catch up (Sachs & Johnson, 1976). Similarly, a study of Dutch children who watched German television every day found that they knew virtually no German (Snow, Arlman, Rupp, Hassing, Jobse, Joosten, & Vorster, 1976).

Attempts to teach chimpanzees human-like language also make the role of conversation salient. Sue Savage-Rumbaugh and her colleagues (Savage-Rumbaugh, Shanker, & Taylor, 1998) have devoted many years to the study of the communication skills of chimpanzees. Since chimpanzees do not have the vocal skills of humans they are taught to place colored shapes on a magnetic board to form meaningful expressions. In the 1980s they began to teach pygmy chimpanzees for the first time. Pygmy chimpanzees are human-like in their use of eye contact and their willingness to temporarily give up the care of infants to friends and relatives. So when Metata give birth to her son Kanzi, she willingly handed him over to a graduate student to play with in her presence during her lessons. The graduate student responded to Kanzi as to a human infant. Of course, as it turned out, the prodigy who best mastered the shape board was the ever-curious little boy Kanzi, who was exposed to it from birth. Kanzi became the first nonhuman to use the shape board to spontaneously communicate requests to his human friends, rather than merely responding to commands with nonverbal actions. Together, the negative example of the Dutch children watching television and the positive example of Kanzi demonstrate that language learning requires a social interaction in which the language is being used purposefully by both the caregiver and infant.

MAKING SENSE OF ADULT SPEECH

Recall from Chapter 5 that fluent speech does not contain clear word boundaries. Normal speech is a jumble of sounds that must be decoded on the basis of knowledge of the language being spoken. But the infant has no such knowledge. So the infant's first task is to learn to segment speech input into individual words.

A convenient methodology for studying what infants hear is the head turn preference task. The researcher turns on a light that is located to the side of the infant. The infant's attention is attracted by the light and when he turns his head toward it a speech passage begins to play from that direction. The infant's interest is measured by how long it is before the infant turns away for at least two seconds. It turns out that infants will listen longer to a familiar passage than to an unfamiliar one. Therefore, to determine whether an infant can hear the word *dog* it is played over and over in the study phase of the experiment. Then, in the test phase, if the infant spends more time listening to a passage that contains repetitions of the word dog than a passage that does not, it implies that the infant recognized the word, which implies that he could hear it in the first place. The late Peter Jusczyk and his colleagues used this method extensively to study how infants come to segment speech into words.

Several cues together make it possible for infants to learn to pick out individual words from speech. The stress pattern is an important segmentation cue. In English, stress is almost always put on the first syllable. By 5-months of age, infants can discriminate between their own language and one that has a different stress pattern (Nazzi, Jusczyk, & Johnson, 2000). Other segmentation cues are very high frequency words (e.g., *a*, *the*). Frequent, distributed repetition is an important determinant of learning. By 6 months of age some infants may know isolated words. Tincoff and Juscyk (1999) showed 24 6-month-old infants side-by-side videos of their parents while listening to the words "mommy" and "daddy." The infants looked significantly more at the video of the named parent. Infants shown videos of unfamiliar parents did not adjust their looking patterns in response to "mommy and "daddy." By 8 months infants can detect frequently repeated words (Saffran, 2001; Saffran, Alsin, & Neewport, 1996) and words segmented by stress (Johnson & Jusczyk, 2001) within the speech stream. By ten and a half months they are segmenting these words correctly when they are heard in fluent speech (Jusczyk, Houston, & Newsome, 1999).

Since the task of segmenting the speech input requires the infant to discriminate different sounds that occur in rapid succession, those infants who are better at rapid auditory discrimination have an advantage in learning spoken language. Benasich and Tallal (2002) tested 7.5-month-old infants on their ability to determine whether two tones were the same or different. The interval between the tones was reduced from 500 milliseconds down to 8 milliseconds to find the minimal interval at which the infant could discriminate them. Those infants that could discriminate the tones at the shortest intervals were the most advanced in language learning at three years of age.

Infants are aided in the speech segmentation task by how they are spoken to. Speakers addressing young children go to great lengths to get the child to attend to what is being said. They use the child's name frequently, particularly at the beginning of an utterance (Shatz & Gelman, 1973). Adults also tend to speak to a young child in particularly high-pitched voices, and they frequently touch the child as they start to talk. These attention-grabbing devices are clearly important, since the child is unlikely to learn the language unless actively processing the speech that is heard. People also simplify their speech when addressing children (Broen, 1972; Phillips, 1973; Sachs, Brown, & Salerno, 1976). They speak more slowly and distinctly, with extra pauses. They use short sentences, with few complex syntactic constructions. Sentence frames like "Look at," "That's a _," and "Here comes _," are repeated over and over. In addition, adults tend to repeat themselves when giving instructions to children, as in the following example (Snow, 1972, p. 563):

Pick up the red one. Find the red one. Not the green one. I want the red one. Can you find the red one?

The net effect of these various modifications is to greatly increase the number of short repeated patterns that are detected at the feature analysis stage and so are perceived as separate word phrases in working memory. This increases the comprehensibility of speech. A psychologist who knew French only imperfectly described this effect from experience (Taylor 1976, p. 231):

I observed a French woman talking to a 10-month-old baby. She would say slowly and clearly, "red," "yellow," "orange," or "look, this one has a hole," holding appropriately colored and shaped toy objects. Furthermore, she repeated the whole sequence two or three times. I could understand everything she said in French to the baby, but could catch only odd words or messages when she was talking to the baby's mother in rapid, normal French.

The effect of adult modifications is to create a distinct representation of a word in working memory that the infant can use as a model for saying the word. At five months of age a cooing baby makes the simplest sounds of all languages. Babies universally begin to babble at about the age of six months. At this point the babbling only consists of the sounds of the language that the baby hears (Jakobson, 1968; Slobin, 1973). First the child produces vowel sounds, like /ah/, and then consonant-vowel combinations.

The first consonant sounds are also highly regular. They are typically sounds like /m/, /b/, and /p/, which are produced by modulating the air at the lips. In fact, in many unrelated languages the first words used as names for the parents sound something like the English *mama* and *papa,* which are easily pronounced by children. Both of these English words illustrate another universal tendency of children—to produce reduplications of consonant-vowel combinations. It is no accident that the words parents are so anxious to hear are designed to be exactly what the infant is naturally most likely to produce.

By saying the word to himself the infant reactivates its representation in working memory and creates permanent representation of it. Alan Baddeley (Baddeley, 1986) called this sequence of events the **phonological loop**. The phonological loop makes it possible to retain unfamiliar sound patterns while more permanent records are being constructed (Baddeley & Gathercole, 1998). Susan Gathercole and Baddeley (Gathercole & Baddeley, 1989) found that the task of repeating a list of nonwords was a good measure of a child's ability to execute her phonological loop. Using this task, they found that up until age 5, the phonological loop plays a crucial role in learning new words. Nonword repetition ability at age 4 predicts vocabulary size at age 5 (Gathercole, 1995). Four-year-old children with better nonword repetition skills also come to have a wider vocabulary, longer average utterances, and more syntactic constructions, than children with poorer nonword repetition skills (Adams & Gathercole, 2000). Subsequently, vocabulary knowledge becomes the major pacemaker in language development and the influence of phonological memory on vocabulary subsides to a nonsignificant level (Gathercole, Willis, Emslie, & Baddeley, 1992).

LEARNING MEANING AND BUILDING VOCABULARY

By six months of age an infant is organizing instances into categories on the basis of their appearance and function. Since the same perceptual features that make instances appear similar to the infants also make them appear similar to their caregivers, a basic level of representation is established through vision that facilitates the naming process in language learning. When a mother says, "See the doggie," she knows that her child will generalize "doggie" to about the same set of furry animals (and possibly toys) that she would. Once the infant gets the idea that things have names, and more generally, that words have meaning, several different systems contribute to her ability to associate words with their meanings. Perceptual, social, and emotional cues all guide the infant to the speaker's intent.

A child's earliest use of language, when his expressive vocabulary is less than ten words, involves a variety of desires, concerns, and comments. These may include sound effects for animals and vehicles, social routines like bye, I, and uh-oh, and names for favorite people (Caselli, Casadio, & Bates, 1999). From the very beginning the child is trying to communicate. However, the child's utterances are limited. A one- or two-word utterance can have many interpretations, so the speaker must rely on the context in which it is uttered, and perhaps on accompanying gestures and inflections, to fill in its meaning and disambiguate it.

Figure 6.7 shows the growth of vocabulary between eight months and sixteen months of year for English-learning infants in the United States and Italian-learning infants in Italy (Caselli, Bates, Casadio, Fenson, Fenson, Sanderl, & Weir, 1993). Vocabulary was measured by having parents fill out a questionnaire on the words that their infant understood and produced. Notice from the figure that early in life comprehension is way ahead of production. Table 6.1 shows the 40 words most frequently understood in this age group for

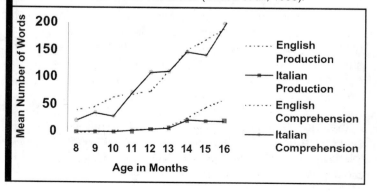

FIGURE 6.7

Growth in productive vs. receptive vocabulary for English and Italian infants between 8 and 16 months (Caselli et al., 1993).

American babies. As can be seen from the table, nouns predominate among the earliest understood words.

Perceptual, social, and emotional cues all continue to guide the infant to the speaker's intent. Recall that the perceptual system directs attention to novel inputs. So an infant will tend to focus on a novel object in her environment. Furthermore, speakers tend to name novel objects when interacting with infants. So when the infant hears the novel name she is likely to already be focusing on the novel object and thus likely to associate them. So the infant will associate a new word with a novel object in a familiar environment. Akhtar, Carpenter, and Tomasello, (1996) had 24-month-olds play with three nameless objects that were later placed in a clear box along with a novel nameless object. When an adult displayed excitement about the contents of the box and said a new word, the children selected the novel object as the referent of the word. However, it is not merely a matter of the infant hearing a new word while looking at a novel object. Recall that the infant is already practiced at communicating nonverbally with the speaker. In a study of social cues (Baldwin, Markman, Bill, Desjardins, & Irwin, 1997) infants 15-20 months of age heard novel labels when they were investigating a single novel object. In one case the label was uttered by a speaker seated within the infant's view and displaying concurrent attention to the novel toy whereas in the other case the speaker was seated out of the infant's view. Only after the former condition, in which they infant was engaged in an episode of shared attention with the adult, did the infant subsequently select the toy in response to the label. Finally, infants can combine social and emotional cues to associate words and objects that are not present together. Sixteen-month-old infants heard a speaker announce her intention to find an unknown object by using a new word. After rejecting one object with obvious disappointment she then gleefully picked up the target object. The infants selected the target object as the referent of the new word heard earlier (Tomasello, Strossberg, & Akhtar, 1996). By 2 years of age, toddlers can combine social and emotional cues to learn words by overhearing others (Akhtar, Jipson, & Callanan, 2001).

Figure 6.8 shows the growth of vocabulary between one and a half and two and a half years of age for English-learning infants in the United States and Italian-learning infants in Italy (Caselli, et al., 1999). The initial set of words an infant understands contains a high proportion of nouns. However, infants in direct cultures, speaking different languages, tend to produce different kinds of words. Korean (Gopnik & Choi, 1990) and Chinese (Tardiff, 1996) infants tend to produce more verbs than American infants do. The details of child rear-

TABLE 6.1

Most frequent words in Comprehension of English for Infants 8 months to 16 months of age (rank order in production list in parentheses).

Rank	Word	% sample
1.	mommy (2)	95.0
2.	daddy (1)	93.5
3.	bye (3)	88.6
4.	no (9)	86.3
5.	peekaboo	84.3
6.	bath (40)	76.2
7.	ball (7)	75.0
8.	bottle (10)	75.0
9.	hi (4)	74.0
10.	allgone	71.9
11.	dog (8)	70.8
12.	book (17)	68.7
13.	night-night (22)	68.5
14.	diaper	67.4
15.	kiss	66.2
16.	uh-oh (5)	65.1
17.	pattycake	62.6
18.	juice (28)	61.9
19.	shoe (24)	61.9
20.	baby (12)	61.6
21.	grandma (30)	61.3
22.	outside	61.0
23.	car (44)	60.1
24.	eat	59.7
25.	kitty (15)	58.8
26.	drink	58.1
27.	keys (41)	56.3
28.	don't	55.8
29.	comb	55.4
30.	nose (35)	55.4
31.	hug	54.9
32.	banana (26)	54.4
33.	cookie (34)	54.2
34.	bathtub	53.2
35.	balloon (20)	52.9
36.	milk	52.9
37.	cat (21)	52.7
38.	cracker (37)	52.7
39.	telephone	52.6
40.	yes (45)	52.6

ing practices that produce these differences are not understood. As the infant's vocabulary grows, the length and grammatical complexity of her utterances increase as well. Some of the kinds of advances in grammatical complexity likely to occur during this period of life are shown in Table 6.2, which shows the simpler and more complex forms of utterances expressing the same grammatical function. Table 6.3 contains some two-word utterances of children a few months older than one year. Figure 6.9 shows grammatical complexity as a function of vocabulary size for English and Italian-speaking infants whose data were also shown in Figure 6.8. Grammatical complexity was measured using a standardized scale in which the mother indicates whether her child is likely to produce the simpler or more complex grammatical construction for pairs including those shown in Table 6.2. Vocabulary size, length of utterance, and grammatical complexity, are all closely connected because grammatical patterns cannot be learned until a sufficient number of words have been learned to notice them.

Children may use correctly whole words and even whole phrases that they hear frequently, including such high-frequency irregular verbs as *came*, *broke*, and *did*. High frequency inflections are detected and encoded. Newport, Gleitman, and Gleitman (1977) found that growth in the child's use of noun inflections (e.g., the plural marker *s*) was positively related to the frequency of deictic utterances in maternal speech; e.g., *That's a truck*. Furthermore, there is cross priming between related words and phrases (e.g., *boys* and *girls*, *talked* and *walked*. So the child generalizes inflections across similar words (Maratsos & Chalkley, 1980). One consequence of this awareness is the phenomenon of overregularization. A child will sometimes regularize an irregular verb. So words like *camed*, *comed*, *goed*, *broked* and *breaked*, are all sometimes produced (Marcus, Pinker, Ullman, Hollander, Rosen, & Xu, 1992).

FIGURE 6.8

Vocabulary size as a function of age in English and Italian children between one and a half and two and a half years of age (Caselli, et al., 1999).

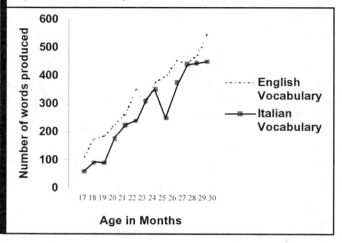

TABLE 6.2

Sample Items from grammatical complexity checklist

Simple	Complex
1. Two shoe	Two shoes
2. Daddy car	Daddy's car
3. I make tower	I making tower
4. Kitty go away	Kitty went away
5. You fix it?	Can you fix it?
6. Where mommy go?	Where did mommy go?
7. Don't read book	Don't want you read that book
8. I want that	I want that one you got
9. We made this	Me and Paul made this

Studies of slightly older children confirm the bias to associate new words with novel objects. Markman and Wachtel (1988) showed 3-year-olds a familiar object (e.g., a cup) and an object that the children did not have a name for (e.g., tongs). The experimenter than asked the children: "Show me a dax." Children chose the object without a name (e.g., the tongs) approximately 80% of the time.

As their knowledge of vocabulary and grammar increases children are increasingly able to use this knowledge to identify the meaning of a new word. Hall, Lee, and Belanger (2001) showed that by two years of age a toddler could recognize a novel word as a proper name by its grammatical context and use it to select the appropriate novel object. The children learned a novel label for a doll or stuffed animal (*This is Zav* or *This is a zav*). The object was then moved to a new location in front of the child and an identical object was placed nearby. The children's task was to choose which of the two identical object's was the zav. The children who heard the proper-name version were significantly more likely to select the named object than the children who heard the count-noun version of the utterance (see also, Jaswal & Markman, 2001).

After the first few hundred, most words are learned the first time they are heard and there is explosive growth in vocabulary. By the time a student enters college he has learned 6-10 words a day between the ages of 5 and 18 and knows about 50,000 words.

FROM WORDS TO SENTENCES

One type of utterance that emerges after three years of age, which is critical for further syntactic development, is the type that describes one thing (the agent) performing some action that affects some other thing (the object). Some examples of agent-action-object utterances are: *The sun melts the ice* and *Laurie broke the doll.* The word order of agent-action-object utterances becomes the model for utterances in general. In some languages word order is more variable than in others, but every language has at least a preferred order for the two nouns and a verb in the basic agent-action-object relationship. The orderings known to exist in different human languages are agent-object-action, agent-action-object, and action-agent-object (Greenberg, 1963; Pullum, 1977). The acquisition of the dominant word order of the language is a gradual process involving generalization from examples. To study this process, Nameera Akhtar (1999) taught English-learning children in three age groups, 2-, 3- and 4-year olds, one novel verb in each of three sentence positions: SVO, SOV, and VSO. The younger children were equally likely to produce the learned non-SVO order as to change it to SVO when they used the verb in speech, whereas the 4-year olds consistently corrected to the SVO order.

TABLE 6.3
Functions of two-word utterances in child speech

Function	Examples
Locate, name	There book That car See doggie
Demand, desire	More milk Give candy Want gum
Negate	No wet No wash Not hungry
Describe	Bambi go Mail come Hit ball
Possession	My shoe Mama dress
Modify	Pretty dress Big boat
Question	Where ball

Source: From Slobin (1979).

FIGURE 6.9
Grammatical complexity as a function of vocabulary size (Caselli, et al., 1999).

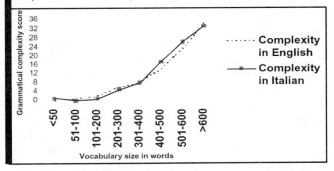

CATEGORIZATION

Infants begin with quite specific and detailed representations but then rapidly begin to generalize. As we have seen, an infant who has been able to move a mobile by kicking will initially only try to move exactly the same mobile in exactly the same location. But given the opportunity to learn that he can move the same mobile in a different location and even different mobiles in different locations, the infant will begin to do so. The infant has not only encoded the representations of one or two specific mobiles but has organized them into a functional category: that of movable mobiles. As they begin to move about it becomes possible to form functional categories such as food. Infants also are born with direct knowledge of social kinship categories like caregiver or mother.

FIGURE 6.10
Examples of test pictures used by Gelman and Markman (1986).

Finally, language provides a powerful tool for forming new categories through verbal labeling. All that is needed to create the category *bird* is to label some instances, e.g., a robin, canary, and pigeon, as birds and then leave it to the listener to infer the common properties of category members from these instances. Categorization provides a powerful learning tool because if you hear that a grackle is a bird then you already know that it has feathers, a beak and lays eggs without ever seeing one. Gelman and Markman (1986) demonstrated that children as young as four years old make some use of language to direct their inference processes. Children were presented with 20 triads of pictures such as the triad shown in Figure 6.10. For this example the experimenter first told the child, "This bird gives its baby mashed-up food" (pointing at the flamingo), and "This bat gives its baby milk" (pointing at the bat). Then the child was asked, "Does this bird (indicating the blackbird) give its baby mashed-up food or milk?"

Even though the critical instance was always more similar visually to the out-of-category instance (the bat), on about 68 percent of test trials the children selected the answer corresponding to the instance of the same category (i.e., they claimed that the new bird would feed its babies mashed-up food). In contrast, control subjects who were asked the question without seeing any prior instances responded at the chance level, with about 50 percent selecting each of the two possible alternatives. Thus even four-year-olds may know that instances of the same categories are likely to share properties that are not readily observable (see also, Gelman & Markman, 1987). (With the same triads but more difficult questions, adults picked the same-category instance over the visually similar instance 86 per cent of the time. So some people never totally rely on category labels to the exclusion of all other information.)

Frank Keil (1979) showed how young children organized concepts into categories, beginning with preschoolers as young as three years old and extending to children in kindergarten and second, fourth and sixth grade. He asked whether sentences such as *The rabbit is sorry* and *The chair is awake* were "okay" or "silly." He used predicates that could be combined with different kinds of category concepts to examine the child's understanding of the meaning of each word. For example, if a child agreed that either *A chair is heavy* or *A chair is light* were "okay," then Keil concluded that the child thought a chair was a physical object. Conversely, if the child thought that *A chair is alive* and *A chair is dead* were both silly, Keil concluded that the child realized that a chair was not a living thing.

Keil tested each child with a variety of nouns and predicates. The youngest children with the most primitive semantic development responded as if all concepts represented physical objects. For example, even if they used the word *idea*, they thought that an idea could be tall and heavy. The children distinguished between only two types of concepts: living (e.g., girl, rabbit) and nonliving (e.g., chair, water, recess, fight, idea). A comparison of the responses of younger and older children revealed the following sequences of steps in conceptual development:

1. Living and nonliving
2. Artifacts (chair) and other nonliving physical objects (water, thunderstorm, fight, love).
3. Events (thunderstorm, fight, love) and physical objects (water).
4. Intentional events (fight, love) and other events (thunderstorm).
5. Abstract concepts (love) and events (fight).

With language it becomes easier to classify instances on the basis of the functions they have or the roles they serve by simply giving them the same name. For example, a tool specifically designed for pounding objects is called a hammer. Objects that satisfy this definition may differ widely in appearance (e.g., from claw hammers to jackhammers). However, even when a category is functionally defined, typical category members often have a characteristic appearance. Most people would probably agree that a claw hammer is a more typical hammer than a jackhammer. But as functional categories become broader (e.g., tool, vehicle, toy), there may no longer be a set of features that define the entire category. The philosopher Ludwig Wittgenstein (1953) demonstrated this point by raising a deceptively simple question: "What is the definition of game?" This question is difficult to answer. Is there really anything in common across such diverse games as professional football, amateur golf, Monopoly, tag, chess, and solitaire? Wittgenstein proposed that the instances of the category *game* are tied together by a principle of family resemblance. Members of a family often look alike in various ways. For example, Susan may look a bit like her brother Jeff and may also look a bit like her cousin Mary. But Jeff and Mary may not really look alike at all. What makes a family resemblance is successive overlap in the features of instances; e.g., Jeff looks like Susan, and Susan looks like Mary, etc. So it seems to be with games. Professional sports resemble amateur sports; team sports resemble team bridge; bridge resembles solitaire. The features of games overlap, even though no feature is necessarily common to all games. If we let letters represent properties, then the following four concepts illustrate a simple family resemblance structure: AB, BC, CD, DA. Other broad functional categories besides game, such as tool and toy, may also be described by the family resemblance principle.

READING

Reading is initially learned through letter-sound conversion, which makes English particularly difficult, but then, as described in Chapter 5, the direct vision-to-meaning route is added. The results of most experiments (e.g., Kleiman, 1975; Levy, 1978) suggest that most of the time the visual representations of words access their meanings directly. Even children in the first grade, just learning to read, do not appear to rely on auditory recoding of print to determine meaning (Barron & Baron, 1977). Only when material is difficult is evidence of auditory recoding obtained (Hardyck & Petrinovich, 1970).

People can read much faster than they can speak, 300 versus 120 words a minute. Also, since writing can be crafted over an extended period of time but speech is spontaneous, writing can contain a much more complicated pattern of phrases than is ordinarily heard in speech. Finally, people must read a great deal to make their way first in school and then in the world. So much knowledge comes through reading. Literacy has a large effect on vocabulary growth, the development of grammar, and general cognitive functioning. Even small differences among individuals in the ability to learn language are revealed and enhanced by the vast amount of language processing that literacy ordinarily entails. These differences were first noticed in regards to the ability to learn to read. Difficulty in learning how to read is called **dyslexia**. Most children who read more poorly than their peers have a more general problem with language processing that is exaggerated by the demands of literacy (Benson, 1975; Mattis, French, & Rapin, 1975; Rourke, 1978; Rutter, 1978; Vellutino, 1979). This more general disorder, which is the most common cause of dyslexia, is called **specific language impairment (SLI)**. SLI is a hereditary (Bishop, North, & Donlan, 1995), lifelong (Scarborough, 1984) disorder.

AUTISM

One of life's continuing tragedies demonstrates the contributions of emotion and attention to early learning and language development. Some infants are born without normal emotions or attention abilities, or lose them after a year of life. The disorder these infants suffer from is called **autism**. Autism is associated with severely impaired language learning and profound cognitive deficits.

General description. Early infantile autism was first identified as a distinct diagnostic entity by Kanner (1943). The distinct behavioral characteristics emerge in infancy and include an inability to develop normal relations with people and situations in life, a delay in speech acquisition, the non-communicative nature of speech if it develops, pronominal reversal, repetitive and stereotyped play activities, a compulsive demand for the maintenance of sameness in the environment, a lack of imagination but a good rote memory, and a normal physical appearance (Dawson, Webb, Schellenberg, Dager, Friedman, Aylward, & Richards, 2002; Schreibman, 1988; Sigman & Capps, 1997). Manifestations of the disorder range from subtle to marked to severe (Meyer & Minshew, 2002).

Arousal. Children with autism appear to suffer from wild fluctuations in arousal that make it impossible for them to selectively attend to informative events in a routine manner. This is evident by under- or over-reaction to various inputs, or even to the same inputs on different occasions (Mundy & Sigman, 1989;

Schreibman, 1988). For example, a child who fails to respond to his or her name or to loud noises may cover his or her ears and scream at the sound of a turning newspaper page or come running at the sound of a soda pop can being opened. This variability of responsiveness has led some researchers to refer to this pattern of responding as "apparent sensory deficit" to convey the idea that the deficit is apparent in behavior but not associated with known deficits at the receptor level (Mundy & Sigman, 1989; Ozonoff, Pennington, & Rogers, 1991; Schreibman, 1988).

Recall that the there is a bias in the normal perceptual system to direct an observer's attention to a novel input, and that this is an important element in early learning. However, possibly because large swings in arousal level make it unpleasant, autistic children shun novelty. They are very sensitive to specific arrangements and to order and may become very upset when the environment is altered. As young children they display limited and rigid play patterns that lack the variety and imagination displayed by normal children. For example, autistic children may play with blocks or toy cars only to the extent of lining them up in neat rows, perhaps by color and size, and become distressed if their orderly arrangement is disturbed. Even the smallest change in the environment or daily routine will be noticed and lead to a tantrum and or attempts to return the situation to its former state (Schreibman, 1988).

Further evidence of an abnormal arousal level comes from the tendency for autistic children to engage in repetitive and even self-injurious behavior that seems to have no other reason than self-stimulation. This behavior is often viewed as a defining characteristic of autism and was noted by Kanner (1943) in his original description of the disorder. The behavior has been variously labeled self-stimulation, stereotypic behavior, or disturbances in motility. At the gross motor level, typical behaviors include rhythmic body rocking, jumping, darting, or pacing, head bobbing, arm or hand flapping, or posturing (Klin, Jones, Schultz, Volkmar, & Cohen, 2002; Schreibman, 1988). At a more subtle level, the behavior may include gazing at lights, staring out of the corner of the eye, moving or rolling the eyes, tensing muscles, finger wiggling, waiving fingers in front of the face, hair twirling, grimacing, and repeatedly uttering a phrase in a stereotypic, non-communicative manner. While much of this behavior provides kinesthetic feedback (i.e., rocking, jumping, flapping), a good deal involves visual and auditory feedback (i.e., gazing at flickering lights, repetitive vocal patterns, tapping objects, or straining to hear particular noises) (Schreibman, 1988). At the most extreme level stereotypic behavior includes such self-injurious behavior as head banging and self-biting of hands or wrists. Other common self injurious behaviors are elbow or leg banging, hair pulling or rubbing, face scratching, and self-slapping of face or sides (Siegel, 1996). Self-injury can vary in intensity and the amount of damage incurred can range from slight to extremely severe.

Emotional and social deficits. Recall that MacLean (1993) suggested that human emotional development begins with the attachment-dependency relationship between a mother and her infant that characterizes all mammals. Severely autistic children completely lack the emotional ability to form this relationship with their parents. Kanner (1943) originally pointed to the child with autism's inability from the beginning of life to relate in a normal manner to people and situations. Numerous researchers have demonstrated that there is a definite lack of attachment to others and a failure to bond with parents (Klin et al., 2002). Typically, the parents of autistic children say they feel the child does not "need" them in the true emotional sense.

It has often been observed that autistic infants do not cry for attention, as do normal infants. Rather, they are perfectly content to lie alone in their crib and seldom cry unless truly uncomfortable (i.e., hungry or wet). They are frequently described as "good babies" because they are content to be left alone and rarely demand attention. They may not display the normal postural anticipation of being picked up when the parent is near and may even cry when approached (Schreibman, 1988). Another very early sign of social impairment, and one that persists throughout their lives, is the failure to establish social eye contact with others (Dawson et al., 2002; Klin et al., 2002). Not only do autistic children not show the normal social response of eye contact when interacting, they very often actively avoid it. This has been called **gaze aversion**.

Many children with autism also display an intolerance, or passive acceptance, of physical contact (Schreibman, 1988). In striking contrast to the intense, dependent, and affectionate emotional attachment demonstrated by non-autistic children, autistic children show minimal involvement with their parents or caregivers. This preference for being alone continues as the child grows older. Autistic children usually avoid play situations with peers and, if in the same area, will engage in solitary activity. Rather, it is frequently reported that autistic children relate to people as "objects" and hence treat them as such. For example, an autistic child may stand on a parent's lap to reach a cookie jar but will do so without establishing eye contact or in any way acknowledging the parent as anything but a piece of furniture, a mere means to an end. A child might also lead people by the hand (without looking at them) to gain access to a desired object or activity.

Children with autism do not display appropriate emotions to situations. Their emotional behaviors may range from complete detachment, to giggling and hysterical laughter, to fury to inconsolable sobbing. These emotional responses often seem to be totally independent of environmental events, and the child can rapidly vacillate from one to the other without apparent reason (Klin et al., 2002; Mundy & Sigman, 1989).

Speech and language. Given the severe impairments in arousal, emotions, and attachment, it should come as no surprise at this point that language learning is also severely impaired. Often it is the child's failure to acquire language that first alerts parents that something is wrong. Kanner (1943) considered the delay or failure in the acquisition of language to be of primary importance in autism. Some children never begin to learn language. Other children begin to speak, learning to say "Mama," or "Dada," and other labels but then suddenly lose the acquired speech and fail to progress linguistically. This language loss tends to occur between 18 and 30 months of age (Schreibman, 1988). Approximately 50% of individuals with autism never develop functional speech and those who do speak characteristically display speech that is qualitatively different than the speech of normal children and children with other language disorders (Schreibman, 1988).

Children with autism who do develop speech commonly display **echolalia**, the repetition of words or phrases spoken by others with no apparent intent to communicate. The only purpose appears to be self-stimulation through sensory feedback (Schreibman, 1988). It should be noted that echolalia is not peculiar to children with autism nor is echoic responding necessarily pathological. However, when this echoing persists past the age of three or four years, it is considered to be pathological (Schreibman, 1988)..

Pronominal reversal is another distinctive characteristic of the speech of children with autism who do speak. Typically, the child will refer to him/herself as "you" or by name. For example, a child named John who has sufficient speech for communicative purposes might ask for a glass of juice by saying "Do you want a glass of juice?" or "Want some juice, John?" This pronominal reversal is undoubtedly related to echolalia, and the reversal of pronouns is not surprising in that other people typically refer to the child as "you" or by name. In the example above, it is likely that the child has heard his mother say, "Do you want a glass of juice?" in a situation associated with obtaining juice (Schreibman, 1988).

The speech of most speaking children with autism is characterized by **dysprosody**. The speech is characterized by inaccurate pitch, rhythm, inflection, intonation, pace, and or articulation. The result is that even children who have relatively sophisticated language skills often sound abnormal when they speak (Schreibman, 1988).

Cognitive deficits. From 65 to 85 percent of children with autism are mentally retarded; that is, they test reliably below IQ 70 on conventional IQ tests (Gillberg & Coleman, 2000; Meyer & Minshew, 2002). (IQ tests will be described in Chapter 12.)

The cognitive impairment associated with autism presents itself in uneven cognitive profiles (Frith, 1991; Shah & Frith, 1992). For example, verbal abilities are usually poorer than performance skills; comprehension is quite often much more impaired than word production; and a variety of measures reflecting rote memory skills demonstrate good or even superior results while working memory may be impaired (Frith, 1991; Shah & Frith, 1992; Zelazo, Jacques, Burack, & Frye, 2002).

Recall that Gelman and Markman (1986) and Keil (1979) found that by age three normal children could use language-defined categories to make inferences and beginning with the living versus nonliving distinction, come to recognize successively more abstract categories. In contrast, many autistic children appear to lack any categorical structure or inferential ability at all (Happe & Frith, 1996; Klinger & Dawson, 2001). The impairment in categorization and inference may be the cause of many of the cognitive social deficits. Autistic individuals rely on individual facial features rather than processing the face as a whole (Meyer & Minshew, 2002). They have a need for rote practice, are inflexible in their behavior, and generally function poorly in social situations. In particular, their use of speech in communication is typically quite limited and they seem to have great difficulty talking about anything outside the immediate situation or events (Schreibman, 1988).

SUMMARY OF LANGUAGE LEARNING

- Around 5 or 6 months of age the learning of spoken language begins.
  - The initial difficulties in establishing communication through speech are daunting and require specialized brain areas. Normal speech is a jumble of sounds that must be decoded on the basis of knowledge of the language being spoken. But the infant has no such knowledge.
  - Speech is learned in the context of communication through emotional utterances so the infant is already focused on the speech input and using it for communication.
  - The infant is aided in segmenting the auditory input into speech sounds by a number of adjustments made by the speaker and the context in which the speech is heard.
    * The speaker speaks slowly with extra emphasis and pauses to aid segmentation.
    * The speech contains a few sounds and sound sequences that are repeated frequently. Since the learning system is sensitive to distributed repetition, the highest frequency sounds are learned first and then used to segment the input into smaller shorter sound sequences.
    * Finally, when an infant attempts to imitate speech she must produce a sequence of discrete vocal sounds through a sequence of vocal movements. By comparing what she hears when she produces speech with what she hears when she listens to speech she can identify the discrete syllables that blend together to form the speech input.

- Early speech perception
  - By 5 months of age, infants can discriminate between their own language and one that has a different stress pattern.
  - By 6 months of age some infants may know isolated words.
  - By 8 months, infants can detect statistical regularities in speech and words segmented by stress.
  - By ten and a half months they are segmenting these words correctly when they are heard in fluent speech.

- Over the next two years the infant is actively learning language. Once the infant gets the idea that things have names, and more generally, that words have meaning, perceptual, social, and emotional cues all guide the infant to the speaker's intent.
  - A basic level of representation is established through vision that facilitates the naming process in language learning.
  - By 2 years of age, toddlers can combine social and emotional cues to learn words by overhearing others.
  - The perceptual system directs attention to novel objects and speakers will tend to name the novel objects.
  - After the first few hundred, most words are learned the first time they are heard and there is explosive growth in vocabulary.
    * Auditory working memory plays a crucial role because the child learns words by using the working memory representation as a model and repeating what she hears. So at age four non-word repetition is a predictor of vocabulary growth.

* By the time a student enters college he has learned 6-10 words a day between the ages of 5 and 18 and knows about 50,000 words.

- Grammar learning begins when there is sufficient knowledge of different word forms.
  - The acquisition of the dominant word order of the language is a gradual process involving generalization from examples.
  - As knowledge of word order stabilizes verbal learning becomes an additional tool for learning the meanings of words.
  - Around three years of age learning assumes a mature form in which learning is the incremental elaboration of a semantic network.

- Reading is initially learned through letter-sound conversion, which makes English particularly difficult, but then, the direct visual whole-word route is added as early as the first grade.
  - Difficulty in learning how to read is called dyslexia.
  - A general problem with language processing, which is the most common cause of dyslexia, is called specific language impairment (SLI).

- Some infants are born without normal emotions or attention abilities, or lose them after a year of life. These deficits result in profound cognitive and language impairments that are called autism.

SUMMARY OF CHAPTER

- The same basic learning system encodes representations in memory throughout a person's life.
  - The recognition system constructs new representations in working memory
  - These representations are made permanent by the medial temporal learning system
    * As the result of action
    * As the result of emotion

- Nevertheless, a distinction may be made between
  - mature learning - based on prior knowledge
  - early learning - there are few or no representations for the input to match.

- Infant Learning
  - Shortly after birth the infant is already able to
    * make emotional responses to orient towards emotional targets
    * recognize basic things such as his caregiver and home.
    * develops the basic attention and motor skills that make learning possible.
    * use the emotional system for communication with the caregiver.
  - After six months the infant is able to
    * sit up, then crawl, walk, explore the world, and learn about it.
    * reach for and grasp objects, and learn through imitation of actions.
  - Some time around ten months she begins to point and understand the function of pointing, hence facilitating learning, including language learning.

- Early Memory During the First Months of Life
  - Detailed visual representations are already being encoded.
  - Generalization and category formation already occurs
  - Retention interval is a function of the number and distribution over time of the training/study materials.

- Around 5 or 6 months of age the learning of spoken language begins.
  - Communication through speech requires specialized brain areas. Normal speech is a jumble of sounds that must be decoded on the basis of knowledge of the language being spoken that the infant does not have.

- Speech is learned in the context of communication through emotional utterances.
- The infant is aided in segmenting the auditory input into speech sounds by a number of adjustments made by the speaker and the context in which the speech is heard.
- Once the infant gets the idea that things have names, and more generally, that words have meaning, perceptual, social, and emotional cues all guide the infant to the speaker's intent.
- Auditory working memory plays a crucial role because the child learns words by using the working memory representation as a model and repeating (i.e., imitating) what she hears. So at age four non-word repetition is a predictor of vocabulary growth.
- Grammar learning begins when there is sufficient knowledge of different word forms.
- Reading is initially learned through letter-sound conversion, which makes English particularly difficult, but then, the direct visual whole-word route is added as early as the first grade.

Chapter 7

SEMANTIC LEARNING

A friend of the author's once heard two students talking after an exam. One student said to the other, "It's amazing how much clearer things are if you study when you are sober." The student had discovered an important fact about alcohol intoxication, its devastating effect on learning. However, it is also interesting that it took a sober episode to produce this insight. Often even good students have no insight into what makes learning easy or difficult.

DECLARATIVE MEMORY

Five overlapping brain mechanisms contribute to declarative learning. The first mechanism is the recognition system (Chapter 5) that terminates in the frontal cortex, specifically the ability to construct novel representations in working memory by associating the perceptual input with structural descriptions in long-term memory. Working memory makes it possible to hear a tune, rather than individual notes. It makes it possible to understand a sentence, to plan an action, and anticipate its consequences. Because working memory is where new representations are constructed it is the engine of learning. However, working memory is of limited capacity. Every time something is brought into working memory, something old is pushed out. Each object and event is almost immediately semantically categorized and any new learning is an elaboration of an existing representation. Furthermore, an individual develops an array of skills, including verbal rehearsal and visual imagery, that make it possible for him to intentionally remember specific objects and events regardless of whether they are novel or routine, salient or mundane.

The second mechanism is the medial temporal cortex, where representations constructed in working memory are made a part of semantic memory (Figure 6.2). However, not every representation in working memory is made a part of semantic memory. Rather, the medial temporal cortex can be activated in any one of three different ways to encode a representation in working memory. First, some events are so important that they must be remembered the first time they are experienced. The first mechanism is the emotional system. Recall from Chapter 4 that the amygdala, which is the switch for emotional input, directly connects with the hippocampus, which regulates the formation of new representations in memory. When an experience produces a high level of emotional arousal, a permanent representation of the event is encoded. That is, you will remember something that terrifies you.

For the structural descriptions of the targets and consequences of actions that do not elicit large emotional responses, there is a lower but nonzero probability of encoding the representation in semantic memory every time the action is performed. As a result, the more often the action is performed and the structural description is constructed the more likely it is to become a part of semantic memory. So, there is a bias in the learning system to retain representations of familiar objects and routine actions. Furthermore, recall that there is an advantage for distributed over massed learning. That is, the longer the interval over which the structural description of a target object is repeatedly constructed, the longer this representation will remain accessible in semantic memory and be recognized. So representations of routine events experienced infrequently remain accessible in semantic memory over long intervals. Hence, even routine events experienced infrequently will be recognized.

Finally, a representation may be encoded as the result of a **mnemonic** action; an action whose specific purpose is to encode that representation. Such actions include verbal rehearsal and visual imagery.

We begin by looking at the role of the medial temporal cortex in learning. We move on to the role of rehearsal, imagery, and knowledge, and conclude with the role of emotion.

THE LEARNING SYSTEM

The mechanism by which new representations are encoded in long-term memory remains obscure. However, rapid progress is being made in this field. The region of the brain that controls the encoding of long-term declarative representations is deep within the center of the brain and includes the medial temporal cortex along with connecting structures in the thalamus and frontal cortex.

In particular, within the medial temporal cortex the hippocampus plays a crucial role in declarative learning. More generally, the hippocampus controls both spatial and associative learning in all mammals, including humans. In animals, these tasks include spatial learning tasks, e.g., remembering the location of a hidden platform in a pool of water and temporal learning tasks, e.g., learning that a tone will be followed by a puff of air blown in your eye. Every day new neurons are produced in the hippocampuses of mammals, including those of humans (Eriksson, Perfilieva, Bjork-Eriksson, Alborn, Nordborg, Peterson, & Gage, 1998). Studies on rats have established that the new neurons born daily in the hippocampus are essential for spatial and temporal learning. Most neurons born each day die, but learning a spatial or temporal task increases the number of new neurons that survive in the rat's hippocampus (Gould, Beylin, Tanapat, Reeves, & Shors, 1999). On the other hand, reducing the number of new neurons (through poisoning them) decreased the rat's ability learn a temporal learning task (Shors, Miesegaes, Beylin, Zhao, Rydel, & Gould, 2001).

While the medial temporal cortex is necessary for learning, it is not sufficient. The medial temporal cortex is part of a circuit that includes nuclei in the front portion of the thalamus (which are different from the nuclei involved in visual and auditory perception) and in the adjacent central region of the frontal lobe (Figure 6.2). As will be discussed below, when any of these areas is damaged, the ability to learn is impaired.

But what role does the medial temporal cortex play in semantic learning and memory? It may be that it functions the way that an index and table of contents function in a book and an index file functions on a computer drive. That is, it provides a map and set of pointers to the various representations that make up semantic memory. Essentially, it consists of the concept nodes and pathways to the various perceptual representations that were described in Chapter 5. It may be that the analogy between the medial temporal cortex and the index file on a computer drive is particularly close. The representations that are encoded elsewhere on a computer drive cannot be retrieved by the operating system unless their locations are entered in the index file. When you delete a file from your computer, all that happens is that its location is removed from the index file. Otherwise, its entire representation remains intact on the drive. Similarly, declarative learning may involve indexing within the temporal cortex perceptual ad motor representations distributed throughout the cortex that would otherwise only be part of procedural memory. Declarative forgetting may often involve losing this index, though the representation it pointed to remains intact and continues to function as part of procedural memory.

DISTRIBUTED VERSUS MASSED REPETITION

Consider an episode in which you see or hear something that requires the construction of a new representation in working memory. At the same time that the representation is encoded in working memory, it may or may not become a part of long-term memory. That is, it is only encoded in long-term memory with some probability. If the representation is not encoded at that time, then when it is displaced from working memory it leaves no trace behind in declarative memory (Nelson & Batchelder, 1969). If it is presented again it is perceived as entirely novel.

It would perhaps be more convenient if everything that entered working memory was also encoded as a long-term declarative representation. But this is simply not the case. Frequency of occurrence is one factor among others (that will be discussed below) that act as a filter for what becomes part of long-term memory. Any input that is part of a routine activity, and hence occurs frequently, has a high cumulative probability of being encoded in long-term memory on some occasion. Furthermore, recall that learning is not only a function of the number of repetitions of the study item but also the interval between the repetitions of the study item. Distributed training results in longer retention than massed trained for study and retention intervals encompassing the entire range of human experience. Recall that over training intervals of days and retention intervals of weeks and months, distributed training of typing produces better performance (Chapter 2) and distributed training moving a mobile produces better recognition (Chapter 6). In fact, in the verbal learning experiments described below, distributed study was superior for study and retention intervals measured in seconds up to study intervals measured in days and retention intervals measured in years.

Short-term distributed repetition. As was the case for perceptual-motor learning and operant learning, for verbal learning distributed repetitions are more effective than massed repetitions (Melton, 1967). For example, if you see an item twice, you will remember it better if the two presentations do not occur one after the other. Figure 7.1 illustrates a typical spacing effect. Madigan (1969) gave students two presentations each of forty-eight words. Each presentation involved showing the word for 1.5 seconds. All the points plotted in Figure 7.1 represent the percentage of words recalled after two presentations. The only difference between the points involves the lag between the introduction of the word and its repetition, i.e., the number of items intervening between the two presentations of the same word. For example, with a lag of 0 the two presentations occur one after the other. At the other extreme, a lag of 40 means that the two presentations were separated by the presentation of 40 other items.

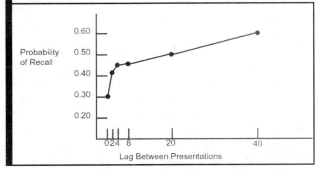

FIGURE 7.1

Probability of recalling a word after two presentations. The probability increases with the lag between the two presentations.

As Figure 7.1 indicates, recall is greatly improved by spacing the presentations rather than massing them together. Most of the advantage due to spacing accrues as long as even two items separate the repeated words; but to some extent the advantage continues to increase even up to a lag of 40. Spaced repetitions increase learning in two ways.

Distributed repetitions allow an input such as a word to be encoded in more than one context. When a word is repeated twice in succession, each representation is encoded in the same context. But as the separation between the items increases, the probability of differences in the encoding context increases as well. Distributed presentations produce additional contextual generation cues that massed presentations lack (Glenberg 1979; McFarland, Rhodes, & Frey, 1979). Differences in encoding context contribute to the increase in recall shown in Figure 7.1, from a separation of 2 to a separation of 40. However, this factor cannot account for the initial large increase in recall between a separation of 0 and a separation of 2, because at this small separation the contexts of both presentations are quite similar.

Long-term retention of a list of words requires that an association between each word and the list representation be encoded in long-term memory. Whenever a list item is presented that is not in working memory there is some probability that an association between it and the list representation will be encoded in long-term memory. However, if the item is already in working memory then no encoding in long-term memory takes place. At a separation of 0 the study item remains in working memory and is matched with the input without being retrieved from long-term memory. However, even at a separation of 2 the study item is out of working memory and hence must be retrieved from long-term memory. It is the generation from long-term memory that encodes the item's association with the list representation in long-term memory. Cuddy and Jacoby (1982) found that factors that reduced the likelihood that the second presentation of an input would be matched with its representation in working memory, thus forcing re-activation of its representation in long-term memory, ultimately enhanced its recall.

Evidence that a massed (i.e., immediate) repetition of a target is recognized in working memory but a distributed (i.e., delayed) repetition of a target is recognized as the result of a response from long-term memory is provided by their different effects on the attention. William Johnston and Charles Uhl (1976) hypothesized that recognition of the immediate repetition of a target would be an automatic perceptual process that would leave an observer free to direct attention to another detection task. In contrast, recognition of the delayed repetition of a target would be a voluntary process involving long-term memory that would interfere with another detection task.

They had students do two tasks at the same time. The first task was to listen to several lists of about a hundred words. The words were presented at the rate of one every 5 seconds. The students heard the words in their right ear (by means of headphones). The students were to study and remember each list for a later recall test. Some of the words were repeated four times in the list. If a word was repeated, it could be presented four times in succession (massed) or at four separate times during the list (distributed). As we would expect, the students recalled more words after distributed than massed presentations.

The real interest in the experiment, however, involves the second task the students had to perform while studying the words. Their second task was to press a button as quickly as possible whenever they heard a faint tone presented to the left ear. The tones occurred at various times throughout the presentation of the study list. The reaction time data from Johnston and Uhl's experiment are presented in Figure 7.2. The points in the graph indicate the average time required to detect the tone when it occurred simultaneously with the first, second, third, or fourth presentation of a word. When the presentations were massed, the tone detection times decreased markedly with each successive presentation of a word. This result suggests that less attention was paid to the study word with each successive massed repetition. On the other hand, with spaced presentations the reaction times actually increased

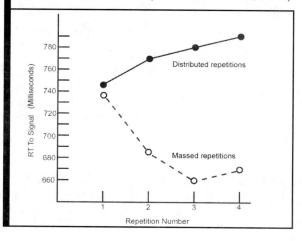

FIGURE 7.2

The time to detect a tone decreases over massed presentations of a word but increases over distributed presentations of a word. (After Johnson & Uhl, 1976.)

over repetitions. So retrieval of the study word from long-term memory interfered with the detection of the tone.

Long-term distributed repetition. Harry Bahrick was interested in performing an experiment in which the effect of verbal learning distributed over days was assessed over a retention interval of years. He was fortunate in being a very clever experimentalist and in having a family of psychologists who would participate, along with him, in the study (Bahrick, Bahrick, Bahrick, & Bahrick, 1993). The task to learn pairs of words in which one word was in English and the other was in French or German (depending on the participant). The foreign word was not known to the participant. Training was by the selective reminding method. That is, each training session began with the participant attempting to recall the English meaning of 50 words. After each word, the participant checked the meaning, and put aside the words he or she had gotten wrong. The participant successively retested all the words whose English meanings had not been recalled on the previous trial until every word's meaning had been recalled once.

Each individual participated in six different schedules of training sessions. A different set of 50 words was used for each schedule. Three of the schedules consisted of 13 sessions and three of the schedules consisted of 26 sessions. Intervals between training sessions were 14, 28, and 56 days, respectively for the three 13-day schedules and the three 26-day schedules. The shorter the interval between training sessions, the more English response words were recalled at the beginning of each session. This difference occurred across all training sessions. At the beginning of the last session, an average of 48 English response words were recalled for the 14-day training interval, an average of 46 English response words were recalled for the 28-day training interval, and an average of 43 English response words were recalled for the 56-day training interval.

Recall of different words was tested at retention intervals of 1, 2, 3, and 5 years. Since the results were the same at all retention intervals, the data shown in Figure 7.3 are collapsed over retention interval and shown for each training schedule. As can be seen from the figure, both number of training sessions and length of training interval increased recall.

REM sleep and distributed learning. REM sleep (Chapter 4) only occurs in mammals.   An animal's maturity at birth is correlated with the amount of REM sleep after birth. Mammals born with well-developed brains (i.e. guinea pigs), spend proportionally less time in REM sleep than mammals born in a

FIGURE 7.3

Mean percentage recall as a function of the interval between training sessions and the number of training sessions (Bahrick, 1993).

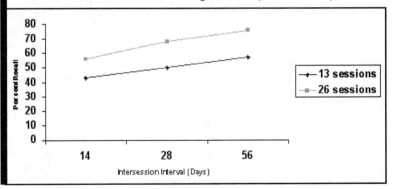

relatively immature state in which the brain is not completely developed at birth, i.e. rats and humans, (Jouvet-Mounier, Astic, & Lacote, 1969). A newborn human infant spends approximately 70% of its total sleep time in REM sleep and this declines to 30% at 6 months of age. By 8 years this has been further reduced to 22% and finally to the adult percentage of 15%. REM sleep may provide a stage for brain growth (Carlson, 2001). When pharmacological suppressions of REM sleep are administered to postnatal rats, it has been found to alter the course of visual system development. In addition, the REM sleep deprived rats were noted to have behavioral, anatomical, and biochemical deficiencies throughout adulthood (Marks, Shaffery, Oksenberg, Speciale, & Roffwarg, 1995; Mirmiran, 1995).

It has been hypothesized that sleep, especially REM sleep, aids in the **consolidation** of memory traces (Kavanau, 1996; Maquet, 2001), thus producing the advantage of distributing training over days. According to this theory, memory traces are vulnerable to interference until after the first post-exposure onset of sleep has occurred (Poe, Nitz, McNaughton, & Barnes, 2000). There have been many experimental findings examining memory and learning that are consistent with this hypothesis. Stickgold, James, and Hobson (2000) found that without any additional training sessions, performance on a visual discrimination task displayed maximal improvement 48-96 hours after an initial training episode. When participants were deprived of sleep for the first 36 hours after training and then allowed to have recovery sleep the next two nights, the improvement of performance on the task was no longer demonstrated. By allowing the participants at least 6 hours of sleep on the first night, participants were able to obtain maximal performance (Stickgold, Whidbee, Schirmer, Patel, & Hobson, 2000). Thus, improvement of task performance is absolutely dependent on the first night of post-training sleep, and subsequent recovery sleep cannot compensate for this initial reduction in memory consolidation.

When recovering from sleep deprivation it has been noted that participants recover very little of stage one and two sleep (7%), while recovering 68% of SWS and 53% of REM sleep (Kales, Tan, Kollar, Naitoh, Preston, & Malmastrom, 1970). These differential amounts of recovery sleep have lead some researchers to focus on REM sleep as a possible stage where memory consolidation occurs. In a perceptual learning task, animals that were deprived of REM sleep did not learn as well as those deprived of slow wave sleep (Karni, Tanne, Rubenstein, Askenasy, & Sagi, 1994). Other researchers have proposed that nREM-REM cycles, rather than the REM state is essential for the consolidation of verbal information. Ficca, Lombardo, Rossi, and Salzarulo (2000) found that morning recall was impaired following a night of disrupted sleep cycles compared to a night with undisturbed sleep cycles. Both experimental groups had a similar amount of REM sleep. Salzarulo and Fagioli (1995) noted a positive correlation between sleep cycles and protein synthesis. A disruption in the sleep cycle could result in a decline of protein synthesis and thus impair processes for consolidating memory.

VERBAL REHEARSAL

Suppose that you meet Jennifer Patel and she tells you that her father is from Bombay and her mother is from Baltimore. You discover that you are both in the same psychology class, so you exchange phone numbers so that if one of you is ever absent that person can get the notes from the other. After your conversation you would be unlikely to practice your new friend's name or personal information, or go over her facial features or appearance, in fear that you would forget them. You have detailed structural descriptions for encoding all kinds of personal information that make such information easy to learn so that you will later recognize Jennifer (though, alas, not necessarily recall her name, as discussed in Chapter 9). However, the meaningless pattern of digits that was her phone number is different. You consciously **rehearsed** it to yourself, or even wrote it down, to be sure that you would remember it. Since it starts out as essentially a random string of numbers, you must devote considerable action to constructing a representation for it. The next part of this chapter will consider the hurdles in learning things like phone numbers for which you cannot retrieve detailed structural descriptions in memory. The second part following it will consider the advantages in learning high imagery, meaningful material.

Rehearsal is the act of attempting to immediately generate from memory a string that you have just heard or seen. Rehearsal is a complex activity. The individual rehearsing repeatedly translates a phonologically represented sequence of items into an articulatory code, and as he articulates them the phonological code is regenerated. Figure 5.3 shows the parietal area where the phonological and articulatory codes are integrated, hence making rehearsal possible. The short-term effect of rehearsal is to maintain the sequence in working memory. The long-term consequence of rehearsal is to **hierarchically organize** the items in the sequence under **category nodes** so that they form a **chunk** and may be retrieved together. This process will be called **pattern learning**. Rehearsal is one of small set of voluntary actions whose only purpose is to learn something.

DEVELOPMENT OF REHEARSAL STRATEGIES

You might think that rehearsal is such an obvious strategy that any children old enough to perform an intentional memory task would automatically use it. It turns out, however, that they do not. Children up to the age of kindergarten or first grade generally do not spontaneously rehearse (Flavell, Beach, & Chinsky, 1966). For example, Keeney, Cannizzo, and Flavell (1967) showed a group of first grade children a set of pictures of common objects. On each trial the experimenter pointed to several of the pictures (the number varied from three to five across trials). The child had to wait 15 seconds (without looking at the pictures) and then had to point to the same pictures in the same order as the experimenter had used. One of the experimenters was a lip-reader and recorded any signs of verbalization during the delay interval. Several striking findings emerged in this study. Children who spontaneously rehearsed remembered the pictures more accurately than did the non-rehearsers. But with a little instruction from the experimenter, the non-rehearsers could also be induced to rehearse; when they did so, their accuracy rose to the same level as that of the spontaneous rehearsers. However, the effect of training was not long lasting. When given the option of either rehearsing or not, more than half of the children who had to be trained abandoned the rehearsal strategy, so their accuracy declined again. Merely having the ability to rehearse is not sufficient for improving learning. Rehearsal must be employed at the appropriate times. An important aspect of development is **metamemory**—the child's understanding of his or her own memory abilities (Flavell & Wellman, 1976). Younger children, for example, will wildly overestimate how many pictures pointed out by the experimenter they will later be able to remember. They do not seem to understand how their own memories operate and the limits on how much information they can encode in a short period of time (Flavell 1984). Metamemory improves with experience, and particularly with schooling.

By the third grade, school children will rehearse if told to do so. But they will use inefficient massed rather than efficient distributed rehearsal. Ornstein, Naus, and Liberty (1975) asked children in grades three, six, and eight to overtly rehearse lists of words that were presented for recall. After the words *yard*, *cat*, *man*, *desk*, … had been presented an eighth grader might be rehearsing, "desk, man, yard, cat;" but third graders would be rehearsing "desk, desk, desk, desk."

IMMEDIATE SUPER-SPAN RECALL

The act of rehearsal brings into working memory more than one kind of representation. To begin rehearsal the articulatory representations of the to-be-rehearsed items must be in working memory. When the items are articulated, not only their phonological representations but their complete semantic representations become part of working memory as well. All three representations influence how many items may be rehearsed and which are learned as the result of rehearsal.

One obvious limiting factor on rehearsal is the number of items that can be maintained in working memory at one time. The capacity of working memory is a positive function of the familiarity of the items and their relatedness to each other. Familiar and related items may already be partly organized in chunks. If several items being rehearsed form a chunk then it is only necessary to maintain the single category node of the chunk in working memory it order to generate all its members. So the apparent span for the chunked items is increased. When asked to repeat a string, the average **span**, i.e., the number of items that can be repeated without error, is 5 for random letters and 7 for random digits (Cavanaugh, 1972) in English. The capacity of working memory is also a negative function of the articulatory similarity of the items. In general, words that have similar articulatory representations are more difficult to articulate and take longer to do so. The extreme case of this is tongue twisters. Digit span is language specific. Digits take longer to articulate in Welsh and less time to articulate in Chinese than in English. Hence, average digit span is only 6 in Welsh but 10 in Chinese (Ellis & Hennelly, 1980; Hoosain & Salili, 1988).

The effects of the articulatory and semantic representations are also evident when a person attempts to repeat a list that exceeds his span and then fails to repeat all the items correctly. The solid circles in Figure 7.4 show the probability of recall at each list position when students were asked to immediately recall a 20-word list in any order. If recall is attempted immediately after the list is presented then working memory usually includes the articulatory representations for the last four items. So people usually first attempt to recall the last four items. The resulting high probability of recall for the last four items is called the **recency effect**. In addition, some earlier items, often including the first one, may have already been encoded semantically and may be generated as well. This is called the **primacy effect**.

Recency effect.   The last words in a list are auditory and/or articulatory representations in working memory. Once the capacity of working memory has been exceeded, as each new

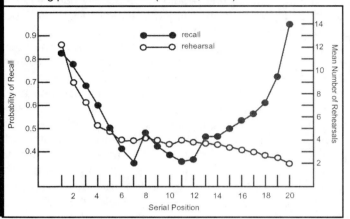

FIGURE 7.4

Serial position curves for immediate free recall and corresponding data on number of rehearsals given items at each position during presentation of list. (Rundus, 1971.)

list item is perceived and enters working memory it eliminates the representation of a previous list item. In an immediate recall task the last items in the list are the ones that subjects usually recall first because articulating other items first would disrupt their representations. Similarly, if subjects are given a distracter task, such as counting backward before they recall the list, the recency portion of the recall curve will suffer substantially (Glanzer & Cunitz 1966; Postman & Phillips, 1965).

Primacy effect.   The words in the beginning and middle of a list must be retrieved from long-term memory. The probability of recalling a word is largely determined by the probability of its being associated with the hierarchical list structure in long-term memory. In order to try to learn the list, the subject repeats as many words as he can. But after the subject hears several words, it becomes impossible to rehearse them all. To obtain a count of the number of rehearsals given each item, Rundus and Atkinson (1970) asked students to rehearse the words on a list aloud and tape-recorded their responses. The open circles in Figure 7.4 show how many times the words at each serial position were rehearsed. As shown in the figure, the early words on the list are given the most rehearsals. Since later words have more items competing for rehearsal at the same time, on average, they receive less total rehearsal than earlier words.   In fact, the primacy and middle portions of the recall curve have virtually the same shape as the plot of the number of rehearsals (Rundus, 1971).

Furthermore, recall that by eighth grade the rehearsals of the earlier words tend to be distributed throughout the list. Further experiments conducted by Modigliani (1980) clearly indicated that what is important about the extra rehearsals that the early list items receive is not their number but where they occur. The later rehearsals for the early list items come in the middle and end of the list. The subject is not just repeating individual list items but is rehearing sub-span sequences of two or three words, so the initial items are repeated. This important aspect of rehearsal will be considered again below.

Serial position curve. To summarize, when subjects are free to rehearse as they please, immediate recall of a super-span list produces a U-shaped serial position function in which the recency portion represents retrieval from auditory short-term memory and the primacy portion represents retrieval from long-term memory. When there is a retention interval filled with a distracter task that eliminates the last items from working memory before retrieval is permitted then the recency effect is eliminated. So in delayed recall there is typically primacy but not recency.   The same variables that affect learning in the laboratory affect it in everyday life as well. Hyman and Rubin (1990) cued 76 undergraduates with the title and first line of one of 64 different Beatles' songs and asked them to write down the entire song. The probability of recalling a line was best predicted by the number of times a line was repeated; thus exhibiting a distributed frequency effect, and how early the line first appeared in the song; thus exhibiting a primacy effect.

When people are encouraged or forced to distribute their rehearsals differently from the usual pattern, so that the first list items do not receive more distributed rehearsals, then the normal serial position function is disrupted. For example, if a feature of an input attracts attention to it and hence increases its rehearsal then it increases the item's memorability regardless of its list position. This result is known as the isolation or Von Restorff (1933) effect, after its discoverer. In one demonstration Douglas Detterman and Norman Ellis (1972) had students recall serially presented lists of line drawings of common objects (e.g., hat, pill, pencil sharpener). Half the lists contained, in the middle position, one of a set of critical items, which were photographs of groups of male and female nudes with exposed genitalia. Their results are shown in Figure 7.5. A dramatic Von Restorff effect can be seen in the figure. In the Von Restorff Effect, the distinctive item receives more rehearsals, at the expense of other items.

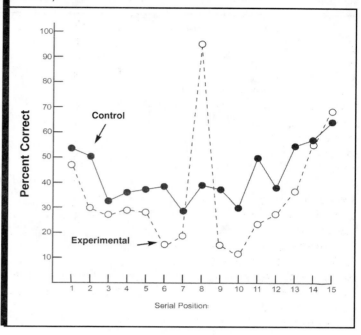

FIGURE 7.5

Percentage of correct recall by serial position (Detterman & Ellis, 1972).

LEARNING A REPEATED LIST

If you rehearse a phone number you have just heard enough times you usually will remember it. But why will you remember it? What are the necessary conditions for learning a phone number so that you will remember it later. Would merely hearing it over and over be sufficient to remember it? Or would it be necessary to say the number over and over? Or is it necessary to repeatedly generate the number from memory through rehearsal? Glass, Krejci, and Goldman (1989) performed an experiment to answer this question. College students shadowed a sequence of about 150 digits presented at the rate of one digit per second. In the continuous condition a string of 9 digits was repeated five times at regular intervals in the sequence, as shown in Figure 7.6. Yet immediately afterwards the students could not recognize the repeated string, indicating that merely hearing and saying a sequence of numbers over and over was not sufficient to encode a representation of the string in declarative memory.

In a segmented condition there was an additional one-second pause after every ninth digit in the sequence, as shown in Figure 7.6. This caused the auditory system to segment the sequence into strings of 9 digits. As a result, representations (i.e., hierarchical patterns) of 9-digit strings were formed in working memory. Immediately after presentation of the entire 150-digit sequence, the students could recognize the repeated string. So merely shadowing a perceptually segmented string over and over was sufficient to encode a representation of the string in working memory. But if recognition was delayed an hour and the interval was filled with listening to other strings, the repeated string was not recognized. The representation of the repeated string could be destroyed by listening to other strings of digits. The destruction of the new representation by the subsequent processing of similar representations is called **Retroactive Interference (RI)**.

In a rehearsal condition there was a five-second pause after every ninth digit in the sequence and the student had to try to repeat the most recent 9-digit string during the pause, as shown in Figure 7.6. These students could recognize the repeated string even after an hour delay filled with listening to other

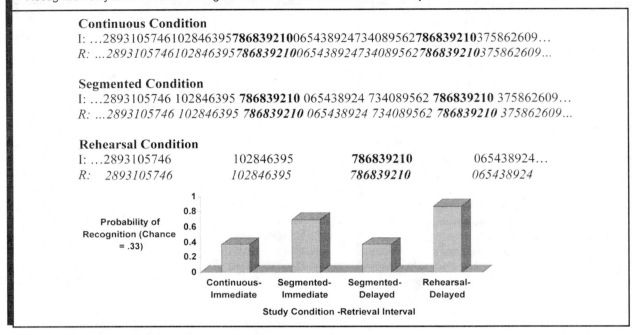

FIGURE 7.6

Experiment of Glass et al. (1989). Input (I) in regular type and responses (R) in italics. Repeated string shown in bold. Recognition only above chance in Segmented-Immediate and Rehearsal-Delayed conditions.

strings. So it is necessary to generate a representation from memory in order to construct within semantic memory a hierarchical category structure for generating it. Notice how important rehearsal was for forming a long-term semantic memory. A working memory auditory or articulatory representation of a list may be a by-product of perception but a long-term semantic representation of it is a by-product of action.

Further evidence of the essential role of rehearsal in learning comes from the RSVP task, in which items are presented too fast to be rehearsed. Recall that Potter (1975, 1976) and Intraub (1980, 1981) had students perform a task in which they had to detect a target among a sequence of pictures presented for 114 milliseconds apiece, pressing a button when the target appeared. Sometimes, the target was defined quite generally, e.g., a picture that is not house furnishings or decorations. Such a definition required the observer to identify *every* picture in the sequence as either an instance or a noninstance of the specified category. Therefore if activation of a logogen was sufficient to leave a memory then an observer should have been able to select most of the pictures just presented in a subsequent recognition test. However, in the recognition test that immediately followed presentation of the sequence, the observer was able to select few, if any, pictures as one that had just been seen. Detection accuracy was almost always much higher than recognition accuracy. Merely attending to an input and being briefly aware of it does not automatically lead to a permanent record of that input in memory.

THE EFFECT OF REHEARSAL ON SEMANTIC REPRESENTATION

Tulving (1962) observed that students tend to recall a set of words in about the same order on successive recall attempts, even if the items are represented in different orders on successive study trials. Herman Buschke (Buschke 1973, 1976, 1977; Fuld and Buschke 1976) carried this analysis further. Buschke asked people to learn lists of random words and examined the precise order in which they recalled list items. He found that successive recall attempts of the same list revealed the same clusters of words, presumably reflecting the chunks into which they were organized. His results suggested that the process of learning a list involved combining smaller chunks into larger ones. In other words, learning a list involves organizing its members into a hierarchical structure. Words tended to cluster semantically. That is, a chunk was more likely to be study words that were similar in meaning than words that occurred together on the study list.

THE PHONOLOGICAL—ARTICULATORY LOOP
AND THE DUAL FUNCTIONALITY OF REHEARSAL

To summarize, verbal rehearsal has two distinct consequences. The first is to maintain the phonological representation of a word sequence in memory by repeatedly re-articulating the words. The second is to build a hierarchical semantic representation of the word sequence. We saw in Chapter 6 that the phonological—articulatory loop plays a role in word learning early in life and we saw in Chapter 5 that it plays a role in the comprehension of long and complex sentences throughout life. Immediately above we saw that hierarchical organization plays an important role in list learning.

It turns out that these two functions are separable. Baddeley, Papagno, and Vallar (1988) found a woman who could no longer repeat phonological sequences, including words and numbers. Though she had suffered damage to all the temporal and parietal language areas, including a deep lesion in the phonological—articulatory integration area, only the functioning of the latter was affected. For her the link between phonology and articulation, indicated by f in Figure 5.6, had been severed. They had her participate in a paired associate learning task. The participant studies pairs of words and then is shown a member of each pair and asked to respond with the other. When both words of the pair were familiar, the woman learned the task normally. But when the response word was an unfamiliar nonword she was unable to perform the task at all.

Hence, though you typically make use of the phonological—articulatory loop to engage in rehearsal, the phonological and articulatory representations are only necessary for those study items for which no other representation exists.

KNOWLEDGE AND LEARNING

Beyond infancy, there are few truly novel inputs. Learning is a bootstrapping process in which each input matches a representation associated with some logogen. So only the differences between the memory representation and the perceptual input need be encoded in an elaborated representation. The more a person knows, the more likely that an input will be very similar to what is in memory. So the more you know, the less there is to add. Furthermore, there will already be a place to add the new information in a detailed structural description. So the more you know, the easier it is to learn more.

As was mentioned in Chapter 5, structural descriptions include visual structural descriptions of scenes, syntactic descriptions of sentences, and schemas of stories. Materials that are associated with such structural descriptions, such as high imagery and meaningful words and pictures of recognizable objects, can be combined into new representations at a more rapid rate than low imagery material like numbers. Even random lists of words are easier to learn than random lists of numbers.

Knowledge can either support or interfere with learning. Its effect depends on the relationship of the old structural description (knowledge) to the new structural description (learning). If the old knowledge is a good part of the new knowledge then learning will be supported and occur rapidly. If the old knowledge is a bad part of the new knowledge then it will interfere with learning, which will proceed more slowly. Most of the time knowledge supports learning. For example, the more words you know, the easier it is to learn more words. This is because most words are made of the same familiar spelling patterns. For example, "st" and "th" may be found at the beginning of words, but virtually never "ts" and "ht." Once you have learned a sufficient number of words, they may be encoded as familiar spelling patterns rather than individual letters, which reduces the number of parts that have to be learned. In contrast, it is difficult to learn a random letter string assigned as a password. In this case, its letters remind you of the familiar letter sequences, which interferes with rehearsal of the novel sequence in the password. Most of this section will be concerned with the supporting effects of knowledge on learning. But at the end we will begin to consider the interfering effects as well.

APPLYING KNOWLEDGE TO WORD-LIST LEARNING

For a list whose items are associated with a structural or category description, the more closely the order of the list items matches the organization of their categorical or structural description, the more rapidly the items are associated with that description, and remembered. For example, Bower, Clark, Lesgold, and Winzenz (1969) found that a list of words was remembered much better when people were aware that the list could be organized hierarchically. They showed students four cards, each of which contained approximately 28 words. The students studied each word set for about a minute and then tried to recall as many as possible of the 112 words. The students were then asked to study and recall the word sets three more times, for a total of four study-test trials. One group (the hierarchical condition) saw the words on each card arranged in a sensible hierarchical classification scheme (Table 7.1). The other group (the random condition) saw each word set randomly scrambled (Table 7.1). The recall results for the two conditions over the four trials are shown in Figure 7.7. As the figure shows, the students in the hierarchical condition consistently recalled many more words than did students in the random condition.

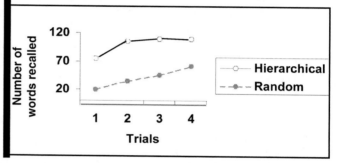

FIGURE 7.7

The effect of hierarchical and random organization on learning lists of words (Bower et al., 1969).

The strategy of organizing a list of items into a hierarchical organization that will be useful for retrieving them requires that the list items already have strong associations among them prior to the study task. More words from a list of high-frequency words are recalled than from a list of low-frequency words because the higher-frequency words have more associations that facilitate their organization into chunks. The associations among the high-frequency items produce faster list learning. Also people are also more accurate at remembering the absolute list positions of items for lists of high-frequency-items than for lists of low-frequency-items (DeLosh & McDaniel, 1996)

TABLE 7.1

Two Levels of Organization

Hierarchical condition

Minerals			**Stones**	
Metals				
Rare	**Common**	**Alloys**	**Precious**	**Masonry**
Platinum	Aluminum	Bronze	Sapphire	Limestone
Silver	Copper	Steel	Emerald	Granite
Gold	Lead	Brass	Diamond	Marble
	Iron		Ruby	Slate

Random Condition

		Knee		
	String		**Ruby**	
Drum	Arm	Lead	Percussion	Head
Flower	Slate	Instrument	Hand	Trumpet
Tuba	Foot	Maple	Rose	Marble
Neck	Piano	Toe	Birch	Aluminum
	Oak		Gold	Violin

because in the high-frequency lists adjacent, associated items form natural clusters. However, associated words cannot be too far apart on the list or they will not be associated in working memory together. When a mixed-list of high and low frequency words is studied, the high-frequency words are no longer more likely to be recalled than the low-frequency words because the low-frequency words break up the chunks of no-longer adjacent high-frequency words (DeLosh & McDaniel, 1996).

VISUAL IMAGERY

You can learn visually as well as verbally by engaging in visual imagery instead of or in addition to verbal rehearsal. Just as was the case with verbal rehearsal, visual imagery creates a pattern out of the individual list items. Bower, Lesgold, and Tieman (1969) showed that interactive imagery could be used to create compound representations containing clusters of targets analogous to the substrings created by rehearsal. They presented subjects with a list of twenty-four nouns in clusters of four at a time. One group of subjects imaged the same clusters of nouns during four successive presentations of the list, while another group imaged the same words clustered differently on each trial. Figure 7.8 presents the recall results for the two groups on the second, third, and fourth trials. As shown, recall improved much more over trials if the same nouns were clustered together on each trial because a single list-representation could be constructed across the four list presentations in the same order.

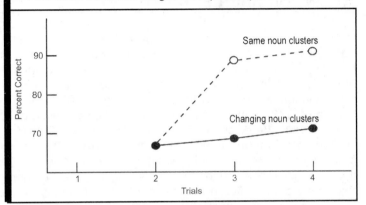

FIGURE 7.8

Imagery and recall. Imagery improves recall over trials much more if the same interactive images are repeated (Bower, et. al., 1969).

In fact, high-imagery list items are more likely to be remembered than low-imagery list items even when explicit instructions to engage in visual imagery are not given. Words such as *tree* that refer to concrete, easily imaged objects are remembered better than words such as *thought* that are abstract and do not refer directly to anything that can be imaged, whether the test is free recall (Stoke, 1929), recognition (Gorman, 1961), or paired-associate learning (Paivio, 1969). Bevan and Steger (1971) presented both children and adults with a list consisting of a mixture of actual objects, pictures of objects, and names of objects. For both age groups recall (always of the names) was best when the input was an object, next best for pictures, and poorest for words. When people are instructed to use imagery to learn high-imagery list items, recall is higher than for rehearsal instructions. Bower (1972) presented twenty consecutive pairs of nouns to students in a paired-associate task in which subjects had to recall the second word in each pair when given the first word as a cue. When the students were instructed to rehearse the pairs, they recalled only 33 percent correctly; but when they were told to form interacting images for each pair, they recalled 80 percent.

Generally, tasks that require visual imagery increase the learning of the imaged items (Johnson-Laird, Gibbs, & deMowbray, 1978; Ross, 1981). For example, Jacoby, Craik, and Begg (1979) found people are better able to recognize and recall the names of animals if they are involved in a difficult mental size comparison (e.g., deciding which is larger, a tiger or a donkey) than an easy comparison (e.g., choosing the larger of a frog and a kangaroo). However, Bower and Winzenz (1970) showed that explicit imagery instructions do not have to be given to induce people to use imagery, and hence to improve recall.

They presented two groups of subjects with thirty pairs of words, such as frog-tree. The subjects' task was to learn to produce the second word in each pair given the first word as a cue. One group was told to form a visual image of the two objects interacting in some way. The other group was told to think of a sentence that contained both words. The imagery group recalled 87 percent of the words and the sentence group 77 percent of the words. Notice that, despite the different instructions, the structural description that is encoded when making up a linking sentence may be exactly the same as the structural description of an interactive image. For example, the meaning of the linking sentence *The frog was sitting under a tree* may simply be an interactive image of a frog sitting under a tree.

Bobrow and Bower (1969) found that a linking sentence is a more effective learning tool when the student makes it up for himself, which is a voluntary action. Bobrow and Bower had two groups of undergraduates learn word pairs through linking sentences. In the experimental group, each student had to make up his or her own linking sentence as each word pair was presented. In the control group a yoked control subject was given each sentence that the experimental student made up. In the test, the first member of each word pair was presented and the student had to respond with the second member. Students in the experimental group recalled 58% of the response words but students in the control group recalled only 29% of the response words.

ATTENTION AND LEARNING

In ordinary life awareness is crowded with more things than you can possible remember. Often only those details to which attention is directed are encoded. If a comment calls attention to a detail of a scene or picture, the witness is more likely to recognize that detail (Loftus & Kallman, 1979), to discriminate it from other pictures lacking the detail (Jorg & Hormann, 1978), and to recognize the similarity of other scenes that contain that detail (Bartlett, Till, & Levy, 1980). The influence of a label can be quite subtle. Jorg and Horman (1978) found that whether a picture was called a fish or a flounder influenced the distracters from which it could be discriminated (also see Nagae, 1980; Warren & Horn, 1982). Carmichael, Hogan, and Walters (1932) found that the verbal label (eye glasses versus dumbbells) influenced how an observer subsequently drew an ambiguous pattern. Bower and Holyoak (1973) found that a verbal label influenced the recognition of a sound. In a wide-ranging review of memory studies, Hasher and Zacks (1979) showed that many of the differences observed in the learning abilities of people of different ages and in different situations were the result of the differing amounts of attention the people could devote to the inputs.

When attention is directed to an aspect of a study item that would not be encoded automatically it influences the learning of that input. For this reason, attention plays a special role in the **dual encoding** of word and pictures through both verbal rehearsal and visual imagery. Pictures automatically activate visual representations and words automatically activate verbal representations, so there is a bias to rely on just visual imagery for pictures and just verbal rehearsal for words. Generally, any task that encourages dual encoding, by encouraging the visual imagining of the referents of words or the naming of pictures, increases learning (D'Agostino, O'Neill, & Paivio, 1977). Durso and Johnson (1980) had students perform either a verbal task (e.g., What is the name of the item?) or an imaginal task (e.g., How long would it take to draw the object?) for words and pictures and then gave them a surprise memory task. They found that both recognition and recall for words was better following the imaginal task than the verbal task but the reverse was true for pictures.

Similarly, to learn unrelated, dissimilar items attention is better directed towards constructing a structural description that includes them. Conversely, to learn related, similar items attention is better directed towards encoding details that distinguish among them. Begg (1978a) found that related words were better remembered if the task drew attention to differences among the words, whereas unrelated words were better remembered if similarity relations were processed. Similarly, Einstein and Hunt (1980) found that pleasantness ratings produced greater recall for lists of related words than a category-sorting task, but that the reverse was true for lists of unrelated words.

STORY LEARNING

Nowhere is the effect of structural descriptions on learning more dramatic than in memory for essays and stories. The better the material is understood, the more of it that is remembered. The role of understanding in learning was demonstrated in a series of ingenious experiments conducted by John Bransford and his colleagues (Bransford, 1979). In a typical experiment students were asked to read the following passage (Bransford and Johnson 1972, p. 722):

> The procedure is actually quite simple. First you arrange things into different groups. Of course, one pile may be sufficient depending on how much there is to do. If you have to go somewhere else due to lack of facilities that is the next step, otherwise you are pretty well set. It is important not to overdo things. That is, it is better to do too few things at once than too many. In the short run, this may not seem important but complications can easily arise. A mistake can be expensive as well. At first the whole procedure will seem complicated. Soon, however, it will become just another facet of life. It is difficult to foresee any end to the necessity for this task in the immediate future, but then one never can tell. After the procedure is completed one arranges the materials into different groups again. Then they can be put into their appropriate places. Eventually they will be used once more and the whole cycle will then have to be repeated. However, that is part of life.

After reading the passage, the students were asked to recall as much as they could. Try recalling the passage yourself right now. You will probably find it difficult to remember very much at all, which was also true for the students in the actual experiment. Because the sentences cannot be easily integrated into an existing conceptual structure, the passage is difficult to remember. Now suppose we tell you that the passage is entitled, "Doing the Laundry." Try reading the passage again. You will find that it suddenly all makes sense. In the actual experiment students who were given the title before they read the passage recalled more of it.

Writers make use of titles, headings, and opening sentences to call up relevant knowledge that can be used to interpret incoming information. The new information is encoded by linking it to the old. Sulin and Dooling (1974) cleverly demonstrated this point. People usually do not confuse facts from different semantic categories. You do not mix up what you read in your psychology text with what you read in your history text. However, Sulin and Dooling showed that when people integrate what they are learning with what they already know, they are soon unable to discriminate the new knowledge from the old. They had one group of students read the following passage, entitled "Carol Harris's Need for Professional Help" (Sulin & Dooling, 1974, p. 256):

> Carol Harris was a problem child from birth. She was wild, stubborn, and violent. By the time Carol turned eight, she was still unmanageable. Her parents were very concerned about her mental health. There was no good institution for her problem in her state. Her parents finally decided to take some action. They hired a private teacher for Carol.

A second group of students read exactly the same passage, except for one change: the name "Helen Keller" was substituted for "Carol Harris." After reading the passage, all the students were given a recognition test. They were presented with a series of sentences and asked to judge whether or not each had been included in the passage. The most interesting part of the experiment focused on the responses given to one critical test sentence: "She was deaf, dumb, and blind." Since this sentence was not in the passage, everyone should have rejected it. In fact, students who had read the Carol Harris version did exactly that; not one of them claimed that the sentence had been presented. However, 20 percent of the students who read the Helen Keller version erroneously indicated that they had read the critical sentence. This difference in mistaken recognition was even more dramatic if the recognition test was postponed a week. Only 5 percent of the Carol Harris subjects misrecognized the critical sentence, but a whopping 50 percent of the Helen Keller students indicated that they had read it (see also Kozminsky, 1977).

EMOTION AND LEARNING

Recall that the amygdala, which extends from the hippocampus, is the primary control center for human emotion. Cahill and McGaugh (1995) used a clever experimental technique to demonstrate the influence of emotional arousal on learning. College students were shown a sequence of a dozen slides while told a story about a mother taking her son to visit his father at work. Two versions of the story accompanied the slides. Half the students heard the emotionally neutral version of the story, in which the boy viewed an accident simulation in which make up artists created realistic looking injuries. The rest of the students heard an emotionally arousing story in which the boy was in an accident and surgeons re-attached his severed feet. In a multiple-choice test given two weeks later, the group of students who heard the emotionally arousing story performed better than the students who heard the emotionally neutral story. Throughout life emotion plays a role in determining which experiences are remembered. The more emotional the experience the more likely elements of it will be encoded in memory (Cahill & McGaugh, 1995).

In contrast to strongly felt emotions of grief and joy, which make an event much more memorable, depression has a negative effect on information processing (Hasher & Zacks, 1979). Depressed people learn less in experimental situations (Watts, Morris, & MacLeod, 1987; Watts, & Sharrock, 1987). Also, profound depression in an elderly person may produce a pseudodementia (Wells, 1979) in which there is a generalized loss in the abilities to learn, recall, comprehend, and reason. The reason that a severely depressed person is impaired in learning may depend on the cause of the depression. In some cases the depressed person may simply not direct attention to the learning task. But in other cases an impairment in brain function may cause both the depression and the learning deficit. Massman, Delis, Butters, Dupont, and Gillin (1992) compared depressed patients with amnesic patients suffering from Alzheimer's disease and Huntington's disease (described below) on a battery of memory tests. They were able to discriminate 70% of the patients from amnesics because their learning deficits were not as profound. However, the learning deficits of 30% of the depressed patients were indistinguishable from the deficits (described below) observed in patients with Huntington's disease, which results from deterioration of the basal ganglia. So there may be more than one cause of depression and they may be distinguishable by the severity of their effects on learning.

In normal cognitive functioning so much is recognized and recalled that the facilitating effect of strong emotion on learning is masked. However, when learning is severely impaired strong emotion can produce little islands of memory in a sea of forgetting (Zola-Morgan & O'Berg, 1980). For example, the author once tested an amnesic patient who had been brought in for testing by his family. The man did not know who had brought him to the office (his wife, son, and daughter), what year it was, or who was president. But he volunteered the information that he had been at the same hospital the previous Friday when his brother died. This lone memory was accurate. Another amnesic man was institutionalized for years when he suffered carbon monoxide poisoning. One day his son and daughter-in-law came to visit, placed a baby in his arms, and told him the baby was his granddaughter. Ever after that he always remembered that child and always asked after her by name. However, he always thought of her as a little baby, even after she was a grown woman who gave him her own infant to hold.

MEMORY AND AGING

Memory is a topic that is of much more concern to the old than to the young. For college students studying cognitive psychology, memory is just one more topic to be studied. Not one student in a hundred worries about his or her own memory. But if a cognitive psychologist says, while in earshot of a group of people past their fifth decade, that he studies memory, inevitably one or more individuals volunteer that their memory is not what it once was and ask if anything can be done.

As people age, there is a general decline in physiological arousal and this decline has a pervasive effect on emotion and cognition. With age an input produces less activation of its perceptual representation (Di Lollo, Arnett, & Kruk, 1982) and hence people are less successful at dividing attention among multiple inputs (Craik, 1977).   Though many small declines in the ability to perform cognitive tasks can be detected by demanding laboratory tasks, virtually no tasks in daily life place sufficient demands on attention so that the decline in awareness affects task performance.   So for the most part, the decline goes unnoticed.   The one task in which the decline in performance has a noticeable effect on ordinary levels of performance is the encoding of new information, and many old people are keenly aware of this decline.

Brain imaging studies indicate that aging is primarily associated with changes in the prefrontal cortex and in the medial temporal cortex (Rabbitt & Lowe, 2000).   First, consider the medial temporal cortex.   Since the medial temporal cortex is important for declarative learning, it seems reasonable to expect a change in declarative learning as a function of age.   In fact, as people age there is a decline in learning ability that is usually detectable in the seventh decade of life (Rabbitt & Lowe, 2000; Sliwinski & Buschke, 1999).   Even when young and old subjects use exactly the same mnemonic strategies (Hulicka & Grossman, 1967; Hulicka, Sterns, & Grossman, 1967; Hultsch, 1971) and when they are given a recognition test, which eliminates any potential retrieval deficit (Erber, 1978; Kausler & Klein, 1978), the young subjects remember more.   People show the most consistent decline on learning tests that have been designed to minimize the effects of processes other than learning and are believed to require medial temporal functioning.   One test in particular that has been shown to be primarily a learning test and to be sensitive to aging is the Cued Category Retrieval Test.   The subject must identify the category for each of the 64 words on the study list.   For example, for *eagle* the response would be *bird*.   There are 4 words each from 16 categories on the list.   This study procedure ensures that all subjects encode each list item in the same way.   During the test, first there is free recall of the list and then each category term is presented and the subject has to report the four instances of the category that were on the study list (Sliwinski & Bushke, 1999).

Next consider the frontal cortex.   The frontal cortex is important for various planning and reasoning functions (that will be discussed in later chapters).   People's abilities in these areas do show declines, but all of the abilities associated with the frontal cortex also require the functioning of other parts of the brain, especially the medial temporal cortex.   The level of ability on tasks associated with the frontal cortex in the elderly is closely associated with their level of performance on all kinds of cognitive tasks.   So it is not clear whether the decline in abilities associated with the frontal cortex are the result of changes in the frontal cortex or in changes in the quality of information that it receives from other areas in the brain (Rabbitt & Lowe, 2000; Sliwinski & Buschke, 1999).

In summary, the seriousness of the age-related decline in encoding should be neither minimized nor exaggerated.   The decline is real and cannot be wished away. As people age, they must put more time into learning.   However, as long as a person is willing to put in the time (Hulicka & Wheeler, 1976; Treat & Reese, 1976), the ability to acquire new information remains more than adequate to keep up with changes in the environment and does not impair performance in most human endeavors.

ANTEROGRADE AMNESIA

Brain damage can produce deficits in the ability to learn new information. **Anterograde** amnesia is defined as an inability to remember events that occurred after a brain injury.   It is contrasted with **retrograde** amnesia, which is the inability to remember events that occurred before a brain injury.   As mentioned above, learning requires a circuit including three adjacent interior brain areas, the medial temporal cortex, the anterior thalamic nuclei, and the basal forebrain.   The temporal lobes are essential to the permanent storage of memory traces.   The storage system is quite robust.   Damage to the medial temporal lobe of one hemisphere leaves, at worst, a mild deficit in the retention of either visual inputs (if the right hemisphere is damaged) or auditory inputs (if the left hemisphere is damaged).   But if certain structures are damaged bilaterally in the interior of the temporal lobes, then anterograde amnesia results.   In a famous surgical disaster, anterograde amnesia resulted from the deliberate bilateral destruction of the hippocampus and surrounding cortex in the medial temporal lobes (Milner, 1975). Anterograde amnesia also results from bilateral destruction of the nuclei of the thalamus that connect with the hippocampus. Since the thalamus is part of the diencephalon this is called diencephalic amnesia. Finally, anterograde amnesia also results when the arteries that supply blood to the basal forebrain are damaged (Gade, 1982).

TEMPORARY AMNESIA

Temporary amnesia is a common consequence of a shock to the brain, which may be caused by a blow to the head. A head injury may produce a temporary amnesia lasting from a few minutes to a few months. One common source of such head injuries is collisions during sports competitions. When Dick (1994) used the NCAA surveillance system to uniformly evaluate head injuries in twelve intercollegiate sports he found a surprisingly uniform rate of head injury across sports. Ice hockey had the highest percentage of head injuries, followed by football and field hockey, women's lacrosse, and men's soccer. An apparently minor head injury can produce a deficit in word-list learning or digit span that can last for weeks (Ruff, Levin, Mattis, High, Marshall, Eisenberg, & Tabaddor, 1989). Otherwise, the individual is unimpaired in daily life. However, a learning deficit that is only detectable by testing may be quite significant if the athlete is a student!

A somewhat mysterious temporary amnesia, called **transient global amnesia,** may occur for from 2 to 12 hours, most commonly in middle-aged to elderly men. For most cases, the cause is unknown, but may be the result of a temporary reduction of blood flow to the medial temporal region of the brain. In a minority of cases, the patient has apparently had a seizure. In these cases the disorder is called **transient epileptic amnesia** (Kopelman, 2002).

Sometimes transient epileptic amnesia is deliberately induced. Depression may be cured by electronic convulsive therapy (ECT). An electric shock is applied to the cortex, which induces a seizure. When the depression is lifted, any pseudodementia caused by depression, which includes a learning deficit among its symptoms, disappears. Ironically, Larry Squire (1981) showed that electric shock itself causes temporary anterograde amnesia. He compared patients who received electric shock with alcoholic Korsakoff patients on a yes-no picture recognition task. Alcoholic Korsakoff's patients have a severe permanent amnesia. Yet Squire found that the patients receiving electric shock showed more forgetting between 2- and 32-hour tests than those with Korsakoff's syndrome. Another source of temporary amnesia is lithium (which relieves manic-depressive mood swings), and the tricyclic antidepressants, like valium (Judd, Squire, Butters, Salmon, & Paller, 1987). Unfortunately, a side effect of the treatment of depression is a temporary impairment in learning ability.

Of special interest among drugs that induce amnesia is Midazolam. Midazolam is a safe, fast-acting drug that produces five minutes after administration an anterograde amnesia lasting about an hour by interfering with normal processing of neurotransmitters in the hippocampus. It leaves other cognitive functions intact. It is used in experimental studies of learning to determine the precise effect a single study episode has on memory by having volunteers perform a study task both under the effect of Midazolam and placebo (Hirshman, Fisher, Henthorn, Arndt, & Passannante, 2002). Such results will be mentioned in Chapter 9.

The most common cause of drug-induced temporary amnesia is alcohol. While a person is drunk, the storage of information in memory is impaired (Hartley, Birnbaum, & Parker, 1978; Ryan & Butters, 1983). The most dramatic aspect of this impairment is the well-known blackout phenomenon. Later when the individual sobers up, he or she is unable to remember what occurred while drunk. This short-term encoding impairment clears up after the alcohol passes through the system if there is only occasional drinking. But frequent drinking results in a deficit even when sober from the poisonous effects of the drug. The effect of alcohol is insidious. The change in memory from day to day is imperceptible. Furthermore, whatever skills people use in their daily activities remain unimpaired. Frequently, years of gradual mental decline go unnoticed. Hence even a superficially healthy person who is addicted to alcohol—someone who may appear to be functioning as a businessperson, college professor, or student—may suffer from a memory disorder. The brains of even young alcoholics in their twenties and thirties show cortical atrophy. Their brains also show abnormal electrical activity during target detection (Ryan & Butters, 1984). These changes cause a variety of nonverbal cognitive deficits. Ryan and Butters (1980) found that detoxified alcoholics performed more poorly than age-matched controls on paired-associate learning tests of unrelated words, and of digits and unfamiliar symbols (see also Ryan & Butters, 1983). There are also deficits involving visuospatial reasoning (Jones & Parsons, 1972) and visuospatial attention (Becker, Butters, Hermann, & D'Angelo, 1983). If at some point the person stops drinking, then there is a gradual improvement in some cognitive functions, although the ability to store new information remains permanently impaired (Brandt, Butters, Ryan, & Bayog, 1983).

PERMANENT AND PROGRESSIVE AMNESIA

When there is bilateral damage to the medial temporal cortex or the pathways to it, a permanent amnesia is the result. Damage can result from trauma, poisoning, anoxia, vascular disorders, or herpes encephalitis. The location and extent of the damage determine the resulting disability. Usually the disorder is a syndrome, which means that there is more than one symptom. Three types of disorders can be distinguished. In the first type of amnesia damage is restricted to the medial portion of the brain and only the process of consolidating new memory traces is impaired. In the second type of amnesia damage to the temporal cortex is more widespread; long-term memory traces are destroyed as well. In the third type of disorder the process of forming associations among memory traces is impaired. First, if only the medial temporal lobes are bilaterally damaged, whether by surgery, or stroke, or encephalitis (a viral infection) then a relatively pure permanent amnesia results in which both recognition and recall of past events are impaired. Other cognitive functions are intact. Similarly, if the connecting thalamic nuclei are damaged the predominant symptom is again a permanent amnesia that is qualitatively indistinguishable from medial temporal amnesia. Second, a disease process may destroy both medial and lateral portions of the temporal cortex and produce both an anterograde amnesia, as described here, and a semantic dementia, as described in Chapter 5. Alzheimer's disease progressively damages many cortical and subcortical brain structures until death results. Along the way there is an increasingly severe semantic dementia as well as an increasingly severe amnesia. Third, Huntington's disease is the result of progressive damage to the basal ganglia, which leads to the loss of voluntary movement in addition to an increasingly severe amnesia. This amnesia is distinguishable from the other anterograde amnesias because recognition is much less impaired than recall.

TABLE 7.2
Impairments that characterize different dementias

Cognitive Function	Example Task	Hippocampal Amnesia	Korsakoff's Dementia	Alzheimer's Dementia	Huntington's Dementia
Motor Skill	pursuit rotor	normal	normal	normal	impaired
Semantic Priming	word completion	normal	normal	impaired	normal
Semantic Memory	verbal fluency	normal	normal	impaired instance	impaired production
Long-term Memory	list recognition	impaired	impaired	impaired	mildly impaired
Working & Long-term Memory	list recall	impaired	impaired	impaired	impaired

Table 7.2 contrasts the performance of patients with different types of amnesic disorders on a variety of cognitive tasks. Huntington's disease is distinguished from the other disorders by impaired motor skills and less impaired recognition. Alzheimer's disease is distinguished from medial temporal/diencephalic amnesia by impaired word finding. Notice that Table 7.2 shows that both recognition and recall are impaired in anterograde amnesia. This would necessarily be the case if nothing of an input is encoded. However, when the learning deficit causing the anterograde amnesia is moderate or mild, recognition may be relatively less impaired than recall (Kopelman, 2002). This is because, as will be described in Chapter 9, recall requires the encoding of more information than recognition does.

MEDIAL TEMPORAL/DIENCEPHALIC AMNESIA

The same dense learning deficit is caused by bilateral damage to either the hippocampus and surrounding area of the medial temporal cortex or to the anterior thalamic nuclei. The first type of injury is the result of rare misfortune but the same type of injury is most often the result of willful self-abuse by the excessive consumption of alcohol.

Medial temporal amnesia. The most famous amnesic in the world is a man known as H. M. He is a man of above-average intelligence who had parts of his hippocampus and the surrounding cortical tissue removed in 1953 to alleviate life-threatening epileptic seizures. He has almost total anterograde amnesia for all events since that time, as has been described in detail by Brenda Milner and her colleagues (Milner, Corkin, & Teuber, 1968). A few other people have disorders like those of H. M. Encephalitis damaged the hippocampus of an optical engineer (S. S.). R. B. was a postal worker who had the blood supply to his brain cut off as the result of an atrial tear that occurred while he was in the hospital recovering from coronary artery bypass surgery (Zola-Morgan, Squire, & Amaral, 1986).

Diencephalic amnesia: Korsakoff's syndrome. Diencephalic amnesia is the result of bilateral damage to the diencephalon, which is comprised of the thalamus and hypothalamus. The most common, hence the most studied, form of diencephalic amnesia is alcoholic Korsakoff's syndrome. This disorder is different from one caused by the diffuse damage that results from alcoholism. In **alcoholic dementia** all cognitive functions are equally impaired as the result of alcoholic poisoning. In alcoholic Korsakoff's syndrome memory is much more severely impaired than other cognitive functions. IQ remains normal.

Alcoholic Korsakoff's syndrome represents the chronic state of what is known as the **Wernicke-Korsakoff disorder**. It is the result of a thiamine deficiency coupled with alcohol abuse. Alcohol consumption causes Alcoholic-Korsakoff's syndrome because the metabolism of alcohol uses up the supply of thiamine, which is an essential nutrient for neurons that make up parts of the diencephalon. When excessive drinking is combined with a thiamine-poor diet, cells in the diencephalon begin to die. However, not all alcoholics develop Korsakoff's syndrome. The necessary conditions for the development of the syndrome include the nutritional factor, lack of thiamine in the diet, and possibly a genetic factor. The onset of the syndrome is signaled by a single traumatic event. This phase is the Wernicke phase of the disorder, named after the German neurologist who first described it. In the initial, acute Wernicke's phase there is confusion and severe motor dysfunction in the eyes and limbs. If the patient is not treated with large doses of thiamine he is in danger of fatal midbrain hemorrhage. If treated with thiamine promptly about 75% of the patients enter the chronic Korsakoff's phase and about 25% recover their intellectual functioning (Butters & Stuss, 1989). The chronic Korsakoff phase of the syndrome is named after the Russian neurologist who first described it.

After several weeks these symptoms are replaced with a permanent anterograde amnesia that is indistinguishable from medial temporal amnesia. This is by far the most obvious and severe symptom. Though 75% of Korsakoff patients show a degree of improvement over time, learning ability does not return to a normal level (Kopelman, 2002). There are other changes in mental status, as well. Not surprisingly, there is a deficit in selective attention (recall from Chapter 4 that selective attention requires the opening and closing of thalamic gates). There are also mood and personality changes. Even when there is a prior history of aggression, patients are described as apathetic, euphoric, and irritable. Finally, there are mild visuospatial deficits. The problem solving, visuoperceptual, attention, and motivational changes that characterize diencephalic amnesia are similar to those reported for patients with damage to the prefrontal cortex (Butters & Stuss, 1989). Hence it may be that many alcoholic Korsakoff patients suffer from alcoholic dementia in addition to Korsakoff's syndrome.

GENERAL CHARACTERISTICS OF MEDIAL TEMPORAL/DIENCEPHALIC AMNESIA

The memory disorder from which these patients suffer combines normal perceptual and motor learning (Corkin, 1968) with an almost complete absence of declarative learning. To get a feeling for just how devastating this memory loss is, let us consider a specific case. Imagine that you are introduced to a pleasant man in his midfifties. A few minutes of conversation indicate that the man is of above average intelligence. To confirm this impression, you could administer an IQ test, on which the man might score well above the normal range. You ask him about himself, and he tells you about his wife, children, and job. There is no apparent memory deficit. At this point you leave him. Five minutes later, you happen to run into the same man again. He shows no sign of knowing you and, in fact, denies ever meeting you before in his life. Now imagine that you continue to meet with this man every day. You rapidly discover that at every meeting you must reintroduce yourself. He never has any memory of the previous meetings. In addition, he was injured years ago and his children are grown up.

IMPLICIT MEMORY IN MEDIAL TEMPORAL/DIENCEPHALIC AMNESIA

Whenever an experience produces an improvement on a task independently of whether the individual remembers the experience, improvement is called **implicit memory**. Like patients with medial temporal anterograde amnesia, only explicit declarative memory is affected in diencephalic amnesia. Procedural memory remains intact and priming is relatively unimpaired.

Skill learning. Alcoholic Korsakoff patients can acquire and retain motor and visuoperceptual skills normally. Patients improve on the pursuit-rotor task, in which a stylus must be maintained on a moving target (Cermak, Lewis, Butters, & Goodglass, 1973), and in the reading of mirror-imaged writing (Cohen & Squire, 1981; Martone, Butters, Payne, Becker, & Sax, 1983). Every day the mirror-tracing apparatus must be shown to the patient as if for the first time, and the patient must be reinstructed in its use. But once he or she takes up the task, the patient shows the same increment in improvement over the previous day's performance as an individual whose memory is unimpaired. Hence, the patient learns the skill normally without having any memory of having ever performed it before.

Priming. In medial temporal amnesia the semantic network is intact and logogen activation is normal. Priming occurs normally, as revealed in a word completion task, even in the absence of explicit declarative learning. If you ask the patient to remember a word, (e.g., *butter*), and ask him to recall it 5 minutes later, he cannot do so. If you give him a recognition test, his ability to select *butter* as the word he heard is at chance. However, if you ask him to say the first word he can think of that begins with bu- he is about as likely to say butter as a normal individual who was asked to remember the word (Graf, Shimamura, & Squire, 1985).

Like patients with medial temporal anterograde amnesia, alcoholic Korsakoff patients have intact semantic networks, as revealed by normal priming. Alcoholic Korsakoff patients have normal implicit memory for word completion, free association, perceptual identification, preference, and judgment tasks. The first demonstration of intact implicit memory in alcoholic Korsakoff patients was provided by Elizabeth Warrington and Lawrence Weiskrantz (1970; 1974). They found that amnesic patients (including alcoholic Korsakoff patients) could exhibit almost normal performance when fragmented words, fragmented pictures, and two-letter word stems were used to cue recall. For example, amnesics who were severely impaired in their intentional recall and recognition of common words from a study list nevertheless evidenced rapid, accurate identification when shown the first two letters of the word. They reported that this priming effect occurred 24 and 72 hours later. Warrington & Weiskrantz tested only with explicit memory instructions but Graf, Squire, and Mandler (1984) used both explicit and implicit procedures. The explicit instructions were to use the three-letter word stems to cue recall of the previously presented words; the implicit instructions were to complete the stems with the first words that came to mind. Alcoholic Korsakoff patients produced significantly fewer of the to-be-remembered words than control subjects with explicit instructions (as well as with free recall and recognition). However the two groups generated the same number of study words in the implicit free-association condition.

Another demonstration of intact implicit memory in alcoholic Korsakoff patients was provided by Gardner and his collaborators (Gardner, Boller, Moreines, & Butters, 1973). After subjects were presented with a list of common words (e.g., tennis, lettuce), belonging to one of six general categories (e.g., sports, vegetables), recall was assessed under three different conditions. In one condition the patients were simply asked to recall the words that had been read to them (i. e., free recall); in another, intentional recall was cued by category (e.g., "A few moments ago I asked you to remember some words. One of them was a sport. What was it?"); in the third condition the subjects were simply given a category name (e.g., vegetables) and asked to produce the first example of this category that came to mind. The results showed that although the Korsakoff patients were significantly impaired in comparison to intact subjects on the first two recall conditions, they did not differ from controls on the third (free association) condition. Both the alcoholic Korsakoff patients and intact controls tended to produce previously presented words (e.g., tennis) when asked to free associate to the category names (e.g., sports). Both Gardner et al. (1973) and Graf et al. (1984) found that alcoholic Korsakoff patients produced the same number of responses with both implicit and explicit instructions but normal subjects produced fewer study items with implicit instructions.

If priming is the result of the activation of associations that already exist in semantic memory then amnesic patients should show normal priming for familiar targets whose representations are already a part of semantic memory but not for novel targets. Gooding, Mayes, and van Eijk (2000) conducted a meta-analysis of 36 studies describing 59 separate measures of implicit memory for familiar versus novel information in amnesic patients and healthy controls that produced results generally consistent with this hypothesis. For the 23 measures of priming for familiar information controls performed better 11 times and patients 12 times, so there was no difference in priming for familiar information (e.g., words, famous faces). For the remaining 36 measures of priming in which the targets e.g., nonwords) or associations between them (e.g., unrelated word pairs) were novel, controls performed better than patients 27 times. The meta-analysis shows that amnesic patients generally show normal priming for familiar information but not for unfamiliar information; however, some studies have not found this result. This may be because assessing priming effects requires a sufficiently difficult test so that healthy controls may perform better than amnesic patients. Otherwise, the failure to find a difference may be a ceiling effect (Ostergaard, 1994).

ALZHEIMER'S DISEASE

Alzheimer's disease eventually comes to include damage throughout the temporal cortex, including the medial cortex, and so includes both semantic dementia and anterograde amnesia among its symptoms. Alzheimer's disease occurs when bits of protein that should be broken down and discarded accumulate as tangles and plaques within and between neurons. The growth is progressive and irreversible and it eventually destroys brain cells. Whereas normal aging is accompanied by a shrinkage of neurons, in Alzheimer's disease there is an actual loss of neurons. The pathological changes tend to appear first in the temporal region and then spread over the temporoparietal cortex, eventually reaching the frontal association cortices. The occipital and motor cortices remain largely intact. In the early stages of Alzheimer's disease most of the basal ganglia and thalamic structures remain relatively unaffected, but in the middle and later stages of the disease changes also occur in these subcortical structures. Some of the cognitive impairment is the result of swelling from the collection of fluid occurs around the plaques. The only effective treatment for the early cognitive symptoms is ibuprofen or some other nonsteroidal medicine that reduces swelling, such as Advil and Motrin.

The severe anterograde amnesia associated with the disease is directly attributable to the fact that the disease affects the medial temporal cortex bilaterally. Indeed, often the first detectable symptom is anterograde amnesia, as measured by the Cued Category Retrieval test (Buschke, Kuslansky, Katz, Sliwinski, Eckholdt, & Lipton, 1999). Typically, amnesia and problem-solving deficits are the first signs of the disorder, followed by anomic aphasia, and still later by visuospatial deficits. However, procedural memory, including motor and visuospatial skills, is preserved.

Patients lose information from working memory extremely rapidly; in fact they forget faster than purely amnesic patients do. They also have anomia, i.e., word finding difficulty (see Chapter 5). They are deficient on picture naming and on verbal fluency tests. A verbal fluency test is one in which all the members of a category must be generated, e.g., words that start with the letter F, or things found in a supermarket. The poor performance on these tasks reflects a breakdown in semantic memory. The breakdown has been described as "bottom up" because patients tend to lose instances while retaining category labels. For example, a patient asked to generate items found in a supermarket may report meat, vegetables, fruits, cereals, etc., but fail to mention instances like steak, beef, potatoes, corn, etc. (Hodges, Salmon, & Butters, 1992).

Since there is damage to semantic memory, patients with Alzheimer's disease do not benefit from semantic priming. Therefore they do not exhibit implicit memory when asked to complete word stems or recognize picture fragments named by words they have studied earlier (Butters, Heindel, & Salmon, 1990).

HUNTINGTON'S DISEASE

The learning disorder in Huntington's disease is different from the other learning disorders described above. Because of the deterioration of the basal ganglia, the ability to make a voluntary response is impaired. So motor skill learning is impaired. Figure 7.9 shows the performance of normal controls, amnesics, Alzheimer's patients, and Huntington's patients on a pursuit-rotor task, in which a stylus must be held on a dot on a rotating turntable. As shown in the figure, all groups learn the task normally, except for HD patients, who fail to learn the task at all (Heindel, Butters, & Salmon, 1988).

The impairment in the ability to act impairs the sophisticated verbal rehearsal and visual imagery strategies necessary to promote recall. Hence patients with Huntington's disease perform much more poorly on recall than recognition tasks. This dissociation is not true of other forms of anterograde amnesia. Since recall is impaired, Huntington's patients are impaired in verbal fluency. But since they do not have anomia, unlike Alzheimer's patients they do not produce an abnormal preponderance of category labels over instances (Troster, Salmon, McCullough, & Butters, 1989).

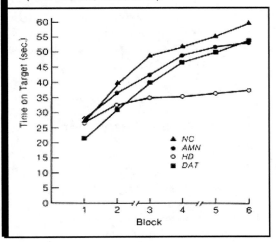

FIGURE 7.9

Performance of Alzheimer's (DAT), Huntington's Disease (HD), and amnesic (AMN) patients and normal controls (NC) on the pursuit-rotor task (from Heindel, et al., 1988).

SUMMARY

- Semantic learning is the result of the successive operation of several distinct systems.
  - The recognition system (Chapter 5) creates a novel representation in working memory by indexing existing representations.
    * Since learning often involves combining existing representations from semantic memory, knowledge plays a role in learning.
  - The medial temporal declarative learning system
    * includes thalamus, hippocampus and ventral medial prefrontal cortex.
    * encodes the indexes, thus making the novel representation permanent.
  - The learning system is activated, thus making the novel representation permanent, in one of three ways.
    * If the emotional system signals that it is important by associating the representation with a strong emotion, then the probability of encoding the representation increases.
    * If the representation is the target or consequence of some voluntary action then the probability of encoding it increases.
    * If the representation is generated by some action whose specific function is mnemonic, i.e., to encode the representation, then the probability of encoding it increases.

- The most common mnemonic action is verbal rehearsal
  - Rehearsal is the result of the phonological – articulatory circuit at the temporal – parietal interface (Figure 5.3)
    * Recall of the last four (hence most recently presented) items is elevated by retrieval from articulatory representations that are part of working memory. This is called the recency effect.
  - The effect of a rehearsal is to construct a new hierarchical representation in memory by combining two existing representations in working memory (organized in the prefrontal cortex) under a common node.
  - Each rehearsal creates a new representation in semantic memory with some probability that is usually less than one.
    * Hence, the probability of encoding a pair of representations in working memory as a new semantic representation increases with the number of distributed rehearsals.
    * Hence, the number of list items that are learned decreases as the rate of presentation of list items increases because there are fewer rehearsals.
    * Also, the first few list items tend to get more rehearsals than later items and therefore are more likely to be encoded in a hierarchical representation of the list. As a result, the beginning list items are more likely to be recalled either immediately or after a delay. This is called the primacy effect.
    * Since there is both a primacy and a recency effect, immediate recall is best for the beginning and end of a list, so immediate recall is a U-shaped function of list position.

- Existing structural descriptions can be used to encode representations of new instances through:
  - Generating visual images
  - High imagery words and nameable pictures

- Anterograde amnesia is the inability to learn new things. It results from bilateral damage to the interior of the temporal cortex; especially the hippocampus or to connecting areas in the thalamus.
  - Declarative memory is impaired.
  - Perceptual-motor skill learning is normal.

Chapter 8

CATEGORIZATION & MNEMONICS

C ategories are such a ubiquitous part of the way we view the world that imagining what the world would be like without them is difficult. For example, imagine that you are shown a set of pictures of common objects spread out in a random order on a table. These pictures may be of such items as a cow, a rose, a desk, a horse, a pansy, and a table. If you were asked to group the picture into sets of items that go together, you would undoubtedly divide them into categories such as furniture, animals, and flowers. That is, you would use the semantic categories of English to perform the task.

But damage to the temporal cortex (Chapter 5) can deprive a person of these natural categories, and in this case the obviousness of these categories disappears. When Shanon (1978) asked a patient to sort pictures he appeared unable to use the obvious categories. Rather, he divided up the pictures according to various idiosyncratic criteria. For example, during one test he put all flowers in a category with domestic animals, justifying his classification of the flowers by noting that "these are small, and are around the house. Therefore, they are domestic animals. They cannot be wild."

Categorization is vital to memory, reasoning, and problem solving. The first part of this chapter will set the stage for the chapters that follow by examining the ways in which categories come to be represented in memory.

People learn of instances as well as categories and sometimes the details of the instances are important. A phone number is useless unless it is remembered perfectly. The specialized procedures used for the encoding of details are called mnemonics. Mnemonics will be the topic of the second part of this chapter.

CATEGORIZATION AND LEARNING

As described in Chapter 6, if an infant learns to do something, like move a mobile, in a specific context, then the infant's memory is initially very specific and context-dependent. However, infants learn to generalize, and generalization becomes the basis for much semantic learning. When an infant is trained, on different occassions, to move two different mobiles through kicking, she will kick to a third, novel mobile as well (Fagen, Morrongiello, Rovee-Collier, & Gekoski, 1984). Two different visual representations of the two training mobiles have been associated with the kicking response. So the perceptual representation of a novel mobile will be compared with the representations of both training mobiles. The response to the novel mobile depends on how closely it matches a single mobile and also its average response to both mobiles. An infant will kick to a novel mobile that shares a different feature with each training mobile, even if it is not highly similar to either one of them. This process of extending a response to a novel object is called **generalization**. Because the two training mobiles were given the same response they are represented in memory as instances of a common category.

Let us consider in more detail, how a category is formed. First there is usually some perceptual similarity among the instances to which the same response it made. An **instance** may be anything that can be recognized. Sometimes there is some obvious feature or good part defined by perceptual organization that makes a set of instances appear similar. For example, a set of instances that have the same structural description and are constructed from the same geons look alike (Chapter 3). For example, most shoes look like other shoes, most chairs look like other chairs, and most birds look like other birds. All the instances of the category have the same basic shape. As a result of the normal perceptual process, both complete perceptual representations of category instances and representations of good parts in common among members are encoded. Representations of the good parts as well as representations of entire instances are associated with the category node controlling the response. Because the representations of the parts are necessarily simpler than complete instance representations, novel instances can be recognized as possible category members much faster by finding a perfect match with a category feature (i.e., a perceptual feature or good part) then by finding a partial match with a complete instance representation. Hence, novel instances may be recognized as members of a category as rapidly as familiar members. This is, of course, an example of perceptual (i.e., procedural) learning.

Second, you may consciously notice the similarity among category instances and verbally label the perceptual features and good parts that they have in common. For example, all your red clothes look somewhat similar by virtue of the fact that they are all red. This makes them easy to sort when you are washing clothes. Many concepts corresponding to concrete objects (e.g., cat, tree, and rock) are basically defined by visual representations. Early in life, categories that arise out of perceptual organization are used for labeling instances and form the basis of more elaborated hierarchical representations as both more instances, and more details of instances, are encoded. This awareness of what makes the category instances similar and the assignment of a verbal label to it is, of course, an example of declarative learning. Furthermore, whenever the perceptual representation of a novel instance is as similar to the representation of the category instances as they are to each other, then you may consciously associate it with the category label so that its perceptual representation is added to those under the category node. In this way, a category may be consciously expanded and altered through learning. When you verbally describe the features that all category instances must have, you explicitly define the category.

Other categories are defined by their characteristic functions, or uses. A weapon, for example, is anything that can serve to inflict injury. Other categories defined by function are tools, furniture, clothing, and jewelry. Occupations, such as doctor, lawyer, employee, and servant, are all functional categories. Finally, kinship terms, such as mother, father, uncle, are all categories. Furthermore, it is possible to create an indefinitely large number of categories. Throughout life the ability to define categories through naming provides a method for directing learning by directing attention to functionally important features that otherwise might not be obvious. When you select the clothes to take when you go away on vacation, you create a category containing the clothes you want.

CREATING CATEGORIES

Categories used by people in everyday life to organize their knowledge and activities. Black, dog, hammer, and father are all categories. One interesting question is where categories come from. Initially, category representations are constructed from the perceptual and social features present in the cortex at birth. Once language is learned they may be defined by merely labeling a few instances. We begin our review of categorization with a set of simple category names that have been studied extensively: the color terms.

Organization of color categories. Perceived color (more specifically, **hue**) is primarily a function of the wavelength of light. As wavelength increases, the color of light moves through the categories violet, blue, green, yellow, orange, and red, in that order. But the boundaries of the color categories are usually difficult to judge. You would probably have trouble deciding whether some hues are better described as orange or red. Anthropologists have found that languages vary considerably in the number of major color categories they have. Whereas English has eleven, the Dani tribe of New Guinea has only two.

Two anthropologists, Berlin and Kay (1969) studied the distribution of color terms across languages. They began by identifying the basic color terms in ninety-eight languages. To be classified as basic, a color term has to satisfy four criteria:

1. It must be expressed as one morpheme, or meaning-bearing lexical unit. This criterion rules out compounds like salmon-colored.
2. Its meaning cannot be included in that of another term. This criterion rules out crimson, which is included in red.
3. It must not be restricted to a small class of objects. This criterion rules out blond, which applies only to hair and perhaps furniture.
4. It must be a common term, like purple, rather than magenta.

Berlin and Kay then proceeded to map out the domain of the basic color terms in twenty languages by interviewing native speakers of each language. They showed each subject a set of 329 different-colored chips and asked the subject to answer two questions about each basic color term in his or her language:

1. What chips would you be at all willing to call by this term?
2. What chips are the best, most typical examples of the term?

The first question was designed to determine the boundaries of the color categories, while the second was designed to pick out the most central example, the focal color.

The results were quite remarkable. People were not at all consistent in drawing boundaries between the basic terms. In contrast, speakers of different languages were very consistent in selecting the focal colors (i.e., the best red, green, blue, etc.). Even though the boundaries of color categories varied from language to language, the focal colors were universal. In fact, speakers of different languages showed no more variability in their placement of focal colors than did speakers of the same language. In addition, by matching focal colors across languages, Berlin and Kay discovered that all languages draw their basic color terms from a set of eleven. In English (which has all of them) these terms are black, white, red, green, yellow, blue, brown, purple, pink, orange, and gray. Furthermore, if a language has only two color terms, they correspond to white and black. If a language has three terms, they always correspond to white, black, and red. If a language has four color terms, the fourth will correspond to green, yellow, or blue. Note that the first six terms to appear are always the primary colors of the visual system.

So apparently, the focal instances of color categories are not determined by the specific language someone speaks. But can focal colors influence cognition even if they do not correspond to linguistic categories? To answer this question, one would like to find people who speak a language that has no basic color terms. Would they nevertheless show superior memory for focal colors? While no language seems to be altogether lacking in color terms, the Dani of New Guinea speak a language that comes close. As mentioned earlier, they have only two basic color terms: mili (roughly "dark") and mola (roughly "light"). Rosch (formerly Heider) performed a number of experiments to investigate the Dani memory for colors. She showed that the Dani remember focal colors better than nonfocal ones (Heider, 1972). The Dani could also learn names for the focal colors more quickly than they could for nonfocal colors (Rosch, 1973). Furthermore, the Dani judge the similarity of colors in very much the same way as English speakers do (Heider & Olivier, 1972).

Rosch's results appeared to demonstrate that focal colors are primary in a way that does not depend on language. However, Lucy and Schweder (1979) examined the set of color chips that Rosch had used in her experiments with the Dani and found that the nonfocal chips were less easily discriminated from others in the set than were focal chips, even when memory was not involved. Thus while focal colors appear to have a special status as the central examples of color categories, as evidenced by the work of Berlin and Kay (1969), whether focality has a direct impact on memorability remains unclear.

However, focal colors do apparently determine color categories, not vice versa. But what determines which colors are focal? The answer lies in the physiology of human color perception. As mentioned in Chapter 3, the opponent process theory of color vision (DeValois & Jacobs, 1968; Hering, 1920; Jameson & Hurvich, 1955) postulates three types of color detectors: one for brightness (black vs. white) and two for hue (red vs. green and yellow vs. blue). This system has six points of maximal response, corresponding to six of the eleven basic color terms: black, white, red, green, yellow, and blue. In the first months of life infants only respond to differences among these broad color categories (Bornstein, 1976).

We still are left with the question of where the remaining five basic color terms come from. An elegant explanation of the development of the later terms was suggested by Kay and McDaniel (1978). Kay and McDaniel's explanation is illustrated in Figure 8.1. The graphs at the top of Figure 8.1 show the hypothetical goodness of the terms yellow and red when they are applied to a range of wavelengths. Each term applies best to its focal color (the peaks of the bell-shaped curves), and it applies less and less well to colors farther from the focal point. Now if this hypothetical language could add one more color category, where would be the most useful place to put the new focal point? Clearly, it is right in the middle of the "valley" between yellow and red. With only yellow and red in the color vocabulary the language has no term that applies well in this region, and speakers would be unsure about what term to use. This situation is remedied at the bottom of Figure 8.1 with the addition of orange to the language. The new focal point is placed so that orange applies best at the very point where

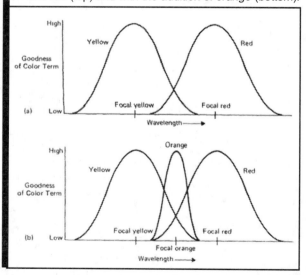

FIGURE 8.1

Hypothetical goodness of color terms with just *yellow* and *red* (top) and with the addition of *orange* (bottom).

yellow and red apply worst. Note that orange is a relatively narrow category, one that fills the gap between yellow and red without competing in the regions in which yellow or else red applies well.

Kay and McDaniel argued that the five later basic colors emerge in this way to fill gaps in the regions in which the first six terms do not apply well. But why only eleven basic terms in all? Actually, this number may only be a kind of accident of the present moment in linguistic history. More basic color terms may yet emerge as languages continue to evolve. In fact, Russian may be developing a twelfth basic term, goluboy ("light blue"). In English, conceivably, a word like turquoise may one day acquire the status of a basic term, filling a gap between blue and green. As you can see, the study of color categories has brought together work in anthropology, linguistics, cognitive psychology, and sensory psychology in an extremely fruitful way—even producing predictions about the future evolution of language.

Basic-level categories. The focal instances of color categories are independent of differences in language and culture because they are closely tied to the physiology of vision. Also, Rosch (1973) found that symmetrical geometric forms are universal focal instances. The existence of focal instances shows how visual organization guides visual category formation. If instances of two different categories differ at any of the four levels of visual organization: feature, geon, object, and scene, then pop-out occurs and the difference between the two categories is obvious. For example, the difference between yellow versus black, yellow-haired heads versus black-haired heads, and yellow cars versus black cars, is obvious.

Categories that are defined by perceptual organization are apparent in a free sorting task. In a free sorting task a person is given a set of instances and asked to sort them into whatever categories seem natural. When the categories are defined by innately specified perceptual features then most people sort the instances into about the same categories. Furthermore, new categories can be learned by merely observing instances. Even when examples of multiple categories are intermixed and subjects are not told the category to which any individual item belongs, distinctive categories can still be learned (Evans, 1967). Fried and Holyoak (1984) performed experiments in which instances of two categories of complex visual patterns were randomly intermixed, without category labels. Even though subjects were not told that they were in a category-learning task until after all the training instances had been presented, they were nonetheless able to classify novel instances in a manner indicating they had learned something about the **central tendencies** and **variability** of the categories. The central tendencies are what most category instances have in common. For example, faces share two eyes, two ears, a nose, and a mouth in specific locations. Variability are how the category instances differ. For example, faces differ on the shapes of the nose and mouth and color of the skin and hair.

One implication of this view that categorization is influenced by visual similarity is that there is a basic level at which people naturally divide the world into alternative categories (Rosch, Mervis, Gray, Johnson, & Boyes-Braem, 1976). This is the object level of visual organization. At this level instances are categorized by comparing them with visual structural descriptions. This level maximizes the perceptual similarities among instances of the same category, which match the same structural description, as well as maximizing the differences between instances of different categories, which match different structural descriptions. For example, consider the hierarchical sequence kitchen table, table, and furniture. Furniture is a functional category. It cannot be defined by a single structural description that is applicable to all instances. Table, on the other hand, has a clear visual structural description ("flat top," "usually four legs," etc.). Also, instances of table are quite distinct from instances of related categories, like chair. What about kitchen table? It has a clear visual representation, but one that is very similar to the representation of close alternatives, like living room table, which match the same structural description. So table is a basic level category. It is the concrete-category level with a structural description that distinguishes it from alternative categories defined by different structural descriptions.

Rosch et al. (1976) found that people can classify pictures most quickly into basic-level categories. For example, suppose people are shown a photograph of a kitchen table. They can classify the photograph as a table faster than they can classify it as either a kitchen table or furniture. This result suggests that basic-level categories correspond to categories that people use in the recognition of objects. Rosch et al. also noted that basic-level categories are the earliest that children use to name or sort objects. Hence, basic level categories provide another cue to the infant for learning the meanings of words, as discussed in Chapter 6. Since the caretaker and infant share the same basic level of representation the infant has a pretty good idea what the caretaker is naming. If pictures of instances are categorized on the basis of their visual structural descriptions, then an instance will be categorized most quickly at the basic level when its perceptual representation is most similar to the structural description. In fact, whereas typical instances are classified most quickly as members of the basic-level category, atypical instances are often classified more readily into subordinate categories. For example, although people can categorize a picture of a robin more quickly as a bird than as a robin, they can categorize a picture of an ostrich more quickly as an ostrich than as a bird (Jolicoeur, Gluck, and Kosslyn, 1984).

Murphy and Smith (1982) replicated Rosch and her colleagues' (1976) natural-category results with categories for four basic kinds of unusual tools, which were invented especially for the experiment. They confirmed that people use visual representations to categorize instances. In their experiments they varied the level at which a single visual representation of the category best discriminated it from its alternatives, and they found that their pictures of tools were categorized most rapidly at this level.

Subcategorizing the basic level. Of course you can elaborate a basic-level structural description into more detailed descriptions and hence elaborate a basic-level category into subcategories. If you categorize things on the basis of perceptual similarity then this brings us back to the question of what makes things look similar to each other, which brings us to the question of how perceived similarity is computed for objects that have similar but not identical structural descriptions. Medin and Schaffer (1978) proposed a detailed model of how the features of an instance are combined during the comparison with a category representation to assess similarity. Essentially, Medin and Schaffer assume that a single bad mismatch greatly diminishes similarity. Suppose we consider instances that can be represented by two feature values, as in Figure 8.2. If face (a) is moderately similar to face (b) on both features, whereas it is highly similar to face (c) on one feature and highly dissimilar to face (c) on the other, then Medin and Schaffer's model predicts that people will judge face (a) to be more similar overall to face (b) than to face (c). If faces (b) and (c) are stored in memory as instances of different categories, and if face (a) is a novel input, then face (a) will tend to be classified into the same category as face (b).

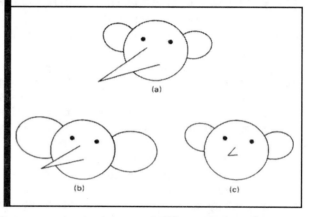

FIGURE 8.2
Instances of feature values.
(a) Large nose, medium ears; (b) medium nose, large ears; (c) small nose, medium ears. Face a) differs from face (b) on two features (its ears are smaller and its nose is larger), and it differs from face (c) on only feature (its nose). Yet face (a) looks more similar to face (b).

GENERALIZING TO NEW INSTANCES

Not all categories defined by a visual structural description or visual features are obvious. A limitless number of **artificial** categories can be defined with reference to perceptible features that are not automatically encoded by the perceptual system. (An **artificial** category is a category that has no functional significance and whose defining perceptual features are not obvious.) For example, Figure 8.3 versus Figure 8.4 contrasts pairs of obvi-

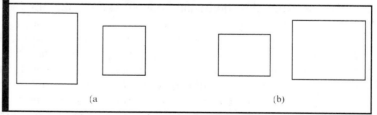

FIGURE 8.3
Two natural categories. Rectangles taller than wide (a) and rectangles wider than tall (b). (After Maddox & Ashby, 1993.)

ous and nonobvious visually-defined categories. The former are defined by whether height is greater than length and the later are defined by whether size is greater than tilt. Notice that at an abstract level the definitions of the pair of categories shown in Figure 8.3 and the pair of categories shown in Figure 8.4 are comparable. However, the pair of categories in Figure 8.3 are organized by the visual system into vertical and horizontal rectangles since orientation is a basic visual feature and it defines the difference between the categories. So people notice the difference between vertical and horizontal rectangles even if they are not labeled as instances of different categories. In contrast, people do not notice any difference between the instances of the categories in 8.4 if they are not labeled as instances of different categories. Nevertheless, such artificial categories can easily be created that a person can only learn with feedback (e.g., McKinley & Nosofsky, 1995; Medin & Schwanenflugel, 1981). That is, a person is told to sort instances into two or more categories. Every time an instance is placed in the wrong category the person is told what category it

FIGURE 8.4

Two artificial categories. Size larger than tilt (a) and tilt larger than size (b). (After Maddox & Ashby, 1993.)

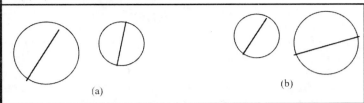

belongs in. Once observers have seen enough instances of each category with feedback they are able to identify new instances by matching them with representations of ones they have previously seen (Estes, 1986; Medin & Schaffer, 1978; Nosofsky, 1986).

Even quite complicated artifical categories can be learned by receiving feedback in an instance sorting task. For example, Arthur Reber (1967) and his colleagues studied artificial category learning by using artificial "languages" composed of letter sequences. Such a language is defined by a grammar that determines which letter strings are category instances. Figure 8.5 illustrates one such grammar, represented in a special kind of flowchart called **a finite-state network**. Category instances are generated by following the arcs from node to node and producing the letter indicated on each arc as it is traversed. An arc that returns to the

FIGURE 8.5

Finite-state grammar for generating artificial language. (From Reber 1967.)

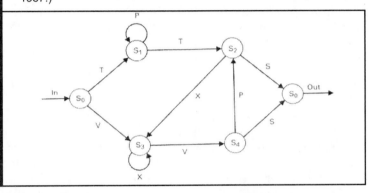

same node can be traversed any number of times in a row. The sequence always begins at the point labeled "in" and ends at the point labeled "out." For example, for the network in Figure 8.5 the sequence TTS is a category instance, as are TPPPTXVS, VXVPS, and WS. In contrast, the sequences TVTS and VXXVP do not correspond to complete paths through the network, and hence they are not category instances.

As you can see, such finite-state grammars can be quite complex. Subjects who do not have the grammar described to them as a network never spontaneously invent such a representation for it. Nonetheless, Reber has demonstrated that people who observe examples of category instances can learn to make judgments about novel strings with reasonable accuracy. More remarkably, Reber (1976) found that subjects were actually more successful in learning a category when they simply memorized sample strings than when they actively examined the same set of sample strings and tried to figure out the rule system.

The roles of procedural and declarative knowledge in categorization. Organizing a set of instances into a category involves both procedural and declarative representation. Both kinds of representations are constructed at the same time. First, a procedural structural description is constructed that organizes the representations of many instances. In the case of the vertical and horizontal rectangles in Figure 8.3 this structural description may be as simple as a vertical or horizontal line of indefinite width. In the case of an artificial language this structural description may be as complicated as the finite-state grammar in Figure 8.5. Once a structural description has been constructed, representations for new instances are constructed more rapidly by first matching them to the structural description and then filling the details. Hence they are easier to learn. In a classic study, Attneave (1957) showed that subjects could perform a memory task involving variants of a visual form more accurately if they had prior experience with the standard they were all similar to. Also, once a structural description has been encoded, an observer notices the instance-parts that are represented in the structural description. For example, the finite grammar in Figure 8.5 describes strings that begin TP..., TT..., VX..., and VV. String parts are described by **cooccurence frequencies**, i.e., T cooccurs with P and V cooccurs with X. Another way of describing string parts is by **transitional probabilities**. For example, an initial T is followed by P with probability p and by another T with probability $1 - p$.

Second, the procedural structural description is used to construct declarative representations of individual instances. When a person is asked to categorize a novel instance, the representation of the novel instance is compared with representations of several instances of different categories. If the match between the representation of the novel instance and the representations of several category instances exceeds a criterion then the new novel instance is categorized with that category. Notice that instances are sorted into categories in the same as they are recognized: when the match between the perceptual input and representation exceeds some criterion, a response is made (Chapter 5).

Because people encode representations of individual instances they learn a great deal about the overall structure of the category. Attneave (1957) anticipated the main conclusions of later work. He found that observers learn three characteristics of a category: (1) its central tendency; (2) the dimensions along which its members differ; and (3) the degree of variability among the category members. Posner and Keele (1968) found that categories based on more variable instances are initially harder to learn than categories based on less variable instances, but that observers are subsequently more likely to classify new inputs (especially highly distorted ones) as category members if the initial training instance is more variable (also see Homa & Vosburgh, 1976).

Fried and Holyoak (1984) had subjects learn two categories of complex perceptual forms, one based on low-variability instances and one based on high-variability instances. In a subsequent transfer test subjects were more likely to classify novel instances into the high-variability category, even for some patterns that were actually more similar to some instance of the low-variability category. The effect of instance variability on category judgment shows that people base category judgments on more than one remembered instance (Brooks, 1978; Elio & Anderson, 1981; Fried & Holyoak, 1984; Medin & Schaffer, 1978). In fact, Light, Kayra-Stuart, and Hollander (1979) demonstrated that people are better able to recognize unusual faces rather than typical faces.

Some instances are perceived as more typical than others. For example, people rate robins as more typical than geese for the category bird. Similarly, when people are asked to list instances of a category, they reliably produce some items both earlier and more frequently than others (Battig & Montague, 1969). Items that are produced most readily tend to be those that people also consider most typical of the category (Rosch, 1973). Both of these measures (typicality ratings and frequency of production) predict the speed with which people classify instances as members of a category. For example, people can verify the truth of the sentence *A robin is a bird* more quickly than they can verify *A goose is a bird* (Glass, Holyoak, & O'Dell, 1974; Rips, Shoben, & Smith, 1973; Wilkins, 1971). Robert Nosofsky and his colleagues (Nosofsky & Johansen, 2000; Palmeri & Nosofsky, 2001) have shown that typicality effects can be precisely accounted for by assuming that an instance is compared with many category members and its similarity is computed by averaging its similarity to all the individual category members. These experiments begin with subjects judging the similarity of pairs of instances. These judgments are used to construct a multidimensional model of how similar the instances are to each other. This measure of similarity predicts how typical each instance is rated. The typicality of each instance is its average similarity to all the other instances in the category.

Mixed definitions. Perceptual and functional categorization are not mutually exclusive. Good examples of categories defined by both perceptual representations and functional procedures are container terms, such as glass, cup, vase, and bowl. All of these terms are in part defined functionally. That is, any instance of a container must be shaped so that it can hold something inside it; e.g., a container requires a solid bottom, solid sides, and an opening at the top. The perceptual features of a container are therefore in part dictated by its function. But what determines the particular category that a container falls into? A glass, for example, used to always be made of glass. But now a glass is often made of some other material, like plastic. You might suspect that a cup is always distinguished by having a handle. But a Chinese teacup, for example, has no handle; neither does a Styrofoam cup. Also, glasses tend to be used for cold liquids, cups for hot. But a "typical" cup (like a coffee cup) is still a cup even if you use it to drink cold lemonade.

Actually, an object can be a certain type of container if it has either the right perceptual representation or the right functional properties. This concept was nicely demonstrated in experiments by William Labov (1973). He showed college students pictures of containers like the pictures in Figure 8.6. All of these drawings resemble cups to some degree,

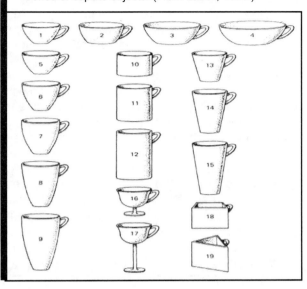

FIGURE 8.6
Series of cuplike objects. (From Labov, 1973.)

but some objects are rather strange. The cups numbered 10 through 19 illustrate a variety of shapes: cylindrical (10-12), conical (13-15), square (18), and triangular (19). Some of these objects might not always be called cup. Object 17, for example, with its long stem, might be referred to as a goblet. The cups of particular interest are numbered 1 through 9. Moving across the top from cup 1 to cup 4, the ratio of the width to the depth increases. The wider cups look more like bowls (with handles) than like cups. Similarly, the ratio of depth to width increases from cup 1 down the left column to cup 9. Here the taller cups look more and more like vases.

Labov set out to answer two questions: (1) How will these shape variations influence the names people use? (2) Will the function of the objects also influence naming? To answer these questions, he presented each of the drawings to his subjects in a random order and asked the subjects to name each object. He did this experiment a number of times for each subject, and each time he varied the instructions slightly. Thus, in the neutral context subjects were told to simply imagine the object in someone's hand. In the food context subjects were asked to imagine the object sitting on a dinner table and filled with mashed potatoes. Finally, in the flowers context they were told to imagine the object on a shelf, with cut flowers in it.

Figure 8.7 shows the results for one group of eleven subjects. Figure 8.7(a) gives the frequencies with which the drawings were called cup or bowl as the relative width increased. In the neutral context (solid lines) the most frequent name was cup, except for the very widest object. But the pattern was very different for the food context (dashed line). The frequencies for cup were quite a bit lower, while bowl was a frequent response for objects of medium or large width. Note that the very "best" cup (width-to-depth ratio of 1.0) was always called cup, even in the food context. But the names for the wider objects were heavily influenced by their imagined function.

FIGURE 8.7
Names applied to cuplike objects. (a) use of names *cup* and *bowl* in food and neutral contexts; (b) use of names *cup* (or *mug*) and *vase* in flowers and neutral contexts. (From Labov, 1973.)

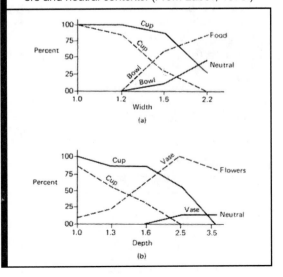

Figure 8.7(b) shows that similar results were obtained for the use of cup versus vase in the neutral and flowers contexts. When subjects imagined the objects holding flowers, use of the name cup (actually either cup or mug) greatly diminished, while use of the name vase greatly increased. But, again the effect of context was much more pronounced for the relatively strangelooking objects (i.e., the deepest ones), while the normal-shaped object was usually called a cup even if it held flowers.

Labov's results clearly show that both perceptual representations (like shape) and functions (such as being used for eating food or displaying flowers) influence the way people categorize objects. His work also shows that no single part of the concept need always be present to make an object a satisfactory category member. For example, something may be called a cup either if it looks like a standard cup or if it has an unusual shape and is used to drink coffee.

Regardless of how the category is defined, anything that is encountered in the world must initially be categorized on the basis of its appearance. While a hammer may be anything good for driving one object through another by pounding, nevertheless an object must be identified as a hammer, at least initially, on whether it looks like it is good for this purpose. So appearance is part of the representation of all categories.

EXPLICIT VERBAL DEFINITION OF CATEGORIES

Natural categories may be learned merely by viewing instances. The observer does not have to be given a verbal definition of the category. Nevertheless, when people are asked to sort instances into categories they often generate a verbal rule that describes the difference between the categories and then use the rule to sort the instances (Medin, Wattenmaker, & Hampson, 1987; Wattenmaker, 1992). Once the rule has been generated, it may be used for classification rather than intuitions of perceptual similarity. For example, when people were asked to categorize vertical and horizontal rectangles like those in Figure 8.3, they were able to state the definitions of the categories after classifying instances of each. Once they were able to state the category definitions their classifications became much faster. Presumably this was because they were no longer comparing the representation of each novel instance with several category instances but instead using the category definitions to check whether it was vertical or horizontal (Maddox & Ashby, 1993).

In fact, words for categories are frequently invented and added to the language. In this case the comparison of novel instance with category members is bypassed entirely. Instances are merely checked against the definition. Often a verb is turned into a noun; thus someone who writes, as an occupation, can be called a writer. Novel categories can readily be created and understood. For example, you can probably form a good idea of what a coconut polisher might be (though it might be either a tool or an occupation). Note that once a new category term arises, its definition can become more specific. For instance, just being able to write doesn't make you a writer; you have to write as a serious professional or creative enterprise (e.g., filling out your income tax form isn't enough).

However, even when categorization is highly accurate, if the features of the structural description are complex and/or obscure then even a practiced observer may never be able to verbalize them Examples of such obscure categories are those formed by the bisected circles in Figure 8.4 (Maddox & Ashby, 1993) and the members of the artificial language defined in Figure 8.5 (Reber, 1967).

FIGURE 8.8
The effect of verbal labeling on reconstructive memory for line drawings (Carmichael et al., 1932).

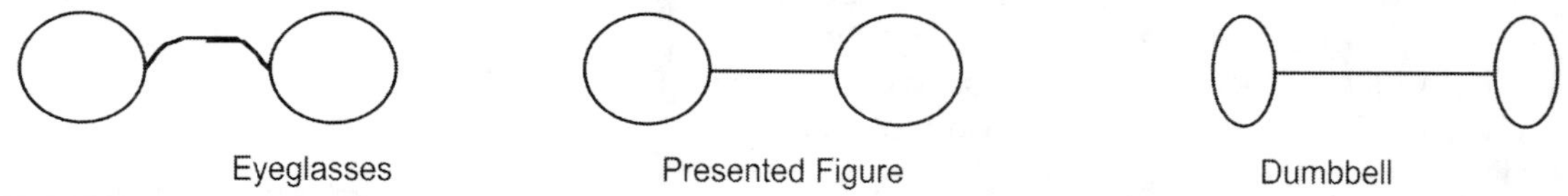

| Eyeglasses | Presented Figure | Dumbbell |

As mentioned in Chapter 5, verbal category labels influence subsequent categorization regardless of whether the category has an explicit verbal definition. Merely labeling an ambiguous instance as a category member influences its representation by determining the structural description to which it is compared and possibly matched. Carmichael, et al. (1932) showed people ambiguous shapes like the one in the center of Figure 8.8 labeled as either a dumbbell or eyeglasses. People who received the dumbbell label were more likely to draw it later as shown on the right in Figure 8.8, while people who received the eyeglass label were more likely to draw it later as shown on the left in Figure 8.8. Holyoak and Bower (1972) showed the same thing for ambiguous sounds. Students heard ambiguous sounds, e.g., heart beating or ball bouncing, which were given an appropriate label either by the experimenter or by the subject. During a subsequent recognition test the students were also asked to provide a label for each sound. The students were more likely to recognize sounds to which they gave the same label that was associated with it at learning.

SUMMARY OF CATEGORIZATION AND LEARNING

- Categories may be defined by
  - a visual representation or other perceptual representation. Most concepts corresponding to concrete objects (e.g., cat, tree, and rock) are basically defined by perceptual representations.
  - a characteristic functions. A weapon, for example, is anything that can serve to inflict injury. Other categories defined by function are tools, furniture, clothing, and jewelry. Occupations, such as doctor, lawyer, employee, and servant, are all functional categories.
  - a social relation. Kinship terms, such as mother, father, uncle, are all such categories.

- Category Learning
  - Procedural
    * The same response is made to more than one target instance. Hence, a single category node marks the perceptual representations of the different instances as targets of the same response. Whenever perceptual input matches any of the instance representations, the category node is activated.
    * As the result of the normal perceptual process, both complete perceptual representations of category instances and representations of the good parts in common among instances, are encoded. Hence, category instances are recognized more rapidly by identifying high frequency parts.
  - Declarative
    * The perceptual similarity among instances is noticed. Verbal labels are assigned to their common good parts.
    * Whenever the perceptual representation of a novel instance is as similar to the representation of the category instances as they are to each other, it may be classified as a category instance.
    * An explicit category definition may be constructed from all the verbally labeled good parts. Subsequently, any novel instance matching the defining features (i.e., good parts) of the category is classified as an instance of the category.

- Attention to Category Learning
  - For natural categories, learning proceeds from the bottom up, when perceptual or functional similarities among instances are first noticed and then labeled.
  - For artificial categories, learning proceeds from the top down, when more than instance is named as a member of the same category, inducing an observer to search for perceptual or functional similarities among them.

MNEMONICS

A technique for learning something is called a **mnemonic** or mnemonic strategy. All mnemonics operate on the same general principal of rapidly associating list items with a hierarchical representation or structural description in memory. Since the items to be remembered have to be instances of the categories contained in the representation, mnemonics are material specific. That is, a mnemonic that is useful for words will be useless for digits or anything else. Today mnemonics are hardly used at all. But before the invention of paper, when writing things down was difficult and expensive, they were an important part of education.

THE METHOD OF LOCI

The method of loci, or mental-walk technique, is the oldest and probably the best-known mnemonic strategy. It has been described so often and so well that we will not try to describe it again; instead, we will quote from others. We use Gordon Bower's (1970, pp. 496-497) description of the method. Bower in turn quotes Frances Yates (1966).

The "method of loci" has been known in Western civilization since ancient Greek times. Cicero (in De Orotore) claimed that the method originated in an observation by a Greek poet, Simonides, about whom he told the following story:

Simonides was commissioned to compose a lyric poem praising a Roman nobleman and to recite this panegyric at a banquet in his honor attended by a multitude of guests. Following his oration before the assembled guests, Simonides was briefly called outside the banqueting hall by a messenger of the gods Castor and Pollux, whom he had also praised in his poem; while he was absent, the roof of the hall collapsed, killing all the celebrants. So mangled were the corpses that relatives were unable to identify them. But Simonides stepped forward and named each of the many corpses on the basis of where they were located in the huge banquet hall. This feat of total recall is said to have convinced Simonides of a basic prescription for remembering—to use an orderly arrangement of locations into which one could place the images of things or people that are to be remembered.

Cicero relates this story about Simonides in connection with his discussion of memory regarded as one of the phases of rhetoric. In ancient times rhetoric teachers provided memory instruction because, in those days before inexpensive paper and writing implements, public speakers had to memorize an entire speech, or at least the main sequence of topics. For this reason most references to the method of loci come down to us from treatises on rhetoric, such as Cicero's De Oratore, the anonymous Rhetorica ad Herennium, and Quintilian's Institutio oratoria. Frances Yates tells the historical story in fascinating detail in The Art of Memory [1966, p. 3] and provides a detailed description of how the method of loci was used in ancient times:

It is not difficult to get hold of the general principles of the mnemonic. The first step was to imprint on the memory a series of loci or places. The commonest, though not only, type of mnemonic place system used was the architectural type. The clearest description of the process is that given by Quintilian. In order to form a series of places in memory, he says, a building is to be remembered, as spacious and varied a one as possible, the forecourt, the living room, bedrooms, and parlours, not omitting statues and other ornaments with which the rooms are decorated. The images by which the speech is to be remembered . . . are then placed in imagination on the places which have been memorized in the building. This done, as soon as the memory of the facts requires to be revived, all these places are visited in turn and the various deposits demanded of their custodians. We have to think of the ancient orator as moving in imagination through his memory building whilst he is making his speech drawing from the memorized places the images he has placed on them. The method ensures that the points are remembered in the right order, since the order is fixed by the sequence of places in the building.

To summarize, the prescription for memorizing a series of items is (1) first to memorize a list of "memory snapshots" of locations arranged in a familiar order; (2) to make up a vivid image representing, symbolizing, or suggesting each of the items of information that is to be remembered; and (3) to take the items in the sequence they are to be learned and to associate them one by one with the corresponding imaginary locations in memory. The associations are to be established by "mentally visualizing" the image of the items placed into the imaginary context of the locational snapshots. The same loci are used over and over for memorizing any new set of items. Without this feature—if an entire new set of loci had to be learned for each new list—the use of the method would be uneconomical.

Over the centuries many different mnemonics have been invented for different purposes. Several additional mnemonics will be described here that were all designed to make it possible to remember a long list of items the very first time that it was seen or heard. In each case, the learner trains himself to associate a list item with a category within a hierarchical organization that already exists in memory.

OTHER WORD MNEMONICS

The pegword method is extremely similar to the method of loci. The only difference is that instead of learning a sequence of locations it involves first learning a series of number-word rhymes. A possible set is as follows: one is a bun, two is a shoe, three is a tree, four is a door, five is a hive, six is sticks, seven is heaven, eight is a gate, nine is a line, and ten is a hen. After this set of rhymes has been thoroughly learned, quickly and accurately learning any new list of ten words is then possible. The technique from this point on is the same as the method of loci. As each new word is presented, you form a vivid image relating the word to one of the pegwords. For example, suppose you wanted to remember the elements in the order of their atomic weights. To memorize the first element, hydrogen, you might imagine a bun rising out of the mushroom cloud of an exploding hydrogen bomb. For the second element, helium, you might image a shoe suspended from a helium balloon, etc. To later recall the list, you would run through the pegwords in order and retrieve the word associated with each. A nice feature of the pegword method is that because the items are numbered, overlooking an item is impossible. For example, when one comes to three-tree, one knows that there is some word that comes with it that must be recalled.

With a little practice both the method of loci and the pegword method produce extremely accurate recall (Roediger, 1980). The methods are limited only by the number of loci or pegwords you have learned. In fact, you can learn several different lists by using the same loci and not confuse them, at least for relatively short retention intervals, just as you would not be likely to confuse events that occurred on two different trips to school (Bower & Reitman, 1972). In each case the new material to be learned is associated with a set of cues that can easily be generated in order. A distinctive retrieval cue for each item is therefore available at the time of recall. However, Bower and Clark (1969) found that an even simpler mnemonic worked nearly as well. They had two groups of subjects learn twelve lists of 10 nouns each, either by rehearsal or by linking all the words together in sentences that formed a story. Notice that the instruction to link the sentences in a story is implicitly a suggestion to organize them hierarchically by phrase, clause, sentence, episode, and story. After the students had been presented with all twelve lists, they were asked to recall all 120 words that had been presented. The difference between the two groups was almost incredible. While the rehearsal group recalled a mere 13 percent of the words, the story group recalled fully 93 percent of them.

NONWORD MNEMONICS

The strategy for learning meaningless items is to associate them with meaningful items. By associating the input with meaningful concepts, the person is able to establish a set of retrieval cues. One such strategy is called natural-language mediation (Montague, Adams, & Kiess, 1966; Prytulak, 1971). Natural-language mediation involves encoding a term by thinking of a real-word association. For example, suppose you had to learn a set of nonsense pairs such as wis-op, cer-val, or klm-ptg. One way to encode the material is by allowing yourself to free-associate while you are studying in order to come up with a more meaningful representation. In our examples, wis-op might remind you of whistle-stop, cer-val might translate into Sir Valiant, and klm-ptg might result in Dutch airline-paper tiger.

Experimental studies have demonstrated the effectiveness of a strategy that combines natural-language mediation with imagery to aid in memorizing the meanings of foreign vocabulary items. In the keyword method subjects are trained to connect a foreign word to its translation in two steps: First, the foreign word is linked to a similar-sounding word in the native language (the keyword). Then the keyword is linked to the translation by a mental image. For example, the Russian word for "building," zdanie, is pronounced somewhat like "zdawn-yeh," with emphasis on the first syllable. One could therefore use dawn as the keyword and then form a mental image of the first light of dawn casting its glow over a large building. Students taught to use the keyword method show improved ability in recalling the definitions of foreign vocabulary items (Atkinson & Raugh 1975; Kasper & Glass, 1982).

NUMBER MNEMONICS

Chunking is the process by which people organize input items into larger units. It occurs whenever several items are matched against a single larger representation in memory. Chunking plays an especially important role in determining how much material can be successfully encoded in one presentation. For example, you could probably repeat a 15-word sentence verbatim, but not 15 random words. Most people can repeat about 7 short words, 7 syllables, or 7 random letters. Yet the 7 words would contain about 35 letters! Clearly, how much is remembered is not equivalent to a simple physical or perceptual characteristic of the input, such as number of letters. Rather, the rate at which information can be encoded into memory depends on the size of the representations that can be formed. A word generally will be encoded as a single unit, or chunk, whereas 7 unrelated letters will be encoded as 7 individual chunks. In general, the larger the unit of encoding, the more material can be encoded in a given period of time.

George Miller (1956) performed a demonstration experiment with one subject to show how the rate at which information can be encoded depends on the size of the chunks formed in memory. He first presented the subject with a series of strings of 1s and 0s (e.g., 10011101101), and for each string he asked the subject to repeat the numbers to him in the same order. Not surprisingly, the subject could not remember very long strings of 1s and 0s in perfect order. In fact, a typical person can remember a string of only nine such digits.

However, Miller then went on to teach his subject a trick for remembering strings of 0s and 1s. The basic idea is to give the person a rule for coding the digits into larger chunks. Miller's rule was to code the digits from base 2 (binary) numbers into base 8 (octal) numbers. This technique increases the size of the chunks because one octal number stands for a unique pattern of three 0s and 1s, as follows: 0 = 000, 1 = 001, 2 = 010, 3 = 011, 4 = 100, 5 = 101, 6 = 110, 7 = 111. After learning this simple coding scheme, one can listen to a series of 0s and 1s and quickly translate it into a much shorter string of octal numbers. For example, 010001111011101110010 becomes 2173562, which is no harder to remember than an ordinary telephone number. To recall the original string, one simply has to translate back from the octal code into 0s and 1s. By using this technique, Miller's subject was able to listen to a string of as many as forty 0s and 1s and repeat them back perfectly.

Twenty-five years later, Chase and Ericsson (1982) performed another experiment demonstrating the role of chunking in mnemonics. However, this time they let the subjects invent their own chunking strategies. Chase and Ericsson monitored the course of learning in a digit span task, in which subjects listen to a series of digits read at the rate of one digit per second and then immediately attempt to report the series in order. Two subjects practiced the digit span task for two years, completing well over two hundred sessions. Figure 8.9 plots the growth in their average digit span with practice. One of the subjects, Steve Faloon, began like any other naive subject, with an initial span of seven digits. Ultimately, he attained truly spectacular levels of recall ability, culminating in a peak performance of eighty-two digits!

What were the mechanisms underlying this tremendous increase in digit span? The factors identified by Chase and Ericsson are entirely consistent with what we have learned about mnemonic strategies. First, the subjects learned to chunk sequences of three or four digits by matching them to representations already stored in long-term memory. Both subjects were runners, and their primary coding device was to relate incoming digits to well-known times of races (e.g., the sequence 351 was coded as the "old world record for the mile for a long time").

Second, the subjects developed a retrieval structure—a device for indexing information in long-term memory, such as the memory locations used in the method of loci. The two subjects both learned to group their low-level digit chunks into larger super groups, hierarchically organized as illustrated in Figure 8.10. By using these retrieval structures, the subjects were able to locate chunks within a long series directly, without necessarily having to repeat the list from the beginning. When the series was being reported, the subjects tended to pause for a longer time between the major boundaries in the retrieval structure. Finally, extensive practice produced an increase in the speed with which the subjects could access the relevant information in long-term memory. These results show how extraordinary memory skill can be produced by learning appropriate strategies and practicing their use.

MINDS OF MNEMONISTS

The kinds of mnemonic strategies we have been discussing can improve anyone's memory performance. However, there are people who are expert mnemonists, masters of mnemonic strategies. Their memory abilities go well beyond anything we have yet considered. When these abilities are displayed for the first time, they seem almost superhuman. But when we consider what we already know about memory, we can understand them as extensions of our own abilities. We will examine the memory feats of three individuals: a mathematician in Scotland, a history graduate student in Washington State, and a reporter in the Soviet Union.

FIGURE 8.9

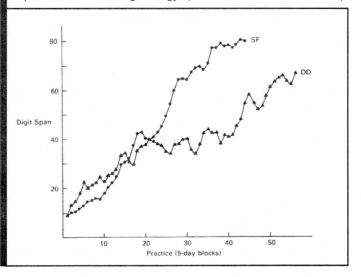

Growth in digit span for two subjects, SF and DD, as a function of practice with recording strategy. (From Chase & Ericsson, 1982).

FIGURE 8.10

Hierarchical organizations used by two subjects in recording digit strings. (From Chase & Ericsson, 1982.)

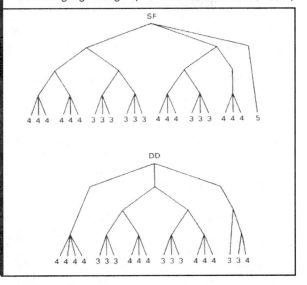

Lightning calculator. For hundreds of years there have been reports of people with exceptional abilities to perform numerical calculations in their heads. Hunter (1962, 1977) presented an interesting case study of one such "lightning calculator," Professor A. C. Aitken of Edinburgh University. Here is one example of his prodigious skill. He was given the task of expressing 4/47 in decimals. After an initial pause of 4 seconds, he began to produce the answer at the rate of about one digit every 4 seconds: ".08510638297872340425531914. . . (a pause of about 1 minute) . . . 191489 . . . (5-second pause) . . . 361702127659574458." At this point he stopped and announced that the decimal pattern repeats itself.

How did Aitken do it? His ability depended on two essential types of knowledge. First, he simply knew an enormous number of facts about numbers. Second, he had many alternative strategies for performing calculations. These strategies in turn relied on the number facts that Aitken knew. He worked a calculation in two steps. First, he examined the problem and decided upon a plan of attack. In doing so, he might translate the problem into a different form that was easier to handle. Second, he actually implemented the method and generated the answer.

Consider a second example, for which Aitken described how he arrived at a solution. The problem was to express 1/851 in decimals. The first thing he did was recall that 851 equals 23 x 37 (a number fact). Then he also recalled that 1/37 equals 0.027027027. . ., repeating. As a result, his chosen plan of attack was to divide 1/37 by 23. At this point Aitken began to produce the answer in the following way:

- 23 into 0.027 = 0.001 with remainder 4:
- 23 into 4027 = 175 with remainder 2;
- 23 into 2027 = 88 with remainder 3;
- 23 into 3027 = 131 with remainder 14;
- 23 into 14,027 = 609 with remainder 20; etc.

In addition, Aitken could easily calculate how far the solution would go before repeating. He knew that 1/37 repeats after 3 places and that 1/23 repeats after 22 places. As a result, 1/851 must start to repeat after 3 x 22 = 66 places.

The basic principle motivating Aitken's choice of a plan of attack was always to minimize the amount of conscious processing he had to do at one time. Most of us have great difficulty with such mental calculations because we have to compute and remember so many partial results as we go along. Aitken minimized this problem of limited capacity by using his enormous repertoire of number facts that were already stored in memory and could be retrieved without computation. We all know, for example, that 8 / 4 = 2. But Aitken also knew all the prime numbers up to 1000 and the factors of all the nonprimes (e.g., 851 = 23 x 37). When the year 1961 was mentioned, for example, he commented that 1961 was 37 x 53, also 44 squared + 5 squared, as well as 40 squared + 19 squared.

Unlike most of us, Aitken thought of large numbers as single chunks rather than as combinations of digits. He said that all numbers up to 1000 seemed like "one idea," while numbers from 1000 to 1 million seemed (regrettably) like "two ideas." As a result of having such compact chunks for numbers, Aitken had no trouble repeating fifteen digits either forward or backward when they were read out to him at the rate of five per second (Baddeley 1976, p.367).

Before the age of electronic calculators and computers, lightning calculation was a very valuable skill for a mathematician. Today it is a dying art. One of the saddest days in Professor Aitken's life was in 1923 when he first used a mechanical calculator. After that first encounter he lost interest in extending his abilities any further, and he believed that his skills deteriorated.

Mnemonist V. P. While Professor Aitken used his memory skills primarily for mental calculation, two other mnemonists were more general. The first of these, known to science as V. P., was born in Latvia but lived for many years in the United States. He was a very intelligent man (with an IQ of 136). When V. P. was tested systematically (Hunt & Love, 1972), he was able to repeat seventeen digits in order. He also recalled a one-page story almost verbatim six weeks after being presented with it. V. P. apparently relied mainly on linguistic and semantic associations to elaborate what he was trying to remember. In doing so, he was aided by an extremely wide knowledge of languages (he could read almost all modern European languages). Since virtually all consonant sequences approximate a word in one language or another, he found it very easy to generate natural-language mediators for any nonsense syllable.

V. P. had his own views about how his skills developed. He regarded his memory abilities as the result of Jewish culture, which valued and encouraged rote memory. He viewed good memorizers such as himself as basically passive individuals who are prepared to devote their energies to encoding the presented material, without being particularly concerned with the purpose of remembering it.

Mnemonist S. The most extensively studied of all mnemonists, known to us as S., was born a few miles from V. P.'s birthplace, shortly before the turn of the past century. In the 1920s he was a newspaper reporter in Russia. When the editor gave out assignments for the day, S. never took notes. One day the editor started to reproach him for being inattentive, but S. repeated the assignment word for word. The editor then sent him to a psychology laboratory. There he met the great Russian psychologist A. R. Luria. Luria studied S.'s memory abilities for almost thirty years, and he published his findings in a fascinating book called The Mind of a Mnemonist (1968).

S.'s abilities were truly astounding. He could repeat seventy or more items in order without error, whether they were words, letters, nonsense syllables, or sounds. He could repeat the series either forward or backward. Furthermore, his recall of such lists was still perfect when tested after fifteen years, despite the fact that by that time S. had become a professional mnemonist, who had learned thousands of similar lists. To recall a particular list, he would carefully reconstruct the situation, as the following example demonstrates (Luria 1968, p. 12):

> "Yes, yes.... This was a series you gave me once when we were in your apartment.... You were sitting at the table and I in the rocking chair.... You were wearing a gray suit and you looked at me like this.... Now, then, I can see you saying.... " And then he would quickly recall the entire list.

How did S. encode the material? In large part he relied on extraordinarily vivid visual imagery. For example, when S. was presented with a list of 50 digits he reported that he could still "see" the numbers even after they were removed. As a result, he was able to rapidly read off the numbers by rows, columns, or diagonals of four. After four months he needed more time to "recapture the situation" before beginning to recall, but then he performed as quickly and accurately as ever.

Part of S.'s encoding ability depended on an extreme form of synesthesia. **Synesthesia** occurs when an input evokes an image in a different sense modality. Many people experience synesthesia occasionally, as when a piece of music arouses visual images. But S. experienced synesthesia in response to virtually any input. For example, Luria (1968) reports S.'s reaction to a particular tone (p. 23): "S. saw a brown strip against a dark background that had red, tongue-like edges. The sense of taste he experienced was like that of sweet and sour borscht, a sensation that gripped his entire tongue." His synesthesia allowed S. to easily form visual images of essentially anything—words, numbers, or nonsense material. Here, for example, is how S. imaged digits (Luria 1968, p. 31): "Take the number 1. This is a proud, well built man; 2 is a high-spirited woman; 3 is a gloomy person (why, I don't know); 6 is a man with swollen feet; 7 a man with a mustache; 8 a very stout woman."

Did S. ever forget? He did occasionally make errors, but these seemed to be not so much defects of memory as defects of perception. For example, a noise during the reading of a list might be imaged as "puffs of steam" or "splashes," which would make it difficult for S. to encode the table. During recall he might do something like "misread" the digit 8 as a 3. He often used the method of loci, which he appeared to have rediscovered for himself. Sometimes, he would omit words during recall because he couldn't "see" them clearly in his image. For example, on one occasion he missed the words pencil and egg in recalling a list by the mental-walk technique. Here is his explanation for the errors (Luria 1968, p.36):

> I put the image of the pencil near a fence . . . the one down the street, you know. But what happened was that the image fused with that of the fence and I walked right on past without noticing it. The same thing happened with the word egg. I had put it up against a white wall and it blended in with the background. How could I possibly spot a white egg up against a white wall?

While S.'s amazing abilities were in some ways an extraordinary benefit, they were also an extraordinary burden. Because everything aroused a distinctive image, he had trouble with any task requiring the ability to think more abstractly. For example, he sometimes had difficulty recognizing faces or voices. For him, a different expression or tone would seem to change the face or voice entirely. His vivid imagery also interfered with his ability to understand metaphorical or abstract language. Each word would conjure up a specific image, and he would have difficulty in ignoring these images to get to the meaning of the entire sentence. For example, consider how much trouble he had with the apparently simple sentence "The work got under way normally" (Luria 1968, p.128):

> I read that "the work got under way normally." As for work, I see that work is going on ... there's a factory.... But there's that word normally. What I see is a big, ruddy-checked woman, a normal woman.... Then the expression got under way. Who? What is all this? You have industry . . . that is, a factory, and this normal woman—but how does all this fit together? How much I have to get rid of just to get the simple idea of the thing!

The power of S.'s imagination was extraordinary. He was able, for example, to make the temperature of his left hand go up while making the temperature of his right hand go down. He did so by imagining his left hand on a hot stove and his right hand holding ice. But his mental powers also created problems. To a large extent he lived in his imagination. He changed jobs dozens of times, working as a reporter, vaudeville actor, efficiency expert, and professional mnemonist. Although his life was rather unstable, he always believed he would somehow achieve greatness. Although he did not really succeed, through Luria he has given us a fascinating look at a phenomenal memory.

Normal and expert memory. There are clearly both similarities and differences among the three mnemonists we have described. One commonality is their use of special encoding strategies. The mnemonists illustrate the general point that learning depends on knowledge. For example, because Professor Aitken knew so much about numbers, he was able to rapidly encode new numerical information.

Also interesting is that all three mnemonists used strategies that improve recall for average individuals as well. But the mnemonists are much more proficient in their use of these strategies. This point raises an interesting question: The abilities of Aitken and V. P. seem to rest on two major factors. First, each stored in memory a vast body of knowledge about a specialized area (numbers for Aitken, languages for V. P.). Second, both were highly practiced in using the knowledge to facilitate encoding. Such knowledge and skills seem to be the kind of thing that could be learned with extensive practice.

Of course, most of us would never achieve their level of performance within a reasonable length of time. For one thing, most people simply would not be willing to devote years of concentrated effort to the task, any more than they would be willing to devote years of practice to becoming a championship bowler. Still, the abilities of Aitken and V. P. do not seem all that mysterious in view of what we know about normal human memory. However, S. is a different case. His extraordinary synesthesia is not the kind of thing we would expect to develop through practice. Although he used some standard mnemonic devices like the method of loci, his encoding processes were generally highly unusual. Instead of abstracting only certain critical features of a sensory input in order to construct a representation of it, as people normally seem to do, he apparently retained a virtually exact representation of the entire experience. As we have seen, this detailed type of encoding affected not only his memory but other aspects of his thought processes as well.

There does not appear to be great practical benefit to being a mnemonist. There are relatively few occupations that put great time pressure on individuals to learn study materials to a high degree of accuracy. Professional actors have to remember a varying number of lines, as well as bits of stage business, accurately. However, they are not under the time pressure to learn their lines during the first reading of the script. Helga Noice (1992) asked seven actors to describe the procedures they used in preparing and learning a role. There was unanimous agreement among the actors that they do not memorize the lines in a rote-type fashion. Nor did they use any of the mnemonics described here. In fact, they did not try to learn their lines at all. Instead they read the script many times, trying to infer the motivation behind each utterance. All of the actors stressed the importance of identifying the underlying meaning and of explaining why the character said those exact words. Apparently this type of active elaboration produces verbatim recall and makes line-for-line memorizing unnecessary.

SUMMARY OF MNEMONICS

- When the purpose of a voluntary action is to learn something it is called a mnemonic. This is done by associating the input with categories in an already learned structural description. Hence mnemonics are material specific. There are well-known mnemonics for
    - Words. Two well-known mnemonics for words are
        - the method of loci
        - the peg-word method
    - Nonwords
    - Numbers

- The extraordinary abilities of famous mnemonists are based on their use of special encoding strategies that improve recall for normal individuals as well. The mnemonists illustrate the general point that learning depends on knowledge.

SUMMARY OF CHAPTER

- Common Types of Categories include
  - Perceptual
  - Functional
  - Kinship

- Category Learning
  - Procedural
    * The same response is made to more than one target instance. Hence, a single category node marks the perceptual representations of the different instances as targets of the same response.
    * As the result of the normal perceptual process, both complete perceptual representations of category instances and representations of the good parts in common among instances, are encoded. Hence, category instances are recognized more rapidly by identifying high frequency parts.
  - Declarative
    * The perceptual similarity among instances is noticed. Verbal labels are assigned to their common good parts.
    * A similar novel instance may be classified as a category member.
    * An explicit category definition may be constructed from all the verbally labeled good parts.

- Attention to Category Learning
  - For natural categories, learning proceeds from the bottom up, when perceptual or functional similarities among instances are first noticed and then labeled.
  - For artificial categories, learning proceeds from the top down, when more than instance is named as a member of the same category, inducing an observer to search for perceptual or functional similarities among them.

- When the purpose of a voluntary action is to learn something it is called a mnemonic.
  - Two well-known mnemonics for words are
    * the method of loci
    * the peg-word method
  - The extraordinary abilities of famous mnemonists are based on their use of special encoding strategies that improve recall for normal individuals as well. The mnemonists illustrate the general point that learning depends on knowledge.

Chapter 9

RETRIEVAL

B efore we went to Paris, I suggested to my eight-year-old son that it would be fun to walk to the top of the Eiffel Tower. At first he was dubious, but when we got there he embraced the task with great enthusiasm. Soon he was bounding up the stairs at rapid clip, and we reached the top far in advance of the rest of our party, who waited for the elevator. Very much pleased with myself, when we returned home I asked him what he enjoyed most about the trip to Paris. He answered, unhesitatingly, "the Empire State Building."

Clearly, this was a retrieval error. It demonstrates that encoding the representation of an object or event is not sufficient to ensure an accurate memory later on. In this chapter we consider how things are recognized and recalled.

OVERVIEW

There are two tasks that require the retrieval of information. A **recognition task** merely requires you to verify something against what you know and hence often only requires a yes/no response; e.g., Was George Washington the first President of the United States? A **recall task** requires you to respond with information not in the question; e.g., Who was the first President of the United States? There are also two mental processes that make information retrieval possible. One is the **recognition process**, described in Chapter 5, which automatically retrieves information directly related to a perceptual target. The success of this recognition process is what convinces you to respond "yes" to "Was George Washington the first President of the United States?" The other is the voluntary act of **generation** by which a person retrieves information related to some cue. You engage in generation when you attempt the recall task of naming all the Presidents of the United States that you can think of. It is convenient to associate **generation** with **recall** and recognition with recognition, but it is not strictly correct to do so. While the more difficult recall task of naming all the presidents requires generation, "first president" always activates "George Washington," so the much simpler recall task, "Who was the first President?" may be answered through the automatic recognition process alone. While the simple recognition task of responding that George Washington was the first President may be accomplished through the automatic recognition of the name, the much more difficult recognition task, "George Washington retired from the presidency in 1796," must in fact require the generation of such information as when he was first elected and how long he served, if it can be answered at all.

Having given this caveat, we will follow the convenient path of using the recognition task to describe the process of recognition in the first half of this chapter, and the recall task to illustrate the act of generation in the second of half of the chapter.

RECOGNITION PROCESS

You walk into class and turn your gaze upon the face of someone already there. The process of recognition has several distinct stages. First, in the feature analysis and perceptual organization stage a perceptual representation of the face is constructed (Chapter 3). Second, in the comparison stage the perceptual representation is compared with logogen face-representations in memory (Chapter 5). Third, in the response stage the logogen whose representation most closely matches the perceptual representation responds, activating information about the person with matching face (Chapter 5). Fourth, in the decision stage, you evaluate the response and decide whether you are looking at an acquaintance or a stranger. In this chapter we continue the description of recognition where we left off in Chapter 5. In particular, the decision stage is described in detail for the first time.

The expanded schematic of recognition is shown in Figure 9.1. Notice the expanded description of the response stage. We have already seen that the match between the perceptual and memory representation activates **semantic information** which produces an **identification response**. That is if the perceptual representation of the face you fixate on matches the representation of your best friend's face then you recognize your best friend. However, identification is only one component of a **four-part recognition response**. The last time you saw your friend it was at a particular place and time. Her representation was encoded as part of a structural description of particular scene and episode; saying good night after going to the movies. If any part of that structural description is activated by seeing her face again, this **contextual information** about when and where you saw her determines the **familiarity response**. That is, the more often you have seen her, hence the more contextual information activated, the more familiar she seems. Third, when a representation becomes part of working

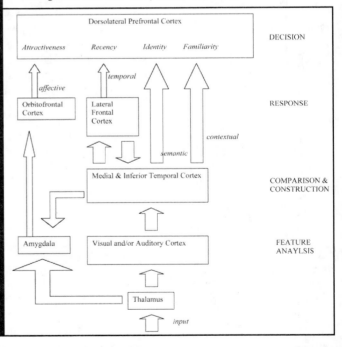

FIGURE 9.1
Recognition has four component responses.

memory it becomes part of a structural description that orders it with respect to what came just before it and what will come right after it (Chapter 4). If you have just seen the same face moments before in the hall it will appear recent when you see it again in the classroom. The short-term temporal information of working memory is experienced as a feeling of **recency**; so the third component of recognition is the recency response. That is, when you see or hear something after a short retention interval you often have a sense of having just seen or heard it. Anyone who has been nagged knows how annoying this can be.

Fourth, the identification of the face is accompanied by an **emotional response** to it (Chapter 6); so it may look attractive, pleasant etc.

So you recognize your friend. But what about that less familiar face beside her? Is that another classmate with a new haircut and makeup or a visitor you have never seen before? Since faces vary in familiarity, recognition must contain a decision criterion for sorting objects into old and new on the basis of their familiarity. But what criterion should you apply? You know that the same people attend class with you and so it is reasonable to set a low criterion and infer that anyone sitting in class with you is someone you have seen before. You might not give the same person a second glance if you passed her on the street. So **inference** and **criterion** are both parts of the recognition process. They are applied in the final decision stage of the recognition process.

GENERATION

Let us consider the task of recalling the names of all the presidents. This is a difficult task that few people can perform whether they know all the names or not. The problem is that in order to generate something that is not in working memory you use an associate that is already in working memory as a **cue**. For example, the cue `president` might give you the names `Washington`, `Lincoln`, `Clinton`, and `Bush`. The problem is that each cue only generates a small cluster of responses. To generate more names you must find different cues that are **specific** for names you haven't generated yet. Hence, "lived in the White House," is of no help, because this just regenerates the names you have, but "came from Massachusetts," might get you Kennedy. When information is not well organized you soon run out of cues and can only generate a small portion of what you actually know.

The situation is quite different when information is well organized. Whether recalling a book you read, a movie, or your last vacation, there is no limit to the number of details you may recall. They are all organized nicely in structural descriptions of scenes and events. You can probably do a pretty good job of recalling your classmates. People usually sit in the same seats and you can use the spatial arrangement of seats to cue the person in each seat (Chapter 8). So people are pretty good at recalling routine events. However, suppose instead you are asked who attended your last class. Now your structural description of class can be as misleading as it is helpful. Do you remember someone because he usually attends class or because you specifically saw him at the last class? A general structural description is not useful for recalling such specific details.

RECOGNITION

Recall from Chapter 5 that the process of recognition involves three different stages that are associated with three different parts of the brain. First, in the feature analysis stage, in the occipital cortex for vision, and the temporal cortex for audition, an input is analyzed as a set of features and organized into successively more complex patterns. In the comparison stage, in the temporal cortex, the representation of the input is compared with many memory representations in parallel. In the response stage, a match activates some representation in the temporal cortex, which is communicated to the prefrontal cortex, which results in an awareness of the input that was called both working memory and declarative memory in earlier chapters (Figure 5.3). Figure 9.2 is a schematic of how the analysis, comparison, and response stages operate together to produce recognition for the word *dog*.

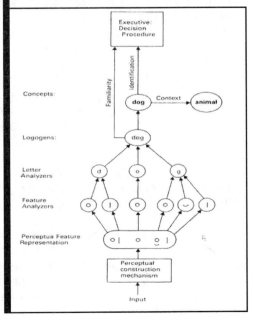

FIGURE 9.2
Recognition process for the word *dog*.

Until now the recognition process has been treated as a means to an end. When you read, the purpose of recognizing the letters is not the end of the process but a stage towards understanding the sentence. Here we consider recognition itself as the end point itself for the processing of an input.

The act of recognition separates the normal individual from the amnesic. It orients you to time as well as to place. It is to know that you are in familiar surroundings, that the person before you is your friend, and that that book on the table is your own, and where you placed it a few minutes before. Recognition occurs when the output of the response and selection stage (Chapter 5) is evaluated against a criterion and determined to be this or that, novel or familiar, recent or routine. This evaluation process in the prefrontal cortex is called the decision stage of recognition. Of course the decision actually made, e.g., whether the object is familiar or novel, is influenced by the processing that occurs during feature analysis and organization, and comparison. So we begin by reviewing the effect of these stages on the recognition decision. However, the main focus of the first half of this chapter is on the decision process itself.

FEATURE ANALYSIS STAGE

The features that an input activates determine its representation; hence the logogen it activates; hence what it is recognized as. So recognition is initially dependent on perceptual organization. For example, Bower and Glass (1976) investigated the ability of college students to recognize patterns such as those depicted in Figure 9.3. Target patterns like that in Figure 9.3 were first presented to the students. A week later the target was presented along

FIGURE 9.3

Examples of the patterns used in a recognition test by Bower and Glass (1976).

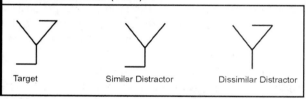

Target   Similar Distractor   Dissimilar Distractor

with one of the two distracter-patterns shown in Figure 9.3. The subject simply had to choose which of the two patterns had been presented a week earlier. This task is called a forced-choice recognition procedure, because the subject is forced to choose one of the alternative test items as the one that had been previously presented.

To understand the logic of the Bower and Glass experiment, look carefully at the target pattern in Figure 9.3. What are the features of the pattern? Most people see this pattern as an open triangle atop a right angle. That is, the target is composed of two corner features. Now look at the two distracter-patterns. In each case they differ from the target by the removal of one horizontal line, which is the same length in both cases. So objectively, the two distracters are equally similar to the target. But if you look at the patterns carefully, you will probably agree with us that the middle pattern seems more similar to the target than does the pattern on the right.

Why do we think this way? Notice that even after the top horizontal line has been removed, the top of the similar distracter can be interpreted as an incomplete triangle. As a result, the distracter is composed of two corner features, just like the target. In contrast, the bottom horizontal line removed to form the dissimilar distracter turned the right angle into a straight line, which is a different feature entirely. So most people perceive the right pattern as less similar to the target than the middle pattern.

FIGURE 9.4

Camouflage. Cover the left sides of symbols to find familiar patterns.

The results of the recognition test performed by Bower and Glass showed a striking effect of distracter similarity. The students erroneously selected a similar distracter instead of the target four times as often as they selected a dissimilar distracter. In addition, nineteen of the twenty students were more confident in choosing between a target and a dissimilar distracter than in choosing between a target and a similar distracter. These results show that the features of perceptual representations are also the critical features for recognition.

Another way to demonstrate the role of features in determining similarity is to camouflage a familiar pattern by embedding it in a larger pattern. In this case the embedded pattern will no longer match its unembedded representation in memory and will no longer be recognized. If you try the exercise in Figure 9.4, you will see that the strange symbols are camouflaging some familiar patterns.

COMPARISON STAGE

Visual memory is remarkable. But it requires experience to be truly useful. Recall that if an infant sees exactly the same mobile again in exactly the same crib in exactly the same room then it is recognized. This ability remains throughout life. So if an adult sees a picture of a face then later that exact picture can be recognized. But the ability to recognize a specific, detailed visual pattern is quite limited. What you want to be able to do is recognize objects and individuals regardless of their orientation to you or their context. In order to do this, several visual patterns must be associated with the same object or individual, which are all compared with an input during the comparison stage. When this occurs, the entity becomes familiar and can be recognized in any context, in a wide variety of poses.

Human beings have a phenomenal capacity to recognize perceptual inputs that they have previously experienced. People can identify thousands upon thousands of different words and objects, often from only a single exposure.

Visual recognition. Table 9.1 summarizes the results of four different studies of picture recognition. In each experiment a single presentation of the study list was followed by presentation of target-distracter pairs. No matter how long the study list, immediate recognition was essentially perfect and remained good for at least a week. Even after

TABLE 9.1
Picture Recognition

Picture Recognition					
Observers	Study Set Size	Immediate Retention	Up to One Week	At least a Month	Study
4-year olds	100	98%	90%	67%	Brown & Scott, 1971
adults	612	97%	87%	58%	Shepard, 1967
adults	2,500		91%		Standing, Conezio, & Haber, 1970
adults	10,000		85%		Standing, 1973
	At least 5-second presentation rate				

six months it remained a little above chance performance. So if a person is shown exactly the same picture he has seen once before he has a very good chance of recognizing it. For example, if you are shown a picture of a person and then the same picture later, you will almost certainly recognize it. However, suppose that instead you are shown a different picture of the same person. Recognizing the person turns out to be considerably more complicated.

Vicki Bruce (1982) performed this experiment. Observers saw 12 pictures of the faces of people who worked in the same department as them and 12 pictures of the faces of strangers. The recognition test consisted of target-distracter pairs in which the target was a picture of one of the twenty-four individuals whose picture was part of the study list. The picture was either the same picture shown at study or a different picture that had been taken at the same time as the study picture. Pictures of the same individual differed on the expression of the individual, whether the pose was frontal or three-quarters, or both. The results are shown in Figure 9.5. The observers were virtually perfect at recognizing faces of familiar individuals whether the same picture or a different picture was shown. The observers were also virtually perfect at recognizing exactly the same picture of the face of a stranger.

FIGURE 9.5
Picture recognition versus face recognition. (After Bruce, 1982.)

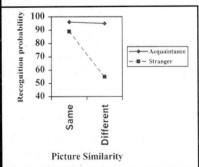

However, recognition of the face of a stranger from a different picture was only slightly above chance. The role of familiarity is also evident in people's ability to recognize the faces of individuals of different races. Both black and white American college students most accurately recognize the faces of the racial types with which they have had the most experience (Bothwell, Brigham, & Malpass, 1989).

Of course, even with familiar objects, if distracters are made sufficiently similar to targets then recognition errors occur. Nickerson and Adams (1979) examined the ability of American college students to recognize the appearance of an object they were extremely familiar with—the head side of a penny. They found that the students were quite poor in selecting the correct version of the coin when it was presented along with fourteen distracters in which various features were omitted or altered.

People's word recognition is also very good. Shepard (1967) showed people a sequence of 540 words and then tested them on sixty pairs of words in which one member of each pair had been shown in the inspection series. The subjects selected the target 88 percent of the time. Though the high average score indicates that performance was generally quite good, off course some people did a little better than others. This raises the question of whether some people are just good recognizers in general, or whether different people are better at recognizing different kinds of things. In fact, there was a dissociation between recognition of words and pictures when individual differences in performance were examined. Woodhead and Baddeley (1981) selected people who had done well (the good recognizers) or badly (the poor recognizers) on a facial recognition task and then gave them three more recognition tests: another involving faces, one involving paintings, and one involving visually presented words. The good recognizers performed better than the poor recognizers on the faces and paintings, but there was no difference between them on the words.

Non-visual recognition. People are quite good at recognition of familiar things in the other sensory domains besides vision. For example, Lawrence and Banks (1973) demonstrated a fairly impressive memory for common sounds. They had subjects listen to tape recordings of 194 common sounds (babies crying, dogs barking, a car starting, etc.). Their subjects were 89 percent accurate in recognizing the sounds that had been presented from a set including similar sounds that had not been presented.

Engen and Ross (1973) found that immediate recognition of 48 smells was only 69 percent correct. However, memory for smell exhibits virtually no decline over fairly long time periods. In the Engen and Ross experiment students were 70 percent correct if the test was a week later and 68 percent correct if the test was given a month later. In fact, a similar experiment showed roughly the same level of performance when the test was given three months after the students sniffed the odors. Subsequent studies using more familiar odors have obtained better initial recognition performance than Engen and Ross did and confirmed the slow decline in performance over long retention intervals (Lawless & Cain, 1975; Rabin & Cain, 1984).

Recognition of emotions. It was mentioned in Chapter 6 that infants are born with the ability to produce and recognize positive and negative emotions. Through learning, children come to be able to recognize the features of more specific emotions, e.g., through the recognition of emotional expressions. Beginning in the second year of life, as situational learning occurs, the distress emotion becomes differentiated into four distinct negative emotions: sadness, disgust, anger, and fear (Ekman, 1992; Izard, 1994). Happiness and surprise also become differentiated. Evidence for the set of six basic adult emotions comes from the ability of adults across different cultures to recognize facial expressions of each of these six emotions.

The representational system supporting emotional recognition is closely integrated with but nevertheless distinct from the general medial temporal system. Hornak, Rolls, and Wade (1996) found that patients with aberrant behavior following lower frontal cortex lesions were generally impaired in their recognition of facial and vocal emotional expressions. Damage to specific parts of the emotional system results in impairments in the recognition of the facial expression of specific emotions. As reviewed by Blair and Curran (1999), damage to the amygdala impaired recognition of fear, damage to the basal ganglia impaired recognition of disgust, and suppression of the functioning of the lower area of the frontal cortex, called the **orbitofrontal** cortex, through the administration of valium, impaired the recognition of anger.

RESPONSE STAGE

In mature recognition, awareness that something has been seen before follows immediately upon a match between a representation in memory and perceptual input. However, in early infancy, after a long retention interval there may be a remarkably long lag between the match and the awareness that something familiar has been seen.

When Carolyn Rovee-Collier trained 3-month old infants to move a mobile by kicking their feet she found an infant remembered the mobile no more than a week (Figure 6.5). At longer retention intervals, when the infant saw the mobile there was neither a glint of recognition nor an immediate effort to get it moving through kicking. Why was that, she wondered? Was it because the representation of the mobile had been lost from the young memory, or was it because after a week, a few minutes of looking were not enough time to gain access to it?

To test the second possibility Rovee-Collier (1993) decided to reactivate the memory of the mobile after 13 days, well after it appeared to be forgotten. To do this she showed different groups of infants the training mobile as a reminder and then returned to test their memories after different intervals. Each infant was shown the training mobile for 3 minutes. The infant wasn't attached to the mobile, so the infant could not move it himself (or herself). But the mobile was shaken to attract the infant's attention and perhaps remind the infant what he could once do. Then the mobile was taken away.

With one group of infants, Rovee-Collier returned 15 minutes later with the training mobile and attached it above the infant. Would the infants recognize the training mobile and kick to it? The infants did not. But maybe 15 minutes was not enough time to retrieve the memory of the training mobile. She waited an hour after the reminder before returning with the training mobile for a second group of infants. But these infants also did not recognize or kick to it. But Rovee-Collier did not give up. She waited 8 hours before returning with the mobile for a third group of infants. These infants kicked a little, but not enough to say that they remembered anything. So she waited 24 hours before returning with the training mobile for a fourth group of infants. These infants did recognize the mobile 24 hours after the reminder and kicked to try to move it, though not quite as much as during the original training session. However, Rovee-Collier was not done. With a fifth group of infants she waited 72 hours after the 3-minute reminder before returning with the training mobile (Figure 9.6). The infants in this group recognized the mobile right away and kicked as vigorously as the last day of training, 16 days ago! The infants' memories of the training mobile were perfect! After a single reminder, the forgetting function for the training mobile was exactly the same as after the original training session (Figure 9.7).

Consider what a remarkable result this is. A 3-minute reminder was sufficient to reactivate the memory of a mobile an infant had learned to control at the age of 3 months. However, such a memory took a very long time to retrieve. It was fully 72 hours after the reminder was shown that the memory was fully reactivated. In a further experiment, Rovee-Collier found that a reminder was effective at retrieving the memory of a training mobile formed at 3 months for up to 27 days after the last training session. Furthermore, once the memory of the training mobile was reactivated, it was forgotten at least as slowly as when the infant had first been trained to recognize it. When presented with a reminder 20 and 27 days after training, an infant could recognize the training mobile 41 days after training. Also, as an infant becomes older, retrieval becomes a much faster process. If a

FIGURE 9.6

Rates of recovery of a forgotten memory at different delays after exposure to a reminder at 3 and 6 months.

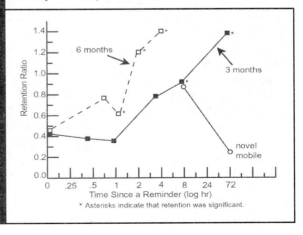

reminder is given for a training mobile that was first seen at 6 months, the training mobile is fully recognized four hours later. By the time a child is a year old, reactivation, or priming, takes less than a second (Hildreth & Rovee-Collier, 1999).

The extraordinarily long time to reactivate a three-month-old infant's memory after a retention interval of more than a week makes it clear that merely matching perceptual input with a representation is not sufficient to produce recognition. The recognition response is distinct from the match itself.

DECISION STAGE

The common case in cognitive psychology is, as we have seen, many different words for exactly the same thing. However, when we come to recognition we have the opposite terminological problem, one word used for many different kinds of judgment. There is not just one kind of recognition decision but many distinct kinds of recognition judgments. You can make a **semantic categorization or identification judgment** of an object (chapters 5 and 8); for example, that's a jacket or that's my jacket. You can make a **familiarity judgment**

FIGURE 9.7

Retention ratio as a function of the retention interval after 2 days of training (original memory: solid line) or 2 days of training plus a reactivation treatment (reactivated memory: broken line). A single reactivation treatment (priming) occurred 13 days for all points connected by broken lines and either 27 or 34 days after training for the single data points at the 28- and 35-day retention intervals. A retention ratio of 1.0 indicates perfect retention; ratios of 0.6 and lower typically indicate complete forgetting. Infants whose memories had been forgotten days or weeks earlier exhibited perfect retention when their memories were primed the day before the 2- or 4-week long-term test, but a single prime before the 5-week test did not alleviate forgetting. Each data point represents an independent group of at least five 3-month-olds who were tested only once.

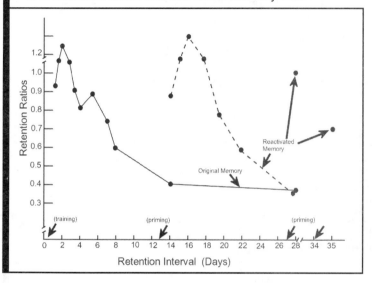

about an object; for example, I've seen you in that jacket before. You can make a **recency judgment** about an object, for example, I saw you in that jacket when you came in. You can make a **frequency judgment**; for example, you wear that jacket a lot. You can make an **episodic judgment**; for example, you wore that jacket to the party last week. Depending on the circumstances, you can make a variety of judgments of varying degrees of specificity about when and where and how often you have seen something before.

There are four kinds of information from the recognition process on which these judgments are based. First, **semantic information** tells you what something is; i.e., it produces an **identity response**. Once a logogen responds to an input, its perceptual representation enters working memory along with additional identifying representations. If you see a penny, you know it is money, but very little money. Second, **contextual information** tells you that you have seen something before, i.e., it produces a **familiarity response.** So a penney looks familiar. Third, **temporal order information** from working memory lets you know whether you have just seen or done something, i.e., it produces a **recency response**. Having just reached into your pocket to retrieve a penney, you are very unlikely to reach into your pocket and do it again. Fourth, **affective information** produces an **emotional response** telling you whether something is good or bad.

It is apparent that semantic judgments are often based on semantic information. However, when it comes to the variety of familiarity, frequency, recency, and episodic judgments that may be made, a mixture of semantic, contextual, temporal, and affective information may be employed, depending on what is appropriate for the specific task. Furthermore, whether a particular task requires a semantic, familiarity, or recency judgment may depend on your state of knowledge. Suppose that you must learn the names of the Confederate States. So you read over the list and then ask a friend to name states and respond whether or not they were in the Confederacy. Initially, you may be making a recency judgment. After awhile it may be a familiarity judgment. With sufficient practice it becomes a semantic judgment.

Semantic identification/categorization judgments were discussed in detail in earlier chapters. Here we consider how various kinds of information are used to make other kinds of recognition judgments.

Recency judgments. Even an apparently very simple recognition judgment may be based on any one of several different kinds of information and involve a sophisticated decision process. Suppose a show you a list of items of items one at a time. The list might be as long as twenty words. Or the list might consist of letters or numbers and be as short as six, four, two, or even one item. Just a few seconds after the last list item is presented you are given a single test item and must respond as fast as possible whether it was on the list. Let us consider all the kinds of information you might use to perform this task. First, you might make use of the perceptual system's ability to detect novel targets. If a test item appeared to be novel you would say that it was not a list item, otherwise you would call it a list item. Second, you might make use of working memory's ability to place a target in a temporal ordering. If a test item appeared to be recent you would call it a list item, otherwise you would say that it was not a list item. Third, you might rely on the retrieval of contextual information. If you remembered seeing the target on the study list then you would call it a list item, otherwise you would say it was not a list item. Fourth, you might rely on semantic information. During the study task you were essentially trying to form an association between each list item, and a mental "list tag." If a test item activated a list tag as part of its semantic representation then you would call it a list item, otherwise you would say that it is not on the list.

There are two points about recognition that this example illustrates: the roles of **inference** and **criterion** in recognition. First consider the role of inference. If you have just seen a list of items and then a test item looks familiar or recent then it is reasonable to infer that you have just seen it on the list. As we shall see, inference plays an important role in both recognition and recall. However, as we shall also see, inferences are not always correct. Second notice that the four different kinds of information imply four different criteria for deciding whether a test item is a list item. How each test item is classified depends on which criterion is used. It may even be that more than one criteria is employed and that different criteria are employed for different test items.

In fact, short-term recognition judgments may be based on either recency responses or on contextual responses. Glass (1993) used a simple recognition task, introduced by Sternberg (1966), to illuminate the conditions under which temporal and contextual responses each contributed to recognition. On each trial an observer saw a set of from one to four items and then a single test item. The study set consisted of either letters randomly drawn from the first ten in the alphabet, letters drawn from among the last ten in the alphabet, or digits. In the varied category-set condition the category of set items was varied so that items from the same category were only presented once every third trial; beginning alphabet set, end of alphabet set, and digit set trials would be repeated in this order throughout the experiment. Response times as a function of study set size for targets and distracters are shown in the top panel of Figure 9.8. As shown in the figure, the increase in response time asymptotes at a study-set size of four. This result indicates that an observer did not have to compare the test item with the study set one item at a time. Instead, it was possible to make a judgment of the test item's perceived recency and this was only slightly affected by the size of the study set.

In the repeated category-set condition the category of set items was kept the same over a long sequence of trials. In the first third of the experiment all study sets were randomly drawn from the beginning of the alphabet; in the middle third of the experiment all study sets were randomly drawn from the end of the alphabet, and in the final third all study sets were randomly drawn from the digits. Response times as a function of study set size for targets and distracters are shown in the bottom panel of Figure 9.8. As shown in the figure, response time is a linear function of study-set size.

This experiment reveals that working memory can only order a limited number of items by recency. In the varied category-set condition, in which a study set from the same category was only presented every third trial, only the individual item representations of the most recently presented study set were part of working memory. Because its representation was part of working memory, a study item presented on the most recent trial seemed more recent than a distracter that was presented no more recently than three trials back as part of that study set. Hence recency was an effective cue for membership in the study set. In contrast, in the repeated category-set condition, in which a study set from the same category was presented on consecutive trials, it was possible for the same item to be presented on successive trials. So a test item might appear recent because it had been presented on the most recent trial or the trial immediately preceding it. Furthermore, priming among all the category members presented on consecutive trials made all the category members equally a part of working memory. So there was a similar degree of recency for all items regardless of how recently a test item had been presented. So a recency judgment was impossible and a contextual judgment was required.

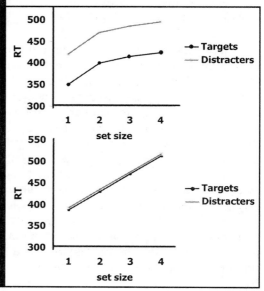

FIGURE 9.8
The effect of study set size response times to targets and targets in the varied category-set condition (top) and the repeated category-set condition (bottom). (Glass, 1993.)

To make a contextual judgment required that the observer bring the representation of the entire study set into working memory and then check whether the test item was in it. To do this the study set must be generated by a motor program that generates; i. e. makes each item in the study set part of working memory, one at a time (Checkosky & Baboorian, 1972). As a result, as shown in the figure, response time is a linear function of study-set size.

Short-term recency judgments (over minutes) require unimpaired frontal lobe functioning. Brenda Milner (1995) showed that prefrontal damage impairs recency judgments. Patients with frontal damage who saw a sequence of pictures and then had to judge which of a pair had been seen more recently performed more poorly than patients with temporal damage (Milner, Corsi, & Leonard, 1991).

Familiarity and frequency judgments. If recognition is no longer immediate but after a retention interval then short-term temporal information can no longer be relied on to make the judgment. Instead it must be based on contextual or semantic information.

When it is available, contextual information plays a dominant role. The more details of the study context that are preserved at test, the more accurate recognition is. People perform much better on recognition tests if the material is tested in the same order as it was originally presented (Jacoby, 1972; Jacoby & Hendricks, 1973). If you study a set of questions in a particular order, random order on the exam will make the test more difficult because it breaks the context in which you originally learned the material.

A finer kind of temporal judgment is a frequency judgment about how often something has occurred within a specified period of time. For example, most people judge that they have seen the word *boy* in their lives more times than the word *lad*. This turns out to be a familiarity judgment based on contextual information. Suppose you are asked how many times you saw a particular friend in the last year. Logically, the most certain answer would be obtained by thinking of every time you saw the friend and counting the instances. However, there is a simpler way of making the judgment. The more contexts that a representation is associated with, the more familiar that a matching input appears. Since frequency influences familiarity a simpler basis for a judgment is to translate the perceived familiarity of the friend into a frequency estimate. In fact, often people appear to base their frequency judgment on a feeling of familiarity (Harris, Begg, & Mitterer, 1980). Hasher and Chromiak (1977) found that students in the second, fourth, and sixth grades and in college were only slightly more accurate at estimating the frequencies of words that appeared in a sequence when they were told they would have to make frequency judgments before viewing the sequence, suggesting that frequency information was accumulated in either case. Greene (1984) found that frequency judgments by college students were equally accurate regardless of whether the subjects were led to expect they would have to make frequency judgments about words or simply that they would be given an unspecified memory test.

Sometimes the information retrieved for an object is very limited. Sometimes contextual information is retrieved without semantic information, so a face looks familiar but you don't know who she is or where you have seen her. Presumably this is because something miscarries in the matching logogen representation and only fragmentary information is activated. In such a situation you know very well that if the person tells you who she is then you will remember her. This is called the **Tip of the Tongue (TOT)** or **Feeling of Knowing (FOK)** state. Even five-year-olds can suffer the frustration of knowing they know something they cannot remember (Wellman, 1977).

A number of psychologists (Brown & McNeill, 1966; Hart, 1965) have studied the TOT experience. For example, Brown and McNeill's (1966) experiment consisted of reading to students a large number of dictionary definitions, such as "an instrument used by navigators to measure the angle between a heavenly body and a horizon." Then after reading each definition, they asked the students to indicate their ability to recall the defined word. Most students either recalled the word or were certain that they had no idea what the word might be. Brown and McNeill were not interested in either of these groups; instead, they focused on the few students that were left. These students indicated that they were certain they knew the word but could not quite recall it. They expressed the feeling that the word was on the tips of their tongues.

Whenever a student suggested that they were in a TOT state, Brown and McNeill proceeded to ask a variety of questions, such as, "What is the first letter? How many letters does the word contain? How many syllables? Can you tell me what the word sounds like?" They found that students in the TOT state could often answer such questions quite accurately. For instance, they might know that the first letter was an s, that the word had two syllables, even that it had seven letters, but they still were unable to produce the name sextant. Instead, they might produce soundalikes, like secant or sextet.

The TOT experience is fortunately sufficiently rare to disrupt everyday recognition. More commonly, semantic information is retrieved but only limited or no contextual information. The amount of contextual information available for a recognition judgment is sometimes plotted along the remember-know continuum. If enough contextual information is retrieved to reconstruct the episode in which an item was encountered, e.g., *I remember that it appeared at the beginning of the list*, this is called a **remember** judgment. When a remember judgment is made in a recognition task the retrieval and decision processes involved in the judgment are indistinguishable from the process of recall, which will be discussed below. The target functions as a retrieval cue for a representation of the context in which it was last encountered. In contrast, if insufficient contextual information is retrieved to reconstruct the episode in which an item was encountered, yet you nevertheless perceive it as somewhat familiar or know something about it, this is called a **know** judgment (Donaldson, 1996; Gardiner, 1988). A know judgment may be based on fragmentary contextual information or on purely semantic information. For example, if know that Virginia was part of the Confederacy then you can infer that you learned this fact sometime in the past. If you are the kind of person who only knows the history she was forced to study in school then you may know that you learned about Virginia in school even though you do not remember learning it. Notice the role that inference plays in a know judgment.

HIT VERSUS FALSE ALARMS IN RECOGNITION JUDGMENTS

We now must consider in more detail the important role that criterion plays in recognition. The perception of recency and familiarity is a matter of degree, but recognition tasks frequently force a choice between two responses: old or new. A decision procedure must use the perception of recency or familiarity to determine whether an item is new or old. The same decision procedure is employed for both recency and familiarity. Familiarity will be used as the example here. A criterion is set so that every item more familiar than the criterion is called "old" and every item less familiar than the criterion is called "new." If the least familiar old input is more familiar than the most familiar new input, then one can set a criterion such that no errors are made. However, if the least familiar old input is perceived as less familiar than the most familiar new input, then no matter where the criterion is set, some errors will be made. For example, suppose I give you a list of names that I culled from your junior high school yearbook intermixed with names from another yearbook, and I ask you which of these people you know. Inevitably, you will make some errors because the familiarity values of the names of the people you have and haven't met will overlap. If you set the familiarity criterion at a high level, you will miss some people you do know. Alternatively, if you set the criterion at a low level, you will false alarm to the names of some people you do not know.

A person's expectations influence the level where the criterion is set. For example, if you are simply given a set of index cards with names on them and asked to pick out the people you know, you will probably use a relatively high criterion. However, if you are handed your yearbook and asked to pick out familiar names, your criterion will be much lower, and you will identify more names as those of people you know. After all, you already know that you know many of these people.

Your ability to select a decision criterion creates a knotty measurement problem for psychologists. Suppose that two alumni pick out different numbers of classmates from high school graduation pictures. Does the person who selected more pictures have more detailed representations of the faces, or does he merely have a more lenient criterion?

Signal detection theory. The solution to the problem is to measure not only a person's hit rate—the number of targets reported as old—but also the false alarm rate—the number of distracters reported as old. If observers have altered their decision criterion, then inevitably both the hit and the false alarm rates will change in the same direction. To determine each person's criterion, they may be asked to assign confidence ratings: certain, probability, just guessing, to their decisions and then using the elegant mathematical theory of signal detection (Banks 1970; Swets, Tanner, & Birdsall, 1961), researchers can describe an observer's judgments in terms of both how sensitive they are to differences between targets and distracters and their criterion for calling an item a target.

For example, suppose a person is given a list of names and asked to identify all those she knows. The subject is asked to perform the task both when she has only one second apiece to decide whether each name is familiar or novel and when she has unlimited time. Figure 9.9 illustrates a signal detection analysis of two possible effects of giving a subject unlimited time on the task of distinguishing known and unknown names. Figure 9.9(a) shows the distributions of familiarity values for unknown and known names in a test taken under time pressure. In accord with most applications of signal detection theory, we assume that both distributions are of the bell-shaped normal form (a form that will be familiar to you if you have had a statistics course). The familiarity distribution for known names is largely to the right of that for unknown names, since known names will, of course, tend to be more familiar. However, the two distributions overlap, indicating that some unknown names will actually seem more familiar than some known names. In this situation perfect performance is impossible. Suppose subjects set a familiarity criterion at point c and respond "known" to all names more familiar than the criterion and "unknown" to those that are less familiar. The shadings in Figure 9.9(a) indicate the proportion of responses that will be of the four types logically possible: hits (correct responses to known names), correct rejections (correct responses to unknown names), misses (erroneous responses to known names), and false alarms (erroneous responses to unknown names).

Figures 9.9(b) and 9.9(c) illustrate two possible ways that giving a participant more time might increase the proportion of hits. Figure 9.9(b) depicts a pure criterion shift. The familiarity distributions are unchanged from those in Figure 9.9(a), but the criterion c has been shifted to a lower level on the familiarity continuum. The result is an increase in hits but also in false alarms. In contrast, Figure 9.9(c) illustrates a pure change in sensitivity. The criterion c is set at the same point as in Figure 9.9(a), but the familiarity distribution for known names has been shifted to the right, indicating that they seem more familiar, presumably because the participant has time to retrieve more details about them. As a result, the proportion of hits increases without any accompanying increase in false alarms.

In signal detection theory sensitivity is measured by the distance between the means of the two distributions, which is termed d'. When the signal and the noise distributions are both normal, then the distance of the criterion from the mean of the noise distribution can be calculated from the false-alarm rate, and its distance from the mean of the signal distribution can be calculated from the hit rate (actually, these calculations were performed long ago, and the answer can be looked up in any table describing the normal distribution). Adding these two distances gives the distance from one mean to the other.

The location of the criterion is measured in signal detection theory by the ratio of the height s of the signal distribution to the height n of the noise distribution at the criterion, a ratio that is called β (Greek letter beta). Again, when the signal and the noise distributions are normal, and if the hit and false alarm rates are known, the height of each distribution can be found in a table describing the normal distribution with these values. By measuring the hit rate and false-alarm rate in a recognition task, and applying the mathematical procedures provided by signal detection theory, we can derive separate estimates of both sensitivity and the decision criterion. Signal detection theory thus provides an extremely valuable tool for investigating recognition performance.

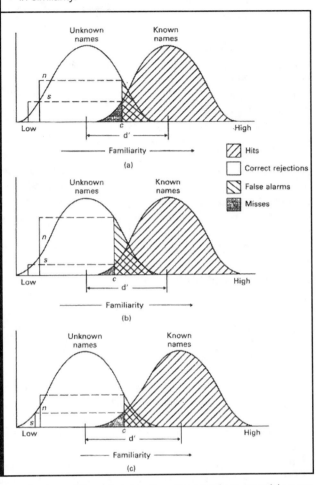

FIGURE 9.9

Signal detection analysis of two possible effects of context on recognition: 9a) baseline; (b) criterion shift; (c) increase in similarity.

Mirror effect. Signal detection theory has been a very useful tool in distinguishing the extent to which recognition judgments are based on general semantic information versus the retrieval of specific contextual information. Recognition of low-frequency words is a little better than recognition for both high-frequency words and very-low-frequency words whether the words appear in homogeneous or mixed-frequency lists (Chalmers, Humphreys, & Dennis, 1998; MacLeod & Kampe, 1996). This is because more specific contextual information from the study task is retrieved for the low-frequency words than the high-frequency words. Notice that since low-frequency words have, by definition, appeared in fewer contexts than high-frequency words, it may be that each appearance is more novel and so learners are more likely to associate distinctive features of the study context with the low-frequency words (Maddox & Estes, 1997). Hence, at test a low-frequency word target is more likely to serve as a cue for the study context and produce a remember response than a high-frequency target is. As a result of the greater number of remember responses for them, hit rates are higher for low-frequency than for high frequency targets (Hirshman, et al., 2002). However, a high frequency distracter will be associated with more nonspecific contextual information in memory than a low frequency distracter from the previous occasions on which it was seen or heard. So a high-frequency distracter is more likely to activate a context representation that is similar to the target context and may be mistaken for it than a low-frequency word is. That is, the false alarm rate is lower for low frequency than for high frequency distracters (Reder, Nhouyvanisvong, Schunn, Ayers, Angstadt, & Hiraki, 2000). To summarize, low frequency words have both higher hit rates and lower false alarm rates than high frequency words. In general, if two kinds of materials or conditions differ in memorability, the better material or condition is associated with both higher hit rates and lower false alarm rates. This ubiquitous aspect of recognition is called the mirror effect (Glanzer & Adams, 1990).

Since know judgments may be based on the semantic information immediately available from the match between the target and its representation but remember judgments require using this representation to generate additional contextual information, Joordens & Hockley (2000) reasoned that a remember judgment should take longer than a know judgment; so that reducing the time for a recognition judgment would eliminate remember judgments but not know judgments. Consistent with this reasoning, when they reduced the time for recognition judgments the difference in hit rates between high and low frequency words was eliminated but the difference in false alarm rates for high and low frequency words remained intact. Since remember judgments are based on representations formed during the presentation of the study list but know judgments are based on representations formed before the presentation of the study list, Hirshman et al. (2002) reasoned that reducing the opportunity for learning during the study task would reduce remember judgments but not know judgments. Consistent with this reasoning, when they reduced the opportunity for learning during study by reducing study time and by administering the amnesia producing drug Midazolam the difference in hit rates between high and low frequency words was eliminated but the difference in false alarm rates for high and low frequency words remained intact.

Eyewitnesses and lineups. We saw above that recognition is considerably better for familiar than for other unfamiliar faces. For ordinary life this is of no matter. It is the familiar people around you that you must recognize. However, the one special circumstance in which an unfamiliar face must be recognized is when an eyewitness must select a perpetrator from a lineup. In this case the probability of a false alarm is of more than academic interest. The fundamental fairness of the criminal justice system requires that the false alarm rate be negligible.

To study the accuracy of eyewitness identification a crime wave hit psychology classrooms in the 1970's that has not abated to this day. For example, in a classic study (Malpass & Devine, 1981) students were assembled in a large lecture hall for a biofeedback demonstration. During a pause in the demonstration a man entered the room, spoke with the instructor, and was asked to wait next to a rack of the apparatus. Instead the man repeatedly changed settings on the rack, though asked by the instructor, with increasing anger, not to. The man responded to the last of these requests by shouting an obscenity, pushing the electronic rack to the floor, and escaping through a rear door. He had been visible to the audience for 85 seconds. Twenty minutes after the vandalism a state police officer arrived and interviewed faculty members and a few persons who were seated close to the vandalism. The audience was then told that the vandalism had been staged and that the vandal was a confederate of the investigators. Members of the audience were asked to volunteer to attend one of the lineups to be held on the following three evenings. One hundred witnesses (74 women, 26 men) appeared to view these lineups.

The lineup contained five participants who were similar in height, body build, hair color and style, and dress. Two instructions, biased and unbiased, were given. The biased instructions read: "We believe that the person who pushed over the electronics equipment during the EEG demonstration is present in the lineup. Look carefully at each of the five individuals in the lineup. Which of these is the person you saw push over the equipment? Circle the number of his position in the lineup below." The eyewitnesses receiving this instruction were provided with five numbers (1-5) from which they could choose. Witnesses who wished to reject all five of the persons in the lineup had to ask how to indicate their judgment because no place was provided for such a response. Those witnesses who did ask were told that "if you believe that the vandal is not one of the people in the lineup, write that on the identification form." The unbiased instruction, however, explicitly provided the witnesses with a "no choice" option. It read: "The person who pushed over the electronics equipment during the EEG demonstration may be one of the five individuals in the lineup. It is also possible that he is not in the lineup. Look carefully at each of the five individuals in the lineup. If the person you saw push over the equipment is not in the lineup, circle 0. If the person is present in the lineup, circle the number of his position." The witnesses receiving this instruction were provided with six numbers from which to choose (0-5). On every other trial the perpetrator was absent and his place in the lineup was taken by an alternate.

The lineup identifications under the various conditions are shown in Table 9.2. Under biased instructions, the misidentification rate was 78% when the perpetrator was absent and 25% when the perpetrator was present. Under unbiased instructions, the misidentification rate was 33% when the perpetrator was absent and 0% when the perpetrator was present. With the perpetrator present under biased instructions all errors were false identifications, whereas under unbiased instructions all errors were false rejections of the lineup. Confidence and accuracy were not related. When the instructions were unbiased and the

TABLE 9.2
Percentage of Identifications for Lineups with Perpetrator Present and Absent under Biased and Unbiased Instructions

	Perpetrator Present Instructions		Perpetrator Absent Instructions	
	Biased	Unbiased	Biased	Unbiased
Perpetrator	75	83		
Other lineup member	25	0	78	33
No choice	0	17	22	67

perpetrator was actually present in the lineup, eyewitness identifications were reliable. However, even under unbiased instructions, if the perpetrator was not present in the lineup there was a 33% chance of a false identification being made.

Lineups of individuals are difficult and time consuming to assemble, so police usually rely on photo lineups. This raises the issue of whether the photos should be presented to the witness one at a time or simultaneously. Lindsay and Wells (1985) suggested that the use of a relative judgment strategy when the photos were presented simultaneously; i.e., selecting the individual most similar in appearance to the perpetrator, would increase false alarms. In contrast, presenting the photos one at time would encourage an absolute judgment strategy. In fact, they found that sequential presentation of photos produced the same number of hits but fewer false alarms than simultaneous presentation, and this result was replicated in further studies (Lindsay & Bellinger, 1999).

In the case of lineup the police already have a perpetrator in mind. Otherwise, an eyewitness may be asked to look through photos from a mug book. This situation is quite different. The eyewitness knows that the perpetrator may not be among the photos. She may say "yes" or "maybe" to more than one photo in order to provide the police with investigative leads. Again the issue arises of how to present the photos, one at a time or in groups. It is obviously not possible to present the hundreds of mug shots simultaneously. When Stewart and McAllister (2001) compared one at time presentation to presentation in groups of 12, they found no difference in hits but fewer false alarms when the pictures were presented in groups. Eyewitnesses shown the pictures in groups tended to pick no more than one per page, but eyewitnesses shown the photos individually would say maybe to photos less than twelve apart, resulting in the higher false alarm rate for individual presentation. The different results for photo lineups and mug books demonstrate how procedural details can influence recognition judgments and the importance of understanding these details to the criminal justice system.

DELUSIONS

In normal cognitive functioning the identification response dominates all the others and absurd conclusions are rejected without a second thought. However, in rare instances not only is the familiarity response impaired but it dominates the identification response. As a result, a delusion takes hold of an individual.

In Capgras delusion a person comes to believe that an exact duplicate has replaced someone close to him. Parents, a spouse, in one instance even a pet dog, have all been believed to be replaced by duplicates in different cases of the disorder. In many cases the belief is restricted to visual appearance. Ramachandran (Ramachandran & Blakeslee, 1998) described a case in which a patient accepted his parents as his parents when he spoke with them on the phone, but not when he was with them. Part of the problem may have been that damage to the amygdala was blocking the normal emotional response the patient should have gotten when he saw his parents. This led to his belief that they were strangers. When Ramachandran measured the patient's GSR response to emotional pictures, consistent with this hypothesis, he found a flat, rather than a normal response (see also Ellis, Lewis, Moselhy, & Young, 2000). However, this cannot be the entire explanation. A flat emotional response, even an unexpected feeling of unfamiliarity, when viewing a loved one may be disquieting, but should not be enough evidence to force the conclusion that the loved one is not who he or she says she is. In addition, in a delusion, the normal evaluation process appears to be turned around so that the impaired familiarity and emotional responses determine the conclusion, rather than being subordinated to the normal identification response.

Reduplicative paramnesia does for familiar locations what Capgras delusion does for familiar faces. The patient believes that a familiar location is in fact a duplicate of the real location. For example, Hudson and Grace (2000) described a 71-year-old woman who believed that her home was a duplicate of her real home.

In Fregoli's Syndrome the patient comes to believe that strangers he sees are actually persons he knows in disguise. Of course, here the response is the opposite of that in Capgras Syndrome. But again, the critical feature of the disorder is not the odd familiarity or emotional response but how it drives the patient's conclusion regardless of other evidence to the contrary.

Perhaps the most extreme delusion is mirrored-self misidentification (Davies & Coltheart, 2000). A patient comes to believe that his own reflection in the mirror is a different person who looks just like him and who silently follows him around. The patient may be aware of how odd his belief is and quite frankly tell you that he would not believe such a story if told it by someone else. He may still remember what a mirror is and what a reflection is. Nevertheless, he may cover up the mirror in his bedroom so that his silent twin cannot look at his wife.

These various delusions may occur in isolation or in combination (Hudson & Grace, 2000). The delusions also vary in severity. The patient may believe that a person or persons close to her have been replaced by robots (Silva & Leong, 1995). The delusions may result from brain injury (Box, Laing, & Kopelman, 1999), from schizophrenia (Edelstyn, Oyebode, Booker, & Humphreys, 1998), or from another psychiatric disorder (McEvedy, Hendry, Barnes, & Thomas, 1996). When the delusion is the result of a brain injury, such as a stroke or head trauma as the result of an automobile accident, it usually dissipates over several weeks (Box et al., 1999). When the delusion is associated with a psychiatric disorder it is usually alleviated by anti-psychotic medication. The disorders are assumed to result from a combination of temporal recognition system and prefrontal evaluation deficits, but a consistent set of damaged locations has not been found across patients. Furthermore, face recognition has not been found to be consistently impaired across patients (Edelstyn, 1998; Edelstyn, Riddoch, Oyebode, Humphreys, & Forde, 1996).

SUMMARY OF RECOGNITION

- A recognition task requires a yes/no or forced-choice judgment.
  - For example, *Was George Washington the first president of the United States?* and *Which is a picture of George Washington?* are both recognition tasks.
  - In the recognition system an input is compared with memory and matched with a representation, which in turn activates additional representations sufficient for a response.

- The process of recognition has several distinct stages.
  - Feature analysis and perceptual organization stage

* The features of an input determine its representation and the logogen it activates; hence what it is recognized as. So recognition is initially dependent on perceptual organization.
  ○ Comparison stage
    * The comparison process is influenced by what is learned from past experiences with the input. For example, when people are shown pictures of familiar and unfamiliar faces and then tested for recognition of exactly the same picture they are equally accurate for both familiar and unfamiliar faces. However, when they are tested with a different picture of the same face then they are much more accurate for familiar than for unfamiliar faces.
  ○ Response stage
    * In early infancy, after a long retention interval a match can take a long time to produce a response
  ○ Decision stage
    * Inference and criterion are both parts of the recognition process.

* The Four-part Recognition Response
  ○ Semantic information produces an identification response.
  ○ Contextual information determines the familiarity response.
  ○ Short-term temporal order information from working memory is experienced as the recency response.
  ○ Affective information produces an emotional response.

* There are different kinds of recognition judgments.
  ○ Semantic categorization or identification judgment
    * That person is your friend
  ○ Familiarity judgment
    * You have seen your friend before
  ○ Recency judgment
    * You have just seen your friend
  ○ Frequency judgment
    * You have seen your friend many times
  ○ Episodic judgment
    * You saw your friend last week in class

* The perception of familiarity is a matter of degree, but recognition tasks frequently force a choice between two alternatives: old or new. As a result, a decision procedure must set a familiarity criterion so that every item more familiar than the criterion is called "old" and every item less familiar than the criterion is called "new."
  ○ Both the environmental context and the person's expectations influence the level where the criterion is set.
  ○ The theory of signal detection compares correct recognitions with false alarms as a means of separately measuring a person's ability to discriminate old from new inputs and the criterion used for calling an input old.
  ○ The role of the decision criterion in recognition memory has an important application in the evaluation of eyewitness testimony.

GENERATION

Who was president during World War II? Name all the states in the United States. What are the primary symptoms of schizophrenia? Can you give directions from where you live to the nearest McDonald's restaurant? Who is the author of this book? Each of these queries is a request to recall some information from memory. A recall task taps the same basic process of accessing information in memory as does a recognition task. However, a recall task requires an additional processing step that is usually not required in a recognition task. In a recognition task the person is presented with a copy of the information to be found in memory. For example, when you recognize the word *Utah*, the input is automatically matched to a representation, and the match automatically activates additional representations, including a categorical representation that identifies Utah as a state. But in a recall task you are not given a copy of the information to be found in memory. Therefore you must begin by generating possible candidate concepts, using the information provided by the question. After each candidate concept is generated, an attempt is made to identify it. For example, suppose you are asked to recall an American state that begins with the letter U. You might begin by generating words that begin with U (e.g., Ulysses, Uganda, Utah), and then you check each word to determine whether it is a state. Or (as is more likely) you might attempt to serially generate the names of states (e.g., Wyoming, Virginia, Indiana, Utah), and then you check whether any of the candidates begins with U.

The processing steps required by a recall task are summarized in Figure 9.10. As the figure indicates, the request that initiates the recall operation contains the information that specifies the goal. Each piece of information that helps to guide the recall process is called a cue. In our example the recall cues are the letter *U* and the word *state*. The representation specified by the cues will again be called the target. Cues play two roles in a recall task. First, one or more cues are used to generate a set of concepts that are potential targets. For example, U may be used to generate Uganda and state may be used to generate Ohio and Utah. Second, the cues are used to identify which, if any, of the generated concepts is the actual target. This involves checking whether the U-generated potential target, Uganda, is a state, and whether either of the state-generated potential targets, Ohio and Utah, begins with U. Selecting the actual target is the same process as the identification process involved in recognition. Recall involves a two-step process often called either generate and identify or generate and recognize (Bahrick, 1970). That is,

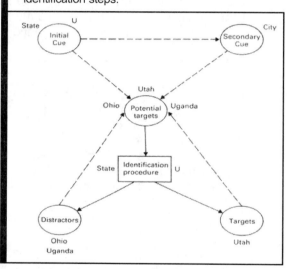

Figure 9.10

Steps in performing a recall task. The dotted arrows indicate generation steps; the solid arrows indicate identification steps.

when you recall something, you generate possible answers and choose among them in much the same way as you would if the alternatives were presented as part of a multiple-choice recognition test.

The area in the prefrontal cortex that selects among possible responses is the response selection area shown in Figure 4.1. This area was identified by using a very simple recall task: saying what was done with a common object. For high agreement objects everyone gives the same response, e.g., knife – cut; but for low agreement objects different people give different responses; e.g., pie – bake, eat, throw, etc. Both healthy individuals and individuals with damage to the late selection area had to generation functions for objects that had high versus low levels of agreement. Low agreement across individuals implies that several of these responses are first generated by a single individual and then one is selected. The individuals with damage to the late selection area were not impaired in generating responses for high agreement objects. But they were impaired at naming low agreement pictures (Thompson-Schill, Swick, Farah, D'Esposito, Kan, & Knight, 1998). Ironically, when more than one response is generated by the comparison process, they may interfere with each other so that the correct response is not produced.

Recognition has already been described in detail. Here generation will be described as well. A variety of factors during learning and test influence an individual's ability to generate potential targets. First factors limiting generation, and then factors enhancing generation, will be described.

PROACTIVE INTERFERENCE

As discussed earlier in the chapter, if you saw a list of ten random words you should have no difficulty a moment later selecting which words you had just seen in a recognition test. Yet you would be unlikely to immediately recall all ten words. The reason is retrieval failure. You would not have sufficient cues for generating the target words. The cue "word list" is just too general. Retrieval failure has been studied in experiments in which a person is prevented from forming specific associations between a study item and information already in memory. So there is only one, very general, retrieval cue. This kind of experiment is called a distracter paradigm because the subject is prevented or distracted from rehearsing the target. It is also sometimes called the Brown-Peterson paradigm, after the first investigators to perform this type of experiment (J. Brown, 1958; L. R. Peterson & M.J. Peterson, 1959).

The distracter paradigm. The task is performed as follows: A subject is presented with a consonant trigram, such as *QBF.* The person repeats it once and at the same time is presented with a three-digit number, such as 687. The person then has to immediately start counting backward by 3s. The only purpose of the counting task is to prevent the person from rehearsing the trigram (i.e., repeating it to himself or herself) or using any other strategy to consciously try to remember it. The counting task distracts the person from learning the trigram. After a specified period of time, which is usually 3-18 seconds, the person is permitted to stop counting and is asked to recall the trigram. The series of events from the presentation of the consonant trigram until the subject is asked to recall it constitutes a single trial. A single experiment consists of many trials, with a different consonant trigram being presented on each one. A person's performance changes from trial to trial in this task. The change in performance over trials was first demonstrated by Keppel and Underwood in 1962. Their results are shown in Figure 9.11 (see also Loess, 1964). Consider how people performed on the very first trial in the experiment, shown by the point farthest to the left in the figure. As the figure shows, on the very first trial a person was almost certain to recall the trigram no matter how long he or she first counted backward. Virtually everyone who had counted backward for 3, 9, or 18 seconds recalled their first trigram correctly. But look what happens on the second and third trial.

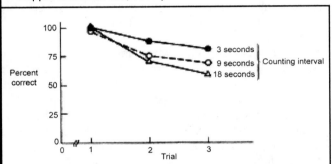

FIGURE 9.11

Experimental results of distractor paradgm. Performance deteriorates after the first trial on a distractor task. (From Keppel & Underwood, 1962.)

The performance of people begins to deteriorate on these trials, and performance is poorer the longer people have to count backward before recalling the trigram. In fact, if the experiment is continued for six trials, correct recall of the trigram averages less than 50 percent after 18 seconds of counting backwards. As mentioned above, the effect of the earlier material on the later material is called proactive interference (PI). As the result of PI, early list-items are more likely to be retrieved, resulting in primacy.

Before we consider why performance drops off so markedly when a person has to count backward for more than 3 seconds, let us consider what a really remarkable result this is. After all, three consonants are not very much information to remember. For example, memorizing someone's phone number, which contains seven digits, is quite easy. But the results in the distracter paradigm demonstrate that a relatively brief period of interference right at the time when a target would normally be associated with other information in memory has a very dramatic effect on later recall.

Why does performance deteriorate so dramatically over successive trials? The distracter task prevents a subject from forming associations between the target and other information in memory that could serve as retrieval cues. So when the subject is asked to recall the target at the end of the first trial, probably only one fact serves as a cue for the target—namely, that it was a consonant trigram. However, since

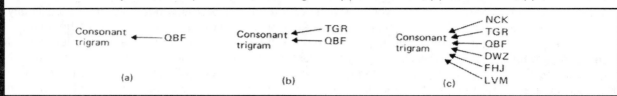

FIGURE 9.12

Associative memory structure for presented constant trigrams: (a) After one trial, (b) after two trials; (c) after six trials.

this association is recent and therefore strong, this one cue will probably be sufficient to generate the target. The memory structure on the first trial is depicted in Figure 9.12(a).

Now consider the situation at the end of the second trial, when the subject has to recall the most recently presented trigram. The subject again only has a single cue: that a consonant trigram has been presented. But now the cue is associated to two recently presented trigrams, as shown in Figure 9.12(b). As a result, there is a significant probability that when the subject tries to use the cue to generate the trigram presented on the second trial, the trigram presented on the first trial will be generated instead. The retrieval cue has been overloaded.

Even if the subject succeeds in generating both trigrams, he or she will still be faced with the task of selecting the more recent of the two. But here the length of the interval spent counting backward will have an effect. If this interval is relatively long, say 18 seconds, the recency of the more recent trigram may have already diminished enough so that it is difficult to discriminate from the earlier trigram. As the number of trials continues to increase, the subject's problems will be further compounded. As Figure 9.12(c) indicates, the recall cue will become associated with more and more trigrams, so the cue becomes increasingly useless. With each additional trial both generating and recognizing the most recently presented trigram become more difficult.

PI only builds up when items from the same category are studied on consecutive trials. If after several trials a study item from a different category is presented, recall on that trial will increase substantially. This result was first demonstrated in 1963 by Wickens, Born, and Allen. In their experiment subjects recalled consonant trigrams, with the usual deterioration in recall performance over trials. Then, on the fourth trial half the subjects were given a digit trigram (e.g., 549) to recall. Figure 9.13 presents the results. As the figure shows, those subjects who were given a consonant trigram on the fourth trial continued to perform poorly. But the subjects given a digit trigram performed virtually as well as they had on the very first trial. Wickens and colleagues obtained the same result when they first presented digit trigrams and then shifted to consonants, and whether the shift occurred on the fourth, seventh, or tenth trial. Performance always returned to the initial level of recall on the shift trial. In later studies Wickens (1972) showed that this effect is obtained with a wide variety of different shifts in inputs. In general, the more dissimilar the new category of targets is from the original category, the more recall improves.

Figure 9.14 illustrates why performance increases in the case of a shift from consonant trigrams to digit trigrams. After the first six trials the memory structure would be as in Figure 9.14(a)—six consonant trigrams all associated with a single cue. As a result, this cue is not effective in generating the last input presented. But on the seventh trial the digit trigram will be associated to an entirely different

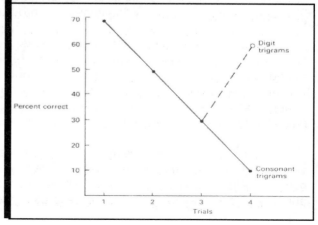

FIGURE 9.13

Recall in distracter paradigm. Recall deteriorates over trials, but it increases when the category of the input is changed (After Wickens, et al., 1963).

cue, as shown in Figure 9.14(b). Since only one target will be associated with the cue *digit trigram*, that cue is effective when the person tries to recall the target.

A recall cue does not have to be noticed at study to be effective at recall. Gardiner, Craik, and Birtwistle (1972) demonstrated this by changing from one kind of target to another in a very subtle way and alerting the subject to the change at recall. The study was done in England, where gardening is a national hobby. Consequently, many people know the names of a great many flowers. When college students were presented with a series of trials on which the items were cultivated flowers (e.g., rose, carnation), followed by a critical trial on which the items were wildflowers (e.g., dandelion), recall did not improve. The students simply did not notice the subtle shift in category. But when the experimenter provided the student at the time of recall on the last trial with the cue *wild*, release from PI occurred (Figure 9.15). Therefore the critical factor causing improvement in recall seems to be the introduction of a new retrieval cue (see also Loftus & Patterson, 1975; Watkins & Watkins, 1975).

FIGURE 9.14

Effect of changing the category of input. Multiple category members associated with a single cue.

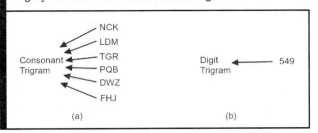

(a)   (b)

FIGURE 9.15

Even when the shift in category is not noticed at study, a recall cue causes release from PI (Gardiner et al., 1972).

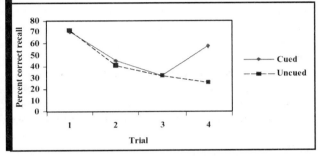

Clustering in recall. When we move from the distracter task to the recall of things you already know the limitation on the number of items that may be generated from a single cue remains the same. Consider the case of someone attempting to think of the names of the states. First, the person attempts to generate the names of states by using the concept *state* as a retrieval cue. Assume the person is a New Jersey resident, so there are associations among New Jersey, New York, and Pennsylvania, causing these state names to enter consciousness. Next, the person attempts to generate more names by tracing more associations from the cue *state*. But the activation levels of New Jersey, New York, and Pennsylvania are now higher than those of the other state logogens, so that another attempt to generate state names from the logogen *state* is most likely to result in retrieval of the same three state names. Each successive attempt to traverse the associations emanating from *state* only maintains the high activation levels of those names already generated—or drives them even higher. In short, after a single use, subsequent attempts to access additional state names from the logogen *state* are likely to fail.

So each recall cue has a dual effect on the recall of a set of targets, such as the members of a category or a list of words. The cue first has a potentially facilitatory effect. It may activate new targets sufficiently for them to enter consciousness. However, once the targets have been activated, the cue has an inhibitory effect because a new cue similar to both the old cue and to a new target will be more likely to reactivate the old targets because of their higher activation levels. Thus cues, targets, and distracters all come to block the retrieval of new targets. For example, A. Brown (1981) found that when students had to name members of a particular category that each began with a particular letter (e.g., for g-animal one answer is giraffe), students took a longer time to produce each successive member. Similarly, when naming a sequence of pictures of members of a category, after three or four items students took a longer time to name each successive picture.

J. Brown (1968) required two groups of subjects to recall as many of the fifty states as they could. For one group he first read the names of twenty-five of the fifty states. This group naturally recalled more of the names of the twenty-five states that had been read aloud than did the group that had not heard the list. However, the former group of subjects recalled fewer of the twenty-five states that had not been read aloud than did the group that had no prior cuing. Slamecka (1968; 1969) introduced the part-list cuing paradigm for studying this effect systematically. People studied a list of words and were then given some of the list words and told to use them as cues to recall the remainder of the list. Fewer list words not used as cues were recalled in this condition than in the condition in which subjects were not given any cues and simply told to freely recall the entire list (also see M. C. Anderson, R. A. Bjork, & E. L. Bjork, 1994; Roediger, 1978).

How, then, does the person generate more state names? (We obviously can recall more than three states at one time.) The answer is that the person uses concepts other than *state* as recall cues. One strategy might be to form a mental image of the map of the United States. Then the person could mentally scan the imaginary map and name each state as its location was encountered. Another strategy might be for the person to think of all the places he or she had visited. What both these strategies have in common is that potential targets are generated in a systematic fashion that prevents the person from generating the same concepts again and again. The map of the United States in the first strategy and the person's own life experiences in the second strategy form the backbone of a chain of associations that prevents the person from getting trapped into repeating the same path.

There are many possible generation strategies for every recall task. Since different people know different things, the choice of strategy is fundamentally idiosyncratic. Thus a sports fan may use the names of sports franchises to cue the states that they are located in. A meteorologist may use the climate type of the region as a cue for the state's name. What cue is effective will depend on how the individual's knowledge is organized. And many different strategies for generating cues may be effective. What is important is that the person must find some strategy or combination of strategies for generating additional recall cues. These additional recall cues, generated from the original recall cue (e.g., state) in the hope that they will be associated to the target, are called **secondary recall cues**. When the target set is large, a person's skill at generating secondary recall cues may often be what determines how many targets are recalled (Rabinowitz, Mandler, & Patterson, 1977).

The generation of targets from cues produces a recall function that has three ubiquitous features. First, the number of additional items recalled decreases over time. Second, the items are recalled in clusters. Third, the clusters usually have no more than three or four items.

For example, following Bousfield and Sedgewick (1944), Gruenewald and Lockhead (1980) gave students either 15 or 30 minutes to generate all the instances of a category. Figure 9.16 shows that a continuous effort yields a lower and lower rate of production (i.e., the curve increases less rapidly as the recall attempt progresses). Figure 9.17 shows that the instances are produced in clusters and Figure 9.18 shows the distribution of cluster sizes. As shown in Figures 9.17 and 9.18, most clusters contain only one or two instances but a few very large clusters, even clusters containing more than ten instances, are observed. Presumably this occurs when a hierarchically organized set of cues is hit upon.

Returning to Figure 9.16, the reason the rate of instance production declines with time is that the rate of cluster production declines with time. Average cluster size remains constant. Suppose, say, a person has 150 animal names stored in memory and embarks on a strategy of first generating secondary recall cues and then using them to generate animal clusters. Furthermore, the secondary recall cues are produced at a constant rate. At the beginning, when virtually no animal names have been generated, the probability of a secondary recall cue adding new animal names will be high, and hence

FIGURE 9.16

Cumulative number of animal names produced by a subject in a 30-minute session. The insert shows those items detailed in Figure 9.17 (From Gruenewald & Lockhead, 1980).

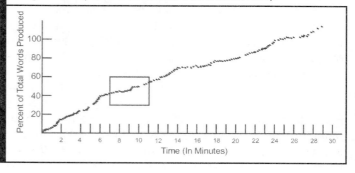

new clusters will be rapidly added. However, as more and more animal names are produced, the probability of a secondary recall cue producing new names decreases, and the person must generate more and more secondary recall cues before a new cluster is produced. As a result, the time between new clusters increases. Therefore if what you know is poorly organized, then the results of an extended recall effort will inevitably diminish with time.

The limit on the number of responses that can be generated from a single cue places a limit on the number of similar targets that can be recalled at one time. For example, Battig and Montague (1969) asked college students to generate instances of fifty-six different categories (e.g., flowers, diseases, ships, metals, toys). The students had 30 seconds to generate instances for each category. Each student was usually able to generate only five or six instances for a category within the 30 seconds. The greatest average number (11) of instances produced was for the category human body parts. Yet many of the categories obviously had more than a hundred familiar instances (e.g., female names, male names, cities).

Fluctuations in recall. The precise items recalled depends on the strength of their associations, their momentary activation levels, and the generation strategy adopted. If you try to recall the same list later you may think of new generation strategies and the activation levels of the targets will be different. So you may generate targets that you didn't generate the first time. For example, W. Brown (1923) gave his college students two chances to recall all the states they could in 5 minutes. The two recall trials were half an hour apart. On their second try the students recalled about five states they had failed to recall on the first trial, but they also failed to recall about two states they had recalled previously. Buschke (1974) found a similar result with successive recall attempts of a list of randomly selected words. An even more striking increase in recall with time is observed with children. Ballard (1913) discovered that a partially learned poem studied by twelve-year-old London schoolchildren was not recalled as well immediately after the learning as it was a day or two later. Ballard named this phenomenon **reminiscence**, which was defined as the opposite of forgetting, that is, as an improvement in the memory for a target over time. Kasper (1983) obtained reminiscence in a paired-associate learning task in which twelve-year-old Brooklyn schoolchildren studied pairs of Spanish words and their English translations and then had to recall the translations when presented with the Spanish words.

FIGURE 9.17

Items produced in a portion of the 30-minute animal recall task (Gruenewald & Lockhead, 1980)

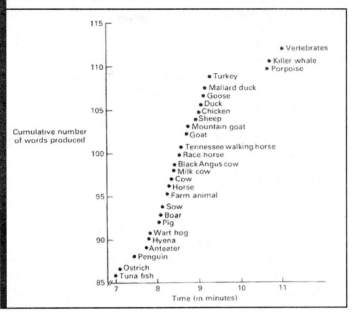

FIGURE 9.18

Relative frequency of occurrence of different-sized clusters from four categories. (From Gruenewald & Lockhead, 1980.)

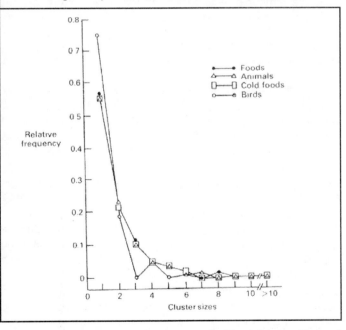

Repeated recall attempts only improve recall when the list or category items have been encoded in sufficient detail to be discriminated during identification. In one experiment, Erdelyi and Kleinbard (1978) presented subjects with sixty pictures of common objects (e.g., watch, fish, feather) or with the names of the objects. Each target was presented for 5 seconds. Afterward, the subjects were asked to recall the list (always by writing the object names). The subjects then continued to try to recall the list, again and again over a period of a week. Figure 9.19 presents the average number of items recalled over time. When the items had been presented as words, average recall stayed fairly constant after the first hour. But when the items were presented as pictures, recall continued to go up for

FIGURE 9.19

Multiple recall attempts. The number of items recalled increases for a longer period of time for pictures than for words. (From Erdelyi & Kleinbard, 1978.)

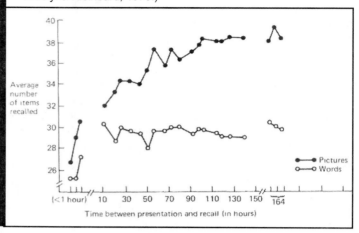

about four days (see also Erdelyi & Becker, 1974). Pictures are recognized more accurately than words, presumably because pictures are more discriminable from one another. People will therefore have less trouble discriminating list pictures from nonlist pictures after many recall trials. However, differences between memory performance with pictures and words depend on the strategies people use to encode the inputs. For example, if subjects are told to form a visual image of each object as its name is presented, recall over trials will increase in much the same way as it does when pictures are presented (Erdelyi, Finkelstein, Herrell, Miller, & Thomas, 1976). Instructions that focus attention on the meaning of the words produce similar effects when the words are easy to image (Roediger & Thorpe, 1978) but not when the words are abstract and hence difficult to image (Belmore, 1981).

FORM, SEMANTIC, AND ASSOCIATIVE CUES

The other side of PI is **cue specificity**. PI causes retrieval failure because a nonspecific cue is associated with too many distracters in order to reliably retrieve the target. Release from PI occurs when a cue is found that is more strongly associated with the target than with any distracter; hence is specific for that target. Here let us consider the various kinds of specific cues that may be found for a target. Recall from Chapter 5 that there are three kinds of primes, form primes, semantic primes and associative primes. As defined above, when a prime does not merely increase the speed with which a target is subsequently recognized, but generates recall of the target, then it is called a cue. That is, if you are asked to generate an animal name and say *dog, animal* is not merely a prime for a *dog*; in this example it is a cue as well.

Form cues. If the perceptual representation of the cue matches some gestalt (good part) of the perceptual representation of the target then the cue is called a **form cue**. The primes that had the same geons as the corresponding targets, described in Chapter 2, would function as form cues. Form cues are often highly specific to their targets and hence highly effective retrieval cues. Consider the pattern shown in Figure 9.20(a). Most people perceive the features of this pat-

FIGURE 9.20

Patterns and components: (a) Basic pattern; (b) a good part of the pattern in (a); (c) bad part of the pattern in (a).

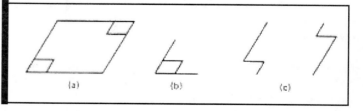

tern as organized into three gestalts (or good parts, see Chapter 3), which in turn form the entire figure. That is, they perceive this pattern as a parallelogram with boxes in the lower left and upper right corners.

So the part of the pattern shown in Figure 9.20(b) is a good part of the pattern, whereas the part shown in Figure 9.20(c) is not. This result is true even though objectively both Figures 9.20(b) and 9.20(c) contain equally large pieces of the pattern in Figure 9.20(a). Bower and Glass (1976) showed a group of undergraduates a series of patterns like the one shown in Figure 9.20(a). The students were then given a piece of each pattern as a cue and asked to draw the complete patterns. If the cue was a good part of the pattern, then the students were able to recall the entire pattern about 90 percent of the time. But if the part of the pattern presented as a cue was not a good part of the pattern, the pattern was recalled only about 20 percent of the time. Form cues mark the border between recall and recognition. If a form cue is replaced with a cue that is identical to the target, then the nominal generation stage disappears and the task becomes a recognition task.

Tip-of-the-tongue phenomenon. Form cues for the unretrieved word may be effective in relieving the tip-of-the-tongue experience. Both the first letter of the word (Freedman & Landauer, 1966; Gruneberg & Monk, 1974) and a rhyming word (Kozlowski, 1977) sometimes help the person remember the word. However, presenting a semantic cue may not help; but only increase PI. Alan Brown (1979) showed students a word followed by a definition and they had to decide whether the two matched. If they did not, the students were to generate the word that matched the definition. Suppose the definition was "to eat greedily," so the word it defined was "gobble." If 'gobble" was not presented then the word shown was either semantically similar (*cram*) orthographically similar (*goggle*) or unrelated (*feud*). The students were most likely to retrieve the correct word when the cued word was orthographically similar, but least likely to recall it when the cue was semantically similar. Presumably the orthographic cues were effective because they were highly specific; they were more similar to the target than to any distracter. In contrast, presumably the semantic cues delayed recall because they were nonspecific and subsequent attempts to find a cue specific to the target instead produced words related to the semantic cue. Roediger, Neely, and Blaxton (1983) showed that the semantic cue reduced recall of the target only when subjects thought that the semantic cue itself might be the target and tested it against the definition.

Semantic cues. A **semantic cue** has some sort of semantic relationship with the target. Semantic relations include any structural description that includes both the cue and target. Semantic cues play the central role in generation since hierarchically organized semantic representations are used to generate most cues. The role of hierarchical organization will be described in detail below. Here, the less obvious role of semantic cues in generating visual representations will be described.

In one experiment people were presented with irregular visual patterns that they later had to either recognize or reproduce. The subjects were also asked to describe the forms in words. Cohen and Granstrom found that the patterns that could be described most accurately were most likely to be reproduced accurately. However, the describability of the form had no influence on recognition performance. This result is exactly what we would expect if the verbal descriptions were used as cues for generating the forms during recall.

In another experiment Cohen and Granstrom (1970) showed people a pattern and then asked them to either recognize or reproduce it after a 7-second delay. During the delay interval either three names or three faces were presented, which the subject also had to remember. The names interfered more with the reproduction task than with the recognition task, suggesting that reproduction was more dependent on verbally generating a representation. In contrast, the faces interfered more with the recognition task, suggesting that visual recognition depended on comparing the input with visual representations of the targets in memory.

Semantic cues are generally more effective in visual recall than cues that were merely associated with the target at study. For example, Figure 9.21(a) depicts three separate objects. Hence each object is merely an associated cue for the others. Figure 9.21(b) shows the same three objects in a single integrated representation that would be encoded as a single visual structural description. So each object is a semantic cue for the entire picture. Studies show that both adults (Wollen, Weber, & Lowry, 1972) and children (Reese, 1965) are better at recalling integrated patterns than separate pictures from cues.

Similarly, Bower (1970) found that interactive imagery instructions improved cued recall with respect to instructions to form separate images. Furthermore, when recognition of the words was tested instructions to form interactive images were no more effective than instructions to form separate images (also see Begg, 1978b). The fact that interactive imagery is only superior to separate imagery for recall, but not for recognition, demonstrates that it has its effect only on the generation stage of recall, not the recognition

FIGURE 9.21

Visual representations. (a) Separated. (b) Integrated.

stage. Presumably interactive imagery encodes the cue-target study pair in a visual structural description. At test the cue primes the target through the structural description, thus increasing the likelihood that it will be generated.

The fact that associative cues are less effective than semantic cues does not mean that they are totally ineffective. When other kinds of cues are not available, such as in a free recall task, associative cues do help generate targets. So when you learn something, everything in the learning context, including the immediate environment and your emotional state, are all potential associative cues for the study materials.

Context-dependent recall. Recall that infant recognition memory is highly specific. If an infant learns to kick to move a specific mobile in a specific context then the infant only recognizes the mobile in that context. But in the second six months of life, when the infant can move around on her own and sees the same toy in different contexts, the context-dependency of memory declines. Recall that list context does influence recognition for list items since the list context consists of other task relevant targets. However, recognition is independent of task-irrelevant context cues. As we shall see, the room in which the list was learned generally does not affect subsequent recognition for the list. However, recall remains context-dependent. In the classic experiment (Godden & Baddeley, 1975) sixteen divers learned a list of forty unrelated words either on the shore or 20 feet under the sea. They were subsequently asked to recall the words in either the same or the alternative environment. Mean free-recall scores were as shown in Figure 9.22. As the figure shows, words were recalled more accurately in the environment in which they were originally learned. Godden and Baddeley also tested divers' recognition of words in different environments. A change in environmental context had no effect on recognition performance.

FIGURE 9.22

Recall scores. Godden and Baddeley (1975) found that word lists were recalled better in the same environment in which they were learned that they were in a different environment.

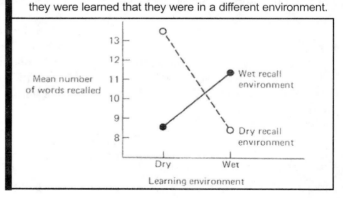

Apparently the environment acts primarily as a generation cue, though a person is usually not aware of it (S. M. Smith, Glenberg, & Bjork, 1978). When people placed in a new environment are instructed to recall the original learning environment just prior to free recall of the list, their recall is as good in the new environment as in the original learning environment (S. M. Smith, 1979). So when people are made aware of the learning context, they can deliberately use it as a secondary recall cue to help generate potential targets. Furthermore, just as in infancy, context-dependent memory in adulthood only occurs when a specific study list is learned in a single discriminable context. S. M. Smith (1982) found that context only facilitated recall when associating a context with a study list was a special event. He had college students perform different study tasks in different rooms of the college. When the students learned two different lists in two different rooms context facilitated recall. But when the number of rooms and study tasks was increased to five recall was no longer facilitated by context. More generally, context-dependent retrieval will not be superior whenever the task demands have discouraged people from encoding details of the study environment.

State-dependent memory. A phenomenon that is related to context-dependent memory is state-dependent memory. This term originally was used to describe the casual observation that heavy drinkers, when sober, were unable to find money or alcohol they had hidden while drunk, but they remembered the hiding places when they were drunk again. To explain this result, researchers assumed that the physiological state of the person acted as a cue for the hiding place. The existence of this phenomenon was unclear until a thoughtful review by James Eich (1980) showed that the tasks for which pharmacological-state-dependent retrieval is observed are the same as for context-dependent retrieval. That is, state-dependent retrieval is generally observed with free recall but not with cued recall or recognition. Apparently, in the latter cases the effects of the more salient retrieval cues obscure the effect of the state cue.

Mood congruency and depression. Related to but subtlely different from state-dependency is the mood congruency effect (Blaney, 1986). You recall memories consistent with the mood you are in. For example, Clark and Teasdale (1982) asked patients who underwent mood swings to produce autobiographical memories in response to neutral words. The patients recalled fewer pleasant memories during their sad phase than their neutral phase. However, depressed patients recall fewer details of their lives in general than normal individuals do (Moore, Watts, & Williams, 1988). Sorting out why this is the case has been difficult experimentally (Bower, Gilligan, & Monteiro, 1981; Isen, Shalker, Clark, & Carp, 1978), possibly because it is not possible to artificially induce intense happiness or sadness in a person in an experimental setting.

THE ROLE OF ORGANZATION IN GENERATION

Given the hit-or-miss nature of cue generation for unorganized material, the basic factor influencing generation is the organization of the targets. Using existing semantic associations to hierachically organize a study list into chunks that are each generated from a unique semantic cue greatly increases the number of targets that can be generated at recall. As discussed in Chapter 7, such organization often takes place at encoding. First, the learner associates subspan segments of the list with cues such that each cue is already strongly associated with all the members of its associated segment. For example, the segment *tree bush fern* might be associated with the cue *plant*. Similarly, the cues for the segments *pony goat lamb*, *shoe belt vest*, *bone skin hair* might be *animal*, *clothes*, and *body parts*, respectively. Hence the list may be organized as a hierarchy. The hierarchy, having been created from the bottom up, may be used to generate the list from the top down. First, a single top-level cue is used to generate the four middle-level cues, and then the middle-level cues are used to generate the chunks containing list members.

Guided generation. John Seamon (Seamon & Chumbley, 1977) tested this retrieval model by cuing retrieval of particular list items with their predecessors and/or successors and measuring reaction time to produce targets. According to the model, to retrieve *fern* from *tree bush* requires two steps: first, accessing the cue *plant* from *tree* and/or *bush*, and second, using the cue to activate a generative procedure for the sequence *tree bush fern*. In contrast, to retrieve *fern* from *pony goat* requires six steps. First, the cue *animal* is accessed from *pony* and/or *goat*. Second, the sequence *pony goat lamb* is generated. This sequence does not contain a target before *pony goat*, so the retrieval process must continue. Third, the cue *animal* is reactivated from *pony goat* and/or *lamb*. Fourth, the top-level cue is activated from *animal*. Fifth, the top-level cue generates the sequence *plant*, *animal*, *clothes*, *body parts*. Sixth, the cue *plant* is used to generate the sequence *tree bush fern*. When Seamon and Chumbley (1977) correlated the predicted number of steps necessary to generate a target from a cue with the observed reaction time, the correlations in three experiments ranged from 93 to 99 percent, providing powerful support for the hierarchical retrieval model.

In this example members of the same chunk were instances of the same category in order to clarify the exposition. However, it was mentioned in Chapter 7 that people also hierarchically organize lists of unrelated words into chunks that may not contain instances of the same category. Seamon and Chumbley showed that hierarchical organization was used to cue the retrieval of lists of unrelated words, though in this case the cues did not correspond to natural categories.

In fact, even if the learner does not notice the hierarchical organization of the list at study it still has some effect as long as the learner becomes aware of it at recall. Santa, Ruskin, Snuttjer, and Baker (1975) had one group of students study lists in hierarchical arrangements, whereas two other groups studied randomly arranged lists. After studying the lists, the students tried to recall as many words as possible. At this point the subjects were given some cues to help them recall more words. The hierarchical group and one of the random groups were given the top three levels of the conceptual hierarchy as cues for further recall. The other random group was given the same cue words, except that the cue words were arranged randomly. Santa et al. then counted how many additional words the subjects were able to recall after receiving the cues. The hierarchy cues improved recall most for the students who originally studied the list in hierarchical form (an extra 19 words recalled). The cue words were next most effective for the group that studied the words in a random arrangement but were cued with the hierarchy (10.2 additional words). The cues were least effective when they were arranged randomly (just 4.8 additional words). This experiment demonstrates that organization is most effective when presented for both study and recall; however, it is an aid even when presented only at the time of recall.

False memories. The effect of semantic organization on generation is generally a blessing; but it is not an unmixed one. Recall from the discussion of recognition, above, that it is not always possible to perfectly discriminate among similar targets and distracters. First Deese (1959) and then Roediger and McDermott (1990) showed that if a person was asked to recall a list of related words he might also recall or recognize a related word that was not on the list. For example, if a group of college students heard a list of words all related to *mountain*, e.g., *hill, valley, summit, peak, ...*, over half the students recalled hearing *mountain* as well. Across several experiments, false recall and recognition for the similar distracter was often about as high as correct recall and recognition for words actually presented in the middle of the list. (Recall that words in the middle of the list are less well remembered than words at the beginning.) Two factors influenced the probabilty of both false recognition and false recall. The first factor was the probability of generating the distracter as an associate of the list item; e. g., the probability of responding *mountain* when asked to give an associate to *hill, valley, summit*, etc. The higher the probability of generating the distracter as an associate of a list item, the more likely it was to be falsely remembered. The second factor was the overall level of recall of the list. The lower the level of list recall, the more likely the associated distracter was to be falsely remembered (Roediger, Watson, McDermott, & Gallo, 2001).

The influence of these two factors on false memory illuminate key steps during the process of learning and remembering. As we have seen, mature learning involves the integration of old and new information and temporal recognition requires discriminating when various experiences occurred. The first factor demonstrates that when you see or hear a list of words, there is some probability that you will think of other associated words. So, if you hear *valley, hill, summit, peak*, etc. there is some probability that you will think of *mountain* as well (Goodwin, Meissner, & Ericsson, 2001). The automatic activation of associates is an aid to list learning because it provides a category (*mountain*) for organizing the list. But later, when you are asked to remember the list, you must discriminate those words you actually heard from those that you merely thought of. This is usually possible because a word that was actually presented may be associated with a representation of the tone of voice in which it was spoken. Presumably, a distracter is not associated with such a specific contextual representation. So contextual information can be used to discriminate targets from distracters. The second factor, the level of recall of the list, demonstrates that when detailed representations of the list items are available, hence recall is high, it is possible to discriminate targets from associated distracters. But when detailed representations of list items are not available, hence recall is lower, it is more difficult to discriminate targets from associated distracters.

We mentioned above that given a sufficient degree of organization, there is no limit on the number of concepts that can be recalled upon request. The downside of associating information learned on different occasions in a single semantic network is losing the contextual details of when each piece of information was learned. Sometimes these details are important. Recall that when Sulin and Dooling (1974) entitled a story, "Helen Keller," the college students who read it subsequently falsely thought that they had read that she was blind.

KNOWLEDGE

With the exception of dropping by a store to pick up a few needed items, recall tasks generally do not involve recalling lists of words as much as useful facts about the world, such as how to get to class, what are the correct answers to the exam questions, and where you can find the phone number of someone you need to call. Semantic organization makes knowledge retrieval very efficient. Not only do you retrieve what you know very rapidly but you also know right away what you do not know. If I ask you a physics question, you do not spend several minutes searching your memory for the answer before you discover that you never took a physics course.

Sentence verification. Inference plays an even more important role in recall than it does in recognition. You can verify that a dog is an animal by retrieving from semantic memory that a dog is, in fact, an animal (Collins & Quillian, 1969). But how do you know that a dog is not a cat? The falsification strategy is to determine that two concepts are mutually exclusive instances of the same superordinate category. Since dogs and cats are different kinds of animals, you can infer that a dog is not cat when you retrieve that they are both animals. When such a contradiction strategy is used, "false" decisions are made relatively quickly when the two concepts shared a highly related superordinate; e.g., *A dog is a cat* (Holyoak & Glass, 1975). Other examples include *Valleys are mountains* and *Fruits are vegetables*.

Holyoak and Glass (1975) also found that instances are used as counterexamples to disconfirm false generalizations such as *All birds are robins* (also see Lorch, 1978). Such sentences are rejected by retrieving an instance of the subject category that is not an instance of the predicate category. For example, a person could retrieve the fact that some birds are canaries; since canaries aren't robins, canary is a counterexample to the claim *All birds are robins*. Counterexamples can also be used to reject some false sentences about properties. For example, you could decide that *All roses are red* is false by thinking of a yellow rose. Counterexamples can include personal experience. Remembering a particular yellow rose you saw last week would be enough to falsify the general claim that all roses are red.

Notice that using a counterexample to determine that something is false is another example of making an inference. The ability to make inferences greatly expands the amount of information a hierarchical organization contains since many positive and negative inferences can be drawn from it. You can know that all roses are not red even if you were never told that before. Similarly, you can infer that squirrels have hearts because they are animals and animals have hearts, but that squirrels do not have gills because they are not fish and only fish have gills, though you probably never thought about this before.

The rapid verification of the almost endless number of statements that comprise an individual's ordinary knowledge of the world make salient the close connection between organization and rapid retrieval. The better that targets are organized in memory, the more targets one will be able to recall. When concepts form statements that form episodes that form stories, people can recall scores of details from a story they have heard once. Given a sufficient degree of organization, there is no limit on the number of concepts that can be recalled upon request.

Semantic cues and visual targets. Is it true that all trees have leaves? Holyoak and Glass (1975) found that most students said yes when asked this question. However, pine trees have needles, not leaves, as the same students agreed when this was pointed out to them. Why then did they get it wrong? When asked the question, the students used the semantic cue to *tree* to generate representations of a few trees.

More specifically, they used the semantic cue to generate a structural description, which in turn was used to construct a representation of one or more tree-instances. However, the structural description was for a tree with leaves and so all the instances generated had leaves.

FIGURE **9.23**

Recall task. An American penny (a) and drawings from students who attempted to reproduce it from memory (b) (from Nickerson & Adams, 1979.)

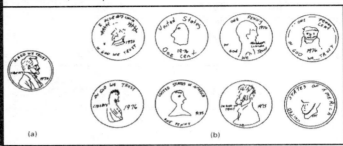

Since structural descriptions are by their nature general, it is difficult to generate accurate detailed visual representations of specific instances. Recall that Nickerson and Adams (1979) examined the ability of American college students to recognize the head side of a penny. The students had even more difficulty when asked to draw the coin. Some of their rather lamentable efforts are displayed in Figure 9.23. You have the impression that your representations are so detailed because the detail is fine enough for what you use it for—reading a page, dialing a phone number, or selecting a penny out of a few coins of various values. Actually, you usually need many fewer features to recognize something than to form a clear mental image of it.

Indeed, Rubin and Kontis (1983) found evidence that people base their recall of all coins on a single structural description. Figure 9.24(a) shows the American coins in use at the time of their study, and Figure 9.24(b) shows versions based on the most frequent features subjects used in drawing each one. The striking result is that all the reconstructed coins tended to be the same except for the identity of the president depicted on each. The subject appeared to know little about the specific details of each type of coin (except for its size and color, presumably), but they did seem to have a clear notion of what coins in general are like.

Distortions in geographic knowledge. The reconstructed coins show the role of inference in visual construction. People infer that coins of different denominations all look like pretty much alike, and so when drawing any one coin, they draw on their pool of features for all coins. This is useful to a point, but where the coins differ in detail errors are introduced into the reconstruction. Inference plays an important role in geographical knowledge. If a detour moves you off a familiar path then you can infer that two left turns or two right turns will get you back on it. However, this inference is only valid if the angles of the two turns add up to 180 degrees. However, mental maps are often simplified and do not contain precise information about the relative location of one familiar place to another. So when you apply your standard rules of inference, the locations of specific places are not exactly where you would expect them to be.

Barbara Tversky (1981) performed a series of experiments on people's memory for real and artificial maps, local environments, and visual patterns. Because remembering the absolute location of places is difficult, people encode places relative to other places or natural directions. They then use the same inferential process described above. Geographical

FIGURE **9.24**

Recall task. Actual American coins (a) and coins reproduced from memory (b) (from Rubin & Kontis, 1983).

regions are commonly viewed as hierarchical structures. Thus a building is in a city, which is in a state, which is in a country, etc. Because you know that the location of a superordinate constrains the location of all the regions within it, distortions caused by misalignment of the larger region are inherited by its subordinate locations. Because most people, quite reasonably but mistakenly, align South America as south of North America, rather than as southeast of it, they infer that Miami is east of Lima. But, as the map in Figure 9.25 reveals, the reverse is true. People are very prone to make such errors based on superordinate locations (Stevens & Coupe, 1978). As another example, most people believe that the Pacific terminus of the Panama Canal is west of the Atlantic terminus. But, as the map in Figure 9.26 reveals, the reverse is true. In this case many people do not have a visuospatial representation of the Panama Canal. However, they reason approximately as follows: The Pacific Ocean is west of the Atlantic Ocean, so the Pacific end of the Panama Canal is west of the Atlantic end. Finally, try answering the following question: Which is further east, Los Angeles, California or Reno, Nevada? Most people who are asked to draw a map of California and Nevada place Los Angeles considerably west of Reno. This location is illustrated in the distorted map in the left panel of Figure 9.27. But as the accurate map in the right panel of 9.27 shows, Los Angeles is actually east of Reno. People think of California as west of Nevada and do have an accurate visuospatial representation of just how far east the Pacific coast is in southern California.

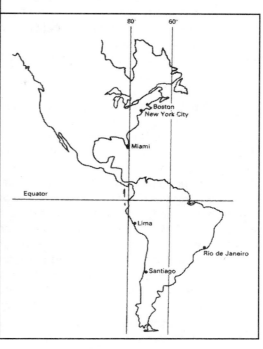

FIGURE 9.25
Western Hemisphere.

Although the studies cited so far illustrate errors in geographical knowledge, they do not demonstrate that such knowledge could not be represented in a single map-like structure. For example, the map in the left panel of Figure 9.27 is perfectly consistent, even though it is wrong. However, other evidence reveals distortions that could not be captured in any single, consistent map. Thus Moar and Bower (1983) had residents in Cambridge, England, estimate the angles formed by each of the three street intersections depicted in Figure 9.28. They found that the estimates were all biased toward 90 degrees. The consequence was that the sum of the three angles exceeded 180 degrees, which would be an impossible tri-

FIGURE 9.26
The Pacific end of the Panama Canal is east of the Atlantic end.

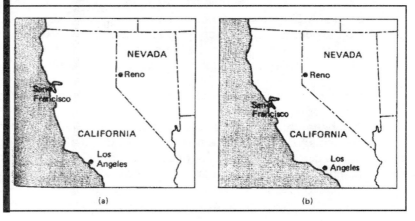

FIGURE 9.27
Geographical disortion: (a) Mental location of Reno as east of Los Angeles; (b) actual location of Reno west of Los Angeles.

angle. In another experiment Moar and Bower had American subjects estimate the relative orientation of pairs of U.S. cities in both directions. For several pairs of cities, including New York and Chicago, the subjects were inconsistent in that the estimated direction from one city to the second was not equivalent to the estimated reverse direction from the second city to the first.

Such spatial inconsistencies suggest that geographical knowledge is often represented in several small mental maps rather than one large map of the entire environment. Because the maps overlap, the environment can be navigated by switching from map to map. Familiar reference locations that appear in many maps can be used to piece together a route from one unfamiliar location to another. For example, a student might not have mental map containing both the chemistry building and the psychology building, but she might have a map containing the dormitory and the chemistry building and another map containing the dormitory and the psychology building. By using the dormitory as a reference point and using both maps that contain it, she could trace a route from the chemistry building to the psychology building. This kind of piecemeal representation may foster the transition from route to survey knowledge.

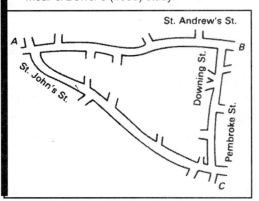

FIGURE 9.28
Intersections in Cambridge, England, for Moar & Bower's (1983) study.

SUMMARY OF RECALL

- A recall task cannot be satisfied with a yes/no or forced-choice judgment.
  - For example, *Who was the first president?* and *Name all the presidents* are recall tasks.
  - Sometimes the response of the recognition system is sufficient for a recall task. For example, *first president* activates *George Washington* as part of the response.
  - However, for many recall tasks there must first be a stage in which potential targets, such as the possible names of presidents, must be generated. So recall responses are often produced through a two-stage, generate and recognize process.

- In a recall task potential targets are generated by cues. Each cue may be used once and retrieves at most a small number of targets.
  - As instances of a very large category, such as animals, are retrieved, they are recalled in small clusters corresponding to distinct cues.
  - Over time fewer cues that retrieve new category members are generated, so fewer targets are retrieved. This negative effect of earlier items on the retrieval of later items is called proactive interference (PI).
  - Not all cues facilitate retrieval. A cue that is similar to the target but does not retrieve it may subsequently block retrieval of the target.
  - Context-dependent memory is the result of the effect of environmental cues on generation. More words can be recalled for a list when it is recalled where it is learned than are recalled in a different location. However, environmental context has no effect on recognition.

- PI does not occur for hierarchically organized lists where each cue uniquely retrieves two or three additional cues or targets.
  - The better that targets are organized in memory, the more targets one will be able to recall. When concepts form statements that form episodes that form stories, people can recall scores of details from a story they have heard once. Given a sufficient degree of organization, there is no limit on the number of concepts that can be recalled upon request. The rapid verification of the almost endless number of statements that comprise an individual's ordinary knowledge of the world make salient the close connection between organization and rapid retrieval.

∘ The downside of associating information learned on different occasions in a single semantic network is losing the contextual details of when each piece of information was learned. The same associations that make a target easier to generate may make it less discriminable from distracters that may have been spontaneously generated during learning.

∘ Recall sometimes requires that inferences be drawn from insufficiently detailed information. In this cases errors may be made.

SUMMARY OF CHAPTER

• Tasks that require the retrieval of information from memory are of two types.
   ∘ A recognition task requires a yes/no or forced-choice judgment.
   ∘ A recall task cannot be satisfied with a yes/no or forced-choice judgment.
      * For many recall tasks there must first be a stage in which potential targets, such as the possible names of presidents, must be generated. So recall responses are often produced through a two-stage, generate and recognize process.

• The process of recognition has several distinct stages.
   ∘ Feature analysis and perceptual organization stage
   ∘ Comparison stage
   ∘ Response stage
   ∘ Decision stage, including
      * inference
      * criterion

• The Four-part Recognition Response
   ∘ Semantic information produces an identification response.
   ∘ Contextual information determines the familiarity response.
   ∘ Short-term temporal order information from working memory is experienced as the recency response.
   ∘ Affective information produces an emotional response.

• There are different kinds of recognition judgments.
   ∘ Semantic categorization or identification judgment
   ∘ Familiarity judgment
   ∘ Recency judgment
   ∘ Frequency judgment
   ∘ Episodic judgment

• The perception of familiarity is a matter of degree, but recognition tasks frequently force a choice between two alternatives: old or new. As a result, a decision procedure must set a familiarity criterion so that every item more familiar than the criterion is called "old" and every item less familiar than the criterion is called "new."
   ∘ Both the environmental context and the person's expectations influence the level where the criterion is set.
   ∘ The theory of signal detection compares correct recognitions with false alarms as a means of separately measuring a person's ability to discriminate old from new inputs and the criterion used for calling an input old.
   ∘ The role of the decision criterion in recognition memory has an important application in the evaluation of eyewitness testimony.

• In a recall task potential targets are generated by cues. Each cue may be used once and retrieves at most a small number of targets.

- Hence, as instances of a very large category, such as animals, are retrieved, they are recalled in small clusters corresponding to distinct cues.
- Over time fewer cues that retrieve new category members are generated, so fewer targets are retrieved. This negative effect of earlier items on the retrieval of later items is called proactive interference (PI).

- PI does not occur for hierarchically organized lists where each cue uniquely retrieves two or three additional cues or targets.
  - When concepts form statements that form episodes that form stories, people can recall scores of details from a story they have heard once. Given a sufficient degree of organization, there is no limit on the number of concepts that can be recalled upon request.
  - The downside of associating information learned on different occasions in a single semantic network is losing the contextual details of when each piece of information was learned. The same associations that make a target easier to generate may make it less discriminable from distracters that may have been spontaneously generated during learning.
  - Recall sometimes requires that inferences be drawn from insufficiently detailed information. In this cases errors may be made.

Chapter 10

EPISODIC MEMORY

O ne night an intruder climbed in the window of a college residence hall and sexually assaulted a student. A few days later she was walking in the nearby town when she saw a person she immediately identified as her attacker. He was convicted and sent to jail on the basis of her testimony. After several years in prison, he was released when DNA evidence proved conclusively that he was not the attacker. This double tragedy, which was repeated many times at the end of twentieth century, makes an important point about the relationship between confidence and accuracy in autobiographical memory.   The core of what we mean by memory are our own autobiographies, which we carry around with us all the time and are constantly updating. You may forget what you learned in school today or what you had for breakfast, but there is almost no chance that you will forgot who you are. As a result people have tremendous confidence in the accuracy of many of the autobiographical details that we all can recall. However, the study by Bruce (1984) described in the Chapter 9 showed that recognition of a person seen only once before may be mistaken. A strong emotional response associated with a representation of that person may greatly increase the confidence in, without increasing the accuracy of, the comparison. The introduction of DNA evidence in the 1990's made clear that confidence is sometimes terribly misplaced.

Autobiographical memory is also called episodic memory. Episodic memory itself has a double meaning. On the one hand, it refers to contextual and temporal judgments that were discussed in the last chapter. On the other hand, it refers to the organization of representations into contextually, temporally, and causally ordered structural descriptions called episodes. Distinguishing between episodic and nonepisodic recall tasks is useful. Episodic recall tasks ultimately require remember recognition responses (Chapter 9); they are about personal experience. Nonepisodic recall tasks ultimately require know recognition responses (Chapter 9); they do not involve personal experience. The contrast is best illustrated by examples. Suppose you are asked what you had for dinner yesterday. This question is about a specific event in your life that took place at a specific time. The recall target is therefore episodic. In contrast, suppose you are asked who the first president was. This question does not ask anything about your own life; rather, it asks about a fact you might have learned at any point in time. This question involves a nonepisodic recall target. Episodic targets, then, in the first sense of the word, are facts about your personal experiences, whereas nonepisodic targets are facts you may know that are not tied to any particular episode in your own life. However, all stories that you hear and tell have the same episodic structure that you use in organizing memories of the events of your lives. Episodic memory in this sense is memory for all stories, not just personal autobiography. Similar mental processes are involved in remembering both the story of one's own life as well as stories of the lives of others. We will therefore begin with a discussion of story recall in general.

STORY RECALL

A simple story called "Circle Island," was written by Dawes (1964), and used by him, Thorndyke (1977), and Buschke and Schaier (1979) to study story recall. The story is shown with each proposition numbered in Table 10.1. Its schema (Chapter 5) is shown in Figure 10.1. You do not need to understand every detail in this figure. It is the overall organization that is important. This organization is hierarchical—more general levels of structure divide into more specific levels, until the actual propositions of the story's schema (represented by the numbers from Table 10.1) appear at the lower levels of the hierarchy.

At the top level of the hierarchy shown in Figure 10.1, the story divides into a setting (where the story takes place), a theme (the basic topic of the story), a plot (the sequence of events that is described), and a resolution (the eventual outcome). Each of these major aspects of the story leads to more specific information that fills in the details. For example, the plot consists of several episodes, each of which can be described in terms of a subgoal (a specific goal), an attempt to reach the goal, and an outcome. Problem-solving behavior can be described in a similar way. This similarity is not surprising, since stories are generally written about problems (Black & Bower, 1980).

Focusing on episode 2, we see that the subgoal of this episode is specified by the information in propositions 25 and 26 of the story; that is, "The senators agreed to build a smaller canal." The attempt to accomplish this goal is specified by propositions 28, 29, and 30: "After starting construction on the smaller canal, the islanders discovered that no water would flow into it." Finally, the outcome of this episode is specified by proposition 31: "The project was abandoned."

FIGURE 10.1
Plot structure for the story "Circle Island."

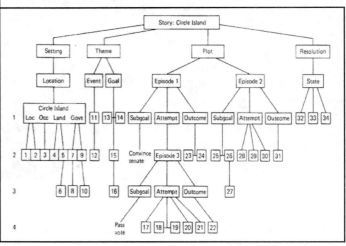

TABLE 10.1
Circle island

(1) Circle island is located in the middle of the Atlantic Ocean, (2) north of Ronald Island. (3) The main occupations on the island are farming and ranching. (4) Circle Island has good soil, (5) but few rivers and (6) hence a shortage of water. (7) The island is run democratically. (8) All issues are decided by a majority vote of the islanders. (9) The governing body is a senate, (10) whose job is to carry out the will of the majority. (11) Recently, an island scientist discovered a cheap method (12) of converting salt water into fresh water. (13) As a result, the island farmers wanted (14) to build a canal across the island, (15) so that they could use water from the canal (16) to cultivate the island's central region. (17) Therefore, the farmers formed a pro-canal association (18) and persuaded a few senators (19) to join. (20) The pro-canal association brought the construction idea to a vote. (21) All the islanders voted. (22) The majority voted in favor of construction. (23) The senate, however, decided that (24) the farmers' proposed canal was ecologically unsound. (25) The senators agreed (26) to build a smaller canal (27) that was two feet wide and one foot deep. (28) After starting construction on the smaller canal, (29) the islanders discovered that (30) no water would flow into it. (31) Thus the project was abandoned. (32) The farmers were angry (33) because of the failure of the canal project. (34) Civil war appeared inevitable.

The hierarchical structure shown in Figure 10.1 has important implications for the way people who hear the "Circle Island" story will remember it. To recall a story, one must do more than recall the individual sentences. One must also recall how the individual propositions relate to one another. Without these relationships there would be no story. For instance, suppose someone took all the sentences of the story, wrote them on index cards, and then shuffled the cards. We certainly would not say that someone reading those index cards was reading the story.

How would a person go about trying to recall a story? By now it should come as no surprise that recall will depend on the way the story is organized in memory. A person generally cannot simply find the beginning of the story and then generate every detail in the order in which it occurred, any more than a person can generate every item of a hundred-word list in the original order. There is no guarantee that all details of the story will be generated, or that all the ideas generated will actually be from the story. Someone trying to recall a story will have to decide which ideas were from the story and how they should be combined to reconstruct the conceptual structure of the original story.

How do we go about selecting and ordering the ideas in a story we are trying to recall? This area is where the hierarchical story organization becomes critical. Note that in 10.1 the individual propositions (represented by numbers) in the "Circle Island" story fall at four levels in the hierarchy. Suppose someone is asked to recall "Circle Island." The person will use his or her general knowledge of stories, encoded in a general story hierarchy, to generate general features like setting and plot. These features, along with the specific cue "Circle Island," will be used to activate propositions at the top level of the "Circle Island" hierarchy. The propositions at higher levels will then be used to cue propositions at lower levels. At lower levels the higher-level propositions are combined with the basic goal-attempt-outcome sequence to generate the story's propositions in the appropriate order.

Notice that story recall is not self-limiting like the free recall of a list. Each higher-level proposition provides a unique cue for the small set of propositions immediately below it in the hierarchy, so there is relatively little cue overload. Also, the sequence of propositions generated from the story hierarchy, e.g., goal-attempt-outcomes, provides a framework that reveals any important gaps in the recall and provides cues for filling those gaps. So unlike the recall of list members, which approaches an asymptote after only a few minutes of effort, the recall of a story has no limit. That is, there is no known limit to the length of a story that can be recalled in a single attempt. However, as mentioned above, people telling a story rarely report every detail they can recall. Rather, they summarize the story at the level of the hierarchy that is appropriate for the listener.

If people actually use the hierarchical story structure in this way to cue information, then clusters of concepts that correspond to clusters of propositions in the story hierarchy (e.g., 1 and 2; 9 and 10; 28, 29, 30) should be recalled together. This clustering is what Buschke and Schaier (1979) found. Furthermore, a higher percentage of propositions high in the hierarchy than propositions low in the hierarchy should be recalled, because the recall of propositions low in the hierarchy is dependent on the prior recall of the propositions that dominate them. For example, proposition 6 should not be recalled until proposition 5 is first recalled and used as a cue to generate it. But the recall of proposition 5 is not dependent on the recall of proposition 6. Consistent with this prediction, Thorndyke (1977) found that the percentage of propositions recalled at each level of the hierarchy decreased monotonically from level 1 to level 4 (also see Rumelhart, 1977).

Notice that the story hierarchy does not contain the exact words spoken, but the meanings of sentences encoded as propositions. Since people reconstruct the story from its hierarchy they are much better at recalling the propositions than the exact words of a story they've heard. Reder (1982) had students read ten stories and then respond, as quickly as possible, whether certain sentences had either appeared in the story (verbatim recall) or seemed true given the story (gist recall). The recall task occurred either immediately after, 20 minutes after, or two days after the stories were read. Judgments about whether sentences had appeared were always less accurate than judgments about whether they were true. Furthermore, the accuracy of the appearance judgments deteriorated considerably at the 20-minute delay and again two days later, while the truth judgments declined only slightly in accuracy. At delays of 20 minutes and two days truth judgments were much faster than appearance judgments. Nevertheless, the exact words spoken were in procedural memory. Both kinds of judgments were faster for sentences that actually had appeared than sentences that had not.

ENCODING AUTOBIOGRAPHICAL MEMORY

The story that you know best is the story of your own life. But you are never finished learning this story and it is constantly being revised. How the story of your life is organized during encoding determines what you are able to remember about yourself. Your autobiography is not merely a recording of things that happened to you. Rather, it is the story of the effect of your actions on the world. It is organized around your intentions, your actions, and finally the events that resulted from them.

ORIENTING TO TIME

You must always know where you are and what you must do. Knowing what you must do implies knowing what time it is. So the day of the week and time of day must be constantly updated in working memory. This information provides the basic set of cues that guide the recall of autobiographical information. This process has been studied by the simple task of answering the question, "What day is today?" (Koriat & Fischoff, 1974; Shanon, 1979). In one study Ben Shanon asked students in the Cambridge, Massachusetts's area to respond, as rapidly as possible, to the question of what day of the week it was (the today question). As Figure 10.2 shows, this question was answered most quickly on the weekends and most slowly in the middle of the week. This result suggests that students use the weekend as a landmark for keeping track of the days. The days in the middle of the week are probably less distinct from each other than are the days of the weekend.

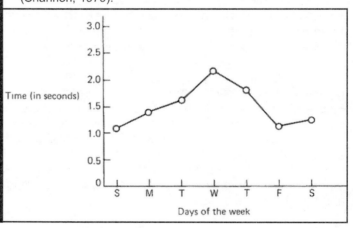

FIGURE 10.2
Time to respond to the question, "What day of the week is it?" (Shannon, 1979).

The landmarks that are most salient and familiar are constantly changing. As new events occur and a person's goals and plans change new recall cues become available. This dynamic aspect of episodic memory was also demonstrated in Shanon's study. He asked people two other questions besides the today question: "What day of the week was yesterday?" (the yesterday question), and "What day of the week will it be tomorrow?" (the tomorrow question). Shanon was interested in how long people took to answer these three questions at different times of the day and week.

As you might expect, at any time the today question was answered more rapidly than the yesterday and tomorrow questions. The times for answering the latter two questions showed a very interesting pattern. In the afternoon the tomorrow question was answered more rapidly than the yesterday question; but in the morning the yesterday question was answered more rapidly than the tomorrow question. Shanon suggested that this result occurred because in the morning we are still reflecting on yesterday's events, while by the afternoon we are already planning tomorrow's activities.

But what about the questions asked at noon? These results are especially interesting. In the first part of the week the yesterday question was answered more quickly than the tomorrow question; but in the later part of the week the reverse was true. Shanon suggested that a similar explanation applies here. At the beginning of the week we are preoccupied with the recent past. On Monday we still vividly recall the weekend; on Tuesday, we recall the start of the new school week or workweek on Monday. In contrast, at the end of the week we are preoccupied with the near future. On Thursday we look forward to Friday. On Friday we look forward to the weekend. Therefore recall of the days of the week is seemingly heavily influenced by recall and anticipation of the weekend. This interpretation is supported by Shanon's finding that all three questions are answered most rapidly on the weekends and most slowly on Wednesday. The idea that the weekend serves as a temporal landmark also fits in with anecdotal reports from people who move to a different country in which the weekend falls on different days. They report finding it very difficult to keep track of what day it is.

You also use cues to estimate the length of durations (Ornstein, 1969). Sometimes, when you wait for a bus, it seems as if the bus comes in 2 minutes, and at other times it seems as if the bus comes in 20 minutes, even though objectively the wait may have been the same length in both cases. The greater the number of events that occur, the longer the interval feels. For example, a piece of music that contains 40 events per minute is experienced as shorter than one with 120 events per minute. Furthermore, the more complex the sequence of sounds, the longer it will seem. Being able to recall more recent memories affects your perception of the passage of time. Suppose that during winter break you go to Fort Lauderdale for a week. On the last day of vacation, you feel as though you've been in Florida for a long time. At this point you can think of many specific events that occurred over the past ten days. Yet a month later back at school, your Florida vacation seems to have come and gone in a flash. Now you no longer easily recall many distinct events. The entire episode has been recoded as "a week in Florida," and as a result, its duration is perceived as shorter.

INTENTIONS AND ACTIONS

Discriminating between a memory of what you actually did and what you only intended to do can be difficult. Examples are remembering that you intended to mail a letter, lock the door, or turn out the lights but not remembering whether you did it. Marcia Johnson and her colleagues (Johnson & Foley, 1984; Johnson & Raye, 1981) found that discriminating between having thought about saying something and actually having said something (i.e., discriminating between an intention and an action) is more difficult than distinguishing between having said something and having heard something (i.e., distinguishing between an action and a perception).

It is not surprising that autobiographical memory should be organized around intentions and actions. Recall that rehearsing items produces much more learning then merely hearing them repeated (Glass, et al., 1989). Hence, memory of what happened is influenced (and in some cases distorted) by memory of what was done. Raye, Johnson, and Taylor (1980) found that students were more accurate at estimating the frequencies with which they had generated words than at estimating the frequencies with which they had studied words. Furthermore, judgments of internally generated words impaired estimates of environmental word frequency more than environmental frequency impaired judgments of internally generated words.

FIGURE 10.3
Proportion of perspective-relevant and perspective-irrelevant information recalled on the first test. (Anderson & Pichert, 1978.)

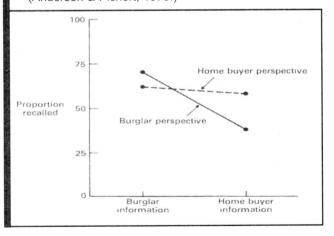

Each person encodes life from his or her own point of view by selectively attending to the most relevant inputs among the many available to awareness. Anderson and Pichert (1978) had college undergraduates read a story about two boys playing hooky from school at one of their homes. The subjects were instructed to take the perspective of either a burglar or a person interested in buying a home. All subjects then recalled the story. Some of the information in the story was particularly relevant to a would-be burglar, whereas other information was particularly relevant to a homebuyer. As Figure 10.3 indicates, those students who had taken the burglar perspective recalled more burglar information than students who had taken the home buyer perspective, whereas those who had taken the homebuyer perspective recalled more homebuyer information than those students who had taken the burglar perspective.

Each person also reconstructs life from his or her own point of view by selecting the most relevant cues to his or her current circumstances. Anderson and Pichert's study also demonstrated the impact of a change in perspective on recall. Subjects were asked to recall the story a second time. Some were told to maintain the same point of view, whereas others were now told to shift (e.g., taking the perspective of a home buyer instead of a burglar). Those subjects who changed perspective on the second recall attempt recalled an additional 7 percent of the information related to their new point of view and 7 percent less of the information related to their former view. A shift in perspective appeared to alter the retrieval cues available for accessing the story information and hence systematically altered the ease of recalling different aspects of the story. Similarly, we would expect a changed perspective on one's own life to affect the recallability of past events, actions, and beliefs.

POST EVENT INFORMATION

Despite the many similarities, there is one critical difference between story recall and autobiographical memory. Once a story is learned, it is not dynamically updated and integrated with new information. In contrast the constant updating of autobiographical memory causes memories of distinct events to become confused. Rand Spiro (1982) showed that stories that people learn as stories are quite resistant to integration with other information, but stories that people encode incidentally as life events are likely to become integrated with other life events and hence are subject to distortion at recall. He had students read a story and then recall it either two days, three weeks, or six weeks later. The story is below. Half the students read the version with the happy ending and half the students read the version with the sad ending:

> This is a story about Bob and Margie. When they met they were both twenty years old and beginning their senior year in college. Bob was majoring in political science and Margie in history. They didn't know each other until they were introduced at a party in a mutual acquaintance's apartment. Since neither of them was particularly extraverted and they knew very few people at the party, they seemed glad to have each other to talk to. They found some interests they had in common, and hit it off fairly well. They soon began to see each other regularly.

> After several months, Bob began to think he would like to marry Margie. He felt he loved her and he believed the feeling was reciprocated. Still, he was not sure how she would react. Finally he asked her to marry him. She agreed and they happily began making plans for their marriage and life together.

> However, Bob's happiness was clouded by his awareness that there was something important he had to discuss with Margie—his strong feeling that he did not want to have children. He avoided bringing the subject up because he didn't want anything to hurt their relationship. However, he soon realized that he could not put off the discussion forever. Filled with apprehension, he told Margie he had a very important matter to discuss with her. He anxiously related to her his strong feelings against having children and awaited her response.

Happy ending: *Margie was elated. Because she wanted to have a career she had also felt that she didn't want to have children. They rejoiced in the dissolution of what would have been a very serious problem for them. A long discussion of the status of their relationship followed.*

Sad ending: *Margie was horrified. She had always wanted to be a mother and had her heart set on having many children. They argued bitterly over what had become a very serious problem for them. A long discussion of the status of their relationship followed.*

Students were either told that they were in a recall experiment (Memory group) or an experiment in which they would have to react to a real-life event at a later time (Interactive group), so that the story they were reading was true. After some of the students had read the story, the experimenter, while collecting the consent forms about 8 minutes later, sometimes mentioned either that Bob and Margie had or had not gotten married. This information was either consistent or inconsistent with what the students had read, depending on whether they had read the happy or sad ending to the story. A third of the time Bob and Margie were not mentioned during the collection of the consent forms.

All subjects had to write down exactly what they had read two days, three weeks, or six weeks later. The results are shown in Figure 10.4. Almost all the students who were told that they were in a memory experiment and would have to recall the story did not make intrusion errors, where they added or changed a proposition, even six weeks later. Similarly, almost all the students who were told that the story was true but were exposed to no or consistent information did not make intrusion errors. In contrast, only students who were told that the story was true and exposed to inconsistent information made intrusion errors when tested only three weeks later. For example, two students who read the unhappy ending but heard that Bob and Margie had married wrote down:

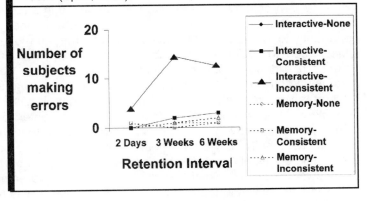

FIGURE 10.4
Effect of no, consistent, and inconsistent post-event information on story memory under memory and interactive instructions (Spiro, 1982).

(1) They separated but realized after discussing the matter that their love mattered more.
(2) They discussed it and decided they could agree on a compromise: adoption.

Two students who read the happy ending but heard that Bob and Margie had separated wrote down:

(1) There was a hassle with one or the other's parents.
(2) They disagreed about having children.

So people are perfectly capable of remembering things they learned with the intention of recalling them later and are not easily confused by post-event information. However, stories about ordinary life events, even about other people, seem to be subject to revision on the basis of post-event information. As a result, a person can have a false memory, i.e., a memory of something that didn't happen. A false memory is called a **confabulation**. Also, people are said to **confabulate**, i.e., generate, false memories.

Eyewitness testimony. Even eyewitness testimony may be influenced by post-event information. The degree of distortion in eyewitness testimony is of particular importance, since the fairness of our justice system depends in large part on its accuracy. Leading questions can influence reports. For example, Loftus and Palmer (1974) showed students a film of a collision between two cars. Later the students were asked one of two questions: "About how fast were the cars going when they hit each other?" or "About how fast were the cars going when they smashed into each other?" Subjects gave higher estimates of the speed when the question contained the word *smashed* instead of *hit*. In addition, after a one-week delay the subjects who had been asked the question containing *smashed* showed a greater tendency to report erroneously that there had been broken glass at the accident scene. In this case the question itself influenced how the person reconstructed a description of the original event..

Child eyewitness testimony.   The effect of leading questions on eyewitness testimony is exacerbated when the eyewitness is a child. This does not mean that children are always unreliable witnesses. In a review of the experimental literature up until that time Stephen Ceci and Maggie Bruck (1993) found a mixed picture. False information rarely appears in preschoolers' spontaneous free recall of a past experience (Goodman & Reed, 1986). However, many children spontaneously recall very little, and have to be prompted by repeated questioning. There is always the danger that subsequent recall reflects the content of the questions. However, research with children of all ages produced mixed results in regard to whether younger children were more susceptible to influence from leading questions than older children or adults. In some studies it appeared that susceptibility decreased with age but increased as the interval between the event and the questioning increased. For example, Ornstein, Gordon and Larus (1992) tested 3- and 6-year-old children's memories of a pediatric exam immediately and either one or three weeks after the exam. Up to one week later the 6-year-old children gave more accurate answers to misleading questions but were no better than the 3-year-old children after three weeks.

When post-event information is introduced in a more substantial way than by a leading question it does affect the recall of many children. Poole and Linday (1995) gave 3- and 4-year-old children the opportunity to interact with Mr. Science and then three months later the children heard their parents read a story about Mr. Science. In a subsequent interview, 41% of the children spontaneously reported that Mr. Science had done something during their meeting that had actually only been mentioned in the story. Also, young children have more difficulty distinguishing pretended events from real events when they do the pretending themselves. Harris, Brown, Marriott, Whittall, and Harmer (1991) found that four of 12 4-year-old children who had been told by an experimenter to pretend that there was a monster in a box would not let her leave them alone in the room even though they had just seen and stated that the box was empty. Finally, as we have seen, a conversation is a social interaction before it is a communicative one. Children usually try to please adults with the right answer to a question, and to the child that means the answer the child thinks the adult wants. When children are asked the same question more than once in a way that implies to them that the previous answer was not what the adult wanted to hear, they often change their answers, presumably because they interpret the repeated question as indicating that their first answer was not correct. Cassel, Roebers, and Bjorklund (1996) asked children about a bicycle theft. When presented with a misleading question; e.g., "The girl was wearing shorts, wasn't she?" when in fact she was wearing jeans, most children rejected the false information. When these children were asked a second misleading question; e.g., "Don't you remember that the girl was wearing shorts?" children in second grade and older continued to reject it. But 42% of kindergarten children changed their answer and now agreed with the false information.

Research on the reliability of child witnesses took on special urgency at the end of the twentieth century. In the 1980's and 1990's nursery school teachers were convicted of child abuse and served long prison terms (before ultimately successful appeals) on the basis of the often fantastic testimony of preschool children. There was never any physical evidence against the defendants or spontaneous accusations against them. Rather the charges emerged only after the children had been repeatedly questioned by agitated parents and prosecutors whose initial reason for the questioning proved irrelevant to the ultimate prosecution. The key elements for obtaining a false allegation for a child 5-7 years appears to be reinforcement of the allegations through social approval and validation of the allegations by referring to the testimony of other witnesses. Garven, Wood, Malpass, and Shaw (1998) found that these interviewing techniques, derived from transcripts of the infamous McMartin Preschool case, induced 58% of the children interviewed to make false accusations against a classroom visitor, compared with 17% of the children who received leading questions. Garven, Wood, and Malpass (2000) found that even when being questioned about fantastic events like being taken from school in a helicopter children receiving social reinforcement made 52% false allegations, compared with 5% made by controls. In a second interview children repeated the allegations even when the reinforcement had been discontinued.

Implanting false memories. The encoding of false memories on the basis of post-event information is not limited to young children. With sufficiently coercive techniques, it is possible to implant false memories in some adults. Even when a false response is initially coerced, it may subsequently affect the memory of an event. Zaragoza, Payment, Ackil, Drivdahl, and Beck (2001) showed college students an 8 minute excerpt from the Disney movie, "Looking for Miracles," which depicted the adventures of two brothers at summer camp. The clip was filled with action and drama, including a fight among the campers and an encounter with a deadly snake. Immediately thereafter, participants were individually interviewed and asked to respond to 14 questions about the film. Of these, 4 were false-event questions about events that were obviously not depicted in the video. Thus, in order to answer the false-event questions, participants had to make up, or confabulate, answers. In fact, students in the control group refused to answer the false-event questions and did not show evidence of distorted memories later. However, students in the forced group were told that they must provide an answer to every question and were explicitly instructed to guess if they did not know an answer. For the forced group, each student received neutral feedback about responses to two false event questions, e.g., okay, and confirmatory feedback about responses to two false event questions, e. g., "that's right, knee is the correct answer." For example, the following is the transcript of the interview for a false-event question with confirmatory feedback for a student in the forced group:

Interviewer:	After he fell, where was Delaney bleeding?
Participant:	He wasn't. He was? I didn't see any blood.
Interviewer:	What's your best guess?
Participant:	Where was he bleeding?
Interviewer:	Yeah.
Participant:	But he wasn't bleeding. Oh … I don't have a best guess. I didn't think he was bleeding. His knee?
Interviewer:	Okay, his knee.
Participant:	It's not his knee!
Interviewer:	That's actually the right answer.
Participant:	Is it? I was just thinking, kid falling, hit his knee on the chair, you know.

One week later, participants were met by a different experimenter, who informed them that the earlier interviewer had made some mistakes and had asked them questions about events that never happened in the video. Their task, they were told, was to indicate which things were in the video and which were not. This was done to eliminate social pressure to respond consistently across test sessions. All students were asked 23 yes/no questions of the form, "When you watched the video, did you see _____?" For the forced group, 27% of the false-event questions that received neutral feedback received "yes" responses and 55% of the false-event questions that received confirmatory feedback received "yes" responses. Some of the students returned four to six weeks later to free recall the video. The students incorporated 13% of the false events that received neutral feedback and 27% of the false-events that received confirmatory feedback in their free recalls.

REMEMBERING YOUR LIFE

When you recall an episode in your life, you often reconstruct it in much the same way as you would reconstruct an episode in a story. However, your own life story is much richer and contains many more details important to you than any story you might read. So you need a much finer system of cues and rules to reconstruct your life than to construct a story. After all, in a very large measure your personal identity depends on what you can recall of your past.

The reconstructive aspect of recall becomes more obvious as the task becomes more difficult. If you are simply asked what you were generally doing two years ago, you may not be conscious of using rules and landmarks to reconstruct the answer. But now suppose you were asked to describe what you were doing and wearing at noon on January 19, 2003. Your initial response might be, "Are you crazy? That was a long time ago." But if you persist, you might begin to think along the following lines:

January 19, 2003, let's see, that was during winter break, so I suppose I was at home. No, wait a minute, that year winter break ended January 18. So, let's see, I must have been back at school. So I assume I was in a class. Let's see, we came back on a Monday, so the nineteenth would have been a Tuesday. What classes was I taking that term? Renaissance poetry, physics—wait, I must have been in statistics because it met over the noon hour on Tuesdays and Thursdays. Now I remember the first class. Dr. Shaw was having trouble with all the nervous students, demanding to know if they were responsible for this or that particular piece of information.

Looking back at this hypothetical recall example, we see a lot of recall activity that resembles logical problem solving. A person figures out the context in trying to deduce what might have happened. All of this activity is setting the stage—trying to establish enough context to make contact with a specific memory. If the problem-solving effort is successful, it leads to an actual memory of the experience, not simply a reconstruction of a possible experience.

The first constructive process to influence recall was finding an appropriate landmark to cue the experience (winter break). How might this construction of a recall cue influence a person's eventual recall? Possibly, the constructive deductions used to find the cue are incorrect (or use information that is itself misremembered). For example, you might have been wrong about Christmas break ending on January 18; perhaps it really ended on January 8. In this case your recall will be completely incorrect. You may well have located some memory, but it would be of the wrong day or perhaps the wrong year. (January 19, 2003, was a Sunday.)

The world is filled with rules, principles, conventions, and traditions that aid in the generation of responses, such as "The sun comes up in the morning and goes down in the evening"; "We are young before we are old." Whenever recall of an extended description is attempted, whether it is a story or an eyewitness report, rules play an important role in cuing and ordering the output. Let us assume that you have succeeded at the first constructive step and managed to locate the correct record of experience in memory. What further influence does the reconstructive process have? In most cases when you manage to locate the representation of an experience, you fail to access many of the details. But you will probably still have pieces of it—some of the general structure and a few very particular details. You can use your knowledge of rules to notice gaps in recall and then fill them in. As you begin recalling, you will also construct plausible connections between the specific things you remember. Sometimes, these constructions will again produce sufficient context to serve as a cue to recall (and recognize) another specific detail from the experience. At other times the constructions will seem correct, but they might not lead to that warm secure feeling of clearly remembering (recognizing) the original input.

However, the use of rules to fill in gaps in recall causes an important problem in determining the veracity of the information you recall. Do you really remember getting dressed this morning or is it obvious that you did because you have clothes on now? People are usually very confident when they try to recall something that they are recalling it accurately. So you might expect that the generation of false memories is relatively rare. However, this task is one in which your intuitions sometimes mislead you. Sometimes, your reconstruction of a story you have heard or an accident you have witnessed is as accurate as you feel it is, but sometimes it is not. In general, whenever a person is asked to recall a story or experience, he or she will produce a mixture of actual memories and logical fabrications that might or might not be correct. This is simply the result of trying to glue together the fragments of memory in the best way possible. Of course, each person constructs an event sequence that is consistent with his or her recollection of what he or she said and did. So if you are mistaken about what you said or did, the error is propagated throughout the recall of the sequence of events that must be made consistent with the initial error.

Moreover, when one is attempting to recall past thoughts and intentions, recalling the thoughts most consistent with current beliefs is easier. This result is an inevitable consequence of the structure of memory. Current thoughts and beliefs will have the highest levels of activation. As a result, your past thoughts and actions will seem to you to be more consistent with your current beliefs than they actually were (Greenwald, 1980). For example, when attitude change was induced in students by having them write an essay in favor of the opposing side, they remembered their old opinion as having been consistent with their new one (Bem & McConnell, 1970; Wixon & Laird, 1976).

The level of accuracy of memory is very much a function of the level of detail that you demand of it. The purpose of memory is to prepare you for the rest of your life by making available in any situation anything that you have learned to that point that might be of use. As will be described immediately below, for this purpose it is a great success. A great deal of general knowledge, including the ability to recognize most everyone you ever met who was somewhat important in your life, is retained for decades. However, it is not the purpose of memory to compile and retain an accurate record of what you have seen and done; i.e., a personal autobiography. As was described above, and will be elaborated below, autobiographical memory is not a record of a life but an imaginative reconstruction of it.

VERY LONG-TERM RECALL OF GENERAL KNOWLEDGE

Extensive research on long-term retention has been performed by Harry Bahrick and his colleagues (Bahrick, 1983, 1984; Bahrick, Bahrick, & Wittlinger, 1975). They (Bahrick et al., 1975) asked groups of alumni to recognize names and pictures from their high school yearbook after intervals ranging up to almost fifty years after their graduation. The results are depicted by the top two lines in Figure 10.5. As the figure shows, ability to recognize classmates' names showed no decline after fourteen years, and ability to recognize classmates' pictures showed no decline after thirty-four years. In contrast, the ability to recall the names of classmates, even when cued by their pictures (not plotted in Figure 10.5), remained constant for only three years before beginning a steady decline with time. Also, reassuringly, students remember much of what they study in college for many years afterwards. Figure 10.6 shows the retention of students who studied Spanish in college. These results confirm the effect of distributed learning on long-term retention, whether it is repeated encounters with classmates or several courses in Spanish.

FIGURE 10.5

Long-term recognition of pictures of high school students by classmates and teachers. (Barick, 1984.)

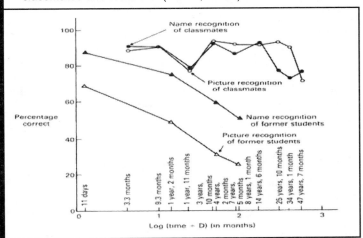

FIGURE 10.6

Long-term recall of Spanish as a function of initial learning (Bahrick, 1984).

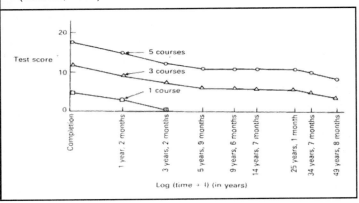

AUTOBIOGRAPHICAL RETENTION FUNCTION

Another way to study long-term memory is to examine the age distribution of memories that are easily available as a function of retention interval. For example, suppose someone is given the cue word "fireworks" and asked to describe a specific event associated with fireworks. Will he mention the last time he saw them or the first time? Will the event recalled be weeks, or months, or years old? Figure 10.7 shows the distribution of the ages of many events recalled in response to different cue words found by Rubin, Wetzler, and Nebes (1986). The function has three main features: First, older memories are less likely to be recalled than more recent ones. Hence, there is a strong recency effect. Second, contrary to this general recency trend, there is a reminiscence bump consisting of a surprisingly large number of memories coming from ages 10-30, particularly between 15 and 25. Third, there is childhood amnesia for the early years of life.

FIGURE 10.7

Long-term autobiographical memory (Rubin, et al., 1986).

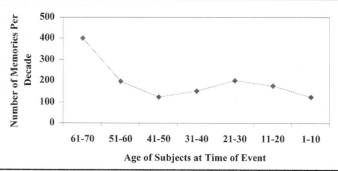

Early childhood amnesia. Specifically, there is childhood amnesia for at least the first three years of life but by age four there is evidence of long-term retention, given sufficient cuing (Sheingold & Tenney, 1982; West & Bauer, 1999; but also see Eacott & Crawley, 1998). Quas, Goodman, Bidrose, Piple, Craw, and Ablin (1999) studied children's long-term memory for a medical procedure from 8 to 69 months after the procedure. Children at the age of 2 when the procedure was performed showed no evidence of remembering the event. Pillemer, Picariello, and Pruett (1994) interviewed three- and four-year –old children two weeks and seven years after an emergency school evacuation. Two weeks after the evacuation there were no significant differences in the amount of information remembered. After seven years children were required to respond to forced-choice questions about the event. The younger children were at chance but the older children were 86% correct.

However, the paucity of early childhood memories later in life does not imply that young children cannot remember events over long periods of time. Hamond and Fivush (1991) found that 4-year-old children could remember a trip to Disney World taken when they were 2 and $\frac{1}{2}$ years old. Why then, do people not recall the events years later? It may be that very young children are not skilled enough at story telling to weave their experiences into their autobiographies, which do become a permanent part of their knowledge until around the age of four. In support of this hypothesis, children of mothers who frequently engage in conversations about the past, provide rich descriptive information about previous experiences, and invite their children to participate in stories about the past later have earlier autobiographical memories than children who do not (Mullen, 1994; Reese, Haden, & Fivush, 1993). By helping their children engage in story telling and life events the mothers help the children to create schemas that are useful for encoding the children's own experiences.

Reminiscence bump. The reminiscence bump occurs because of the large number of first time experiences that occur during those years. First time and unique experiences generate stronger emotions and hence are more memorable. A total of 93% of vivid life memories are either unique events or first-time experiences (Rubin, et al., 1986). When alumni were asked to recall 4 memories from their first year of college, more than 20 years previously, 41% of the memories came from September. If the reminiscence bump is the result of people having their most memorable experiences between 10 and 30 years then individuals who have memorable experiences at other ages should show reminiscence bumps for those periods as well. Conway and Haque (1999) confirmed this prediction. They plotted the autobiographical retention functions for Bangladeshi participants. Participants of all ages showed the usual reminiscence bump between 10 and 30 years of age. In addition, participants who were 35 years or older during the period when Bangladesh achieved its independence from Pakistan showed a reminiscence bump for this period as well.

Recency. Your memories are constantly being updated so that more recent events are more accessible. When people are asked to recall things or events from throughout their lives, a greater number of recent events are recalled (Crovitz & Quina-Holland, 1976; Crovitz & Schiffman, 1974; Franklin & Holding, 1977; Squire & Slater, 1975; Warrington & Sanders, 1971). Different cues are most effective for memories of different ages (Robinson 1976; Rubin 1982), and apparently few cues are immediately available for older memories. Furthermore, when Whitten and Leonard (1981) asked college students to name teachers from each of grades one through twelve, more students who were told to search backward from grades twelve to one completed the task than students who were told to search forward from grades one to twelve. Thus older memories can be recovered best through a secondary cuing strategy that successively activates older and older memories.

RECONSTRUCTION AND ACCURACY

Autobiographical memory is vulnerable at many points to distortion. Since new information is integrated with old, the representations from which all memories are retrieved change over time. Alterations in the recollection of stories and events are evident over retention intervals of days and weeks. If you remember the same event differently at different times and the inconsistencies are great enough then some of your memories must be false. How much greater are the differences between the event and recall when measured over retention intervals of years? This question was not studied at all until the end of the twentieth century. Partly this was because studies that measure retention intervals over years are difficult to do. Also, the topic was neglected because psychologists, like everyone else, have a high degree of subjective confidence in their own memories. They expected to find the forgetting of accurate memories, rather than the reconstruction of entirely false ones. However, now the question is being addressed with a variety of methodologies.

False retrieval cues. One method has been to attempt to create a false memory in a person through suggestion. Pezdek and Hodge (1999) found that 36% of children aged 5 to 12 claimed to remember an event alleged to have occurred when they were 4 years old that had been made up by the experimenter. Loftus and Pickrell (1995), asked older relatives of 24 adults, ages 18 to 53, about three events that happened to the subjects between the ages of 4 and 6. When the 72 events reported by their relatives were told to them the 24 subjects remembered 49 (68%) of the events. Each of the 24 subjects was also told that their relative reported that they had been briefly lost in a shopping mall at age 5. Six of the subjects (25%) claimed that they remembered this event, albeit they reported less clarity and confidence than for memories of events that actually happened. Similarly, Hyman, Husband and Billings (1995) also found that 20% of college students claimed to remember a made-up event they were told of.

Self-deception. A second method has been to have diarists record plausible imaginary events at the same time that they record real ones and then later ask them to distinguish between the two. Essentially, the subject was asked to implant a false memory in himself. Again, though some false memories were identified as true 7 months later, Conway, Collins, Gathercole, and Anderson (1996) found that they were distinguished from memories of real events by a lower level of recollective experience or familiarity.

The third method is to check whether the episodes that people report in response to minimum cuing did in fact take place as reported. In this case it is useful to have two eyewitnesses to the event. If they agree then both their memories may be true. But if they disagree then at least one person's memory must be false. When Mercedes Sheen, Simon Kemp and David Rubin (2001) asked 20 pairs of twins to recall life events in response to cue words they found convincing evidence of false autobiographical memories. Fourteen pairs of twins both recalled at least one event that only one of them had actually experienced! Some of these events are mentioned in Table 10.2. The fourteen pairs of twins disputed a

TABLE 10.2

Descriptions of Memories in Response in Cue Words that were Disputed Between Twins

Age at Test	Age at Memory	Cue Word	Description of Memory
21	5	Bicycle	Both believe they were pushed off bike by their cousins
21	11	Fair	Both think they came 12th in an international cross country race
21	14	Restaurant	Who went for lunch with their mum and had a worm in her meal
21	12	Boat	Who was in boat with father when they saw a tiger shark
20	8	Accident	Who got nail in their foot
20	8	Accident	Both say the other ate half the contents of mustard jar and got sick
17	9	Car	Who on a trip in a car threw up on everyone
16	9	Fair	Who went on a roller coaster at a fairground

total of 36 events, because 7 pairs of twins had more than one disputed memory. In fact, one pair of twins had 14 disputed memories! A further experiment found disputed memories between nontwin siblings and friends, as well.

Flashbulb memories. You might think that anything worth remembering was worth remembering well. However, this does not seem to be the case, as the memories disputed between twins demonstrate. In this case, a person comes to believe that something he or she only heard about actually happened to them because the story is filled with personal details of their own life and could have happened to him or her. Coming to believe something that didn't happen, but could have, leaves open the question of how well remembered is something that actually did happen.

We have already seen that details of an emotion-inducing story are less likely to be forgotten than a mundane one (Cahill & McGaugh, 1998). Perhaps novel and unique events are so well remembered, thus producing the reminiscence bump, because they generate stronger emotions than repeated events. Memories of events that evoked strong emotions and are recalled with special vividness are called **flashbulb memories**. It is difficult to study flashbulb memories of personal events because there are not detailed records of them. This is not a problem for public events.

In the modern world, a particularly emotional public event can become the common memory of an entire generation (e.g., Kennedy assassination, Challenger space shuttle explosion, destruction of Twin Towers on 9/11). People tend to remember flashbulb memories with a high degree of confidence. In 1977, if you asked any American old enough to remember where they were when they heard that President John F. Kennedy had been assassinated, they could tell you (Brown & Kulik, 1977). However, just because someone is confident, does not necessarily mean that the person is accurate. For a long time Ulric Neisser wondered about the accuracy of flashbulb memories. When the Challenger space shuttle exploded on take-off he had his chance. Within 24 hours of the explosion he and Nicole Harsch were interviewing students at Emory University about how they heard of the explosion. They then re-interviewed the students up to two and a half years later. While the students remained confident in their recollections, for 40 per cent of the students the recollections changed (Neisser & Harsch, 1992). Several other studies have confirmed these results. Michael McCloskey and his colleagues (McCloskey, Wible, & Cohen, 1988) also studied recall of the Challenger disaster. Martin Conway and his colleagues (Conway, Anderson, Larsen, Donnelly, McDanieal, McClelland, & Rawles, 1994) investigated recall of the resignation of Prime Minister Margaret Thatcher in England. Neisser and his colleagues (Neisser, Winograd, Bergman, Schreiber, Palmer, & Weldon, 1996) looked at memory for the Loma Pieta earthquake in California. Also, Larry Squire and his colleague (Schmolck, Buffalo, & Squire, 2000) recorded recollections of the O. J. Simpson verdict. One general finding is that memories of an event tend to be accurate for about one year, but are likely to be distorted after about two and a half years, as Neisser and Harsch (1992) had found. Schmolck et al. found 11% of 15-month reports but 43% of 32-month reports contained major distortions, such as incorrectly reporting from where the verdict was first heard (television, radio, a friend, etc.). However 61% of the participants who gave grossly distorted reports remained highly confident. So while flashbulb memories are recalled with confidence, that confidence does not necessarily imply that the recall is accurate.

PTSD. Everyone alive then has a flashbulb memory of 9/11. Yet there can be doubt that the memories of the day of those individuals who lost close loved ones on 9/11 differ in the intensity of the emotional response from the rest of us. Unfortunately, a strong emotional experience can seriously distort autobiographical memory in **posttraumatic stress disorder (PTSD)**. PTSD is the result of an unexpected horrifying or terrifying event, such as a car crash, flood, or violent attack. So the disorder is found among war veterans as well as attack victims and the survivors of natural disasters. The most prominent complaint is of an intrusive, vivid memory of the precipitating event that interferes with normal memory and attention, thus disabling normal daily activity (Bower & Sivers, 1998; Brewin, 1998, Witvliet, 1997). Such memories can persist for months or years. There is more to PTSD than the intrusive memory. PTSD patients have much in common with depressed patients in general. Like other depressed patients, PTSD patients recall fewer details of autobiographical events other than the precipitating event (Harvey, Bryant, & Dang, 1998). Like PTSD patients, depressed patients in general tend to report an intrusive memory of a distressing event (Reynolds & Brewin, 1999). Just because the precipitating event is intrusive and vivid does not mean that its recall is particularly accurate. In fact, when tested in an experimental situation, the memories of PTSD patients appear to be less accurate than others. Recall that if a list of words related to a common word are presented (e.g., hill, valley, summit, peak,...), a person may falsely remember hearing the related word, i.e., mountain. Zoellner, Foa, Brigidi, and Przeworski (2000) found that PTSD patients are more susceptible to this kind of false memory than normal individuals.

Brainwashing rationalized as therapy. The evidence of the existence of false memories has raised concern that some people may construct memories of events that never happened at the repeated suggestion of and reinforcement by a therapist in clinical settings. Recall how Zaragoza, et al. (2001) were able to induce a false memory of a video clip only a week later through repeated questioning and social approval. Consider instead the power of a respected therapist to induce a false memory of event that allegedly took place years earlier through repeated questioning, suggestion, and reinforcement, over many counseling sessions. This is especially the case when hypnosis is used as a therapeutic technique because hypnosis seems to be a particularly powerful technique for implanting false memories. The use of repeated suggestion and reinforcement to get an individual to remember something that they initially did not was first popularized in the 1950's. At that time it was called 'brain washing" and not considered to be a good thing. However, the repeated interrogation methodology was reintroduced in the 1980s as a legitimate clinical technique for recovering repressed memories of trauma. This rationale flew in the face of the overwhelming evidence from PTSD that memories of traumatic events are not and cannot be repressed. To the contrary, memories of traumatic events are intrusive precisely because they are difficult to forget.

Nevertheless, the combination of repeated interrogation and approval is effective for generating new memories regardless of the actual experiences of the individual doing the remembering.

When the repeated interrogation technique is used clinically a patient who "recovers" a memory always remembers the kind of event that the therapist expects to find, regardless of how implausible or even impossible it may be. So clients of therapists who believe that people repress memories of sexual abuse only recover memories of sexual abuse. However, clients of therapists who believe that past lives are disturbing them recover memories of past lives. Finally, clients of therapists who believe that a memory of an alien encounter has been repressed recover memories of their encounter with aliens (Lindsay & Read, 1994; Spanos, Burgess, & Burgess, 1994).

RETROGRADE AMNESIA

Retrograde amnesia refers to the loss of information learned normally prior to the onset of the memory disorder. Retrograde amnesia is a retrieval disorder. Not all retrograde amnesia is the result of brain injury.

PSYCHOGENIC AMNESIA

Sometimes retrograde amnesia is the result of motivated forgetting caused by a personal crisis, such as a marital or financial crisis. This is also called a fugue state. A fugue state consists of a sudden loss of personal identity and is usually associated with a period of wandering, which lasts a few hours or days and for which there is a virtually complete amnesic gap upon recovery. The individual may be oriented to time and place but either fails to recall his or her identity or confabulates a false identity. Essentially, though the individual knows the date and where he or she is, they deny knowing who they are. Kopelman, Christensen, Puffett, and Stanhope (1994) reported the following case history.

A. T. reported that she "came round" on the London Underground railway between Liverpool Street and Bethnal Green stations. On video-tape a month later, she explained:

> I woke up on the tube at the Liverpool Street station. The train was just pulling into the Liverpool Street station. It seemed as if I'd been asleep because I woke up and found myself on the train and I didn't know where I was—where I was going, or where I was supposed to be, and everyone was getting off and I was alone. It was almost midnight, and I was very frightened. When we got to the Bethnal Green station, I got out. I asked the ticket agent if there was a phone I could use to call the police department and he told me that it was just about 50 yards down the road, so I walked over there and they eventually got someone to get me in hospital.

She did not know who she was. She was carrying a bag and at the police station it was opened and found to contain a few clothes and an envelope addressed to Alice Thornton. She was admitted to the Royal London Hospital on 13 March 1990. Two weeks later she was oriented in time and place and had apparently retrieved a number of memories, usually of a macabre quality; e.g., that her ex-husband and son had been killed in a traffic accident the previous December. The administration of 500 mg of sodium amytal produced a flow of memories, almost all of which turned out to be false. Subsequently, A. T. was discharged from hospital and seen as an outpatient. She proved to be very resourceful. She soon had paid employment and a boyfriend. She had a North American accent, and so the United States and Canadian embassies were contacted.

A. T. was identified on 24 July 1991 after her relatives in the United States had sent Scotland Yard a missing person poster. In fact, she had a living husband and three children. After a second amytal administration on 16 September 1991 she recalled a considerable amount of her past, including her name, her home town, and the names and ages of her three children. She subsequently reported that [My husband] would drink quite heavily and he'd get very violent with his drinking... I think that I—I would if I were in that kind of a situation, now I would, I would try and get out of it somehow." She said that the last thing that she could recall was taking her children to school and dropping them off. "I remember being very sad, but I don't know why, unless maybe that's when I was planning to leave, I don't know." After her identification A. T. obtained a divorce from her husband and married her English boyfriend. She consistently reported complete amnesia for the period from 6 March to 13 March 1990; the time from her disappearance in the United States to her appearance in the London tube.

Because fugue states are rare and frequently associated with criminal activity or some degree of dishonesty, whether they should be considered a genuine disorder is controversial (Coons, 1999). It later emerged that 3 months after her arrival in England, when she was disclaiming all knowledge of her identity, A. T. had written to her 11-year-old daughter in the United States saying that she had cancer of the cervix and that she had left home to spare the family the misery of her illness. A year later she sent the family a typewritten letter, apparently from a friend, saying that she had died and had been buried in Devon, England. Kopelman et al. (1994) concluded their report of A. T. as follows: "Finally, readers may care to note that the travel agency from which A. T. purchased her airline ticket was called "Great Escapes Travel" and, perhaps appropriately, it carried a hot air balloon as its emblem."

ORGANIC RETROGRADE AMNESIA

Usually, retrograde amnesia is the result of bilateral injury to the medial temporal cortex. If a person receives some kind of shock to the brain, such as a severe blow, he or she may forget events that occurred during some time period leading up to the moment of the trauma. Though no longer oriented to place and/or time, the person remembers his or her identity. In general, the more severe the shock, the longer is the time period that is forgotten. Thus football players who are stunned by a hard tackle may forget a few seconds of their lives. But a patient who receives electroconvulsive shock treatment (ECT) in a mental hospital or a survivor of a severe auto accident with a major skull injury may forget months or even years.

Evidence suggests that immediately after the shock some memories that will later be lost are still available. In one interesting study Lynch and Yarnell (1973) attended football practices and games in the hopes that they would be in attendance when players received minor head impacts. When players appeared dazed, Lynch and Yarnell would immediately ask them the play they had just run. Players could usually recall the play at this point, but 3 to 20 minutes later they usually could not. Retrograde amnesia therefore seems to develop after a blow, but it does not appear to be an instantaneous consequence of the blow.

Retrograde amnesia inverts the normal recall function. Recent memories are least likely, rather than the most likely, to be recalled. For example, in the first half of 1974, Larry Squire and his colleagues (Squire & Slater, 1975; Squire, Slater, & Chace, 1975 gave depressed patients a multiple-choice recognition test for television shows that had been on for only one season between 1957 and 1972. The tests were given before and after electroconvulsive shock was administered. The results are shown in Figure 10.8. Before ECT the patients showed the normal recency effect: The most recent shows were among the best remembered. After ECT recognition of shows seen two years previously was severely depressed, but recognition of older shows remained unchanged. Why a shock reverses the recency effect is not known. However, different cues are most effective for recent and remote events (Robinson, 1976; Rubin, 1982). Perhaps the shock disturbs the cues for recent events while leaving the cues for remote events intact.

FIGURE 10.8
Results of TV show questionnaire administered to depressed psychiatric patients receiving a course of bilateral ECT. Testing was done before the first treatment and 1 hour after the fifth treatment. (After Squire, et al., 1975.)

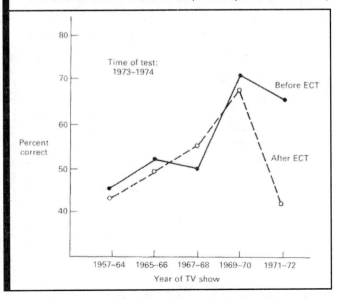

When the memories of a person suffering from severe retrograde amnesia begin to return, the pattern in which they do so is quite disorganized. At first only a few memories are recovered, and the person may be unable to place them in the right temporal order. Two separate events may be combined into one.

As more and more events are recalled, the person is able to create islands of remembering; that is, a series of related events may be placed together in their correct chronological order. As more events are recalled, the islands become bigger and the gaps between them become smaller, until finally the islands merge and the complete episodic record is restored.

In rare cases a large temporal gap never closes, and the person in effect loses a few years from his or her life. Permanent temporal gaps may be induced by ECT, stroke, encephalitis, or trauma. A particularly striking case, in which a large temporal gap occurred in the absence of other cognitive deficits, was reported by Goldberg, Hughes, Mattis and Antin (1982). A thirty-six-year-old, college-educated man suffered a skull fracture that initially caused severe impairments in motor movements, language, learning, and memory. In particular, he could only remember something for a few minutes, so he could not recall where he was. The patient maintained that he was sixteen to eighteen years old and mentioned his parents' address as his address. He revealed no knowledge of his subsequent life history, his marriage, children, or past employment. His command of general information was equally impaired.

During the next two years the motor, linguistic, and learning deficits virtually disappeared. The patient again began orienting to the world and became aware of events since the injury from newspapers and television. However, he had no parallel recovery from the twenty-year-deep retrograde amnesia. Though told about his past, he did not remember it. He also failed to recall anything he had learned during the period within the gap. He could not answer questions like "Who wrote Hamlet?" or "What is the capital of France?"

This disorder suggests that episodic memories are stored adjacent to each other in the brain in the sequence in which they were encoded, like books on a shelf. Consequently, an injury that damages that particular part of the brain wipes out a particular period of time.

The dementias associated with both Alzheimer's disease and Huntington's disease always include a retrograde amnesia that increases in severity as the disease progresses. Finally, the dementia associated with alcoholic Korsakoff's syndrome always includes a stable retrograde amnesia. Albert, Butters, and Levin (1979) demonstrated that patients with alcoholic Korsakoff's syndrome exhibit the reversed recency effect; older memories were better preserved. They gave both 60-year-old patients with Korsakoff's disease and normal controls three different memory tests. One hundred photographs of famous individuals from the 1920s to the 1970s were used in a test of face recognition. A questionnaire was administered that consisted of 132 questions about public events and people famous from 1920 to 1975. Finally, a 132-item, multiple choice recognition test was given for events in the same period. The results for patients with alcoholic-Korsakoff's syndrome and for normal subjects on the faces and the verbal-recall tests are shown in Figure 10.9. (The tests were scaled so that normal individuals would achieve equal recall scores for all decades.) A similar but milder gradient was observed for the recognition task. Alcoholics (non-Korsakoff's) are also impaired on facial and verbal recall in comparison with normal controls, and they also exhibit a mild gradient (Albert, Butters, & Brandt, 1981a; 1981b).

Butters (1984) found the reversed recency effect in the memory of an individual whose learning history was known in detail. This patient (P. Z.), was an eminent scientist and university professor who developed alcoholic Korsakoff's syndrome at

FIGURE 10.9

Overall performance of alcoholic Korsakoff's syndrome patients and normal controls on famous-faces test and verbal-recall questionnaire. (From Albert, et al., 1978.)

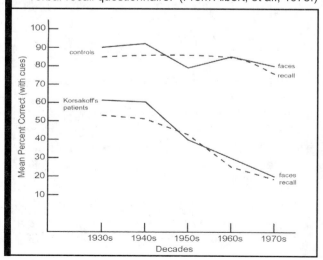

the age of sixty-five. He had written several hundred research papers and numerous books and book chapters, including an extensive autobiography written three years prior to the acute onset of the disorder in 1982.

P. Z.'s amnesia was assessed through the construction of two special tasks: a famous-scientists test and an autobiographical-information test. The famous-scientists test consisted of the names of seventy-five famous investigators and scholars in P. Z.'s scientific specialty, all of whom should have been well known to P. Z. The vast majority of these names were mentioned prominently in one or more of P. Z.'s books or major scholarly papers. Other names were chosen because of their documented professional interactions with P. Z. Twenty-eight of these scholars were prominent before 1965, twenty-four made major contributions before and after 1965, and twenty-three attained visibility after 1965. P. Z. was presented with each name and asked to describe the scholar's area of interest and major contribution. P. Z.'s recognition failure rate doubled from about 40 to 80 percent from pre-1965 to post-1965.

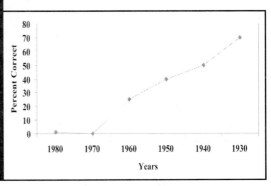

FIGURE 10.10
P.Z.'s recall of information from autobiography. (Butters, 1984.)

The autobiographical-information test consisted of questions about relatives, colleagues, collaborators, conferences, research assistants, research reports, and books mentioned prominently in P. Z.'s autobiography. The results, shown in Figure 10.10, show a steeply graded retrograde amnesia, which cannot be the result of a failure of original learning. The fact that all questions were drawn from P. Z.'s autobiography eliminates the possibility that the information was never acquired. Just three years prior to the onset of the Korsakoff's syndrome, P. Z. could retrieve this information and considered it to be important in his professional and personal life.

CONFABULATION

A certain amount of confabulation is a part of the functioning of normal memory, as studies of eyewitness testimony and autobiographical memory have revealed. It occurs when the representation of an autobiographical episode is constructed from insufficiently specific information about separate episodes, so that details of separate episodes are combined into one. In retrograde amnesia, in which the amount of information that can be retrieved is decreased., there should be a corresponding increase in normal confabulation. In fact, normal confabulation is a part of retrograde amnesia. However, damage to the prefrontal cortex produces another kind of confabulation. Normal confabulation produces a plausible memory that neither the speaker nor listener has any reason to doubt. Abnormal confabulation produces an implausible false memory whose implausibility is apparent to a normal listener but not to the individual producing it. Johnson and Raye (1998) listed several vivid examples of patient confabulation:

"Benson et al. reported a patient who gave detailed descriptions of conversations with physicians that she had never met and trips she had made out of the hospital that had not occurred. Stuss et al. reported a patient who fabricated a story of a drowning accident in which he rescued one of his children and another patient who fabricated stories about how members of his family had been killed before his eyes." (p. 140)

Implausible confabulations do not require severe retrograde amnesia. In fact, one confabulating patient had quite good recognition inabilities (Dab, Claes, Morais, & Shallice, 1999). Rather the source of the confabulation appears to be decision making system of the brain in the prefrontal cortex (Chapter 9). Damage to the prefrontal cortex impairs the ability to monitor reality regardless of whether memory is impaired. Delusions not involving memory were described in Chapter 9. So it is not surprising that damage to the frontal cortex produces confabulations as well (Mattioli, Miozzo, & Vignolo, 1999; Papagno & Baddeley, 1997). Schnider (Schnider & Ptak, 1999; Schnider, .Ptak, von Däniken, & Remonda , 2000) found that all the subjects who produced spontaneous confabulation (defined below), had damage to the basal forebrain or the medial orbitofrontal cortex.. Causes of confabulation include anything that is likely to damage the inferior prefrontal cortex, including alcoholism, and damage to the anterior communicating artery, which supplies this region of the brain with blood. In a post-mortem study looking at the possible anatomical sources of alcohol dementia as a whole, Brun and Andersson (2001) found damage to the ventral area of the frontal lobes. Similarly, damage to anterior communicating artery cause lesions in the ventromedial frontal lobes and the basal forebrain (Shallice, 1999, p. 588).

Recall that the prefrontal cortex is involved in both recency and familiarity judgments. Schnider (2001) suggests that one source of confabulation is an impaired sense of familiarity and recency, so that episodes that occurred long ago are perceived as recent and details from episodes that occurred at different times are combined. He calls examples that conform to this pattern **spontaneous confabulation** to distinguish it from normal confabulation, which results from retrieving insufficiently specific details. He (Schnider, 2001, p. 151) cites the following example:

> *A 58-year-old woman hospitalized following rupture of an anterior communicating artery aneurysm was convinced that she was at home and had to feed her baby; but her 'baby' was over 30 years old at the time...a tax accountant with extensive traumatic destruction of the orbitofrontal cortex inadvertently left the hospital in the conviction that he had a meeting with the county's financial director...*

Schnider also pointed out that people who suffer from spontaneous confabulation often have no comprehension of their memory loss, or of their dissociation from current reality. Thus the mother was agitated – not relieved – on being told her baby was actually 30, and calmed down only when she was told that someone else was caring for the baby while she remained in the hospital.

The results of various experimental studies also suggest that spontaneous confabulation arises from impaired perceptions of familiarity and recency. Schnider and Ptak, (1999) presented randomized runs of pictures to patients and asked them to respond when they saw a target picture. The presentations were repeated after five minutes, and after 30 minutes. The targets changed for each run, while the overall set of pictures remained the same. The patients who had shown spontaneous confabulation were more likely to indicate previous targets as current targets than were non-confabulating amnesiacs and healthy controls, especially in the runs that occurred after a lapse of time. Also, Schnider (2000) asked patients to indicate which square of two on a computer screen stayed dark longer. He varied independently when each square turned dark and returned to light. So observers had to track and remember two different durations that did not have a common onset or offset. Spontaneous confabulators were worse at choosing which square stayed dark longer.

Shallice (1999) pointed out that impaired perceptions of familiarity and recency cannot be the sole source of all abnormal confabulations. First, semantic knowledge, which does not depend on recency or familiarity, may also be confabulated (Diamond, DeLuca, & Fisher, 2000; Moscovitch & Melo, 1997). Second, some confabulations are too unrealistic to be based on memories of real events, such as a memory of being a space pirate, or of having had a detailed conversation with the Prime Minister. Third, though the retrograde amnesia of the patient remains unchanged, his or her confabulation is often a transient disorder, which improves along with tests of frontal lobe functioning (Benson, Djederedjian, Miller, Pachana, Chang, Eng, & Mena, 1996; Fischer, Alexander, D'Esposito & Otto, 1994). Fourth, some confabulations include a compulsion to do something. Examples are the patient who believed she had to feed her baby (Schnider, 2001) and the patient who believed he had to go somewhere that required him to dress formally every morning (Shallice, 1999). At some point confabulations become false beliefs, i.e., delusions.

SUMMARY OF CHAPTER

- Many memories are hierarchically organized into event sequences called episodes. These episodes are further hierarchically organized into stories.
  - Most stories are not constantly updated and their recall is not affected by post event information
  - One story that everyone knows is the story of his or her own life. This story is called autobiographical memory. So your autobiographical memory has the same structure, and is subject to the same retrieval and decision processes, as other stories that you know. But unlike other stories, autobiographical memory is constantly being updated in order to keep you oriented to place and time.

- Recall of life events is a process of reconstruction based on general rules of how things must go together.
  - It is organized around your intentions and actions.
  - Unfortunately, it is not easy to discriminate between a memory of intending to do something and of actually doing it. In reconstructing a memory of a past event, representations encoded at different times may be combined to form a single description of the event.
  - As a result, autobiographical memory may change as the result of post-event information. So the things that are most important to you, such as who said what to whom of a personal nature, are the things that you are least likely to remember accurately.
    * Because of the reconstructive nature of memory, even memories for highly emotional, unforgettable, events change over time. An emotionally charged memory is no more likely to be accurate than a mundane memory though it is likely to be associated with a higher degree of confidence in its accuracy.
    * When a memory is recovered after repeated interrogation, suggestion, or hypnosis, there is no reason to consider it accurate.

- Recall of ordinary knowledge, such as the names and faces of classmates, and the subject matter of topics studied over a few years, remains at a high level for decades.
  - The long-term recall of autobiographical events is described by a three-part function. First there is a recency effect. The number of autobiographical memories recalled declines as a function of retention interval back to the age of thirty.
  - From thirty to fifteen there is a reminiscence bump. Autobiographical memories, particularly of unique or first-time events, are over-represented from this time period.
  - Finally, there is childhood amnesia for memories below the age of four and a half. No autobiographical memories are reported from this period.

- Retrograde amnesia is the failure to retrieve memories that were encoded normally. There are two entirely different disorders of this type.
  - In psychogenic amnesia an individual is oriented to time and place but doesn't know who he or she is. This disorder is very rare and highly controversial since it is associated with lying on the part of the patient.
  - More common is organic retrograde amnesia as the result of bilateral damage to the medial temporal cortex.
    * The individual knows who he or she is but has forgotten everything for some time period up to the moment of the injury. Hence, the patient is initially not oriented to time or place.
    * If there is also damage to the prefrontal cortex then the patient may also suffer from confabulation. That is, entirely false memories may take the place of real ones.

Chapter 11

REASONING

Y ou know a lot of things that you have never learned. If a pair of jeans is too small for you, then you will try on a larger size, not a smaller size, because you know that an even smaller size cannot fit you. Such a deduction is obvious, but it is not trivial. After all, it provides you with a strategy for finding a pair of jeans that fit. The logical system that makes such deductions possible terminates in the upper portion of the prefrontal cortex. It consists of procedures that make it possible to extract information from representations. For example, the procedures directed by the prefrontal cortex make it possible to determine that a square contains two pairs of parallel lines, one horizontal pair and one vertical. It also makes it possible to determine that a square does not contain a diagonal line. These procedures make it possible to extract information contained in an individual's total knowledge that are not available from any single experience. As theses examples indicate, logical reasoning relies heavily on structural description and comparison. However, language also plays a role in reasoning. Verbal labels may be substituted for visual structural descriptions. Procedures that make use of these verbal labels can be executed much faster than the visual structural descriptions can be constructed and extend reasoning to cases that can't be visualized. Hence, when you search for a pair of jeans you merely have to check the size on the label, you don't have to visualize each pair on you. The first part of this chapter is concerned with logical reasoning.

As in the jeans example, reasoning may be involved in selecting a course of action from more than one alternative. It supplies the "why" to the "what" of the temporal cortex and the "how" of the parietal cortex. However, there are many choices for which logic has no immediate answer or no answer at all. Suppose the sky is cloudy and there is some chance of rain. Your expectation of rain is not based on a logical analysis of weather conditions but on your past experience with the weather. Suppose you are trying to decide whether to go on a picnic or to a movie. You really would prefer the picnic, but if you chose the picnic and it rains then you will be left with nothing. The decision to select among several possible actions often rests on two kinds of information: what are the likely outcomes of each action and which outcome is preferred? The logical system cannot determine whether or not it rains and how much you prefer a picnic over movies. Instead, the intuitive system that terminates in the lower prefrontal cortex (Figure

4.1) rapidly generates an intuition about the likelihood of an outcome along with a degree of preference for it. It relies on automatic processing. The intuitive system is a heuristic system. It is fast because it makes use of a limited amount of information. It usually generates a reasonably accurate intuition of the likelihood of an outcome, but because it relies on a limited amount of information, drawn from personal experience, it may be wrong, particularly in novel situations. The second part of the chapter is concerned with intuitive decision-making.

DEDUCTION

Logical reasoning has two processing steps. The first step is forming an initial representation of a situation defined by statements called the **premises**. The second step is to manipulate the representation in some way to reach a **conclusion**. The **conclusion**, also called a **deduction**, is a statement that must be true if the premises are true. A **statement** is a simple sentence whose semantic representation is a single proposition (Chapter 5). In fact, the terms statement and proposition are used interchangeably. For example, if you are reading this book (premise 1), and anyone reading this book is a student of psychology (premise 2) then you are a student of psychology (conclusion). Some deductions, like the one in the last sentence, are obvious. Another way of saying this is that you have logical intuitions that certain deductive inferences have to be true. However, as will be discussed below, other deductions are not obvious. What separates the obvious from the non-obvious deductions is whether the representation defined by the premises is correctly constructed in working memory. The likelihood of correctly representing the premises in working memory determines the probability that the correct conclusion will be drawn from them.

Deduction has a linguistic component. As mentioned above, premises and conclusions are statements, which are defined by propositions, which of course are semantic representations that are part of language. However, this is not the whole story. Furthermore, deduction also has a visuospatial component. As will be discussed below, the ability to generate visuospatial representations in working memory is an essential part of logical intuition.

TRANSITIVE INFERENCES BASED ON LINEAR ORDERINGS

One important type of deductive inference is based on the transitivity of comparative relations. A basic transitive inference is the following:

> A is greater than B.
> B is greater than C.
> Therefore A is greater than C.

This is a very simple deduction. Nevertheless, the mental machinery necessary to make it is considerable.

Working memory. Suppose you were presented with the premises *Ann is taller than Beth* and *Beth is taller than Carol*. How do you draw the conclusion *Ann is taller than Carol*? This case is easy because you just form a new representation containing the first and last names in the inference chain. Four-year-old children can do this. But suppose we reverse the premises, so we have *Beth is taller than Carol* and *Ann is taller than Beth*. Now you must find the two, no longer adjacent terms that are identical and use that information to reorder the two premises. This is a job for working memory. That is where you detect the identical terms through a recency judgment and then reorder the statements through verbal rehearsal. However, as discussed in Chapter 4, the rehearsal skills of young children are poor. Children cannot reliably draw the correct conclusion from the reversed premises until the age of 5 (Halford, 1984). Working memory is essential for all except the simplest deductions. Adults who had brain damage restricted to the upper part of the prefrontal cortex were tested on transitive chains of up to four premises by Waltz, Knowlton, Holyoak, Boone, Mishkin, de Menzies Santos, Thomas, & Miller, 1999). The individuals still had normal intelligence and memory.   They could still make deductions for the transitive chains when they were ordered from largest to smallest:

> Ann is taller than Beth
> Beth is taller than Carol
> Carol is taller than Debby
> Debby is taller than Eve

However, they were unable to make the correct deduction when the order of the premises was scrambled. All but the simplest deduction requires the construction of some sort of representation in working memory. Human deduction is just another voluntary action. Like all novel actions, it is constrained by the limits on the number of novel representations that may be part of working memory.

Linear orderings. If the premises are not scrambled then almost anyone can make the correct inference from a transitive chain. Suppose someone is given the following information as a set of premises: "Bill is taller than Sam," "Sam is taller than Dave," "Dave is taller than Bob," "Bob is taller than Pete." Now the person is asked to decide as quickly as possible whether the conclusion "Bill is taller than Pete" is valid. One way to formulate the process of reaching a decision as a series of inference steps is as follows:

> 1. Bill is taller than Sam.
> Sam is taller than Dave.
> Therefore Bill is taller than Dave.
>
> 2. Dave is taller than Bob.
> Bob is taller than Pete.
> Therefore Dave is taller than Pete.
>
> 3. Bill is taller than Dave.
> Dave is taller than Pete.
> Therefore Bill is taller than Pete.

This procedure produces the correct solution, but it requires three inference steps. In general, the further apart in the ordering two terms are, the more inferences will be required to evaluate the relation between them. Thus if people used this inference-chaining procedure to derive conclusions, their decision time would be expected to increase with the "distance" between the terms in the conclusion to be evaluated.

George Potts (1972, 1974) performed the first studies that used longer series. In a typical experiment he first taught subjects an arbitrary ordering by presenting them with sentences describing the relation between pairs of adjacent items, as illustrated in the sequence just given. The entire ordering contained six terms. After subjects had learned the ordering, they made true or false judgments about sentences describing all possible pairs of items. The results were dramatically different from those inference chaining would predict. Reaction time actually decreased with the distance between the items. Sentences based on a pair of remote items (e.g., "Bill is taller than Pete") were evaluated more quickly than the sentences based on adjacent items (e.g., "Dave is taller than Bob"), even though only the latter sentences had actually been presented during learning.

People learn an ordered list by creating a visual representation of the items in a linear array. As a result, the time to make comparisons depends not on the specific sentences used to learn the ordering but on the ease with which the items can be accessed in a linear array. In general, the terms at the two ends of the array (often called "end anchors") are accessed very quickly, whereas terms near the center of the array are accessed much more slowly. Since remote pairs tend to be nearer the ends of the list, more remote inferences can be made relatively quickly. This basic pattern has been obtained for linear orderings containing as many as sixteen items (Woocher, Glass, & Holyoak, 1978).

A similar reaction time pattern is found when people judge the relative position of items in a perceptual array, e.g., a series of lines ordered from left to right (Holyoak & Patterson, 1981). Therefore, it may be that the process used to make transitive inferences may include representing the elements being compared in the kind of spatial structural description used in perception. Perhaps for this reason even children as young as five or six years old seem to be able to use mental arrays to represent the relations between ordered items and hence make transitive inferences (Trabasso, Riley, & Wilson, 1975).

Similar processes appear to be used to make comparative judgments about well-learned concepts. Across many different types of concepts, reaction time measures show a **symbolic-distance effect**: The further apart the items are on the relevant dimension, the faster a comparative judgment can be made. For example, people are faster to choose the larger animal of the pair horse and cat than of the pair horse and goat (Moyer, 1973) and they are faster to choose the larger digit of the pair 2 and 8 than of the pair 2 and 3 (Moyer & Landauer, 1967). Symbolic-distance effects have also been found in judgments of animal intelligence (Banks & Flora, 1977); e.g., people can decide that horses are smarter than sheep.

Even with abstract dimensions, memory for subjective magnitude can be quite detailed. Holyoak and Walker (1976) had subjects perform mental comparisons with pairs of words from semantic orderings, such as quality terms (e.g., poor, fair) and temperature terms (e.g., cool, hot). One group of subjects was asked to rate the psychological distance between the terms in each ordering. These ratings were used to derive a scale for each set of terms. Figure

FIGURE 11.1
Scales showing psychological differences among terms for quality and for temperature. (From Holyoak & Walker, 1976.)

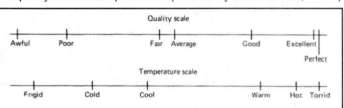

11.1 shows how the quality and temperature terms were placed. As the figure shows, the terms are not spaced evenly. For example, the two central terms in the quality scale, fair and average, are very close. In contrast, the central terms in the temperature scale, cool and warm, are very far apart (i.e., people feel that the temperature difference between cool and warm is greater than that between, say, cold and cool).

A different group of subjects then performed a reaction time task in which they chose the better of each possible pair of quality terms and the warmer of each possible pair of temperature terms. A symbolic-distance effect was found for each scale: The greater the distance between the terms, the faster the comparison was made. The exact spacing of the terms affected decision time. For example, the "close" pair fair-average was compared very slowly, whereas the more "distant" pair cool-warm was compared rapidly. These results indicate that not only does the order of the terms matter but also the psychological distance between them on the scale.

EVALUATING CONDITIONAL RULES

Deductive reasoning requires that the reasoner integrate two or more separate assertions in order to deduce a new assertion as a necessary consequence. If your classmate says, "Tomorrow is Wednesday. On Wednesday, we have psychology." Together, the premises and conclusion form a **deductive argument**:

> Tomorrow is Wednesday
> <u>Wednesday, we have psychology</u>
> Tomorrow, we have psychology

Above the line are the premises, which are assumed to be true. Below the line is the conclusion. The argument is valid if and only if the truth of the premises guarantees the truth of the conclusion. Note that validity is not the same thing as truth. An argument is valid if and only if the truth of the conclusion depends only on the truth of the premises and the form of the argument.

Some deductive arguments, like the one above, correspond to familiar, frequently used structural descriptions that can easily be retrieved into working memory. Their conclusions are obvious. Other deductive arguments require the construction of novel structural descriptions that describe a relationship specific to the premises. Their conclusions are not obvious. An interesting comparison between an obvious and nonobvious argument involves two inference rules based on conditional statements of the form "If p, then q." In standard logic two rules follow from this fact, which are traditionally called by the Latin names **modus ponens** and **modus tollens**. Modus ponens has the following form:

If p, then q.
p.
Therefore q.

Modus tollens is as follows:

If p, then q.
Not q.
Therefore not p.

Both of these rules are clearly valid. For example, suppose our initial premise is "If it is Wednesday, then we have psychology." Modus ponens then gives the following:

If it is Wednesday, then we have psychology. It is Wednesday. Therefore we have psychology today.

Modus tollens gives the following:

If it is Wednesday, then we have psychology. We do not have psychology today. Therefore it is not Wednesday.

But while both rules are valid, you have probably already noticed that they do not seem of equal difficulty. Modus ponens is immediately obvious, whereas modus tollens seems to require careful thought. And, in fact, studies have shown that whereas virtually all college students endorse modus ponens as valid, a substantial proportion fail to endorse modus tollens (Taplin, 1971; Taplin & Staudenmayer, 1973). Seemingly modus ponens is an intuitive rule of logic, whereas modus tollens is not.

Modus ponens can be verified through a straightforward matching strategy. If the second premise matches the first term of the first premise, then the conclusion is true. However, modus tollens involves negation, which inevitably increases processing difficulty (Clark & Chase, 1972). Probably the clearest justification of modus tollens is to reason as follows (using our earlier example):

I know that if it is Wednesday, then we have psychology. I also know that we do not have psychology today. Now suppose it were Wednesday. Then (by modus ponens) we would have psychology today. But that contradicts the fact that we do not have psychology today. So my supposition must be false: It is not Wednesday.

Although most people find this justification of modus tollens compelling, it clearly involves several inference steps. In contrast, the simple matching operation for modus ponens is easily applied so that the deduction is immediately recognized as valid. This discussion suggests that modus ponens is part of our cognitive repertoire of rules for everyday reasoning, whereas modus tollens is not.

Why should modus tollens be so difficult? One possibility is that in order to solve a logical reasoning problem you construct a structural description of the scene described by the premises, called a **mental model**. That is, you imagine a scene consistent with the premises and then scan the scene to determine what is true about it. This heuristic works much better for positive assertions than negative ones. First consider modus ponens. The mental image of "if p then q" is an image of a p followed by a q. The mental image of "p," "therefore q" is exactly the same. So it seems obvious by matching in working memory that "if p then q" and "p," "therefore q" are the same thing. So if "if p then q" and "p" are true then "therefore q" must also be true.

Next consider modus tollens. Again the mental image of "if p then q" is an image of a p followed by a q. But how can you make an image of "not q?" How would this image be different from the image of "not p" or "not r?" So instead you have to fall back on the extended verbal reasoning described above.

The bead problem. Because modus ponens is easy to visualize and to verify by verbal chaining, its transitive nature is apparent. If we add the premise, if we have psychology, then we meet in Cattel auditorium, to the premises above, then it obviously follows from *today is Wednesday*, that we meet in Cattel auditorium. In contrast, if even two arguments having negation in them, hence requiring modus tollens to evaluate, are combined, the resulting problem requires such a long train of reasoning that for most individuals it is initially unsolvable.

Consider the following problem:

> Only one of the following two statements is true:
> >   At least some of the plastic beads are not red
> >   None of the plastic beads are red.
> Is it possible that none of the plastic beads are red?

What do you think the answer is? A total of 77% of the responses of Princeton undergraduates were yes. But the answer is no. Suppose that we assume that the second statement is true and the first statement is false. If the first statement, that at least some of the plastic beads are not red, is false then it must be that all of the plastic beads are red, which contradicts the second statement that none of the plastic beads are red. So it cannot be the case that the second statement is true and the first statement is false. So it must be the case that the first statement is true and the second statement is false. If the second statement, none of the plastic beads are red, is false, then the answer to the question, "Is it possible that none of the plastic beads are red?" is no.

What made this problem so difficult for the poor muddled Princeton undergraduates? To begin, the students cannot imagine the correct models because only true cases, not false or negative cases, can be imagined (Yang & Johnson-Laird, 2000). Furthermore, errors of reasoning can be related to the number of steps involved in applying the few basic intuitions people have to problems that exceed the capacity of working memory. Solving the problem above, as we have just seen, involves so many steps that it is not possible to keep them all in working memory through the phonological – articulatory loop. If some part of one the propositions, perhaps a *some* or a *not*, is not integrated into the representation of the problem then an error will be made (O'Brien, Braine, & Yang, 1994).

Wason's selection task. The problem of modus tollens, imagining a negative case, makes other apparently simple problems difficult. The most famous is Wason's selection task, named after its originator, Peter Wason (1966,1968). In its original version the task is deceptively simple. Wason presented his subjects with four cards, which were placed in front of them, showing symbols such as the following:

    A   M   6   3

They were told that each card has a letter on one side and a number on the other. Then they were given a rule: "If a card has a vowel on one side, then it has an even number on the other side." The subjects' task was to name those cards, and those cards only, that needed to be turned over in order to determine whether the rule was true or false.

What do you think is the correct answer? Almost all the subjects in Wason's experiment said either "A and 6" or "only A." But the correct answer is "A and 3." If you think about the problem carefully, you will see why this answer is correct. Card "6" is incorrect because even if there isn't a vowel on the other side, it would not falsify the rule. The rule says only that if a card has a vowel, then it will also have an even number. But the "3" is a critical card. For if a card with an odd number turns out to have a vowel on the other side, the rule will have been falsified.

The solution to Wason's selection task is closely related to the two inference rules for conditional statements we discussed above. The rule to be tested has the conditional form "If p, then q." As we saw earlier, conditionals are falsified just in case p occurs without q. Modus ponens implies that if we have established p, we need to check that q holds. So in the selection task we have to check the "A" card. Modus tollens implies that if q does not hold, p must not hold either. Accordingly, we need to check the "3" card (i.e., the noneven number) to ensure there is not a vowel on its back. Subjects' failure to select the "3" card (or, more generally, the not q case) thus confirms that modus tollens is not a readily available inference rule.

Since the selection task basically involves the evaluation of a conditional statement, one can construct a host of logically equivalent problems. As it turns out, performance on the task can be radically altered by varying the content of the rule. Figure 11.2 illustrates two versions of selection problems studied by Johnson-Laird, Legrenzi, and Legrenzi (1972). One condition used a meaningful rule, and another used an arbitrary rule.

In the meaningful condition the subjects were told to imagine they were postal workers engaged in sorting letters. They were to decide if the following rule was being followed: "If a letter is sealed, then it has a 5d stamp on it." (The experiment was conducted in England, and d is the symbol for "pence.") The choices were the four envelopes shown at the top of Figure 11.2: a closed envelope (p), an open envelope (not p), a 5d stamp (q), and a 4d stamp (not q).

FIGURE 11.2

Materials used in meaningful and arbitrary conditions. (From Wason & Johnson-Laird, 1972.)

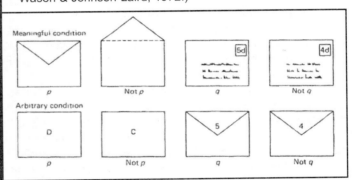

In the arbitrary condition the rule was stated as follows: "If a letter has a D on one side, then it has a 5 on the other." The choices shown at the bottom of Figure 11.2 corresponded to the four alternatives in the arbitrary version.

The logic of the rule was exactly the same in both the meaningful and the arbitrary conditions. The two relevant cases to check were always p and not q, i.e., the closed envelope and the 4d stamp in the former version, and the D and the 4 in the latter version. However, performance on the two versions was strikingly different. In the meaningful condition twenty-one of the twenty-four subjects were correct, whereas in the arbitrary condition only two of the same twenty-four subjects were correct. Moreover, no transfer occurred between the two conditions: Getting the correct solution to the meaningful version did not improve performance on the arbitrary version.

The results of Johnson-Laird et al. thus indicated that people are much more successful at reasoning about a meaningful rule than a logically equivalent arbitrary rule. The reason is not simply that meaningful rules involve more concrete objects, since not all concrete versions produce facilitation (Griggs

& Cox, 1982; Manktelow & Evans, 1979; for reviews see Evans, 1982; Griggs, 1983; Wason, 1983). Indeed, Johnson-Laird and colleague's postal rule version does not always produce the good performance it did in the original experiment. Griggs and Cox (1982) failed to find facilitation for American subjects.

At the time of the original Johnson-Laird et al. study, there was, in fact, an actual British postal rule of this sort: A sealed envelope signified first-class mail, which required more postage. The postal rule version of the selection task was thus very similar to a rule with which the subjects were familiar. Since no such rule existed in the United States at the time of the Griggs and Cox study, their results suggested that direct prior experience might be essential to produce facilitation. A study by Golding (1981) provided further support for this possibility. Golding found that the postal rule version produced facilitation for older British subjects who were familiar with the rule, which was by then defunct, but not for younger British subjects who were not familiar with it.

Such evidence suggested that everyday reasoning is highly dependent on memories of specific experiences. If the experience is encoded in a schema that provides a representation for deducing the conclusion then there is no need to maintain the premises through the phonological – articulatory loop. The critical information provided by the postal schema for solving the problem was the counterexample to the rule, a first class letter with insufficient postage.

Cheng and Holyoak (1985) gave the postal rule problem both to students in the United States, who were unfamiliar with it, and to students in Hong Kong, where the post office still enforced such a rule. As would be expected given earlier results, the Hong Kong subjects selected the correct alternatives more often than did the American subjects. However, Cheng and Holyoak also tested conditions in which a rationale was provided along with the rule. Subjects in the rationale condition were simply told that the post office defined sealed mail as first class. When the rationale was provided, students in the United States performed just as well as Hong Kong students with prior familiarity with the rule.

Essentially, Cheng and Holyoak (1985) provided the students in the rationale condition with the schema for deducing the conclusion. One thing we learn about regulations is how to check that they are followed. Many regulations, like the postal rule, have the form "If a certain action (such as sealing an envelope) is to be taken, then a certain condition (such as providing adequate postage) must be met." If the action is taken, we need to check that the condition was met; and if the condition wasn't met, we need to check that the action wasn't taken. This kind of regulation schema thus permits inferences equivalent to both modus ponens and modus tollens, in effect providing a shortcut procedure for deriving the latter inference, which is otherwise very difficult.

To sum up, in the Wason selection task, there are four possible cards. Three are consistent with the rule and one is a counterexample to it. In difficult versions of the problem, consistent with modus tollens, naïve individuals tend to think of three cards consistent with the rule but not the counterexample. This makes for a lot to keep track of in working memory through the phonological – articulatory loop, and creates the likelihood that the counterexample will be missed.

Concrete situations and rationales make the problem easier because they make the counterexample to the rule part of the person's mental model. Using this principle, investigators have become highly inventive at creating versions of the selection problem that suggest a counterexample and hence are easy to solve. Almor and Sloman (1996) used the quality-control rule, "If the product breaks then it must have been used under abnormal conditions" and found that people were most likely to select the correct p and not-q cards (the product broke and it was used under normal conditions). Presumably the quality-control context elicited counterexamples, products that were bad despite correct usage (see also, Green, 1995; Green & Larking, 1995; Sperber, Cara, & Girotto, 1995).

Part of the difficulty of the original abstract version of the Wason selection problem is that the mental model it describes has quite a lot of information to represent in working memory. The mental model for the conditional statement: If a card has vowel on one side then it can only have an even number on the other side, contains three cards: 1) vowel-even number, 2) consonant-even number, 3) consonant-odd number. Few, if any, individuals begin by imagining these three possibilities. Rather, they consider each of the four pictured cards in conjunction with the verbal statement and construct a part of the mental model of the statement for each card (Gigerenzer & Hug, 1992; Manktelow & Over, 1991). When Staller, Sloman, and Ben-Zeev (2000) included in the statement of the problem the three cards described by the rule, correct performance was 50%.

THE THREE-CARD PROBLEM AND THE THREE-DOOR PROBLEM

The research on the Wason selection problem demonstrates that the failure to imagine all the possibilities is often what leads to error in deduction. This is confirmed by research on other deductive problems. Even when there are only a few possibilities it may not be easy to differentiate and count them. Suppose you are told that there are three cards in a hat. One card is red on both sides (the all-red card). One card is white on both sides (the all-white card). One card is red on one side and white on the other (the red-white card). You close your eyes, pick a single card randomly, and put it down on the table. The drawn card has a red side up. What is the probability that this is the all-red card? If your answer is one-half then you responded like 35 of 53 of students in an experiment by Bar-Hillel and Falk (1982). Most people reason as follows: The red face means that we can exclude the all-white card from consideration. This means that the card can either be the all-red or the red-white one, each with a 50-50 chance. However, this response is incomplete and leads to the wrong conclusion. There are three possible surfaces that are red. Two of these are on the all-red card and one on the red-white card. So the correct answer is two-thirds.

Even a lot of experience with a problem will not necessarily guarantee the correct representation or the correct answer. For many years a popular show on television was "Let's Make a Deal." At the end of the show a contestant was given a choice of three doors by the host, Monty Hall. Behind one door was a valuable prize, behind a second door a lesser prize, and behind one door a prize of little or no value. Suppose that the contestant chose door number 1. Sometimes Monty Hall would increase the suspense by showing that the booby prize was behind door number 3 and then giving the contestant the chance to switch from door number 1 to door number 2 if he wished. On September 9, 1990, this problem appeared in Marilyn Vos Savant's column in *Parade* magazine who asked, "Is it to your advantage to switch your choice?"

What happened next was quite remarkable.   Vos Savant gave the correct answer, that the contestant should switch. The contestant has only a one-third chance of his initial choice being the one with the big prize since he selected from among three doors. But if he did not select the correct door, then the one that remains must have the big prize since the one that was eliminated did not. Hence if the contestant sticks with his original door he has only a one-third chance of winning the big prize, but if he switches then he has a two-thirds chance of winning it. In response, came a cascade of mail from readers of all levels of education arguing that Vos Savant was wrong and it made no difference whether the contestant stayed or switched.   Vos Savant replied as follows:

"Yes, you should switch. The first door has a 1/3 chance of winning, but the second door has a 2/3 chance. Here's a good way to visualize what happened. Suppose there are a million doors, and you pick door No. 1 then the host, who knows what's behind the door and will always avoid the one with the prize, opens them all except for door No. 777,777. You'd switch to that door pretty fast, wouldn't you?"

The difficulty appears to be the same in both the three-card and three-door problems. The statement of the problem encourages the reasoner to collapse two of the possible outcomes together, so that what should be visualized as three outcomes is imagined as only two.

WILLIAM'S SYNDROME

The research on deduction problems demonstrates that the ability to construct representations in working memory is a limiting factor in deductive reasoning. Another question is the extent to which deductions are based on visual and/or verbal representation in working memory. The relationship is murky, but logical intuition appears to be related to a general ability to manipulate visuospatial representations. A rare genetic disorder, called William's Syndrome, destroys this one ability was leaving all others reasonably intact. The effect on reasoning is devastating.

William's syndrome was described in detail by Ursula Bellugi and her colleagues (Bellugi, Lichtenberger, Jones, Lai, & St. George, 2000). To begin, children with Williams syndrome have excellent visual recognition skills, as measured by standardized face recognition tests. Their performance is just below, or even above, normal performance (Rossen, Jones, Wang, & Klima, 1995). Though language learning is initially delayed, children with William's syndrome rapidly catch up for awhile to same-age normal children in vocabulary (Karmiloff-Smith, Grant, Berthoud, Davies, Howlin, & Udwin, 1997). As mentioned in Chapter 6, verbal working memory plays an important early role in language learning and children with Williams syndrome have excellent verbal working memories. The preserved abilities of Williams syndrome children result in an atypical pattern of language learning and ultimately an uneven level of linguistic performance (Bishop, 1999; Paterson, Brown, Gsodl, Johnson, & Karmiloff-Smith, 1999). When asked to produce instances of a category like animals (the verbal fluency test) they produce more words than age matched controls and more rare words than age matched controls (Bellugi, et al., 2000). Furthermore, they show good understanding of the words they know. Also, the syntactic complexity of their spontaneous speech is excellent and knowledge of syntax is generally good (Bellugi, Klima, & Wang, 1996; Karmiloff-Smith, 1998). In general, conversational communication is excellent and individuals with William's syndrome are excellent storytellers (Jones, et al., 2000). Many become avid readers (Howlin, Davies, & Udwin, 1998). For all these reasons, it was once thought that the general linguistic abilities of individuals with William's syndrome are normal. However, this is sadly not the case. Ultimately, the distribution of vocabulary scores for individuals with Williams syndrome is below that for normal individuals (Bellugi, et al., 2000).

In contrast, the performance of children with William's syndrome on any task that requires any degree of visualization is extremely poor. When asked to compare a standard with a set of lines in different orientations, they cannot find the line in the same orientation as the standard (Bellugi, et al., 2000). Their ability to copy a pattern or picture is also poor. It does not exceed the level of a normal 5-year-old. Even their use of spatial prepositions is impaired. Prepositions like on, in, in front of, etc. may be misused in describing scenes, despite otherwise appropriate syntactic and semantic constructions (Bellugi, et al., 2000). The effect of this deficit on cognitive development is severe. On general cognitive tasks, individuals with Williams syndrome rank in the mild to moderate mentally retarded range (Bellugi, et al., 1996). Adults have a conceptual understanding of basic biological categories of living things, such as people, animals, and plants, that is only equivalent to that of normal 6-year-olds (Carey, 1985).

Individuals with William's syndrome have severely deficient computational skills. Only a few master addition. Fewer still master subtraction and division. Finally, the ability to make inferences is absent. When asked to estimate the sizes of familiar objects, many responses were far off the mark. The length of a dollar bill was estimated to be five feet by an 18-year-old and one inch by a 20-year-old. The length of a bus was estimated at 30 inches by a 12-year-old (Kopera-Frye, Dehaene, & Streissguth, 1996). Since much of daily conversation requires the making of what are normally obvious inferences, this leaves individuals with Williams syndrome with an inordinately concrete view of the world. A 21-year-old woman with Williams syndrome had read several books on her favorite topic: vampires. When she was asked what a vampire is, she responded that a vampire is "a man who climbs into ladies' bedrooms at night and sinks his teeth into their necks." When asked why vampires do that, she thought for a bit, and then said, "Vampires must have an inordinate fondness for necks" (Johnson & Carey, 1998).

CAUSATION AND DEDUCTION

The poor understanding of individuals with Williams syndrome reveals the connection between deduction and intuitions about causality. Without the ability to make deductions there is no way to fully appreciate the relationship between cause and effect. For example, the woman with Williams syndrome was unable to infer from their behavior, a vampire's fondness for necks, not blood. In contrast, Michael Waldman (Waldmann & Holyoak, 1992; Waldmann, 2001) showed that the deductions of college students about events were guided by causal relations. Waldmann (2001) presented students with a description of a box with various lights and lighted buttons. In the critical learning condition the students saw that when two lights, A and B, on one side of the box were lit, light C on the opposite was also lit. The students were then asked how certain they were that light C was lit if they only knew whether light A or B were lit. Half the students were told that pressing buttons A and B caused them to become lit, as well as possibly having an effect on C. So the lighting of C was a possible consequence of A and B being lit. In this condition, the students had a mean confidence rating of 70 out of 100 that C was on if either A or B was lit, presumably because they were uncertain whether the other light was lit and what would happen if only one button were pressed. The other half of the students were told that pressing C caused it to light up, as well as possibly having an effect on A and/or B. So the lighting of A and/or B was a possible consequence of the lighting of C. These students had a mean confidence rating of 100 that C was on if they saw that either A or B was on, presumably because since the lighting of both A and B were consequences of the lighting of C, the lighting of either was sufficient to indicate that C was lit.

HEURISTIC INDUCTION OF EXPECTATION

Recall from Chapter 9 that a familiarity response can be used to make a frequency estimate. For example, *boy* is more familiar than *lad* and so it is judged to be more frequent. The use of a familiarity response to make a frequency judgment is called a **heuristic**. That is, information about one kind of variable (e.g., familiarity) is used to make a judgment about another kind of variable (e.g., frequency). The use of a heuristic is based on the assumption that values on the two variables are positively correlated; e.g., that more frequent words are more familiar. Amos Tversky and Daniel Kahneman (1973) suggested another heuristic for making a frequency comparison they called the **availability** heuristic. This is to generate a few examples and then extrapolate from them. For example, to determine whether more people die of cancer or heart disease you would notice whether more people immediately came to mind who died of cancer or heart disease. Whichever illness was a cue for more examples would be judged as a greater cause of fatalities. (Heart disease produces many more deaths than cancer.)

Expectations of the future are based on past experiences. The same heuristics produce intuitions about the both the past and future. The familiarity and availability heuristics do not only determine intuitions about how often something as occurred in the past but how likely it is in the future. That is, if asked whether in the next year more books will contain the word *boy* or *lad* or whether more people will die of cancer or heart disease, in all probability you will rely on your intuitions about the past frequencies of the events and the assumption that the recent past is an accurate guide to the immediate future.

REPRESENTATIVENESS AND INDUCTION

One of the basic laws of probability is that increasing the specificity of an event or outcome can only decrease its probability. For example, the probability that a person is both a lawyer and a tennis player must be less than the probability that the person is a lawyer. More generally, the probability that both condition A and condition B are met can only be less than the probability of meeting condition A alone.

Even though this normative principle is one that most people find intuitive when it is directly stated, Tversky and Kahneman (1983) were able to demonstrate that college students—including statistically sophisticated graduate students in the Stanford Business School—systematically violate it when using the representativeness heuristic. One of Tversky and Kahneman's demonstrations involved having subjects read the following brief personality sketch (1983):

Linda is 31 years old, single, outspoken, and very bright. She majored in philosophy. As a student, she was deeply concerned with issues of discrimination and social justice, and also participated in anti-nuclear demonstrations.

After they had read the description, the subjects were asked to rank order the probabilities that various statements about Linda were true. Among these statements were the following two:

1. Linda is a bank teller.
2. Linda is a bank teller and active in the feminist movement.

If you understood the law of probability described above, you realize that the second of these statements, which is a conjunction that includes the first statement, can only be less probable. However, over 80 percent of the students Tversky and Kahneman tested said that the conjunctive statement was more probable—a clear violation of the normative model of probability. Furthermore, students with statistical training were just as prone to this conjunction fallacy as were students who lacked such training.

Why did the judgments of so many people violate the normative principle? The first thing to note is that the description of Linda seems to "fit" very well with her being a feminist but not particularly well with her being a bank teller. To use Kahneman and Tversky's (1972, 1973) term, Linda seems more **representative** of the category "feminist" than of the category "bank teller." That is, Linda is more similar to a typical feminist than to a typical bank teller. As a result, students rated her as more similar to the compound "feminist bank teller" than to "bank teller." Apparently, then, the students who made probability judgments based their assessments on implicit similarity judgments; i.e., since Linda was viewed as more similar to a feminist bank teller than to a bank teller, students judged the conjunction to be more probable. Under this interpretation the conjunction fallacy reveals that people use the **representativeness heuristic** to make probability judgments. You tend to judge probability on the basis of similarity, even though the two concepts are by no means equivalent.

Generalization fallacy. Relying on representativeness can also make a generalization to a larger category seem more plausible than to a smaller category that it contains. Osherson, Smith, Wilkie, Lopez, and Shafir (1990) had people judge which of two generalizations they thought followed more strongly from an observation. They found that when people were told that *robins secrete uric acid crystals* they thought that the generalization *all birds secrete uric acid crystals* followed more strongly than *ostriches secrete uric acid crystals*. It is easy to see where these intuitions come from. When you think of birds you think of typical birds like robins, so the similarity between robin and other instances is highlighted. However, ostriches have several salient differences from robins that lower the strength of the generalization. Nevertheless, since all birds includes ostriches it makes no logical sense for the generalization to all birds to be stronger than the generalization for ostriches alone. Similarly, Sloman (1993) found that people prefer to generalize from animals to mammals than from animals to reptiles, though anything true of animals is obviously equally true of both mammals and reptiles. Also, Sloman (1998) found that people prefer to generalize from birds to sparrows than from than from animals to sparrows though anything true of either animals or birds must be true of sparrows.

Furthermore, the typicality of the instance within the category influences the degree of generalization. A property observed in a typical bird like a robin is perceived as more likely to be true for other birds than a property observed in an atypical bird like an ostrich. On the other hand, we have so far only considered generalization from a single instance. Of course, the more instances a property is observed in, the more confidence people have in the generalization. Furthermore, the generalization is stronger if it is observed with more diverse instances in a category. Lopez (1995) told people that lions had some property and then asked whether they would test leopards or goats to see whether it generalized to mammals. Goats was the preferred choice. So when generalization from multiple instances is considered, the generalization may be stronger when less representative instances are included in the set that the generalization is based on to maximize its diversity.

Similarity judgments. A representativeness judgment is based on the similarity of one representation to another. The assessment of similarity depends on the decomposition of the comparison concepts into their component features. The similarity of concepts increases with the number of shared features—features that are true of both concepts. So the concepts robin and sparrow are similar because they share many features (e.g., flies, small size); in contrast, robin and penguin are relatively dissimilar because they share fewer features.

Note that number of shared features is always independent of the order of the two concepts. By definition, robin shares as many features with sparrow as sparrow does with robin. If similarity depended only on shared features, similarity would be a symmetrical relation. In fact, however, similarity is not always symmetrical.   Note that in the expression A is similar to B, the concepts A and B serve different roles. A has the role of subject, while B is the referent; i.e., A is being compared with B, not vice versa. The difference between the roles of the subject and the referent is a source of potential asymmetry in the similarity relation. This is particularly striking in figurative uses of language, such as metaphor or simile. For example, the simile A rattlesnake is like lightning suggests that rattlesnakes share some of the salient features of lightning (rapid motion, sudden extension). But the reversed simile, Lightning is like a rattlesnake, suggests that lightning shares some of the salient features of rattlesnakes (potentially deadly, unpredictable, striking suddenly). In each case the simile asserts that some salient features of the referent are also true of the subject. When two concepts have different salient features, the interpretation differs depending on which term fills which role.

Tversky (1977) developed a detailed theory of how people use features to judge the similarity between two concepts that explains why similarity is asymmetrical in more detail. Figure 11.3 depicts the relation between the features of two concepts, A and B, using Venn diagrams. The features of each concept are represented by a circle. The features can be partitioned into three sets. The area where the circles overlap represents the shared features of the concepts. This set is referred to as "A ∩ B" (read "A and B"); i.e., these are features that are true of both A and B. The other two sets represent distinctive features. "A – B" is the set of distinctive features of concept A (i.e., those true of A but not of B); similarly, "B – A" is the set of distinctive features of concept B.

FIGURE 11.3

A graphical illustration of the relations between the features of two concepts (After Tversky, 1977.)

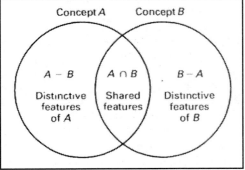

The three types of features affect similarity judgments in the following way:

1. Increasing A ∩ B increases similarity.

2. Increasing A – B decreases similarity.

3. Increasing B – A decreases similarity.

In other words, increasing the shared features of two concepts increases their similarity, whereas increasing their distinctive features decreases their similarity. How can asymmetries in similarity arise? This is quite simple: the distinctive features of the subject are usually given more weight than the distinctive features of the referent. That is, similarity is reduced more by the unique features of the subject than by the unique features of the referent.

In addition, if one concept is more **salient** (more familiar or more informative) than another, the distinctive features of the more salient item will receive greater weight. As a result, the similarity of two items will be reduced if the more salient concept is placed in the subject position, in which its distinctive features will be weighted heavily. For example, Tversky and Gati (1978) selected pairs of countries in which one was more familiar than the other (e.g., China-North Vietnam, Belgium-Luxembourg, Russia-Poland). They asked two groups of college students to rate how similar each pair of countries was. For each pair, one group was asked to compare the more familiar country with the less familiar one (e.g., "How similar is Russia to Poland?"), whereas the other group was asked to compare the less familiar country with the more familiar one (e.g., "How similar is Poland to Russia?") As predicted, the less familiar country was usually judged to be more similar to the familiar country than vice versa.

Also, the judged degree of difference between items is not necessarily the same as similarity in reverse. Tversky argued that whereas similarity judgments primarily stress shared features, difference judgments stress distinctive features. This change in focus can have striking effects on people's judgments. For example, do you think it is possible for one pair of items to be both more similar and more different than another pair? Figure 11.4 illustrates the way this possibility might arise. China and Japan are two prominent countries that most people know a lot about. As a result, each country has many features. On the other hand, Ceylon and Nepal are two countries that most people know relatively little about. As a result, the two prominent countries have more shared features than do the less prominent ones (i.e., A ∩ B is larger than A' ∩ B'). But in addition, the more prominent countries also have more distinctive features (i.e., A – B plus B – A is larger than A' – B' plus B' – A'). In other words, people can think of many similarities between Japan and China, and also many differences. But since people do not know very much about Ceylon and Nepal, those countries do not seem either as similar or as different Japan and China.

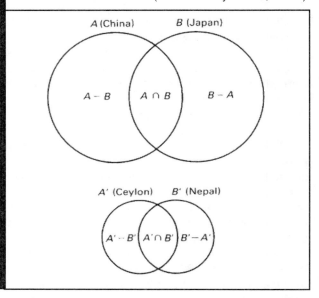

FIGURE 11.4
Similarity v. differences. China and Japan are perceived as both more similar to and more different from each other than Ceylon and Nepal are similar to or different from each other. (After Tversky & Gati, 1978.)

Another factor influencing a similarity judgment is the purpose for which the judgment is made. In making a similarity judgment for a specific purpose some features may be irrelevant. For example, in deciding whether it will rain today, the day of the week is an irrelevant feature. Instead of making an overall similarity judgment between the subject and referent of comparison, you judge whether the subject shares those characteristic of the referent relevant to your purpose. People have some ability to ignore irrelevant features. Heit and Rubinstein (1994) found that people preferred to generalize from chicken to hawk than from tiger to hawk the property of a two-chambered liver. However, they preferred to generalize from tiger to hawk than from chicken to hawk the property prefers to feed at night. Clearly, the first property cued anatomical similarity but the second property cued (predatory) behavior (See also Ross & Murphy, 1999). Hence, the two different judgments were based on different features.

REPRESENTATIVENESS AND EXPECTATION

Representativeness is such a compelling heuristic that people fail to distinguish between categorization and prediction when they use it. People are just as confident about predictions as categorizations. For example, Tversky and Kahneman (1974) presented subjects with several paragraphs, each describing the performance of a student teacher during a particular practice lesson. Some subjects were asked to evaluate the quality of the lesson. Other subjects were asked to predict the standing of each student teacher five years after the practice lesson. The judgments made under the two conditions were identical. In another experiment (Kahneman & Tversky, 1973) a group of sixty-five college students were presented with the following personality sketch:

Tom W. is of high intelligence, although lacking in true creativity. He has a need for order and clarity, and for neat and tidy systems in which every detail finds its appropriate place. His writing is rather dull and mechanical, occasionally enlivened by somewhat corny puns and by flashes of imagination of the sci-fi type. He has a strong drive for competence. He seems to have little feel and little sympathy for other people and does not enjoy interacting with others. Self-centered, he nonetheless has a deep moral sense.

The subjects were asked to rate how similar Tom W. seemed to the typical graduate student in either computer science or the humanities. Overwhelmingly, they thought that Tom W. was more similar to a typical computer science student.

The same sketch was then given to a different group of 114 psychology students, along with the following additional information:

The preceding personality sketch of Tom W. was written during Tom's senior year in high school by a psychologist, on the basis of projective tests. Tom W. is currently a graduate student.

Subjects were then asked to predict whether Tom W. was more likely to be in computer science or in the humanities. Overwhelmingly, they decided on computer science. Well, you might ask, what's surprising about that? After all, people think the sketch of Tom W. fits a computer science student. Three things make the result remarkable. First, yet another group of subjects simply estimated the relative frequencies of the two types of graduate students. Humanities students were judged to be about three times more numerous. So the **prior odds**—the odds based simply on this background information—were rather heavily against Tom W. being in computer science. Second, the same subjects who made the predictions were also asked how reliable they thought projective tests (e.g., inkblot tests) were. They thought projective tests—the source of Tom W.'s personality sketch—were very unreliable. Third, even if the description were valid when Tom W. was in high school, everyone would agree he might well be very different by the time he is in graduate school. So seemingly, in making their predictions, subjects ignored the prior odds and based their decisions entirely on information they would readily admit was very likely wrong. The sketch was considered highly "representative" of the personality of a computer science student, and this high degree of representativeness appeared to overwhelm all other considerations.

Causal interpretation of prior odds. You should not think, however, that people never integrate prior odds in making decisions. In studies that have involved categorization rather than prediction, subjects have taken base rate information into account. Evans, Handley, Over, and Perham (2002) asked students to judge how likely various kinds of students were to be members of different student societies; e.g., how likely an engineering student would be to be a member of the chess club, drama club, etc. The prior odds were manipulated by stating the percent of students at the university in each major; e.g., the percent of students who were engineers. They were able to manipulate how much their subjects took base rate information into account by how salient they made that information.

In particular, prior odds are considered in situations in which they seem to plausibly cause variations in the outcome (Ajzen, 1977; Tversky & Kahneman, 1978). For example, Tversky and Kahneman told subjects that a particular town had two cab companies, the Blue Company and the Green Company. An accident had taken place, and a witness made an uncertain judgment about whether the cab involved was blue or green (visibility had been poor). One group of subjects was told that 85 percent of the cabs in town were blue and 15 percent were green. These subjects, like those in the studies discussed above, largely ignored the base rates and based their decision about which company was involved in the accident primarily on the apparent reliability of the witness. A second group received base rate information in a different way. They were told that although the blue and green cabs were equal in number, 85 percent of all accidents involving cabs were due to blue cabs and only 15 percent were due to green cabs. In this case the prior odds had a clear causal interpretation: The drivers of the blue cabs were more careless. This second group of subjects was heavily influenced by the base rate information.

ACCESSIBILITY

Since expectations are based on the retrieval of information, anything that affects retrieval may affect expectation.   This effect of priming and cuing on expectation is called the effect of **accessibility**. Accessibility is not itself a heuristic but describes how the representativeness and availability heuristics are influenced by the retrieval of specific bits of information.

Frequency and likelihood estimation. Since familiarity does increase with frequency, the availability heuristic is often quite accurate. But familiarity is affected by any cue that matches contextual details. Sometimes, functionally irrelevant features influence a likelihood judgment. Certain features of a novel situation may serve to remind the person of a superficially similar prior situation, which will in turn influence the decision. A study by Gilovich (1981) provides an interesting demonstration of this possibility. Gilovich pointed out that modern American foreign policy has been heavily influenced by two salient historical analogies: the Munich analogy, in which misguided attempts were made to appease Hitler prior to World War II, and the Vietnam analogy, in which American interference in a foreign country led to disaster. Gilovich reasoned that if a new crisis situation contained cues associated with Munich, people would tend to advocate intervention; whereas if the crisis cued Vietnam, people would tend to favor a hands-off policy.

To test this hypothesis, he gave students in a political science course (dealing with conflict from World War I to the present) a description of a hypothetical crisis. The crisis involved a threatened attack by a large totalitarian country, country A against a small democratic country, country B. The subjects were asked to select an option for the United States to follow, ranging from extreme appeasement of country A to direct military intervention.

Two versions of the crisis were constructed, which were intended to cue either the Munich or the Vietnam analogy. For example, the Munich version referred to the impending invasion as a "blitzkrieg," whereas the Vietnam version referred to it as a "quickstrike." The Munich version described how minority refugees were fleeing from country A, in boxcars on freight trains, to country G. In contrast, the Vietnam version indicated that minority refugees were fleeing from country A in small boats that sailed up the "Gulf of C" to country G. These alternative descriptions thus made the crisis seem superficially similar to either the situation in World War II or Vietnam.

These cues have no functional relevance to a decision about how the United States should respond to the hypothetical crisis. After all, why should it matter whether refugees are fleeing in boxcars or small boats? Nevertheless, Gilovich's subjects tended to make decisions of a more interventionist nature when they read the Munich version rather than the Vietnam version. So functionally irrelevant features guided the selection of the analogy. Accessibility operated together with representativeness to determine the judgment.

Probably the most striking demonstrations of accessibiltiy involve the real life impact of salient events. Your subjective estimate of the probability of a car accident is likely to shoot up after seeing an overturned car beside the road. For many people, stepping onto an airplane calls to mind memories of airplane crashes, leading to overestimation of the danger. One consequence of the availability heuristic, observed by Lichtenstein, Slovic, Fischhoff, Layman, and Combs (1978), is that people overestimate the frequency of well publicized causes of death while underestimating the frequency of less notorious causes. For example, Lichtenstein et al. found that homicides are judged to be about as frequent as death by stroke in the United States population, whereas in fact stroke is over ten times more common than homicide as a cause of death.

The availability heuristic has important implications for clinical judgment. For example, suppose a clinician encounters a depressed man and wishes to estimate how likely it is that the patient will attempt suicide. What are the relevant instances? Clearly, the clinician should recall previous instances of depressed patients and determine how many attempted suicide. However, the clinician may well find it easier to recall previous instances of suicidal patients, since suicide is a much more striking occurrence than simple depression. Very probably, all previous suicidal patients were depressed, even though in fact few of the previous depressed patients attempted suicide. In this case availability may lead to a logical error and consequent overestimation of the probability that a particular depressed patient will attempt suicide. The logical error is to assume that if A implies B, then B implies A (i.e., confusing a conditional statement with a biconditional). In other words, just because all suicidal patients were depressed (A implies B), one can't conclude that all depression leads to suicide (B implies A). By the same erroneous logic, if all suicidal patients ate mashed potatoes, then mashed potatoes lead to suicide.

Simulation and regret. The availability and representativeness heuristics are based on the retrieval of examples from memory. However, one can also base decisions on examples or scenarios that are constructed by the reasoner. This basis is especially evident in reasoning about counterfactual statements—claims made about what would have been true had conditions been otherwise. Compare the following two counterfactual statements:

1. If Hitler had had the atomic bomb in 1943, Germany would have won World War II.

2. If Hitler had had one more airplane in 1943, Germany would have won World War II.

Both of these statements make claims based on an overtly false premise —Hitler had neither the atomic bomb nor an extra airplane in 1943. Nevertheless, we feel confident that statement 1 is highly plausible whereas statement 2 is almost certainly false.

How do we make such judgments? One general hypothesis involves what Kahneman and Tversky (1982) call the simulation heuristic. We can form a general mental model of the situation at the height of World War II, and then we imagine the different outcomes that various changes in the situation would produce. We know that possession of the atomic bomb would yield an enormous shift in the balance of military strength, whereas one more airplane would yield only a tiny change. Our mental simulation thus indicates that statement 1 is a much more believable claim than 2, even though both are counterfactual.

Kahneman and Tversky (1982) provide an illuminating illustration of the emotional consequences of the simulation heuristic. Consider the following scenario:

Mr. Crane and Mr. Tees are scheduled to leave the airport on different flights at the same time. They travel from town in the same limousine, are caught in a traffic jam, and arrive at the airport 30 minutes after the scheduled departure time of their flights. Mr. Crane is told that his flight left on time. Mr. Tees is told that his flight was delayed, but it left 5 minutes ago. Who will be more upset?

Virtually everyone agrees that Mr. Tees will be more upset. But notice that objectively the two unfortunate travelers suffered exactly the same fate. Both presumably expected to miss their planes because of the slow limousine trip, and both did so. Why should Mr. Tees be more disappointed than Mr. Crane? The difference is that he will find it easier to imagine how the mishap could have been avoided. If only the limousine had been a little faster, or the plane had been delayed just a bit more, he would have caught his flight. Because the simulation heuristic indicates that small changes in reality would have produced a dramatically better outcome, Mr. Tees suffers greater disappointment. In general, defeats almost avoided and victories almost gained are the sources of life's most trying moments.

The belief that if the limousine had gone a little faster everything would have turned out better is called a hindsight bias (perhaps there would have been a disastrous crash). This is the bane of every football coach who had his team go for it in a fourth-down-and-one-yard situation only to have the effort fail. In retrospect, the risky decision tends to seem just plain stupid, since the negative actual outcome is now by far the most available. People tend to neglect the fact that the outcome could have been quite different and that the calculated risk was perhaps justified.

The simulation heuristic can be used to evaluate the probability of an event by the ease with which you can construct a plausible scenario leading to that outcome. For example, one way a clinician might estimate the likelihood of a suicide attempt is by trying to imagine a chain of events that might occur in the patient's life to worsen the depression. If such a causal scenario is easy to imagine (e.g., the patient's wife is ready to leave him, or he is in danger of losing his job), the clinician may conclude that a suicide attempt is relatively likely. The simulation heuristic plays a role in many kinds of situations in which people are trying to understand events happening around them.

NORMATIVE VERSUS INTUITIVE REASONING

The limitations of working memory on deductive reasoning can be overcome by recoding the features of the assertions through Venn diagrams or truth tables. Using these tools, the validity of syllogisms like modus ponens and modus tollens can be verified. Once a syllogism has been verified and memorized, future encounters with the syllogism no longer involve reasoning but are straightforward retrieval tasks. You recognize the problem as an instance of a syllogism that you know and respond with the answer. A sequence of steps that gives the correct (or at least the best answer) to some kind of problem is called a **normative** model or theory.

Similarly, Bayes Theorem provides a normative model for predicting a statistically uncertain event, such as whether it will rain today. By learning Bayes Theorem, you can improve your ability to predict certain kinds of events. Nevertheless, intuitive reasoning is still with us. People who have learned normative rules often fail to recognize situations in which they apply (Kahneman, Slovic, & Tversky, 1982; Nisbett & Ross, 1980). In their very first study of human judgment, Tversky and Kahneman (1971) found that professional statisticians did not apply their knowledge of statistics to solving simple statistics puzzles presented to them at a statistics convention! Rather, they relied on the same erroneous intuitions that they shared with other human beings.

Another example of the imperviousness of intuition to knowledge comes from physics instruc-

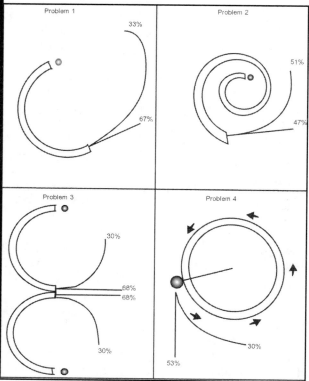

FIGURE 11.5

Motion intuitions. In problems 1-3 students had to draw the path a ball would follow when it came out of the tube. In problem 4, students had to draw the path of the ball spun round on the string when the string broke. The most common responses are shown with the percentage that gave that response: (McCloskey et al., 1980).

tion. Anyone who has ever thrown a ball, or seen it thrown, is familiar with the curved path that it follows. However, Newton's great discovery was that when the ball initially leaves your hand it is traveling in a straight line. The curved motion observed is the result of the two forces exerted on it, yours and the force of gravity. This is taught in every introductory college physics course. Michael McCloskey was interested in how effective such normative instruction in physics was in affecting a person's beliefs about motion.

Figure 11.5 shows a curved tube with its entrance marked with an arrow. McCloskey and his colleagues (McCloskey, Caramazza, & Green, 1980) asked students who had completed a college physics course to draw the trajectory of a ball shot through the tube at high speed. The figure shows the two most common responses, a curved or a straight trajectory. The students who chose the curved trajectory made the intuitive response. In a subsequent study, McCloskey and Kohl, (1983) found that even when students had the opportunity of interacting with actual objects, such as a puck exiting from a curved tube, many still indicated that it followed a curved path when it exited the tube. Some beliefs are so accessible, that they are not easily overcome by knowledge of a normative theory.

SUMMARY OF HEURISTIC INDUCTION OF EXPECTATION

- In making predictions about the future people rely on representations of the past in memory. In general it is assumed that the future will be like the past.
  - Heuristics are used to predict the likelihood of future events:
    * Familiarity
    * Availability
    * Representativeness
  - Priming and cuing influence expectation by influencing the accessibility of the information in memory that influences expectation

PREFERENCE

Much of human cognition is about knowing what you want and getting it. Knowing what you want is about having preferences and making choices. In general, you want to make choices that minimize your loss and maximize your gain. When preferences can be ordered along a single dimension, like monetary value, there is a logic to preference. Just as in the three-term series problems that began this chapter, normative unidimensional preference judgments are transitive. If you would prefer a quarter to a dime, and a dime to a nickel, then logically you should prefer a quarter to a nickel. However, human preference judgments are often not unidimensional and hence not transitive. For example, it is possible for a person to prefer steak to potatoes, potatoes to peas, and peas to steak. It may be that the individual prefers both good tasting and low fat food. The person considers steak tastier than potatoes and so chooses steak even though it is a little more fattening. The person also considers potatoes more tastier peas so chooses potatoes even though they are a little more fattening. However, the person considers steak a lot more fattening than peas and so chooses peas, even though they are less tasty. The choice of a different single feature for different comparison pairs leads to the intransitivity (Slovic, 1975; Tversky, 1972).

Prospect theory. Notice that preferences are motivated both by possible gains and losses. Fatty foods offer the immediate gain of tastiness but also the loss of weight gain. According to **prospect theory** (Kahneman & Tversky, 1979), people's preferences are affected by whether problems are framed in terms of gains or losses. Consider the following problems to different groups of subjects:

Problem 1. You are given $1,000. In addition, you may choose between a) a 50% chance of an additional $1,000 or b) a 100% chance of an additional $500.

Problem 2. You are given $2,000. However, you must chose between c) a 50% chance of losing $1,000 or d) a 100% chance of losing $500.

Notice that outcome a) is the same as outcome c) a 50% chance each of either $1,000 or $2,000; and outcome b) is the same as outcome d) a 100% chance of $1,500. Nevertheless, most people selected b) over a) and also selected c) or d). Most people prefer sure gains and also prefer to avoid sure loses. So people demonstrate **preference reversal**. When a pair of choices is expressed as gains, one of the alternatives is selected. However, when the same pair of choices is expressed as losses, the other alternative is selected. Why should this be the case? There are two parts to the answer.

First, because of the limits of imagination, the subjective magnitude of a number is less than its arithmetic magnitude. The arithmetic magnitude of a number is determined by the rules of arithmetic. For example, arithmetic magnitude of 1000 is twice that of 500 because 2 x 500 = 1000. But can you really imagine how much 500 is and how much 1000 is? Would you really want $1000 exactly twice as much as you would want $500? As numbers get larger, the difference between arithmetic magnitude and subjective magnitude becomes obvious. Does 10 million really seem ten times larger than one million and 1 billion a thousand times larger, or are all these numbers simply too large to subjectively comprehend? So the subjective magnitude of 1000 is not twice the subjective magnitude of 500. The subjective magnitude function falls beneath the arithmetic function, as shown in Figure 11.6.

Second, according to prospect theory the values of possible outcomes are represented as gains or losses from what you have before you act. The amount you have before you act is the **zero reference point**. So if you start with $1000 that is the zero reference point in Figure 11.6 and whatever you end up with as the result of a choice is represented as a gain or loss over the $1000 you began with. How a problem is framed determines where the rea-

FIGURE 11.6

A gain of $1000 (from $1,000 to $2,000 in 1a) is not twice as desirable as a gain of $500 (from $1,500 in 1b) and a loss of a $1000 (from $2,000 to $1,000 in 2c) is not twice as undesirable as a loss of $500 (from $2,000 and $1,500 in 2d). See text for problem (Kahneman & Tversky, 1979.)

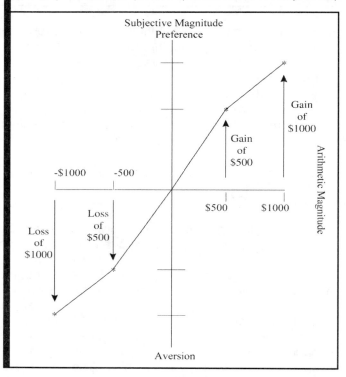

soner places the zero reference point, hence how the outcomes are valued. In Problem 1 the participant has $1,000, hence the zero point is here. As shown in Figure 11.6, a subjective gain of $1,000 is less than twice a subjective gain of $500 so only a 50% chance of gaining an additional $1,000 is not preferable to a 100% of gaining an additional $500. In fact, 84% of the participants selected the sure gain of $500. In Problem 2 the participant has $2,000, hence the zero point is here. As shown in Figure 11.6, a subjective loss of $1,000 is less than twice as undesirable as a loss of $500; so a 50% chance of losing $1,000 is preferred to a 100% chance of losing only $500. In fact, 69% of the participants selected the 50% chance of a $1000 loss.

The decision does not have to be stated in terms of monetary gain or loss to obtain the preference reversal. Tversky and Kahneman (1981) were able to restate the problems as medical dilemmas.

Problem 1. Imagine that the United States is preparing for the outbreak of an unusual Asian disease, which is expected to kill 600 people. Two alternative programs to combat the disease have been proposed.
If Program A is adopted, 200 people will be saved.

If Program B is adopted, there is a one-third probability that 600 people will be saved, and two-thirds probability that no people will be saved.
Which of the two programs would you favor?

Problem 2. Imagine that the United States is preparing for the outbreak of an unusual Asian disease, which is expected to kill 600 people. Two alternative programs to combat the disease have been proposed.
If Program C is adopted, 400 people will die.
If Program D is adopted, there is a one-third probability that no people will die, and two-thirds probability that 600 people will die.
Which of the two programs would you favor?

Again notice that Program A is the same as Program C a 100% chance of 200 people living and 400 people dying; and Program B is the same as Program D a one-third chance of all 600 people living and a two-thirds chance of all 600 people dying. Nevertheless 72% of the participants selected Program A over Program B but 78% of the participants selected Program D over program C. Again most people preferred sure gains and also preferred to avoid sure loses.

In the examples above, stated probabilities were held constant across problem pairs to determine the effect of gain versus loss desirability. However, since probabilities are stated in numbers, the subjective magnitude of probabilities is distorted in the same way as for numerically stated outcomes.
As a result, Kahneman and Tversky (1979) found that people tend to perceive small probabilities as greater than they actually are and large probabilities, with exception of 1.0, as less than they actually are.

Complex judgments. The existence of preference reversal leads to the peculiarity of human behavior that people sometimes will only sell something for more than they themselves would pay for it. For example, suppose you had to choose between two gambles:

Bet A: 29/36 probability of winning 40¢   7/36 probability of losing 20¢
Bet B: 7/36 probability of winning $1.80 29/36 probability of losing 10¢

Which bet would you chose? Your preference is determined by combining the desirability of the outcome with its probability to determine the value of that choice. Most of the subjects chose Bet A. Now suppose that you owned a ticket for each bet. How much would you sell each ticket for? Most of the participants wanted more money for bet B, showing what is known as **preference reversal** (Lichtenstein & Slovic, 1971). According to Tversky, Sattath, and Slovic (1988) how the problem is framed influences which feature is most important to the reasoner; hence which choice is made. When individuals are asked to make a simple choice the probability of the gain tends to be valued more than the amount; the person doesn't want to come away with nothing. But when the problem is framed in terms of selling one of the chances attention is focused on the dollar amounts rather than the chance of winning. Of course the larger dollar amount is valued more.

Emotion. Where do preferences come from in the first place? It seems likely that preference is part of the emotional response mediated by the amygdala. Despite the differentiation into more specific emotions, the basic distinction between withdrawal-related negative emotion and approach-related positive emotion observed in infancy extends into adulthood and is reflected in their organization in the frontal cortex. In normal individuals, during the experimental arousal of emotion, elation is associated with increased left hemisphere activity and depression is associated with increased right hemisphere activity as measured by an EEG (Davidson, 1993). Furthermore, left frontal damage tends to produce depression, while right frontal damage tends to produce elation. As a result, patients with right hemisphere damage often appear to be either inappropriate or very courageous, depending upon ones interpretation, when compared with patients with left hemisphere damage. If you can no longer move the right side of your body, and are uncertain whether you will ever be better, then depression may seem appropriate. But if you are unconcerned by the fact that you can not move the left side of your body or by whether you will ever get better, that can seem very inappropriate. The moral is that bad feelings may have good consequences. A person who can no longer worry, and is no longer risk averse, may instead be indifferent to the point of apathy.

Without emotional cues an individual may be unable to accurately evaluate the value of the outcomes of their actions and undertake risky actions that they otherwise would not. Bechara, Damasio, and Damasio (2000) found that when the connection between the amygdala and the lower part of the prefrontal cortex is severed a person no longer considers the consequences of his or her actions; so judgment is severely impaired (Figure 4.1 and Figure 4.23). They developed a card game in which different stacks of cards (face down) represented a more or less risky choice. Over many studies they found that patients with damage to the lower part of the prefrontal cortex from a variety of causes, including alcohol and other drugs, make more risky and less advantageous choices than normal individuals when playing the card game. For example, Bechara, Tranel, and Damasio (2000) found that ten patients with lower prefrontal lesions performed a version of the game where advantageous decks yielded high immediate losses but even higher future gains and disadvantageous decks yielded low immediate losses but even lower future gains. The patients consistently chose the disadvantageous decks. They appeared insensitive to future consequences, positive or negative, and instead were guided by immediate prospects. They persisted despite the increasing losses they incurred following the short-term strategy.

Why did the patients with damage to the amygdala – prefrontal emotional system perform poorly on the gambling task? One possibility is that they were no longer averse to loss and another possibility that their feelings remained the same but could no longer determine the best course of action. Bechara, Damasio, Damasio, and Lee, (1999) found evidence for both impairments, associated with different areas of damage. Both patients with lower prefrontal damage and patients with amygdala damage made disadvantageous choices in the card game compared with normal individuals. However, they appeared to differ in how they felt about their choices. When a normal individual chose to turn over a card that represented a risky choice, the person sweated in anticipation of the result, indicating he or she appreciated the possible consequences. Patients with lower prefrontal damage also sweated, indicating that they also appreciated the possible consequences. But patients with damage to the amygdala coolly made a choice without the anticipatory sweating response.

SUMMARY OF PREFERENCE

- In choosing among alternatives people try to maximize gains and minimize losses. However, the subjective magnitude of larger gains is skewed so that larger gains and losses are perceived as less than they actually are.
    - Hence people tend to over value small gains and losses and tend to follow a strategy in which certain small gains are preferred to larger more speculative gains but larger speculative losses are preferred to smaller certain losses. As a result of this strategy, people's choices display preference reversal when the same problem is framed two ways: in terms of gains and in terms of losses.
    - Preference is probably an emotional response. When the connection between the amygdala and the lower portion of the prefrontal cortex was damaged patients no longer showed the anxiety of normal individuals in making a risky choice.

SUMMARY OF CHAPTER

- The logical system terminates in the upper portion of the prefrontal cortex. It consists of procedures that make it possible to exact information from representations. The use of these procedures is called reasoning.

- The process of reasoning has two major steps.
    - Forming an initial representation of a situation defined by conditions called the premises.
    - Manipulate the representation in some way to reach a conclusion.

- There are two procedures for deducing a conclusion from premises
    - Positive inference is called modus ponens.
    - Negative inference is called modus tollens.
    - There is no satisfactory way to construct a representation in working memory based on a negative inference.
    - As a result, reasoning requiring a negative inference is much more likely to produce a misstep and an error.

- Logical reasoning relies heavily on both visual and verbal structural description and comparison.
    - Children with a genetic disorder called William's syndrome have no visual or spatial imagery though they have normal perceptual skills. Such children are severely deficient in mathematics and reasoning.

- In making predictions about the future people rely on heuristics based on representations of the past in memory:
    - Familiarity
    - Availability
    - Representativeness
    - Priming and cuing influence expectation by influencing the accessibility of the information in memory

- In choosing among alternatives people try to maximize gains and minimize losses. However, the subjective magnitude of larger gains is skewed so that larger gains and losses are perceived as less than they actually are.

Chapter 12

PROBLEM SOLVING & INTELLIGENCE

A t an intuitive level everyone knows what a problem is; we all have them from time to time. Consider a few examples:

> Deciding how to lose weight   Building a spaceship
> Designing a house   Selecting a good chess move
> Solving a crossword puzzle   Writing a play

While problems can be extremely diverse, all have a goal, or a description of what would constitute a solution to the problem. What makes a problem, a problem, is that the statement of the goal does not act as a cue for its own solution. If your friend asks you to get her a can of diet Coke from the refrigerator in your room, that is not a problem. But if your friend asks you to get her something to drink, that is a problem statement because there are several ways that you can formulate and solve your task.

THE THREE STEPS IN PROBLEM SOLVING

The process of solving a problem has three major steps (Figure 12.1). The first step is forming an initial representation of the problem. A major dimension along which problems vary is the extent to which they are well defined (Newell, 1969; Reitman, 1964; Simon, 1973). In a well-defined problem, such as solving a crossword puzzle, the components are all completely specified. Ill-defined problems, on the other hand, are those for which the problem solver has more uncertainty concerning the operations that can be used and many solutions are possible. Unfortunately, the term ill-defined problem has a slightly negative ring to it. In fact, however, many ill-defined problems are very creative tasks. When people

FIGURE 12.1
Schematic outline of problem solving process

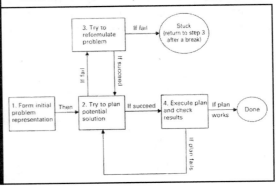

decide to paint pictures, write books, or perform experiments, they are all undertaking ill-defined but creative tasks. Virtually all real-life problems are actually ill-defined in one way or another. Take an apparently simple problem like preparing dinner. The available objects may not be precisely determined (Shall I use whatever is in the house or go shopping in a gourmet food store?), nor the possible operations (Shall I fry hamburgers or use a recipe in my Tibetan cookbook?), nor the goal state (Do I really need dessert?). Preparing a meal illustrates a basic characteristic of problem solving. Each problem begins with a **goal**; e.g., eating something for dinner. In order to solve the problem it may be necessary to break it down into smaller, well-defined, problems, each with is own **subgoal**. Before you can eat, you must decide what to make and where to obtain the ingredients and utensils to make it.

The second step is generating and evaluating potential solutions for each subgoal. We have already discussed generation in the context of recall. In fact, a recall task may be considered a specific kind of problem. The generate and recognize strategy of recall is a special case of the generate and test strategy used in problem solving. As its name implies, the generate-test method has two steps: 1. Generate a candidate for a solution. 2. Test to see whether it is actually a solution. If the candidate fails the test, another candidate is generated, and the cycle repeats until a solution is found. The third step is executing a procedure to carry out a planned solution. It has already been discussed in Chapters 2 and 4 and will only be briefly further considered here.

THE PREFRONTAL CORTEX

The representation of the problem, the generation of a solution, and the execution of the solution plan requires the entire system for performing voluntary action. In particular, the prefrontal cortex directs all aspects of problem solving (Figure 12.2). The relationship of the prefrontal cortex to problem solving is complicated by the fact that the prefrontal cortex does not act in isolation but directs the retrieval of task relevant information in the medial temporal cortex. The entire process of problem solving is a sequence of voluntary actions; hence, it takes place within working memory. The ability to find a solution to the problem may require the consideration of several solutions. Each one must be brought into working memory, evaluated, and replaced by

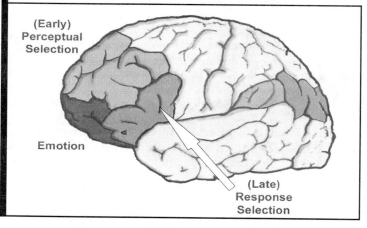

FIGURE 12.2
Areas of neocortex incolved in problem solving

(Early) Perceptual Selection

Emotion

(Late) Response Selection

another possible solution if it is found inadequate. The prefrontal cortex performs two different functions that are essential to problem solving: generation and temporal order judgment. First each possible solution must be generated through semantic cuing. If it is rejected then its representation must be inhibited, so that another solution can be generated in its place. Finally, it is necessary to be able to keep track of which solutions have already been tried and which subgoals have been achieved.

The importance of all three functions is illustrated by the **verbal fluency task**. The task is to generate as many instances of a category in a specified time period, usually a minute. For example, in Chapter 9 the generation of animal names was described. Another version of the task requires generating words that begin with a particular letter, e.g., the letter f. This task is usually impaired by damage to the left prefrontal cortex and so is used to assesses its functioning. Damage produces a failure to respond. That is, the patient produces one or two responses, e.g., *fix, fish*, …, but no more (Tucha, Smely, & Lange, 1999; Baldo & Shimamura, 1998). Furthermore, it is useful when generating instances of a category to be able to keep track of which ones have already been generated. However, damage to the prefrontal cortex may impair this ability independently of whether generation is impaired. Recall from Chapter 9 patients with prefrontal damage performed poorly in judging which of a pair of pictures they had seen more recently (Milner, et al., 1991). When generation and temporal order impairments are combined the patient can not monitor his own responses and so there is **perseveration** of the initial response, e.g., *fix, fish, fix, fix, …*(Crowe, 1992). When the frontal cortex is not functioning properly, the results are more catastrophic than an inability to generate lists of words. It is not possible to efficiently generate subgoals or to effectively keep track of them. When it is impossible to keep track of subgoals, even simple problems, such as cooking or shopping (Shallice & Burgess, 1991) become impossible.

FORMING AN INITIAL REPRESENTATION

Consider the following well-defined problem:

The price of a notebook is four times that of a pencil. The pencil costs 30¢ less than the notebook. What is the price of each?

This problem is presented in a purely verbal form. However, this form is not a very good representation for solving it. If you are like most people who have learned algebra, you will probably translate the problem into a different representation, perhaps as follows:

Let n = notebook and let p = pencil.

Initial state: n = 4p, and p = n − 30; hence, by adding 30 to both sides, p + 30 = n.

Substitute for n: p + 30 = 4p.

Subtract p from both sides: 30 = 3p.

Divide each side by 3: 10 = p.

Substitute for p in n = 4p: n = 4*10 = 40.

Therefore p = 10 and n = 40.

An algebraic representation makes use of both the verbal and the visuospatial representations to bring into play a set of operations for manipulating equations, making the problem quite simple to solve. Algebra makes use of naming to identify variables, but it also makes use of the visuospatial code in substituting variables and moving them from one side of the equation to the other. Problem formulation takes place within working memory. So the number of representations that can be maintained in working memory is a determiner of problem solving ability. Passolunghi, Cornoldi, and De Liberto (2000) divided fourth grade children into good and poor problems solvers on the basis of their ability to perform simple mathematics word problems like:

On Pascoli Street there are 45 shops. 3/5 of them sell clothes. How many clothes shops are there on Pascoli Street?

The poor problem solvers also performed more poorly on the Daneman and Carpenter (1983) test of working memory. In general, poor problem solvers were less able to inhibit the task irrelevent information in the word problems.

Sometimes there is more than one way to formulate a problem in order to reach a solution. One can also translate the verbal representation directly into the visuospatial code. When this problem was given to S., the remarkable mnemonist studied by Luria, S. reported imagining a series of visual equations, as illustrated in Figure 12.3. In Figure 12.3(a) he imagined a notebook beside four pencils. Then in Figure 12.3(b) he mentally pushed three pencils aside and replaced them with 30¢, since one pencil plus 30¢ equals the value of the notebook. Since 30¢ therefore is equivalent to three pencils, S. immedi-

FIGURE 12.3

Visual equations that S. used to solve pencil and notebook problem. (a) Original equation. (b) Substituting 30 cents for three pencils. (From Luria, 1968.)

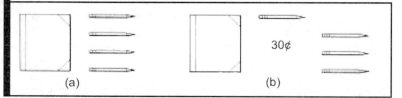

ately realized (presumably by simple arithmetic) that one pencil was worth 10¢ and the notebook was worth 40¢. Some of S.'s major problem solving operations were thus manipulations of visual images.

The example of the algebra problem illustrates the fact that a problem can have more than one representation because the person often defines the problem in his or her own way. Is there a best way to think of a problem in order to solve it more easily? Here we find some individual differences; e.g., some people claim they usually think visually. However, some problems can be solved much more easily with one form of representation than another.

One common example of a dramatic shift in representation is the game of number scrabble (Newell & Simon, 1972), which can be described as follows:

Each of the digits 1 through 9 is written on a separate piece of paper. Two players draw digits alternately. As soon as either player gets any three digits that sum to 15, that player wins. If all nine digits are drawn without a win, then the game is a draw.

FIGURE 12.4

Equivilence of number scrabble and tic-tac-toe

8	1	6
3	5	7
4	9	2

Most people who play this verbally encoded game a few times are still surprised when told that it is actually equivalent to the visuospatially encoded game tic-tac-toe. Figure 12.4 illustrates why they are equivalent. The nine digits can be placed on the squares in such a way that each horizontal, vertical, or diagonal row sums to 15. As a result, the rule for winning number scrabble (select three digits that add to 15) is equivalent to the rule for winning tic-tac-toe (occupy three squares in a row).

Even though the two games are equivalent, so that we can represent one in terms of the other, most people find tic-tac-toe easier. For one thing, the digits disappear; we no longer have to compute sums of numbers, as in number scrabble. Also, in tic-tac-toe scanning all possible solutions is easier. If players actually discover that number scrabble can be represented as tic-tac-toe, this insight may substantially alter the way they play the game. For example, many people know that a good strategy in tic-tac-toe is to occupy the corner squares. The equivalent strategy in number scrabble is to select even digits. This strategy might not occur to you unless you thought about it in terms of tic-tac-toe. This point is a general point about problem-solving strategies: the kind of representation will affect the strategies chosen.

TASK ANALYSIS

Another example of how problem representation can affect the ease of solution is the Buddhist monk problem. This problem, like many of those commonly discussed by psychologists, originated with the Gestalt psychologists of the early twentieth century (in this case, Karl Duncker). The problem is as follows:

One morning, exactly at sunrise, a Buddhist monk began to climb a tall mountain. A narrow path, no more than a foot or two wide, spiraled around the mountain to a glittering temple at the summit. The monk ascended at varying rates of speed, stopping many times along the way to rest and eat dried fruit he carried with him. He reached the temple shortly before sunset. After several days of fasting and meditation he began his journey back along the same path, starting at sunrise and again walking at variable speeds, with many pauses along the way. His average speed descending was, of course, greater than his average climbing speed. Show that there is a spot along the path that the monk will occupy on both trips at precisely the same time of day.

People who think about this problem verbally or algebraically are unlikely to solve it. They may conclude that it would be an improbable coincidence for the monk to find himself at the same spot at the same time on two different days. But one can actually visualize the solution, as the following report by a young woman suggests (Koestler, 1964, p. 184):

I tried this and that, until I got fed up with the whole thing, but the image of the monk in his saffron robe walking up the hill kept persisting in my mind. Then a moment came when, superimposed on this image, I saw another, more transparent one, of the monk walking down the hill, and I realized in a flash that the two figures must meet at some point in time—regardless of what speed they walk and how often each of them stops. Then I reasoned out what I already knew: whether the monk descends two days or three days later comes to the same; so I was quite justified in letting him descend on the same day, in duplicate so to speak.

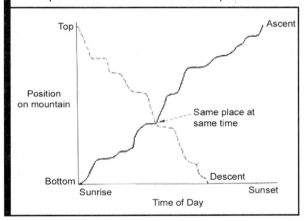

FIGURE 12.5
Graphical solution to Budhist monk problem.

Figure 12.5 provides a somewhat more abstract, visual solution to the problem. This graph plots the altitude of the monk on the mountain as a function of time of day, for both his ascent and his descent. We see that the two paths must cross, regardless of the monk's variable rates of progress. The point of intersection is the point on the path that the monk will occupy at the same time of day on both trips.

In the report quoted above the problem solver experiences a flash of insight when she visualizes the solution. Insight, a concept stressed by Gestalt psychologists who investigated problem solving, seems to involve a rapid reorganization of a problem representation that proceeds finding a solution. We will encounter other illustrations of insight as our discussion proceeds.

The successful visual solution to the Buddhist monk problem can be contrasted with the solution to the following mental paper-folding problem (from Adams, 1974, p. 63):

Picture a large piece of paper, 1/100 of an inch thick. In your imagination, fold it once (now having two layers), fold it once more (now having four layers), and continue folding it over on itself 50 times. It is true that it is impossible to fold any actual piece of paper 50 times. But for the sake of the problem, imagine that you can. About how thick would the 50-times-folded paper be?

At first glance this problem might seem like another problem requiring a visual solution. But in fact a visual solution is impossible. Note that the first fold will result in 2 times the original thickness, while the second fold will result in 2 x 2 = 4 times the original thickness. In fact, each fold increases the thickness by a factor of 2. So 50 folds will increase the paper's thickness by a factor of 2 multiplied by 2 exactly 50 times, or 2^{50}. This number works out to about 1,100,000,000,000,000, a number so large that the resulting thickness of the folded paper would approximate the distance from the earth to the sun. Obviously, visual imagery cannot produce this result. People who try to visualize a few folds and then extrapolate to estimate the thickness resulting from fifty folds invariably wildly underestimate the correct answer. In this case only a mathematical representation can easily produce an accurate solution.

The contrast between the Budhist monk problem and the mental paper folding problem highlights the importance of **task analysis**. Understanding the nature of the task and defining what is necessary for a solution is usually a major step toward finding a representation that can be used effectively to solve the problem.

We see, then, that a major part of forming an initial problem representation is selecting the best way to represent it. This selection process requires making implicit information explicit, weeding out irrelevant information, and noting what is forbidden and what is permitted by the problem.

REFORMULATING PROBLEM REPRESENTATIONS

When the initial problem representation is not adequate for the task of planning a solution it must be somehow reformulated (step 3 in the overall problem-solving process in Figure 12.1). In many ways the reformulation process resembles the process of forming an initial representation; in fact, in extreme cases the problem solver may essentially discard the initial representation and construct a new one.

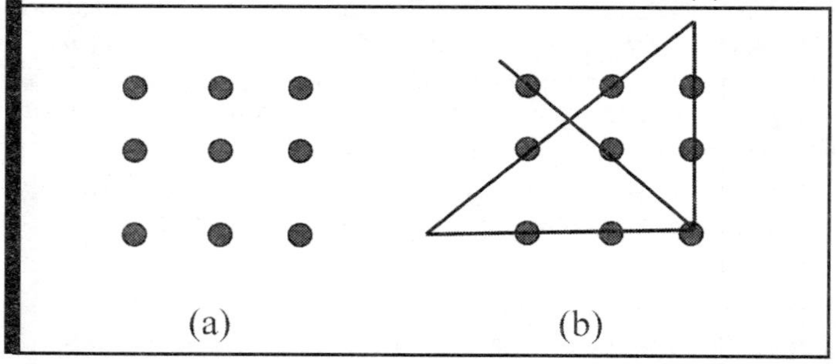

In other cases, however, the initial representation may undergo much more subtle changes. An example is provided by the

FIGURE 12.6

Nine-dot problem: (a) Configuration of nine-dots; (b) solution

(a)   (b)

well-known nine-dot problem. The problem is to draw four straight lines through all the nine dots depicted in Figure 12.6(a) without lifting the pencil from the paper. The Gestalt psychologists noticed that people see a square boundary around the nine dots. As a result, when most people are given this problem, they tend to assume that the four lines can't go outside the imaginary boundary. But, in fact, the problem can be solved only by extending some of the lines beyond the boundary, as in Figure 12.6(b). Weisberg and Alba (1981) enhanced problem reformulation by instructing some subjects, after they had made several

unsuccessful attempts, that it was necessary to draw lines outside the boundary to solve the problem. Although the problem still proved far from easy, about 25 percent of these subjects eventually solved the problem, whereas subjects in a control condition that did not receive such a hint invariably failed.

Knoblich, Ohlsson, and Raney (2001) used three matchstick arithmetic problems, shown in Figure 12.7, to study problem reformulation. In matchstick arithmetic the problem solver is faced with an incorrect arithmetic statement expressed in Roman numerals constructed out of matchsticks. The goal is to correct the arithmetic statement by moving a single matchstick from one position in the statement to another. Try to solve the problems before going on. Problem A is the easiest of the three. The matchstick in the 4 is moved to the right of the V to form a six and solve the problem. In

FIGURE 12.7

Make each arithmetic statement correct by moving one matchstick (Knoblich, et al., 2001).

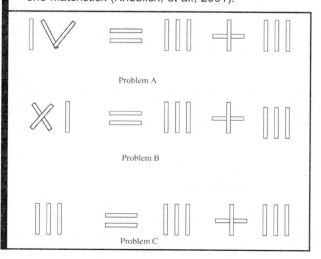

Problem A

Problem B

Problem C

Problem B one stick in the X must be moved to change it to a V. Knoblich et al. (2001) suggest that this problem is more difficult because the reformulation involves decomposing what is normally taken as a "chunk," the presentation of the X as a single character. In problem C one stick in the plus must be moved to change it to an equals, giving 3 equals 3 equals 3. Again this reformulation is difficult because it not only requires the decomposition of a chunk but the reformulation of constraints. The problem solver must focus on an operator rather than the numbers and must consider the possibility that it does not involve two numbers producing a third result. Knoblich et al. (2001) recorded the eye movements of problem solvers. People who eventually solved problem C had longer and longer fixations on the operators until they had the "aha" insight reaction, reformulated the problem, and solved it. In contrast, people who did not solve the problem did not show the pattern of increasing fixations on the operators.

Where does that reformulated representation of the problem that produces the "aha" insight come from? In the case of a **novice**, i.e., someone who has not worked on that kind of problem before, it must come from his general knowledge. In the case of the expert, it is domain specific knowledge from similar problems. First novice problem representation, and then expert problem solving, will be described.

NOTICING AND APPLYING ANALOGIES

Often a problem must be reformulated by modeling its representation after that of some structurally similar or analogous problem. An analogy can result in the reformulation of a problem such that the solution to a known problem can be used to plan a solution to the new one. Useful analogies can sometimes be found between concepts that are superficially very different. Gick and Holyoak (1980, 1983) investigated the use of such analogies in solving relatively ill-defined problems. Their results indicate that analogies from other knowledge domains are only occasionally useful in reformulating problems because the problem solver rarely notices their relevance. The problem they studied most extensively was the radiation problem made famous by the Gestalt psychologist Karl Duncker (1945). The problem runs as follows:

Suppose you are a doctor faced with a patient who has a malignant tumor in his stomach. To operate on the patient is impossible, but unless the tumor is destroyed, the patient will die. A kind of ray, at a sufficiently high intensity, can destroy the tumor. Unfortunately, at this intensity the healthy tissue that the rays pass through on the way to the tumor will also be destroyed. At lower intensities the rays are harmless to healthy tissue but will not affect the tumor, either. How can the rays be used to destroy the tumor without injuring the healthy tissue?

This problem is reasonably realistic, since it describes a situation similar to what actually arises in radiation therapy. Most of the problem components are reasonably well specified; however, the operations are extremely vague. The problem solver might imagine the possibilities of altering the effects of the rays or of avoiding contact between the rays and the healthy tissue. However, none of these operations immediately specify realizable actions; they remain at the level of wishful thinking.

Gick and Holyoak (1980) wanted to find out whether college students could use a remote analogy to develop a clearer problem representation and hence solve the problem. To provide the students with a potential analogy, the experimenters first had them memorize a story about the predicament of a general who wished to capture a fortress located in the center of a country. Many roads radiated outward from the fortress, but these roads were mined so that although small groups could pass over them safely, any large group would detonate the mines. Yet the general needed to get his entire large army to the fortress in order to launch a successful attack. Thus the general's situation was analogous to that of the doctor in the radiation problem.

The correspondences between the convergence version of the military story and the radiation problem are shown in Table 12.1. Even though the particular objects involved (e.g., army and rays, fortress and tumor) are very different, the basic relations that make the convergence solution possible are present in both. The goal, resources (and other objects), operations, and constraints are structurally similar, and

TABLE 12.1

Correspondences Between Two Convergence Problems and Their Schema (From Gick & Holyoak, 1983.)

Military problem

Representation:
Goal: Use army to capture fortress.
Resources: Sufficiently large army.
Operators: Divide army, move army, attack with army.
Constraint: Unable to send entire army along one road safely.
Solution plan: Send small groups along multiple roads simultaneously.
Outcome: Fortress captured by army.

Radiation Problem

Representation:
Goal: Use rays to destroy tumor.
Resources: Sufficiently powerful rays.
Operators: Reduce ray intensity, move ray source, administer rays.
Constraint: Unable to administer high-intensity rays from one direction safely.
Solution plan: Administer low-intensity rays from multiple directions simultaneously.
Outcome: Tumor destroyed by rays.

Convergence schema

Representation:
Goal: Use force to overcome a central target.
Resources: Sufficiently great force.
Operators: Reduce force intensity, move source of force, apply force.
Constraint: Unable to apply full force along one path safely.
Solution plan: Apply weak forces along multiple paths simultaneously.
Outcome: Central target overcome by force.

they can be matched, or "mapped," from one problem to the other. Because the military story provides clear operations (e.g., "divide the army"), subjects are able to use the mapping to construct corresponding operators (e.g., "reduce ray intensity") that can be used to solve the ray problem. The abstract structure common to the two problems can be viewed as a schema for convergence problems. The schema is described at the bottom of Table 12.1.

After the students memorized the story of the general's predicament, they were given the ray problem to solve. Twelve students were given the hint that the story they memorized would help them solve it. Eleven of these students found the analogy and suggested the simultaneous application of weak rays to solve the ray problem. However, only one of fifteen students who did not receive the hint thought of this solution.

Other experiments by Gick and Holyoak (1983) further demonstrated that subjects often fail to make use of a potentially helpful analogy unless its relevance is pointed out to them. The difficulty of noticing distant analogies is perhaps not surprising, since the underlying similarity is quite abstract, whereas the many superficial differences between the two cases are very obvious.

Sometimes, people are explicitly taught to think about one domain in terms of a very different one so that the problem of noticing the analogy is avoided. For example, students are often told that electricity behaves like a hydraulic system. As depicted in Figure 12.8, electricity is analogous to water flowing through a pipe; batteries act like reservoirs, and resistors act like constrictions in the pipe. Gentner and Gentner (1983) have demonstrated that the ease with which high school and college students solve particular types of electricity problems depends on the degree to which the analogy they have been taught generates correct inferences about the relevant electrical concepts.

FIGURE 12.8

Example of analogy: Electric current and water system.

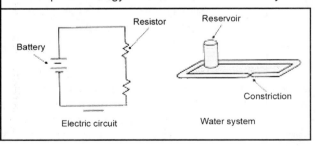

Another way in which the difficulty of noticing distant analogies can be overcome is by encouraging abstraction of the underlying general similarities. Gick and Holyoak (1983) demonstrated this by having subjects first read two convergence stories, such as the military story and a story about fire fighting (e.g., a story in which the hero extinguished an oil well fire by using multiple small hoses). The subjects were asked to describe ways in which the stories were similar, thus encouraging them to combine the common elements into a single prototype. When such subjects subsequently attempted to solve the radiation problem, they were much more likely to generate the parallel solution (either with or without a hint to use the stories) than were subjects who received just one prior story.

These results suggest that analogical mapping is used not only to reformulate novel problems but also to construct more abstract problem representations that can be stored in memory and later retrieved and applied.

The consideration of enough similar problems can lead to the construction of an efficient schema for encoding the problem and generating potential solutions. Expertise in a problem domain is based in part on knowledge of a specialized schema.

PROBLEM SCHEMAS IN PHYSICS

In domains such as physics, in which knowledge is highly systematized, the role of specialized problem schemas is especially apparent (Larkin, McDermott, Simon, & Simon, 1980). A major factor differentiating experts from novices is that experts have both more and better problem schemas, which allow them to rapidly classify problems and retrieve relevant solution procedures.

A study of experts and novices in the domain of physics problems by Chi, Feltovich, and Glaser (1981) is especially illuminating. When subjects were asked to sort problems into clusters on the basis of similarity, novices tended to form categories based on relatively surface features of the problem statements (e.g., inclined-plane problems). In contrast, experts sorted the problems with respect to applicable physical laws (e.g., problems solvable by the principle of conservation of energy). If you compare the problem pairs depicted in Figure 12.9, which were grouped together by novices, with those depicted in Figure 12.10, which were grouped by experts, you will get a sense of the greater degree of abstraction involved in the experts' problem categories. Further differences were apparent in protocols in which subjects described their problem categories. The experts were able to articulate rules for realizable actions—i.e., explicit solution procedures for problems of a given type. The novices' protocols, on the other hand, even when they mentioned abstract problem features, usually did not reveal such rules for action. Rather, their rules seemed to set further abstract subgoals that lacked specific solution procedures.

FIGURE 12.9

Diagrams of two problems categorized together by novices and samples of explanations given (from Chi, et al., 1981.)

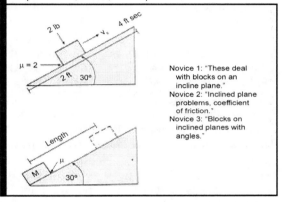

Novice 1: "These deal with blocks on an incline plane."
Novice 2: "Inclined plane problems, coefficient of friction."
Novice 3: "Blocks on inclined planes with angles."

FIGURE 12.10

Diagrams of two problems categorized together by experts and samples of explanations given (from Chi, et al., 1981.)

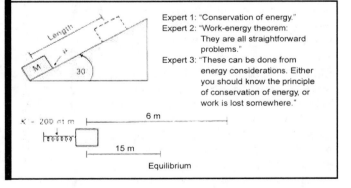

Expert 1: "Conservation of energy."
Expert 2: "Work-energy theorem: They are all straightforward problems."
Expert 3: "These can be done from energy considerations. Either you should know the principle of conservation of energy, or work is lost somewhere."

EXPERTISE IN CHESS AND GO

The most detailed studies of what a problem schema is were done on the game of chess. The pioneering work on chess skills was done by De Groot (1965). His basic question was simple: What makes a master chess player better than a weaker player? To investigate this question, he collected protocols from some of the best chess players in the world as they selected chess moves. De Groot's findings were quite different from what most people might expect. The master chess players did not seem to reason in any unusual ways. Nor did the masters search through more possible moves before selecting one. In fact, if anything, the masters considered fewer alternatives than did ordinary players. The difference was that the masters explored particularly good moves, whereas weaker players spent more time considering bad moves. Somehow, the good moves seemed to be immediately apparent to the master players.

The most striking difference between masters and weaker players emerged in a test of perceptual and memory abilities. In this test a chess position, such as the middle game (board position in the middle of an actual game) shown in Figure 12.11(a), was displayed for 5 seconds and then removed. The player then had to reconstruct the board position from memory. Chase and Simon (1973) performed this experiment with a master player (an expert), a class A player (a very good player), and a beginning (B) player. Figure 12.12 (a) plots the number of pieces correctly recalled by each player over seven trials. As shown, memory performance is ordered in the same way as the level of chess skill: the master recalled the most pieces, followed by the class A player and the beginner.

This result might suggest that master players simply have the best memories. But this conclusion is not quite right. Chase and Simon also performed the memory test with positions in which the pieces were arranged randomly, as in Figure 12.11(b). With these random games the superiority of the master player completely disappeared. In fact, as Figure 12.12(b) indicates, the master actually tended to recall fewer correct pieces than the weaker players.

Apparently, then, the master players are especially good at a very specialized task—encoding actual chess positions. You might wonder whether the master players perform so well because they can recognize large meaningful chunks in board positions. Chase and Simon (1973) found evidence that this recognition is indeed the case. They timed how long the subjects paused between each placement of a piece as they recalled the positions on the first trial. If the pause was less than 2 seconds long, the two successive pieces were defined as belonging to the same chunk. If the pause was longer than 2 seconds, the two pieces were defined as belonging to different chunks. Chase and Simon found that pieces belonging to the same chunk tended to be recalled together on both the first and second trials, even though the order of recall within a cluster varied. This result suggests that each chunk is stored in memory as a single compound representation.

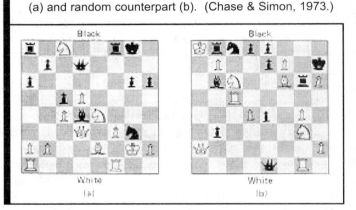

FIGURE 12.11
Examples of chess configurations from real middle game (a) and random counterpart (b). (Chase & Simon, 1973.)

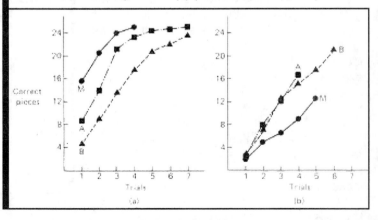

FIGURE 12.12
Number of pieces recalled correctly by master (M); class A player (A), and beginner (B) over trials for actual board positions (a); for random board positions (b) (Chase & Simon, 1973).

If the unitization hypothesis is correct, the master should have recalled larger chunks than the weaker players, and the master did. In addition to recalling larger chunks, the master also recalled more chunks. This result suggests that the master is able to establish more associations in memory between chunks, so that one chunk can serve as a retrieval cue for another.

Recall that only a limited number of representations can be maintained in awareness. Britton and Tesser (1982) hypothesized that if experts activated more knowledge when performing a problem-solving task, they would be slower to detect a target that was part of a secondary task. Both expert and novice chess players were given chess problems to solve, but they were also told to press a telegraph key when they heard a click. The expert took longer than the novices to respond to the clicks. Finally, Gobet and Simon (1996) compared the hypothesis that a chess master automatically recognizes useful game positions with the hypothesis that a chess master engages in deliberate search. To compare these hypotheses they rated the performance of the word chess champion, Gary Kasparaov, both in normal chess matches and when playing multiple opponents. They reasoned that going from an average time of 3 minutes to 30 seconds per move should disrupt the generation process more than it would automatic recognition. They found only a small reduction in Kasparov's performance in the multiple matches, which they interpreted as supporting the automatic recognition hypothesis.

What is the basis for the perception of a chunk? One might expect that two pieces would be united together if they were related in some way that was important to the game. Chase and Simon (1973) examined five relations between two pieces that are important in chess:

1. One piece can attack another.
2. One piece can defend another.
3. Two pieces can be on adjacent squares.
4. Two pieces can have the same color.
5. Two pieces can be of the same type (e.g., both pawns).

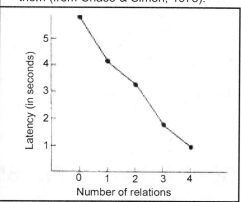

FIGURE 12.13
Average latency between two pieces as a function of a number of relations between them (from Chase & Simon, 1973).

Figure 12.13 plots the length of the pause between the recall of one piece and the next as a function of the number of relations between them. As the figure shows, the more relations there were between the two pieces, the shorter was the pause. This result suggests that the more ways two pieces are related, the more likely they are to be coded into a single chunk. Chunks therefore contain information about important relations between pieces that will make this information readily available to help plan the next move.

Simon and Gilmartin (1973) developed a computer program that simulated the way chess players store board positions in memory. The program contained information about many familiar patterns of pieces. Simon and Gilmartin used the performance of their program to estimate how many patterns a master chess player has stored in memory. Their estimate was 30,000. This estimate may seem like a very large number of patterns, but it is less than the number of words (another type of meaningful pattern) that a good reader can recognize. And a master chess player will have spent as much time studying chess positions as a good reader will have spent reading. In fact, the most basic requirement for becoming a master player appears to be an incredible amount of practice: as many as 50,000 hours spent working with chess positions. As a result of this practice, the master is able to recognize complex chess patterns as chunks, just as a skilled reader recognizes words as chunks.

The fact that skilled chess players seem to have their knowledge of board positions organized into large perceptual chunks has important consequences for how they select moves. Good players often seem to know immediately after looking at a board what the best move is. Simon (1973) suggests that the selection of chess moves is partly based on a set of rules, built up through years of experience. These rules can be stated in an if-then form: "If a particular board configuration is present, then a particular move should be taken." In other words, perception of a familiar perceptual chunk leads directly to an appropriate action.

Related evidence has been found with another complex board game, the oriental game of go. The game involves placing black and white stones on a grid and fighting for territory on the board. A player can capture an enemy stone by surrounding it with his or her own pieces. Judith Reitman (1976) studied a go master and a beginner, using the kinds of memory tests used earlier with chess players. As in chess, the go master player showed superior memory for real go positions but not for random positions.

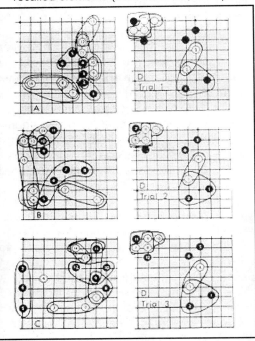

FIGURE 12.14
Examples of go master's penciled partitioning of meaningful patterns and orders in which he recalled elements (from Reitman, 1976).

The go master also tended to recall pieces in clusters. Figure 12.14 shows several examples of board positions (labeled A through D) that were presented to the master. The circles show how the master himself partitioned the pieces into chunks. Notice that the go master saw the chunks as overlapping in many different ways. That is, the same piece was often included in several different clusters. The numbers on the pieces in Figure 12.14 give the order in which the pieces were recalled on that trial (if there is no number, the piece was not recalled). As shown, pieces that were part of the same pattern had a very strong tendency to be recalled together.

The study of chess and go reveals that the perceptual skills that support expertise in problem solving rely on the same kinds of operations and procedures as other perceptual skills, such as reading and face recognition. The only difference is that other perceptual skills are an end in themselves, while the perceptual skills that support expertise serve a function within the problem schema. Recognizing clusters of chess pieces is only meaningful within the context of planning a move, it has no function by itself.

GENERATING A PROBLEM SOLUTION

The process of generating a problem solution can be viewed as a search through a space of possible solutions (Newell & Simon, 1972). In many problems a major difficulty is that the space to be searched is potentially enormous. This feature is the principle behind the use of combination locks. If a lock on a bank vault has ten dials, each of which can be set at any number from 00 to 99, then there are 100^{10}, or 100 billion billion, combinations. Since only one randomly chosen combination will open the lock, the sheer size of the search space will protect the bank vault from a thief who tries to use the generate-test method to discover the correct combination.

Another example of a large problem space is the problem of winning a game of chess. The course of a chess game can be represented as a tree similar to the one shown in Figure 12.15. The top node in the tree represents the initial position on the chessboard. Each of the possible alternative moves will lead to a different new position. At an average choice point a chess player may have twenty or thirty possible alternatives; for simplicity only three alternatives are shown at each choice point in the figure. At the second level in the tree the opponent will select a move, again changing the board position. The first player then chooses one of the next set of possible moves, etc. As Figure 12.15 illustrates, the final positions at the bottom of the tree determine how the game ends—whether the first player wins, ties, or loses. The dark line in the figure shows a path through the tree (i.e., a sequence of moves) that leads to a win. Only a few of the possible paths are shown in Figure 12.15, and all the paths are just four moves long. An actual chess game will often be fifty or more moves long.

FIGURE 12.15

Hypothetical decision tree for a game showing path of moves leading to win for first player.

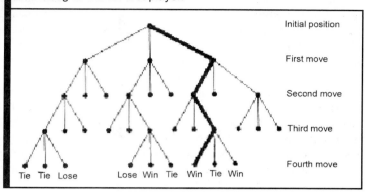

There is a clear way to win a game that can be represented as a decision tree, as in Figure 12.1. This method is to explore every possible path in the tree to determine its final outcome and then to always select a move that sends the game along a path that cannot end in a win for the opponent. The problem with this approach is that the number of paths that would have to be considered at each choice point may be astronomical. An astronomical number will certainly arise in a complex game like chess, in which the tree of possible moves is both very wide (many alternatives at each choice point) and very deep (many moves to complete a game). As a result, the only effective way to play a good chess game—even for a computer—is to use a problem-solving method that sharply restricts the search space.

PLANNING

Chess also illustrates the general usefulness of breaking down a problem into parts, sometimes called the problem reduction approach (Nilsson, 1971). In this approach the original problem is broken down into subproblems, or subgoals, so that a solution to all the subproblems implies a solution to the overall problem. In chess it is usual easier to first take other pieces as steps along the path to capturing the king. A set of subgoals constitutes a plan for finding a problem solution. Reducing a problem to a hierachically organized set of subgoals is called **planning**. The hierarchically organized subgoals are called the **plan**. In planning you must substitute imagination for action in order to prepare for action. A plan is a procedure for a sequence of actions that implicitly makes a prediction: "If I take the following actions, then I will achieve a solution." One of the most basic aspects of problem solving is that a plan is created and then mentally tested before overt actions are taken.

A heuristic strategy for finding subgoals is **means-ends analysis**. This procedure requires problem solvers to determine the ends they are trying to achieve and the means that will serve to reach these ends. In doing so, problem solvers set up subgoals. Means-ends analysis is used frequently in everyday life. Consider the problem of cooking a Chinese dinner. You might work through this problem by using means-ends analysis and by thinking approximately as follows: "What's the difference between what I have now (my initial state) and dinner (the goal state)? A cooked meal. What is needed to cook a meal? Food, an oven. I have an oven. I also have some food, but not Chinese food. What do I do to get Chinese food? Go to the grocery store. The grocery store is down the street. How can I get there? Walk." And so on.

As you can see from this example, a major component of means-ends analysis consists of two steps applied repeatedly: (1) identifying the differences between the current state and the desired goal, and (2) applying an operation to reduce one of these differences. This two-step procedure is often called difference reduction. The method can be illustrated by using a simple algebra problem: Solve the equation ax - b = x for x. The steps to a solution are outlined in Table 12.2. The goal state for this problem can be described as "term x on the left-hand side of the equation; all other terms on the right." At each step the current known version of the equation is compared with the goal state and differences are noted. Then an algebraic operation (e.g., "add a term to both sides of the equation"), which will eliminate one of the differences, is selected and applied. The process is then repeated until no differences remain.

Note that a major difference between the algebra problem and the dinner problem is that the algebra problem does not require subgoals. Everything needed to solve the algebra problem is available from the start, which was not the case in the example of cooking dinner. Since the required

TABLE 12.2
Method of Difference Reduction Applied to Simple Algebra Problem

Problem: Solve the equation ax - b = x for x.

Goal state: Term x on the left-hand side of the equation; all other terms on the right.

Steps

1. Current state: ax - b = x.
   Differences: a on left, b on left, x on right.
   Apply operation: Add b to both sides.

2. Current state: ax = x + b.
   Differences: a on left, x on right.
   Apply operation: Subtract x from both sides.

3. Current state: ax - x = b.
   Differences: a on left, x on left twice.
   Apply operation: Factor x on left.

4. Current state: x(a -1) = b.
   Differences: (a - 1) on left.
   Apply operation: Divide both sides by (a -1).

5. Current state: x = b/ (a -1).
   Differences: None.
   Problem solved.

food was not immediately available, we had to set up a subgoal of getting food, etc. Problems that require subgoals are often difficult because they require extra information to be stored in memory. The person has to remember what the subgoals are and the reasons for achieving them. If we didn't remember why the subgoals were established in the first place, we might find ourselves in the position of going to the bank and then forgetting why we went there.

A more complex problem that illustrates the importance of planning and setting up subgoals in the strategy of means-ends analysis is the well-known Tower of Hanoi puzzle depicted in Figure 12.16. A number of disks (three in Figure 12.16) must be moved from peg A to peg C. Only one disk (the top disk on a peg) can be moved at a time, and no disk can ever

FIGURE 12.16
Initial state for three-disk Tower of Hanoi

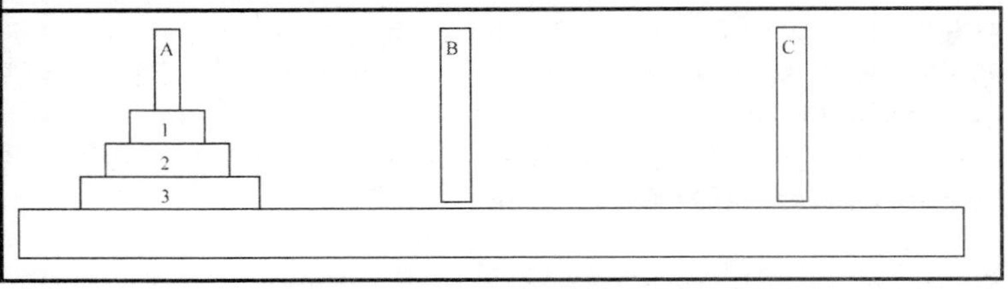

be placed on top of a disk smaller than itself. This puzzle derives its name from a legend that a group of monks near Hanoi are working on a version of the puzzle that uses sixty-four disks. The legend says that the world will end when they finish the puzzle, which at the rate of one perfect move every second, will take them about a trillion years (Raphael, 1976).

The three-disk version of the puzzle is considerably more tractable, but it still requires a degree of planning in selecting moves and generating subgoals that will bring the problem closer to a solution. For example, clearly the solution to the puzzle in Figure 12.16 requires that the largest disk (disk 3) be placed on peg C first. (This approach is an illustration of working backward from the goal to solve a problem.) Therefore we begin by setting up a subgoal of getting disk 3 to peg C. Also clear is that disks 1 and 2 have to be moved from disk 3 before the latter can be moved. This step results in a further subgoal of moving disks 1 and 2, which in turn sets up a subgoal of first moving disk 1.

But should disk 1 go to peg B or peg C? Here looking ahead a few moves will help. For if we move disk 1 to peg B, then disk 2 will have to go on peg C. But then disk 3 won't be able to go on peg C. On the other hand, if we begin by moving disk 1 to peg C, the following sequence will accomplish the subgoal of moving disk 3 to peg C:

Disk 1 to peg C;
Disk 2 to peg B;
Disk 1 to peg B;
Disk 3 to peg C.

Having completed the initial subgoal, we can set up the next subgoal, getting disk 2 onto peg C. This step is easily accomplished:

Disk 1 to peg A;
Disk 2 to peg C.

Then a final move (disk 1 to peg C) completes the puzzle.

Notice that this approach to the Tower of Hanoi puzzle involves formulating a hierarchy of subgoals (e.g., the subgoal "move disk 3 to peg C," generates the subgoal "move disk 2 off disk 3," which in turn generates the subgoal "move disk 1 off disk 2"). This puzzle becomes increasingly difficult when more disks are used, because the subgoal hierarchies get deeper. Thinking far enough ahead in planning moves and remembering how all the subgoals that are generated relate to each other becomes difficult. Egan and Greeno (1974) observed subjects as they worked on a six-disk Tower of Hanoi problem. They found that the probability of a subject's making an error on a move increased with the number of subgoals that had to be set up between moves. Ward and Allport (1997) found that the most difficult moves in the development of a solution were those that initiated a subgoal where there were alternative moves available. In addition to the Tower of Hanoi puzzle (Egan & Greeno, 1974), the Water Jugs puzzle (Atwood & Polson, 1980), and the Missionaires and Cannibals puzzle (Jeffries, Polson, Razran, & Atwood, 1977), as well as chess problems, have been used to study planning.

Once all the steps of a problem cannot be held in working memory people do not plan more than one or two moves ahead when trying to solve a multi-step problem (Simon, 1975). In selecting the next step, a novice problem solver first relies on recognition in working memory to avoid returning to solutions to subproblems he or she has already tried (Atwood & Polson, 1970). However, in a complicated problem in which there are many subgoals with many possible solutions, working memory may be inadequate for recognizing all attempted solutions. So in planning a move the problem solver may test it by using the rules of the problem and the generation process to retrospectively reconstruct whether it has been tried before (Davis, 2000).

PROACTIVE INTERFERENCE

As the flowchart in Figure 12.1 indicates, the first two steps of the problem solving process do not follow each other in a fixed order. Rather, the problem solver is basically trying to plan a potential solution (step 2). However, if no plan can be constructed (perhaps because the representation is inadequate in some way), an attempt will be made to reformulate the representation (step 3), after which step 2 will be repeated. Once a plan is actually constructed, it can be tested (step 4). If the plan fails, the process cycles back to step 2 to generate a new plan. In this section we will consider how a solution plan can be generated (step 2) when the problem representation is adequate.

The generation of potential solutions may involve both verbal generation and imagination. Proactive interference from the earlier, discarded, potential solutions makes reformulating a problem difficult. Generating the first few candidates is usually easy, but then thinking of new possibilities becomes quite difficult. Since discarded solutions are likely to be associated with many of the same cues as new solutions, they are a source of proactive interference in producing new solutions. Within the problem solving situation PI manifests itself in two ways, called problem solving set and functional fixedness.

Problem-solving set. As we saw in the last chapter, the availability of representations influences reasoning. Availability influences problem solving as well. In the case of problem solving people often exhibit a problem-solving set—a tendency to repeat a solution process that has been previously successful.

The classic demonstration of a problem-solving set (einstellung in German) was a series of experiments by Luchins (1942; Luchins & Luchins, 1950). Luchins tested over nine thousand subjects, ranging in age from elementary school children to adults, on water jar problems. A typical series of problems is shown in Table 12.3. The subject is asked to imagine three jars of various specified capacities and told to find a way to get a required amount of water. For the first problem in Table 12.3 the solution is to fill jar B, then to take out the volume of jar A, and then to take out the volume of jar C twice. The series of problems is set up so that this same general solution (B - A - 2C) works for the first five problems. This series is designed to establish a problem-solving set.

On trials 6 and 7 there are two possible solutions: the previously successful formula and also a simpler one. One measure of the effect of a set is how often people discover the simpler solution. Finally, trial 8 is a problem for which the earlier formula won't work but a simpler one (A - C) will. Luchins found that subjects very often failed to notice the simpler solutions to problems 6 and 7 and sometimes failed to solve problem 8 at all. Seemingly, an initially successful solution procedure tends to be repeated, blocking discovery of alternative solutions.

The set effect is hardly surprising given what we know about learning and memory. Attempting to apply previously successful solution procedures to similar new problems is only reasonable. Educators can minimize the negative aspects of set by carefully selecting the examples used to teach skills in solving a particular type of problem. To begin by exposing the students to only a narrow range of examples is unwise. Although the students may learn how to solve the initial examples, the limited problem-solving rules that they acquire may actually interfere with their ability to solve a wider range of problems.

Functional fixedness. Another kind of negative influence of memory on problem solving is illustrated by the following experiment. Duncker (1945) presented subjects with several objects lying on a table and asked them to find a way to use them to support a board. The available objects included two iron joints and a pair of pliers. The solution to the problem was to use the iron joints to support one end of the board and the pliers to support the other. In one condition the subject first had to use the pliers to free the board. Duncker found that the subjects who began the

TABLE 12.3

Typical Series of Water Jar Problems (Source: based on Luchins, 1942).

	Capacity of given jars (in quarts)			
Problem	A	B	C	Amount of quarts to get
1	21	127	3	100
2	14	163	25	99
3	18	43	10	5
4	9	42	6	21
5	20	59	4	31
(B – A – 2C is the solution to the first five problems.)				
6	23	49	3	20
(A – C also works.)				
7	15	39	3	18
(A + C also works.)				
8	28	76	3	25
(A – C works, but B – A – 2C doesn't.)				

experiment by using the pliers to free the board were less likely to find the solution of using the pliers as a support. He called this phenomenon **functional** fixedness: If an object has one established use in a situation, subjects have difficulty in using the object in another way.

Functional fixedness, like set, is a block to effective problem solving resulting from prior experience. But whereas set is a tendency to repeat previously successful problem-solving operations, functional fixedness is a tendency to think of past uses of an object to the exclusion of novel potential uses. Functional fixedness can also be understood in terms of memory processes. The most familiar functions of objects are likely to be directly stored with the concept in the semantic network (e.g., the concept pliers might be associated with the function "used for grasping objects"). These familiar uses will be the most available ones, especially if they have already been activated in the current context (as occurred when the pliers were used to free the board). But the perceptual attributes of an object (e.g., its shape, size, or weight) may be compatible with other potential uses, sometimes called affordances (J. J. Gibson, 1966). A pair of pliers can therefore be used as a support. However, these potential uses are usually harder to think of than functions that have already been stored in memory.

Perceptual set and functional fixedness are the downside of semantic priming. Whatever functions of objects are activated in a given context will be most readily available for generation of a solution to a problem. Indeed, Per Saugstad showed that success in generating a problem solution can be predicted by measures of the availability to the problem solver of the functions required for a solution.

Saugstad (1955) showed 57 college students objects to be used later in a problem in which some hollow tubes and putty had to be used to blow out a candle 6 feet away. Nothing was mentioned of the problem itself. Subjects were simply instructed to list all the possible functions that the objects might serve. All 13 subjects who listed functions for the objects that were later necessary to solve the problem did, in fact, solve the problem. In contrast, only 58% of the remaining subjects solved the problem. In another experiment, Saugstad and Raaheim (1960) demonstrated the functions of some objects, which turned out to be critical to the solution of a problem, to 20 male high school students. Nineteen of the boys later solved the problem. In contrast, only 10 of 45 boys who had not seen the demonstration were able to solve the problem.

Another task that illustrates functional fixedness is the so-called candle problem (Duncker, 1945). In this problem subjects are given the task of affixing a candle to a wall and lighting it. The objects available for use are some matches, a candle, and a matchbox filled with thumbtacks. The optimal solution, as defined by Duncker, is to use the tacks to fix the matchbox to the wall, put the candle on the box, and then light it with the matches. Duncker found that more subjects used the box as a candle holder when it was presented empty than when it was full of tacks. He considered functional fixedness to be a perceptual problem. Seeing the box as a container for tacks makes it difficult for subjects to see it also as a platform. Presenting it empty makes it easier for them to perceive the box as a candle holder.

Sam Glucksberg, Robert Weisberg, and their colleagues (Glucksberg & Danks, 1968; Glucksberg & Weisberg, 1966; Weisberg & Suls, 1973) performed several experiments that illustrate how subtle changes in the experimental situation can affect how the candle problem is solved. For example, sometimes the experimenter would name the box while giving instructions to the subject, while sometimes he only named the tacks. More subjects solved the problem by using the box as a platform (the box solution) when the box itself was labeled. One way to interpret this result is to suppose that when only the tacks are labeled, the box that holds them is not really "seen" as a separate object. But once the name box is heard, the subjects become aware not only of the box as an object but also of the various familiar uses of boxes that are stored in the conceptual network. Since these familiar uses are likely to include the use of boxes to support other objects, hearing the name box makes it easier to find the solution.

Glucksberg and Danks (1968) also found cases where hearing the name of an object actually hindered problem solving. In this experiment the subject's task was to complete an electric circuit. The objects provided were batteries, a bulb, a switch, and a wrench. The solution was to use the wrench to complete the circuit. In this case subjects were more likely to find the solution when they were required to refer to the wrench by a nonsense name such as vorpin rather than by the familiar name wrench.

Why did the name wrench interfere with solving this problem, whereas the name box facilitated the process in our previous example? The critical difference is that the box had to be used in a relatively familiar way (as a support), whereas the wrench had to be used in a more novel way (to conduct electricity). The name wrench therefore activated known uses stored in memory that actually conflicted with the critical potential use, which could be discovered by exploring the perceptual properties of the object.

Functional fixedness requires that you know and pay attention to an object's typical use. When given a box of tacks that actually had to be used as a support to a solve a problem, six-year-old children showed functional fixedness but five-year old children did not. The five-year-old children were insufficiently influenced by the typical use of the tack box to impair their performance (German & Defeyter, 2000).

Problem-solving behavior requires such extensive conscious manipulation of representations that we would not expect to find much evidence of it in nonhuman species. In fact, only a few animals engage in anything that closely resembles human problem-solving behavior. In particular, the classic studies of the Gestalt psychologist Wolfgang Kohler (1925) demonstrated that chimpanzees can sometimes overcome functional fixedness. In one sequence the chimp Sultan was in a cage and noticed a banana lying outside out of reach. In the cage was a bushy tree. Sultan suddenly went to the tree, broke off a branch, ran back to the bars and used the branch to bring the banana into reach. What was at first not even a separate object was suddenly recognized as a potential tool.

INTELLIGENCE AND TALENT

Suppose the entire senior class at a high school were given a bunch of different cognitive tests, measuring as many different abilities as you could think of; visual recognition and recall, auditory recognition and recall, drawing ability, musical ability, logical reasoning, etc. Scores on all the different tests are correlated across individuals. What patten of correlations would you expect? You might expect that performance on some tests would be positively correlated. For example, you might expect that students who did well on visual recognition would do well on visual recall. You might expect that there would be no correlation between some tests. For example, you might expect no correlation between visual and auditory acuity. You might even expect there to be a negative correlation between some tests because people who relied heavily on one kind of ability might not develop another ability. However, when the mathematical techniques for computing correlations were first invented a little over a hundred years ago, and this kind of comparison was tried, the results were surprising. In general, across all kinds of cognitive tests, Charles Spearman (1927) found that the correlations were positive. Some people tended to do better on all the tests and other people tended to do worse on all the tests. Similarly, students tend to do about the same in all their subjects in school. An A student tends to get all As and Bs, a B student tends to get all Bs and Cs, etc. Spearman attributed the correlation in test performance to some general ability, g, that some people had more of than others. Of course, each test also required specific abilities, s_1, s_2, etc.

INTELLIGENCE TESTING

The tests that are today called intellignce tests have two origins (Tuddenham, 1962). At the beginning of the twentieth century, the Binet-Henri test was a collection of simple skill tests developed as a predictor of scholastic achievement to determine which French school children required special education. This test was translated into English by Lewis B. Termin of Stanford University and hence is known in the United States as the Stanford-Binet (the Stanford revision of the Binet test.) David Wechsler was a clinical neuropsychologist who had the task of evaluating whether people brought to Bellevue Hospital in New York City were mentally competent. He collected the scores of normal adults on a battery of simple cognitive tests measuring such things as vocabulary, analogies, and arithmetic.   Hence, the Wechsler Adult Intelligence Test (WAIS) gave a **deviation score.**   The score indicated how far the individual's score deviated (above or below) the mean of the normal population.   The mean is set at 100.   So a score above a hundred is better than average and less than 100 is worse than average.   Since intelligence tests are collections of simple subtests they provide a good way of measuring g. However, intelligence tests do not measure learning ability.

The concept of a hypothetical general ability g has long been bound up with the question of the extent to which g, if it exists, is determined by a person's heredity or their environment.   Obviously, performance on an intelligence test is partly influenced by environment.   Someone who has never learned to read or do arithmetic is not going to do very well.   Scores on intelligence tests do not become stable over time until school age.   Furthermore, as education improved in the twentieth century, the population mean on intelligence tests increased by about 3 points per decade (Flynn, 1987).   However, the effect of the environment does not rule out an effect of heredity.   Studies of identical twins reared together have found correlations of 0.80 in their test performance, which is higher than for nontwin siblings or for unrelated individuals (Bouchard, Lykken, McGue, Segal, & Tellegen, 1990; Plomin & Loehlin, 1989).   This works out to IQ being about 50% the result of genetics for whites living in the relatively homogeneous educational environments of the United States and Great Britain.   The percent of the variance due to genetics is less among members of population groups living in less homogeneous educational and social environments (Ceci, 1993).   Rowe, Jacobson, and van der Ord (2000) compared the per cent of variability in IQ due to genetics in adolescents raised by highly educated versus poorly educated parents.   Presumably, all highly educated parents provide their children with rich educational environments, so the level of eduction all the children in this group received was uniformly high.   However, presumably the levels of education that the poorly educated parents provided their children were more variable.   For the adolescents raised by the highly educated parents 79% of the variance was attributed to heredity and 0% to environment.   But for the adolescents raised by poorly educated parents 26% of the variance was attributed to heredity and 23% to environment.

GENERAL ABILITY

How genetics exerts its influence on IQ is not known.   It appears to be mediated by environmental factors that influence the development of IQ over time.   The correlation between the IQs of children and their biological parents is low at birth and does not become significant until 16 years of age (Plomin, Faulker, Corley, & DeFries, 1997).   As we have seen, newborn infants can already recognize things they have seen (or heard).   Furthermore, when given a choice between a novel or familiar input, they spend more time looking at the familiar input.   Also, when the same pattern is shown to an infant repeatedly the infant spends less time looking at it on each trial.   Infants differ in the amount of novelty preference they show.   In a classic study, Joseph Fagan (Fagan & Singer, 1983) showed that the stronger an infant's novelty preference was at 3 to 7 months the higher their IQ score was up to 7 years later (see also Bornstein & Sigman, 1986).   These results suggest that some people from the very beginning of life are more efficient at learning than others and this leads to a greater growth in IQ.   However, whether there is a single factor underlying this efficiency, such as a preference for novely, or an ability to inhibit processing irrelevant inputs, or some combination of factors, has not been determined.   All of these hypotheses refer to some ability associated with a function of the prefrontal cortex.   In fact, tests that require higher levels of g are associated with a higher level of activity in the lateral prefrontal cortex (Duncan, Seitz, Ruediger, Kolodny, Bor, Herzog, Ahmed, Newell, & Emslie, 2000).

However, the prefrontal cortex has several different functions, each of which also requires the functioning of some other brain area.   Both autistic individuals and individuals with Williams syndrome have impaired abilities associated with prefrontal functions.   However, both types of individuals have very specific impairments, in social and linguistic communication, and visual comparison, respectively, rather than a general decline in g.   For both groups the most prominent congenital defect in brain anatomy is not the prefrontal cortex but the medial temporal cortex for autistic individuals (Dawson, et al., 2002) and in other areas of the brain for individuals with Williams syndrome. If the functioning of the prefrontal cortex was the basis of single, general ability, which contributed to the learning of all other abilities, then one would expect different tests of prefrontal functioning would correlate more highly with one another and with g than tests of other brain functions. However, Rabbitt and Lowe (2000) pointed out that neither was the case.

In fact, what intelligence (or g) is is unclear, except in the statistical sense of the correlation about the scores of different tests. Whether g reflects a single cognitive ability or the effects of several abilities has always been controversial. Thurstone (1938) defined intelligence by seven primary abilities: verbal comprehension, verbal fluency, number, space, memory, inductive reasoning, and perceptual speed. Many modern theorists have also redefined intelligence as sets of specialized abilities, rather than as a single general ability (Ceci, 1996; Gardner, 1983; Sternberg, 1985).

Whether or not there is some general ability g, it is clear that more specific abilities are important for intelligent behavior. Children with Williams syndrome, who have a severe deficit in basic visual comparison, are also severely deficient in mathematics and logical reasoning. After a lifetime of research, Witken, Goodenough and Oltman (1979) found that visual comparison was a necessary component of mathematical ability in all individuals. In their studies, people were consistent in their ability to detect or attend to camouflaged targets across a variety of tasks. People better at attending to targets in the presence of distracters were more likely to study math and science and were less sensitive to social inputs than people who were more influenced by the distracters. Males tend to perform better at selective visual attention tasks and at mathematics than females do. This difference is most noticeable at the highest levels of ability. Twenty years of research by Camilla Benbow and her colleagues (Benbow, Lubinski, Shea, & Eftekhari-Sanjani, 2000) has confirmed that at all ages the top 1% of individuals on tests of mathematical reasoning ability are predominantly male. However, there are no differences in verbal ability. This difference accounts for the predominance of males in science and engineering.

TALENT

As we move from adequate performance across many tasks to exceptional performance in some task, general ability becomes less important and specific abilities become more important. Some people are born with extraordinary abilities to draw lifelike pictures, remember musical compositions, solve mathematical problems, etc. Many outstanding figures in these areas were child prodigies who exhibited their talent at an early age before they had received much formal training. However, talent in one area does not guarantee ability in other areas. On the one hand, Leonardo Da Vinci coupled an extraordinary drawing ability with a variety of superior skills. On the other hand, Louis Pasteur was a mediocre student, and Thomas Edison was learning disabled. The success of Pasteur and Edison demonstrates that specific cognitive abilities may be more important for creative solutions to important specific kinds of problems than some general problem solving ability. Academically gifted children often have lower correlations among different cognitive subtests than other children (Benbow & Minor, 1990). Similarly, adults with high IQs have lower correlations among the subtests of the IQ than do those with ordinary IQs (Detterman & Daniel, 1989). Since g is determined by the size of the correlation among cognitive subtests, the reduced correlations for intelligent individuals suggest a limited role of g in outstanding performance.

Some children are idiot savants who combine an extraordinary drawing, musical, or mnemonic ability with a profound retardation in language and reasoning. So extraordinary ability in one area may not be dependent on general intelligence at all. Unfortunately, there have been few detailed studies of idiot savants published, which is why Selfe's (1977) study of Nadia, an autistic child with extraordinary drawing ability, is so important.

Nadia was born in Nottingham, England, in 1967. From the first her development was slow. As an infant she was unresponsive and would not turn at her mother's approach. Her first words appeared at nine months; but at eighteen months, two-word utterances, which normally appear, did not develop, and she used the single-word utterances she had acquired less and less frequently. During this time she became increasingly isolated emotionally, and her family began to worry that her development was not proceeding normally.

Nadia entered a special school for severely subnormal children in 1972. She was physically large for her age, but she was slow and lethargic in her movements. Her typical behavior exhibited passivity and excessive slowness, and she was mute and inactive. She had an effective vocabulary of less than ten words. She could not dress herself without assistance.

When she was 3 years old, Nadia suddenly displayed an extraordinary drawing ability. Over the next three years she created many striking drawings. From the beginning her drawings were three-dimensional, lifelike, and quite beautiful. Nadia drew pictures of horses, with and without riders, of birds, of other animals, of trains, and of people. Her drawings were based on both pictures she had seen and solid objects, but her drawings were not copies. Rather, elements of what she had seen appeared in drawings done weeks later in new and original perspectives. Her drawings were not wooden portraits but contained scenes of vigorous action, sometimes containing strange, new creatures. For example, one of her animals looks part giraffe and part donkey. A comparison of Nadia's drawings with 24,000 "pictures of mommy" from a local newspaper contest made it clear how unique Nadia was. A further search of the psychological literature revealed no documented case of such exquisite drawing ability emerging at such an early age.

Nadia was left-handed and drew with a ballpoint pen, which she held firmly and comfortably. She rapidly executed strokes with the kind of command that suggests years of training. She could stop a line exactly where it met another even while drawing quite rapidly. She could change the direction of a line and draw lines at any angle toward or away from the body. She could draw a small but perfect circle in one movement and place a dot in the center.

Nadia drew intensively for varying intervals of time up to a minute and then usually sat back to survey the effect, moving her head perhaps to vary the viewing angle. This study usually gave her great pleasure, and after surveying intently what she had drawn, she often smiled, babbled, and shook her head and knees in glee. During her most productive period she drew four or five times a week.

Nadia entered a school for autistic children when she was seven, and in the next two years her sociability and language improved greatly. However, she virtually stopped drawing spontaneously, though she would produce a recognizable sketch of a classmate upon request.

PRACTICE

Finally, though talent is necessary, it is not sufficient for outstanding performance. From simple motor skills like reaching and grasping to complex cognitive skills like mastery of chess, expertise requires encoding a huge number of representations to cover every possible situation. Ericsson, Krampe, and Tech-Romer (1993) demonstrated that the level of achievement in piano, violin, ballet, chess, bridge, and athletics is predicted by sheer amount of deliberate practice. After thorough review, both Simonton (1999) and Winner (2000) concluded that talent plus practice was essential for an individual to reach an exceptional level of performance in a specialized field.

SUMMARY OF CHAPTER

- The process of solving a problem has three major steps.
  - Forming an initial representation of the problem.
  - Generating and testing potential solutions (The generate and recognize strategy of recall is a special case). It has two steps:
    * 1. Generate a candidate for a solution.
    * 2. Test to see whether it is actually a solution. If the candidate fails the test, another candidate is generated, and the cycle repeats until a solution is found.
  - Executing a procedure to carry out a planned solution and checking the results.

- The initial representation of the problem is different for novices versus experts.
  - A novice may employ either of two strategies for representing the problem.
    * Task analysis, in which the overall problem is broken down into subproblems that the novice can solve.
    * Applying an analogy; i.e., retrieve a representation of some other problem previously solved. However, novices are poor at finding analogies because a novice is more likely to retrieve a representation with common superficial features instead one for a structurally similar problem with a similar solution.
  - In contrast, an expert is likely to retrieve the representation of a structural similar problem that has a similar solution.

- Generation
  - Problem solving set. PI from previously generated potential solutions during generation.
  - Functional fixedness. Superficial features can interfere with generating potential solutions.
  - The number of subgoals that comprise the solution plan is limited by constraints on working memory.

- Intelligence. When people perform a variety of different tasks, task performance is positively correlated across tasks.
  - One possible explanation is that there is a single general ability, g, that is applied in all tasks.
  - Alternatively, there may be a small set of basic abilities that are applied across tasks.
  - Since intelligence tests are collections of subtests they are good measures of g.
  - In addition to g, specific visual and verbal abilities are also required for task performance. These talents are independent of g.

BIBLIOGRAPHY

Abrams, R. L., Greenwald, A. G. (2000). Parts outweigh the whole (word) in unconscious analysis of meaning. *Psychological Science, 11*, 118-124.

Adams, A..M., & Gathercole, S. E. (2000). Limitations in working memory: Implications for language development. *International Journal of Language & Communication Disorders, 35*, 95-116.

Adams, J. A. (1976). *Learning and memory: An introduction*. Homewood, Ill.: Dorsey Press.

Adams, J. A., Goetz, E. T., & Marshall, P. H. (1972). Response feedback and motor learning. *Journal of Experimental Psychology, 92*, 391-397.

Adams, M. J. (1979). Models of word recognition. *Cognitive Psychology, 11*, 133-176.

Adler, S. A., & Rovee-Collier, C. (1994). The memorability and discriminability of primitive perceptual units. *Vision Research, 34*, 449-459.

Afifi, A. K., & Bergman, R. A. (1980). *Basic neuroscience*. Baltimore: Urban & Schwarzenberg.

Ajzen, 1. (1977). Intuitive theories of events and the effects of base-rate information on prediction. *Journal of Personality and Social Psychology, 35*, 303-314.

Akhtar, N. (1999). Acquiring basic word order: Evidence for data-driven learning of syntactic structure. *Journal of Child Language, 26*, 339-356.

Akhtar, N., Carpenter, M., & Tomasello, M. (1996). The role of discourse novelty in early word learning. *Child Development, 67*, 635-645.

Akhtar, N., Jipson, J., & Callanan, M. A. (201). Learning words through overhearing. *Child Development, 72*, 416-430.

Albert, M. S., Butters, N., & Brandt, J. (1981a). Memory for remote events in alcoholics. *Journal of Studies on Alcohol, 41*, 1071-1081.

Albert, M. S., Butters, N., & Brandt, J. (1981b). Patterns of remote memory in amnesic and demented patients. *Archives of Neurology, 38,* 495-500.

Albert, M. S., Butters, N., & Levin, J. (1979). Temporal gradients in the retrograde amnesia of patients with alcoholic Korsakoff's disease. *Archives of Neurology,* **36,** 211-216.

Alexander, M. P., Benson, D. F., & Stuss, D. T. (1989). Frontal lobes and language. *Brain and Language,* **37,** 656-691.

Almor, A., & Sloman, S. A. (1996). Is deontic reasoning special? *Psychological Review,* **103,** 374-380.

Amabile, T. A., & Rovee-Collier, C. (1991). Contextual variation and memory retrieval at six months. *Child Development,* **62,** 1155-1166.

Anderson, B. L., & Nakayama, K. (1994). Toward a general theory of stereopsis: Binocular matching, occluding contours, and fusion. *Psychological Review,* **101,** 414-445.

Anderson, J., & Revelle, W. (1982). Impulsivity, caffeine, and proofreading: A test of the Easterbrook hypothesis. *Journal of Experimental Psychology: Human Perception and Performance,* **8,** 614-624.

Anderson, M. C., Bjork, R. A., & Bjork, E. L. (1994). Remembering can cause forgetting: Retrieval dynamics in long-term memory. *Journal of Experimental Psychology: Learning, Memory and Cognition,* **20,** 1063-1087.

Anderson, R. C., & Pichert, J. W. (1978). Recall of previously unrecallable information following a shift in perspective. *Journal of Verbal Learning and Verbal Behavior,* **17,** 1-12.

Anzola, G. P., Bertoloni, G., Buchtel, H. A., & Rizzolatti, G. (1977). Spatial compatibility and anatomical factors in simple and choice reaction time. *Neuropsychologia,* **15,** 295-302.

Arnett, J. L., & Di Lollo, V. (1979). Visual information processing in relation to age and to reading ability. *Journal of Experimental Child Psychology,* **27,** 143-152.

Atkinson, R. C., & Raugh, M. R. (1975). An application of the mnemonic keyword method to the acquisition of a Russian vocabulary. *Journal of Experimental Psychology: Human Learning and Memory,* **104,** 126-133.

Attneave, A. (1957). Transfer of experience with a class schema to identification learning of patterns and shapes. *Journal of Experimental Psychology,* **54,** 81-88.

Atwood, M. E., & Polson, P. G. (1976). A process model for water jug problems. *Cognitive Psychology,* **8,** 191-216.

Baddeley, A. D. (1972). Selective attention and performance in dangerous environments. *British Journal of Psychology,* **63,** 537-546.

Baddeley, A. D. (1976). *The psychology of memory.* New York: Basic Books.

Baddeley, A.D. (1986). *Working memory.* Oxford: Oxford University Press.

Baddely, A. D. (1992). Working memory. *Science,* **255,** 556-559.

Baddeley, A. D., & Gathercole, S. E. (1998). The phonological loop as a language learning device. *Psychological Review,* **105,** 158-173.

Baddley, A. D., & Longman, D. J. A. (1978). The influence of length and frequency of raining sessions on the rate of learning to type. *Ergonomics,* **21,** 627-635.

Baddeley, A. D., Papagno, C., & Vallar, G. (1988). When long-term learning depends on short-term storage. *Journal of Memory and Language*, **27**, 586-595.

Bahrick, H. P. (1970). Two-phase model for prompted recall. *Psychological Review*, **77**, 215-222.

Bahrick, H. P. (1983). Memory and people. In J. Harris (Ed.), *Everyday memory, actions, and absentmindedness*. New York: Academic Press.

Bahrick, H. P. (1984). Semantic memory content in permastore: Fifty years of memory for Spanish learned in school. *Journal of Experimental Psychology: General*, **113**, 1-29.

Bahrick, H. P., Bahrick, P. 0., & Wittlinger, R. P. (1975). Fifty years of memory for names and faces: A cross-sectional approach. *Journal of Experimental Psychology: General*, **104**, 54-75.

Bahrick, L. E., & Pickens, J. N. (1995). Infant memory object motion across a period of three months: Implications for a four-phase attention function. *Journal of Experimental Child Psychology*, **59**, 343-371.

Bakker, D. J. (1970). Ear asymmetry with monaural stimulation: Relations to lateral dominance and lateral awareness. *Neuropsychologia*, **8**, 103-117.

Baldo, J. V., & Shimamura, A. P. (1998). Letter and category fluency in patients with frontal lobe lesions. *Neuropsychology*, **12**, 259-267.

Baldwin, D. A., Marman, E. M., & Melartin, R. L. (1993). Infants' ability to draw inferences about nonobvious prop-erties: Evidence from exploratory play. *Child Development,*, **64,** 711-728.

Ballard, P. B. (1913). Oblivescence and reminiscence. *British Journal of Psychology Monograph Supplement*, **1**, No. 2.

Baluch, B., & Besner, D. (1991). Visual word recognition: Evidence for strategic control of lexical and nonlexical rou-tines in oral reading. *Journal of Experimental Psychology: Learning, Memory, & Cognition*, **17,** 644-652.

Banks, W. P. (19 70). Signal detection theory and human memory. *Psychological Bulletin*, **74**, 81-99.

Banks, W. P., & Flora, J. (1977). Semantic and perceptual processes in symbolic comparisons. *Journal of Experimental Psychology: Human Perception and Performance*, **3**, 278-290.

Barber, T. X. (1969). *Hypnosis: A scientific approach.* New York: Van Nostrand Reinhold.

Barber, T. X., & Glass, L. B. (1962). Significant factors in hypnotic behavior. *Journal of Abnormal and Social Psychology*, **64**, 222-228.

Bar-Hillel, M., & Falk, R. (1982). Some teasers concerning conditional probabilities. *Cognition*, **11,** 109-122.

Baron- Cohen, S. (1995). *Mindblindness*. Boston: MIT Press.

Barr, R. Dowden, A., & Hayne, H. (1996). Developmental changes in deferred imitation by 6- to 24-month-old infants. *Infant Behavior and Development*, **19**, 159-179.

Barron, R. W., & Baron, J. (1977). How children get meaning from printed words. *Child Development*, **48**, 587-594.

Bartlett, J. C., Till, R. E., & Levy, J. C. (1980). Retrieval characteristics of complex pictures: Effects of verbal encoding. *Journal of Verbal Learning and Verbal Behavior*, **19**, 430-449.

Bartolo, A. Cubelli, R. Della Sala, S. Drei, S., & Marchetti, C. (2001). Double dissociation between meaningful and meaningless gesture reproduction in apraxia. *Cortex*, **37**, 696-699.

Battig, W. F., & Montague, W. E. (1969)* Category norms of verbal items in 56 categories: A replication and extension of the Connecticut category norms. *Journal of Experimental Psychology*, **80**, 1-46.

Bauer, P. J. (2002). Early memory development. In U. Goswami (Ed.), *Blackwell handbook of childhood cognitive development*. Malden, MA: Blackwell (pp. 127-146).

Bechara, A., Damasio, H., & Damasio, A. R. (2000). Emotion, decision making, and the orbitofrontal cortex. *Cerebral Cortex,* **10**, 295-307.

Bechara, A., Tranel, D., & Damasio, H. (2000). Characterization of the decision-making deficit of patients with ventromedial prefrontal cortex lesions. *Brain*, **123**, 2189-2202.

Bechara, A., Damasio, H., Damasio, A. R., & Lee, G. P. (1999). Different contributions of the human amygdala and ventromedial prefrontal *Cortex* to decision-making. *Journal of Neuroscience*, **19**, 5473-5481.

Becker, J. T., Butters, N., Hermann, A., & D'Angelo, N. (1983). A comparison of the effects of long-term alcohol abuse and aging on the performance of verbal and nonverbal divided attention tasks. *Alcoholism: Clinical and Experimental Research*, **7**, 213-219.

Becker, W. (1991). Saccades. In, R. H. s. Carpenter (Ed.) *Vision and visual dysfunction (Vol. 8)Eye movements*. Boca Raton: CRC Press.

Begg, I. (1978a). Similarity and contrast in memory for relations. *Memory & Cognition*, **6**, 509-517.

Begg, I. (1978b). Imagery and organization in memory: Instructional effects. *Memory & Cognition,* **6**, 174-183.

Behrmann, M., Moscovitch, M., & Winocur, G. (1994). Intact visual imagery and impaired visual perception in a patient with visual agnosia. *Journal of Experimental Psychology: Human Perception & Performance*, **20**, 1068-1087.

Bellugi, U., Klima, E. S., & Wang, P. P. (1996). Cognitive and neural development: Clues from genetically based syndromes. In D. Magnussen (Ed.), *The life-span development of individuals: Behavioral, neurobiological, and psychosocial perspectives*. The Nobel Symposium. New York, NY: Cambridge University Press, pp. 223-243.

Bellugi, U., Lichtenberger, L., Jones, W., Lai, Z., & St. George, M. (2000). The neurocognitive profile of Williams syndrome: A complex pattern of strengths and weaknesses. *Journal of Cognitive Neuroscience (Supplement)*, **12**, 7-29.

Belmore, S. M. (1981). Imagery and semantic elaboration in hypermnesia for words. *Journal of Experimental Psychology: Human Learning and Memory*, **7**, 191-203.

Bem, D. J., & McConnell, H. K. (1970). Testing the self-perception explanation of dissonance phenomena: On the salience of premanipulation attitudes. *Journal of Personality and Social Psychology*, **14**, 23-31.

Benasich, A. & Tallal, P. (2002). Infant discrimination of rapid auditory cues predicts later language impairment. *Behavioural Brain Research*, **136**, 31-49.

Benbow, C. P., Lubinski, D., Shea, D. L, & Eftekhari-Sanjani, H. (2000). Sex differences in mathematical reasoning ability at age 13: Their status 20 years later. *Psychological Science,* **11**, 474-480.

Benbow, C. P., & Minor, L. L. (1990). Cognitive profiles of verbally and mathematically precocious students: Implications for identification of the gifted. *Gifted Child Quarterly,* **34**, 21-26.

Ben-Shakhar, G., Lieblich, L., & Bar-Hillel, M. (1982). An evaluation of polygraphers' judgments: A review from a decision theoretic perspective. *Journal of Applied Psychology, 87,* 701-713.

Benson, D., Djenderedjian, A., Miller, B., Pachana, N., Chang, L., Itti, L., & Mena, I. (1996). Neural basis of confabulation. *Neurology*, **46**, 1239-1243.

Benson, D. F., & Greenberg, J. P. (1969). Visual form agnosia. *Archives of Neurology, 20,* 82-89.

Benton, A. L. (1968). Differential behavioral effects in frontal lobe disease. *Neuropsychologia*, **6**, *53-60.*

Benton, A. L. (1975). Developmental dyslexia: Neurological aspects. In W. J. Friedlander (Ed.), *Advances in Neurology. (Vol. 7).* New York: Raven Press.

Benton, A., L., & Tranel, D. (1993). Visuoperceptual, visuospatial, and visuoconstructive disorders. In, K. M. Heilman & E. Valenstein (Eds.), *Clinical neuropsychology.* New York: Oxford University Press.

Bergum, B. O., & Lehr, D. J. (1964). Monetary incentive and vigilance. *Journal of Experimental Psychology,* **67**, 197-198.

Berlin, B., & Kay, P. (1969). *Basic color terms: Their universality and evolution.* Berkeley and Los Angeles: University of California Press.

Best, C. T., Morrongiello, B., & Robson, R. (1981). Perceptual equivalence of acoustic cues in speech and nonspeech perception. *Perception & Psychophysics*, **29**, 191-211.

Bevan, W., & Steger, J. A. (1971*).* Free recall and abstractness of stimuli. *Science*, **172**,597-599.

Bever, T. G., & Chiarello, R. J. (1974*).* Cerebral dominance in musicians and nonmusicians. *Science*, **185**, 137-139.

Bhatt, R. S., & Rovee-Collier, C. (1994). Perception and 24-hour retention of feature relations in infancy. *Developmental Psychology*, **30**, 142-150.

Bhatt, R. S., Rovee-Collier, C., & Weiner, S. (1994). Developmental changes in the interface between perception and memory retrieval. *Developmental Psychology,* **30**, 151-162.

Biederman, I. (1985). Human image understanding: Recent research and a theory. *Computer Vision, Graphics, and Image Processing,* **32**, 29-73.

Biederman, I., & Bar, M. (1999). One-shot viewpoint invariance in matching novel objects. *Vision Research*, **39**, 2885-2899.

Biederman, I., & Checkosky, S. F. (1970). Processing redundant information. *Journal of Experimental Psychology*, **83**, 486- 490.

Biederman,I., & Cooper, E. E. (1991). Priming contour-deleted images: Evidence for intermediate representations in visual object recognition. *Cognitive Psychology*, **23**, 393-419.

Biederman, I., Mezzanotte, R. J., & Rabinowitz, J. C. (1982). Scene perception: Detecting and judging objects undergoing relational violations. *Cognitive Psychology,* **14**, 143-177.

Bishop, D. V., North, T., & Donlan, C. (1995). Genetic basis of specific language impairment: evidence from a twin study. *Developmental Medicine and Child Neurology*, **37**, 56-71.

Bisiach, E., Capitani, E., Luzzatti, C., & Perani, D. (1981). *Brain* and conscious representation of outside reality. *Neuropsychologia,* **19**, 543-551.

Bisiach, E., Rusconi, M. L., & Vallar, G. (1992). Remission of somatophrenic delusion through vestibular stimulation. *Neuropsychologia, 29,* 1029-1031.

Black, J. B., & Bower, G. H. (1980). Story understanding as problem solving. *Poetics, 9,* 223-250.

Blair, R. J. R. (1995). A cognitive developmental approach to morality: investigating the psychopath. *Cognition,* **57,** 1-29.

Blair, R. J. R. & Curran, J. V. (1999). Selective impairment in the recognition of anger induced by diazepam. *Psychopharmacology,* **147,** 335-338.

Blaney, P. H. (1986). Affect and memory: A review. *Psychological Bulletin,* **99,** 229-246.

Bobrow, S. A., & Bower, G. H. (1969). Comprehension and recall of sentences. *Journal of Experimental Psychology,* **80,** 455-461.

Bogen, J. E., & Bogen, G. M. *(1976).* Wernicke's region-where is it? *Annals of the New York Academy of Sciences,* **280,** 834- 843.

Bothwell, R. K., Brigham, J. C., & Malpass, R. S. (1989). Cross-racial identification. *Personality & Social Psychology Bulletin,* **15,** 19-25.

Bouchard, T. J., Jr., Lykken, D. t., McGue, M., Segal, N. L., & Tellegen, A. (1990). Sources of human psychological differences: The Minnesota study of twins reared apart. *Science,* **250,** 223-228.

Bousfield, W. A., & Sedgewick, H. W. (1944). An analysis of sequences of restricted associative responses. *Journal of General Psychology,* **30,** 149-165.

Bower, G. H. (1970). Analysis of a mnemonic device. *American Scientist,* **58,** 496-510.

Bower, G. H. (1972). Mental imagery and associative learning. In L. W. Gregg (Ed.), *Cognition* in Learning and Memory. New York: Wiley.

Bower, G. H., & Clark, M. C. (1969). Narrative stories as mediators for serial learning. *Psychonomic Science,* 14, 181-182.

Bower, G. H., Clark, M. C., Lesgold, A. M., & Winzenz, D. (1969). Hierarchical retrieval schemes in recall of categorized word lists. *Journal of Verbal Learning and Verbal Behavior,* **8,** 323-343.

Bower, G. H., Gilligan, S. G., & Monteiro, K. P. (198 1). Selective learning caused by affective state. *Journal of Experimental Psychology: General,* **110,** 451-473.

Bower, G. H., & Glass, A. L. (1976). Structural units and the reintegrative power of picture fragments. *Journal of Experimental Psychology: Human Learning and Memory,* **2,** 456-466.

Bower, G. H., & Holyoak, K. J. (1973). Encoding and recognition memory for naturalistic sounds. *Journal of Experimental Psychology,* **101,** 360-366.

Bower, G. H., Lesgold, A. M., & Tieman, D. (1969). Grouping operations in free recall. *Journal of Verbal Learning and Verbal Behavior,* **8,** 481-493.

Bower, C. H., & Reitman, J. S. (1972). Mnemonic elaboration in multilist learning. *Journal of Verbal Learning and Verbal Behavior,* **11,** 478-485.

Bower, G. H., & Sivers, H. (1998). Cognitive impact of traumatic events. *Development & Psychopathology,* **10**, 625-653.

Bower, G. H., & Winzenz, D. (1970). Comparison of associative learning strategies. *Psychonomic Science,* **20**, 119-120.

Bradley, D. C., Garrett, M. F., & Zurif, E. B. (1980). Syntactic deficits in Broca's aphasia. In D. Caplan (Ed.), Biological Studies *of* Mental Processes. Cambridge, Mass.: MIT Press.

Brebner, J., Shephard, M., & Cairney, P. T. (1972). Spatial relationships and S-R compatibility. *Acta Psychologica,* **36**, 1-15.

Box, O., Laing, H., & Kopelman, M. (1999). The evolution of spontaneous confabulation, delusional misidentification and a related delusion in a case of severe head injury. *Neurocase,* **5,** 251-262.

Braitenberg, V. (1967). Is the cerebellar *Cortex* a biological clock in the millisecond range? *Progress in Brain Research,* **25**, 334-346.

Brandt, J., Butters, N., Ryan, C., & Bayog, R. (1983). Cognitive loss and recovery in long-term alcohol abusers. *Archives of General Psychiatry,* **40**, 435-442.

Bransford, J. D. (1979). *Human Cognition. Learning, understanding and remembering.* Belmont, Calif.: Wadsworth.

Bransford, J. D., & Johnson, M. K. (1972). Contextual prerequisites for understanding: Some investigations of comprehension and recall. *Journal of Verbal Learning and Verbal Behavior,* **11**, 717-721.

Bransford, J. D., & Johnson, M. K. (1973). Consideration of some problems of comprehension. In W. C. Chase (Ed.), Visual Information Processing. New York: Academic Press.

Bregman, A. S. (1981). Asking the "what for" question in auditory perception. In M. Kubovy & J. R. Pomerantz (Eds.), *Perceptual organization.* Hillsdale, N.J.: Erlbaum.

Brewin, C. R. Intrusive autobiographical memories in depression and post-traumatic stress disorder. *Applied Cognitive Psychology,* **12**, 359-370.

Broadbent, D. E. (1958). *Perception and communication.* London: Pergamon Press.

Broadbent, D. E. (1971). *Decision and stress.* London: Academic Press.

Broadbent, D. E. (1978). The current state of noise research: Reply to Poulton. *Psychological Bulletin,* **85**, 1052-1067.

Broadbent, D. E., & Broadbent, M. H. P. (1987). From detection to identification: Response to multiple targets in rapid serial visual presentation. *Perception & Psychophysics,* **42**, 105-113.

Broen, P. (1972). The verbal environment of the language-learning child. *Monographs of the American Speech and Hearing Association,* **17**.

Brockmole, J. R., Wang, R. F., & Irwin, D. E. (2002). Temporal integration between visual images and visual percepts. *Journal of Experimental Psychology: Human Perception & Performance,* **28**, 315-334.

Brooks, L. R. (1968). Spatial and verbal components of the act of recall. *Canadian Journal of Psychology,* **22**, 349-368.

Brooks, L. R. *(*1978). Nonanalytic concept formation and memory for instances. In E. Rosch & B. B. Lloyd (Eds.), *Cognition and categorization.* Hillsdale, N.J.: Erlbaum.

Brown, A. L., & Scott, M. S. (1971). Recognition memory for pictures in preschool children. *Journal of Experimental Child Psychology*, **11**, 401-412.

Brown, A. S. (1979). Priming effects in semantic memory retrieval processes. *Journal of Experimental Psychology: Human Learning and Memory*, **5**, 65-77.

Brown, A. S. *(198 1).* Inhibition in cued retrieval. *Journal of Experimental Psychology: Human Learning and Memory*, **7**, 204- 215.

Brown, E. L., & Deffenbacher, K. (1979). *Perception and the senses.* New York: Oxford University Press.

Brown, J. *(1958).* Some tests of the decay theory of immediate memory. *Quarterly Journal of Experimental Psychology*, **10**, 12-21.

Brown, J. *(1968).* Reciprocal facilitation and impairment of free recall. *Psychonomic Science*, **10**, 41-42.

Brown, R., & Kulik, J. (1977). Flashbulb memories. *Cognition*, **5**, 73-99.

Brown, R., and Lenneberg, E. H. (1954). A study in language and *Cognition. Journal of Abnormal and Social Psychology*, **49**, 454-462.

Brown, R., & McNeill, D. (1966). The "tip of the tongue" phenomenon. *Journal of Verbal Learning and Verbal Behavior*, **5**, 325-337.

Brown, W. (1923). To what extent is memory measured by a single recall? *Journal of Experimental Psychology*, **6**, 377-382.

Bruce, V. (1982). Changing faces: Visual and non-visual coding processes in face recognition. *British Journal of Psychology*, **73**, 105-116.

Brun, A. & Andersson, J. (2001) Frontal dysfunction and frontal cortical synapse loss in alcoholism – the main cause of alcohol dementia? *Dementia and Geriatric Cognitive Disorders* **12**, 289-294.

Bryden, M. P., & Allard, F. (1976). Visual hemifield differences depend on typeface. *Brain and Language*, **3**, 191-200.

Bugelski, B. R., & Alampay, D. A. (1961). The role of frequency in developing perceptual set. *Canadian Journal of Psychology*, **15**, 205-211.

Buschke, H. (1973). Selective reminding for analysis of memory and learning. *Journal of Verbal Learning and Verbal Behavior*, **12**, 543-550.

Buschke, H. (1974). Spontaneous remembering after recall failure. *Science*, **184**, 579-581.

Buschke, H. (1976). Learning is organized by chunking. *Journal of Verbal Learning and Verbal Behavior*, **15**, 313-324.

Buschke, H. (1977). Two-dimensional recall: Immediate identification of clusters in episodic and semantic memory. *Journal of Verbal Learning and Verbal Behavior*, **16**, 201-215.

Buschke, H., Kuslansky, G., Katz, M., Steward, W. F., Sliwinski, M. J., Eckholdt, H. M, Lipton, R. B, (1999). Screening for dementia with the Memory Impairment Screen. *Neurology*, **52**, 231-238.

Buschke, H., & Schaier, A. H. (1979). Memory units, ideas, and propositions in semantic remembering. *Journal of Verbal Learning and Verbal Behavior*, **18**, 549-563.

Butler, J., & Rovee-Collier, C. (1989). Contextual gating of memory retrieval. *Developmental Psychobiology,* **22***,* 533-552.

Butters, N. (1984). Alcoholic Korsakoff's syndrome: An update. *Seminars in Neurology,* **4***,* 226-244.

Butters, N., Heindel, W. C., & Salmon, D. P. (1990). Dissociation of implicit memory in dementia: Neurological implications. *Bulletin of the Psychonomic Society,* **28***,* 359-366.

Butters, N., & Stuss, D. T. (1989). Diencephalic amnesia. In F. Boller & J. Grafman (Eds.) *Handbook of neuropsychology, Vol. 3,* New York: Elsevier.

Butterworth, G., & Itakura, S. (2000). How the eyes, head and hand serve definite reference. *British Journal of Developmental Psychology,* **18***,* 25-50.

Butterworth, G., & Morissette, P. (1996). Onset of pointing and the acquisition of language in infancy. *Journal of Reproductive & Infant Psychology,* **14***,* 219-231.

Cahill, L., & McGaugh, J. L. (1998). A novel demonstration of enhanced memory associated with emotional arousal. *Consciousness and Cognition,* **4***,* 410-421.

Camras, L. a. (1977). Facial expressions used by children in a conflict situation. *Child Development,* **48***,* 1431-1435.

Caplan, D. (1972). Clause boundaries and recognition latencies for words in sentences. *Perception & Psychophysics,* **12***,* 73- 76.

Caramazza, A., & Berndt, R. S. (1978). Semantic and syntactic processes in aphasia: A review of the literature. *Psychological Bulletin,* **85***,* 898-918.

Caramazza, A., & Zurif, E. B. (1976). Dissociation of algorithmic and heuristic processes in language comprehension: Evidence from aphasia. *Brain and Language,* **3***,* 572-582.

Carey, S. (1985). *Conceptual change in childhood.* Cambridge, MA: MIT Press.

Carlsson, A. (1988). Speculations on the control of mental and motor functions by dopamine-modulated cortico-striato-thalamo-cortical feedback loops. *The Mount Sinai Journal of Medicine,* **55***,* 6-10.

Carlson, N. R. (2001). *Physiology of Behavior* (7th ed.). Boston: Allyn and Bacon.

Carmichael, L., Hogan, H. P., & Walter, A. A. (1932). An experimental study of the effect of language on the reproduction of visually perceived form. *Journal of Experimental Psychology,* **15***,* 73-86.

Carpenter, P. A., & Daneman, M. (1981). Lexical retrieval and error recovery in reading: A model based on eye fixations. *Journal of Verbal Learning and Verbal Behavior,* **20***,* 137-160.

Cassel, W. S., Roebers, C. E. M., & Bjorklund, D. F. (1996). Developmental patterns of eyewitness responses to increasingly suggestive questions. *Journal of Experimental Child Psychology,* **61***,* 116-133.

Caselli, M. C., Bates, E., Cadadio, P., Fenson, J., Fenson, L., Sanderl, L. Weir, J. (1995). A cross-linguistic study of early lexical development. *Cognitive Development,* **10***,* 159-199.

Caselli, C., Casadio, P., & Bates, E. (1999). A comparison of the transition from first words to grammar in English and Italian. *Journal of Child Language,* **26***,* 69-111.

Cavanaugh, J. P. (1972). Relation between the immediate memory span and the memory search rate. *Psychological Review,* **79***,* 525-530.

Ceci, S. J. (1996). *On intelligence: A bio-ecological treatise on intellectual development.* Cambridge, MA: Harvard University Press.

Ceci, S. J; Bruck, M. (1993). Suggestibility of the child witness: A historical review and synthesis. *Psychological Bulletin*, **113**, 403-439.

Cermak, L. S., Lewis, R., Butters, N., & Goodglass, H. (1973). The role of verbal mediation in performance of motor tasks by Korsakoff patients. *Perceptual and Motor Skills*, **37**, 259-262.

Chalmers, K. A., Humphreys, M. S., & Dennis, S. (1997). A naturalistic study of the word frequency effect in episodic recognition. *Memory & Cognition*, **25**, 780-784.

Chase, W. G., & Ericsson, K. A. (1980). Skilled memory. In J. R. Anderson (Ed.), *Cognitive skills and their acquisition*. Hillsdale, N.J.: Erlbaum.

Chase, W. G., & Simon, H. A. (1973). *The mind's eye in chess*. In W. G. Chase (Ed.), Visual Information Processing. New York: Academic Press.

Chastain, G. (1977). Feature analysis and the growth of a percept. *Journal of Experimental Psychology: Human Perception and Performance*, **3**, 291-298.

Checkosky, S. F., & Baboorian, N. (1972).   Memory search for CVC and CCC trigrams. *Journal of Experimental Psychology*,.**96**, 158-163.

Cheng, P. W., & Holyoak, K. J. (1985). Pragmatic reasoning schemas. *Cognitive Psychology*, **17**.

Cherry, E. C. (1953). Some experiments on the recognition of speech, with one and two ears. *Journal of the Acoustical Society of America*, **25**, 975-979.

Chi, M. T. H., Feltovich, P. J., & Glaser, R. (1981). Categorization and representation of physics problems by experts and novices. *Cognitive Science*, **5**, 121-152.

Chomsky, N. (1975). *Reflections on language*. New York: Pantheon Books.

Cirilo, R. K., & Foss, D. J. (1980). Text structure and reading time for sentences. *Journal of Verbal Learning and Verbal Behavior*, **19**, 96-109.

Clark, D. M., & Teasedale, J. D. (1982). Diurnal variations in clinical depression and accessibility of memories of positive and negative experiences. *Journal of Abnormal Psychology*, **91**, 87-95.

Clark, H. H., & Chase, W. G. (1972). On the process of comparing sentences against pictures. *Cognitive Psychology*, **3**, 472- 517.

Cohn, J. F., & Tronick, E. Z. (1983). Three-month-old infants' reaction to simulated maternal depression. *Child Development*, **54**, 185-193.

Colavita, F. B. (1974). Human sensory dominance. *Perception & Psychophysics*, **16**, 409-416.

Cherry, E. C. (1953). Some experiments on the recognition of speech, with one and two ears. *Journal of the Acoustical Society of America*, **25**, 975-979.

Cohen, N. J., & Squire, L. R. (1981). Retrograde amnesia and remote memory impairment. *Neuropsychologia*, **19**, 337-356.

Cohen, R. L., & Granstr6m, K. (1970). Reproduction and recognition in short-term visual memory. *Quarterly Journal of Experimental Psychology*, **22**, 450-457.

Cohn, N. B., Dustman, R. E., & Bradford, D. C. (1984). Age-related decrements in Stroop color test performance. *Journal of Clinical Psychology,* **40***,* 1244-1250.

Cole, R. A., (1973). Listening for mispronunciations: A measure of what we hear during speech. *Perception & Psychophysics,* **11***,* 153-156.

Collins, A. M., & Loftus, E. F. (1975). A spreading-activation theory of semantic processing. *Psychological Review,* **82***,* 407-428.

Collins, A. M., & Quillian, M. R. (1969). Retrieval time from semantic memory. *Journal of Verbal Learning and Verbal Behavior,* **8***,* 240-248.

Coltheart, M., & Rastle, K. (1994). Serial processing in reading aloud: Evidence for dual route models of reading. *Journal of Experimental Psychology: Human Perception & Performance,* **20***,* 1197-1211.

Comalli, P. E., Jr. Wapner, S., & Werner H. (1962). Interference effects of Stroop color-word test in childhood, adulthood, and aging. *Journal of Genetic Psychology,* **100***,* 47-53.

Conrad, R. (1964). Acoustic confusion in immediate memory. *British Journal of Psychology,* **55***,* 75-84.

Conway, M. A., Anderson, S. J., Larsen, S. F., Donnelly, C. M., McDaniel, M. A., McClelland, A. G. R., & Rawles,R. E., 1994). The formation of flashbulb memories. *Memory & Cognition,* **22***,* 326-343.

Conway, M. A., Collins, A. F., Gathercole, S. E., & Anderson, S. J. (1996). Recollections of true and false autobiographical memories. *Journal of Experimental Psychology: General,* **125***,* 69-95.

Conway, M. A., & Haque, S. (1999). Overshadowing the reminiscence bump: Memories of a struggle for independence. *Journal of Adult Development,* **6***,* 35-44.

Coons, P. M. (1999). Psychogenic or dissociative fugue: A clinical investigation of five cases. *Psychological Reports***,** **84***,* 881-886.

Cooper, a. C. G., & Humphreys, G. W. (2000). Coding space within but not between objects: Evidence for Balint's syndrome. *Neuropsychologia,* **38***,* 723-733.

Corcoran, D. W. J. (1966). An acoustic factor in letter cancellation. *Nature,* **210***,* 658.

Corcoran, D. W. J. (196 7). Acoustic factor in proofreading. *Nature,* **214***,* 851-852.

Corcoran, D. W. J., & Weaning, W. J. (1968). Acoustic factors in visual search. *Quarterly Journal of Experimental Psychology,* **20***,* 83-85.

Corkin, S. (1968). Acquisition of motor skills after bilateral medial temporal-lobe excision. *Neuropsychologia,* **6***,* 255-265.

Craik, F. 1. M. (1977). Age differences in human memory. In J. E. Birren & K. W. Schaie (Eds.), *Handbook of the psychology of aging.* New York: Van Nostrand Reinhold.

Crossman, E. R. F. W. (1959). A theory of the acquisition of speed-skill. *Ergonomics,* **2***,* 153-166.

Crovitz, H. F., & Quina-Holland, K. (1976). Proportion of episodic memories from early childhood by years of age. *Bulletin of the Psychonomic Society,* **7***,* 61-62.

Crovitz, H. F., & Schiffman, H. (1974). Frequency of episodic memories as a function of their age. *Bulletin of the Psychonomic Society,* **4***,* 517-518.

Crowder, R. G. (1982). *The Psychology of reading*. New York: Oxford University Press.

Crowe, S. F. (1992). Dissociation of two frontal lobe syndromes by a test of verbal fluency. *Journal of Clinical & Experimental Neuropsychology, 14*, 327-339.

Crowe, S. F. (1996). The performance of schizophrenic and depressed subjects on tests of fluency: Support for a compromise in dorsolateral prefrontal functioning. *Australian Psychologist, 13*, 204-209.

Cubelli, R., Marchetti, C., Boscolo, G., & Della Sala, S. (2000). Cognition in action: Testing a model of limb apraxia. *Brain and Cognition, 44*, 144-165.

Cuddy, L. J., & Jacoby, L. L. *(1982).* When forgetting helps memory: An analysis of repetition effects. *Journal of Verbal Learning and Verbal Behavior, 21*, 451-467.

Currie, C. B., McConki, G. W., Carlson-Radvansky, L. A., Irwin, D. E. (2000). The role of the saccade target object in the perception of a visually stable world. *Perception & Psychophysics, 62*, 673-683.

Cutting, J. (1976). Auditory and linguistic processes in speech perception: Inferences from fusions in dichotic listening. *Psychological Review, 83*, 114-140.

Dab, S., Claes, T., Morais, J., Shallice, T. (1999). Confabulation with a selective descriptor process impairment. *Cognitive Neuropsychology, 16*, 215-242.

D'Agostino, P. R., O'Neill, B. J., & Paivio, A. (1977). Memory for pictures and words as a function of level processing: Depth or dual coding? *Memory & Cognition, 5*, 252-256.

Dagenbach, D., Carr, T. H., & Wilhelmsen, A. (1989). Task-induced strategies and near-threshold priming: Conscious influences on unconscious perception. *Journal of Memory and Language, 28*, 412-443.

Dalrymple-Alford, E. C., & Budayr, D. (1966). Examination of some aspects of the Stroop color-word test. *Perceptual & Motor Skills, 23*, 1211-1214.

Daneman, M., & Carpenter, P. A. (1983). Individual differences in integrating information between and within sentences. *Journal of Experimental Psychology: Learning, Memory and Cognition, 9*, 561-584.

Darley, C. F., & Glass, A. L. (1975). Effects of rehearsal and serial list position on recall. *Journal of Experimental Psychology: Human Learning and Memory, 104*, 453-458.

Damasio, H., Tranel, D., Grabowski, T., Adolphs, R., & Damasio, A. (2004). Neural systems behind word an concept retrieval. *Cognition, 92*, 179-229.

Darwin, C. T., Turvey, M. T., & Crowder, R. G. (1972). An auditory analogue of the Sperling partial report procedure: Evidence for brief auditory storage. *Cognitive Psychology, 3*, 255-267.

Davidson (1993). Neuropsychology of emotion and affective style. In M. Lewis and J. M. Haviland (Eds.), *Handbook of Emotions*: New York: Guilford Press.

Davies, D. R., & Tune, G. S. (1969). *Human vigilance performance*. New York: Elsevier.

Davies, M., & Coltheart, M. (2000). Introduction: Pathologies of belief. In M. Coltheart & M. Davies (Eds.), *Pathologies of Belief*. Malden, MA: Blackwell, pp. 1-46.

Davies, S. P. (2000). Memory and planning processes in solutions to well-structured problems. *The Quarterly Journal of Experimental Psychology, 53A*, 896-927.

Dawes, R. (1964). Cognitive distortion. *Psychological Reports*, **14**, 443-459.

Dawson, G., Webb, S., Schellenberg, G. D., Dager, S., Friedman, S., Aylward, E., & Richards, T. (2002). Defining the broader phenotype of autism: Genetic, brain, and behavioral perspectives. *Development and Psychopathology,* **14**, 581-611.

Deese, J. (1959). On the prediction of occurrence of particular verbal intrusions in immediate recall. *Journal of Experimental Psychology*, **58**, 17-22.

De Groot, A. D. (1965). *Thought and choice in chess*. The Hague: Mouton.

DeLosh, E. L., & McDaniel, M. A. (1996). The role of order information in free recall: Application to the word-frequency effect. *Journal of Experimental Psychology: Learning, memory, & Cognition,* **22**, 1136-1146.

De Mornay Davies, P. (1998). Automatic semantic priming: the contribution of lexical- and semantic-level processes. *European Journal of Cognitive Psychology,* **10**, 389-412.

Dennis, M. (1980). Capacity and strategy for syntactic comprehension after left or right hemi-decortication. *Brain and Language*, **10**, 287-317.

Dennis, M., & Kohn, B. (1975). Comprehension of syntax in infantile hemiplegics after cerebral hemi-decortication: Left hemisphere superiority. *Brain and Language*, **2**, 475-486.

Desimone, R. Chelazzi, L. Miller, E. K., & Duncan, J. (1995). Neuronal mechanisms of visual attention. In, T. V. Papathomas (Ed.) *Early vision and beyond*. Cambridge MA: MIT Press.

Detterman, K. K., & Daniel, M. H. (1989). Correlations of mental tests with each other and with cognitive variables are highest for low IQ groups. *Intelligence,* **15**, 349-359.

Detterman, D. K., & Ellis, N. R. (1972). Determinants of induced amnesia in short term memory. *Journal of Experimental Psychology*, **95**, 308-316.

De Valois, R. L., & Jacobs, G. H. (1968). Primate color vision. *Science*, **162**, 533-540.

Diamond, A. (1995).. Evidence of robust recognition memory early in life even when assessed by reaching behavior. *Journal of Experimental Child Psychology*. **59**, 419-456.

Diamond, B.J., DeLuca, J., and Fisher, C. (2000). Confabulation and memory in anterior communicating artery aneurysm. *Abstracts/Archives of Clinical Neuropsychology*, **15**, 721-722.

Dick, R. W. (1994). A summary of head and neck injuries in collegiate athletics using the NCAA surveillance system. In, E. F. Horner (Ed.), *Head and neck injuries in sports*. Philadelphia: ASTM

Di Lollo, V., Arnett, J. L., & Kruck, R. V. (1982). Age-related changes in rate of visual information processing. *Journal of Experimental Psychology: Human Perception and Performance,* **8**, 225-237.

Doty, R. W., & Overman, W. H., Jr. (1977). Mnemonic role of forebrain commissures in macaques. In S. Harnad, R. W. Doty, L. Goldstein, J. Jaynes, & G. Krauthamer (Eds.), *Lateralization in the nervous system*. New York: Academic Press.

Dronkers, N. F. (1996). A new brain region for coordinating speech articulation. *Naure*, **384**, 159-161.

Dronkers, N. F., Wilkins, D. P., Van Valin Jr., R. D., Redfern, B. B., & Jaeger, J. J. (2004). Lesion analysis of the brain areas involved in language comprehension. *Cognition*, **92**, 145-177.

Druker, J. F., & Hagen, J. W. (1969). Developmental trends in the processing of task-relevant and task irrelevant information. *Child Development, 40,* 371-382.

Duncan, J. (1980). The locus of interference in the perception of simultaneous stimuli. *Psychological Review, 87,* 272-300.

Duncan, J., & Humphreys, G. W. (1989). Visual search and stimulus similarity. *Psychological Review, 96,* 433-458.

Duncan, J., & Humphreys, G. W. (1992). Beyond the search surface: Visual search and attentional engagement. *Journal of Experimental Psychology: Human Perception and Performance, 18,* 578-588.

Duncan, J., & Nimmo-Smith, I. (1996). Objects and attributes in divided attention: Surface and boundary systems. *Perception & Psychophysics, 38,* 1076-1084.

Duncan, J., Sietz, R. J., Kolodny, J., Bor, D., Herzog, H., Ahmed, A. Newell, F. N., & Emslie, H. (2000). A neural basis for general intelligence. *Science, 289,* 457-560.

Duncker, K. (1945). On problem solving. *Psychological Monographs,* **58** (No. 270).

Dunlap, G. L., & Dunlap, L. L. (1979). Manipulating the word frequency effect in free recall. *Memory & Cognition,* 7, 420-425.

Durso, F. T., & Johnson, M. K. (1980). The effects of orienting tasks on recognition, recall, and modality confusion of pictures and words. *Journal of Verbal Learning and Verbal Behavior,* 19, 416-429.

Dyer, F. N., & Severance, L. J. (1973). Stroop interference with successive presentations of separate incongruent words and colors. *Journal of Experimental Psychology, 98,* 438-439.

Eacott, M. J; & Crawley, R. A. (1998). The offset of childhood amnesia: Memory for events that occurred before age 3. *Journal of Experimental Psychology: General,* 127, 22-33.

Easterbrook, J. A. (1959). The effect of emotion on cue utilization and the organization of behavior. *Psychological Review, 66,* 183-201.

Easton, R., & Moran, P. W. (1978). A quantitative confirmation of visual capture of curvature. *Journal of General Psychology,* 98, 105-112.

Edelstyn, N. M. J., Oyebode, F. Booker, E., & Humphreys, G. W. (1998). Facial processing and the delusional misidentification syndromes. *Cognitive Neuropsychiatry,* **3,** 299-314.

Edelystyn, N. M. J., Riddoch, M. J., Oyebode, F., Humphreys, G. W., & Forde, E. (1996). Visual processing in patients with Fregoli syndrome. *Cognitive Neuropsychiatry,* **1,** 103-124.

Efron, R., Bogen, J. E., & Yund, E. W. (1977). Perception of dichotic chords by normal and commissurotomized human subjects. *Cortex,* 13, 137-149.

Efron, R., & Yund, E. W. (1974). Dichotic competition of simultaneous tone bursts of different frequency. I. Dissociation of pitch from lateralization and loudness. *Neuropsychologia,* **12,** 149-156.

Egan, D., & Greeno, J. (19 74). Theory of inductive learning: Knowledge acquired in concept identification, serial pattern learning, and problem solving. In L. Gregg (Ed.), *Knowledge and Cognition.* Hillsdale, N.J.: Erlbaum.

Egeth, H. E., & Sager, L. C. (1977). On the locus of visual dominance. *Perception & Psychophysics, 22,* 77-86.

Ehrlich, S. F., & Rayner, K. (1981). Contextual effects on word perception and eye movements during reading. *Journal of Verbal Learning and Verbal Behavior,* 20, 641-655.

Eich, J. E. *(1980)*. The cue-dependent nature of state dependent retrieval. *Memory & Cognition*, **8**, 157-173.

Eijkman, E., & Vendrik, A. J. H. (1965). Can a sensory system be specified by its internal noise? *Journal of the Acoustical Society of America*, **37**, 1102-1109.

Einstein, G. 0., & Hunt, R. R. (1980). Levels of processing and organization: Additive effects of individual-item and relational processing. *Journal of Experimental Psychology: Human Learning and Memory*, **6**, *588-598.*

Ekman, P. (1992). Facial expressions of emotion: New findings, new questions. *Psychological Science,* **3**, 34-38.

Elio, R., & Anderson, J, R. *(1981)*. The effects of category generalizations and instance similarity on schema abstraction. *Journal of Experimental Psychology: Human Learning and Memory*, **7**, 397-417.

Ellis, A. W. (1984). Introduction to Bramwell's (1897) case of word meaning deafness. *Cognitive Neuropsychology*, **1**, 245-258.

Ellis, H. D., Lewis, M. B., Moselhy, H. F., Young, A. W. (2000). Automatic without autonomic responses to familiar faces: Differential components of covert face recognition in a case of Capgras delusion. *Cognitive Neuropsychiatry,* **5**, 255-269.

Ellis, N. C., & Hennelly, R. A. (1980). A bilingual word-length effect: Implications for intelligence testing and the relative ease of mental calculation in Welsh and English. *British Journal of Psychology*, **71**, 43-52.

Engen, T., & Ross, B. M. (1973). Long-term memory of odors with and without verbal descriptions. *Journal of Experimental Psychology*, **100**, 221-227.

Enns, J. T., & Resnick, R. A. (1990). Sensitivity to tree-dimensional orientation in visual search. *Psychological Science,* **1**, 323-326.

Epstein, E. J. (1994). Why spy? *The New York Times Magazine,* May 22, 42-43.

Erber, J. T. (1978). Age differences in a controlled-lag memory test. *Experimental Aging Research*, **4**, 195-205.

Erdelyi, M. H., & Becker, J. (1974). Hypermnesia for pictures: Incremental memory for pictures but not words in multiple recall trials, *Cognitive Psychology*, **6**, 159-171.

Erdelyi, M. H., Finkelstein, S., Herrell, N., Miller, B., & Thomas, J. (1976). Coding modality vs. input modality in hypermnesia: Is a rose a rose a rose? *Cognition*, **4**, 311-319

Ericsson, K. A., Krampe, R., & Tesch-Romer, C. (1993). The role of deliberate practice in the acquisition of expert performance. *Psychological Review,* **100**, 363-406.

Eriksson, P. S., Perfilieva, E. Bjork-Eriksson, T., Alborn, A. M., Nordborg, C., Peterson, D. A., & Gage, F. H. (1998). Neurogenesis in the adult human hippocampus. *Nature Medicine*, **4**, 1313-1317.

Eriksen, C. W., & Collins, J. F. (1967). Some temporal characteristics of visual pattern perception. *Journal of Experimental Psychology*, **74**, 476-484.

Erdelyi, M. H., & Kleinbard, J. *(1978)*. Has Ebbinghaus decayed with time? The growth of recall (hypermnesia) over days. *Journal of Experimental Psychology: Human Learning and Memory*, **4**, 275-289.

Estes, W. K. (1986). Array models for category learning. *Cognitive Psychology,* **18**, 500-549.

Estes, W. K., Allmeyer, D. H., & Reder, S. M. (1976). Serial position functions for letter identification at brief and extended exposure durations. *Perception & Psychophysics*, **19**, 1-15.

Evans, S. H. (1967). A brief statement of schema theory. *Psychonomic Science, 8*, 87-88.

Evans, J. St. B. T., Handley, S. J., Over, D. E., & Perham, N. (2002). Background beliefs in Bayesian inference. *Memory & Cognition*, **30**, 179-190.

Eysenck, H. J. (1967). *The biological basis of personality.* Springfield: Thomas.

Eysenck, M. W. (1982). *Attention and arousal.* Berlin: Springer-Verlag.

Fagen, J. W., Morrongiello, B. A., Rovee-Collier, C., & Gekoski, M. J. (1984). Expectancies and memory retrieval in 3-month-old infants. *Child Development*, **55**, 936-943.

Fagan, J. W., Rovee, C. K., & Kaplan, M. G. (1976). Psychophysical scaling of stimulus similarity in 3-month-old infants and adults. *Journal of Experimental Child Psychology, 22*, 272-281.

Fantz, R. L. (1958). Pattern vision in young infants. *Psychological Record*, **8**, 43-47.

Fernald, A. (1993). Approval and disapproval: Infant responsiveness to vocal affect in familiar and unfamiliar languages. *Child Development, 64*, 657-674.

Ferrand, L., & Grainger, J. (1994). Effects of orthography are independent of phonology in masked form priming. *Quarterly Journal of Experimental Psychology, 47A*, 365-382.

Ficca, G., Lombardo, P., Rossi, L., & Salzarulo, P. (2000). Morning recall of verbal material depends on prior sleep organization. *Behavioural Brain Research, 112*, 159-163.

Fischer, B., & Breitmeyer, B. (1987). Mechanisms of visual attention revealed by saccadic eye movements. *Neuropsychology, 25*, 73-84.

Fischer, R., Alexander, M., D'Esposito, M., & Otto, R. (1995). Neuropsychological and neuroanatomical correlates of confabulation. *Journal of Clinical and Experimental Neuropsychology*, **17**, 20-28.

Fischler, I. (1977). Semantic facilitation without association in a lexical decision task. *Memory & Cognition, 5*, 335-339.

Fitts, P. (1954). The information capacity of the human motor system in controlling the amplitude of movement. *Journal of Experimental Psychology*, **47**, 381-391.

Fitts, P. M., & Deininger, R. L. (1954). S-R compatibility: Correspondence among paired elements within stimulus and response codes. *Journal of Experimental Psychology*, **48**, 483-491.

Fitts, P. M., & Posner, M. 1. (1967). *Human performance.* Belmont, Calif.: Brooks/ Cole.

Fitts, P. M., & Seegar, C. M. (1953). S-R compatibility: Spatial characteristics of stimulus and response codes. *Journal of Experimental Psychology*, **46**, 199-210.

Flavell, J. H. (1984). *Cognitive development*, 2nd ed. Englewood Cliffs, N.J.: Prentice-Hall.

Flavell, J. H., Beach, D. H., & Chinsky, J. M. (1966). Spontaneous verbal rehearsal in a memory task as a function of age. *Child Development*, **37**, 283-299.

Flavell, J. H., & Wellman, H. M. (1976). Metamemory. In R. V. Kail & J. W. Hagen (Eds.), *Memory in cognitive development*. Hillsdale, N.J.: Erlbaum.

Fleishman, E. A., & Parker, J. K. (1962). Factors in the retention and relearning of perceptual-motor skills. *Journal of Experimental Psychology*, **64**, 215-226.

Flowers, J. H., Warner, J. L., & Polansky, M. L. (1979). Response and encoding factors in ignoring irrelevant information. *Memory & Cognition, 7,* 86-94.

Flynn, J. R. (1987). Massive IQ gains in 14 nations: What IQ tests really measure. *Psychological Bulletin, 101,* 171-191.

Forster, K. I., & Chambers, S. M. (1973). Lexical access and naming time. *Journal of Verbal Learning and Verbal Behavior, 12,* 627-635.

Forster, K. I., & Davis, C. (1991). The density constraint on form-riming in the naming task: Interference effects from a masked prime. *Journal of Memory and Language, 30,* 1-25.

Forster, K. I., & Taft, M. (1994). Bodies, antibodies, and neighborhood density effects in masked form priming. *Journal of Experimental Psychology: Learning, Memory & Cognition, 20,* 844-863.

Franco, F., & Butterworth, G. (1996). Pointing and social awareness: Declaring and requesting in the second year. *Journal of Child Language, 23,* 307-336.

Franklin, H. C., & Holding, D. H. (1977). Personal memories at different ages. *Quarterly Journal of Experimental Psychology*, **29**, 527-532.

Franklin, S. S., & Erickson, N. L. (1969). Perceived size of off-size familiar objects under normal and degraded viewing conditions. *Psychonomic Science*, **15**, 312-313.

Freedman, J. L., & Landauer, T. K. (1966). Retrieval of long-term memory: "Tip-of-the-tongue" phenomenon. *Psychonomic Science*, **4**, 309-310.

Fried, L. S., & Holyoak, K. J. (1984). Induction of category distributions: A framework for classification learning. *Journal of Experimental Psychology: Learning, Memory, and Cognition*, **10**, 234-257.

Frith, U. (1991). *Autism and Asperger syndrome*. Cambridge: Cambridge University Press.

Fuld, P. A., & Buschke, H. (1976). Stages of retrieval in verbal learning. *Journal of Verbal Learning and Verbal Behavior*, **15**, 401-410.

Gade, a. (1982). Amnesia after operations on aneurysms of the anterior communicating artery. *Surgical Neurology*, **18**, 46-49.

Gardiner, J. M., Craik, F. 1. M., & Birtwistle, J. (1972). Retrieval cues and release from proactive inhibition. *Journal of Verbal Learning and Verbal Behavior*, **11**, 778-783.

Gardner, E. (1994). *Fundamentals of neurology*. Philadelphia: Saunders.

Gardner, H. (1976). *The shattered mind*. New York: Vintage Books.

Gardner H. (1983). *Frames of mind: The theory of multiple intelligences*. New York: Basic Books.

Gardner, H., Boller, F., Moreines, J., & Butters, N. (1973). Retrieving information from Korsakoff patients: effects of categorical cues and reference to the task. *Cortex, 9,* 165-175.

Garven, S., Wood, J. M., & Malpass, R. S. (2000). Allegations of wrongdoing: The effects of reinforcement on children's mundane and fantastic claims. *Journal of Applied Psychology, 85,* 38-49.

Garven, S., Wood, J. M., Malpass, R. S., & Shaw, J. S. III (1998). More than suggestion: The effect of interviewing techniques from the McMartin Preschool case. *Journal of Applied Psychology*, **83**, 347-359.

Gathercole, S. E. (1995). Is nonword repetition a test of phonological memory or long-term knowledge? It all depends on the nonwords? *Memory & Cognition*, **23**, 83-94.

Gathercole, S. E., & Baddeley, A. D. (1989). Development of vocabulary in children and short-term phonological memory. *Journal of Memory and Language*, **28**, 200-213.

Gathercole, S. E., & Broadbent, D. E. (1984). Combining attributes in specified and categorized target search: Further evidence for strategic differences. *Memory & Cognition*, **12**, 329-337.

Gathercole, S. E., Willis, C. S., Emslie, H., & Baddeley, A. D. (1992). Phonological memory and vocabulary development during the early school years: A longitudinal study. *Developmental Psychology*, **28**, 887-898.

Gazzaniga, M. S. (1970). *The Bisected Brain*. New York: Appleton-Century-Crofts.

Gazzaniga, M. S. (1983), Right hemisphere language following brain bisection. *American Psychologist*, **38**, 525-537.

Gazzaniga, M. S., & Hillyard, S. A. (1971). Language and speech capacity of the right hemisphere. *Neuropsychologia*, **9**, 273-280.

Gazzaniga, M. S., Ivry, R. B., & Mangun, G. R. (1998). *Cognitive neuroscience*. New York: Norton.

Gelman, S. A., & Coley, J. D. (1990). The importance of knowing a dodo is a bird: Categories and inferences in 2-year-old children. *Developmental Psychology*, **26**, 796-804.

Gelman, S. A., & Markman, E. M. (1986). Categories and induction in young children. *Cognition*, **23**, 183-209.

Gelman, S. A. & Markman, E. M. (1987). Young children's inductions form natural kinds: The role of categories and appearances. *Child Development*, **58**, 1532-1541.

Gentner, D., & Gentner, D. R. (1983). Flowing waters or teeming crowds: Mental models of electricity. In D. Gentner & A. L. Stevens (Eds.), *Mental models*. Hillsdale, N.J.: Erlbaum.

Georgopoulos, A. P. (1995). Motor cortex and cognitive processing. In M. S. Gazzaniga (Ed.), *The Cognitive Neurosciences* (pp. 507-517). Cambridge MA, MIT Press.

German, T. P., & Defeyter, M. A. (2000). Immunity of functional fixedness in young children. *Psychonomic Bulletin & Review*, **7**, 707-712.

Gerhardstein, P., Renner, P., & Rovee-Collier, C. (1999). The roles of perceptual and categorical similarity in colour pop-out in infants. *British Journal of Developmental Psychology*, **17**, 405-420.

Gescheider, G. A., Sager, L. C., & Ruffolo, , L. J. (1975). Simultaneous auditory and tactile information processing. *Perception & Psychophysics*, **18**, 209-216.

Geschwind, N. (1970). The organization of language and the brain. *Science*, **170**, 940-944.

Gibson, J. J. (1966). *The senses considered as perceptual systems*. Boston: Houghton Mifflin.

Gick, M. L., & Holyoak, K. J. (1980). Analogical problem solving. *Cognitive Psychology*, **12**, 306-355.

Gick, M. L., & Holyoak, K. J. (1983). Schema induction and analogical transfer. *Cognitive Psychology*, **15**, 1-38.

Gillberg, C., & Coleman, M. (2000). *The biology of the autistic syndromes* (3rd ed.). Cambridge: Cambridge University Press.

Gilovich, T. (1981). Seeing the past in the present: The effect of associations to familiar events on judgments and decisions. *Journal of Personality and Social Psychology*, **40**, 797-808.

Glanzer, M., & Adams, J. K. (1990). The mirror effect in recognition memory. *Memory & Cognition*, **13**, 8-20.

Glanzer, M., & Cunitz, A. R. (1966). Two storage mechanisms in free recall. *Journal of Verbal Learning and Verbal Behavior*, **5**, 351-360.

Glass, A. (1993). The role of generation in recognition. *Scandinavian Journal of Psychology*, **34**, 255-267.

Glass, A. L., & Holyoak, K. J. (1975). Alternative conceptions of semantic memory. *Cognition*, **3**, 313-339.

Glass, A. L., Holyoak, K. J., & Kiger, J. I. (1979). Role of antonymy relations in semantic judgments. *Journal of Experimental Psychology: Human Learning and Memory*, **5**, 598-606.

Glass, A. L., Holyoak, K. J., & O'Dell, C. (19 74). Production frequency and the verification of quantified statements. *Journal of Verbal Learning and Verbal Behavior*, **13**, 237-254.

Glass, A. L., Krejci, J. & Goldman, J. (1989). The necessary and sufficient conditions for motor learning, recognition and recall. *Journal of Memory, and Language*, **28**, 189-199.

Glenberg, A. M. (1979). Component-levels theory of the effects of spacing of repetitions on recall and recognition. *Memory & Cognition*, **7**, 95-112.

Gloning, K. (1977). Handedness and aphasia. *Neuropsychologia*, **15**, 355-358.

Glucksberg, S., & Cowen, G. N., Jr. (1970). Memory for nonattended auditory material. *Cognitive Psychology*, **1**, 149-156.

Glucksberg, S., & Danks, J. (1968). Effects of discriminative labels and of nonsense labels upon availability of novel function. *Journal of Verbal Learning and Verbal Behavior*, **7**, 72-76.

Glucksberg, S., & Weisberg, R. W. (1966). Verbal behavior and problem solving: Some effects of labeling in a functional fixedness problem. *Journal of Experimental Psychology*, **71**, 659-664.

Godden, D. R., & Baddeley, A. D. (1975). Context-dependent memory in two natural environments: On land and underwater. *British Journal of Psychology*, **66**, 325-332.

Godijn, R., & Theeuwes, J. (2002). Programming of endogenous and exogenous saccades: Evidence for a competitive integration model. *Journal of Experimental Psychology: Human Perception & Performance*, **28**, 1039-1054.

Goldberg, E., Hughes, J. E, Mattis, S., & Antin, S. P. (1982). Isolated retrograde amnesia: Different etiologies, same mechanisms? *Cortex*, **18**, 459-462.

Goldberg, G. (1985). Supplementary motor area structure and function: Review and hypothesis. *Behavior and Brain Science*, **8**, 567-616.

Golding, E. (1981). The Effect of Past Experience on Problem Solving. Paper presented at the Annual Conference of the British Psychological Society, Surrey University.

Goodale, M. A., & Humphrey, G. K. (1998). The objects of action and perception. *Cognition*, **67**, 181-207.

Goodglass, H. (1968). Studies on the grammar of aphasics. In S. Rosenberg & J. Kaplin (Eds.), *Developments in applied psycholinguistic research*. New York: Macmillan.

Goodglass, H. (1976). Agrammatism. In H. Whitaker & M. A. Whitaker (Eds.), *Perspectives in neurolinguistics and psycholinguistics*. New York: Academic Press.

Goodglass, H., & Berko, J. (1960). Aphasia and inflectional morphology in English. *Journal of Speech and Hearing Research*, **10**, 257-262.

Goodglass, H., Fodor, I., & Schulhoff, S. (1967). Prosodic factors in grammar-evidence from aphasia. *Journal of Speech and Hearing Research*, **10**, 5-20.

Goodglass, H., & Geschwind, N. (1976). Language disorders (aphasia). In E. C. Carterette & M. Friedman (Eds.), *Handbook of Perception (Vol., 8)*. New York: Academic Press.

Goodglass, H., & Hunt, J. (1958). Grammatical complexity and aphasic speech. *Word*, **14**,197-207.

Goodglass, H., Quadfasel, F. A., & Timberlake, W. H. (1964). Phrase length and the type and severity of aphasia. *Cortex*, **1**, 133-158.

Gooding, P. a., Myes, A. r., & van Eijk, R. (2000). A meta-analysis of indirect memory tests for novel material in organic amnesics. *Neuropsychologia*, **38**, 666-676.

Goodman, G. S., & Reed, R. S. (1986). Age differences in eyewitness testimony. *Law and Human Behavior*, **10**, 317-322.

Goodwin, K. A., Meissner, C. A., & Ericsson (2001). Toward a model of false recall: Experimental manipulation of encoding context and the collection of verbal reports. *Memory & Cognition,* **29,** 806-819.

Gopnik, A., & Choi, S. (1990). Do linguistic differences lead to cognitive differences? A cross-linguistic study of semantic and cognitive development. *First Languaguage*, **10**, 99-215.

Gordon, H. W. (1970). Hemispheric asymmetries in the perception of musical chords. *Cortex*, **6**, 387-398.

Gordon, H. W. (19 74). Hemispheric asymmetry and musical performance. *Science*, **189**, 68-69.

Gordon, H. W. (1980). Degree of ear asymmetries for perception of dichotic chords and for illusory chord localization in musicians of different levels of competence. *Journal of Experimental Psychology*: *Human Perception and Performance*, **6**, 516-527.

Gorman, A. M. (1961). Recognition memory for nouns as a function of abstractness and frequency. *Journal of Experimental Psychology*, **61**, 23-29.

Gould, E., Beylin, A., Tanapat, P., Reeves, A., & Shors, T. J. (1999). Learning enhances adult neurogenesis in the hippocampal formation. *Nature Neuroscience*, **2**, 260-265.

Graf, P., Shimamura, A., & Squire, L. R. (1985). Priming across modalities and priming across category levels: Extending the domain of preserved function in amnesia. *Journal of Experimental Psychology: Learning, Memory, & Cognition*, **11**, 386-396.

Graf, P., Squire, L. R., & Mandler, G. (1984). The information that amnesic patients do not forget. *Journal of Experimental Psychology:, Learning, Memory, and Cognition*, **10**, 164-178.

Graham, K. R. (1977). Perceptual processes hypnosis: Support for a cognitive-state theory based on laterality. *Annals of the New York Academy of Sciences,* **296**, 274-283.

Graham, K. S., Lambon, Ralph, M. A.., & Hodges, J. R. (1997). Determining the impact of autobiographical experience on "meaning": new insights from investigating sports-related vocabulary and knowledge in two cases with semantic dementia. *Cognitive Neuropsychology*, **14**, 801-837.

Grainger, J., & Ferrand, L. (1996). Masked orthographic and phonological priming in visual word recognition and naming. Cross-task comparison. *Journal of Memory and Language, 35, 623-647.

Grandstaff, N. W., & Pribram, K. H. (1975). Habituation: Electrical changes in the visual system. *Neuropsychologia, 10, 125-132.

Green, D. W. (1995). Externalization, counter-examples, and the abstract selection task. *Quarterly Journal of Experimental Psychology*, **48A**, 424-446.

Green, D. W., & Larking, R. (1995). The locus of facilitation in the abstract selection task. *Thinking & Reasoning, 1, 183-199.

Greenberg, J. H. (1963). Some universals of grammar with particular reference to the order of meaningful elements. In J. H. Greenberg (Ed.), *Universals of language*. Cambridge, Mass.: MIT Press.

Greene, R. L. (1984). Incidental learning of event frequency. *Memory & Cognition*, **12**, 90-95.

Greenwald, A. G. (1980). The totalitarian ego: Fabrication and revision of personal history. *American Psychologist*, **35**, 603- 618.

Gregory, R. L. (1997). *Eye and brain: The psychology of seeing.* Princeton: Princeton University Press.

Griggs, R. A. (1983). The role of problem content in the selection task and in the THOG problem. In J. St. B. T. Evans (Ed.), *Thinking and reasoning: psychological approaches*. London: Routledge & Kegan Paul.

Griggs, R. A., & Cox, J. R. (1982). The elusive thematic-materials effect in Wason's selection task. *British Journal of Psychology*, **73**, 407-420.

Grison, S., & Strayer, D. L. (2001). Negative priming and perceptual fluency: More than what meets the eye. *Perception & Psychophysics*, **63**, 1063-1071.

Gruenewald, P. J., & Lockhead, G. R. (1980). The free recall of category examples. *Journal of Experimental Psychology: Human Learning and Memory*, **6**, 225-240.

Gruneberg, M. M., & Monks, J. (1974). Feeling of knowing and cued recall. *Acta Psychologica*, **38**, 257-265.

Guridi, J., Rodriguez-Oroz, Lozano, A. M., Moro, E., Albanese, A., Nuttin, B., Gybels, J., Ramos, E., & Obeso, J. A. (2000). Targeting the basal ganglia for deep brain stimulation in Parkinson's disease. *Neurology*, **55** (Supplement 6), s21 – s28.

Guttman, N., & Julesz, B. (1963). Lower limits of auditory periodicity analysis. *Journal of the Acoustical Society of America, 35, 610.

Haber, R. N., & Hershenson, M. (1965). The effects of repeated brief exposures on the growth of a percept. *Journal of Experimental Psychology*, **69**, 40-46.

Haber, R. N., & Schindler, R. M. (1981). Error in proofreading: Evidence of syntactic control of letter processing? *Journal of Experimental Psychology*: *Human Perception and Performance*, **7**, 573-579.

Haberlandt, K., Berian, C., & Sandson, J. (1980). The episodic schema in story processing. *Journal of Verbal Learning and Verbal Behavior*, **19**, 635-650.

Hadani, I., Ishai, G., Frisch, H. L., & Kononov, A. (1994). Two metric solutions to the three-dimensional reconstruction for an eye in pure rotations. *Journal of the Optical Society of America,* **11**, 1564-1574.

Hagen, J. W., Meacham, J. A., & Mesibov, G. (1970). Verbal labeling, rehearsal, and short-term memory. *Cognitive Psychology,* **1**, 47-58.

Halford, G. S. (1984). Can young children integrate premises in transitivity and serial order tasks? *Cognitive Psychology*, **16**, 65-93.

Hall, D. G., Lee, S. c., & Belanger, J. (2001). Young children's use of syntactic cues to learn proper names and count nouns. *Developmental Psychology,* **37,** 298-307.

Hamers, J. F. & Lambert, W. E. (1972). Bilingual interdependencies in auditory perception. *Journal of Verbal Learning and Verbal Behavior,* **11**, 303-310.

Hamilton, C. R. (1977). An assessment of hemispheric specialization in monkeys. *Annals of the New York Academy of Sciences*, **299**, 222-232.

Hammerton, M. (1963). Retention of learning in a difficult tracking task. *Journal of Experimental Psychology*, **66**, 108- 110.

Hamond, N. R; & Fivush, R. (1991). Memories of Mickey Mouse: Young children recount their trip to Disneyworld. *Cognitive Development.* **6**, 433-448

Hanna, E., & Meltzoff, A. N. (1993). Peer imitation by toddlers in laboratory, home, and day-care contexts: Implications for social learning and memory. *Developmental Psychology,* **29**, 701-710.

Hansen, R. M.,& Skavenski, A. A. (1985). Accuracy of spatial localization near the time of saccadic eye movements. *Vision Research,* **25**, 1077-1082.

Happe, F., & Frith, U. (1996). The neuropsychology of autism. *Brain,* **119**, 1377-1400.

Hardyck, C. D., & Petrinovich, I. F. (1970). Subvocal speech and comprehension level as a function of the difficulty level of the reading material. *Journal of Verbal Learning and Verbal Behavior*, **9**, 647-652.

Harris, G., Begg, L, & Mitterer, J. (1980). On the relation between frequency estimates and recognition memory. *Memory & Cognition*, **8**, 99-104.

Harris, P., Brown, E., Marriott, c., Whittall, s., & Harmer, s. (1991). Monsters, ghosts, and witches. Testing the limits of the fantasy reality distinction in young children. *British Journal of Developmental Psychology,* **9**, 105-123.

Hart, J. T. (1965). Memory and the feeling of knowing experience. *Journal of Educational Psychology*, **56**, 208-216.

Hartley, J. T., Birnbaum, I. M., & Parker, E. S. (1978). Alcohol and storage deficits: Kind of processing? *Journal of Verbal Learning and Verbal Behavior*, **17**, 635-647.

Hartshorn, K., & Rovee-Collier, C. (1997). Infant learning and long-term memory at 6 months: A confirming analysis. *Developmental Psychobiology,* **30**, 71-85.

Hartshorn, K., Wilk, A. E., Muller, K. L., & Rovee-Collier, C. (1998). An expanding training series protracts retention for 3-month-old infants. *Developmental Psychobiology,* **33**, 271-280.

Harvey, A. G., Bryant, R. A., Dang, S. T. (1998). Autobiographical memory in acute stress disorder. *Journal of Consulting & Clinical Psychology,* **66**, 500-506.

Hasher, L., & Chromiak, W. (1977). The processing of frequency information: An automatic mechanism? *Journal of Verbal Learning and Verbal Behavior*, **16**, 173-184.

Hasher, L., & Zacks, R. T. (1979). Automatic and effortful processes in memory. *Journal of Experimental Psychology*: *General*, **108**, 356-388.

Hatfield & Rapson (1993), Love and attachment processes. In, M. Lewis and J. M. Haviland (Eds.), *Handbook of Emotions*: New York: Guilford Press.

Hay, J. C., Pick, H. L., & Ikeda, K. (1965). Visual capture produced by prism spectacles. *Psychonomic Science*. **2**, 215-216.

Hayne, H. Boniface, J. & Barr, R. The development of declarative memory in human infants: Age-related changes in deferred imitation. *Behavioral neuroscience*, **114**, 77-83.

Hayne, H., Greco, c., Earley, L., L, Griesler, P., & Rovee-Collier, C. (1986). Ontogeny of early event memory II. Encoding and retrieval by 2- and 3-month-olds. *Infant Behavior and Development*, **9**, 461-472.

Hayne, H., Rovee-Collier, C., & Borza, M. A. (1991). Infant memory for place information. *Memory & Cognition*, **19**, 378-386.

Hayward, W. G. & Tarr, M J. (1997). Testing conditions for viewpoint invariance in object recognition. *Journal of Experimental Psychology: Human Perception and Performance*, **23**, 1511-1521.

Healy, A. F. (1976). Detection errors on the word the: Evidence for reading units larger than letters. *Journal of Experimental Psychology*: *Human Perception and Performance*, **2**, 235-242.

Healy, A. F. (1980). Proofreading errors on the word the: New evidence on reading units. *Journal of Experimental Psychology*: *Human Perception and Performance*, **6**,45-57.

Healy, A. F. (1981). The effects of visual similarity on proofreading for misspellings. *Memory & Cognition*, **9**, 453-460.

Heathcote, A., Brown, S., & Mewhort, D. J. K. (2000). The power law repealed: The case for an exponential law of practice. *Psychonomic Bulletin & Review*, **7**, 185-207.

Heider, E. R. (1972). Universals in color naming and memory. *Journal of Experimental Psychology*, **93**, 10-20.

Heider, E. R., & Olivier, D. (1972). The structure of the color space in naming and memory for two languages. *Cognitive Psychology*, **3**, 337-354.

Heilman, K. M., Rothi, L. I., & Valenstein, E. (1982). Two forms of ideomotor apraxia. *Neurology*, **32**, 342-346.

Heilman, K. M., Watson, R. T., Valenstein, E. (1993). Neglect and related disorders. In, K. M. Heilman & E. Valenstein (Eds.), *Clinical neuropsychology*. New York: Oxford.

Heindel, W. C., Butters, N., Salmon, D. P. (1988). Impaired learning of a motor skill in patients with Huntington's disease. *Behavioral neuroscience*, **102**, 141-147.

Heit, E. (2000). Properties of inductive reasoning. *Psychonomic Bulletin & Review*, **7**, 569-592.

Heit, E., & Rubinstein, J. (1994). Similarity and property effects in inductive reasoning. *Journal of Experimental Psychology: Learning, Memory, & Cognition*, **20**, 411-420.

Hellige, J. B. (1980). Effects of perceptual quality and visual field of probe stimulus presentation on memory search for letters. *Journal of Experimental Psychology*: *Human Perception and Performance*, **6**, 639-651.

Hellige, J. B., Cox, P. I., & Litvac, L. (1979). Information processing in the cerebral hemispheres: Selective hemisphere activation and capacity limitations. *Journal of Experimental Psychology*: *General*, **108**, 251-279.

Hering, E. (1964). *Outlines of a theory of the light sense*. Cambridge, Mass.: Harvard University Press.

Hiatt, S., Campos, J. J., & Emde, R. N. (1979). Facial patterning an infant facial expression: Happiness, surprise, and fear. *Child Development,* **50**, 1020-1035.

Hickok, G., & Poeppel (2004). Dorsal and ventral sreams: a framework for understanding aspects of the functional anatomy of language. *Cognition*, **92**, 67-99.

Hildreth, K., & Rovee-Collier, C. (1999). Decreases in the response latency to priming over the first year of life. *Developmental Psychobiology,* **35**, 276-290.

Hilgard, E. R., & Hilgard, J. R. (1975). *Hypnosis in the relief of pain.* Los Altos CA: Kaufman.

Hinrichs, J., & Craft, J. L. (1971). Stimulus and response factors in discrete choice reaction time. *Journal of Experimental Psychology*, **91**, 305-309.

Hirshman, E., Fisher, J., Henthorn, T., Arndt, J., & Passannante, A. (2002). Midazolam amnesia and dual-process models of the word-frequency mirror effect. *Journal of Memory & Language*, **47**, 499-516.

Hodges, J. R., Patterson, K., Oxbury, S., & Funnel, E. (1992). Semantic dementia: progessive fluent aphasia with temporal lobe atrophy. *Brain*, **115**, 1783-1806.

Hodges, J. R., Salmon, D. P., & Butters, N. (1992). Semantic memory impairment in Alzheimer's disease: Failure of access or degraded knowledge? *Neuropsychologia*, **30**, 301-314.

Holbrook, M. B. (1978). Effect of subjective interletter similarity, perceived word similarity, and contextual variables on the recognition of letter substitutions in a proofreading task. *Perceptual and Motor Skills*, **47**, 251-258.

Holmes, G. (193). The cerebellum of man. *Brain*, **62**, 1-30.

Holmes, D. S. (1984). Meditation and somatic arousal reduction: A review of the experimental evidence. *American Psychologist,* **39**, 1-10.

Holyoak, K. J., & Glass, A. L. (1975). The role of contradictions and counterexamples in the rejection of false sentences. *Journal of Verbal Learning and Verbal Behavior*, **14**, 215-239.

Holyoak, K. J., & Patterson, K. K. (198 1). A positional discriminability model of linear-order judgments. *Journal of Experimental Psychology*: *Human Perception and Performance*, **7**, 1283-1302.

Holyoak, K. J., & Walker, J. H. (1976). Subjective magnitude information in semantic orderings. *Journal of Verbal Learning and Verbal Behavior*, **15**, 287-299.

Homa, D., & Vosburgh, R. (1976). Category breadth and the abstraction of prototypical information. *Journal of Experimental Psychology: Human Learning and Memory*, **2**, 322-330.

Hoosain, R., & Salili, F. (1988). Language differences, working memory, and mathematical ability. In M. M. Gruneberg, P. E. Morris, & R. N. Sykes (Eds.), *Practical aspects of memory: Current research and issues, Vol. 2: Clinical and educational implications*. Chichester: Wiley.

Hornak, J., Rolls, E. T., & Wade, D. (1996). Face and voice expression identification in patients with emotional and behavioral changes following ventral frontal lobe damage. *Neuropsychologia*, **34**, 247-261.

Horne, J.A. (1988). *Why We Sleep: The functions of sleep in humans and other mammals.* Oxford: Oxford University Press.

Horne, J.A., & Moore, V. J. (1985). Sleep EEG effects of exercise with and without additional body cooling. *Electroencephalography and Clinical Neurophysiology,* **60**, 33-38.

House, E. L., & Pansky, B. (1967). *A functional approach to neuroanatomy.* New York: McGraw-Hill.

Hudson, A. J., & Grace, G. M. (2000). Misidentification syndromes related to face specific area in the fusiform gyrus. *Journal of Neurology, Neurosurgery & Psychiatry,* **69,** 465-468.

Hudson, J. A., & Sheffield, E. G. (1998). Déjà vu all over again: Effects of reenactment on toddlers' event memory. *Child Development*, **69**, 51-67.

Humphreys, G. W., & Price, C. J. (1994). Visual feature discrimination in simultanagnosia: A study of two cases. *Cognitive Neuropsychology,* **11**, 393-434.

Howlin, P., Davies, M., & Udwin, O. (1998). Cognitive functioning in adults with Williams syndrome. *Journal of Child Psychology and Psychiatry,* **39**, 183-189.

Hulicka, I. M., & Grossman, J. L. (1967). Age-group comparisons for the use of mediators in paired-associate learning. *Journal of Gerontology*, **22**, 46-51.

Hulicka, 1. M., Sterns, H., & Grossman, J. (1967). Age-group comparisons of paired associate learning as a function of paced and self-paced association and response times. *Journal of Gerontology*, **22**, 274-280.

Hulicka, I. M., & Wheeler, D. (1976). Recall scores of old and young people as function of registration intervals. *Educational Gerontology*, **1**, 361-372.

Hultsch, D. F. (1971). Adult age differences in free classification and free recall. *Developmental Psychology*, **4**, 338-342.

Humphreys, G. W., & Rumiata, R. I. (1998). Agnosia without prosopagnosia or alexia: Evidence for stored visual memories specific to objects. *Cognitive Neuropsychology,* **15**, 243-277.

Hunt, E., & Love, T. (1972). How good can memory be? In A. W. Melton & E. Martin (Eds.), *Coding Processes in Human Memory.* Washington, D. C.: Winston/Wiley.

Hunter, I. M. L. (1962). An exceptional talent for calculative thinking. *British Journal of Psychology*, **53**, 243-258.

Hunter, I. M. L. (1977). Mental calculation. In P. N. Johnson-Laird & P. C. Wason (Eds.), *Thinking.* New York: Cambridge University Press. (Originally published, 1966.)

Hyman, I. E., Husband, T. H., & Billings, F. J. (1995). False memories of childhood experiences. *Applied Cognitive Psychology,* **9**, 181-197.

Hyman, I. E, & Rubin, D. C. (1990). Memorabilia: A naturalistic study of long-term memory. *Memory & Cognition.* **18**, 205-214.

Hyona, J., & Bertram, R. (2004). Do frequency characteristics of nonfixated words influence the processing of fixated words during reading? *European Journal of Cognitive Psychology.* **16**, 104-127.

Intraub, H. (1980). Presentation rate and the representation of briefly glimpsed pictures in memory. *Journal of Experimental Psychology: Human Learning and Memory, 6,* 1-12.

Intraub, H. (1981). Rapid conceptual identification of sequentially presented pictures. *Journal of Experimental Psychology: Human Perception and Performance, 7,* 604-610.

Intraub, H. (1985). Visual dissociation: An illusory conjunction of pictures and forms. *Journal of Experimental Psychology: Human Perception & Performance, 11,* 431-442.

Isen, A. M., Shalker, T. E., Clark, M., & Carp, L. (1978). Affect, accessibility of material in memory and behavior: A cognitive loop. *Journal of Personality and Social Psychology, 36,* 1-12.

Ivry, R. B., & Keele, S. W. (1989). Timing functions of the cerebellum. *Journal of Cognitive neuroscience, 1,* 136-152.

Izard, C. E. (1994). Innate and universal facial expressions: Evidence from developmental and cross-cultural research. *Psychological Bulletin, 115,* 288-299.

Jacoby, L. L. (1972). Effects of organization on recognition memory. *Journal of Experimental Psychology, 92,* 325-331.

Jacoby, L. L., & Hendricks, R. L. (1973). Recognition effects of study organization and test context. *Journal of Experimental Psychology, 100,* 73-82.

Jakobson, R. (1968). *Child language, aphasia, and phonological universals.* The Hague: Mouton.

Jameson, D., & Hurvich, L. M. (1955). Some quantitative aspects of an opponent-colors theory. Chromatic responses and spectral saturation. *Journal of the Optical Society of America, 45,* 546-552.

Jarvella, R. J. (1970). Effects of syntax on running memory span for connected discourse. *Psychonomic Science, 19,* 235-236.

Jarvella, R. J. (1971). Syntactic processing of connected speech. *Journal of Verbal Learning and Verbal Behavior, 10,* 409- 416.

Jaswal, V. K., & Markman, E. M. (2001). Learning proper and common names in inferential versus ostensive contexts. *Child Development, 72,* 768-786.

Jeannerod, M. (1994). The representing brain. Neural correlates of motor intention and imagery. *The Behavioral and Brain Sciences, 17,* 187 –245.

Jeffries, R., Polson, P., Razran, L., & Atwood, M. E. (1977). A process model for missionaries-cannibals and other river crossing problems. *Cognitive Psychology, 9,* 412-440.

Jerison, H. J. (1977). Vigilance: Biology, psychology, theory, and practice. In R. R. Mackie (Ed.), *Vigilance: Theory, Operational Performance, and Physiological Correlates.* New York; Plenum.

Jersild, A. T. (1927). Mental set and shift. *Archives of Psychology, 14,* 81.

Johnson, E. K., & Jusczyk, P. W. (2001). Word segmentation by 8-month-olds: When speech cues count more than statistics. *Journal of Memory & Language, 44,* 548-567.

Johnson, M. K., & Raye, C. L. (1981). Reality monitoring. *Psychological Review, 88,* 67-85.

Johnson, M.K., & Raye, C.L. (1998) False memories and confabulation. *Trends in Cognitive Sciences* 2, 137-145.

Johnson, S. C., & Carey, S. (1998). Knowledge enrichment and conceptual change in folk biology: Evidence from Williams syndrome. *Cognitive Psychology,* **37**, 156-200.

Johnson-Laird, P. N., Gibbs, G., & de Mowbray, J. (1978). Meaning, amount of processing, and memory for words. *Memory & Cognition*, **6**, 372-375.

Johnson-Laird, P. N., Legrenzi, P., & Legrenzi, M. (1972). Reasoning and a sense of reality. *British Journal of Psychology*, **63**, 395-400.

Johnston, W. A. (1978). The intrusiveness of familiar nontarget information. *Memory & Cognition,* **6**, 38-42.

Johnston, W. A., & Dark, V. (1986). Selective attention. *Annual Review of Psychology,* **37**, 43-75.

Johnston, W. A., & Heinz, S. P. (1979). Depth of nontarget processing in an attention task. *Journal of Experimental Psychology: Human Perception and Performance,* **5**, 168-175.

Johnston, W. A., & Uhl, C. N. (1976). The contributions of encoding effort and variability to the spacing effect on free recall. *Journal of Experimental Psychology: Human Learning and Memory*, **2**, 153-160.

Johnston, W. A., & Wilson, J. (1980). Perceptual processing of nontargets in an attention task. *Memory & Cognition,* **8**, 372-377.

Jolicoeur, P., Gluck, M., & Kosslyn, S. M. (1984). Pictures and names: Making the connection. *Cognitive Psychology*, **16**, 243-275.

Jones, B. M., & Parsons, 0. A. (1972). Specific vs. generalized deficits of abstracting ability in chronic alcoholics. *Archives of General Psychiatry*, **26**, 380-384.

Jones, W., Bellugi, U., Lai, Z., Chiles, M., Reilly, J., Lincoln, A., & Adolphs, R. (2000). Hypersociability in Williams syndrome. *Journal of Cognitive neuroscience (Supplement)*, **12**,30-46.

Joordens, S., & Hockley, W. E. (2000). Recollection and familiarity through the looking glass: when old does no mirror new. *Journal of Experimental Psychology: Learning, Memory, and Cognition*, **26**, 1534-1555.

Jorg, S., & Hormann, H. *(1978).* The influence of general and specific verbal labels on the recognition of labeled and unlabeled parts of pictures. *Journal of Verbal Learning and Verbal Behavior*, **17**, 445-454.

Jouvet-Mounier, D., Astic, L., & Lacote, D. (1969). Ontogenesis of the states of sleep in rat, cat, and guinea pig during the first postnatal month. *Developmental Psychobiology, 2,* 216-239.

Judd, L. L., Squire, L. R., Butters, N., Salmon, D. P., & Paller, K. A. (1987). Effects of psychotropic drugs on cognition and memory in normal humans and animals. In, H. &. Meltzer, Ed., *Psychopharmacology: The Third Generation of Progress.* New York: Raven Press.

Julesz, B. (1971). *Foundations of cyclopean perception.* Chicago: University of Chicago Press.

Julesz, B. (1981). Textons, the elements of texture perception and their interactions. *Nature,* **290**, 91-97.

Jusczyk, P. W., Houston, D. M., & Newsome, M. (1999). The beginnings of word segmentation in English-learning infants. *Cognitive Psychology,* **39,** 159-207.

Just, M. A., & Carpenter, P. A. *(1980).* A theory of reading: From *eye fixations* to comprehension. *Psychological Review,* **87***,329-354.*

Kahneman, D. (1973). *Attention and effort.* Englewood Cliffs, NJ: Prentice-Hall.

Kahneman, D., & Tversky, A. (1972). Subjective probability: A judgment of representativeness. *Cognitive Psychology,* **3**, 430-454.

Kahneman, D., & Tversky, A. (1973). On the psychology of prediction. *Psychological Review,* **80**, 237-251.

Kahneman, D., & Tversky, A. (1979). Prospect theory: An analysis of decision under risk. *Econometrica* **47**, 263-291.

Kahneman, D., & Tversky, A. (1982). The simulation heuristic. In D. Kahneman, P. Slovic, & A. Tversky (Eds.), *Judgment under uncertainty: heuristics and biases.* (pp. 201-208). New York: Cambridge University Press.

Kales, A., Tan, T.-L., Kollar, E., Naitoh, P., Preston, T., & Malmastrom, E. (1970). Sleep patterns following 205 hours of sleep deprivation. *Psychosomatic Medicine,* **32**, 189-200.

Kanner, L. (1943). Autistic disturbances and affective contact. *Nervous Child,* **2**, 217-250.

Karmiloff-Smith, A. (1998). Development itself is the key to understanding developmental disorders. *Trends in Cognitive Sciences,* **2**, 289-298.

Karmiloff-Smith, A., Grant, J., Berthoud, J., Davies, M., Howlin, P., & Udwin, O. (1997). Language in Williams syndrome: How intact is "intact?" *Child Development,* **68**, 246-262.

Karni, A., Tanne, D., Rubenstein, B., Askenasy, J., & Sagi, D. (1994). Dependence on REM sleep of overnight improvement of a perceptual skill. *Science,* **265**, 679-682.

Kasper, L. F. *(1983).* The effects of linking sentence and inter active picture mnemonics on the acquisition of Spanish nouns by middle school children. *Human Learning,* **2**, 141-156.

Kasper, L. F., & Glass, A. L. (1982). The role of the keyword method in the acquisition of Spanish nouns. *Human Learning* **1**, 235-250.

Kattler, H., Dijik, D., & Borbely, A. (1994). Effect of unilateral somatosensory stimulation prior to sleep on the sleep EEG in humans. *Journal of Sleep Research,* **3**, 159-164.

Kausler, D. H., & Klein, D. M. (1978). Age differences in processing relevant versus irrelevant stimuli in multiple-item recognition learning. *Journal of Gerontology,* **33**, 87-93.

Kavanau, J. (1996). Memory, sleep, and dynamic stabilization of neural circuitry: Evolutionary perspectives. *Neuroscience and Biobehavioral Reviews,* **20**, 289-311.

Kay, P., & McDaniel, C. K. (1978). The linguistic significance of the meanings of basic color terms. *Language,* **54**, 610-646.

Keeney, T. J., Cannizzo, S. R., & Flavell, J. H. (1967). Spontaneous and induced verbal rehearsal *in* a recall task. *Child Development,* **38**, 953-966.

Keppel, G., & Underwood, B. J. (1962). Proactive inhibition in short-term *reten*tion of single terms. *Journal of Verbal Learning and Verbal Behavior,* **1**, *153-161.*

Kiger, J. I., & Glass, A. L. (1983). The facilitation of lexical decisions by a prime occurring after the target. *Memory & Cognition,* **11**, 356-365.

Kihlstrom, J. F. (1977). Models of posthypnotic amnesia. *Annals of the New York Academy of Sciences,* **296***,* 284-301.

Kimura, D. (1961). Cerebral dominance and the perception of verbal stimuli. *Canadian Journal of Psychology*, **15**, 166- 171.

Kimura, D. (1967). Functional asymmetry of the brain in dichotic listening. *Cortex*, **3**,163-178.

Kimura, D. (1974). Left-right differences in the perception of melodies. *Quarterly Journal of Experimental Psychology*, **16**, 355-358.

Kinney, J. A. S., & Luria, D. M. (1970). Conflicting visual and tactual-kinesthetic stimulation. *Perception & Psychophysics*, **8**, 189-192.

Kirsch, I., & Braffman, W. (2001). Imaginative suggestibility and hypnotizability. *Current Directions in Psychological Science,* **10***,* 57-61.

Kleiman, G. M. (1975). Speech recoding in reading. *Journal of Verbal Learning and Verbal Behavior*, **14**, 323-329.

Klein, G. S. (1964). Semantic power measured through the interference of words with color-naming. *American Journal of Psychology,* **77***,* 576-588.

Kleinmuntz, B., & Szucko, J. J. (1982). On fallibility of lie detection. *Law and Society Review,* **17***,* 85-104.

Klin, A., Jones, W., Schultz, R., Volkmar, F., & Cohen, D. (2002). Visual fixation patterns during viewing of naturalistic social situations as predictors of social competence in individuals with autism. *Archives of General Psychiatry,* **59***,* 809-816.

Klinger, L. G., & Dawson, G. (2001). Prototype formation in autism. *Development and Psychopathology,* **13***,* 111-124.

Kluver, H., & Bucy, P. C. (1937). "Psychic blindness" and other symptoms following bilateral temporal lobectomy. *American Journal of Physiology,* **119***,* 352-353.

Knierim, J. J., & Van Essen, D. C. (1992). Neuronal responses to static texture patterns in area V1 of the alert Macaque monkey. *Journal of Neurophysiology,* **67***,* 961-980.

Knight, R. T., Hillyard, S. A., Woods, D. L., & Neville, H. J. (1981). The effects of frontal cortex lesions on event-related potentials during auditory selective attention. *Electroencephalography & Clinical Neurophysiology*, **52**, 571-582.

Knight, R. T., Scabini, D., & Woods, D. L. (1989). Prefrontal cortex gating of auditory transmission in humans. *Brain Research*, **504**, 338-342.

Knoblich, G., Ohlsson, S., & Raney, G. E. (2001). An eye movement study of insight problem solving. *Memory & Cognition,* **29***,* 1000-1009.

Kolb, B., & Whishaw, I. Q. (1980). *Fundamentals of human neuropsychology.* San Francisco: Freeman.

Kolers, P. A. (1976). Reading a year later. *Journal of Experimental Psychology: Human Learning and Memory,* **2***,* 554-565.

Kohler, W. (1925). *The mentality of apes.* London: Routledge & Kegan Paul.

Kohn, S. E., & Friedman, R. B. (1986). Word-meaning deafness: A phonological-semantic dissociation. *Cognitive Neuropsychology*, **3**, 291-308.

Kopelman, M. D. (2002). Disorders of memory. *Brain*, **125**, 2152-2190.

Kopelman, M. D., Christensen, H., Puffett, A., Stanhope, N. (1994). The great escape: A neuropsychological study of psychogenic amnesia. *Neuropsychologia, 32,* 675-691.

Kopera-Frye, K., Dehaene, S., Streissguth, A. P. (1996). Impairments of number processing induced by prenatal alcohol exposure. *Neuropsychologia, 34,* 1187-1196.

Koriat, A., & Fischoff, B. (1974). What day is today? An inquiry into the process of time orientation. *Memory & Cognition*, **2**, 201-205.

Kozlowski, L. T. (1977). Effects of distorted auditory and of rhyming cues on retrieval of tip-of-the-tongue words by poets and nonpoets. *Memory & Cognition*, **5**,477-481.

Kozminsky, E. (1977). Altering comprehension: The effect of biasing titles on text comprehension. *Memory & Cognition*, **5**, 482-490.

Kroll, N. E. A., Parks, T., Parkinson, S. P., Bieber, S. L., & Johnson, A. L. (1970). Short-term memory while shadowing: Recall of visually and aurally presented letters. *Journal of Experimental Psychology*, **85**,220-224.

Krose, B. J. A., & Julesz, B. (1989). The control and speed of shifts attention. *Vision Research, 29,* 1607-1619.

Kubovy, M., & Howard, F. P. (1976). Persistence of a pitch segregating echoic memory. *Journal of Experimental Psychology: Human Perception and Performance, 2,* 531-537.

Labov, W. (1973). The boundaries of words and their meanings. In C.-J. N. Bailey & R. W. Shuy (Eds.), *New ways of analyzing variation in English.* Washington, D.C.: Georgetown University Press.

Lane, D. M. (1980). Incidental learning and the development of selective attention. *Psychological Review, 87,* 316-319.

Larkin, J. H., McDermott, J., Simon, D. P., & Simon, H. A. (1980). Expert and novice performance in solving physics problems. *Science*, **208**, 1335-1342.

Lawless, H. T., & Cain, W. S. (1975). Recognition memory for odors. *Chemical Senses and Flavor*, **1**, 331-337.

Lawrence, D. M. (1971). Two studies of visual search for word targets with controlled rates of presentation. *Perception & Psychophysics, 10,* 85-89.

Lawrence, D. M., & Banks, W. P. (1973). Accuracy of recognition memory for common sounds. *Bulletin of the Psychonomic Society*, **1**, 298-300.

Lederman, S. J., & Abbott, S. G. (1981). Texture perception in studies of intersensory organization using a discrepancy paradigm and visual versus tactual psychophysics. *Journal of Experimental Psychology*: *Human Perception & Performance*, 7, 902-915.

LeDoux J. E. (1993). Emotional networks in the brain. In, M. Lewis and J. M. Haviland (Eds.), *Handbook of Emotions*: New York: Guilford Press.,

Leeper, R. (1935). A study of a neglected portion of the field of learning-the development of sensory organization. *Journal of Genetic Psychology*, **46**, 41-75.

Levinthal, C. F. (1983). *Introduction to physiological psychology.* Englewood Cliffs, NJ: Prentice-Hall.

Levitt, D. R., & Teitelbaum, P. (1975). Somnolence, akinesia, and sensory activation of motivated behavior in the lateral hypothalamic syndrome. *Proceedings of the National Academy of Sciences, 72,* 2819-2823.

Levy, B. A. (1978). Speech analysis during sentence processing: Reading versus listening. *Visible Language*, **12**, 81-101.

Levy, J., & Trevarthan, C. (1976). Metacontrol of hemispheric function in human split-brain patients. *Journal of Experimental Psychology: Human Perception and Performance*, **2**, 299-312.

Levy, J., & Trevarthan, C. (1977). Perceptual, semantic and phonetic aspects of elementary language processes in split-brain patients. *Brain*, **100**, 105-118.

Levy, J., Trevarthan, C., & Sperry, R. W. (1972). Perception of bilateral chimeric figures following hemispheric deconnexion. *Brain*, **95**, 61-78.

Lewis, M., Alessandri, S. M., & Sullivan, M. W. (1990). Violation of expectancy, loss of control and anger expressions in young infants. *Developmental Psychology*, **26**, 745-751.

Liberman, A. M. (1982). On finding that speech is special. *American Psychologist*, **37**, 148-167.

Liberman, A. M., Cooper, F. S., Shankweiler, D. P., & Studdert-Kennedy, M. (1967). Perception of the speech code. *Psychological Review*, **74**, 431-461.

Liberman, A. M., Isenberg, D., & Rakerd, B. (1981). Duplex perception of cues for stop consonants: Evidence for a phonetic mode. *Perception & Psychophysics*, **30**, 133-143.

Lichtenstein, S., & Slovic, P. (1971). Reversals of preference between bids and choices in gambling decisions. *Journal of Experimental Psychology*, **89**, 46-55.

Lichtenstein, S., Slovic, P., Fischhoff, B., Layman, M., & Combs, B. (1978). Judged frequency of lethal events. *Journal of Experimental Psychology: Human Learning and Memory*, **4**, 551-578.

Light, L. L., Kayra-Stuart, F., & Hollander, S. (1979). Recognition memory for typical and unusual faces. *Journal of Experimental Psychology: Human Learning and Memory*, **5**, 212-228.

Lindsay, D. S., & Read, J. D. (1994). Psychotherapy and memories of childhood sexual abuse: a cognitive perspective. *Applied Cognitive Psychology*, **8**, 281-338.

Lindsay, R. C. L, & Bellinger, K. (1999). Alternatives to sequential lineup: The importance of controlling the pictures. *Journal of Applied Psychology*, **76**, 796-802.

Lindsay, R. C. L, & Wells, G. L. (1985). Improving eyewitness identification from lineups: Simultaneous versus sequential lineup presentation. *Journal of Applied Psychology*, **70**, 556-564.

Loess, H. (1964). Proactive inhibition in short-term memory. *Journal of Verbal Learning and Verbal Behavior*, **3**, 362-368.

Loftus, E. F.. & Palmer, J. C. (1974). Reconstruction of automobile destruction: An example of the interaction between language and memory. *Journal of Verbal Learning and Verbal Behavior*, **13**, 585-589.

Loftus, E. F., & Pickrell, J. E. (1995). The formation of false memories. *Psychiatric Annals*, **25**, 720-725.

Loftus, G. R., & Kallman, H. J. (1979). Encoding and use of detail information in picture recognition. *Journal of Experimental Psychology: Human Learning and Memory*, **5**,197-211.

Loftus, G. R., & Patterson, K. K. (1975). Components of short-term proactive interference. *Journal of Verbal Learning and Verbal Behavior*, **14**, 105-121.

Lopez, A. (1995). The diversity principle in the testing of arguments. *Memory & Cognition, 23*, 374-382.

Lorch, R. F., Jr. (1978). The role of two types of semantic information in the processing of false sentences. *Journal of Verbal Learning and Verbal Behavior*, 17, 523-437.

Lorch, R. F., Jr. (1981). Effects of relation strength and semantic overlap on retrieval and comparison processes during sentence verification. *Journal of Verbal Learning and Verbal Behavior*, 20, 593-610.

Lucas, M. (2000). Semantic priming without association: A meta-analytic review. *Psychonomic Bulletin & Review, 7*, 618-630.

Luchins, A. (1942). Mechanization in problem solving. *Psychological Monographs*, 54(No. 248).

Luchins, A., & Luchins, E. (1950). New experimental attempts at preventing mechanization in problem solving. *Journal of General Psychology*, 42, 279-297.

Lucy, J. A., & Schweder, R. A. (1979). Whorf and his critics: Linguistic and nonlinguistic influences on color memory. *American Anthropologist*, 81, 581-615.

Lupker, S. J. (1979). On the nature of perceptual information during letter perception. *Perception & Psychophysics*, 25, 303-312.

Lupker, S. J., & Katz, A. N. (1981). Input decision and response factors in picture-word interference. *Journal of Experimental Psychology: Human Learning and Memory, 1*, 269-282.

Luria, A. R. (1968). *The mind of a mnemonist*. New York: Basic Books.

Lykken, D. T. (1981). *A tremor in the blood: Uses and abuses of the lie detector.* New York: McGraw-Hill.

Lynch, S., & Yarnell, P. R. (1973). Retrograde amnesia: Delayed forgetting after concussion. *American Journal of Psychology*, 86, 643-645.

MacDonald, M. C., Pearlmutter, N., & Seidenberg, M. S. (1994). The lexical nature of syntactic ambiguity resolution. *Psychological Review*, 101, 676-703.

MacKay, D. G. (1968). Phonetic factors in the perception and recall of spelling errors. *Neuropsychologia*, 6, 321-325.

MacKay, D. G. (1973). Aspects of the theory of comprehension, memory, and attention. *Quarterly Journal of Experimental Psychology*, 25, 22-40.

Mackie, R. R. (Ed.) (1977). *Vigilance: Theory, Operational performance, and physiological correlates.* New York: Plenum.

Mackworth, J. F. (1964). Performance decrement in vigilance, threshold, and high-speed perceptual motor tasks. *Canadian Journal of Psychology, 18*, 209-223.

Mackworth, N. H. (1948). The breakdown of vigilance during prolonged visual search. *Quarterly Journal of Experimental Psychology, 1*, 6-21.

MacLean, P. D. (1993). Cerebral evolution of emotion. In M. Lewis and J. M. Haviland (Eds.), *Handbook of emotions*: New York: Guilford Press.

MacLeod, C. M. (1991). Half a century of research on the Stroop effect: An integrative review. *Psychological Bulletin, 109*, 163-203.

MacLeod, C. M., & Kampe, K. E. (1996). Word frequency effects on recall, recognition, and word fragment completion tests. *Journal of Experimental Psychology: Learning, Memory, & Cognition, 22*, 132-142.

Maddox, W. T., & Ashby, F. G. (1993). Comparing decision bound and exemplar models of categorization. *Perception & Psychophysics, 53*, 49-70.

Maddox, W. T., & Estes, W. K. (1997). Direct and indirect effects of stimulus frequency effects in recognition. *Journal of Experimental Psychology: Learning, Memory, & Cognition, 23*, 539-559.

Madigan, S. A. (1969). Intraserial repetition and coding processes in free recall. *Journal of Verbal Learning and Verbal Behavior, 8*, 828-835.

Malley, G. B., & Strayer, D. L. (1995). Effect of stimulus repetitionon on positive and negative identity priming. *Perception & Psychophysics, 57*, 657-667.

Malpass, R. S., & Devine, P. G. (1981). Eyewitness identification: Lineup instructions and the absence of the offender. *Journal of Applied Psychology, 66*, 482-489.

Manktelow, K. I., & Evans, J. St. B. T. (1979). Facilitation of reasoning by realism: Effect or non-effect? *British Journal of Psychology, 70*, 477-488.

Maquet, P. (2001). The role of sleep in learning and memory. *Science, 294*, 1048-1052.

Maratsos, M., & Chalkley, A. (1980). The internal language of children's syntax: The ontogenesis and representation of syntactic categories. In K. E. Nelson (Ed.), *Children's language (Vol. 2)*. New York: Gardner Press.

Marcus, G., Pinker, S., Ullman, M., Hollander, M., Rosen, T. J., & Xu, F. (1992). Overregularization in language acquisition. *Monographs of the Society for Research in Child Development, 57*, (4, Serial No. 228).

Markman, E. M., & Wachtel, G. F. (1988). Children's use of mutual exclusivity to constrain the meaning of words. *Cognitive Psychology, 20*, 121-157.

Marks, G., Shaffery, J., Oksenberg, A., Speciale, S., & Roffwarg, H. (1995). A functional role for REM sleep in brain maturation. *Behavioural Brain Research, 69*, 1-11.

Marslen-Wilson, W. D., & Welsh, A. (1978). Processing interactions and lexical access during word recognition in continuous speech. *Cognitive Psychology, 10*, 29-63.

Martone, M., Butters, N., Payne, M., Becker, J. T., & Sax, D. S. (1984). Dissociations between skill learning and verbal recognition in amnesia and dementia. *Archives of Neurology, 41*, 965-970.

Massman, P. J., Delis, D. C., Butters, N., Dupont, r. M., Gillin, J. C. (1992). The subcortical dysfunction hypothesis of memory deficits in depression: Neuropsychological validation in a subgroup of patients. *Journal of Clinical and Experimental Neuropsychology, 14*, 687-706.

Mattioli, F., Miozzo, A., Vignolo, L. A. (1999). Confabulation and delusional misidentification: A four year follow-up study. *Cortex, 35*, 413-422.

Mattis, S., French, J. H., & Rapin, 1. (1975). Dyslexia in children and young adults: Three independent neuropsychological syndromes. Developmental Medicine and *Child Neurology, 17*, 150-163.

McCann, R. S., & Besner, D. (1987). Reading pseudohomophones: Implications for models of pronunciation and the locus of word frequency effect in word naming. *Journal of Experimental Psychology: Human Perception & Performance, 13*, 14-24.

McClain, L. (1984a). Effects of response type and set size on Stroop color-word performance. *Perceptual and Motor Skills,* **56***,* 735-743.

McClain, L. (1984b). Stimulus-response compatibility affects auditory Stroop interference. *Perception and Psychophysics,* **33***,* 266-270.

McCloskey, M., Caramazza, A., & Green, B. (1980). Curvilinear motion in the absence of external forces: Naive beliefs about the motion of objects. *Science,* **210***,* 1139-1141.

McCloskey, M., & Glucksberg, S. (1979). Decision processes in verifying category membership statements: Implications for models of semantic memory. *Cognitive Psychology*, **11**, 1-37.

McCloskey, M., & Kohl, D. (1983). Naïve physics: The curvilinear impetus principle and its role in interactions with moving objects. *Journal of Experimental Psychology: Learning, Memory, & Cognition,* **9***,* 146-156.

McCloskey, M., Wible, C. G., & Cohen, N. J. (1988). Is there a special flashbulb-memory mechanism? *Journal of Experimental Psychology: General,* **117***,* 171-181.

McConkie, G. W., & Rayner, K. (1975). The span of the effective stimulus during a fixation in reading. *Perception & Psychophysics*, **17**, 578-586.

McFarland, C. E., Jr., Rhodes, D. D., & Frey, J. J. (1979). The spacing effect. *Journal of Verbal Learning and Verbal Behavior*, **18**, 163-172.

McKinley, S. C., & Nosofsky, R. M. (1995). Investigations of exemplar and decision bound models in large-size, ill-defined category structures. *Journal of Experimental Psychology: Human Perception and Performance,* **21***,* 128-148.

McLean, J. P., Broadbent, D. E., & Broadbent, M. H. P. (1982). Combining attributes in rapid sequential visual presentations. *Quarterly Journal of Experimental Psychology,* **35a***,* 171-186.

Medin, D. L., & Schaffer, M. M. (1978). A context theory of classification. *Psychological Review*, **85**, 207-238.

Medin, D. L., & Schwanenflugel, P. J. (1981). Linear separability in classification learning. *Journal of Experimental Psychology: Human Learning and Memory,* **1***,* 335-368.

Medin, D. L., Wattenmaker, W. D., & Hampson, S. E. (1987). Family resemblance, conceptual cohesiveness, and category construction. *Cognitive Psychology,* **19***,* 242-279.

Melton, A. W. (1967). Repetition and retrieval from memory. *Science*, **158**, 532.

Meltzhoff, A. N. (1988). Immediate and deferred imitation in fourteen- and twenty-four-month-old infants. *Child Development*, **56**, 62-72.

Meyer, D. E., & Schvaneveldt, R. W. (1971). Facilitation of recognizing pairs of words: Evidence of a dependence between retrieval operations. *Journal of Experimental Psychology,* **90***,* 227-234.

Meyer, J. A., & Minshew, N. J. (2002). An update on neurocognitive profiles in Asperger syndrome and high-functioning autism. *Focus on Autism and Other Developmental Disabilities,* **17***,* 152-160.

Meyerowitz, B. E., & Chaiken, S. (1987). The effect of message framing on breast self-examination attitudes, intentions, and behavior. *Journal of Personality and Social Psychology,* **52,** 500-510.

Miller, E. A. (1972). Interaction of vision and touch in conflict and nonconflict form perception tasks. *Journal of Experimental Psychology*, **96**, 114-123.

Miller, G. A. (1956). The magical number seven, plus or minus two: Some limits of our capacity for processing information. *Psychological Review*, **63**, 81-97.

Miller, G. A. (1981). *Language and speech*. San Francisco: Freeman.

Milner, B. (1975). Psychological aspects of focal epilepsy and its neurological management. *Advances in Neurology*, **8**, 299-321.

Milner, B. (1995). Aspects of human frontal lobe function. *Advances in Neurology*, **66**, 67-84.

Milner, B., Corkin, S., & Teuber, H. L. (1968). Further analysis of the hippocampal amnesic syndrome: 14 year follow-up study of H. M. *Neuropsychologia*, **6**, 215-234.

Milner, B., Corsi, P., & Leonard, G. (1991). Frontal-lobe contributions to recency judgements. *Neuropsychologia*, **29**, 601-618.

Milner, B., Taylor, L., & Sperry, R. W. (1968). Lateralized suppression of dichotically presented digits after commissural. section in man. *Science*, **161**, 184-185.

Mirmiran, M. (1995). The function of fetal/neonatal rapid eye movement sleep. *Behavioural Brain Research*, **69**, 13-22.

Moates, D. R., & Schumacher, G. M. *(1980). An introduction to cognitive psychology*. Belmont, Calif.: Wadsworth.

Mohr, J. P. (1973). Rapid amelioration of motor aphasia. *Archives of Neurology*, **28**, 77-82.

Mohr, J. P. (1976). Broca's area and Broca's aphasia. In H. Whitaker & M. A. Whitaker (Eds.), *Studies in neurolinguistics (Vol. 1)*. New York: Academic Press.

Molfese, D. L., Nunez, V., Seibert, S. M., & Ramanaiah, N. V. *(1976).* Cerebral asymmetry: Changes in factors affecting its development. *Annals of the New York Academy of Sciences*, **280**, 821-833.

Montague, W. E., Adams, J. A., & Kiess, H. 0. (1966). Forgetting and natural language mediation. *Journal of Experimental Psychology*, **72**, 829-833.

Moore, J. J., & Massaro, D. W. (1973). Attention and processing capacity in auditory recognition. *Journal of Experimental Psychology*, **99**, 49-54.

Moore, R. G., Watts, F. N., & Williams, J. M. G. (1988). The specificity of personal memories in depression. *British Journal of Clinical Psychology*, **27**, 275-276.

Moray, N. (1959). Attention in dichotic listening: Affective cues and the influence of instructions. *Quarterly Journal of Experimental Psychology*, **11**, 56-60.

Moray, N., Fitter, M., Ostry, D., Favreau, D., & Nagy, V. (1976). Attention to pure tones. *Quarterly Journal of Psychology*, **28**, 271-283.

Morton, J. (1969). Interaction of information in word recognition. *Psychological Review*, **76**, 165-178.

Morton, J. (1979). Facilitation in word recognition: Experiments that cause changes in the logogen model. In P. A. Kolers, M. E. Wrolstad, & H. Bouma (Eds.), *Processing of visual language (Vol. I)*. New York: Plenum.

Moscovitch, M., & Melo, B. (1997) Strategic retrieval and the frontal lobes: evidence from confabulation and amnesia. *Neuropsychologia*, **35**, 1017-1034.

Moss, C. S. (1972). *Recovery with aphasia*. Urbana, Ill.: University of Illinois Press.

Moyer, R. S. (1973). Comparing objects in memory: Evidence suggesting an internal psychophysics. *Perception & Psychophysics*, **13**, 180-184.

Moyer, R. S., & Landauer, T. K. (1967). Time required for judgments of numerical inequality. *Nature*, **215**, 1519-1520.

Mullin, J., & Corcoran, D. W. J. (1977). Interaction of task amplitude with circadian variation in auditory vigilance performance. *Ergonomics, **20**, 193-200.*

Mundy, P., & Sigman, M. (1989). The theoretical implications of joint-attention deficits in autism. *Development and Psychopathology, **3**, 173-183.*

Murphy, G. L., & Smith, E. E. *(1982).* Basic-level superiority in picture categorization. *Journal of Verbal Learning and Verbal Behavior*, **21**, 1-20.

Murray, J. E., Yong, E., & Rhodes, G. (2000). Revisiting the perception of upside-down faces. *Psychological Science, **11**, 492-496.*

Myers, J. J. (1984). Right hemisphere language: Science or fiction? *American Psychologist*, **39**, 315-320.

Myerson, R., & Goodglass, H. (1972). Transformational grammars of three agrammatic patients. *Language and Speech*, **15**, 40-50.

Nachreiner, F. (1977). Experiments on the validity of vigilance experiments. In R. R. Mackie (Ed.), *Vigilance: Theory, operational performance, and physiological correlates.* New York: Plenum.

Nagae, S. (1980). *Nature* of discriminating and categorizing functions of verbal labels on recognition memory for shape. *Journal of Experimental Psychology: Human Learning and Memory*, **6**, 421-429.

Nakayama, K., & He, Z. J. (1995). Attention to surfaces: Beyond a Cartesian understanding of focal attention. In, T. V. Papathomas (Ed.) *Early vision and beyond.* Cambridge MA: MIT Press.

Nazzi, T., Jusczyk, P. W., Johnson, E. K. (2000). Language discrimination by English-learning 5-month-olds: Effects of rhythm and familiarity. *Journal of Memory & Language, **43**, 1-19.*

Neely, J. H. (1977). Semantic priming and retrieval from lexical memory: Role of inhibitionless spreading activation and limited capacity attention. *Journal of Experimental Psychology: General*, **106**, 226-254.

Neill, W. T., & Joordens, S. (2002). Negative priming and multiple repetition: A reply to Grison and Strayer (2001). *Perception & Psychophysics*, **64**, 855-860.

Neisser, U. (1963). Decision-time without reaction-time: Experiments in visual scanning. *American Journal of Psychology, **76**, 376-385.*

Neisser, U., & Harsch, N. (1992). Phantom flashbulbs: False recollections of hearing the news about Challenger. In E. Winograd and U. Neisser (Eds.), *Affect and accuracy in recall: Studies of "flashbulb" memories* (pp.9-31). New York: Cambridge University Press.

Neisser, U. Winograd, E., Bergman, E. T., Schreiber, C. A., Palmer, S. E., & Weldon, M. S. (1996). Remembering he earthquake: Direct experience versus hearing the news. *Memory, **4**, 337-357.*

Nelson, T. O., & Batchelder, W. H. (1969).   Forgetting in short-term recall: All-or-none or decremental?   *Journal of experimental Psychology,* **82**, 96-106.

Newell, A., & Simon, H. (1972).   *Human problem solving.* Englewood Cliffs, N.J.: Prentice-Hall.

Newport, E. L., Gleitman, H., & Gleitman, L. R. (1977). Mother, I'd rather do it myself: Some effects and noneffects of maternal speech style. In C. E. Snow & C. A. Ferguson (Eds.), *Talking to children: Language input and acquisition.* Cambridge: Cambridge University Press.

Nickerson, R. A., & Adams, M. J. (1979). Long-term memory for a common object. *Cognitive Psychology*, **11**, 287-307.

Nilsson, N. J. (1971). *Problem solving methods in artificial intelligence.* New York: McGraw-Hill.

Noice, H. (1992).   Elaborative memory strategies of professional actors. *Applied Cognitive Psychology,* **6**. 417-427.

Norman, D. A. (1969).   Memory while shadowing. *Quarterly Journal of Experimental Psychology,* **21***,* 85-93.

Norman, D. A., & Bobrow, D. G. (1975). On data-limited and resource-limited processes. *Cognitive Psychology*, **7**, 44-64.

Norman, D. A., Rumelhart, D. E., & the LNR Research Group. (1975). *Explorations in cognition.* San Franciso: Freeman.

Northdurft, H. C. (1993).   The role of features in preattentive vision: Comparison of orientation, motion, and color cues. *Vision Research,* **33***,* 1937-1958.

Nosofsky, R. M. (1986).   Attention, similarity, and the identification-categorization relationship. *Journal of Experimental Psychology: General,* **115***,* 39-57.

Nosofsky, R. M., & Johansen, M. K. (2000).   Exemplar-based accounts of "multiple-system" phenomena in perceptual organization. *Psychonomic Bulletin and Review,* **7,** 375-402.

Nottebohm, F. (1977). Asymmetries in neural control of vocalization in the canary. In S. Harnad, R. W. Doty, L. Goldstein, J. Jaynes, & G. Krauthamer (Eds.), *Lateralization in the nervous system.* New York: Academic Press.

Notterman, J. M., & Tufano, D. R. (1980). Variables influencing outflow-inflow interpretations of tracking performance: Predictability of target motion, transfer function, and practice. *Journal of Experimental Psychology: Human Perception and Performance,* **6**, 85-88.

Obeson, J. A., Rodriguez-Oroz, M. C., Rodriguez, M., Macia, R., Alvarez, L, Guridi, J., Vitek, J., & DeLong, M. R. (2000).   Pathophysiologic basis of surgery for Parkinson's disease. *Neurology*, **55** (Supplement 6), s8 –s12.

O'Brien, D. P., *Brain*e, M. D. S., Yang, Y. (1994).   Propositional reasoning by mental models? Simple to refute in principle and in practice. *Psychological Review,* **101**, 711-724.

Obusek, C. J., & Warren, R. M. (1973). Relation of the verbal transformation and the phonemic restoration effects. *Cognitive Psychology*, **5**, 97-107.

Ojemann, G. A. (1977). Asymmetric function of the thalamus in man. *Annals of the New York Academy of Sciences*, **299**, 380-396.

Orne, M. T. (1959).   The nature of hypnosis: Artifact and essence. *Journal of Abnormal and Social Psychology,* **58***,* 277-299.

Orne, M. T. (1966). Hypnosis, motivation and compliance. *American Journal of Psychiatry*, **122**, 721-726.

Orne, M. T. (1977). The construct of hypnosis: Implications of the definition for research and practice. *Annals of the New York Academy of Sciences*, **296**, 14-33.

Ornstein, P. A., Gordon, B. N., & Larus, D. (1992). Children's memory for a personally experienced event: Implications for testimony. *Applied Cognitive Psychology, 6,* 49-60.

Ornstein, P. A., Naus, M. J., & Liberty, C. (1975). Rehearsal and organizational processes in children's memory. *Child Development,* **46,** 818-830.

Ornstein, R. E. (1969). *On the experience of time*. Baltimore: Penguin Books.

Osherson, D. N., Smith E. E., Wilkie, O., Lopez, A., & Shafir, E. (1990). Category-based induction. *Psychological Review,* **97**, 185-200.

Ostergaard, A. L. (1994). Dissociations between word priming effects in normal subject and patients with memory disorders: mltiple memory systems or retrieval? *Quarterly Journal of Experimental Psychology A*, **47**, 331-364.

Ozonoff, S., Pennington, B. F., & Rogers, S. J. (1991). Executive function deficits in high-functioning autistic individuals: Relationship to theory of mind. *Journal of Child Psychology and Psychiatry,* **32**, 1081-1105.

Packard, V. (1957). *The hidden persuaders.* New York: McKay.

Paivio, A. (1969). Mental imagery in associative learning and memory. *Psychological Review*, **76**, 241-263.

Palmeri, T. J., & Nosofsky, r M. (2001). Central tendencies, extreme points, and prototype enhancement effects in ill-defined perceptual categorization. *The Quarterly Journal of Experimental Psychology,* **54A,** 197-235.

Papagno, C., & Baddeley, A. (1997). Confabulation in a dysexecutive patient: Implication for models of retrieval. *Cortex, 33,* 743-752.

Papp, K. R., Newson, S. L., McDonald, J. E., & Schvaneveldt, R. W. (1982). An activation-verification model for letter and word recognition: The word-superiority effect. *Psychological Review, 89,* 573-594.

Passolunghi, M. C., Cornoldi, C., & De Liberto, S. (1999). Working memory and intrusions of irrelevant information in a group of specific poor problem solvers. *Memory & Cognition, 27,* 779-790.

Pavlov, I. P. (1927). *Conditional reflexes: An investigation of the physiological activity of the cerebral cortex*. Oxford: Oxford University Press.

Penfield, W., & Rasmussen, T. (1950). *The cerebral cortex of man: A clinical study of localization and function.* New York: Macmillan.

Perea, M., & Gotor, A. (1997). Associative and semantic priming effects occur at very short SOAs in lexical decision and naming. *Cognition, 67,* 223-240.

Perea, M., & Rosa, E. (2000). Repetition and form priming interact with neighborhood density at a brief stimulus onset asynchrony. *Psychonomic Bulletin & Review, 7,* 668-677.

Peterson, L. R., & Peterson, M. J. (1959). Short-term retention of individual items. *Journal of Experimental Psychology*, **58**, 193-198.

Pezdek, K., & Hodge, D. (1999). Planting false childhood memories in children: The role of event plausibility. *Child Development, 70,* 887-895.

Phillips, J. R. (1973). Syntax and vocabulary of mothers' speech to young children: Age and sex comparisons. *Child Development*, **44**, 182-185.

Pillemer, D. B., Picariello, M. L., & Pruett, J. C. (1994). Very long-term memories of a salient preschool event. *Applied Cognitive Psychology*, **8**, 95-106.

Pilleri, G. (1979). The blind Indus dolphin. *Platanista indi. Endeavours*, **3**, 48-56.

Plomin, R., & Loehlin, J. C. (1989). Direct and indirect IQ heritability estimates: A puzzle. *Behavior Genetics*, **19**, 331-342.

Poe, G., Nitz, D., McNaughton, B., & Barnes, C. (2000). Experience-dependent phase-reversal of hippocampal neuron firing during REM sleep. *Brain Research*, **855**, 176-180.

Poltrock, S. E., Lansman, M., & Hunt, E. (1982). Automatic and controlled attention processes in auditory target detection. *Journal of Experimental Psychology: Human Perception and Performance*, **8**, 37-45.

Pomerantz, J. R. (1981). Perceptual organization in information processing. In M. Kubovy & J. R. Pomerantz (Eds.), *Perceptual organization*. Hillsdale, NJ: Erlbaum.

Poole, D. A., & Lindsay D. S. (1995). Interviewing preschoolers: Effects of nonsuggestive techniques, parental coaching, and leading questions on reports of nonexperienced events. *Journal of Experimental Child Psychology*, **60**, 129-154.

Posner, M. I., & Cohen, Y. (1984). Components of performance. In, H. Bouma & D. Bowhuis (Eds.) *Attention and performance X*. Hillsdale, NJ: Erlbaum.

Posner, M. I., & Keele, S. W. (1968). On the genesis of abstract ideas. *Journal of Experimental Psychology*, **77**, 353-363.

Posner, M. I., Nissen, M. J., & Klein, R. M. (1976). Visual dominance: An information-processing accounts of its origins and significance. *Psychological Review*, **83**, 157-171.

Posner, M. I., & Petersen, S. E. (1990). The attention system of the human brain. *Annual Review of neuroscience*, **13**, 25-42.

Postman, L., & Phillips, L. W. (1965). Short-term temporal changes in free recall. *Quarterly Journal of Experimental Psychology*, **17**, 132-138.

Potter, M. C. (1975). Meaning in visual search. *Science*, **187**, 965-966.

Potter, M. C. (1976). Short-term conceptual memory for pictures. *Journal of Experimental Psychology: Human Learning and Memory*, **2**, 509-522.

Potts, G. R. (1972). Information processing strategies used in the encoding of linear orderings. *Journal of Verbal Learning and Verbal Behavior*, **11**, 727-740.

Potts, G. R. (1974). Storing and retrieving information about ordered relationships. *Journal of Experimental Psychology*, **103**, 431-439.

Povel, D. J., & Collard, R. (1982). Structured factors in patterned finger tapping. *Acta Psychologia*, **2**, 107-123.

Proteau, L., Marteniuk, R. G., Levesque, L. (1992). A sensorimotor basis for motor learning: Evidence indicating specificity of practice. *Quarterly Journal of Experimental Psychology*, **44A**, 557-575.

Prinzmetal, W., & Silvers, B. (1994). The word without the tachistiscope. *Perception & Psychophysics*, **56**, 495-500.

Proctor, R. W., & Van Zandt, T. (1994). *Human factors in simple and complex systems*. Needham Heights, MA: Allyn & Bacon.

Prytulak, L. S. *(1971)*. Natural language mediation. *Cognitive Psychology*, **2**, *1-56*.

Pullum, G. K. (1977). Word order universals and grammatical relations. In P. Cole & J. M. Sadock (Eds.), *Syntax and semantics. Vol. 8, Grammatical Relations*. New York: Academic Press.

Quas, J. A., Goodman, G. S., Bidrose, S., Piple, M., Craw, S., & Ablin, D. S. (199). Emotion and memory: children's long-term remembering, forgetting, and suggestibility. *Journal of Experimental Child Psychology*, **72**, 235-270.

Rabbitt, P. M. A. (1967). Time to detect errors as a function of factors affecting choice-response time. *Acta Psychologica*, **27**, 131-142.

Rabbitt, P. M. A. (1968). Three kinds of error-signaling responses in a serial choice task. *Quarterly Journal of Experimental Psychology*, **20**, 179-188.

Rabbitt, P., & Lowe, C. (2000). Patterns of cognitive ageing. *Psychological Research*, **63**, 308-316.

Rabin, M. D., & Cain, W. S. *(1984)*. Odor recognition: Familiarity, identifiability, and encoding consistency. *Journal of Experimental Psychology: Learning, Memory, and Cognition*, **10**, 316-325.

Rabinowitz, J. C., Mandler, G., & Barsalou, L. W. *(1979)*. Generation-recognition as an auxiliary retrieval strategy. *Journal of Verbal Learning and Verbal Behavior*, **18**, 57-72.

Ramachandran, V. S. (1988). Perceiving shape from shading. *Scientific American*, **259**, 76-83.

Ramachandran, V. S., & Blakeslee, S. (1998). *Phantoms in the brain*. New York: William Morrow.

Ramachandran, V. S., Rogers-Ramachandran, D., & Stewart, M. (1992). Perceptual correlates of massive cortical reorganization, *Science*, **258**, 1159-1160.

Ramachandran, V. S., Rogers-Ramachandran, D., & Cobb, s. (1995). Touching the phantom limb. *Nature*, **377**, 489-490.

Rand, T. C. (1974). Dichotic release from masking for speech. *Journal of the Acoustical Society of America*, **55**, 678-680.

Rapcsak, S. Z., Cimino, C. R., & Heilman, K. M. (1988). Altitudinal neglect. *Neurology*, **38**, 277-281.

Raphael, B. (1976). *The thinking computer*. San Francisco: Freeman.

Rasmussen, T., & Milner, B. (1977). The role of early left-brain injury in determining lateralization of cerebral speech functions. *Annals of the New York Academy of Sciences*, **299**, 355-369.

Rastle, K., & Coltheart, M. (1998). Whammies and double whammies: The effect of length on nonword reading. *Psychonomic Bulletin& review*, **5**, 277-282.

Rastle, K., & Coltheart, M. (1999a). Lexical and nonlexical phonological priming in reading aloud. *Journal of Experimental Psychology: Human Perception & Performance*, **25**, 461-481.

Rastle, K., & Coltheart, M. (1999b). Serial and strategic effects in reading aloud. *Journal of Experimental Psychology: Human Perception & Performance, 25,* 482-503.

Raye, C. L., Johnson, M. K., & Taylor, J. H. (1980). Is there something special about memory for internally generated information? *Memory & Cognition,* 8,141-148.

Reber, A. S. (1967). Implicit learning of artificial grammars. *Journal of Verbal Learning and Verbal Behavior, 5,* 855-863.

Reber, A. S. (1976). Implicit learning of synthetic languages: The role of instructional set. *Journal of Experimental Psychology: Human Learning and Memory, 2,* 88-94.

Reder, L. M. (1982). Plausibility judgments versus fact retrieval: Alternative strategies for sentence verification. *Psychological Review, 89,* 250-280.

Reder, L. M., Nhouyvanisvong, A., Schunn, C. D., Ayers, M. S., Angstadt, P., & Hiraki, K. (2000). A mechanistic account of the mirror effect for word frequency: a computational model of remember-know judgments in a continuous recognition paradigm. *Journal of Experimental Psychology: learning, Memory, and Cognition, 26,* 294-320.

Reese, E., Haden, C. A., & Fivush, Robyn. (1993). Mother-child conversations about the past: Relationships of style and memory over time. *Cognitive Development. 8,* 403-430.

Reese, H. W. (1965). Imagery in paired associate learning in children. *Journal of Experimental Child Psychology, 2,* 290- 296.

Reicher, G. M. (1969). Perceptual recognition as a function of meaningfulness of stimulus material. *Journal of Experimental Psychology, 81,* 275-280.

Reisberg, D., Baron, J., & Kemler, D. G. (1980). Overcoming Stroop interference: The effects of practice on distractor potency. *Journal of Experimental Psychology, 81,* 275-280.

Reitman, J. S. (1976). Skilled perception in Go: Deducing memory structures from inter-response times. *Cognitive Psychology, 8,* 336-356.

Remington, R. (1980). Attention and saccadic eye movements. *Journal of Experimental Psychology: Human Perception and Performance, 6,* 726-744.

Rescorla, R. A., & Wagner, A. R., (1972). A theory of Pavlovian conditioning: Variations in the effectiveness of reinforcement and nonreinforcement. In A. H. Black & W. F. Prokasy, (Eds.), *Classical conditioning II: Current research and theory* (pp. 64-99). New York: Appleton-Century-Crofts.

Revelle, W., Humphreys, M. S., Simon, L., & Gilliland, K. (1980). The interactive effect of personality, time of day and caffeine: A test of the arousal model. *Journal of Experimental Psychology: General, 109,* 1-31.

Reynolds, B. (1945). The acquisition of a trace conditioned response as a function of the magnitude of the stimulus trace. *Journal of Experimental Psychology, 35,* 15-30.

Reynolds, M., & Brewin, C. R. (1999). Intrusive memories in depression and posttraumatic stress disorder. *Behavior Research & Therapy, 37,* 201-215.

Riggs, L. A. (1971). Vision. In J. W. Kling & L. A. Riggs (Eds.), *Experimental Psychology.* New York: Holt, Rinehart and Winston.

Rips, L. J., Shoben, E. J., & Smith, E. E. (1973). Semantic distance and the verification of semantic relations. *Journal of Verbal Learning and Verbal Behavior, 12,* 1-20.

Robinson, G. M., & Solomon, D. J. (1974). Rhythm is processed in the speech hemisphere. *Journal of Experimental Psychology*, **102**,508-511.

Robinson, J. A. (1976). Sampling autobiographical memory. *Cognitive Psychology*, **8**,578-595.

Rock, I., & Victor, J. (1964). Vision and touch: An experimentally created conflict between the two senses. *Science*, **143**, 594-596.

Roediger, H. L. (1978). Recall as a self limiting process. *Memory & Cognition*, **8**, 54-63.

Roediger, H. L. (1980). The effectiveness of four mnemonics in ordering recall. *Journal of Experimental Psychology: Human Learning and Memory*, **6**, 558-567.

Roediger, H. L., & McDermott, K. B. (1995). Creating false memories: Remembering words not presented in lists. *Journal of Experimental Psychology: Learning, Memory, & Cognition*, **21**, 803-814.

Roediger, H. L., & Neely, J. M. (1982). Retrieval blocks in episodic and semantic memory. *Canadian Journal of Psychology*, **36**, 213-242.

Roediger, H. L., Neely, J. H., & Blaxton, T. A. (1983). Inhibition from related primes in semantic memory retrieval: A reappraisal of Brown's (1979) paradigm. *Journal of Experimental Psychology: Learning, Memory, and Cognition*, **9**, 478- 485.

Roediger, H. L., Watson, J. M., McDermott, & Gallo (2001). Factors that determine false recall: A multiple regression analysis. *Psychonomic Bulletin & Review,* **8***,* 385-407.

Roediger, H. L., & Thorpe, L. A. (1978). The role of recall time in producing hypermnesia. *Memory & Cognition*, **6**, 296- 305.

Rogers, R. D., & Monsell, S. (1995). Costs of a predictible switch between simple cognitive tasks. *Journal of Experimental Psychology: General*, **124**, 207-231.

Rosch, E. (1973). On the internal structure of perceptual and semantic categories. In T. E. Moore (Ed.), *Cognitive development and the acquisition of language*. New York: Academic Press.

Rosch, E. (1975). Cognitive representations of semantic categories. *Journal of Experimental Psychology: General*, **104**, 192-233.

Rosch, E., Mervis, C. B., Gray, W., Johnson, D., & Boyes-Braem, P. (1976). Basic objects in natural categories. *Cognitive Psychology*, **8**, 382-439.

Rose, S. A., Gottfried, A. W., Melloy-Carminar, P., & Bridger, W. H. (1982). Familiarity novelty preferences in infant recognition memory: Implications for information processing. *Developmental Psychology* **18**, 704-713.

Rosenbaum, D. A., Loukopoulos, L. D., Meulenbrock, R. G. J., Vaughn, J., & Engelbrecht, S. E. (1995). Planning reaches by evaluating stored postures. *Psychological Review*, **102**, 28-67.

Ross, B. H. (1981). The more the better? Number of decisions as a determinant of memorability. *Memory & Cognition*, **9**, 23-33.

Ross, B. H., & Murphy, G. L. (1999). Food for thought: Cross-classification and category organization in a complex real-world domain. *Cognitive Psychology,* **83***,* 495-553.

Rossen, M. L., Jones, W., Wang, P. P., & Klima, E. S. (1995). Face processing: Remarkable sparing in Williams syndrome. Special Issue, *Genetic Counseling,* **6***,* 138-140.

Rothi, L. J. G., Ochipa, C., & Heilman, K. M. (1997). A cognitive neuropsychological model of limb praxis and apraxia. In Rothi L. J. G. & Heilman, K. M. (Eds.) *Apraxia, the Neuropsychology of Action* (pp. 29-49). Hove, UK: Psychology Press.

Rothwell, J. C., Traub, M. M., Day, B. L., Obeso, J. A., Thomas, P. K., & Marsden, C. D. (1982). Manual motor performance in a deafferented man. *Brain, 105,* 515-542.

Rourke, B. P. (1978). Neuropsychological research in reading retardation: A review. In A. L. Benton & D. Pearl (Eds.), *Dyslexia.* New York: Oxford University Press.

Rovee, C. K., & Rovee, D. T. (1969). Conjugate reinforcement of infant exploratory behavior. *Journal of Experimental Child Psychology, 8,* 33-39.

Rovee-Collier, C. (1993). The capacity for long-term memory in infancy. *Current Directions in Psychological Science, 2,* 130-135.

Rovee-Collier, C., & Dufault, D. (1991). Multiple contexts and memory retrieval at three months. *Developmental Psychobiology, 24,* 39-49.

Rovee-Collier, C., Earley, L., & Stafford, S. (1989). Ontogeny of early event memory: III. Attentional determinants of retrieval at 2 and 3 months. *Infant Behavior and Development, 12,* 147-161.

Rovee-Collier, C., Griesler, P. C., & Earley, L. A. (1985). Contextual determinants of retrieval in three-month-old infants. *Learning and Motivation, 16,* 139-157.

Rovee-Collier, C., Hankins, E. M., & Bhatt, R. S. (1992). Textons, visual pop-out effects, and object recognition in infancy. *Journal of Experimental Psychology: General, 121,* 436-446.

Rowe, D. C., Jacobson, K. C., Van den Oord, Edwin, J. C. G. (1999). Genetic and environmental influences on vocabulary IQ: Parental education level as moderator. *Child Development, 70,* 1151-1162.

Rubin, D. C. (1982). On the retention function for autobiographical memory. *Journal of Verbal Learning and Verbal Behavior, 21,* 21-38.

Rubin, D.C., Wetzler, S.E., & Nebes, R.D. (1986). Autobiographical memory across the life span. In D.C. Rubin (Ed.) *Autobiographical memory.* Cambridge: Cambridge University Press.

Ruff, R. M, Levin, H. S., Mattis, S., High, W. M. Jr., Marshall, L. F., Eisenberg, H. M., & Tabaddor, K. (1989). Recovery of memory after mild head injury: A three-center study. Mild head injury in sports: Neuropsychological sequelae and recovery of function. In, H. S. Levin, H. M. Eisenberg, & A. L. Benton (Eds.), *Mild head injury.* New York: Oxford University Press.

Rumelhart, D. E. (1977). Understanding and summarizing brief stories. In D. Laberge & S. J. Samuels (Eds.), *Basic processes in reading: Perception and comprehension.* Hillsdale, N.J.: Erlbaum.

Rundus, D. (1971). Analysis of rehearsal processes in free recall. *Journal of Experimental Psychology, 89,* 63-77.

Rundus, D. (1973). Negative effects of using list items as recall cues. *Journal of Verbal Learning and Verbal Behavior, 12,* 43-50.

Rundus, D., & Atkinson, R. C. (1970). Rehearsal processes in free recall: A procedure for direct observation. *Journal of Verbal Learning and Verbal Behavior, 9,* 99-105.

Russell, W. R., & Espir, M. L. E. (1961). *Traumatic aphasia-A study of aphasia in war wounds of the brain.* London: Oxford University Press.

Ruthruff, E., Pashler, H. E., Klaassen, A. (2001). Processing bottlenecks in dual-task performance: Structural limitations or strategic postponement? *Psychonomic Bulletin & Review, 8*, 73-80.

Rutter, M. (1978). Prevalence and types of dyslexia. In A. L. Benton & D. Pearl (Eds.), *Dyslexia*. New York: Columbia University Press.

Ryan, C., & Butters, N. (1980). Learning and memory impairments in young and old alcoholics: Evidence for the premature- aging hypothesis. *Alcoholism, 4*, 288-293.

Ryan, C., & Butters, N. (1983). Cognitive deficits in alcoholics. In B. Kissin & H. Begleiter (Eds.), *The pathogenesis of alcoholism (Vol. 7)*. New York: Plenum.

Ryan, C., & Butters, N. (1984). Alcohol consumption and premature aging: A critical review. In M. Galanter (Ed.), *Recent developments in alcoholism* (Vol. 1). New York: Plenum.

Sachs, J. S., Brown, R., & Salerno, R. A. (1976). Adults' speech to children. In W. van Raffler Engel & Y. Lebrun (Eds.), *Baby talk and infant speech (Neurolinguistics 5)*. Amsterdam: Swets & Zeitlinger.

Sachs, J. S., & Johnson, M. (1976). Language development in a hearing child of deaf parents. In W. van Raffler Engel & Y. Lebrun (Eds.), *Baby talk and infant speech (Neurolinguistics 5)*. Amsterdam: Swets & Zeitlinger.

Saffran, J. R. (2001). Words in a sea of sounds: The output of infant statistical learning. *Cognition, 8,* 149-169.

Saffran, J. R., Aslin, R. N., & Newport, E. L. (1996). Statistical learning by 8-month-old infants. *Science, 274,* 1926-1928.

Salzarulo, P., & Fagioli, I. (1995). Sleep for development or development for waking? Some speculations from a human perspective. *Behavioural Brain Research, 69,* 23-27.

Sanders, M. S., & McCormick, E. J. (1993). *Human factors in engineering and design.* New York: McGraw-Hill.

Sarbin, J. R., & Coe, W. C. (1972). *Hypnosis: A social psychological analysis of influence communication.* New York: Holt, Rinehart and Winston.

Saugstad, P. (1955). Problem-solving as dependent on availability of functions. *British Journal of Psychology, 46,* 191-198.

Saugstad, P., & Raaheim., K. (1960). Problem-solving, past experience and availability of functions. *British Journal of Psychology, 51,* 97-104.

Savage-Rumbaugh, S., Shanker, S. G., Taylor, T. J. (1998). *Apes, language, and the human mind.* New York: Oxford.

Scarborough, H. S. (1984). Continuity between childhood dyslexia and adult reading. *British Journal of Psychology, 75,* 329-348.

Scarr, S., & Salapatek, P. (1970). Patterns of fear development during infancy. *Merrill-Palmer Quarterly, 16,* 53-90.

Schatz, C. D. (1954). The role of context in the perception of stops. *Language, 30,* 47-56.

Schiffman, H. R. (1967). Size estimation of familiar objects under informative and reduced conditions of viewing. *American Journal of Psychology, 80,* 229-235.

Schiller, P. H. (1966). Developmental study of color-word interference. *Journal of Experimental Psychology, 72,* 105-108.

Schmitt, V. & Davis, R. (1974). The role of hemispheric specialization in the analysis of the Stroop stimuli. *Acta Psychologica, 18*, 149-158.

Schmolck, H., Buffalo, E. A., & Squire, L. R. (2000). Memory distortions develop over time: Recollections of the O. J. Simpson trial verdict after 15 and 32 months. *Psychological Science, 11*, 39-45.

Schneider, W., & Shiffrin, R. M. (1977). Controlled and automatic human information processing. I. Detection, search, and attention. *Psychological Review, 84*, 1-66.

Schnider, A. (2000). Spontaneous confabulations, disorientation, and the processing of 'now.' *Neuropsychologia, 38*, 175-185.

Schnider, A. (2001).   Spontaneous confabulation, reality monitoring, and the limbic system – a review. *Brain Research Reviews, 36*, 150-160.

Schnider, A., & Ptak, R. (1999). Spontaneous confabulators fail to suppress currently irrelevant memory traces. *Nature Neuroscience, 2*, 677-681.

Schnider, A., Ptak, R., von Däniken, C., & Remonda, L. (2000). Recovery from spontaneous confabulations parallels recovery of temporal confusion in memory. *Neurology, 55*, 74-83.

Schreibman, L. (1988). *Autism* (Vol. 15). London: Sage Publications.

Schuell, H. (1974). *Aphasia theory and therapy: Selected lectures and papers of Hildred Schuell.* Baltimore: University Park Press.

Schumacher, E. H., Seymour, T. L., Glass, J. M., Fencsik, D. E., Lauber, E. J., Kieras, D. E., & Meyer, D. E. (2001). Virtually perfect time sharing in dual-task performance: Uncorking the central cognitive bottleneck. *Psychological Science, 12*, 101-108,

Schvaneveldt, R. W., Durso, F. T., & Mukerji, B. R. (1982). Semantic distance effects in categorization tasks. *Journal of Experimental Psychology: Human Learning and Memory, 18*, 1-15.

Schwartz, M. F., Saffran, E. M., and Marin, O. S. (1980). The word order problem in agrammatism: I. Comprehension. *Brain and Language, 10*, 249-262.

Scott, S. K., & Wise, R. J. S. (2003). PET and fMRI studies of the neural basis of speech perception. *Speech Communication, 4*, 7-21.

Scott, S. K., & Wise, R. J. S. (2004). The functional neuroanatomy of prelexical processing in speech perception. *Cognition, 92*, 13-45.

Seidenberg, M. S., Tanenhaus, M. K., Leiman, J. M., & Bienkowski, M. (1982). Automatic access of the meanings of ambiguous words in context: Some limitations of knowledge-based processing. *Cognitive Psychology, 14*, 489-537.

Seidenberg, M. S., Waters, G. S., Barnes, M. A., & Tanenhaus, M. K. (1984). When does irregular spelling or pronunciation influence word recognition? *Journal of Verbal Learning & Verbal Behavior, 23*, 383-404.

Selfe, L. (1977). *Nadia: A case of extraordinary drawing ability in an autistic child.* New York: Harcourt Brace Jovanovich.

Shah, A., & Frith, U. (1992). Why do autistic individuals show superior performance on the block design task? *Journal of Child Psychology and Psychiatry, 34*, 1351-1363.

Shallice, T. (1999). The origin of confabulations. *Nature Neuroscience*, **2**, 588-590.

Shallice, T., & Burgess, W. (1991). Deficits in strategy application following frontal lobe damage in man. *Brain,* **114**, 727-741.

Shanon, B. (1978). Classification and identification in an aphasic patient. *Brain and Language*, **5**, 188-194.

Shanon, B. (1979). Yesterday, today, and tomorrow. *Acta Psychologica*, **43**, 469-476.

Shatz, M., & Gelman, R. (1973). The development of communication skills: Modifications in the speech of young children as a function of listener. *Monographs of the Society for Research in Child Development*, **38** (Serial No. 152).

Shaver, P. R., Wu, S., & Schwartz, J. C. (1992). Cross-cultural similarities and differences in emotion and its representation. In M. S. Clark (Ed.), *Review of Personality and Social Psychology Vol. 13: Emotion* (pp. 175-212). Newbury Park, CA: Sage.

Shaw, M. L. (1984). Division of attention among spatial locations: A fundamental difference between detection of letters and detection of luminance increments. In H. Bouma & D. Bowhuis (Eds.) *Attention and performance X.* Hillsdale, NJ: Erlbaum.

Sheen, M., Kemp, S., & Rubin, D. (2001). Twins dispute memory ownership: A new false memory phenomenon. *Memory & Cognition,* **29,** 779-788.

Shelton, P. A., Bowers, D., & Heilman, K. M. (1990). Peripersonal and vertical neglect. *Brain,* **113**, 191-205.

Shepard, R. N. (1967). Recognition memory for words, sentences, and pictures. *Journal of Verbal Learning and Verbal Behavior*, **6**, 156-163.

Shiffrin, R. M., & Schneider, W. (1977). Controlled and automatic human information processing. II. Perceptual learning, automatic attending, and a general theory. *Psychological Review,* **84**, 127-190.

Shor, R. E., & Orne, E. C. (1962). *The Harvard group scale of hypnotic susceptibility: Form A.* Palo Alto CA: Consulting Psychologists Press.

Shors, T. J., Miesegaes, G., Beylin, Zhao, M., Rydel, T., & Gould, E. (2001). Neurogenesis in the adult is is involved in the formation of trace memories. *Nature*, **410**, 372-376.

Siegel, B. (1996). *The autistic child.* New York: Oxford University Press.

Sigman, M., & Capps, L. (1997). *Children with autism.* London: Harvard University Press.

Silva, J. A., & Leong, G. B. (1995). Visual-perceptual abnormalities in delusional misidentification. *Canadian Journal of Psychiatry,* **40,** 6-8.

Simon, H. (1973). The structure of ill structured problems. *Artificial Intelligence*, **4**, 181-201.

Simon, H. (1975). The functional equivalence of problem solving skills. *Cognitive Psychology,* **7**, 268-288.

Simon, H., & Gilmartin, K. (1973). A simulation of memory for chess positions. *Cognitive Psychology*, **5**, 29-46.

Simonton, D. K. (1999). Talent and its development: An emergenic and epigenetic model. *Psychological Review,* **106**, 435-457.

Skavenski, A. A., & Hansen, R. M. (1978). Role of eye position information in visual space perception. In J. Senders, D. Fisher, & R. Monty (Eds.), *Eye movements and the higher psychological functions*. Hillsdale NJ: Erlbaum.

Slachevsky, A., Pillon, B., Fourneret, P., Renie, L., Levy, R., Jeannerod, M., & Dubois, B. (2003). *Neuropsychologia*, **41**, 655-665.

Slack, C. W. (1956). Familiar size as a cue to size in the presence of conflicting cues. *Journal of Experimental Psychology*, **52**, 194-198.

Slamecka, N. J. (1968). An examination of trace storage in free recall. *Journal of Experimental Psychology*, **76**, 504-513.

Slamecka, N. J. (1969). Testing for associative storage in multitrial free recall. *Journal of Experimental Psychology*, **81**, 557-560.

Sliwinski, M., & Buschke, H. (1999). Cross-sectional longitudinal relationships among age, cognition,and processing speed. *Psychology & Aging*, **14**, 18-33.

Slobin, D. 1. (1966). Grammatical transformations and sentence comprehension in childhood and adulthood. *Journal of Verbal Learning and Verbal Behavior*, **5**, 219-227.

Slobin, D. 1. (1973). Cognitive prerequisites for the acquisition of grammar. In C. A. Ferguson & D. I. Slobin (Eds.), *Studies of Child Language Development*. New York: Holt, Rinehart and Winston.

Sloman, S. A. (1993). Feature-based induction. *Cognitive Psychology*, **25**, 231-280.

Sloman, S. A. (1998). Categorical inference is not a tree: The myth of inheritance hierarchies. *Cognitive Psychology*, **35**, 1-33.

Slovic, P. (1975). Choice between equally valued alternatives. *Journal of Experimental Psychology: Human Perception & Performance*, **1**, 280-287.

Smith, E. E., Shoben, E. J., & Rips, L. J. (19 74). Structure and process in semantic memory: A featural model for semantic decisions. *Psychological Review*, **81**, 214-241.

Smith, S. M. (1979). Remembering in and out of context. *Journal of Experimental Psychology: Human Learning and Memory*, **5**, 460-471

Smith, S. M. (1982). Enhancement of recall using multiple environmental contexts during learning. *Memory & Cognition*, **10**, 405-412.

Smith, S. M., Glenberg, A., & Bjork, R. A. (1978). Environmental context and human memory. *Memory & Cognition*, **6**, 342-353.

Smith, S. M., & Vela E. (2001). Environmental context-dependent memory: A review and meta-analysis. *Psychological Bulletin & Review*, **8**, 203-220.

Smith, M. C., & Magee, L. E. (1980). Tracing the time course of picture-word processing. *Journal of Experimental Psychology: General*, **109**, 373-392.

Snow, C. E. (1972). Mothers' speech to children learning language. *Child Development*, **43**, 549-565.

Snow, C. E. (1977). The development of conversation between mothers and babies. *Journal of Child Language*, **4**, 1-22.

Snow, C. E., Arlman-Rupp, A., Hassing, Y., Jobse, J., Joosten, J., & Vorster, J. (1976). Mothers' speech in three social classes. *Journal of Psycholinguistic Research*, **5**, 1-20.

Snowden, J. S., Goulding, P. J., & Neary, D. (1989). Semantic dementia: a form of circumscribed cerevral atrophy. *Behavioral Neurology*, **2**, 167-182.

Snowden, J. S., Griffiths, H. L., & Neary, D. (1995). Autobiographical experience and word meaning. *Memory*, **3**,225-246.

Somberg, B. L., & Salthouse, T. A. (1982). Divided attention abilities in young and old adults. *Journal of Experimental Psychology: Human Perception and Performance, **8***, 651-663.

Sorce, J. F., Emde, R. N., Campos, J., & Klinnert, M. D. (1985). Maternal emotional signaling: Its effect on the visual cliff behavior of 1-year-olds. *Developmental Psychiatry*, **21**, 195-200.

Spanos, N. P., Burgess, C. A., & Burgess, M. F. (1994). Past-life identities, UFO abductions, and satanic ritual abuse: the social construction of memories. *International Journal of Clinical and Experimental Hypnosis*, **42**, 433-446.

Sparks, R., & Geschwind, N. (1968). Dichotic listening in man after section of neocortical commissures. *Cortex*, **4**, 3 -16.

Spearman, C. (1927). *The abilities of man.* New York: Macmillan.

Spector, A., & Biederman, I. (1976). Mental set and mental shift revisited. *American Journal of Psychology*, **89**, 669-679.

Spence, M. J. (1996). Young infants' long-term auditory memory: Evidence for changes in preference as a function of delay. *Developmental Psychobiology*, **29**, 685-695.

Sperber, D., Cara, F., Girotto, V. (1995). Relevance theory explains the selection task. *Cognition*, **57,** 31-95.

Sperling, G. (1960). The information available in brief visual presentations. *Psychological Monographs, **74***, 1-29.

Sperling, G., & Weichselgartner, E. (1995). The episodic theory of the dynamics of spatial attention. *Psychological Review*, **102**, 503-532.

Spiro, R. J. (1980). Accommodative reconstruction in prose recall. *Journal of Verbal Learning and Verbal Behavior*, **19**, 84-95.

Squire, L. R. (1981). Two forms of human amnesia: An analysis of forgetting. *Journal of Neuroscience*, **1**, 635-640.

Squire, L. R., & Slater, P. C. (1975). Forgetting in very long-term memory as assessed by an improved questionnaire technique. *Journal of Experimental Psychology: Human Learning and Memory*, **1**, 50-54.

Squire, L. R., Slater, P. C., & Chace, P. M. (1975). Retrograde amnesia: Temporal gradient in very long-term memory following electroconvulsive therapy. *Science*,**187**,77-79.

Staller, A., Sloman, S. A., & Ben-Zeev, T. (2000). Perspective effects in nondeontic versions of the Wason selection task. *Memory & Cognition, **28***, 396-405.

Standing, L. (1973). Learning 10,000 pictures. *Quarterly Journal of Experimental Psychology*, **25**, 207-222.

Standing, L., Conezio, J., & Haber, R. N. (1970). Perception and memory for pictures: Single-trial learning of 2560 visual stimuli. *Psychonomic Science*, **19**, 73-74.

Sternberg, S., Knoll, R. L., & Gates, B. A. (1971). Prior Entry Reexamined: Effect of Attentional Bias on Order Perception. Paper presented at the Psychonomic Society meeting, San Antonio.

Stewart, H. A., & McAllister, H. A. (2001). One-at-a-time versus grouped presentation of mug book pictures: Some surprising results. *Journal of Applied Psychology*, **86**, 1300-1305.

Stickgold, R., James, L., & Hobson, J. (2000). Visual discrimination learning requires sleep after training. *Nature Neuroscience, 3, 1237-1238.*

Stickgold, R., Whidbee, D., Schirmer, B., Patel, V., & Hobson, J. (2000). Visual discrimination task improvement: A multi-step process occurring during sleep. *Journal of Cognitive Neuroscience, 12*, 246-254.

Stoke, S. M. (1929). Memory for onomatapes. *Journal of Genetic Psychology*, **36**, 594-596.

Stratton, G. M. (1897). Vision without inversion of the retinal image. *Psychological Review*, **4**, 341-360.

Strayer, D. L., Drews, F. A., & Albert, R. W. (2002). Negative priming and stimulus repetition: A reply to Neill and Joordents (2002). *Perception & Psychophysics*, **64**, 861-865.

Strayer, D. L., & Grison, S. (1999). Negative identity priming is contingent on stimulus repetition. *Journal of ExperimentalPsychology: Human Perception & Performance*, **25**, 24-38.

Strayer, D. L., & Johnston, W. A. (2001). Driven to distraction: Dual-task studies of simulated driving and conversing on a cellular telephone. *Psychological Science, 12*, 462-466.

Stroh, C. M. (1971). *Vigilance: The problem of sustained attention.* Oxford: Pergamon.

Stroop, J. R. (1935). Studies of interference in serial verbal reactions. *Journal of Experimental Psychology, 18*, 643-662.

Sulin, R. A., & Dooling, D. J. (1974). Intrusions of a thematic idea in retention of prose. *Journal of Experimental Psychology*, **103**, 255-262.

Sternberg, R. J. (1988). *The triarchic mind: A new theory of human intelligence.* New York: Viking.

Swets, J. A., Tanner, W. P., & Birdsall, T. G. (1961). Decision processes in perception. *Psychological Review*, **68**, 301-340.

Tanenhaus, M. K., Leiman, J. M., & Seidenberg, M. S. (1979). Evidence for multiple stages in the processing of ambiguous words in syntactic contexts. *Journal of Verbal Learning and Verbal Behavior*, **18**, 427-440.

Taplin, J. E. (1971). Reasoning with conditional sentences. *Journal of Verbal Learning and Verbal Behavior*, **10**, 219-225.

Taplin, J. E., & Staudenmayer, H. (1973). Interpretation of abstract conditional sentences in deductive reasoning. *Journal of Verbal Learning and Verbal Behavior*, **12**,530-542.

Tardiff, T. (1996). Nouns are not always learned before verbs: evidence from Mandarin speakers' early vocabularies. *Developmental Psychology*, **32**, 492-504.

Taylor, I. (1976). *Introduction to psycholinguistics.* New York: Holt, Rinehart and Winston.

Teghtsoonian, R., & Teghtsoonian, M. (1970). Two varieties of perceived length. *Perception & Psychophysics*, **8**, 389-392.

Theeuwes, J., Kramer, A., & Atchley, P. (1998). Visual marking of old objects. *Psychonomic Bulletin & Review*, 5, 130-134.

Theeuwes, J., Kramer, A., & Atchley, P. (1999). Attentional effects on preattentive vision: Spatial precues affect the detection of simple features. *Journal of Experimental Psychology: Human Perception & Performance*, **25**, 341-347.

Theeuwes, J., Kramer, A., Hahn, S., Irwin, D. E. (1998). Our eyes do not always go where we want them to go: Capture of the eyes by new objects. *Psychological Science*, **9**, 379-385.

Thompson, P. (1980). Margaret Thatcher: A new illusion. *Perception*, **9**, 483-484.

Thompson-Schill, S. L., Swick, D., Farah, M. J., D'Esposito, M., Kan, I. P., & Knight, R. T. (1998). Verb generation in patients with focal frontal lesions: A neurolopsychological test of neuroimaging findings. *Proceedings of the National Academy of Sciences of the United States of America*, **26**, 14792 – 14797.

Thorndyke, P. W. (1977). Cognitive structures in comprehension and memory of narrative discourse. *Cognitive Psychology*, **9**, 77-110.

Thurstone, L. L. (1938). *Primary mental abilities*. Chicago: University of Chicago Press.

Titchener, E. B. (1908). *Lectures on the elementary psychology of feeling and attention*. New York: Macmillan.

Tincoff, R., & Jusczyk, P. W. (1999). Some beginnings of word comprehension in 6-month-olds. *Psychological Science*, **10**, 172-175.

Tipper, S. P. (2001). Does negative priming reflect inhibitory mechanisms? A review and integration of conflicting views. *The Quarterly Journal of Experimental Psychology*, **54A**, 321-343.

Tippett, L. J., Miller, L. A., & Farah, M. J. (2000). Prosopamnesia: A selective impairment in face learning. *Cognitive Neuropsychology*, **17**, 241-255.

Toma, R. J. & Tsao, Y.-C. (1985). Interference effects in the picture-word Stroop task. *Perceptual and Motor Skills*, **61**, 223-228.

Tomasello, M., Strosberg, R., & Akhtar, N. (1996). Eighteen-month-old children learn words in non-ostensive contexts. *Journal of Child Language*, **23**, 157-176.

Townsend, D. J., & Bever, T. G. (2001). *Sentence comprehension*. Cambridge, MA: MIT Press.

Trabasso, T., Riley, C. A., & Wilson, E. G. (1975). The representation of linear order and spatial strategies in reasoning: A developmental study. In R. Falmagne (Ed.), *Psychological studies of logic and development*. Hillsdale, N.J.: Erlbaum.

Trainor, L. J., Austin, C. M., and Desjardins, R. N. (2000). Is infant-directed speech prosody a result of the vocal expression of emotion? *Psychonomic Science*, **11**, 188-195.

Treat, N. J., & Reese, H. W. (1976). Age, pacing, and imagery in paired-associate learning. *Developmental Psychology*, **12**, 119-124.

Treisman, A. M. (1964). Verbal cues, language, and meaning in selective attention. *American Journal of Psychology*, **27**, 215-216.

Treisman, A. M. (1991). Search, similarity, and the integration of features between and within dimensions. *Journal of Experimental Psychology: Human Perception and Performance*, **17**, 252-276.

Treisman, A. M. (1992). Spreading suppression or feature integration? A reply to Duncan and Humphreys. *Journal of Experimental Psychology: Human Perception and Performance,* **18**, 589-593.

Treisman, A. M., & Davis, A. (1973). Divided attention to ear and eye. In S. Kornblum (Ed.) *Attention and performance IV.* New York: Academic Press.

Treisman, A. M., & Gelade, G. (1980). A feature-integration theory attention. *Cognitive Psychology,* **12**, 97-136.

Treisman, A. M., & Gormican, S. (1988). Feature analysis in early vision: Evidence from search asymmetries. *Psychological Review,* **95**, 15-48.

Treisman, A. M., & Riley, J. G. A. (1969). Is selective attention selective perception or selective response? A further test. *Journal of Experimental Psychology,* **79**, 27-34.

Treisman, A. M., & Schmidt, H. (1982). Illusory conjunctions in the perception of objects. *Cognitive Psychology,* **14**, 107-141.

Troster, A. I., Salmon, D. P., McCullough, D., & Butters, N. (1989). A comparison of the category fluency deficits associated with Alzheimer's and Huntington's disease. *Brain and Language,* **37**, 500-513.

Tsotsos, J. K. (1995). Toward a computational model of visual attention. In, T. V. Papathomas (Ed.) *Early vision and beyond.* Cambridge MA: MIT Press.

Tucha, O., Smely, C., & Lange, K. W. (1999). Verbal and figural fluency in patients with mass lesions of the left or right frontal lobes. *Journal of Clinical & Experimental Neuropsychology,* **21**, 229-236.

Tuddenham, R. D. (1962). The nature and measurement of intelligence. In L. Postman (Ed.) *Psychology in the making,* (pp. 469-525) New York: Alfred A. Knopf.

Tulving, E. (1962). Subjective organization in free recall of "unrelated" words. *Psychological Review,* **69**, 344-354.

Tulving, E. (1981). Similarity relations in recognition. *Journal of Verbal Learning and Verbal Behavior,* **20**, 479-496.

Turkewitz, G., & Birch, H. G. (1971). Neurobehavioral organization of the human newborn. In J. Hellmuth (Ed.), *Exceptional infant (Vol. 2).* New York: Brunner/Mazel.

Tversky, A. (1972). Elimination by aspects: A theory of choice. *Psychological Review,* **79,** 281-299.

Tversky, A. (1977). Features of similarity. *Psychological Review,* **84**, 327-352.

Tversky, A., & Gati, 1. (1978). Studies in similarity. In E. Rosch & B. B. Lloyd (Eds.), *Cognition and categorization.* Hillsdale, N.J.: Erlbaum.

Tversky, A., & Kahneman, D. (1971). Belief in the law of small numbers. *Psychological Bulletin,* **76**, 105 –110.

Tversky, A., & Kahneman, D. (1973). Availability: A heuristic for judging frequency and probability. *Cognitive Psychology,* **5**, 207-232.

Tversky, A., & Kahneman, D. (1974). judgments under uncertainty: Heuristics and biases. *Science,* **185**, 1124-1131.

Tversky, A., & Kahneman, D. (1978). Causal schemata in judgments under uncertainty. In M. Fishbein (Ed.), *Progress in social psychology.* Hillsdale, N.J.: Erlbaum.

Tversky, A., & Kahneman, D. (1981). The framing of decisions and the psychology of choice. *Science,* **211**, 453-458.

Tversky, A., & Kahneman, D. (1982). Evidential impact of base rates. In D. Kahneman, P. Slovic, & A. Tversky (Eds.), *Judgment under uncertainty: Heuristics and biases* (pp. 153-160). New York: Cambridge University Press.

Tversky, A., & Kahneman, D. (1983). Extensional versus intuitive reasoning: The conjunction fallacy in probability judgment. *Psychological Review*, **90**, 293-315.

Tversky, A., Sattath, S., & Slovic, P. (1988). Contingent weighting in judgment and choice. *Psychological Review,* **95,** 371-384.

Tyler, C. W. (1995). Cyclopean riches: Cooperativity, neurontropy, hysteresis, stereoattention, hyperglobality, and hypercyclopean processes in random-dot stereopsis. In, T. V. Papathomas (Ed.) *Early vision and beyond.* Cambridge MA: MIT Press.

Ulvund, S. E., & Smith, L. (1996). The predictive validity of nonverbal communicative skills in infants with perinatal hazards. *Infant Behavior & Development*, **19**, 441-449.

Unger, S. M. (1964). Habituation of the vasoconstrictive orienting reaction. *Journal of Experimental Psychology,* **67,** 11-18.

Ungerleider, L. G., & Mishkin, M. (1982). Two cortical visual systems. In D. J. Engle, M. A. Goodale, and R. J. Mansfield (Eds.), *Analysis of Visual Behavior* (pp. 549-586). Cambridge MA: MIT Press.

Vellutino, F. R. (1979). *Dsylexia: Theory and research.* Cambridge, MA.: MIT Press.

Vokey, J. R., & Read, J. D. (1985). Subliminal messages: Between the devil and the media. *American Psychologist,* **40**, 1231-1239.

Von Noorden, G. K. (1995). Binocular vision and ocular motility: Theory and management of strabismus (5th Ed.). Toronto:Mosby.

Von Restorff, H. (1933). Uber die Wirkung von Bereichsbildungen im Spurenfeld. *Psychologisch Forschung*, **18,** 299-342.

Wade, J. A. (1977). Prelanguage and fundamental asymmetry of the infant brain. *Annals of the New York Academy of Sciences*, **299**, 370-379.

Wagner, D. A. (1974). The development of short-term and incidental memory: A cross-cultural study. *Child Development*, **45,**389-396.

Walden, T. A., & Ogan, T. A. (1988). The development of social referencing. *Child Development,* **59**, 1230-1240.

Waldmann, M. R. (2001). Predictive versus diagnostic causal learning: Evidence from an overshadowing paradigm. *Psychonomic Bulletin & Review,* **8**, 600-608.

Waldmann, M. R., & Holyoak, K. J. (1992). Predictive and diagnostic learning within causal model: Asymmetries in cue competition. *Journal of Experimental Psychology: General,* **121,** 222-236.

Walker-Andrews, A. S. (1986). Intermodal perception of expressive behaviors: Relation of eye and voice? *Developmental Psychology,* **22**, 373-377.

Waltz, J. A., Knowlton, B. J., Holyoak, K. J., Boone, K. B., Mishkin, F. S., de Menezes Santos, M., Thomas, C. R., & Miller, B. L. (1999). A system for relational reasoning in human prefrontal cortex. *Psychological Science*, **10**, 119-125.

Wang, Q., Cavanaugh, P., & Green, M. (1994). Familiarity and pop-out in visual search. *Perception & Psychophysics,* **56**, 495-500.

Ward, G., & Allport, A. (1997). Planning and problem-solving using the five disc Tower of London. *The Quarterly Journal of Experimental Psychology,* **50A**, 49-78.

Warner, J., & Glass, A. L. (1987). Context and distance-to-disambiguation effects in ambiguity resolution: Evidence from grammaticality judgments of garden path sentences. *Journal of Memory and Language*, **26**, 714-738.

Warren, D. H., & Cleaves, W. T. (1971). Visual-proprioceptive interaction under large amounts of conflict. *Journal of Experimental Psychology*, **90**, 206-214.

Warren, J. M. (1977). Functional lateralization. of the brain. *Annals of the New York Academy of Sciences*, **299**,273-280.

Warren, L. R., & Horn, J. W. (1982). What does naming a picture do? Effects of prior picture naming on recognition of identical and same-name alternatives. *Memory & Cognition*, **10**, 167-175.

Warren, R. M., & Obusek, C. J. (1971). Speech perception and phonemic restorations. *Perception & Psychophysics*, **9**, 358-362.

Warren, R. M., & Warren, R. P. (1970). Auditory illusions and confusions. *Scientific American*, **223**, 30-36.

Warrington, E. K. (1975). The selective impairment of semantic memory. *Quarterly Journal of Experimental Psychology*, **27**, 635-657.

Warrington, E. K., & Sanders, H. (1971). The fate of old memories. *Quarterly Journal of Experimental Psychology*, **23**, 432-442.

Warrington, E. K., & Weiskrantz, L. (1970). Amnesic syndrome: consolidation or retrieval? *Nature,* **228**, 628-630.

Warrington, E. K., & Weiskrantz, L. (1974). The effect of prior learning on subsequent retention in amnesic patients. *Neuropsychologia,* **12**, 419-428.

Wason, P. C. (1966). Reasoning. In B. M. Foss (Ed.), *New horizons in psychology*. Harmondsworth: Penguin,

Wason, P. C. (1968). Reasoning about a rule. *Quarterly Journal of Experimental Psychology*, **20**, 273-281.

Wason, R. A. (1983). Realism and rationality in the selection task. In J. St. B. T. Evans (ed.), *Thinking and reasoning: Psychological approaches,* London: Routledge & Kegan Paul.

Watkins, 0. C., & Watkins, M. J. (1975). Buildup of proactive interference as a cue-overload effect. *Journal of Experimental Psychology: Human Learning and Memory*, **104**, 442-452.

Wattenmaker, W. D. (1992). Relational properties and memory-based category construction. *Journal of Experimental Psychology: Learning, Memory, and Cognition,* **15**, 282-304.

Watts, F. N., Morris, L., & MacLeod, A. (1987). Recognition memory in depression. *Journal of Abnormal Psychology,* **96**, 273-275.

Watts, F. N., & Sharrock, R. (1987). Cued recall in depression. *British Journal of Clinical Psychology,* **26**, 149-150.

Weeks, D. J., & Proctor, R. W. (1990). Compatibility effects for orthogonal stimulus-response dimensions. *Journal of Experimental Psychology: General*, **119**, 355-366.

Weekes, B. (1997). Differential effects of number of letters on word and nonword naming latency. *Quarterly Journal of Experimental Psychology,* **50A,** 439-456.

Weichselgartner E., & Sperling, G. (1987). Dynamics of automatic and controlled visual attention. *Science,* **238,** 778-780.

Weisberg, R., & Suls, J. (1973). An information-processing model of Duncker's candle problem. *Cognitive Psychology,* **4,** 255-276.

Weiskrantz, L. (1956). Behavioral changes associated with ablation of the amygdaloid complex in monkeys. *Journal of Comparative and Physiological Psychology,* **49,** 381-391.

Weiskrantz, L., Warrington, E. K., Sanders, M. D., & Marshall, J. (1974). Visual capacity in the hemianopic field following a restricted occipital ablation. *Brain,* **97,** 709-728.

Weitzenhoffer, A. M., & Hilgard, E. R. (1959). *Stanford hypnotic susceptibility scale: Forms A and B.* Palo Alto CA: Consulting Psychologists Press.

Weitzenhoffer, A. M., & Hilgard, E. R. (1962). *Stanford hypnotic susceptibility scale: Form C.* Palo Alto CA: Consulting Psychologists Press.

Wellman, H. M. (1977). Tip-of-the-tongue and the feeling of knowing experience: A developmental study of memory monitoring. *Child Development,* **48,** 13-21.

Wells, C. E. (1979). Pseudodementia. *American Journal of Psychiatry,* **136,** 895-900.

Weltman, G., Smith, J. E., & Egstrom, G. H. (1971). Perceptual narrowing during simulated pressure-chamber exposure. *Human Factors,* **13,** 99-107.

West, L. J. (1967). Vision and kinesthesis in the acquisition of typewriting skill. *Journal of Applied Psychology,* **51,** 161- 166.

West, T. A., & Bauer, P. J. (1999). Assumptions of infantile amnesia: Are there differences between early and later memories? *Memory.* **7,** 257-278.

Wheeler, D. D. (1970). Processes in word recognition. *Cognitive Psychology,* **1,** 59-85.

Whitten, W. B., & Leonard, J. M. (1981). Directed search through autobiographical memory. *Memory & Cognition,* **9,** 566-579.

Wickens, D. D. (1972). Characteristics of word encoding. In A. W. Melton & E. Martin (Eds.), *Coding processes in human memory.* Washington, D.C.: Winston.

Wickens, D. D., Born, D. G., & Allen, C. K. (1963). Proactive inhibition and item similarity in short-term memory. *Journal of Verbal Learning and Verbal Behavior,* **2,** 440-445.

Wilkins, A. T. (1971). Conjoint frequency, category size, and categorization time. *Journal of Verbal Learning and Verbal Behavior,* **10,** 382-385.

Wilkins, A. J., Binnie, C. D., & Darby, C. E. (1981). Interhemispheric differences in photosensitive epilepsy: 1. Pattern sensitivity thresholds. *Electroencephalography and Clinical Neuropsychology,* **52,** 461-468.

Wilkins, A. J., & Lewis, E. (1999). Covered overlays, text, and texture. *Perception,* **28,** 641-650.

Wilkins, A. J., & Nimmo-Smith, M. I. (1987). The clarity and comfort of printed text. *Ergonomics,* **30,** 1705-1720.

Windes, J. D. (1968). Reaction time for numerical coding and naming of numerals. *Journal of Experimental Psychology,* **78**, 318-322.

Winner, E. (2000). Giftedness: Current theory and research. *Current Directions in Psychological Science,* **9**, 153-156.

Wise, L. A., Sutton, J. A., & Gibbons, P. D. (1975). Decrement in Stroop interference time with age. *Perceptual and Motor Skills,* **41**, 149-150.

Witkin, H. A., Goodenough, D. R., Oltman, P. K. (1979). Psychological differentiation: Current status. *Journal of Personality & Social Psychology,* **37**, 1127-1145.

Wittgenstein, L. (1953). *Philosophical investigations.* New York: Macmillan.

Witvliet, C. V. (1997). Traumatic intrusive imagery as an emotional memory phenomenon: A review of research and explanatory information processing theories. *Clinical Psychology Review,* **17**, 509-536.

Wixon, D. R., & Laird, J. D. (1976). Awareness and attitude change in the forced compliance paradigm: The importance of when. *Journal of Personality and Social Psychology,* **34**, 376-384.

Wollen, K. A., Weber, A., & Lowry, D. (1972). Bizarreness versus interaction of mental images as determinants of learning. *Cognitive Psychology,* **3**, 518-523.

Woodhead, M. M., & Baddeley, A. D. (1981). Individual differences and memory for faces, pictures, and words. *Memory & Cognition,* **9**, 368-370.

Woods, B. T., & Teuber, H. L. (1978). Changing patterns of childhood aphasia. *Annals of Neurology,* **3**, 273-280.

Woods, D. L., Knight, R. T., & Scabini, D. (1993). Anatomical substrates of auditory selective attention: Behavioral and electrophysiological effects of temporal and parietal lesions. *Cognitive Brain Research,* **1**, 227-240.

Woodworth, R. S., & Schlosberg, H. (1954). *Experimental psychology.* New York: Holt, Rinehart and Winston.

Yamaguchi, S., & Knight, R. T. (1990). Gating of somatosensory inputs by the prefrontal cortex. *Brain Research,* **521**, 281-288.

Yang, Y., & Johnson-Laird, P. N. (2000). Illusions in quantified reasoning: How to make the impossible seems possible, and vice versa. *Memory & Cognition,* **28**, 452-465.

Yarbus, A. L. (1967). *Eye movements and vision.* New York: Plenum.

Yates, F. A. (1966). *The art of memory.* London: Routledge & Kegan Paul.

Yerkes, R. M., & Dodson, J. D. (1908). The relation of strength of stimulus to rapidity of habit-formation. *Journal of Comparative Neurology and Psychology,* **18**, 459-482.

Zahn-Waxler, C. Radke-Yarrow, M., Wagner, E., & Chapman, M. (1992). Development of concern for others. *Developmental Psychology,* **28**, 126-136.

Zaidel, E. (1976). Auditory vocabulary of the right hemisphere following brain bisection or hemidecortication. *Cortex,* **12**,191-211.

Zaidel, E. (1978a). Lexical organization in the right hemisphere. In P. Buser & A. Rougel-Buser (Eds.), *Cerebral correlates of conscious experience.* Amsterdam: North Holland.

Zaidel, E. (1978b). Concepts of cerebral dominance in the split brain. In P. Buser & A. Rougel-Buser (Eds.), *Cerebral correlates of conscious experience*. Amsterdam: North Holland.

Zaidel, E. (1983). A response to Gazzaniga. Language in the right hemisphere, convergent perspectives. *American Psychologist*, **38**, 542-546.

Zakay, D., & Glicksohn, J. (1985). Stimulus congruity and S-R compatibility as determinants of interference in a Stroop-like task. *Canadian Journal of Psychology*, **39**, 414-423.0

Zaragoza, M. S., Payment, K. E., Ackil, J. K., Drivdahl, S. B., & Beck, M. (2001). Interviewing witnesses: Forced confabulation and confirmatory feedback increase false memories. *Psychological Science*, **12**, 473-477.

Zelazo, P. D., Jacques, S., Burack, J. A., & Frye, D. (2002). The relation between theory of mind and rule use: Evidence from persons with autism-spectrum disorders. *Infant and Child Development*, **11**, 171-195.

Zelniker, T. (1971). Perceptual attenuation of an irrelevant auditory verbal input as measured by an involuntary verbal response in a selective-attention task. *Journal of Experimental Psychology*, **87**, 52-56.

Zigmond, M. J., & Stricker, E. M. (1989). Animal models of Parkinsonism using selective neurotoxins: Clinical and basic implications. *International Review of Neurobiology*, **31**, 1-78.

Zoellner, L. A., Foa, E. B., Brigidi, B. D., & Przeworski, A. (2000). Are trauma victims susceptible to "false memories?" *Journal of Abnormal Psychology*, **109**, 517-524.

Zola-Morgan, S. M., & Oberg, R. G. (1980). Recall of life experiences in an alcoholic Korsakoff patient: A naturalistic approach. *Neuropsychologia*, **18**, 549-557.

Zola-Morgan, S., Squire, L. R., Amaral, D. G. (1986). Human amnesia and the medial temporal region: Enduring memory impairment following a bilateral lesion limited to field CA1 of the hippocampus. *The Journal of Neuroscience*, **6**, 2950-2967.

Zurif, E. B., Caramazza, A., Meyerson, R., & Galvin, J. (1974). Semantic feature representations for normal and aphasic language. *Brain and Language*, **1**, 167-187.

Zurif, E., Swinney, D., Prather, P., Solomon, J., and Bushnell, C. (1993). An on-line analysis of syntactic processing in Broca's and Wernicke's aphasia. *Brain and Language*, **45**, 448-464.

A

abilities   1, 3, 82, 154-155, 191, 194, 212-216, 222-224, 248, 284, 301, 316-318
   attention   169, 173
   auditory recognition 129
   basic   320
   cognitive   41
   drawing 67, 318-319
   imagery 67
   inferential   172
   language 160, 284
   learning 188, 191-192
   mathematical   318
   memory   181, 214, 308
   mnemonic 318
   musical 316
   problem solving   301, 318
   reasoning   150
   speech production   135
   verbal   171, 318, 320
   visual   41
action   1-66, 71-74, 93-112, 115-161, 167-176, 184-258, 261, 263, 275, 282, 296, 307, 311
   pathway 66
   system   15, 20-21, 23-24, 30-31, 73, 97
affect   110, 156, 182, 191
affordances 315
agnosia   66, 125, 150
   apperceptive   67, 115, 125
   associative visual   67, 123
   auditory 124
   verbal   124
   visual   31, 66-67, 124-132, 147
agraphia   124
alert 91-94, 108, 113
alexia   124-125, 146
Alzheimer's disease   150, 190, 193-197, 270
ambiguities 57-59, 140-144, 152
amnesia   192-193
   anterograde   191-198
   childhood   264, 273
   diencephalic   192-195
   drug-induced temporary   192
   medial temporal   193-195
   psychogenic   268, 273
   retrograde   191, 197, 268-273
   transient epileptic 192
   transient global   192
amygdala   10-13, 109-111, 154, 175, 190, 224, 234, 295-296
analogies   150, 152, 176, 290-306, 317, 320
anomia   146, 197
anosognosia 96, 147
anterior thalamic nuclei   191, 194
aphasia   132, 146-151, 161
   anomic   146, 197
   Broca's 146-149

conduction   146-147
   fluent   147, 150
   nonfluent   147
   transient   149
   Wernicke's   146-149
apraxia   30-32, 39
arousal   10, 104-108, 111, 113, 169, 171, 190, 295
arousal system   105-106
associations   124-125, 146, 155, 186, 196, 211, 237, 239-241, 251-252, 309
   inter-modal   116
   polymodal   120
   semantic   147
   sound-image   160
ataxia   27
   visual   66-67, 69
attention   3, 12-13, 17, 32, 71-79, 83-84, 87, 91, 93-96, 104-107, 111-112,
125, 132, 141, 153, 155, 165, 169-172, 178, 183, 188, 190-191, 195, 200, 209,
217, 267, 316
   auditory 81
   divided 83-84, 87-88
   infant's 156, 162
   selective   73-74, 77-78, 88-89, 91, 95, 112, 194
   selective auditory   92
   visual   78, 80-81, 87-88, 91
   visuospatial   193
attention system   2-3, 10, 73, 155, 161
auditory pathway 94, 118, 130
auditory perception   176
auditory recognition   131, 316
auditory system   78, 129
auditory whole-word pathway   121, 151
autism   169-171, 173
autobiographical memories   245, 264-265, 273
awareness   4, 7, 16, 18, 43-44, 71-72, 81, 86, 93, 106, 115, 128, 154, 166,
200, 221, 225, 258, 309

B

basal ganglia   10-11, 19-32, 39-76, 83-106, 109-110, 190, 193, 197, 224
belief   1, 17, 159, 234, 263-293
bottom-up process 73
brainstem   9-10

C

camouflage 57
Capgras delusion 234
categories 32, 74, 138, 141, 146, 149, 164, 168, 191, 196-211, 217, 227-228,
238-241, 246, 284, 286, 300, 307
   abstract 172
   artificial   204-205, 209, 217
   basic biological   284
   basic-level   203-204
   color   201-203
   natural 199, 208-209, 217, 246
   phonemic 140
   semantic 189, 199

      social kinship 167
causal scenario   292
cell 49-50, 106-107, 122, 194
    4b 49-50
    bipolar 45
    blob   50
    brain 196
    cone   45
    ganglion 45
    interblob   50
    LGN   50
    light-sensitive   42
    photoreceptor 49, 68
central nervous system 1-3, 6, 8-17, 19, 131
cerebellum 10, 16, 19-21, 24, 26-29, 31, 39, 73, 87
chess 168, 307, 309-311, 319
chimpanzees 162, 316
chunk 34, 37, 180-181, 184-187, 212-213, 245-246, 305, 308-310
cingulate gyrus   11
cluster   184, 187, 240, 255, 307-308, 310
    animal   240
    consonant   123
    initial letter 88
    natural 187
code 6-8, 13, 131, 146
    articulatory   124, 180
    auditory 146
    octal   212
    phonological   124, 180
    visuospatial   301
cognition   1, 3, 5-6, 8-9, 12-13, 109, 190
cognitive system 12, 105
color 10, 43-45, 50, 76-79, 81, 85, 100-101, 170, 201, 203, 248, 309
    focal   201-202
color pathway   77
comparison 55, 62, 64, 74, 77, 80, 82, 87-91, 112, 116, 118, 120, 123, 127,
135, 140, 148, 151-152, 168, 196, 204, 208, 220-222, 253, 270, 275, 277-278,
288, 316, 319
    visual   317-318
    process 74, 80, 89, 93, 112, 120, 123-236
    stage   120, 127, 136, 221, 223
comprehension   88, 118, 135, 140-141, 144, 146-152, 185, 272
    language 12, 129, 139, 141, 144, 146
    sentence 144, 146, 149, 151
    process 140
    system   142, 144
computation 2, 7-8, 11-13, 43-44, 63, 93, 110, 214
concept   125, 168, 200, 207, 209, 236, 240, 247, 250, 252, 255, 278, 287-288,
303, 305, 315, 317
confabulation   259, 271-273
conjunction fallacy   286
consciousness   4, 10, 12, 72, 74, 86, 91, 95, 239
construction stage   45, 48, 68, 130
context-dependent recall   244
control   2-3, 10, 19, 21-23, 28-33, 39, 47, 53, 73, 75, 91-95, 110-111, 122,
131-136, 188, 196, 261, 284
    bilateral   23

   cerebellum   10
   conscious   93
   cortical 47, 91
   hemispheric   135
   heterarchical 25
   motor   15, 25-26, 30, 75
   proprioceptive 28
   sensory 13
   visual   28-29, 36, 45, 66, 98
   voluntary   26, 87, 93
corpus callosum   11, 28, 132-133, 135
counterexample   247, 282
cued recall 244-245
cues 54, 56, 69, 75, 110, 163, 211, 221, 236, 240, 242-246, 250-251, 255-256, 261, 265, 269, 290, 314
   associative   242, 244
   binocular   55-56, 69
   depth   59
   emotional   164-165, 172, 174, 296
   form   242-243
   monocular   54-56, 59, 65, 69
   orthographic   243
   recall   236, 240-241, 256
   retrieval   211, 237, 242, 245, 258
   semantic   243-244
   social   165

D

decision criterion   221, 230-231, 235, 251
decision procedure   230, 235, 251
decision process 102-104, 222, 227, 229, 273
decision stage   104, 118, 220-222, 226
declarative pathway   46, 49, 65, 68-69, 118, 130
deduction 275-277, 279, 283-285
delusion   233-234, 271-272
  Capgras 233-234
dementia   270
  alcohol 195, 272
  fronto-temporal   150
  semantic 150, 193
detector
  edge   51
  orientation   51
  shape   51-52, 58
diencephalon   10, 192, 194
distributed rehearsal   181, 183, 198
distributed repetition 163, 172, 177-178
dopamine   106-107
dyslexia   124, 169, 173
dysprosody 171

E

echolalia   171
einstellung 314
electroconvulsive shock treatment   269

emotion   3, 9, 11-12, 108-156, 159-160, 169, 171, 173, 176, 190, 224, 295
emotional response   11-12, 109-110, 155, 161, 171-235, 251-296
emotional system 3, 10, 108-111, 154-155, 160-161, 173, 175
encoding process 216
episode   145, 165, 177, 211, 220, 229, 253-254, 261, 265, 272-273
   autobiographical   271
evaluation process   222, 234
expectation 47, 49, 69-75, 230, 235, 251, 275, 285, 288, 290, 293, 297
extraversion   108
eye fixation   47, 98, 141
eye-fields 47, 49, 69
eye-fixation system   87
eyeball   16, 42-44
eyes 3, 8-9, 12, 15-17, 22, 43-49, 55, 64, 68-72, 75, 83, 88-89, 94, 96, 130, 170, 194, 271, 283
eyewitness 232-233, 260
eyewitness identification   232-233

F

face recognition 234, 270, 310
false memories   246, 259, 261-262, 265, 267, 273
familiarity 72, 79, 81, 91, 94, 117, 146, 157-230, 235, 251, 265, 272, 282, 285, 290, 293
familiarity criterion   230, 235, 251
familiarity judgment   226-228, 272
familiarity response   220, 226, 233, 285
feature   48, 51-52, 56-58, 63-69, 73, 78-80, 82, 85, 90, 96, 99, 112, 118-119, 123, 168-169, 183, 200, 204, 208, 211, 221-224, 235, 240, 242, 248, 255, 287-288, 292, 295, 310
   basic   51, 56
   category 200
   corner   54, 58, 60, 222
   emotional   161
   facial   125, 172, 180
   orientation   50-51, 54-55
   perceptual   76-77, 164, 203, 207
   shape   51, 57-58
   visual   50, 54, 56-78, 80-81, 158, 203-204
feature analysis stage 48-49, 68-69, 76, 119, 127, 150, 152, 221
feedback   4, 18-19, 21, 27-30, 32, 36, 39, 205
   auditory 93, 170
   kinesthetic   170
   long loop   29-30, 32
   proprioceptive 21, 28-29, 32, 34, 36, 39
   short loop   29, 32
   vestibular   21
   visual   21, 28, 36-37
fixation   12, 21, 48, 55, 75, 88-89
flashbulb memories   266-267
forebrain   9-11, 13, 109
   basal   191-192, 272
foveal image   56
free recall 187, 191, 196, 245, 255, 260-261
Fregoli's delusion   234
frequency judgment   226, 228-229, 285
frontal lobe   11-12, 19, 133, 176, 228, 272

functional fixedness   314-316, 320

G

gate 75-77, 89-91, 112, 211
generalization   37, 167, 173, 247-287
generate   73, 178, 219-221, 235-236, 240, 243, 245-246, 250, 262, 300-301, 309, 314-315, 320
generation stage 243-244
generation strategies 240-241
generative procedure   245
geon 60, 62-63, 65, 69, 74, 85, 203, 242, 284
gestalt   57
gestures   160, 164
gist recall 255
grammar   137, 166, 169, 205
   finite-state   205

H

habituation 94
hemidecortication 162
hemiplegia 26
heterarchy 39, 50, 68, 79
   motor   21, 28
   recognition   121
heuristic   280, 285, 290-291, 297
   simulation   291-292
hierarchical organization   185-186, 211, 243-247, 255
hippocampus 10, 109-110, 154, 176, 190-192, 194, 198
Huntington's disease   27, 190, 193-194, 197, 270
hypnosis   94-95, 267, 273
hypnotic susceptibility 94-95
hypothalamus   10, 109, 194

I

icon 85
identification   63-64, 80, 120, 141, 161, 220-221, 242
identification process 236
identification response 220, 233
illusion   13, 59, 79-80
illusory conjunction   79-80
imagination 13, 169-170, 210, 216, 289, 294, 303, 311, 314
imitation   31, 159-161, 173
immediate recall 181-182, 198
immediate recognition   223-224
induction   285, 293
inference   172, 221, 227, 235, 247-248, 251-252, 277, 284
   deductive   276
   transitive   276, 278
inference process 168, 248
inferior colliculus   9-10, 17, 94, 130
information 1-3, 5-13, 16, 18-19, 21, 28-29, 33, 43-44, 47-48, 50, 56, 59, 66, 68, 73-74, 82-83, 110-111, 115-116, 120, 131, 133, 136, 139, 144-145, 147, 168, 181, 190-192, 194, 197, 211-213, 219-221, 226-227, 229, 235-237, 247, 251-259, 262, 264, 268, 271, 275-276, 285, 289-290, 293, 297, 309

affective   160, 226, 235, 251
associating   247, 251-252
auditory   10-11
autobiographical   256
base rate   289-290
contextual   220, 226-229, 231-232, 235, 246, 251
depth   55
event   109, 258
frequency   229
monocular   56
object   11
personal   180
semantic   220, 226-232
sensory   4, 8-9, 29
tactual   11, 19-20, 45, 66
temporal order 226
visual   3, 11, 21, 31, 45, 49, 59, 69, 83
inhibition   26-27, 105
insight   175, 302-303
instruction 7, 156, 160, 163, 207, 232-233, 242, 315
    explicit imagery   187, 244
    explicit memory   196
    implicit 196
insula   20
intelligence   194-195, 277-278, 289, 316, 318, 320
intention   9, 21, 47, 73, 136, 256-257, 259, 263, 273
interference   73, 97-102, 107, 179, 237
introspection   43-44, 87
introversion   108
intuition   208, 262, 276, 285, 292
    logical   276, 284

J

judgment   63, 66, 133, 135, 205-206, 226-229, 232, 255-257, 278, 285-291, 296
    identification 226, 235
    recognition   226-227, 229, 231-232
    representativeness   287
    semantic 226-227
    similarity   146, 287-288
    size   59
    temporal 228, 253, 300

K

kinesthetic system   21
Korsakoff's syndrome   192, 194-195, 270-271

L

language   6, 11-12, 98, 115, 124, 129, 131-140, 142, 145-147, 150-152, 155-
156, 160-164, 167-173, 201-203, 205, 208, 214, 216, 270, 275-276, 287, 318-319
    artificial   205, 208
    chimpanzee   162
    spoken   124, 137, 160-162, 172-173
    written   124, 137
language perception   129, 136

lateral geniculate nucleus   46, 49-50, 130
learning process 125
learning system   172-173, 176, 198
left hemisphere   12, 20, 23, 45, 67-135, 150-162, 191
letter-sequence pathway 64, 82, 121-122, 129
limbic system   10, 67
lineup   232-233
locomotion system 22
logogen   119-120, 123-129, 137-185, 220, 222, 226, 235, 239
logogen system   120, 146
long-term recall 182, 263, 273
long-term retention   35-36, 263-264

M

massa intermedia 10, 28
massed repetition 177
medial geniculate nucleus   10, 130
medial temporal lobe   191-193
meditation 108, 303
medulla   12
memory   7, 72, 97, 109, 159, 181, 225-269, 272-273, 282, 290, 308
memory consolidation   179-180
memory process   315
mental image   98, 212, 240, 280
mental rotation process 63
metamemory 181
midbrain   9-10, 12, 27, 47, 105-106, 130
mirrored-self misidentification   234
mnemonic   198-199, 209-217
mnemonic strategies   191, 209-210, 213-217
modus ponens   279-280, 282, 292
modus tollens   279-282, 292
mood 147, 194, 245
mood congruency   245
morpheme   201
motor 2, 9, 21-22, 25, 33, 73, 119, 146, 270
motor plan 10, 19-24, 26-27, 32-74, 146
motor program   2-3, 19-20, 23, 27, 34, 37, 228
motor system   2-4, 8, 10, 16-22, 26, 28, 32, 37, 39, 50, 75
motor units 15, 18, 20, 27, 29, 37, 132
movement   1-2, 4, 10-11, 13, 16, 18-32, 34, 36, 39, 47, 71, 87, 106, 136, 142, 153, 319
    eye   10, 23, 27, 36-48, 68, 75, 83, 87, 91, 100, 305
    finger 22
    hand   5, 28-29
    limb   26, 29, 31, 45
    saccadic 47-48, 79
    vocal   135, 172

N

naming process   164, 172
natural-language mediation   211-212, 214
necessary   4, 31, 39, 76, 99, 162, 185
    procedures   131
    sequential muscle movements   31

  temporal schedules   21
neglect syndrome   95-96, 105
neocortex   9-12, 19, 148, 154
neuron   7-10, 16, 21, 26, 28-29, 43-44, 49-50, 53-55, 66-67, 94, 96, 131, 133, 176, 194, 196
    cone   45
    feature-detector   50, 52-53
    LGN   50, 52
    magnocellular 49
    motor   8, 15-18, 27, 29
    parvocellular 49
    rod   45
    sensory 8, 16, 18, 28-29

O

occasion   41, 125, 153, 177, 215
    different   169, 247, 251-252
    previous 4, 231
    prior   117
occipital   13
    adjacent 45, 49
occipital lobe   11, 13, 45, 49
occlusion   55, 58
optic pathway   43-45, 49, 56-69
organization   8-9, 12, 78, 123, 125, 128, 138, 155, 186, 201, 222, 245-247, 250, 252-254, 295
orienting response   74, 87, 90-91, 93-94, 112
overregularization   166

P

parietal lobe   11-13, 23, 30, 45, 66, 68, 92, 95, 130, 135
Parkinson's disease   27, 106-107
pegwords   211
perception 3-4, 11-13, 18, 42-45, 49, 55-56, 59, 62, 64-66, 68-69, 73, 98, 109, 111, 120, 122, 126, 131, 133, 137, 140, 155, 184, 215, 229-230, 235, 251, 257, 278, 309-310
    depth   55
    face   64
    form and/or color   50, 202
    object   62
    pattern 42
    scene   127
perceptual organization 73, 90, 93, 112, 200, 203, 220, 222
perceptual pathway   65-66, 72
perceptual process   178, 200, 209, 217
perceptual system 2-3, 18, 23, 41, 47-80, 94, 99, 116, 123, 155, 165, 172, 204
peripheral nervous system   8, 94
perseveration   301
perspective 54, 72, 96, 258, 319
phantom limb   29
phoneme identification system 137
phonemes   118, 136, 140
phonemic restoration   139
phonological - articulatory loop   124, 147, 164, 185, 280, 282
phonology   185

photoreceptors   45, 49, 68
picture recognition   223
plan 1, 4-5, 9, 13, 20-21, 23, 26-33, 37, 39, 74, 87, 89, 100, 103-104, 112-
113, 214, 258, 284, 291, 302, 308, 310-311, 313
    solution 300, 307-313, 320
polygraph 83
Ponzo illusion   54
positron emission tomography 133
post-event information 259-261, 273
posture   23-25, 31-33, 39
    arm   24
    body   21, 25
    final   23-25, 32, 39
    grasping 24, 31
    limb   37
practice, distributed 36, 38-39, 117, 159
preference 82, 171, 195, 276, 293, 295-296, 317
premotor cortex   21, 30-31
primacy   60, 62, 74-75, 101, 122, 127, 237, 242
priming   62, 122, 126-127, 242
proactive interference 237, 250, 252-314
problem solving process 304, 313
procedural pathway   46, 65-66, 68-69, 130
procedure   5, 7-9, 13, 60, 68, 106, 157, 189, 216, 264, 275, 277, 297, 310-311
    solution 307, 314
prodigies   162, 318
pronunciation system   121
proposition 140, 143-146, 254-255, 259, 276, 280
prosopagnosia   125
prototype   306
pseudodementia   190, 192
PTSD 267
pulvinar nucleus 45, 65, 83

R

recall   23, 34, 58, 64-80, 96-125, 133-148, 154-198, 211-262, 265-268, 272-
273, 285-301, 308-309, 316, 320
recall process   236
recency   182, 220, 226-230, 238, 251, 265, 272
    judgment   226-228, 235
    response   220, 226-227
recognition 11, 13, 16, 31, 62-69, 75, 82, 115-125, 127, 129, 134, 151, 177-178,
183, 187-188, 193-196, 203, 219-236, 243-247, 250-251, 253, 269, 308, 313
    pathway 122-123
    process 116, 122, 127, 131-222, 226, 235
    system 115, 118, 121, 123, 154, 175, 198, 234, 250
reconstruction   248, 262, 265, 273
reduplicative paramnesia   234
reflex   9-10, 16-18, 21, 27, 73, 91, 94, 106, 109
    cerebellar   21
    conditioned   16-17, 109
    flexor 16, 94
    startle 93
    swimming 18
    vestibular-ocular   16, 21, 27, 47
rehearsal 98, 124, 180-187, 198, 211

reinforcement   260-261, 267
remember judgment 229, 232
reminiscence   241, 264
reminiscence bump 264-266, 273
repetition 34, 122-123, 126, 162-179
representation   2, 4-13, 18, 20, 23-24, 31-33, 37, 39, 46, 48-50, 54, 56-65, 69, 72-76, 79-81, 84, 88-94, 97, 99, 101, 104, 109-110, 112, 115-123, 125, 127-129, 131, 136-146, 150-155, 157, 164, 167, 172-185, 196, 198, 200, 203, 205-213, 216-222, 225-229, 232, 234, 236, 243, 246-248, 253, 262, 265, 271, 273, 275-277, 280, 282, 284, 287, 293, 297, 300-305, 309, 313, 316, 320
    action   99
    articulatory   118, 124, 181-182, 184-185, 198
    associated   115, 119, 128-129, 131
    auditory 119-121, 124, 131, 137, 156, 182
    categorical   201, 236
    declarative   32, 34, 118, 176-177, 205-206
    hierarchical   185, 198, 200
    letter   64, 78-79, 123
    linguistic   120, 134
    memory   59, 64, 116, 131, 220-221
    motor   9, 97, 99, 116, 119, 124
    object   57, 60, 73, 110
    perceptual   4, 13, 74, 90, 97, 112-113, 115-120, 136, 143, 150, 176, 190, 200, 203, 208-209, 217, 220, 222, 226, 242
    phonological   118, 124, 181, 185
    posture   23, 32, 35, 37
    problem   302-304, 305, 307, 313
    procedural   32-34
    semantic 89, 140, 143, 151-152, 181, 184, 198, 227, 243, 276
    sentence 141, 150, 152
    shape   45, 58, 67, 80
    spatial   26, 37-39, 63, 66, 68, 99, 129, 151
    speech   136, 140
    temporal 26, 39, 129, 151
    three-dimensional   43-44, 49-50, 53, 56, 58-59, 65, 68-69, 130
    verbal   116, 143, 188, 284, 301
    visual   7, 46, 59, 63-65, 69, 74, 99, 116-119, 121, 124-125, 128, 145, 158, 169, 188, 200, 203, 243, 248, 277
    visuospatial   96, 249, 276, 284
    whole-word   64, 82, 121
    working memory 172, 174
representativeness   285-286, 288-290
repressed memories   267
response   1-2, 7-9, 15-17, 21, 27, 36, 39, 50, 71-74, 79, 81, 83, 85-87, 89, 91-113, 118, 120, 122, 125-127, 131, 134-135, 140, 146-147, 154, 159, 163, 165, 168, 178, 182, 191, 196, 200, 206, 209, 215, 217, 220-222, 227, 230, 232, 234, 236, 241, 245, 250, 258, 261-265, 280, 283-284
    motor   2, 103, 110, 134
response bottleneck   96, 98
response conflict 100-102
response selection stage   118, 136
response stage   104, 120, 122-221, 225, 235
reticular activating system   105-107
reticular formation   10, 95, 105-106
retina   2, 12, 16-17, 42-47, 49-50, 53, 56, 68, 77
retinal image   42-44, 46, 49-55, 68

retrieval   72, 104, 123, 147, 179, 182, 198, 219, 225, 227, 229, 231, 239, 245-247, 250-252, 273, 290-291, 300
    context-dependent   245
    pharmacological-state-dependent 245
    state-dependent   245
retrieval process 245
retroactive interference   183
right hemisphere 12, 45, 67-96, 132-135, 150-162, 191
Ritalin   108
rods 45, 77
RSVP 79, 121

S

S.   185, 215-216, 316
saccade   12, 46-48
scanning plan   88, 90
schema   145-146, 185, 254, 264, 282, 306
    problem 307, 310
    story   145, 254
schizophrenia   234-235
search stage   74, 77, 80, 89, 112
selection 2, 31, 37-38, 72-73, 75, 80, 90-92, 110, 112, 141, 143, 145, 290, 310
    bottom-up   73
    early   76-82, 84, 91, 94
    late   76-77, 80-81, 84, 90-91, 94, 112
    late auditory 80
    late visual   81
    perceptual   76
    response 73, 76, 118, 135-136
    top-down 73
selection process 57, 73, 143, 304
selection stage   89, 112, 222
selective interference 98
semantic categorization 226, 235, 251
semantic organization   246-247
semantic relationship   74, 126, 142, 144, 243
sensation   8, 12, 28-29, 215
    peripheral   7
    retinal 43-44
sensory registration   45, 49, 130
sensory registration stage   43-44, 68
shape pathway   56, 69
signal detection 230, 235, 251
simultanagnosia   67
skill 5, 32, 35-37, 87, 98, 102, 175, 195, 214, 216, 314
    chess   307-308
    memory   213-214
    motor   32, 35, 116-117, 155, 161, 173, 194, 319
    particular visual scanning 88
    perceptual   32, 65, 116-117, 151, 297, 310
    perceptual-motor   32, 88, 124, 158
sleep 10, 105-106, 142, 179-180
    nREM   105, 179-180
    slow wave   105-106, 180
sleep cycle 105, 180

span   149, 181, 192, 212-213, 267
    digit   181, 192, 213
speech   20, 22-23, 78, 93, 118, 129, 131-137, 143, 146-152, 156, 162-163,
167, 169, 171-174, 210
    fluent   162-163, 172
speech perception 136-140
speech production system   132, 150
speech recognition   151-152
speech spectrogram   136
spinocerebellum   27
stage 32-33, 105, 179-180, 199, 222, 250-251
    associative   32-33, 37
    declarative   32-33, 37
    motor   98
    perceptual   97, 234
    procedural   39
    recognition   244
    sentence construction   136
    target detection   112
stimulus-response compatibility   99
story recall   254-255
strategies 34, 133, 186, 211-212, 214, 216, 240, 275, 296, 300, 302, 312, 320
    chunking 212
    cuing   265
    problem-solving   302
    rehearsal   181
striatum   27, 106
subgoals   301, 307, 311-313, 320
subliminal perception   126
substantia nigra 27, 105-106
superior colliculus   9-10, 17, 45, 47-69, 75, 83, 87, 94, 130
suspense   283
synesthesia 215
syntax   137, 144, 284

T

target detection 73, 84, 86, 90, 102, 112, 193
target-response compatibility 99, 101
temporal lobe   11-12, 45-46, 118, 124, 130, 132, 191
thalamic gate   75, 80, 83, 90-91, 106, 194
thalamus   10-13, 26-28, 43-46, 49-50, 65-69, 73-76, 95-106, 109-110, 130, 154,
176, 192, 194, 198
tip-of-the-tongue phenomenon   243
transfer   37-38, 101, 281
typicality 206, 286

U

utterance   146, 151-152, 163, 166-167, 217
    agent-action-object 167
    deictic 166
    emotional   161, 172
    one-word 162, 319
    sarcastic   161
    two-word 164, 166, 318

V

verbal fluency   197, 318
verbal rehearsal 92, 97, 125, 147, 180-188, 198, 276
vergence   55-56
vestibular system 21
vestibulocerebellum   27
vigilance   82
vision   3, 42-45, 50, 56-67, 75-88, 96-119, 129-130, 134, 141, 146, 150, 152, 155, 164, 172, 203, 206, 221, 224, 284, 297
visual image   2, 96, 98, 100-176, 187-188, 215, 242, 302, 304
visual organization   52, 203
visual pathway   11, 45, 69, 129
visual perception 41, 43-44, 49, 59, 68, 78, 95, 116, 118, 140
visual recall   243, 316
visual recognition   66, 115, 121, 125, 223, 243, 316
visual scanning plan   88
visual stress   53
visual system   6, 21, 43-44, 47-54, 56-59, 63-69, 73-79, 81, 87, 97, 116, 118, 122, 131, 201, 204
visuomotor pathway   66
visuomotor system 22
vocabulary 164-167, 172, 317
   color   202
vocalization   36, 98, 161
   involuntary   27
vocalization/ingestion system 22
voluntary movement   15-16, 19, 21, 27, 65, 73, 87, 106, 193
voluntary response   71-72, 84-87, 98, 105-127, 129, 151, 197
Von Restorff   183

W

WAIS 142, 317
whole-face pathway   64, 125
whole-word pathway   64, 82, 121-123, 129, 151
Williams syndrome 284-285, 317-318